The Pyrenees

THE ROUGH GUIDE

D1325227

There are more than one hundred and fifty Rough Guide titles
covering destinations from Amsterdam to Zimbabwe

Forthcoming titles include

Cuba • Dominican Republic • Las Vegas • Sardinia • Switzerland

Rough Guide Reference Series

Classical Music • Drum 'n' Bass • European Football • House
The Internet • Jazz • Music USA • Opera • Reggae
Rock Music • World Music

Rough Guide Phrasebooks

Czech • Dutch • European • French • German • Greek • Hindi and Urdu
Indonesian • Italian • Mandarin Chinese • Mexican Spanish • Polish
Portuguese • Russian • Spanish • Swahili
Thai • Turkish • Vietnamese

Rough Guides on the Internet
http://www.roughguides.com

ROUGH GUIDE CREDITS

Text editor: Paul Gray
Series editor: Mark Ellingham
Editorial: Martin Dunford, Jonathan Buckley, Samantha Cook, Jo Mead, Kate Berens, Amanda Tomlin, Ann-Marie Shaw, Sarah Dallas, Chris Schüler, Helena Smith, Julia Kelly, Caroline Osborne, Judith Bamber, Kieran Falconer, Olivia Eccleshall (UK); Andrew Rosenberg (US)

Production: Susanne Hillen, Andy Hilliard, Judy Pang, Link Hall, Nicola Williamson, Helen Ostick
Cartography: Melissa Flack, Maxine Burke
Picture research: Eleanor Hill
Online Editors: Alan Spicer (UK); Geronimo Madrid (US)
Finance: John Fisher, Celia Crowley, Catherine Gillespie
Marketing & Publicity: Richard Trillo, Simon Carloss, Niki Smith (UK); Jean-Marie Kelly, SoRelle Braun (US)
Administration: Tania Hummel, Alexander Mark Rogers

ACKNOWLEDGEMENTS

The editor would like to thank: Nicky Young for typesetting; Nicola Williamson, Andy Hilliard and Helen Ostick for production; and Eleanor Hill for picture research.

Marc Dubin would like to thank Michael Peters at La Miana; Nicola Forsyth and Richard Cash in Hecho for help with the lead-free crisis and for reviewing parts of the manuscript; Andrea Trey in Barèges for thorough updates; and last but not least, Pamela for accompanying me during the latter half of an often very stressful research trip and tolerating my non-domesticity during the writing of this book. Continued thanks also to all those who smoothed the way on the previous edition. The author would like to acknowledge the contribution of the authors of the *Rough Guides* to Spain and France, and that of Paul Jenner and Christine Smith, responsible for the first edition of this guide. Thanks also to Melanie Ross and Narrell Leffman for their updates from America and Australia respectively; to Jennifer Speake for proofreading; to Kingston Presentation Graphics for brand-new cartography; and last but not least to Paul Gray for level-headed editing under pressure.

Sarah McAlister would like to thank Pat and Ken Jobson, and Valerie and Jean-Marie Rumiel for hospitality; Christine Hicks of the Prades tourist office for information and inspiration; and Jean-Luc and Martine Gibaud for good company.

PUBLISHING INFORMATION

This third edition published March 1998 by Rough Guides Ltd, 62–70 Shorts Gardens, London WC2H 9AB. Reprinted September 1999.
Distributed by the Penguin Group:
Penguin Books Ltd, 27 Wrights Lane, London W8 5TZ
Penguin Books USA Inc., 375 Hudson Street, New York 10014, USA
Penguin Books Australia Ltd, 487 Maroondah Highway, PO Box 257, Ringwood, Victoria 3134, Australia
Penguin Books Canada Ltd, 10 Alcorn Avenue, Toronto, Ontario, Canada M4V 1E4
Penguin Books (NZ) Ltd, 182–190 Wairau Road, Auckland 10, New Zealand
Typeset in Linotron Univers and Century Old Style to an original design by Andrew Oliver.
Printed in England by Clays Ltd, St Ives PLC.
Illustrations in Part One & Part Three by Edward Briant; illustration on p.1 by Tommy Yamaha and on p.453 by Simon Fell.

No part of this book may be reproduced in any form without permission from the publisher except for the quotation of brief passages in reviews.
© Marc Dubin 1998
528pp, includes index
A catalogue record for this book is available from the British Library.
ISBN 1-85828-308-6

The Pyrenees

THE ROUGH GUIDE

written and researched by

Marc Dubin

with additional contributions by

Sarah McAlister and Lance Chilton

THE ROUGH GUIDES

THE ROUGH GUIDES

TRAVEL GUIDES • PHRASEBOOKS • MUSIC AND REFERENCE GUIDES

 We set out to do something different when the first Rough Guide was published in 1982. Mark Ellingham, just out of university, was travelling in Greece. He brought along the popular guides of the day, but found they were all lacking in some way. They were either strong on ruins and museums but went on for pages without mentioning a beach or taverna. Or they were so conscious of the need to save money that they lost sight of Greece's cultural and historical significance. Also, none of the books told him anything about Greece's contemporary life – its politics, its culture, its people, and how they lived.

So with no job in prospect, Mark decided to write his own guidebook, one which aimed to provide practical information that was second to none, detailing the best beaches and the hottest clubs and restaurants, while also giving hard-hitting accounts of every sight, both famous and obscure, and providing up-to-the-minute information on contemporary culture. It was a guide that encouraged independent travellers to find the best of Greece, and was a great success, getting shortlisted for the Thomas Cook travel guide award, and encouraging Mark, along with three friends, to expand the series.

The Rough Guide list grew rapidly and the letters flooded in, indicating a much broader readership than had been anticipated, but one which uniformly appreciated the Rough Guide mix of practical detail and humour, irreverence and enthusiasm. Things haven't changed. The same four friends who began the series are still the caretakers of the Rough Guide mission today: to provide the most reliable, up-to-date and entertaining information to independent-minded travellers of all ages, on all budgets.

We now publish 100 titles and have offices in London and New York. The travel guides are written and researched by a dedicated team of more than 100 authors, based in Britain, Europe, the USA and Australia. We have also created a unique series of phrasebooks to accompany the travel series, along with an acclaimed series of music guides, and a best-selling pocket guide to the Internet and World Wide Web. We also publish comprehensive travel information on our web site:

http://www.roughguides.com/

HELP US UPDATE

We've gone to a lot of effort to ensure that this third edition of **The Rough Guide to the Pyrenees** is as up-to-date and accurate as possible. However, if you feel there are places we've under-rated or over-praised, or find we've missed something good or covered something which has now gone, then please write; suggestions, comments or corrections are much appreciated.

We'll credit all contributions, and send a copy of the next edition (or any other Rough Guide if you prefer) for the best letters. Please mark letters: "Rough Guide Pyrenees Update" and send to:

Rough Guides, 62–70 Shorts Gardens, London WC2H 9AB, or Rough Guides, 375 Hudson St, New York NY 10014.

Or send email to: mail@roughguides.co.uk

Online updates about this book can be found on Rough Guides' web site (see above for details)

THE AUTHOR

Marc Dubin first went to the Pyrenees in 1986 – and thigh-deep in snowmelt, discovered why most facilities are shut in May. Since then he has returned several times to both sides of the range, on one visit toting a 23-kilo pack through the mountains in the course of researching a hiking guide to Spain. He is now thoroughly hooked, not least on the mountain cuisine, and has seen his waist size increase alarmingly after the most recent trip.

READERS' LETTERS

Thanks to those who wrote in with comments on the last edition

David Bays & Maureen Colledge, Steven Bees, Roger L. Blin, Jon Brown, A. Cant & O. Edwards, Billie Catherine, Jan Danilo-Garbacks, Rob Dixon, Richard Eatough, Barbara Engel, John Henderson, Peter Hore, Martin Peeters & Ellen Vogel, Marjory Piggott, N. K. Rayner, A. Redpath, David Sugarman, Mrs David Trollope, and A.J. Wake. Apologies to anyone whose name has been misspelt.

CONTENTS

PART THREE CONTEXTS 453

MAPS

MAP SYMBOLS

━━━	Railway	▲	Mountain Peak
══	Road	⸝⸍	Pass
═══	Track	⸝⸟	Gorge
─ ─	Footpath	◠	Cave
∼∼∼	Waterway	⫽	Waterfall
━ ━	Chapter division boundary	▨	National Park
━•━	International borders	━	Wall
⌂	Refuge	ⓘ	Tourist Office
🏛	Château	⊠	Post Office
♥	Castle	▪	Building
⌂	Abbey	➕	Church
⚓	Church or Monastery	▨	Park
⟁	Campsite	ⓒ	Telephone
✈	Airport	℗	Parking
⚕	Spa	★	Bus stop
⛷	Ski Resort		

INTRODUCTION

A nyone could find their perfect place of exile in the **Pyrenees**, a range that encompasses in its four-hundred-kilometre length a diversity of landscapes rarely equalled in Europe. Between the balmy beaches of the Mediterranean and the more turbulent Atlantic coast lie regions of lush meadowland, peaks clad permanently in ice, sun-blasted canyons of bare rock, swathes of dense forest, weirdly eroded limestone pinnacles and valleys so sheer and overgrown that scarcely a ray of light penetrates them.

These mountains challenge and invite rather than intimidate. Generally rounded and crumbling, most of the peaks are attainable even to people with little experience of such terrain. **Aneto**, at 3404 metres the highest summit of the Pyrenees, stands within reach of any determined and properly equipped walker, as do all the next ranking peaks – **Posets**, **Monte Perdido** and **Vignemale**. Other natural wonders of the range are also accessible to the averagely fit. The **Valle de Ordesa**, the most spectacular of many canyons, can be traversed on nearly level footpaths, as can the great glaciated amphitheatre of the **Cirque de Gavarnie**, just to the north. The stalactite-draped cavern of **Lombrives** is the largest cave in Europe to which there's unrestricted public access, while a visit to the **Sala de la Verna**, the largest chamber in one of the world's deepest cave systems – the Gouffre Pierre-Saint-Martin – requires no great physical effort. And if you join an organized group, you can raft down the fiercest river of the Pyrenees, the **Noguera Pallaresa** in Catalunya, as well as several tamer ones on the French side.

Walking the entire range from end to end has become a classic endeavour, and thousands of people have followed the **Haute Randonnée Pyrénéenne** (HRP) along the watershed, or the more circuitous, but less demanding, **Grande Randonnée 10** (GR10) entirely within France. These long-established footpaths were supplemented during the 1980s by the equally spectacular Spanish trans-Pyrenean **Gran Recorrido 11** (GR11); maps for every part of the Pyrenees show numerous other, briefer itineraries, planned for hikers of all abilities.

The **wildlife** of the Pyrenees is exceptionally rich, despite the devastating impact of human activity on many of its most engaging species. Populations of deer and wild boar hide in the forests, and in some dense woodlands a dwindling number of **brown bears** still manages to survive despite the depredations of hunters and developers. In contrast, the **izard** – or Pyrenean chamois – is on the increase; **marmots** are plentiful; and majestic **birds of prey** circle in the skies. The **capercaillie**, a game bird now extinct in the French Alps, still thrives in the Pyrenees, and the tiny **desman**, a sort of aquatic mole, is unknown anywhere else in western Europe, except the Picos de Europa.

Traces of **human habitation** in the Pyrenees predate recorded history by thousands of years. At **Tautavel**, not far from Perpignan, are displayed some of the earliest human remains ever discovered on the continent, and the prehistoric painted caves around **Tarascon-sur-Ariège** are rivalled only by those of the Dordogne and the Spanish province of Cantabria. The finest cave paintings of the region, at **Niaux**, are the best examples open to public view anywhere in the world.

Architectural highlights of the Pyrenees are its extraordinary **Romanesque churches**, of which there are literally hundreds, including such renowned examples as Saint-Martin-de-Canigou, Serrabonne, Santa Maria de Ripoll, Sant Climent at Taüll and a host of others in the Noguera de Tort valley, San Juan de la Peña, and Saint-Engrâce in the Haute-Soule. Towards the western sector of the range, numerous monuments bear testimony to the thousands of pilgrims who during the Middle Ages followed the

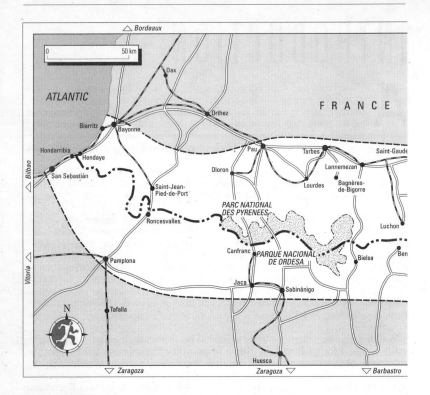

pilgrimage trail to Santiago de Compostela in Galicia via the fabled Puerto de Ibañeta near Roncesvalles, or the nearby Col de Somport. At the eastern end, from the Mediterranean to the Ariège, the strength of the heretical **Cathar** sect is reflected in many immensely evocative ruined **castles**, notably the crag-top citadel of Montségur, site of the faith's effective extinction.

The **people** of the Pyrenees are as disparate as the landscape. The east and west regions of the range are the respective homelands of the Catalans and the Basques, each with a tenaciously preserved cultural vitality, as embodied in the sombre *sardana*, the Catalan communal dance, or the lightning-quick and potentially lethal Basque game of *jaï alaï* (pelota). As you traverse the Pyrenees you'll certainly hear Catalan, Aranese, Aragonese and Euskera (the Basque tongue), not to mention a host of other dialects not accorded the status of distinct languages. For centuries before the final unifications of France and Spain, virtually every valley constituted a mini-republic with its own argot and traditions, jealously guarding customary privileges against encroachment from distant central governments, and defying them further with a thriving trade in **smuggling**. Remoteness and neglect long made the mountains a refuge for political as well as religious dissidents, most recently during the Spanish Civil War and World War II when thousands of **refugees** took advantage of the shepherds' and smugglers' knowledge to evade capture – and again after 1968, when hundreds of disillusioned French protesters took up residence in the back country, swelling the traditional local vote for the political left. Indeed the Pyreneans' historical disregard for the often-altered boundaries

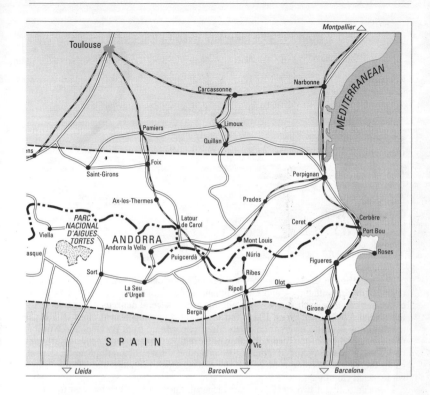

between France and Spain has been vindicated and accentuated by the post-1993 European single market, as old border posts lie abandoned and a strong regional identity bridging the watershed seems set to reassert itself.

When and where to go

There's something to do in the Pyrenees at all times of the year. Snowfall permitting, the **ski season** gets seriously under way in February, while spring sees high-level ski touring. With the thaw, **rafting** and **canoeing** become practicable, and then the long summer **walking** season begins – also a good time for riding, cycling, and the more hair-raising pursuits of **canyoning** and **parapente**, the latter a sort of cross between hang-gliding and parachuting. In autumn the crowds depart and the mountain trails are left to solitary walkers not afraid of the odd snow flurry.

The optimum time to visit obviously depends on what you want to do, but if possible you should **avoid the French and Spanish national summer holidays**, which run from mid-July to the end of August. It's preferable to come after this lemming-stampede rather than before: spring and autumn offer equal solitude, but high passes may still be blocked until July; and in September you'll have the freedom of all the mountains. Besides the crowds, **thunderstorms** cause problems in high summer: the Pyrenees are very prone to them and during July and August several storms a week can be guaranteed. If you are out on the high peaks during summer you should always aim to be well down by early afternoon, when the storms tend to break.

AVERAGE TEMPERATURES (°C)						
	Jan	Mar	May	July	Sept	Nov
Perpignan (Mediterranean coast)	12.4	12.5	20.1	28.4	26.1	15.8
Olot (Inland Catalunya)	4.4	9	14.3	20.7	17.7	7.7
Ransol (Andorra)	-2.1	1.4	7.3	13.6	10.9	2
Tarbes (Midi-Pyrénées)	10	12.3	19.1	27.6	25	15.5
Panticosa (Mountain Aragón)	0.1	2.6	8.2	15.5	12.3	4.1
Bayonne (Atlantic coast)	10	12.2	18	27.2	24.2	15.4

The **weather** in the Pyrenees resists generalization, as temperatures can be erratic owing to marine influences, and microclimates abound. In summer, the cooling action of the sea can give each coastal strip a temperature several degrees lower than a few miles inland, while for every 100–200m of ascent, the temperature often falls by as much as one degree Celsius. Thus a summer train-ride up from Barcelona to Núria in Catalunya might take you through a drop of more than ten degrees. Conversely, there's the common phenomenon of temperature inversion (especially on the French slopes), when the valleys become colder than the peaks, which protrude like islands from a white sea of cloud.

If you've only got two weeks at your disposal, the Pyrenees are too vast to tour in their entirety, but in places **public transport** is good enough to explore a region roughly corresponding to one of the chapters in this book. The rail networks will get you within striking distance of the most interesting areas, and buses are often available to take you deeper into the mountains. A circuit of the eastern Pyrenees, for example, could begin at Perpignan, continue south by train along the Mediterranean coast, move west by road through the verdant Garrotxa to the Ripollès valleys; then north by rail to the sunny plain of the Cerdanya/Cerdagne, and finally return to Perpignan by another train through the dramatic Têt valley. Circular itineraries such as this can be constructed in many other parts of the range – around Andorra or in the Basque country, for example – and even isolated, underpopulated zones such as the central Maladeta and Posets massifs lend themselves to loops on foot from trailheads served by buses.

If you want to concentrate on one area, the **Ariège** will suit most tastes with its fabulous scenery, cave art, ruined castles and almost every form of outdoor activity. Over the border in Catalunya, the **Parc Nacional de Aigües Tortes i Sant Maurici**, easily accessible from the Vall d'Aran, makes an excellent introduction to the glacial glories of the higher peaks. Gavarnie or Cauterets in France, and Torla or Bielsa in Spain, are comfortable gateways for the best of the **Parc National des Pyrénées** and the **Parque Nacional de Ordesa y Monte Perdido**, the great, contiguous national parks in the heart of the range. For walks and climbs on the highest summits further east, make the all-purpose resorts of **Benasque** or **Bagnères-de-Luchon** your bases.

Towards the west end of the range, **Pau** is the largest and most cosmopolitan city of the Pyrenees, and one of several gateways to the karst country at the head of the French **Vallée d'Aspe** and the Spanish valleys of **Hecho** and **Ansó**, the latter also accessible from **Jaca**, "capital" of the Aragonese mountains. Inland from the surf-pounded Atlantic coast, with its elegant resorts of **San Sebastián** and **Biarritz**, the seductively green horizons and sumptuous domestic architecture of the **Basque country** beckon, with graceful **Bayonne** and atmospheric **Saint-Jean-Pied-de-Port** as focuses. The Mediterranean beaches are more varied and – especially at the picturesque port-resorts of **Collioure** or **Cadaqués** – more beautiful, the climate dependably sunny; here there are also opportunites for forays inland to the mysterious, volcanic **Garrotxa basin** in Catalunya or to the gorge-slashed foothills of the **Canigou massif** in Rousillon. Whichever part of the range you decide to visit, take the opportunity to sample both sides of the border if at all possible – the change of landscape, climate and culture is one of the delights of the Pyrenees.

PART ONE

THE

BASICS

randonnées
pyrénéennes
GITE D'ETAPE

GETTING THERE FROM BRITAIN

The most convenient way of getting to the Pyrenees is to fly – flights from London Gatwick, for example, take just under two hours to Barcelona, less to Perpignan or Lourdes, compared with a minimum of 24 hours by train to Barcelona or San Sebastián. Taking the train – and driving – to the Pyrenees has become easier, though, since the opening of the Chunnel and Le Shuttle cross-Channel services, and there are also two ferry services direct to northern Spain, bypassing France.

BY AIR

There are a certain number of scheduled and charter flights from Britain to Pyrenean foothill airports throughout the year, with a concentration in the summer walking and winter skiing seasons. During late spring or late autumn you may find some routes cancelled or dormant; summer flights of any sort – at £150–250 – tend to be more expensive than ski-season charter deals, which on routes like Manchester/Gatwick–Lourdes can be had for as little as £98.

CHARTER FLIGHTS

The number of charter flights from Britain into the Pyrenean region is limited; usual departure airports in the UK are London Gatwick, Birmingham and Manchester. In season, **Girona** is both the cheapest and most convenient destination airport for the eastern part of the range; otherwise aim for **Perpignan** or **Barcelona**. For the central part of the range there's the additional option of a seat on one of the pilgrimage or ski-season flights to **Lourdes/Tarbes** – most travel agents have details. The western part of the range isn't popular enough in Britain for there to be really good deals to **Biarritz/Bayonne**. You sometimes see fares at about £100 return to Lourdes and Girona in particular, but in summer more realistic prices run to around £180 for Perpignan or Toulouse.

Charters are usually block-booked by package holiday firms, but even in the middle of August they're rarely completely full and spare seats are often sold off at discounts. For an idea of current prices and availability, contact any high-street travel agent, or a specialist agency or operator. It helps if you do a little homework beforehand – the assistants sometimes don't know which airports or services are cheapest and the computers may not be programmed to show the lowest price. The widest selection of ads for London departures is invariably found in the classified pages of the London listings magazine *Time Out*. For departures from other British airports check the travel supplements of local evening papers and *The*

AGENTS AND TOUR OPERATORS IN BRITAIN

Allez France 7 West St, Storrington, W Sussex RH20 4DZ (☎01903/745793). *Fly-drive accommodation packages (no flight-only) from London Gatwick to Perpignan or Toulouse with BA or Air France; for example, £345 for a week's cottage stay in July, plus £200 per person for the car and flight.*

Alto Aragón Stilehouse Yard, Deddington, Banbury, Oxfordshire OX15 0SR (☎01869/337339). *Excellent 10- to 15-day walking holidays in the Spanish Pyrenees between Maladeta and the Basque country. Prices from £500 for 10 days.*

Campus Travel 52 Grosvenor Gardens, London SW1 (☎0171/730 3402); 541 Bristol Rd, Selly Oak, Birmingham (☎0121/414 1848); 39 Queen's Rd, Clifton, Bristol (☎0117/929 2494); 5 Emmanuel St, Cambridge (☎02123/324 283); 53 Forest Rd, Edinburgh (☎0131/668 3303); 166 Deansgate, Manchester (☎0161/273 1721); 13 High St, Oxford (☎01865/242 067); also in YHA shops and on university campuses throughout Britain. *Youth/student specialist.*

Chambres d'Hôtes/Gîtes de France Ltd c/o Sally Lines (☎0990/360360). *Houses and cottages in the Pyrenean foothills; rates often include ferry crossings.*

Eclipse Reservations Astral Towers, Bettsway, London Rd, Crawley, West Sussex (☎0293/554444). *Charter flights, for 1-2 weeks only, to the Costa Brava.*

Exodus Expeditions 9 Weir Rd, London SW12 0LT (☎0181/675 5550). *Walking, mountain-biking and cycle-touring on both sides of the Pyrenees; mostly centre-based tours include day walks from a farmhouse, caving and canyoning in Aragón, and a winter snowshoe trek.*

Fly-Sky Travel 258 Vauxhall Bridge Rd, London SW1 (☎0171/976 5833). *Good prices on scheduled flights and charters to Girona and Bilbao.*

Individual Travellers Bignor, Pulborough, W Sussex RH20 1Q (☎01798/869461). *Farmhouses, cottages and village houses all over Spain.*

Inntravel Hovingham, Yorkshire Y06 4JZ (☎01653/628862). *Supported, 7- and 11-night traverses in the Cerdagne, both low- and high-altitude, with half-board hotel accommodation and picnic lunches.*

Magic of Spain (☎01233/211611). *High-quality, out-of-the-way hotels and paradors.*

Mundi Color 276 Vauxhall Bridge Rd, London SW1 (☎0171/828 6021). *Spanish specialists for scheduled flights, with upmarket packages on the Costa Brava.*

Sunday Times, The Independent on Sunday or *The Observer*. The agents and operators listed in the box above make a good start.

The major disadvantage of charter flights is the **fixed return date** – a maximum of four weeks from the outward journey, though rarely six or even eight weeks can be arranged for a surcharge. Some return charters are good value even if you only use half, but for more flexibility you'll probably want to buy a ticket for a scheduled flight.

SCHEDULED FLIGHTS

Scheduled flights are rarely the cheapest option but some of their special promotional offers can be highly competitive. Also available are **open-jaw flights** (fly in to one airport, back from another – expensive but ideal if you're intent on a traverse of the range), Fly-Drive deals, and inexpensive connections from most regional UK airports. The cheapest tickets go by various, constantly changing names at different times of the year, but they are usually valid for seven to ninety days, require you to stay at least one Saturday night, and don't allow for change or cancellation. Consequently there's no great difference between the prices of these and a charter ticket. More flexible tickets, such as BA's Excursion fare, are valid up to six months, can be upgraded and are fully refundable, though you'll pay much more for such privileges.

Spain's national airline, Iberia, and British Airways together have the widest range of scheduled flights to destinations **south of the Pyrenees**, the nearest airports being Bilbao, Zaragoza and Barcelona. Iberia also flies direct from Manchester into Barcelona, with BA offering flights from Birmingham to Barcelona. Fares **from London to Barcelona** range from £170 to £235 depending on season and day of the week, while to **Bilbao**, west of the range, ticket prices are comparable at £160–225. **From Manchester** you're looking at £190–235 to Barcelona, and much the same to Bilbao. Iberia flies two to three times weekly year-round from **London Gatwick to Zaragoza**, with fares much the same as to Bilbao.

Nouvelles Frontières 11 Blenheim St, London W1Y (☎0171/629 7772). *France-based agency that's a good bet for competitive flights to France.*

Panorama 29 Queen's Rd, Brighton BN1 3YN (☎01273/206531). *Andorra ski-package specialists, featuring the major resorts, with prices from £369 (excluding skiing costs) for a week in a good-standard hotel.*

Pyrenees Adventures (☎01433/621498). *Guided mountain walks in the French Basque Pyrenees, based in a restored eighteenth-century farmhouse.*

Sherpa Expeditions 131a Heston Rd, Hounslow, Middlesex TW5 0RD (☎0181/577 2717). *Trekking in the Pyrenees, in particular a spectacular high-level traverse.*

Ski Miquel Holidays 33 High Street, Uppermill, near Oldham, OL3 6HS (☎01457/820200). *1- or 2-week packages, with English-speaking instructor, at Baqueira-Beret in the Vall d'Aran.*

STA Travel, 86 Old Brompton Rd, London SW7 3LH, 117 Euston Rd, London NW1 2SX, 38 Store St London WC1E 7BZ (☎0171/ 361 6161); 25 Queens Rd, Bristol BS8 1QE (☎0117/929 4399); 38 Sidney St, Cambridge CB2 3HX (☎01223/366966); 88 Vicar Lane, Leeds LS1 7JH (☎0113/244 9212); 75 Deansgate, Manchester M3 2BW (☎0161/834 0668); 36 George St,

Oxford OX1 2OJ (☎01865/792800); and branches in Birmingham, Canterbury, Cardiff, Coventry, Durham, Glasgow, Loughborough, Nottingham, Sheffield and Warwick. *Worldwide specialists in low-cost flights and tours for students and under-26s, though other customers welcome.*

STS Travel 138 Eversholt St, London NW1 (☎0171/387 5337). *Spanish flight specialists.*

Trailfinders 215 Kensington High St, London W6 6BD (☎0171/937 5400); 22–24 The Priory, Queensway, Birmingham B4 6BS (☎0121/236 1234); 48 Corn St, Bristol BS1 1HQ (☎0117/929 9000); 254–284 Sauchiehall St, Glasgow G2 3EH (☎0141/353 2224); and 58 Deansgate, Manchester M3 2FF (☎0161/839 6969). *One of the best-informed and most efficient agents for independent travellers; all branches open daily.*

Waymark Holidays 44 Windsor Rd, Slough SL1 2EJ (☎01753/516477). *Walking holidays along the Spanish Camino de Santiago, as well as centre-based and mountain-hut traverse tours of 7-14 days; cross-country ski tours in winter.*

Wildwings International House, Bank Rd, Kingswood, Bristol BS15 2LX (☎0117/984 8040). *Sharply discounted fares to Bilbao, Zaragoza and Barcelona with Iberia, but these must be used in conjunction with a minimum of three nights' hotel accommodation (booked with whomever you like).*

North of the Pyrenees, Perpignan, Toulouse, Tarbes/Lourdes, Pau and Bayonne/Biarritz all have scheduled flights from Britain most of the year. British Airways flies thrice daily in summer to **Toulouse** and once weekly to **Perpignan** at civilized departure times **from London Gatwick**. In summer, APEX fares are £219 to Toulouse, and £279 to Perpignan. **From Manchester**, BA flies daily to Toulouse (£337 summer APEX) and weekly to Perpignan (£397 summer APEX). With Air France out of **London Heathrow**, you have a greater range of choice in destination airports, though many flights go via Paris, where you'll probably change terminals from De Gaulle to Orly (free shuttle bus) and airlines, to Air France's subsidiary Air Inter. **Promotions** such as the sporadically available "Discover France" fare typically cost £140–150 to **Toulouse**, which compares favourably with the standard £219 conventional APEX fare; both are valid for up to ninety days but unchangeable once purchased. The "Discover France" fares to Tarbes/Lourdes, Pau and Bay-

onne/Biarritz are typically much the same at £160–170.

DISCOUNT AND YOUTH FARES

Students and anyone **under 26** can also take advantage of special discount flights, most commonly into Barcelona or Toulouse. The best firms for these are independent travel specialists **STA Travel** and **Campus Travel** (see box for addresses). Student-union travel bureaux can usually fix you up with flights through one of these operators, whether you're a student or not. Student or youth tickets, most often on British Airways, tend to be quite flexible, too: they are often valid for up to a year, and the return date – while you must specify one upon purchase – is changeable for little or no penalty. You can expect to pay around £108 return to Toulouse; £120–140 to Barcelona; or £120–156 to less popular Bilbao. If you don't meet the age or student-status requirement for these budget fares, the specialist agents are still well worth a call: they can get you to Toulouse on

Air France for £150 (as against £141 for under-26s), though Barcelona and Bilbao work out more expensive at £180 on a non-direct carrier such as Sabena. These sorts of tickets, although open to anyone, tend to have fairly inflexible conditions.

PACKAGES

Package holiday deals can be worth looking at, especially if you book early, late, or off-peak season. While the cheaper, mass market packages might seem to restrict you to some of the tackier parts of the Costa Brava, there's no compulsion to stick around your hotel. It's often worth taking the package for the flight alone, using the nominated hotel perhaps only for the first and last nights – with airport transfers all organized. Bargains can be found at virtually any high-street travel agent. **Fly-Drive** deals are well worth considering, too, as a combined air ticket and car rental arrangement can be excellent value.

BY TRAIN

From London to the extreme west or east of the Pyrenees takes just under 24 hours by train, though by using services from London to Paris through the Channel Tunnel (see below) you can shave a few hours off this total. Currently, connecting departures are from Victoria Station around 9am, changing trains (and stations, from Nord to Austerlitz) in Paris around 6–8pm. You reach **Hendaye** on the Atlantic coast or **Perpignan** or **Cerbère** on the Mediterranean coast around dawn; if you continue further into Spain there's another change of stations at Hendaye/Irún or Cerbère/Port Bou.

TRAIN INFORMATION IN BRITAIN

British Rail European information line (☎0990/848848)

Eurostar EPS House, Waterloo Station, London SE1 (☎0345/303030)

Eurotrain 52 Grosvenor Gardens, London SW1 (☎0171/730 3402)

Wasteels Victoria Station, London SW1 (☎0171/834 7066)

BUS INFORMATION IN BRITAIN

Eurolines c/o National Express, 164 Buckingham Palace Rd, London SW1 (☎0990/808080)

In addition to these, there are a couple of other routes. British Rail will sell you a ticket (about £150 return) that takes you by rail to **Oloron-Sainte-Marie** in France, where you must buy a rail-bus ticket on to the Spanish railhead at **Canfranc**. If you want to visit the Aspe/Ossau region of the French Pyrenees or the Aragonese Pyrenees, this route makes sense. A second alternative, a fraction cheaper, is via Foix to **Bourg-Madame** in the French Cerdagne; again BR fares are quoted only up to there, where you must change trains and buy another ticket for the Spanish network, entering Spain at Puigcerdà. This is the closest you can get to Andorra (which has no trains) and also gives handy direct access to the Ariège and the Carlit massif.

EUROSTAR

High-speed **Eurostar** trains from Waterloo International in London serve Paris via Ashford in Kent and the Channel Tunnel in just over three hours, cutting a good five hours off travel time to the Pyrenees. Frequencies and **prices** change regularly and must be checked each time. Standard second-class return fares range from £99–£155 but frequently advertised special offers can get as low as £59; cheaper APEX fares apply if you book two weeks in advance. Inter-Rail passes give discounts on Eurostar service.

You can get **through-ticketing** from mainline train stations in Britain, including the tube journey to Waterloo International; typical add-on prices for a return ticket to Paris from Edinburgh or Glasgow is £30, from Manchester £20 and Birmingham £13.50. As of 1998, night sleeper services should start running directly from Manchester, Edinburgh, Glasgow, Swansea and Plymouth direct to the Continent.

TICKETS AND PASSES

A **standard rail ticket** from London to Perpignan currently costs £149 return, to Pau £146 return, and to San Sebastián £171 return. Tickets are bookable through certain travel agents or at London's Victoria Station.

The only alternative for **under-26s** – though they are hardly any different in price – is a discounted **BIJ** ticket from Eurotrain (through Campus Travel) or Wasteels. These can be booked for journeys from any British station to any major station in Europe; like full-price tickets, they remain valid for two months and allow as many stopovers as you want along a pre-specified route (which can be different going out and coming home). The current BIJ return fare from London to Girona (via Perpignan) is £140, to San Sebastián £183 (via Hendaye), and to Pau (via Dieppe) £137.

If you plan to travel extensively in France or Spain by train, there's a better-value option than simply buying a return ticket to a Pyrenean gateway city. Under-26s can invest in an **InterRail pass** from British Rail or a travel agent; the only restriction is that you must have been resident in Europe for at least six months. This comes in two forms: either an InterRail Global pass, valid for one month's unlimited travel in 26 European countries including France and Spain (£275), or an InterRail Zonal pass, whereby the 26 countries are split into seven zones and you choose which countries you want the pass to be valid for. A fifteen-day pass for any one zone costs £185; any two contiguous zones (which would get you Spain and France), valid for one month, costs £220; any three, also for one month, costs £245. In addition all InterRail passes offer discounts on rail travel in the UK and on cross-Channel ferries. Since both France and Spain have extensive rail networks this is basically a bargain, though be prepared (see "Getting Around") to pay various and unpredictable supplements on some of the Spanish services; there are also one or two private rail lines (Núria, La Rhune) on which passes are not valid.

BY BUS

There are two regular **direct bus routes** from Britain to either end of the Pyrenees: London–Perpignan–Girona (24hr) and London–Bordeaux–San Sebastián (24hr). Both of these routes are operated by Eurolines in Britain and by Iberbus/Linebus and Julia in Spain. In both Britain and Spain tickets are bookable through most major travel agents; Eurolines sells tickets, and through transport to London, at all National Express bus terminals. In summer there are three departures weekly to the Atlantic coast, and five weekly departures to the Mediterranean, falling out of season to two a week to San Sebastián and three weekly to Girona. Fares start at around £68 one-way, £121 return (to Perpignan or San Sebastián), with a ten percent reduction if you're under 26.

The big advantage of the bus ticket is that you can have an **open return** at no extra cost. The disadvantage is that it's slow and tiring, and you may well find that air tickets compare very

favourably in price. To San Sebastián or Girona the journey is long enough but quite bearable – just make sure you take along enough to eat, drink and read, and a small amount of French and Spanish currency for meal breaks. There are stops for around twenty minutes every four to five hours and the routine is also broken by the Dover–Calais/Boulogne ferry (which is included in the cost of a ticket).

BY CAR, FERRY AND LE SHUTTLE

The bus routes follow the most direct road routes from London to the Pyrenees: if you plan to drive them yourself, unless you're into non-stop rally motoring, you'll need to roughly double their times. In addition to the time-honoured French services, there are now two direct ferry sailings to Bilbao and Santander from Britain. See the box on p.8 for ferry company addresses, or contact your local travel agent for the latest ticket and sailing details.

LE SHUTTLE AND CROSS-CHANNEL SERVICES

The opening of the Channel Tunnel hasn't affected travel times to the Pyrenees for drivers as much as for rail passengers, though it has of course speeded up the cross-Channel section of the journey. **Le Shuttle** operates trains 24 hours a day (except midnight to 6am Mon), carrying cars, motorcycles, buses and their passengers, and taking 35 minutes between Folkestone and Calais. At peak times, services operate every 30 minutes, making advance bookings unnecessary; during the night, services are hourly. Return fares have recently plunged dramatically in an attempt to compete with the ferries – count on £149 per vehicle (passengers included) during the day, dropping to £129 between 10pm and 6am.

Traditional cross-Channel options are the **ferry** or **hovercraft** links between Dover and Calais or Boulogne, or, if you're headed for the western portion of the mountains, ferries to Le Havre (from Portsmouth), Cherbourg (from Portsmouth and Weymouth), St Malo (from Portsmouth) or even Roscoff (from Plymouth). Any of these latter routes cuts out the trek around or through Paris, and opens up some interesting detours around Brittany and the French Atlantic coast. Ferry **prices** vary according to the time of year and, for motorists, the size of your car. The Dover–Calais/Boulogne runs, for example, start at about £750 one-way for a car, two adults and two

FERRY COMPANIES AND LE SHUTTLE

Brittany Ferries Millbay Docks, Plymouth; New Harbour Rd, Poole; Wharf Rd, Portsmouth (information & ticket sales ☎0990/360360). *To Santander, St Malo, Roscoff, Cherbourg, Caen.*

Hoverspeed International Hoverport, Dover, Kent (☎01304/240241); also in London (☎0181/554 7061). *To Boulogne and Calais.*

Le Shuttle Customer Services Centre, information & ticket sales ☎0990/353535.

P&O European Ferries Channel House, Channel View Road, Dover; Continental Ferry Port,

Mile End, Portsmouth; also in London (information & ticket sales ☎0990/980980). *To Calais, Cherbourg, Le Havre and Bilbao.*

Sally Line Argyle Centre, York St, Ramsgate, Kent (information & ticket sales ☎0990/595522). *To Dunkerque.*

Stena Sealink Line Charter House, Park St, Ashford, Kent (information & ticket sales ☎0990/353535). *To Calais, Cherbourg and Dieppe.*

children, but this figure doubles in high season. Foot passengers should be able to cross for £20–30.

TO SANTANDER AND BILBAO

Direct car and passenger ferry services from England to Spain are convenient but expensive. The ferry from **Plymouth to Santander** (three to four hours' drive from the west end of the Pyrenees) is operated by Brittany Ferries, takes 24 hours and runs twice weekly for most of the year (less often from Dec to mid-March). Ticket prices vary enormously according to the season, the number of passengers carried and the length of time you want the ticket to be valid; a return ticket for a car and two adults costs £189–343 in low season,

£262–478 in shoulder season, and £327–595 in peak season. Foot passengers will pay £50–80 one way, and everyone has to book some form of accommodation; cheapest is a pullman seat (from £4 off season), and two- and four-berth cabins are available for around £50–70 each. Tickets are best booked in advance, through any major travel agent.

P&O provides a twice-weekly ferry service from **Portsmouth to Bilbao**, two hours closer to the mountains than Santander. The journey takes approximately 30 hours and leaves Portsmouth on Saturdays and Tuesdays. Typical peak-season return fares for a car and two passengers are £270–485; foot passengers pay £80. Cabin fares are extra: prices for a two-berth start at £60.

GETTING THERE FROM IRELAND

If you want to fly directly to the French Pyrenees from Dublin or Belfast you'll be limited pretty much to Lourdes. Alternatives via London are unlikely to prove attractive, considering the additional time factor and the cost of a flight from Ireland to Britain. Year-round scheduled air services operate from Ireland to Barcelona, and there are a few summer charters to Girona. However, other package holidays or city breaks are again often routed via London, with an add-on fare from Ireland for the connection.

Students, and anyone under the age of 31, should contact USIT, which generally has the best discount deals on flights and train tickets. For InterRail details, see "Getting There from Britain" (p.7).

Iberia has daily direct **scheduled flights** from **Dublin to Barcelona** costing from £IR200 (Jan–Feb) to £IR225 (July–Aug). These cheapest fares have several restrictions – you must stay at

---

AIRLINES IN IRELAND

Aer Lingus Northern Ireland reservations ☎0645/737 747; 40–41 O'Connell St, Dublin 1, 13 St Stephen's Green, Dublin 2, and 12 Upper St George's St, Dun Laoghaire all use centralized reservations at Dublin airport (☎01/844 4777); 2 Academy St, Cork (021/327 155); 136 O'Connell St, Limerick (☎061/474 239).

British Airways 9 Fountain Centre, College St, Belfast BT1 6ET (☎01232/899 131 or 0345/222 111); reservations in the Republic ☎1800/626 747. BA doesn't have a Dublin office; Aer Lingus acts as their agents.

Iberia 54 Dawson St, Dublin 2 (☎01/677 9846).

Ryanair Phoenix House, Conyngham Rd, Dublin 8 (☎01/609 7800).

AGENTS IN IRELAND

Aran Travel 58 Dominick St, Galway (☎091/562595).

CIE Tours International 35 Abbey St Lower, Dublin 1 (☎01/703 1888).

Co-op Travel Care 35 Belmont Rd, Belfast 4 (☎01232/471717).

Discount Travel 4 South Great Georges St, Dublin 2 (☎01/679 5888).

Fahy Travel 3 Bridge St, Galway (☎091/563055).

Joe Walsh Tours 34 Grafton St, Dublin 2 (☎01/671 8751); 69 Upper O'Connell St , Dublin 2 (☎01/872 2555); 8–11 Baggot St, Dublin 2 (☎01/676 3053); 117 St Patrick St, Cork (☎021/277 959).

Lee Travel 23 Princes St, Cork (☎021/277111).

Student & Group Travel First Floor, 71 Dame St, Dublin 2 (☎01/677 7834).

Thomas Cook 11 Donegall Place, Belfast (☎01232/242341); 118 Grafton St, Dublin 2 (☎01/677 1721).

Trailfinders 4–5 Dawson St, Dublin 2 (☎01/677 7888).

USIT Fountain Centre, College St, Belfast BT1 6ET (☎01232/324073); 10–11 Market Parade, Patrick St, Cork (☎021/ 270900); 33 Ferryquay St, Derry (☎01504/371888); Aston Quay, Dublin 2 (☎01/602 1600); Victoria Place, Eyre Square, Galway (☎091/565177); Central Buildings, O'Connell St, Limerick (☎061/415064); 36–37 Georges St, Waterford (☎051/872601).

least one Saturday night, and can only stay for a maximum of one month – and if you want to change your departure date you can do so only once by paying an upgrade fee of £IR40. From **Dublin to Lourdes**, you're best off with one of the pilgrimage charters available between early May and the end of October, operating every five to seven days. If you want to stay longer than a week, you can request (at no extra cost) an open-ended ticket, confirming the return date – subject strictly to availability – with the tour reps in Lourdes. Basic fare is about IR£185, plus about IR£20 in governmental taxes, and compulsory travel

insurance (your own or purchased through the travel agent).

If you're really trying to get to the Pyrenees in the cheapest possible way, you might find that budget flights from Dublin (with Aer Lingus, Ryanair and British Midland) or Belfast (British Airways and British Midland) to London, plus a last-minute London charter flight, will save you a few pounds, but don't count on it. Buying a Euro-train ticket (from USIT) from Dublin to London will slightly undercut the plane's price, but by this time you're starting to talk about a journey of days and not hours.

GETTING THERE FROM NORTH AMERICA

Being mountainous and remote, the Pyre-nean region isn't a major air destination, although there are several secondary air-ports on either side of the range. Whether you fly straight into one of these airports, or fly to Paris or Madrid and travel overland from there, will depend on your budget and your schedule.

If you don't mind spending a few days in a city first, or if you were planning to visit other parts of Europe anyway, it might not be worth knocking yourself out over airfares to the Pyrenees. Instead, you might consider buying a cheap transatlantic flight, and sorting out your onward travel when you get there.

If you're looking to regroup somewhere in Europe before continuing on to the Pyrenees, **London** is a good place to aim for: there are plenty of flights and other overland options from there. If you plan to do the cross-Europe journey **by train** with a Eurail pass, see "Rail Passes" on p.13; for advice on getting from London to the Pyrenees, see "Getting There from Britain," pp.3–8.

SHOPPING FOR TICKETS

On high-traffic routes, discount outlets – adver-tised in Sunday newspaper travel sections such as the *New York Times* – are usually your best bet for cheap tickets. They come in several forms. **Consolidators** buy up large blocks of tickets that airlines don't think they'll be able to sell at their published fares, and unload them at a discount. Many advertise fares on a one-way basis, enabling you to fly into one city and out from another without penalty. Consolidators normally don't impose advance purchase requirements (although in busy times you'll want to book ahead just to be sure of getting a ticket), but they do often charge very stiff fees for date changes. Also, these companies' profit margins are pretty tiny, so they make their money by dealing in vol-ume – don't expect them to entertain lots of ques-tions. **Discount agents** also deal in blocks of tickets offloaded by the airlines, but they typical-ly offer a range of other travel-related services like travel insurance, rail passes, youth and stu-

AGENTS, CONSOLIDATORS & TRAVEL CLUBS IN NORTH AMERICA

Council Travel Head Office: 205 E 42nd St, New York, NY 10017 (☎1-800/226-8624). *Nationwide US student travel organization with branches (among others) in San Francisco, Washington DC, Boston, Austin, Seattle, Chicago, Minneapolis.*

New Frontiers/Nouvelles Frontières 12 E 33rd St, New York, NY 10016 (☎1-800/366-6387); 1221 Rue St Hubert, Ste 100, Montréal H2L3Y8 (☎514/288-4800). *French discount travel firm. Other branches in LA, San Francisco and Québec City.*

STA Travel (☎1-800/777-0112; nationwide). *Worldwide specialist in independent travel with offices in Los Angeles, San Francisco, Boston.*

Travel Cuts Head Office: 187 College St, Toronto, ON M5T 1P7 (☎416/979-2406). *Canadian student travel organization with branches all over the country.*

Travelers Advantage 49 Music Square West, Nashville, TN 37204 (☎1-800/344-2334). *Reliable travel club.*

Travac 989 Sixth Ave, New York NY 10018 (☎1-800/872-8800). *US consolidator.*

Unitravel 1177 N Warson Rd, St Louis, MO 63132 (☎1-800/325-2222). *US consolidator.*

Worldwide Discount Travel Club 1674 Meridian Ave, Miami Beach, FL 33139 (☎305/534-2082). *Florida-based travel club.*

dent ID cards, car rentals and tours. These agencies tend to be most worthwhile to students and under-26s, who can often benefit from special fares and deals. **Travel clubs** are another option – most charge an annual membership fee, which may be worth it for their discounts on air tickets and car rental. You should also check the travel section in your own major local newspaper for current bargains, and consult a good travel agent. Some agencies specialize in **charter flights**, which may be even cheaper than anything available on a scheduled flight, but again there's a trade-off: departure dates are fixed, and withdrawal penalties are high (check the refund policy).

For destinations not handled by discounters – which applies to all but one of the Pyrenean airports – you'll have to deal with airlines' published fares. The cheapest way to go is with an **APEX** (Advance Purchase Excursion) ticket. This carries certain restrictions: you have to book – and pay – at least 21 days before departure and spend at least seven days abroad (maximum stay three months), and you're liable to penalties if you change your schedule. There are also winter **Super APEX** tickets, sometimes known as "Eurosavers" – slightly cheaper than an ordinary APEX, but limiting your stay to between 7 and 21 days. Some airlines also issue **Special APEX** tickets to those under 24, often extending the maximum stay to a year.

Note that transatlantic fares are heavily dependent on **season**, and are highest from early June to the end of August, when everyone wants

to travel; they drop during the "shoulder" seasons, September–October and April–May, and you'll get the best deals during the low season, November through March (excluding Christmas). Note that flying on weekends ordinarily adds $50 to the round-trip fare; **price ranges quoted in the following sections assume midweek travel**.

PYRENEAN AIR CONNECTIONS

Flying into the Pyrenean region, your choices are Perpignan, Toulouse or Lourdes (in France) or Barcelona, Zaragoza, Pamplona or Bilbao (in Spain). Of these, **Barcelona** is by far the biggest place, and therefore the most economical choice – Iberia has the widest selection of transatlantic routes into Barcelona, and discount outlets can put you on any of a dozen other airlines that fly there via Madrid or other European capitals (see box above). Fares to Barcelona are very much in line with those to Madrid: figure around $600 from New York in low season, $900 in high season (on TWA); from Miami, $770/990; from LA, $900/1200; from Toronto or Montréal, CDN$1000/1340.

Discount travel agents won't be able to sell you a ticket directly to any of the other Pyrenean destinations, and for these you'll be partially reliant on the domestic services of Air France or Iberia. (Other airlines serving Paris or Madrid may be able to ticket you the rest of the way on an Air France or Iberia internal flight, although this is unlikely to produce any savings.) In the case of

AIRLINES IN NORTH AMERICA

Only gateway cities are listed for each airline; other routings are always possible using connecting flights.

Air Canada (☎1-800/776-3000). Montréal, Toronto and Vancouver to Paris.

Air France (☎1-800/237-2747). New York, Washington, Miami, Montréal, Toronto, Chicago, Houston, San Francisco and Los Angeles to Paris; connections to Toulouse and Lourdes.

American Airlines (☎1-800/433-7300). New York, Miami, Dallas-Fort Worth, Chicago and Los Angeles to Paris and Madrid; connections to Barcelona.

British Airways (☎1-800/247-9297; in Canada ☎1-800/668-1080). Many North American cities to London; connections to Toulouse, Barcelona and Bilbao.

Canadian Airlines (☎1-800/426-7000). Montréal, Toronto and Vancouver to Paris.

Continental Airlines (☎1-800/231-0856). Newark, Houston and Denver to Paris and Madrid.

Delta Airlines (☎1-800/241-4141). Atlanta, Cincinnati and New York to Paris and Madrid; connections to Barcelona.

Iberia (☎1-800/772-4642). New York, Miami, LA, Toronto and Montréal to Madrid and Barcelona; connections to Bilbao, Zaragoza, Pamplona.

KLM (☎1-800/374-7747). Many North American cities to Amsterdam; connections to Barcelona.

Lufthansa (☎1-800/645-3880). Many North American cities to Frankfurt; connections to Barcelona and Bilbao.

Northwest Airlines (☎1-800/225-2525). Los Angeles, Minneapolis and Detroit to Paris.

PIA Pakistan International Airways (☎1-800/221-2552). New York to Paris.

Sabena (☎1-800/955-2000). East Coast cities to Brussels; connections to Barcelona and Bilbao.

TAP Air Portugal (☎1-800/221-7370). New York and Boston to Lisbon; connections to Barcelona.

TWA (☎1-800/892-4141). New York, Boston, St Louis and Washington to Paris and Barcelona.

United Airlines (☎1-800/538-2929). Chicago and Washington to Paris.

Iberia, you can get a round-trip add-on flight from Madrid or Barcelona to **Bilbao** for $170 extra, and flying to **Zaragoza** or **Pamplona** adds about $140 to the Madrid or Barcelona fare. North of the range, Air France charges $120 one-way from Paris to **Toulouse** or **Lourdes** (year-round). For airfares to Paris, figure $460 in the low season, $800 in the high season from New York (though Air Pakistan has a particularly low-priced high-

season flight at the time of writing of $575); from Toronto or Montréal, CDN$890/$1190; from Chicago, $500/$1020; and from LA or San Francisco, $600/$1040. Flying from Vancouver to Paris, Canadian Airlines charge around CDN$1460 low season, CDN$2050 high season.

For a **round-the-world ticket** which stops at **Toulouse**, Air France has a $3100 fare which requires at least three stops and has no maximum

---

TOUR OPERATORS IN NORTH AMERICA

Abercrombie & Kent, 1520 Kensington Rd, Oak Brook, IL (☎1-800/323-7308). Hiking in the Pyrenees.

Butterfield & Robinson, 70 Bond St, Toronto, ON M5B 1X3 (☎1-800/678-1147). Hiking in the French Pyrenees.

Camino Tours, 7044 18th Avenue NE, Seattle, Washington, 98115 (☎1-800/938-9311). Hiking and biking in the Pyrenees.

Himalayan Travel, 110 Prospect St, Stamford, CT 06901 (☎1-800/225-2380). Hiking in the Pyrenees.

La Corsa Tours, Lacorsa@lacorsa.com (☎1-800/522-6772). Customized biking tours in the Pyrenees.

Mountain Travel/Sobek, 6420 Fairmount Ave, El Cerrito, CA 94530 (☎1-800/227-2384). Hiking in the Basque Pyrenees.

Saranjan Tours, 12865 North East 85th Street #102, Kirkland WA 98033 (☎1-800/858-9594). Walking and hiking tours in the Pyrenees.

Wilderness Travel, 801 Allston Way, Berkeley, CA 94710 (☎1-800/368-2794). Hiking in the Pyrenees.

number of stops. The ticket also requires movement in a continual global direction with no backtracking.

PACKAGE TOURS

Package tours may not sound like your kind of travel, but don't dismiss the idea out of hand. If you really want to get up into the Pyrenees, you might find it worthwhile to have a company make the arrangements for you – especially if your time is limited. A package trip can also be great for your peace of mind, if only to ensure a worry-free first week while you're finding your feet on a longer tour.

That said, not many American companies go to the Pyrenees. Most of those that do specialize in **hiking** (backpacking) trips, which cost $500–1000 a week due to all the logistics involved.

RAIL PASSES

A **Eurail Pass** is not likely to pay for itself if you're planning to stick to the Pyrenees. The pass, which must be purchased before arrival in Europe, allows unlimited free train travel in Spain, France and fifteen other countries. The **Eurail Youthpass** (for under-26s) costs $578 for one month or $768 for two; if you're 26 or over you'll have to buy a first-class pass, available in 15-day ($498), 21-day ($648), one-month ($798), two-month ($1098) and three-month ($1398) increments. You stand a better chance of getting your money's worth out of a Eurail **Flexipass**, which is good for a certain number of travel days in a two-month period. This, too, comes in under-26 and first-class versions: 5 days cost $255/348; 10 days, $398/560; and 15 days, $540/740. A further alternative is to attempt to buy an InterRail pass in Europe (see "Getting There From Britain") – most agents don't check residential qualifications, but once you're in Europe it'll be too late to buy a Eurail Pass if you have problems.

North Americans are also eligible to purchase more specific passes valid for travel in France or Spain only (see "Getting Around," pp.27–28 and p.32). All these passes can be reserved through Rail Europe (☎1-800/848-7245) – with a half-dozen branches across North America – or youth-oriented travel agents.

GETTING THERE FROM AUSTRALIA & NEW ZEALAND

There are no direct flights to the Pyrenees from Australia or New Zealand, and you'll have to aim initially for Paris, Barcelona or Madrid. Stopovers mean a journey of around 24 hours' flying time via Asia – not counting time spent waiting for connections – though this is a good way to see places on the way if you're not rushed for time. Air France's services to Paris from Sydney or Auckland include a return "side trip" with the main ticket which can get you to Perpignan or Toulouse for about A$2199–2599 or NZ$2399–2799. The lowest fares to Paris and Madrid are with Garuda via either a transfer or stopover in Denpasar or Jakarta starting at A$1500 /NZ$1899 low season, and JAL via an overnight's stop in either Tokyo or Osaka (included in the fare) from A$1899/NZ$2199.

As destinations in Europe are "common rated" – you pay the same fare whatever your destination – some airlines offer free flight coupons, car rental or accommodation if you arrange these extras with your ticket. Choose carefully, though, as these perks are impossible to alter later. Alternatively, you could buy the cheapest possible flight to anywhere in Europe and make your way

Aeroflot 388 George St, Sydney (☎02/9262 2233). *Twice-weekly flights to Paris via Bangkok and Moscow from Sydney; from Moscow there are also onward connections to Madrid.*

Air France 12 Castlereagh St, Sydney (☎02/9321 1000); 57 Fort St, Auckland (☎09/303 3521). *Daily from Sydney to Paris via Tokyo or Singapore, with onward connections to Madrid, Barcelona, Perpignan and Toulouse.*

British Airways 64 Castlereagh St, Sydney (☎02/9259 7843 or 1800/251 321); Dilworth Building, corner of Queen St and Customs St, Auckland (☎09/356 8690). *Use the free European flight included in the London ticket price to reach Barcelona, Toulouse or Bilbao. Daily to London from Sydney; code share with Qantas to provide a RTW fare.*

Garuda 175 Clarence St, Sydney (☎02/9334 9944 or 1800/800 873); 20 Albert St, Auckland (☎09/366 1855). *Brisbane, Sydney, Perth and Auckland to Paris three times a week and to Madrid twice weekly, via a transfer in Jakarta or Denpasar.*

Japanese Airlines 17 Bligh St, Sydney (☎02/9272 1111); 12/120 Albert St, Auckland (☎09/379 9906). *Flies several times a week from Sydney, Brisbane, Cairns and Auckland to Tokyo*

and then on to Madrid via Amsterdam and to Paris direct; includes an overnight stop in Tokyo or Osaka.

Lauda Air/Lufthansa 11/143 Macquarie St, Sydney (☎02/9251 6155 or 9367 3888); 36 Kitchener St, Auckland (☎09/303 1529). *Several flights a week from Sydney, Brisbane and Melbourne to Vienna with onward connections to destinations in France and Spain; use the free flight coupons (which must be booked with the main ticket and are not alterable) to reach either Spain or France.*

Malaysia Airlines 388 George St, Sydney (☎13 2627); 12/12 Swanson St, Auckland (☎09/373 2741). *Twice weekly, to Madrid via Kuala Lumpur and Istanbul and to Paris via Kuala Lumpur and Munich, from Brisbane, Sydney, Melbourne, Perth and Auckland.*

Qantas 70 Hunter St, Sydney (☎13 1211); 154 Queen St, Auckland (☎09/357 8900 & 0800/808 767). *Three times a week from Auckland via Rome to Madrid; no connection to Paris.*

Thai Airways 75 Pitt St, Sydney (☎13 1960); 22 Fanshawe St, Auckland (☎09/377 3886). *Three flights a week to Paris via Bangkok and to Madrid via Bangkok and Rome, from Sydney, Melbourne, Brisbane, Perth and Auckland.*

to Pyrenean gateway cities by standby flight, train or bus. For extended trips, **"Round the World"** (RTW) flights, valid for up to a year, are a good option – especially from New Zealand, where airlines offer fewer bonuses to fly with them on return tickets. The Qantas/BA "Global Explorer" ticket allows six stopovers anywhere except South America for A$2499/NZ$3089.

Fares are **seasonally adjusted** with high season approximately from mid-May to end-Aug (the European summer) and Dec to mid-Jan, shoulder seasons March to mid-May and Sept, and low season the rest of the year (seasons vary slightly depending on the airline). Tickets purchased direct from the airlines tend to be expensive; **travel agents** offer much better deals and have the latest information on limited specials and stopovers, with the best discounts being through Flight Centres and STA, who can also advise on visa regulations. Students and under-26s are usually able to get at least ten percent off published prices.

Flights are pricier **via North America**, with United Airlines offering the cheapest deal from Australia via LA and either New York, Washington or Chicago, ranging from A$2299–2899. From New Zealand the best deals are with Air New Zealand via LA and Canadian Airlines via Toronto or Vancouver, both around NZ$2299–2999.

RAIL PASSES

If you're planning to visit the Pyrenees as part of a longer European trip, it may be worth buying a **Eurail** pass, which would need to be bought in your home country before you leave. The terms and conditions for Australian and New Zealand travellers are much the same as for Americans and Canadians (see p.13).

The **Eurail Youthpass** (for under-26s) costs A$510 for 15 days, $665 for 21 days, $825 for one month or $1165 for two months. If you're 26 or over you'll have to buy a **first-class pass**, available in 15-day ($730), 21-day ($950), one-month

DISCOUNT AGENTS IN AUSTRALIA AND NEW ZEALAND

Anywhere Travel 345 Anzac Parade, Kingsford, Sydney (☎02/9663 0411).

Brisbane Discount Travel 260 Queen St, Brisbane (☎07/3229 9211).

Budget Travel 16 Fort St, Auckland, plus branches around the city (☎09/366 0061 or 0800/808 040).

Destinations Unlimited 3 Milford Rd, Auckland (☎09/373 4033).

Flight Centres
Australia: 82 Elizabeth St, Sydney, plus branches nationwide (☎13 1600).

New Zealand: 205 Queen St, Auckland (☎09/309 6171), plus branches nationwide.

Northern Gateway 2 Cavenagh St, Darwin (☎08/8941 1394).

STA Travel
Australia: 702 Harris St, Ultimo, Sydney; 256 Flinders St, Melbourne; other offices in state capitals and major universities (nearest branch ☎13 1776, fastfare telesales ☎1800/360 960).

New Zealand: 10 High St, Auckland (☎09/309 0458, fastfare telesales ☎09/366 6673), plus branches in Wellington, Christchurch, Dunedin, Palmerston North, Hamilton and at major universities.

YHA Travel Centre
Australia: 422 Kent St, Sydney (☎02/9261 1111); 205 King St, Melbourne (☎03/9670 9611); 38 Stuart St, Adelaide (☎08/8231 5583); 154 Roma St, Brisbane (☎07/3236 1680); 236 William St, Perth (☎08/9227 5122); 69a Mitchell St, Darwin (☎08/8981 2560); 28 Criterion St, Hobart (☎03/6234 9617).

New Zealand: 36 Customs House, Auckland (☎09/379 4224).

SPECIALIST AGENTS AND OPERATORS

Adventure Specialists 69 Liverpool St, Sydney (☎02/9261 2927). *A good selection of adventure holidays in the Pyrenees.*

Adventure World 73 Walker St, North Sydney (☎02/9956 7766 or 1800/221 931), plus branches in Brisbane and Perth; 101 Great South Rd, Remuera, Auckland (☎09/524 5118). *Agents for a vast array of international adventure travel companies that operate trips to the Pyrenees.*

France Unlimited 16 Goldsmith St, Elwood, Melbourne (☎03/9531 8787). *All French travel arrangements, including cycling tours.*

Peregrine Adventures 258 Lonsdale St, Melbourne (☎03/9663 8611), plus offices in Brisbane, Sydney, Adelaide and Perth. *Guided walking and biking holidays in the Pyrenees.*

Top Deck Adventure 8th Floor, 350 Kent St, Sydney (☎02/9299 8844). *Walking trips in the central Pyrenees.*

Walkabout Gourmet Adventures PO Box 52, Dinner Plain, Melbourne (☎03/5159 5556). *Food- and wine-oriented walking tours in the Pyrenees.*

($1170), two-month ($1665) and three-month ($2050) increments.

The **Eurail Flexipass** is good for a certain number of travel days in a two-month period and also comes in youth/first-class versions: ten days cost $605/$860; and 15 days, $790/$1140. A scaled-down version of the Flexipass, the **Europass** allows travel in France, Germany, Italy, Spain and Switzerland for $295/$440 for five days in two months, on up to $700/$1030 for 15 days

in two months; there's also the option of adding adjacent "associate" countries (Austria, Hungary, Benelux, Portugal and Greece).

Passes are available through CIT, 123 Clarence St, Sydney (☎02/9299 4754; other branches in Melbourne, Brisbane, Adelaide and Perth, but no NZ office); or Thomas Cook Rail Direct (in Australia, ☎1300/361 941; in New Zealand, ☎09/263 7260).

RED TAPE AND VISAS

For EU citizens there is no problem moving around in the Pyrenees, since the range straddles two member nations, and for most other nationals life has been made easier by the relaxation of various tourism restrictions. If you're making a brief excursion across the border in the mountains, it is still advisable to carry a passport or other ID, since hotels and refuges often demand identification – in particular Spain, where non-EU citizens must fill out a registration card at every lodging.

FRANCE

Citizens of **EU countries**, **Canada**, the **USA**, **New Zealand** and **Norway** do not need any visa to enter France, and can stay for up to ninety days. All other passport holders (including Australians and British Travel Document holders) must obtain a visa before arrival in France. Obtaining one from your nearest French consulate is fairly automatic, but check their hours before turning up, and leave plenty of time, since there are often queues (particularly in London during the summer). Australians can obtain a visa on the spot in London.

Three types of visa are currently issued: a transit visa, valid for two months; a short-stay (*court séjour*) visa, valid for ninety days after date of issue and good for multiple entries; and a long-stay visa (*long séjour*), which allows for multiple stays of ninety days over three years, but only issued after examination of individual circumstances.

EU citizens (and other non-visa nationals) who

FRENCH EMBASSIES AND CONSULATES

AUSTRALIA 31 Market St, Sydney, NSW 2000 (☎02/9261 5779); 492 St Kilda Rd, Melbourne, VIC 3001 (☎03/9820 0921).

BRITAIN Consulate General (Visa Section), 21 Cromwell Rd, London SW7 (☎0171/838 2051); 7–11 Randolph Crescent, Edinburgh (☎0131/225 7954).

CANADA 42 Promenade Sussex, Ottawa ONT K1M 2C9 (☎613/789 1795). There are consulates in Montréal, Québec, Toronto and Vancouver.

IRELAND 36 Ailesbury Rd, Dublin 4 (☎01/694 777).

NEW ZEALAND Corner Princes St and Eden Crescent, Auckland (☎09/302 7629).79 9788); 1 Williston St, PO Box 1695, Wellington (☎04/472 0200).

USA Embassy: 4101 Reservoir Rd NW, Washington DC 20007 (☎202/944-6000). Consulates: Park Square Building, Suite 750, 31 St James Ave, Boston MA 02116 (☎617/542 7374); 737 North Michigan Ave, Olympia Centre, Suite 2020, Chicago, IL 60611 (☎312/787 5359); 10990 Wilshire Blvd, Suite 300, Los Angeles CA 90024 (☎310/235 3200); 934 Fifth Ave, New York NY 10021 (☎212/606 3688); 540 Bush St, San Francisco, CA 94108 (☎415/397 4330).

stay longer than three months are officially supposed to apply for a *Carte de Séjour*, for which you'll have to show proof of income at least equal to the minimum wage. However, EU passports are no longer stamped, so there is no evidence of how long you've been in the country. If your non-EU passport is stamped, cross the border – a highly likely event anyway if you're in the Pyrenees – and re-enter for another ninety days legitimately.

SPAIN

Citizens of most **EU countries** (and of Norway and Iceland) need only a valid national identity card to enter Spain for up to ninety days. Since Britain has no identity-card system, however, **British** citizens do have to take a passport. **US**

SPANISH EMBASSIES AND CONSULATES

AUSTRALIA 15 Arkana St,Yarralumla, ACT 2600 (☎02/6273 3555); 4th Floor, 540 Elizabeth St, Melbourne VIC 3000 (☎03/9347 1966); 24th Floor, St Martin Tower, 31 Market St, Sydney, NSW 2000 (☎02/9261 2433).

BRITAIN 20 Draycott Place, London SW3 (☎0171/581 5921); Suite 1a, Brook House, 70 Spring Gardens, Manchester M22 2BQ (☎0161/236 1233).

CANADA 350 Sparks Street, Suite 802, Ottowa, Ontario K1R 7S8 (☎613/237 2193 or 237 219474 Stanley Ave, Ottawa, ONT K1M 1P4 (☎613/747-2252).

IRELAND 17a Merlyn Park, Ballsbridge, Dublin 4 (☎01/691640 or 692597).

NEW ZEALAND 253 Cambridge Terrace (PO BOX 13637), Christchurch (☎03/366 0244).

USA 2700 15th St NW, Washington DC 20009 (☎202/265-0190); 150 East 58th St, New York, NY 10155 (☎212/355-4080); 545 Boylston St #803, Boston, MA 02116 (☎617/536-2506); 180 North Michigan Ave #1500, Chicago, IL 60601 (☎312/782-4588); 1800 Berins Drive #660, Houston, TX 77057 (☎713/783-6200); 5055 Wiltshire Blvd #960, Los Angeles, CA 90036 (☎213/938-0158); 2102 World Trade 2 Canal St, New Orleans, LA 70130 (☎504/525-4951); 2080 Jefferson St, San Francisco, CA 94123 (☎415/922-2995Center, 2 Canal St, New Orleans, LA 70130 (☎504/525-7920); 1405 Sutter St, San Francisco, CA 94109 (☎415/922-2995).

citizens require a passport but no visa and can stay for up to six months; **other European, Canadian and New Zealand** citizens also only require a passport and can stay for up to ninety days. **Australians** need to obtain a visa in advance of travelling, which entitles them to stays of ninety days. Under the Schengen agreement a visa valid for France will also do for Spain under the same ninety-day period, and vice versa.

To stay longer, EU nationals (and citizens of Norway and Iceland) can apply for a *permiso de residencia* (residence permit) once in Spain. You'll either have to produce proof that you have sufficient funds (officially 5000ptas a day) to be able to support yourself without working – easiest done by keeping bank exchange forms every time you change money – or you'll have to have a contract of employment (*contrato de trabajo*) or become self-employed (for example as a teacher), which involves registering at the tax office. Other nationalities will either need to get a special visa from a Spanish consulate before departure (see below for addresses), or can apply for one ninety-day extension, showing proof of funds.

CUSTOMS LIMITS

With the advent of the Single European Market, you can take most articles across EU borders as long as you have paid tax on them in an EU country and they are for personal consumption. Customs will only get suspicious if it's obvious that you're going to try and resell things. Limits still apply to drink and tobacco bought in duty-free shops: 200 cigarettes, 250gm of tobacco or 50 cigars; one litre of spirits, two litres of fortified wine or two litres of sparkling wine; two litres of table wine; 50gm of perfume and 250ml of toilet water.

Residents of the USA can bring home up to $400 worth of overseas goods duty-free, including a litre of alcohol or wine, 200 cigarettes and 100 cigars. If you carry back between $400 and $1000 worth of stuff you'll have to go through the red lane and pay ten percent of the value in duty. **Canadians** are exempt from paying duty on up to $300 worth of goods after a seven-day absence from the country. These may include up to 1.14 litres of spirits or wine, 24 x 355ml bottles of beer and 200 cigarettes.

Travellers returning to **Australia** can bring in $400 worth of "gifts" duty-free (for under-18s this is reduced to $200), not including clothing, plus 250 cigarettes or 250gm tobacco, and one bottle of any alcohol. **New Zealand** permits $700 worth of "gifts", plus six 750ml bottles of wine or beer (4.5 litres total), 1.12 litres of spirits, 200 cigarettes or 250gm tobacco or 50 cigars, or a mixture of these not exceeding 250gm. In both countries, artefacts containing wood or other plant material, fresh produce and cordless phones are prohibited.

COSTS, MONEY AND BANKS

Prices in the Pyrenees don't differ greatly from those in towns and cities away from the mountains. If you do spend less than you budget for on a Pyrenean holiday, it will be because there aren't a great deal of ways to go financially wild once you're off the beaten track.

There are a couple of things to bear in mind before you go if you're really trying to keep costs down. Transport is likely to be a major cost in both countries, but with the limited rail network in the mountains, any rail pass is unlikely to pay for itself unless you travel in the flatlands as well. However, if you're entitled to one, be sure to carry an ISIC (International Student Identity Card) – it will get you free or reduced entry to many museums and sites as well as occasional other discounts; a FIYTO youth card (available to anyone under 26) is almost as good. As always, if you're **travelling alone** you'll end up spending much more than you would in a group of two or more – sharing rooms saves greatly.

FRANCE

Because of the relatively low cost of accommodation and eating out, at least by northern European standards, France is not an outrageously expensive place to visit. **On average**, by staying at a hostel or refuge, or camping, and being strong-willed about denying yourself cups of coffee and culture, you could just about survive on 250F (£25/US$41), including an inexpensive restaurant meal. For a more comfortable existence, including

hotel room and restaurant or café stops, you need to allow about 350–400F (£35–40/$56–64) per person per day; while if you were planning to stay in fancier lodgings, and eat and drink to your heart's content, 550F (£55/$88) per day wouldn't be an unreasonable estimate.

Two or more people will probably find that sharing **hotel accommodation** can occasionally be as cheap as staying at hostels or at a *gîte d'é-tape*, though a sensible average estimate for a double room would be around 170F (£17/$27). There are large numbers of good **restaurants** with three- or even four-course menus for 80–110F (£8–11/$13–17.50). **Picnic food**, obviously, is much less costly, while more sophisticated, but reasonably priced, **take-away** meals – salads and ready-to-reheat dishes – can be put together at *charcuteries* (delis) and the equivalent counters of many supermarkets. Note that **museums, theme parks and monuments**, at 25–50F entrance, can eat into a daily budget.

Transport will inevitably be a large item of expenditure if you're not on a walking tour. The standard tariff for **trains** is about 70 centimes per kilometre (sample fare: Bayonne to Perpignan, over 500km, 330F). **Buses** are less expensive though prices vary enormously from one operator to another. Rental **bikes** cost about 70F per day.

CURRENCY AND THE EXCHANGE RATE

French currency is the **franc**, abbreviated as F or sometimes FF. It is divided into 100 centimes and comes in notes of 500, 200, 100, 50 and 20F, and coins of 10, 5, 2 and 1F, and 50, 20, 10 and 5 centimes. The current **exchange rate** for the franc is about 10F to the pound sterling, just over 6F to the US dollar – as weak as it's been for years against these currencies, and likely to firm up a bit in the future.

TRAVELLERS' CHEQUES AND EUROCHEQUES

Travellers' cheques are one of the safest ways of carrying your money, available from almost any major bank (whether you have an account there or not), usually for a service charge of one to two percent of the amount purchased. Your own bank may offer cheques free of charge provided you meet certain conditions – it's always worth asking first. Thomas Cook, Visa and American Express are the most widely recognized brands in France. Obtaining **French franc travellers' cheques** at the outset could be worthwhile: they can often be used as cash, and French banks are supposed to give you the face value of the cheques when you change them, so commission is only paid on purchase.

Europeans can also use **Eurocheques**, backed up by a guarantee card for which there is a small annual fee. Charges work out roughly similar to those for travellers' cheques, but you write them for the exact amount you wish and it usually takes three to four weeks for the money to be debited from your account. However, no French bank counter currently accepts them, so they can only be used for paying shop and restaurant bills in the same way as an ordinary cheque at home. You can, however, still use the guarantee card in many ATMs, provided you know the PIN number. Also worth considering are post office **International Giro Cheques**, which work like ordinary bank cheques except that you can cash them at post offices, which are more common and have longer opening hours than banks.

CREDIT/DEBIT CARDS

Credit/debit cards are widely accepted; it's always worth asking beforehand, however, in smaller hotels and restaurants. Transactions are debited with immediate effect, the waiter or desk clerk running your card through an on-line swipe reader without use of the PIN number. Visa/Barclaycard – known as the *Carte Bleue* in France – is almost universally recognized; American Express and Mastercard – sometimes called Eurocard – rank considerably lower, with only Crédit Agricole and the Crédit Mutuel providing facilities for the latter. Cash advances on credit cards can be obtained at most bank counters, but with a PIN number you can take advantage of the numerous electronic cash-dispensing machines dotted across the Pyrenean foothills. Many of these – in particular autotellers attached to post offices (*La Poste*) – also accept debit cards of the Cirrus and/or Plus systems, but the machines have been known to eat incompatible or overdrawn cards. **Lost or stolen cards** should be reported on one of the following hotlines: *Carte Bleue* (Visa) ☎01.42.77.11.90; American Express ☎01.47.77.72.00; Mastercard (Eurocard) ☎01.45.67.84.84.

CHANGING MONEY

Standard **banking hours** are Monday to Friday 9am–4 or 5pm, many closing at midday (noon–2pm or 12.30–2.30pm). A few are open Saturday 9am–noon, but all close on Sundays and holidays. **Rates of exchange** and **commissions** vary from bank to bank. The Crédit Mutuel usually offers the best rates and takes the least commission; it also keeps Saturday-morning hours.

There are **money-exchange counters** at the train stations of all big cities, and usually a few in the town centre as well. However, their rates tend to be poor and the commission high, so it would be a sensible precaution to buy some French francs before arriving in France.

SPAIN

Although people still think of Spain as a budget destination, hotel prices have increased considerably since the late 1980s, and in towns especially, you can expect to spend easily as much as you would at home, if not more. However, there are still few places in Europe where you'll get a better deal on the cost of simple meals and drink, and sharp devaluations of the peseta in recent years have cushioned the impact of rising prices – for outsiders anyway.

On average, if you're prepared to buy your own picnic lunch, stay in inexpensive *pensiones* and hotels, and stick to local restaurants and bars, you could get by on £20–25/US$32–40 a day. If you intend to upgrade your accommodation, experience town nightlife and eat fancier meals then you'll need more like £40/$64 a day. On £50–60/$80–96 a day and upwards you'll only be limited by your energy reserves – though of course if you're planning to stay in four- and five-star hotels, or Spain's magnificent *paradores*, this figure won't even cover your room.

Room prices vary considerably according to season, but in the Pyrenees you'll find little below 1800ptas (£7/$11) single, 3200ptas (£13/$20.50) double – 2400ptas single (£9.50/$15), 4500ptas double (£18/$29) might be a more realistic average. Campsites start at around 400ptas (£1.50/$2.50) a night per person (sometimes 600ptas in some of the major resorts), plus a similar charge for a tent.

The cost of **eating** can vary wildly, but in most Pyrenean towns there'll be restaurants offering a basic three-course meal for somewhere between 1000 and 1800ptas (£4–7/$6.50–11). As often as not, though, you'll end up wandering from one bar to the next sampling *tapas* without getting round to a real sit-down meal – though this is rarely any cheaper. Drink, and wine in particular, costs ridiculously little: £3/$5 will see you through a night's very substantial intake of the local vintage.

Long-distance **transport**, if used extensively, may prove a major expense. Although per-kilometre prices compare well with the rest of Europe, Spain is a very large country. Even rural Pyrenean journeys between nearby places tend to be long because of the tortuous routings. Urban transport almost always operates on a flat fare of 150–250ptas.

All of the above, inevitably, are affected by **where you are and when**. The big towns and tourist resorts are invariably more expensive than remoter areas, and certain regions tend also to have higher prices – notably the industrialized lowlands of Euskadi, Catalunya and Aragón. Prices are hiked up, too, to take advantage of special events. Despite official controls, you'd be lucky to find a room in Pamplona for the running of the bulls at less than double the usual rate.

One thing to look out for on prices generally is the addition of sales tax – **IVA** – which may come as an unexpected extra when you pay the bill for food or accommodation. The magic words, often in small print at the bottom of the menu, are *IVA (no) incluido* in Castilian or *IVA (no) inclós* in Catalan. Even fairly modest restaurants and hotels often add seven percent IVA to the total after the fact.

CURRENCY AND THE EXCHANGE RATE

The **Spanish currency** is the **peseta**, indicated in this book as "pta(s)". **Coins** come in denominations of 1, 5, 10, 25, 50, 100, 200 and 500 pesetas; **notes** as 1000, 2000, 5000 and 10,000 pesetas. The only oddity is that in a shop when paying for something, you'll often be asked for a *duro* (5ptas) or *veinte duros* (100ptas). Older-style coins, which will not work in pay phones, have pretty much been withdrawn from circulation.

The **exchange rate** for the Spanish peseta is currently around 250 to the pound sterling, 160 to the US dollar. You can take in as much money as you want (in any form), although amounts over a million pesetas must be declared, and you can only take up to 500,000 pesetas out unless you can prove that you brought more with you in the first place. Not, perhaps, a major holiday worry.

CHEQUES AND CREDIT/DEBIT CARDS

In Spain, too, the easiest way for non-European nationals to carry funds is in **travellers' cheques**

(see "France" section above), though you should watch out for occasionally outrageous commissions; 500–600ptas per transaction isn't unusual. If you have an ordinary British bank account (or virtually any European one), you may prefer to use **Eurocheques** with a Eurocheque card in many banks; you can also write out cheques in pesetas in shops and hotels. In addition, most Eurocheque cards, many Visa and Mastercard (Access) cards, and any electronic debit cards that are part of the Cirrus or Plus systems, can be used for **withdrawing cash** from the numerous ATMs in the Pyrenean foothills and resorts. Check with your bank to find out about these arrangements, which usually carry a modest surcharge of up to two percent – as in France, the system is highly sophisticated and will give instructions in a variety of languages.

Leading **credit cards** are also recognized by merchants: American Express, and Visa, which has an arrangement with the Banco Bilbao Vizcaya, are the most useful; Mastercard is less widely accepted.

CHANGING MONEY

Spanish **bancos** (banks) and **cajas de ahorro** (savings banks) have branches in all but the smallest towns, and many of them are prepared to change travellers' cheques (albeit often with reluctance for certain brands). The Banco Central Hispano and Banco Bilbao Vizcaya are two of the most efficient and widespread; elsewhere you may have to queue up at two or three windows, a twenty-to-thirty-minute process. Both these banks handle Eurocheques, change most brands of travellers' cheques, and give cash advances on credit cards; commissions at the Banco Central Hispano are generally the lowest around.

Banking hours are Mon–Fri 9am–2pm, Sat 9am–1pm (except from June to Sept when banks close on Sat). Outside these times, it's usually possible to change cash at larger hotels (generally bad rates, low commission) or with travel agents, who may initially grumble but will eventually concede a rate with the commission built in – useful for small amounts in a hurry.

In tourist areas you'll also find specialist **casas de cambio**, with more convenient hours (though the rates vary), and most branches of El Corte Inglés, a major department store found throughout Spain, have efficient exchange facilities open throughout store hours and offering competitive rates and generally a much lower commission than the banks (though they're worse for cash).

INSURANCE

Some form of travel insurance is highly recommended. Besides covering medical
emergencies and the cost of any drugs prescribed by pharmacies (see over), policies
also cover loss or theft of luggage, tickets,
money and other property. Note that claims
for theft can only be dealt with if a report is
made to the local police within 24 hours and
a copy of the report sent with the claim. Also
very few insurers will arrange on-the-spot
payments in the event of a major expense or
loss; you will usually be reimbursed only
after going home.

Bank and credit cards (particularly American Express) often have certain levels of medical
or other insurance included, especially if you use
them to pay for your trip. It can be quite comprehensive, anticipating anything from lost or stolen
baggage and missed connections to charter companies going bankrupt; however, certain policies
only cover medical costs.

BRITISH AND IRISH COVER

If you have a good "all risks" **home insurance
policy** it may well cover your possessions
against loss or theft even when overseas, or you
can extend cover through your household contents insurer. Many **private medical schemes**
also cover you when abroad – make sure you
know the procedure and the helpline number.

In Britain and Ireland, dedicated **travel insurance schemes** (standard cover from around £19
a month for Europe) are sold by almost every trav-

el agent or bank, and by specialist insurance companies. Cover varies, but a standard policy will
cover the cost of cancellation of flights, medical
expenses, travel delay, accident, missed departures, lost baggage, lost passport, personal liability and legal expenses. Good-value policies are
issued by Campus Travel or STA (see pp.4–5 for
addresses), Columbus Travel Insurance (17
Devonshire Square, London EC2M 4SQ; ☎0171/
375 0011), Worldwide (Elm Lane, Tonbridge, Kent
TN10 3XS; ☎01732/773366), and Endsleigh Insurance (97–107 Southampton Row, London WC1B
4AG; ☎0171/436 4451).

NORTH AMERICAN COVER

In the US and Canada, insurance tends to be
much more expensive, and may offer medical
cover only. Before buying a policy, check that
you're not already covered by existing insurance
plans. **Canadians** are usually covered by their
provincial health plans. Holders of **ISIC cards**
and some other student/teacher/youth cards are
entitled to $3000 worth of accident coverage and
sixty days ($100 per diem) of hospital in-patient
benefits for the period during which the card is
valid. **Students** will often find that their student
health coverage extends during the vacations
and for one term beyond the date of last enrol-
ment. **Homeowners' or renters' insurance**
often covers theft or loss of documents, money
and valuables while overseas, though conditions
and maximum amounts vary from company to
company.

After exhausting the possibilities above you
might you want to contact a specialist **travel
insurance** company; your travel agent can usually recommend one. Travel insurance offerings are
quite comprehensive, anticipating everything
from charter companies going bankrupt to
delayed or lost baggage, by way of sundry illnesses and accidents.

The best **premiums** are usually to be had
through student/youth travel agencies – ISIS policies (sold by STA Travel, see p.11), for example,
cost $48–69 for fifteen days (depending on level
of coverage), $80–105 for a month, $149–207 for
two months, $510–700 for a year. Other insurance
companies worth trying include Access America
(☎1-800/284-8300), Carefree Travel Insurance

(☎1-800/323-3149), Desjardins Travel Insurance (Canada only; ☎1-800/463-7830), Travel Guard (☎1-800/826-1300) and Travel Insurance Services (☎1-800/937-1387).

AUSTRALASIAN COVER

In Australia and New Zealand, travel insurance is available from most **travel agents** (see p.15) or direct from **insurance companies**, for periods ranging from a few days to a year or even longer.

Insurance companies worth contacting direct include Cover More, 9/32 Walker St, North Sydney (☎02/9202 8000 & 1800/251 881) and Ready Plan, 141 Walker St, Dandenong, Melbourne (☎03/9791 5077 & 1800/337 462) and 10/63 Albert St, Auckland (☎09/379 3208). Most policies are similar in **premium** and coverage; a typical policy for Europe will cost A$100/NZ$110 for two weeks, A$170/NZ$190 for one month, A$250/NZ$275 for two months.

EXTRA COVER

You should bear in mind that ordinary travel insurance policies are rarely valid for **sporting activities** such as skiing, trekking, climbing or horse-riding and certainly not for *parapente*, canyoning or caving. For these two latter categories you'll have to take out **extra cover** such as that supplied by the French Carte Neige, which can be obtained in sports centres, equipment shops and clubs. It's inexpensive, valid Europe-wide and lasts a year, but basically meets just the cost of recovery, offering only limited medical expenses and no property protection. Members of diving clubs or other comparable organizations might be covered by their ordinary annual policy. In Britain, Snowcard Insurance Services (☎01327/262 805) specializes in mountaineering and activity holiday travel insurance.

Otherwise inform your travel insurer of your intentions, who will then attach a "dangerous sports" rider to the basic policy and then charge you an extra premium – probably thirty to fifty percent more. If you are taking a package holiday that might involve participating in some hazardous recreation, be sure to inform the travel agent at the time of booking, so that enquiries can be made on the spot.

HEALTH MATTERS

Citizens of all EU countries are entitled to take advantage of each other's health services under the same terms as the residents of the country, provided they have the correct documentation. So British or Irish citizens in France and Spain may expect to receive medical attention on the same terms as a French or Spanish national, if they have form E111 with them. To apply for this, you must first fill in form SA30, which you get over the counter at any main post office; they will then issue you an E111.

Only citizens of EU member states are covered under the scheme; anyone else is strongly advised to take out travel insurance with medical cover (see above), and supplementary health insurance for EC nationals is highly advisable in any case.

FRANCE

General health care in France is of the highest standard, and no vaccinations are required when entering the country. A peculiarity of the French social security system is that every hospital visit, doctor's consultation and prescribed medicine incurs a charge (though not up front in an emergency). While all employed French people are entitled to a refund of 75–80 percent of medical expenses, this can still leave a hefty shortfall, especially after a stay in hospital (accident victims even have to pay for the ambulance that takes them there).

PHARMACIES, DOCTORS AND HOSPITALS

To find a **doctor** stop at any *pharmacie* and ask for an address. Consultation fees for a visit should be between 100 and 150F and in any case you'll be given a *Feuille de Soins* (Statement of Treatment) for later documentation of private or social insurance claims. Prescriptions should be taken to a *pharmacie* which is also equipped – and obliged – to give first aid (for a fee). For minor illnesses pharmacists will dispense free advice and a wide range of medication. The medicines you buy will have little stickers (*vignettes*) attached to them, which you must remove and stick to your *Feuille de Soins* together with the prescription itself. In serious **emergencies** in France you will always be admitted to the **local hospital** (*Centre Hospitalier*) – a fire-brigade ambulance can be summoned by dialling ☎18. Another useful phone number is ☎17, the police/rescue service.

Since complicated bureaucracy is involved in getting a refund through your social security department back home, it's better to have ordinary travel insurance, which usually allows almost full reimbursement, and covers the cost of repatriation. If you're travelling in your own vehicle, you may want to have breakdown cover which includes return of the vehicle if you're incapacitated.

SPAIN

No inoculations are required for Spain; the worst that's likely to happen to you is that you might fall victim to an upset stomach. Wash fruit and avoid *tapas* that look like they were cooked last week.

PHARMACIES, DOCTORS AND HOSPITALS

For minor complaints, it's easiest to go to a **farmacia** – they're listed in the phone book in major towns and you'll also find one in virtually every village. Pharmacists are highly trained, willing to give advice (often in English) and able to dispense many drugs which would be available only on prescription in most other countries. They keep usual shop hours (9am–1pm & 4–8pm), but some open late and at weekends while a rota system keeps at least one open 24 hours. The rota is displayed in the window of every pharmacy, or check in one of the local newspapers under *Farmacias de guardia*.

In more serious cases you can get the address of an English-speaking doctor from the nearest relevant consulate, or with luck from a *farmacia*, the local police or tourist office. In **emergencies** dial ☎091 for the *Servicios de Urgencia*, or look up the *Cruz Roja Española* (Red Cross) which runs a national ambulance service. Treatment at public hospitals for ECU citizens in possession of form E111 is free; otherwise you'll be charged at private hospital rates, which can be 14,000ptas per visit. Accordingly, it's essential to have some kind of comprehensive travel insurance.

INFORMATION AND MAPS

The national tourist organizations of both France and Spain have numerous overseas outlets, well stocked with literature, and are also conspicuously represented in towns at home. Both sides of the Pyrenean range itself are also meticulously mapped, though so far French products often have a slight edge over Spanish in terms of quality.

FRENCH INFORMATION OFFICES

Branches of the **French Government Tourist Office** overseas give away large quantities of maps and glossy brochures for every region of France, including useful lists of hotels and campsites and festival programmes.

In the French Pyrenees you'll find a tourist information centre – **Office du Tourisme**, as it's usually called – in practically every town and many villages. From these you can get specific local information – including, most importantly, the **météo** or daily weather report, posted in the window – and you should always ask for the free town plan. Many bureaux also publish hotel and restaurant listings, bus and train timetables and local car and walking itineraries. In mountain regions they are often right next door to local trekking and climbing organizers.

SPANISH INFORMATION OFFICES

The **Spanish National Tourist Office** (SNTO) similarly produces and gives away an impressive variety of maps, pamphlets and special interest leaflets. Visit one of their offices before you leave home and stock up, especially on city plans, as well as province-by-province lists of hotels, *hostales* and campsites. Or tap into their website at *www.here-i.com/spain/*.

In Spain itself you'll find SNTO offices in virtually every major town (addresses are detailed in the guide) and from these you can usually get more specific local information. In many towns, the SNTO office is supplemented by a separately administered provincial or municipal **Turismo** (*Turisme* in Catalan). These vary enormously in quality – those of the Basque country and Catalunya are usually excellent – but while they are generally extremely useful for regional information and local maps, they cannot be relied on to know anything about what goes on outside their patch. Like their French counterparts, they post **weather reports**, often for three days at a time, on their windows.

Spanish tourist office **hours** are usually Mon–Fri 9am–1pm and 3.30–6pm, Sat 9am–1pm; but you can't always rely on the official hours, especially in the more out-of-the-way places, where hours of Mon–Fri 9am–2.30pm are more representative.

FRENCH GOVERNMENT TOURIST OFFICES ABROAD

Australia BNP House, 12 Castlereagh St, Sydney NSW 2000 (☎02/9231 5244, fax 9221 8682).

Britain 178 Piccadilly, London W1V 0AL (☎0891/244 123, fax 0171/493 6594).

Canada 30 St Patrick St, Suite 700, Toronto ONT M5T 3A3 (☎416/593 6423, fax 979 7587); 1981 av McGill College, Suite 700, Montréal, QC H3A 2W9 (☎514/288 4264, fax 845 4868).

Ireland 35 Lower Abbey St, Dublin 1 (☎01/703 4046, fax 874 7324).

USA 444 Madison Ave, 16th Floor, New York, NY 10020 (☎212/838-7800, fax 838-7855); 676 North Michigan Ave, Chicago, IL 60611 (☎312/751-7800, fax 337-6339); 9454 Wilshire Blvd, Suite 715, Beverly Hills, CA 90212 (☎310/271-6665, fax 276-2835).

SNTO OFFICES ABROAD

Australia No SNTO office; the best resource is Spanish Tourism Promotions, 1st Floor, 178 Collins St, Melbourne, VIC (☎03/9650 7377, toll-free ☎1800/817 855).
Britain 23 Manchester Square, London W1M 5AP (☎0891/669920, fax 0171/486 8034).
Canada 2 Bloor St W, 34th Floor, Toronto, ONT M4W 3E2 (☎416/961-3131).

USA 665 Fifth Ave, New York, NY 10022 (☎212/265-8822); 8383 Wilshire Blvd, Suite 960, Beverly Hills, CA 90211 (☎213/658-7188); Water Tower Place, Suite 915 E, 845 N Michigan Ave, Chicago, IL 60611 (☎312/642-1992); 1221 Brickell Ave #1850, Miami, FL 33131 (☎305/358-1992).

PYRENEAN TREKKING MAPS

Maps specifically dedicated to the Pyrenees are a problem if you want to trek through the entire range. A scale of at least 1:50,000 is essential, and the 1:25,000 Série Bleue published by the French **Institut Géographique National** (IGN) would be better for the northern slopes. Apart from the enormous expense of 25-odd sheets at that scale, they're tedious to carry. In principle, it would be better to buy maps as you go, because of the stiff mark-up overseas; in practice, however, you would be wise to buy most maps before arrival, as they're often sold out in their area of use.

A compromise for the GR10/HRP traverse on **the French side** would be the eleven Série Verte 1:50,000 **Cartes de Randonnées** published jointly by the IGN and Randonnées Pyrénéennes, covering the range from coast to coast, with *gîtes d'étape*, refuges and recommended GR and *Tour* routes highlighted (the 1:25,000 series also includes locally marked trails featuring on tourist-board-recommended walks). At about 57F apiece (£8.95 in the UK) though, the complete set of 1:50,000 sheets still represents a substantial investment. For both IGN and Cartes de Randonnées maps, relevant titles are quoted throughout the text. For just the GR10 you could manage with the single-volume book, *Walking the Pyrenees* (see "Books" in *Contexts*), which includes very old, un-updated 1:50,000 maps, but you don't get much surrounding terrain.

The most widely available Spanish productions for the **Spanish side** of the range are the maps of Catalunya-based **Editorial Alpina** – some 1:25,000, some 1:40,000 – covering the most popular walking areas between the Catalan coast and Navarra (relevant titles are quoted throughout the text). The accompanying booklets (in Castilian or Catalan) supply useful information about accommodation, walking routes, winter mountaineering and caves, but the maps themselves don't cover the Basque country and trail tracings are often woefully inaccurate, scarcely changed since the maps appeared in the late 1940s. You should always buy Editorial Alpina titles in Spain: not only are they much cheaper there but you'll want the most current cartography, which improves with painful slowness over time – overseas stocks are often even more out of date. In 1997 their booklet format was changed to 20cm x 13.5cm, the maps made waterproof and detail on the French side of the border (where present) improved.

Where necessary, Alpinas can be supplemented by the full range of **topographical maps** issued by two Spanish government agencies: the Instituto Geográfico Nacional (IGN) and the Servicio Geográfico del Ejército (SGE). They are available at scales of 1:100,000, 1:50,000 and occasionally 1:25,000. Though neither series is up to the standard of French products, the IGN's has recently taken a quantum leap in quality, replacing Castilian with local place names, indicating magnetic declination from true north and including useful regional language vocabularies in the margins. Moreover, a blue-jacketed folding series, analogous to the French Serie Bleue and produced together by IGN and MOPU (the ministry of public works), has recently appeared for many areas at scales of 1:50,000 and occasionally 1:25,000. Many bookshops in Spain, and a few specialist overseas stores, stock these governmental maps, though as with the Editorial Alpina products, you'll find them cheaper on arrival – and less accurate than the French equivalents.

When using a **compass** in the Pyrenees, the magnetic declination from true north is about 3° west.

MAP OUTLETS IN BRITAIN AND IRELAND

Most of the outlets listed here offer a mail order service.

London

Daunt Books, 83 Marylebone High St, W1M 3DE (☎0171/224 2295); 193 Haverstock Hill, NW3 4QL (☎0171/794 4006).

National Map Centre, 22–24 Caxton St, SW1 0QU (☎0171/222 2466).

Stanfords, 12–14 Long Acre, WC2E 9LP (☎0171/836 1321). Other branches in London are located at 52 Grosvenor Gardens, SW1W 0AG (☎0171/730 1314) and 156 Regent St, W1R 5TA (☎0171/434 4744).

The Travel Bookshop, 13–15 Blenheim Crescent, W11 2EE (☎0171/229 5260).

The rest of England and Wales

Austick's City Bookshop, 91 The Headrow, **Leeds** LS1 6OJ (☎0113/243 3099).

Blackwell's Map and Travel Shop, 53 Broad St, **Oxford** OX1 3BQ (☎01865/792792). Also 13–17 Royal Arcade, **Cardiff**, CF1 2PR (☎0122/395036) Blackwell's University Bookshop, Alsop Building, Brownlow Hill, **Liverpool**, L3 5TX (☎0151/709 8146); Blackwell's, 156–160 West St, **Sheffield**, S1 3ST (☎0114/273 8906); 32 Stonegate, **York** YO1 2AP (☎01904/624531).

Call of the Wild, 21 Station St, **Keswick**, Cumbria CA12 5HH (☎01768/771014).

Heffers Map Shop, in Heffer's Stationery Department, 19 Sidney St, **Cambridge**, CB2 3HL (☎01223/568467).

Latitude, 34 The Broadway, Darkes Lane, **Potters Bar**, Herts EN6 2HW (☎01707/663090).

The Map Shop, 30a Belvoir St, **Leicester**, LE1 6QH (☎0116/247 14000).

The Map Shop, 15 High St, **Upton-upon-Severn**, Worcestershire WR8 0HJ (☎01684/593146).

Newcastle Map Centre, 55 Grey St, **Newcastle upon Tyne**, NE1 6EF (☎0191/261 5622).

Waterstone's, 91 Deansgate, **Manchester**, M3 2BW (☎0161/832 1992).

Whiteman's Bookshop, 7 Orange Grove, **Bath**, BA1 1LP (☎0225/464029).

Scotland

Aberdeen Map Shop, 74 Skene St, **Aberdeen**, AB10 1QE (☎01224/637999).

John Smith and Sons, 57–61 St Vincent St, **Glasgow**, G2 5TB (☎0141/221 7472).

James Thin Melven's Bookshop, 29 Union St, **Inverness**, IV1 1QA (☎01463/233500).

Ireland

Easons Bookshop, 40 O'Connell St, **Dublin** 1 (☎01/873 3811).

Fred Hanna's Bookshop, 27–29 Nassau St, **Dublin** 2 (☎01/677 1255).

PYRENEAN ROAD MAPS

In terms of **road maps**, the Spanish-produced Firestone "Pireneos" 1:200,000 map is the only one covering **the entire range**, showing both sides of the border at the same level of detail and even indicating parts of the French GR10 and Spanish GR11. Although two-sided, it's very easy to unfold and use, but available only in Spain (about 700ptas) – look for the blue-fringed red livery. The 1:400,000 "Pireneos/Pyrénées", issued jointly by the IGNs of France and Spain in cooper-

ation with Randonées Pyrénéennes, is a distinct second choice if still available.

For the **French side** only, two one-sided IGN Série Rouge 1:250,000 maps document the entire range: no. 113, "Pyrénées Languedoc Roussillon", and no. 114, "Pyrénées Occidentales". A better French production, and perhaps a good compromise – especially for **cyclists** – between a vague road map and a tall stack of *randonnée* maps, is the IGN 1:100,000 Série Verte. This shows contours and the GR10, covering the whole French side (and some of Spain) in four

Hodges Figgis Bookshop, 56–58 Dawson St, **Dublin** 2 (☎01/677 4754).

Waterstone's, Queens Bldg, 8 Royal Ave, **Belfast**

BT1 1DA (☎01232/247355); 7 Dawson St, **Dublin** 2 (☎01/679 1260); 69 Patrick St, **Cork** (☎021/ 276 522).

MAP OUTLETS IN NORTH AMERICA

USA

Adventurous Traveler Bookstore, PO Box 1468, **Williston**, VT 05495 (☎1-800/282-3963).

Book Passage, 51 Tamal Vista Blvd, **Corte Madera**, CA 94925 (☎415/927-0960).

Map Link, 30 S La Patera Lane, Unit #5, **Santa Barbara**, CA 93117 (☎805/692-6777).

The Map Store Inc., 1636 1st St, **Washington DC** 20006 (☎202/628 2608).

Phileas Fogg's Books & Maps, #87 Stanford Shopping Center, **Palo Alto**, CA 94304 (☎1-800/533-FOGG).

Rand McNally, 444 N Michigan Ave, **Chicago**, IL 60611 (☎312/321-1751); 150 E 52nd St, **New York**, NY 10022 (☎212/758-7488); 595 Market

St, **San Francisco**, CA 94105 (☎415/777-3131); call ☎1-800/333-0136 (ext 2111) for other locations, or for maps by mail order.

Sierra Club Bookstore, 6014 College Ave, **Oakland**, CA 94618 (☎510/658-7470).

Travel Books & Language Center, 4931 Cordell Ave, **Bethesda**, MD 20814 (☎1-800/220-2665).

Traveler's Bookstore, 22 W 52nd St, **New York**, NY 10019 (☎212/664-0995).

Canada

Open Air Books and Maps, 25 Toronto St, **Toronto**, ON M5R 2C1 (☎416/363-0719).

World Wide Books and Maps, 736 Granville St, **Vancouver**, BC V6Z 1E4 (☎604/687-3320).

MAP OUTLETS IN AUSTRALASIA

Australia

Bowyangs, 372 Little Bourke St, **Melbourne** (☎03/9670 4383).

The Map Shop, 16a Peel St, **Adelaide** (☎08/8231 2033)

Perth Map Centre, 891 Hay St, **Perth** (☎08/9322 5733).

Travel Bookshop, 20 Bridge St, **Sydney** (☎02/9241 3554).

Worldwide Maps and Guides, 187 George St, **Brisbane** (☎07/3221 4330).

New Zealand

Specialty Maps, 58 Albert St , **Auckland** (☎09/307 2217).

one-sided sheets: no. 69 "Pau Bayonne", no. 70 "Tarbes Bagnères-de-Luchon", no. 71 "Saint-Gaudens Andorre" and no. 72 "Perpignan Béziers".

A useful **free map** for drivers, obtainable from filling stations and traffic information kiosks in France, is the *Bison Futé* (Crafty Buffalo) map, showing alternative secondary routes to the congested main highways; it's keyed to special green *Bison Futé* road signs.

Road maps for the **Spanish side** of the range are best bought in bookshops (*librerías*), street

kiosks or service stations in Spain itself. Among the best are those published by Editorial Almax, which also produces reliable indexed **street plans** for the main cities. A passably accurate second choice, especially if you're shopping before arrival – though almost impossible to use effectively in a car – is the double-sided 1:300,000 "Costa Brava/Pyrenees/Basque Country, Aragón, Navarra, Catalonia, Andorra" map published by Euro-Map and distributed through GeoCenter International in both the UK and the US.

GETTING AROUND

If you're not driving a car, cycling or walking, getting around in the Pyrenees takes a bit of organization and attention to detail. There are surprisingly good bus services (and sometimes trains) along the main valley floors and between major centres, but timings are often geared to school and officework hours. Approximate journey times and frequencies can be found in the "Travel Details" at the end of each chapter, and local peculiarities are also pointed out in the text of the guide.

If you intend to **hitch** in the Pyrenees, it's always safest to try and arrange a lift in advance by asking at your hotel or refuge. However, this guide **does not recommend hitching** as a general means of transport, especially for lone women travellers.

FRANCE

France has the most extensive **rail network** in western Europe, although rural services have been severely cut back in recent years. Trains are an excellent way of travelling parallel to the line of the mountains and along the coasts, but the lines tend to give out as the gradients increase and the populations dwindle. However, where the train stops an **SNCF** (the French rail company) **bus** often continues the route. The private bus services are confusing, uncoordinated and often poorly publicized – where possible, it is much simpler to use the SNCF. If you have the time and the vehicles, **driving** or **cycling** are both excellent ways of seeing the Pyrenean foothills.

TRAINS

SNCF **trains** are by and large clean, fast and frequent, and their staff, with a few exceptions, both courteous and helpful. All but the smallest stations have an information desk and *consignes automatiques* – coin-operated lockers big enough to take a rucksack. Many rent out bicycles, sometimes of rather doubtful reliability. **Fares** are reasonable, at an average – off peak – of about 70 centimes per kilometre. The ultra-fast TGVs (*Trains à Grande Vitesse*) require a supplement at peak times and compulsory reservation costing 20F and up. Slower trains, stopping at most stations, are often marked with a bicycle symbol in the timetable – on these you can travel with a bike as free accompanied luggage (see below for details).

Regional **rail maps** and complete **timetables** are on sale at tobacconist shops. Leaflet time tables for a particular line are available free at stations. *Autocar* at the top of a column means it's an SNCF bus service, on which train tickets and passes are valid.

All **tickets** – though not passes – must be **date-stamped** in the orange machines at station platform entrances or foyers. It is an offence if you don't "*compostez votre billet*", and people caught riding without tickets are liable to a 150-franc spot fine. Train journeys may be broken any time, anywhere, but after a break of 24 hours you must date-stamp your ticket again upon resuming your journey.

While **InterRail** (p.7) and **EurRail** (p.14) **passes** and **BIJ** tickets are valid on all trains, and worth investigating before you leave home, the SNCF itself offers a whole range of **discount fares** on *Période Bleue* (Blue Period) days – in effect, most of the year. A leaflet showing the blue, white (smaller discount) and red (peak) periods is given out at train stations.

One of the most valuable passes is the **Euro Domino**, which for use in France has to be purchased outside the country. It offers unlimited rail travel on any three, five or ten days in a month; the only extra charges are for TGV reservations and any sleeping accommodation. Adult rates in second class are £105 for three days, £135 for five and £205 for ten; under-26s pay respectively, £85, £110 and £175. The pass also entitles you to a reduction on Eurostar (ask for details at time of booking). Note, however, that you probably won't get full value out of it unless you're planning to reach the Pyrenees by train from the UK, as well as travelling a few days along the foothills.

Other SNCF discount cards are available only in France, from travel agents or mainline stations. **Couples** can have a free Carte Couple, entitling one of them to a half-fare if they travel together and start their journey on a blue-period day. You do, however, have to provide proof of marriage or cohabitation, plus photos of each person. If you're **over 60**, you can get the Carte Vermeille in two versions: the Quatre Temps, which costs 152F and covers four journeys, and the Plein Temps, which costs 288F for unlimited travel. Both are valid for one year and offer up to fifty percent off tickets on TGVs, subject to space, or other journeys starting in blue or white periods. The same percentage reductions are available for **under-26s** with a Carissimo pass, which costs around 200F for four journeys, 315F for eight, and is valid for a year. This pass also entitles the card-holder to secure the same reductions for up to three travelling companions aged between 12 and 25. **Families** of up to five can use a Carte Kiwi for which one child under 16 is the holder, securing the above-cited discounts for the rest of the family. The card costs 300F for four journeys, or 470F for unlimited travel.

BUSES

With the exception of SNCF services, **buses** play a generally minor role, even in the Pyrenees. The most frustrating thing about them is that they rarely serve the regions outside the SNCF network – which is precisely where you need them. Where they do exist (mostly in the foothills) timetables are constructed to suit working, school and market hours – it will be a real stroke of luck if one is going where and when you want. Buses are, generally speaking, cheaper and slower than trains.

Larger towns usually have a **gare routière** (bus station), often next to the train station. However, this is not always the case, as the private bus companies have difficulty coordinating their efforts and tend to leave from an array of different points. Their locations, as well as schedule booklets, are often available from tourist offices, or at the very least there will be a timetable posted at the stop.

DRIVING AND VEHICLE RENTAL

Taking a car gives you enormous advantages of access to remote areas. If you're camping or trekking, the ability to carry equipment can make driving an attractive proposition, but you will only save money – especially with a rented vehicle – if there are several of you to share the costs. Breakdown liability and insulation from the feel of the country and its people are other minuses.

Car rental costs upwards of £180/$290 per week; you need to be at least 21 (or 23, depending on which category of car you want to rent). Most travel agents can arrange Fly-Drive packages, which often let you pick the car up on arrival at one airport and leave it at another at the end of your holiday – though you'll pay an extra fee for this facility. Or contact one of the rental agencies listed p.30 – Holiday Autos usually has particularly good rates.

British, EU and US drivers' licences are valid in France, but an **International Driver's Licence** (available from the AA or RAC in Britain, from the AAA in the US) makes life easier. The vehicle registration document and the insurance papers must be carried. If your car is right-hand drive, have your headlight dip adjusted to the right before you go – it's a legal requirement, as is a GB sticker – and, as a courtesy, change or paint them to yellow or stick on black glare deflectors. All the major car manufacturers have service stations in France – get a list of addresses from the manufacturers before you go. If you have an accident or break-in, make a report to the local police (and keep a copy) in order to make an insurance claim.

The main **rule of the road** to remember in France is that you must often give way to traffic coming from your right, even when it is coming from a minor road. This is the law of *priorité à droite*. Because it has been a major cause of accidents, it is being phased out, and so only applies in built-up areas, where you have to be vigilant – watch the roadside for signs with a **yellow diamond** on a white background, which means that you have the right of way; such a diamond with an oblique black line through it means you must yield to right-hand traffic. Signs saying *STOP* or *CEDEZ LE PASSAGE* also mean you must give way. **Roundabouts**, of which there are many in Pyrenean towns, work just like those in Britain, except in the opposite direction: signs always warn you *VOUS N'AVEZ PAS LA PRIORITÉ*.

Fines for driving violations are paid on the spot in cash or French-franc travellers' cheques; if you don't have the funds, you and the vehicle can be locked up immediately. The main N-numbered highways swarm with *gendarmes* (see p.67) manning checkpoints and speed traps; failure to wear a seatbelt (required) nets you a 150F spot fine.

CAR RENTAL AGENCIES ABROAD

UK

Avis	☎0990/900 500	Hertz	☎0990/996 699
Budget	☎0800/181 181	Holiday Autos	☎0990/300 400
Eurodollar	☎0990/365 365	Sun Cars	☎0990/335 588
Europcar/InterRent	☎0345/222 525	Transhire	☎0171/978 1922

Republic of Ireland

Avis ☎	01/874 5844	Hertz	☎01/676747
Budget	☎0800/973159	Holiday Autos	☎01/454 9090
Europcar	☎01/874 5844		

North America

Auto Europe	☎1-800/223-5555	Hertz in US	☎1-800/654-3001;
Avis	☎1-800/331-1084	in Canada	☎1-800/263-0600
Budget	☎1-800/527-0700	National	☎1-800/CAR-RENT
Dollar	☎1-800/421-6868	Thrifty	☎1-800/367-2277

Australia

Avis	☎1800/225 533	Hertz	☎13 3039
Budget	☎13 2727		

New Zealand

Avis	☎09/526 2847	Hertz	☎09/309 0989
Budget	☎09/375 2222		

The minimum fine for speeding is 1300F. **Speed limits** are: 130kph/80mph on toll highways; 110kph/68mph on divided highways; 90kph/56mph on other roads; 50kph/37mph in towns. For all drivers in bad weather, and those with less than two years' experience, the out-of-town limits are 110kph, 100kph and 80kph. For information on **road conditions** call Inter Service Route on ☎02.48.58.33.33 (24hr) or the multilingual Autoroutel (☎08.36.68.09.79).

Motorway – **autoroute** – driving, though fast, is very boring when it's not hair-raising, and the **tolls** are expensive: Paris to Perpignan, for example, costs about 400F. On the whole, it's best not to waste your money on the toll routes, of which there are few in this book anyway; a French N road is the equal of a good UK A road, or a well-maintained state highway in the US. Use the Bison Futé map (see p.27) to avoid the endless traffic jams that build up over the weekends between July 15 and August 15. **Fuel** (*essence*) prices are among the highest in Europe at just over 6F a litre for leaded, just under 6F for unleaded, and about 4F a litre for diesel – though it's

often better value if you buy it at out-of-town supermarkets. Four-star is *super*, lead-free is *sans plomb*, diesel is *gasoil*.

Mopeds and **scooters** are relatively easy to find and although they're not built for any kind of long-distance touring, they're ideal for exploring the environs of foothill towns. Places which rent out bicycles (see below) usually have motorized vehicles, too; expect to pay 160F a day for a 50cc Suzuki, or 200F a day for an 80cc scooter. **Crash helmets** are compulsory only on machines over 125cc, but it's not worth the risk going bare-headed even on a moped.

CYCLING

Bicycles have high status in France. All the car ferries from Britain carry them for nothing; SNCF makes minimal charges; and individual French people respect cyclists. Restaurants and hotels along the way are nearly always obliging about looking after your bike, even to the point of allowing it into your room. Local motorists normally give you plenty of room – it's the lumbering foreign camper van you have to watch out for.

You can normally load your bike straight onto the train at your **ferry port of disembarkation**, but remember that you must first go to the ticket office of the station – don't just try to climb on the train with it. In addition to the ferries, British Airways and Air France both take bikes free within the normal baggage weight allowance. You may have to box them, though, and you should contact the airlines for details.

Lately more and more cyclists are using **mountain bikes** (*VTT* or *Vélo Touts Terrains* in French) for touring holidays. However, it's actually less strenuous, and much quicker, to cycle long distances on asphalt and carry luggage on a traditional touring or racing model.

Most sizeable foothill towns have well-stocked **retail and repair shops**, where parts are normally cheaper than in Britain or the US. However, with a foreign-made bike it's wise to carry spare tyres, as French sizes differ. It's still not that easy, either, to find parts for mountain bikes, with French enthusiasm mainly directed toward highly geared road racers. Inner tubes are not a problem, as they adapt to either tyre size, though make sure you have the right valves.

The **SNCF** runs various schemes for cyclists, all detailed in the free leaflet *Train et Vélo*, available from most train stations. Trains marked with a bicycle in the timetable are usually the only ones on which you can travel with a bike as free accompanied luggage. Otherwise, you have to send your bike as registered luggage (135F parcelled up, 180F unparcelled; 15F for packaging). Although it may well arrive in less time, the SNCF won't guarantee delivery in under five days, and very occasionally bicycles disappear altogether.

At most French train stations, **rental bikes** are also available. At a cost of around 70F per day, you get the use of what is normally an averagely well-maintained Peugeot, and this can be returned to any other station (as long as you specify which when renting). The SNCF does not ask for a deposit, but does require a guarantee such as a credit-card number. You can also rent better bikes from campsites, youth hostels and *gîtes d'étape*, as well as from some tourist offices and a fair number of bike shops (which are more likely to have mountain bikes). Most rental bikes are **not insured**, however, and you will be presented with the bill for its replacement or repair if it's stolen or damaged. Check in advance whether your travel insurance policy covers these contingencies.

SPAIN

Despite their relative remoteness, the Spanish Pyrenees are often as well (or as poorly) served by public transport as the French. However, there are no trains into the settlements of the central Pyrenees; the rail lines consist, on the whole, of a chain of services connecting the towns of the Atlantic and Mediterranean coasts. On shorter or less obvious routes buses tend to be quicker anyway, and will also normally take you closer to your destination; some train stations are several kilometres from the town or village they serve and there's no guarantee of a connecting bus. Car rental may also be worth considering, with costs among the lowest in Europe.

TRAINS

RENFE, the Spanish rail company, operates a horrendously complicated variety of train services. An ordinary train, much the same speed and cost as the bus, will normally be described as an *expreso* or *rapido*. *Semi-directos* and *tranvías* (mostly short-haul trains) are somewhat slower. Intercity expresses, in ascending order of speed and luxury, are known as Electrotren, Talgo or Pendular. The latter two categories, complete with muzak and air-conditioning, cost as much as sixty to seventy percent more than you'd pay for a standard second-class ticket; Electrotren tickets cost forty to fifty percent more.

In recent years many bona fide train services have been phased out in favour of buses operated jointly by RENFE and a private bus company. This is particularly the case when the connection is either indirect or the daily train or trains leave(s) at inconvenient times. On some routes the rail buses outnumber the conventional departures by a ratio of four to one. Prices are the same as on the trains, and these services usually leave and arrive from the bus stations/stops of the towns concerned.

Tickets can be bought at the stations between sixty days and fifteen minutes before the train leaves, from the *venta anticipada* window, or in the final two hours from the *venta inmediata* window. Don't leave it to the last minute, as there are usually long lines. There may also be separate windows for *largo recorrido* (long-distance) trains and *regionales* or *cercanías* (locals). If you board the train without a ticket the conductor may charge you up to double the normal fare; if you don't have the cash, they'll call the police.

Most larger towns have a RENFE office in the centre as well, which will sell **tickets in advance** and dish out schedule pamphlets; you can also buy the *Guía RENFE* timetable there (and at major stations) – useful if you plan to travel extensively by train. You can also buy tickets at travel agents which display the RENFE sign – they have a sophisticated computer system which can also make seat reservations; the cost is the same as at the station. For long journeys, a reserved seat is a worthwhile precaution, as many trains are very crowded.

You can change the departure date of an electronically issued, reserved-seat, long-distance (*largo recorrido*) ticket without penalty up to fifteen minutes before your originally scheduled departure. A full cancellation of the same sort of ticket entails losing fifteen percent of the purchase price if it's done more than 24 hours in advance.

InterRail (see p.7) and **Eurail** (p.14) **passes** and **BIJ** tickets are valid on all RENFE trains (though not on private lines such as the Núria *cremallera*), but there's a supplement payable for travelling on any of the intercity expresses, and sometimes on *expresos* and *rapidos* too. The apparently random nature of these **surcharges** – which seem to depend on the individual train guard – can be a source of considerable irritation. It's better to know what you're letting yourself in for by reserving a seat in advance, something you'll be obliged to do in any case on some trains. For 400ptas (including a 200ptas *suplemento fijo*), you'll get a large, computer-printed ticket which will satisfy even the most unreasonable of guards.

If you're using the trains extensively in Spain, but not outside the country, you might consider a RENFE **Tarjeta Turistica**, accepted on all trains – and currently the only pass available within Spain. You can buy three- to ten-day passes, valid for rail travel on the chosen number of days within a one-month period. Three days' second-class travel costs about 19,000ptas (£76/$122), five days 25,000ptas (£100/$160) and ten days about 48,000ptas (£192/$307). First-class passes are also available, costing around another thirty percent more.

British and Irish residents can buy a **Spanish Freedom** pass before arrival, allowing three, five or ten days' travel in one month within Spain. Youth prices are £69 for three days, £109 for five days, £199 for ten days; over-26 prices are £89,

£139 and £249. North Americans can buy a similar **Spain Flexipass** before arrival, allowing three days' ($145–180) or five days' ($225) unlimited travel in a month, or ten days in two months ($345). A second traveller on the same pass travels half-price.

RENFE also offers a whole range of **discount fares** on its *días azules* ("blue days"), which cover most of the year, with the exception of peak holiday weekends. If you're over 65, travelling with children under 12, in a group of eleven or more, or planning a return to be done on the same or a separate "Blue Day", you can get between twelve and fifty percent off.

BUSES

Buses will probably meet most of your transport needs; most small Pyrenean villages are accessible only by bus, almost always originating in the capital of their province. Service varies in quality, but on the whole the buses are reliable enough, with prices pretty standard at around 600ptas per 100 kilometres. The only real problem is that many towns still have no main bus station, and buses may leave from a variety of places (even if they're heading in the same direction, since some destinations are served by more than one company). Where a new terminal has been built, it's often on the outer fringes of town. As far as possible, departure points are detailed in the text.

One important point to remember is that all public transport, and the bus service especially, is drastically reduced on **Sundays and holidays** – it's best not even to consider travelling to out-of-the-way places on these days. The Castilian words to look out for on timetables are *diario* (daily), *laborables* (workdays, including Saturday) and *domingos y festivos* (Sundays and holidays). On Catalan timetables, the equivalent expressions are *diari* (daily), *feiners* (workdays), *festius* (holidays), *dissabtes* (Saturdays) and *diumenges* (Sundays).

DRIVING

While getting around on public transport is easy enough, you'll obviously have a great deal more freedom with your own car. Major river-valley roads are generally good, the mountain corniches more than serviceable, and traffic, while a little hectic in the cities, is mostly well behaved – though Spain does have one of the highest traffic-accident rates in Europe. But you'll be spending more (even with a full car): fuel prices are only marginally lower than in Britain (almost double North American prices), and in the big cities at least you'll probably want to pay extra for a hotel with parking, or be forced to stay on the outskirts. Also, vehicle crime is rampant – never leave anything of value visible in the car.

Most foreign **driver's licences** are honoured in Spain – including all EU, US and Canadian ones – but an International Driver's Licence (available in Britain from the AA or RAC, in the US from the AAA) is an easy way to set your mind at rest. If you're bringing your own car, you no longer require a **Green Card** from your insurers, or the infamous **bail bond** or extra coverage for legal costs, since a recent EU directive stipulates that insurance contracted in any EU member state is valid in any other state. However, you are automatically entitled only to statutory minimum coverage – that is, third-party insurance. To make sure that you are fully protected, you may have to pay a top-up premium to get comprehensive pan-European coverage.

Away from main roads you yield to vehicles approaching from the right, but rules are not too strictly observed anywhere. **Speed limits** are posted – the maximum on urban roads is 60kph, other roads 90kph, motorways 120kph – and (on the main highways at least) speed traps are common. If you're stopped for any violation, the Spanish police can and usually will levy a stiff **on-the-spot fine** before letting you go on your way, especially since as a foreigner you're unlikely to want, or be able, to appear in court.

Spanish mechanics are most familiar with what the locals drive – small Fords, Renaults, Opels, Citroens, Peugeots, Fiats/Seats – so with a larger or more unusual model you may have some problems should you **break down**.

Fuel currently costs about 125ptas per litre for either Super 98 or *Sin Plomo* (Lead-Free) 95. The latter is hard to come by in villages off the main routes, where limited pump space is dedicated instead to diesel (*gasoleo*). **Credit cards** are accepted at almost all stations on main highways. They are also always taken at the motorway toll gates either side of Girona, though the amount is often trivial; stick the card in the reader and the bar opens. Otherwise you must have exact change for the coin slots, or go to the few attended gates. The **tolls** themselves add up – 1400ptas from the border to points south of Girona – so these motorways are best avoided unless you're in a hurry.

VEHICLE RENTAL

You'll find a choice of **car rental** companies in any major city, with the biggest ones – Hertz, Avis and Europcar – represented at most airports as well as in town centres. You'll need to be 21 (and have been driving for at least a year), and you're looking at from 6000ptas per day for a small car (less by the week, special rates over weekends). **Fly-Drive deals** with Iberia and other operators can be good value if you know in advance that you'll want to rent a car. The big companies all offer schemes, but you'll often get a better deal through someone who deals with local agents. Holiday Autos and Transhire (see box on p.30) are two of the best, substantially undercutting the large companies. If you're going in high season, it's best to try and reserve well in advance.

Renting **motorcycles** (from 3000–4000ptas a day, cheaper by the week) is also possible. You have to be 14 to ride a machine under 75cc, 18 for one over 75cc and production of a driving licence is extremely useful. Crash helmets, incidentally, have been obligatory since 1982, though they're often of the "derby" type usually worn by cyclists in Britain. Note that mopeds and motorcycles are often rented out with insurance that doesn't include theft – always check with the company first. You will generally be asked to produce a driving licence as a deposit.

CYCLING

Taking your own bike can be an inexpensive and flexible way of getting around, and of seeing a great deal of the country that would otherwise pass you by. Do remember, though, that even just the foothills of the Pyrenees are often horrifically steep – and torrid in summer. In the wake of Miguel Indurain's multiple Tour de France triumphs, the Spanish are keen cycle fans – which means that you'll be well received and find reasonable facilities.

There are bike shops in the larger towns and parts can often be found at auto repair shops or garages: look for Michelin signs. Cars tend to toot horns before they pass, which can be alarming at first but is useful once you're used to it. Cycle-touring guides to most of the Pyrenees can be found in good bookshops – written in Spanish, Catalan or Euskera, of course.

Getting your bike there should present few problems. Most airlines are happy to take them as ordinary baggage provided they come within your allowance (though it's sensible to check first; crowded charters may be less obliging). Deflate the tyres to avoid explosions in the unpressurized hold. Spanish trains are also reasonably accessible, though bikes can only go on a train with a guard's van (*furgón*) and must be registered – go to the *Equipajes* or *Paquexpres* desk at the station. If you are not travelling with the bike you can either send it as a package or buy an undated ticket and use the method above. Most *hostales* seem able to find somewhere safe for overnight storage.

ACCOMMODATION

This book details where to find accommodation throughout the Pyrenees, and gives a price range for each establishment, from the most basic rooms to luxury hotels.

FRANCE

During spring or autumn it's possible to turn up in any Pyrenean town and find a room, or a place in a campsite. However, reserving a couple of nights in advance can be reassuring; it saves the effort of trudging around and ensures that you know what you'll be paying. Many hoteliers and campsite managers – and almost all youth hostel managers – will speak some English. In most towns you'll be able to find a double for 130–190F (£13–19/$21–30.50), or a single for 110–160F (£11–16/$18–26).

Problems arise in the mountains mainly during the **February** skiing rush and **between July 15 and August 15**, when the French take their own vacations en masse. The first weekend of August is the busiest time of all. During this period, hotel and hostel accommodation can be hard to come by – particularly in the coastal resorts – and you may find yourself falling back on local tourist offices for help and ideas. With campsites, you can be more relaxed, unless you're touring with a caravan or camper van.

Full **accommodation lists** for each province are available from any French Government Tourist Office (see p.24) or from local tourist offices. If you're travelling in peak season, especially, it is

---

FRANCE: ACCOMMODATION PRICE CODES

All the French accommodation establishments listed in this book have been price-graded according to the following scale. The prices quoted are for the **cheapest available double room** in each hotel **in high season**. Effectively this means that anything in the ② category will be without private bath, though there's usually a washbasin and/or a bidet in the room. In the ③ category you will probably be getting at least a shower, and everything in category ④ and up should have full en-suite facilities, better beds, and perhaps a TV and phone. Remember, though, that many of the budget ② and ③ places will also have more expensive rooms with full en-suite facilities. **Youth hostels**, **mountain refuges** and **gîtes d'étape** are graded as ① since the price per person is about half of the category's upper limit.

① Under 100F	③ 140–200F	⑤ 260–340F
② 100–140F	④ 200–260F	⑥ 340F and upwards

worth getting hold of these, together with a handbook for the *Logis et Auberges de France* – independent hotels, renowned for their consistently good food and reasonably priced rooms (each one is surveyed annually); they're recognizable on the spot by a green-and-yellow logo of a hearth.

HOTELS AND CHAMBRES D'HÔTE

All French **hotels** are graded from zero to three stars. The price more or less corresponds to the number of stars, though the system is a little haphazard, having more to do with ratios of bathrooms-per-guest, and the presence or absence of lobbies, than with genuine quality; renovated and single-star hotels are often very good. At the budget level, what makes a difference in cost is whether a room contains a shower: if it does, the bill will be around 30–50F more. If your room does not have en-suite facilities, an extra charge of about 10F is often made for taking a shower. A **taxe de sejour** of 1–4F per person, according to the star rating, may be added to the final bill.

Breakfast, too, can add 24–35F per person to a bill – though there is no obligation to take it and you will nearly always do better at a café. Officially it is illegal for hotels to insist on your taking **meals** – but they often do, and in busy resorts you may not find a room unless you agree to *demi-pension* (half-board). This often works in your favour, however, as *demi-pension* (often not available for stays of less than three days) often save you twenty percent of the cost of room and board taken separately. Single rooms – or more usually, rooms considered most suitable for a lone person – are only marginally less expensive than more generously proportioned quarters,

so sharing always slashes costs. Most hotels willingly provide rooms with extra beds, for three or more people, at good discounts.

Many Pyrenean hotels take a month or so off per year – usually sometime between November and March, unless they're in a major skiing area. You may also find that their restaurants – often the reception too – may close one night a week. It's always best to phone ahead to check.

In country areas, in addition to standard hotels, you will come across **chambres d'hôte**, bed-and-breakfast accommodation in someone's house or farm. These vary in standard but are certainly affordable, falling mostly into the ③ category; in many instances they are good sources of traditional home-cooking. Leaflets available in tourist offices list most of them.

HOSTELS, GÎTES D'ÉTAPE AND REFUGES

At between 45F and 85F per night for a dormitory bunk, *Auberges de Jeunesse* – **youth hostels** – are invaluable for single budget travellers. For couples, however, and certainly for groups of three or more people, they'll not necessarily be cheaper than hotels – though many of the newer hostels offer double rooms for couples. Stays are usually limited to three consecutive nights maximum, though you may be able to negotiate longer stays in off-peak times. Another drawback is that you might have to share the place with large, raucous school parties. However, many hostels are beautifully sited, and they allow you to cut costs by preparing your own food in their kitchens, or eating in inexpensive canteens. In the more popular regions, advance reservations may be necessary. You are supposed to be a member of the

International Youth Hostel Federation, but you can often join on the spot. There are two rival French youth hostel associations: the Fédération Unie des Auberges de Jeunesse (27 rue Pajol, 75018 Paris), whose hostels are detailed in the *International Handbook*, and the Ligue Française pour les Auberges de Jeunesse (38 bd Raspail, 75007 Paris). IYHF membership covers both associations.

Another hostel-type alternative – the **gîte d'étape** – exists in the countryside, especially in trekking or cycling areas. In the Pyrenees *gîtes* are administered under the umbrella of the publishing and outdoors activities organization Randonnées Pyrénéennes, which was originally established to create a chain of medium-category hostelries for trekkers, cyclists and horse-riders. All *gîtes* must have self-catering kitchen facilities, some form of heating, supposedly a minimum of 15 bunks in dormitories or private rooms (bedding is not provided), laundry, shower and toilet facilities, and may be open year-round. Hot meals are sometimes provided, and re-provisioning might be possible. A bed will be between 60F and 90F, and a meal will rarely cost more than 80F – thus all *gîtes* in the *Guide* are rated as ①. Although *gîtes* must give priority to long-distance travellers on a traverse, it is sometimes possible to use one as a base for several nights; if you do this, the manager will almost certainly be able to share an intimate knowledge of the region. The large-scale IGN walkers' maps show the location of *gîtes*, and they are noted in the individual GR *topoguides*.

Most mountain **refuge huts** are open only in summer, though in winter there is nearly always at least a simple annexe with sleeping platforms and perhaps a fireplace or stove. Many refuges are extremely basic and antiquated, others are passably comfortable and modern – with hot showers in a few cases. Almost all of them have cooking facilities and offer meals, though these are often not the best value (60–85F for emphasis on wine and carbohydrates), the price reflecting the fact that foodstuffs have to be brought in by mule or helicopter. Especially in or around the Parc National des Pyrénées, refuges are often packed to the seams in summer, and there have been reports of trekkers having to sleep on and under tables – for the normal fee. Costs range from 55 to 75F for the night, less if you're a member of a climbing organization affiliated to the Club Alpin Français; either a membership card or your passport will be held as security against payment.

A complete list of all French *gîtes d'étape*, refuges and hostels is included in the publication *Gîtes et Refuges en France* (Éditions Créer, rue Jean-Amariton, Nonette, 63340 St-Germain Lambron); more specific for the Pyrenees is *Gîtes d'Étape, Refuges: France et Frontières*, available from Éditions Lacadole, 74 rue Albert Pedreaux, 78140 Vélizy.

RENTED ACCOMMODATION

If you are planning to stay a week or more in any one place it might be worth considering **renting a house**. You can do this through one of the holiday firms in Britain which market accommodation/travel packages (see pp.4–5); or use the official French government service, the **Gîtes de France** (59 rue St-Lazare, 75009 Paris, ☎01.48.70.75.75; or in the UK through Brittany Ferries, ☎0990/360360). A small membership fee gets you a copy of their handbook which features properties all over France, listed by *département*. The houses vary in size and comfort, but all are basically acceptable holiday homes. There is a photograph and description of each one and the computerized booking service means that you can instantly reserve one for any number of full weeks. The cost varies with the season, from around 800F to 1600F per week – and may include concessionary ferry rates.

CAMPING

Practically every village and town in the Pyrenees has at least one **campsite** to cater for the thousands of French people who spend their holiday under canvas. The cheapest – at around 25F per person per night – is usually the **camping municipal**, run by the local municipality. When officially open, they are always clean, and often situated in prime locations, though hot water can be unreliable. Out of season, many of them don't even bother to have someone there to collect the overnight charge.

On the coast especially, there are **superior categories** of campsite, where you'll pay prices similar to those of a *gîte d'étape* or hostel for the facilities: bars, restaurants, sometimes swimming pools. These have rather more permanent status than the *campings municipals*, with people often spending a whole holiday in one place. If you plan to do the same, and particularly if you have a caravan or camper, or a substantial tent, it's wise to reserve in advance. Count on 35F a head all-in with a tent, 40F with a camper van.

Inland, **camping à la ferme** – on somebody's farm – is another possibility, though facilities often leave much to be desired. Lists of sites are detailed in the *Accueil à la Campagne* booklet, sold by the French Government Tourist Office. With these you should make sure of what you'll be charged before you pitch up – it's easy to get stung the following morning.

Lastly, a **word of caution**: never camp rough (*camping sauvage*, as the French call it) on any-one's land without first asking permission. If the dogs don't get you, the guns might – farmers have been known to shoot before asking any questions. In many parts of the Pyrenees *camping sauvage* on public land – including the beaches – is not tolerated, or is subject (as in the Parc National des Pyrénées) to severe restrictions.

SPAIN

Simple, reasonably priced rooms are still very widely available in Spain, and in almost any inland Pyrenean town you'll be able to find a double room for as little as 3000–4500ptas (£12–18/$19–29), or a single for 1800–2500ptas (£7–10/$11–16). Only in major coastal resorts, particularly in San Sebastián or some of the Costa Brava ports, might you have to pay more. Festivals tend to result more in accommodation filling quickly rather than outrageous rate hikes, though during Pamplona's *San Fermín* festival, rooms do double in price and are virtually sold out months before.

In Spain, unlike most countries, you don't seem to pay any more for a central location, though you do tend to get a comparatively bad deal if you're travelling on your own as there are relatively few single rooms. Much of the time you'll have to negotiate a reduction from the price of a double. In Catalunya, **half-board** at *hostals* with restau-rants is often encouraged or obligatory, and often very good value.

Otherwise, there seems little scope for gen-uine **bargaining** over room prices in the Pyre-nees. High season is construed as August 1–23 and Easter week, when peak prices are adhered to; during the rest of the year, official rates (always posted in the entry hall) may be half to two-thirds as much, and that's your "bargain". If there are more than two of you, most places have rooms with three or four beds at not a great deal more than the double-room price – a good deal, especially if you are travelling with children. Remember always to establish whether quoted rates include seven-percent IVA (Value Added Tax) or not; usually they don't, but proprietors may waive it as a small concession.

FONDAS, PENSIONES, HOSTALES AND HOTELES

The one thing all travellers need to master is the elaborate variety of types and places to stay. Least expensive of all, though just about extinct in the Pyrenees, are **fondas** (identifiable by a square blue sign with a white **F** on it, and often posi-tioned above a bar), closely followed up the price scale by the equally rare **casas de huéspedes** (**CH** on a similar sign), and **pensiones** (*pensió* in Catalan singular; **P**) . Of late, most surviving *fon-das* have reinvented themselves as one- or two-star *pensiones*; the original meaning of *fonda*, now being reverted to, is a roadside taverna in an isolated area (not offering beds). *Pensiones* usu-ally serve food, and a few may offer rooms only on a meals-inclusive basis.

SPAIN: ACCOMMODATION PRICE CODES

All the Spanish accommodation establishments listed in this book have been price-graded according to the following scale. The prices quoted are for the **cheapest available double room** in each hotel **in high season**. Effectively this means that anything in the ② category will be without private bath, though there's usually a washbasin in the room. In the ③ category and above you will probably be get-ting private facilities. Remember, though, that many of the budget places will also have more expen-sive rooms including en-suite facilities. **Youth hostels**, **mountain refuges** and **albergues** are graded as ① since the price per person is approximately half of the category's upper limit.

The categories below include seven-percent IVA where applied.

① Under 2500ptas	③ 3500–5000ptas	⑤ 7000–10,000ptas
② 2500–3500ptas	④ 5000–7000ptas	⑥ 10,000ptas and upwards

Slightly more expensive but far more common are **hostales** (*hostals* in Catalan; marked **Hs**) and **hostal-residencias** (**HsR**). These are categorized from one to three stars, but even so prices vary enormously according to location and facilities – a place in a slightly down-at-heel medieval quarter with no car-parking facilities is bound to cost less than new premises on a suburban street or the town's access road. Most *hostales* offer good, if functional rooms, often with private shower, and, for doubles at least, they can be excellent value. The *residencia* designation means that no meals other than perhaps breakfast are served.

Moving up the scale you finally reach fully-fledged **hoteles** (**H**), again star-graded by the authorities (from one to five). One-star hotels cost no more than three-star *hostales* – sometimes they're actually less expensive, and remain officially graded as *hostales* – but at three stars you pay a lot more, and at four or five you're in luxury facilities with prices to match. Near the top end of this scale there are also state-run **paradores**: beautiful places, often converted from castles, monasteries and other minor Spanish monuments. Even if you can't afford to stay, the buildings are often worth a look in their own right, and usually have pleasantly classy bars.

Outside all these categories you will sometimes find **camas** (beds) and **habitaciones** (rooms) advertised in private houses or above bars, often with the phrase "*camas y comidas*" (beds and meals). If you're travelling on a very tight budget these can be worth looking out for – particularly if you're offered one at a bus station and the owner is prepared to bargain with you.

In addition, each of the autonomous communities featured in this book – Catalunya, Aragón, Navarra and Gipuzkoa – has its own equivalent of the French *chambres d'hôte* or *gîtes de France*. In the Spanish version, they are either a private residence where extra rooms are rented out, self-contained flats or cottages, or even bed-and-breakfast-type farmhouse stays. In Catalunya they are known as **cases de pagès**; in Aragón and Navarra they are called **casas de payés**, **casas rurales** or **viviendas de turismo rural**; while in Gipuzkoa they are identified by a red-and-green circular sign with the word **nekazal-turismoa**. All of these *agroturismo* (agrarian tourism) programmes enjoy strong governmental support and promotion, and the best – sometimes the only – way of contacting proprietors is

through local tourist offices, which print and distribute exhaustive booklets detailing premises. However, most of these establishments (usually category ③, a few ④) are more than happy to host short-term, walk-in trade, and where appropriate this guide lists them as alternatives to conventional accommodation.

YOUTH HOSTELS, MOUNTAIN REFUGES AND MONASTERIES

Spanish **albergues juveniles** (youth hostels) are rarely of much use except for solo, short-term travellers who may not find any other kind of vacancy during the Pyrenean summer. The handful of useful ones is detailed in the guide, or you can get a complete list (with opening times and phone numbers) from your home hostelling association. Be warned that most of the hostels tend to have curfews, are often block-reserved by school groups, and demand production of a membership card (though this is generally available on the spot if you haven't already bought one from your national organization). At 1000–1300ptas a person, too, you can quite easily pay as much as for sharing an inexpensive double room in a *fonda* or *casa de huespedes*.

There are, however, a number of privately run, similarly priced but less institutional **albergues** conforming to the notion of a French *gîte d'étape*, strategically sited in select mountain villages.

In addition, in the high Pyrenees the Federación Aragonesa de Montañismo the Federación Navarra de Montaña, plus three Catalunyan clubs – the FEEC, the CEC and the UEC – and a handful of private individuals all run a number of **refugios** (refuges; *refugís* in Catalan). Like their French counterparts, these are simple, inexpensive dormitory huts for climbers and trekkers, generally equipped with bunk-beds, a common room and cooking space (except in the CEC huts where self-catering is forbidden). As in France, some sort of emergency adjacent shelter is sometimes open all year, and the most popular refuges are generally staffed from mid-June to late September, plus selected snowy weeks and holidays (Christmas, Easter) during the colder months. The cost of accommodation is 1000ptas (the cheaper private refuges) to 1400ptas (the fanciest Catalan ones), unless you are a member of a reciprocally recognized alpine club, in which case you'll get half off at the club-affiliated refuges. At about 1500ptas, **meals** cost a bit less than in French refuges, and have improved recently in quality:

word has gone out from Spanish alpine club head-quarters that they must consist of at least three courses – soup and/or salad, a meat dish, dessert or fruit, and wine.

Again off the beaten track, it is sometimes possible to stay at Spanish **monasterios** or **conventos**. Often severely underpopulated, these may let empty cells for a small charge; in other cases, wings have been renovated expressly as *hostales*, with prices to match, whether or not the monastery or convent is still functioning as a religious community. You can just turn up and ask – many will take visitors regardless of sex – but if you want to be sure of a good reception it's best to approach the local tourist office first, and phone ahead. There are some particularly wonderful monastic locations in Aragón and Catalunya. Those following the **Camino de Santiago** can also take advantage of monastic accommodation specifically reserved for pilgrims along the route; the best places are detailed in the text.

Monasteries and youth hostels aside, if you have any **problems** with Spanish rooms – over-charging, most obviously – you can usually pro-duce an immediate resolution by asking for an *hoja de reclamaciones* (complaints sheet). By law all establishments must stock these and provide them on demand to an unhappy customer. Once filled out, you send it off to the government of the province or autonomous region – not as futile an exercise as it may sound, as we know of at least one hotel in Aragón which was prosecuted in response to a foreigner's complaint.

CAMPING

There are almost four hundred authorized **camp-sites** in Spain, predominantly on the coast. They usually work out at about 400ptas (£2/$3.50) plus as much again for a tent and a similar amount for each car or caravan – the majority of sites are biased towards use by caravans. Only a few of the best-sited or most popular sites are significantly more expensive. The most useful ones in the Pyrenees are described in the text, but if you plan to camp exten-sively then pick up the free *Mapa de Campings* from the Spanish tourist board, which marks and names virtually all of them. A complete *Guía de Campings*, listing full prices, facilities and exact locations, is available at most Spanish bookshops.

Camping outside campsites is legal – but with certain restrictions. There must be fewer than ten people in your group, and you're not allowed to camp "in urban areas, areas prohibit-ed for military or touristic reasons, or within 1km of an official campsite". What this means in prac-tice is that you can't camp on tourist beaches (though you can, discreetly, nearby) but with a lit-tle sensitivity you can set up a tent for a short period almost anywhere in the mountains. (Con-spicuous exceptions are the Ordesa/Monte Perdi-do and Aigües Tortes national parks, where camp-ing is prohibited outside designated areas.) Whenever possible ask locally first.

EATING AND DRINKING

Not surprisingly, the best Pyrenean restaurant food tends to be based on what's available locally, which means a preponderance of river trout, salmon, fresh chestnuts, wild mushrooms, horse and goat meat, and game such as wild boar, rabbit, grouse and pigeon. In the mountains, ordinary restaurants often rely on a small fixed menu, with little in the way of à la carte dishes, though special requests for vegetarian meals should produce some response. Self-catering is a splendid (and if you're trekking a lot, necessary) alternative, with a vast choice of seasonal specialities.

FRANCE

Mountain restaurants within easy reach of major centres can be very popular and consequently expensive, but elsewhere, except in peak holiday season, most restaurants are low-key, informal and very reasonable. If you've just arrived and are looking for a good place to eat, go wherever the largest numbers of locals go – the favourites will be particularly easy to locate on a Sunday lunchtime, when whole families turn out for the traditional weekly get-together. Except in the major towns, which often have at least one Chinese and Moroccan eatery apiece, you'll find little in the way of ethnic food.

BREAKFAST, SNACKS AND PICNICS

A croissant, *pain au chocolat* or a sandwich in a bar or café, with a hot chocolate or coffee, is gen-erally the best way to eat **breakfast** – at a fraction of the price charged by most hotels, where all you'll get for 25F and up is a pile of stale bread and foil-sealed jam, plus a pot of tea or coffee. *Brasseries* – which serve full meals (see below) – are also possibilities for a coffee and a quick bite. If you're standing at the counter, which is cheaper than sitting down, you may see a basket of croissants or some hard-boiled eggs (usually gone by 9.30 or 10am). Help yourself – the waiter will keep an eye on how many you've eaten and bill you accordingly.

At **midday** you may find cafés offering a *plat du jour* (chef's daily special) for between 40F and 75F, or *formules*, a limited or no-choice menu. *Croque-Monsieurs* or *Croque-Madames* (variations on the grilled-cheese sandwich) are on sale at cafés, brasseries and many street stalls, along with *frites*, *crêpes*, *galettes* (wholewheat pancakes), *gauffres* (waffles), *glaces* (ice creams) and all sorts of sandwiches. For variety, there are exotic treats like the North African *brik à l'oeuf* (pastry with an egg inside), *merguez* (spicy sausages), Greek *souvlaki* (kebabs) or Lebanese *falafel* (deep-fried chick-pea balls).

Crêpes or filled pancakes, which have spread all over France from their original home in Brittany, are also popular for light meals, at between 15 and 40F each. The more expensive savoury buckwheat variety (*galettes*) are served as a main course; the sweet light-flour ones are for dessert. **Pizzerias**, often *au feu du bois* (wood-fired oven), are also common and somewhat better value in that you can fill up for 50–70F, though quality varies widely – check for a surplus of empty seats before nosing your way in the door.

For **picnics**, the local *halle* (covered produce market) or supermarket will provide anything you want in the way of cheese, paté and salad ingredients. For more elaborate **takeaway food**, there's nothing to beat the *charcuteries* (delicatessens) which you'll find everywhere, even in small villages. These sell meat dishes – mostly pork-based – salads and fully prepared main courses. These are also available less expensively at supermarket *charcuterie* counters. You buy by weight, or you can ask for *une tranche* (a slice), *une barquette* (a carton), or *une part* (a portion). *Boulangeries* or **bakeries** often sell not just bread but an array of baked snacks with meat or cheese in them, such as *quiche*, eminently suitable for a lunch on the hoof.

MEALS AND RESTAURANTS

There's little or no difference between **restaurants** (or *auberges* or *relais* as they sometimes call themselves) and **brasseries** in terms of quality or price range. The distinction is that *brasseries*, which resemble cafés, serve quicker meals at most hours of the day, while restaurants tend to stick to the traditional meal times of noon–2pm (or 2.30pm in the larger towns) and 7–9pm (or 10pm in towns). After 9pm or so, restaurants may serve only à la carte meals – invariably more expensive than the set *menu fixe*. Serving **hours** tend to be extremely inflexible, to the sorrow of many unaware visitors; even if a place is still packed at its 10pm closing time, you won't be seated or served if you arrive at 10.01, or even at 9.50 for that matter. Even if you're staying in a particular hotel-restaurant, they will be loath to reopen their kitchen, and will demand to know from 7pm on whether you're planning to dine there that night. The *Guide* makes a point of highlighting establishments whose kitchen functions later than usual. In small towns it will be impossible to get anything other than a bar sandwich after 9.30pm; in major cities or busy resorts, town-centre *brasseries* will serve until 11pm or midnight and one or two may stay open all night.

For the more upmarket places it's wise to make **reservations** – easily done on the same day. Don't forget that hotel restaurants are open to non-residents, and often very good value; in many small Pyrenean villages, the sole hotel may also have the only restaurant. As noted in the "Accommodation" section, *Logis de France* are almost always good value. Otherwise, when hunting for a restaurant, avoid places that are half-full at peak time, be suspicious of over-long menus and use your instinct; asking locals for recommendations – the French equivalent of commenting on the weather – will usually net strong views and sound advice.

Prices and menus are posted outside. Normally there is a choice between one or more **menus fixes** – often just referred to in the guide as the *menu* – where the number of courses has already been determined and the choice is limited. At the bottom of the price range, *menus fixes* revolve around standard dishes such as steak (*steack frites*) and chicken (*poulet frites*) served with fries, or various concoctions involving innards. Look for the *plat du jour* which may be a regional dish and more appealing. Increasingly, however, restaurants are offering a range of *menus fixes*, the more expensive of which offer quite a wide choice, and run to four or five courses. For 115F and up, you should expect an array of regional dishes, or at least generic *haute cuisine* that will have you leafing through the menu master (see below) for translations.

Going **à la carte** is always more expensive but does, however, offer greater flexibility and, in the better restaurants, unlimited access to the chef's specialities. A simple and perfectly legitimate tactic is to have just one or two courses instead of the expected three or four. You can share dishes or just have several starters – a useful strategy for vegetarians (see below for more on this). There's no minimum charge.

In the French **sequence of courses**, any salad – sometimes vegetables, too – arrives separately from the main dish, and cheese precedes – or is the alternative to – a dessert. You will be offered coffee, which always costs extra, to finish off the meal. The waiter/waitress will approach with the words *Ça-y-etait?* to take finished plates away, which inevitably throws some people as the expression isn't in most phrasebooks. Incidentally, you address staff as *monsieur* or *madame*, *mademoiselle* if a young woman, not by the school-French *garçon*.

On menus or bills, *TTC* means that all local **taxes** and sales tax (IVA) is included (the rule); *service compris* or *s.c.* means the **service charge** is included (less common). *Service non compris*, *s.n.c.* or *servis en sus* means that it isn't and you need to calculate an additional fifteen percent. Wine (*vin*) or a drink (*boisson*) may be included, though rarely on menus under 120F. When ordering wine, ask for *un quart* or *un pichet* (250ml), *un demi-litre* (half a litre) or *une carafe* (a litre). You'll normally be given the house wine unless you specify otherwise; if you're worried about the cost ask for *vin ordinaire* or *vin du pays*.

The French are well-disposed towards **children** in restaurants, not merely in offering the ubiquitous, cut-price *menu enfants* but by fostering an atmosphere – even in otherwise fairly snooty establishments – that positively welcomes kids. It is regarded as self-evident that large family groups should be able to eat together. More difficult to swallow may be the idea of **dogs** in the dining room, considered quite normal; the French are absolutely besotted with their pooches, and it can come as a surprise in provincial (and urban) restaurants to realize that a significant number of your fellow diners are concealing pets under the table.

VEGETARIANS AND VEGANS

Vegetarians should expect a somewhat lean time in the French Pyrenees. *Crêperies* and pizzerias can be good standbys; elsewhere you'll either have to hope for a sympathetic proprietor willing to replace a meat dish on a *menu fixe* with an omelette, resign yourself to combing the *carte* for something acceptable, or (literally) swallow your principles and eat fish or shellfish.

Vegans should probably forget altogether about eating in French restaurants – since "no animal products" means it's still considered all right to douse everything in butter – and resort to self-catering. Many French health shops stock vegan margarine, plus the usual instant meals and supplements; the La Vie Claire health chain has branches all over France, but be prepared to pay over the odds.

> The magic words are *je suis végétarien(ne); est-ce qu'il y a des plats sans viande ou poisson?* (I'm a vegetarian; are there any dishes without meat or fish?)

ALCOHOLIC DRINKS

Where you can eat you can invariably drink, and to a certain extent the reverse is true. **Drinking** is done at a leisurely pace whether it's a prelude to food (*apéritif*), a sequel (*digestif*), or the accompaniment, and **cafés** are the standard places to do it. Every bar or café has to display its full price list (usually without a fifteen-percent service charge added), with the cheapest drinks at the bar (*au comptoir*), and progressively increasing prices for sitting at a table inside (*la salle*), or on the terrace (*la terrasse*). You pay when you leave, and it's quite acceptable to sit for an hour over one cup of a coffee.

Wine – *vin* – is drunk at just about every meal or social occasion. Red is *rouge*, white *blanc*, or there's *rosé*. *Vin de table* or *vin ordinaire* – table wine – is generally drinkable and always cheap; it may be disguised and marked up as the house wine, or *cuvée*. In wine-producing areas the **local**

vin du pays can be very good indeed. In bars you normally buy wine by the glass – just ask for *un rouge* or *un blanc* – though as in restaurants you can also get *un pichet*, a 250-ml, 500-ml or 1-litre jug.

A.C. (*Appellation d'Origine Contrôlée*) wines are another matter. They can be excellent value at the lower end of the price scale, where favourable French taxes keep prices down to £2/$3 or so a bottle retail, but move up and you're soon paying serious prices; restaurant mark-ups of A.C. wines can be well over 100 percent. Popular **A.C. wines** found on most restaurant lists include Côtes du Rhône (from the Rhône valley), St-Emilion and Médoc (from Bordeaux), Beaujolais and very upmarket Burgundy. Peculiar to the central Pyrenees is Madiran, a high-tannin red used also in cooking. The basic terms are *brut*, very dry; *sec*, dry; *demi-sec*, sweet; *doux*, very sweet; *mousseux*, sparkling; *méthode champenoise*, mature and sparkling. **Cider** (*cidre*) is fairly common in the Pyrenees, and also comes as *brut* or *doux*.

Alsatian brands such as Kanterbrau, Karlsbrau and Kronenbourg account for virtually all of the **beer** served in the Pyrenees. Draught (*à la pression*) is the cheapest drink you can have next to coffee and wine – although the smallest glass, *un demi* (250ml) rarely costs less than 10F.

Stronger alcohol is consumed from as early as 5am as a pre-work fortifier, and right through the day according to inclination. **Cognac** or **Armagnac** brandies and the dozens of *eaux de vie* (brandy distilled from fruit) and **liqueurs** are favourite sips. In the centre and west of the range, **sweet dessert** wines such as Jurançon and Murançon are popular. A Pyrenean speciality is the green or yellow **Izarra** liqueurs, strong and bitterly herbal. Measures are generous, but they don't come cheap; the same applies for imported spirits like whisky, always called *Scotch.* Pastis, aniseed-flavoured drinks such as Pernod or Ricard, are served diluted with water and ice (*glaçons*) – very refreshing and not expensive. Two drinks designed to stimulate the appetite are **Pineau**, cognac and grape juice, and **Kir**, white wine with a dash of blackcurrant syrup, or with champagne for a *Kir Royal.*

SOFT DRINKS AND HOT DRINKS

You can buy cartons of unsweetened **fruit juice** in supermarkets, although in cafés bottled

FRENCH FOOD AND DISHES

Basics

Pain	Bread	*Huile*	Oil	*Vinaigre*	Vinegar	*Couteau*	Knife
Beurre	Butter	*Poivre*	Pepper	*Bouteille*	Bottle	*Cuillère*	Spoon
Oeufs	Eggs	*Sel*	Salt	*Verre*	Glass	*Table*	Table
Lait	Milk	*Sucre*	Sugar	*Fourchette*	Fork	*L'addition*	The bill

Typical French snacks

Un sandwich/ une baguette	A sandwich	*au sucre*	with sugar
jambon	with ham	*au citron*	with lemon
fromage	with cheese	*au miel*	with honey
saucisson	with sausage	*à la confiture*	with jam
à l'ail	with garlic	*aux oeufs*	with eggs
au poivre	with pepper	*à la crème de marrons*	with chestnut
pâté (de campagne)	with pâté (country-style)		purée
Croque-monsieur	Grilled cheese and ham sandwich	**Other fillings/salads:**	
		Anchois	Anchovy
Croque-madame	Grilled cheese and bacon, sausage, chicken or an egg	*Andouillette*	Tripe sausage
		Boudin	Black pudding
		Coeurs de palmiers	Hearts of palm
Oeufs	Eggs	*Epis de maïs*	Corn on the cob
au plat	fried	*Fonds d'artichauts*	Artichoke hearts
à la coque	boiled	*Hareng*	Herring
durs	hard-boiled	*Langue*	Tongue
brouillés	scrambled	*Poulet*	Chicken
Omelette . . .	Omelette . . .	*Thon*	Tuna fish
nature	plain	**And some terms:**	
aux fines herbes	with herbs	*Chauffé*	Heated
au fromage	with cheese	*Cuit*	Cooked
Salade de . . .	Salad of . . .	*Cru*	Raw
tomates	tomatoes	*Emballé*	Wrapped
betteraves	beets	*À emporter*	Takeaway
concombres	cucumber	*Fumé*	Smoked
carottes rapées	grated carrots	*Salé*	Salted/spicy
Crêpe	Pancake	*Sucré*	Sweet

Soups (*Soupes*)

Bisque	Shellfish soup	*Pistou*	Parmesan, basil and garlic paste, sometimes added to soup
Bouillabaisse	Marseillais fish soup		
Bouillon	Broth or stock	*Potage*	Thick soup, usually vegetable
Bourride	Thick fish soup	*Rouille*	Red pepper, garlic and saffron mayonnaise served with fish soup
Consommé	Clear soup		
		Velouté	Thick soup, usually fish or poultry

Starters (*Hors d'oeuvres*)

Assiette anglaise or de charcuterie	Plate of cold meats	*Hors d'oeuvres variés*	Combination of the previous two plus smoked or marinated fish
Crudités	Raw vegetables with dressings		

Fish (*Poisson*), Seafood (*Fruits de mer*) and Shellfish (*Crustacés* or *Coquillages*)

Anchois	Anchovies	*Hareng*	Herring
Anguilles	Eels	*Homard*	Lobster
Baudroie	Monkfish, anglerfish	*Huîtres*	Oysters
Brème	Bream	*Langouste*	Spiny lobster
Bulot	Whelk	*Langoustines*	Saltwater crayfish
Cabillaud	Cod	*Limande*	Lemon sole
Calmar	Squid	*Lotte de mer*	Monkfish
Carrelet	Plaice	*Loup de mer*	Sea bass
Claire	Type of oyster	*Louvine*	Similar to sea bass
Colin	Hake	*Maquereau*	Mackerel
Congre	Conger eel	*Merlan*	Whiting
Coques	Cockles	*Morue*	Salt cod
Coquilles Saint-Jacques	Scallops	*Moules (marinière)*	Mussels (with shallots in white wine sauce)
Crabe	Crab		
Crevettes grises	Shrimps	*Palourdes*	Clams
Crevettes roses	Prawns	*Poulpe*	Octopus
Dorade, daurade	Sea bream	*Praires*	Small clams
Ecrevisse	Freshwater crayfish	*Raie*	Skate
Éperlan	Smelt or whitebait	*Rouget*	Red mullet
Escargots	Snails	*Saumon*	Salmon
Favou(ille)	Tiny crab	*Saint-Pierre*	John Dory
Flétan	Halibut	*Sole*	Sole
Friture	Assorted fried fish	*Thon*	Tuna
Gambas	King prawns	*Truite*	Trout
Grenouilles (cuisses de)	Frogs (legs)	*Turbot*	Turbot

Terms (Fish)

Aïoli	Garlic mayonnaise served with salt cod and other fish	*Fumet*	Fish stock
		Gigot de mer	Large fish baked whole
Béarnaise	Sauce made with egg yolks, white wine, shallots and vinegar	*Grillé*	Grilled
		Hollandaise	Butter and vinegar sauce
Colbert	Fried in egg and breadcrumbs	*À la meunière*	In a butter, lemon and parsley sauce
Darne	Fillet or steak		
La douzaine	A dozen	*Mousse/mousseline*	Mousse
Frit	Fried	*Pané*	Breaded
Friture	Deep-fried small fish	*Quenelles*	Light dumplings
Fumé	Smoked	*Tourte*	Tart or pie

Meat (*Viande*) and Poultry (*Volaille*)

Agneau	Lamb	*Chevreau*	Kid goat
Andouille, andouillette	Tripe sausage	*Contrefilet*	Sirloin roast
Bavette d'échalote	Cheap steak fried with shallots	*Coquelet*	Cockerel
		Dinde, dindon, dindonneau	Turkey of different ages and genders
Boeuf	Beef		
Bifteck	Steak	*Entrecôte*	Ribsteak
Boudin blanc	Sausage of white meats	*Faux filet*	Sirloin steak
		Foie	Liver
Boudin noir	Black pudding	*Foie gras*	Fattened liver of duck or goose
Caille	Quail		
Canard	Duck	*Fraises de veau*	Veal testicles
Caneton	Duckling	*Cervelle*	Brains

Châteaubriand	Porterhouse steak	*Os*	Bone
Cheval	Horse meat	*Porc, pieds de porc*	Pork, pig's trotters
Fricadelles	Meatballs	*Poulet*	Chicken
Gibier	Game	*Poulette*	Young chicken
Gigot (d'agneau)	Leg of lamb	*Poussin*	Baby chicken
Gigot de . . .	Leg of another meat	*Ris*	Sweetbreads
Graisse	Fat	*Rognons*	Kidneys
Grillade	Grilled meat	*Rognons blancs*	Testicles
Hâchis	Chopped meat or hamburger	*Sanglier*	Wild boar
		Steack	Steak
Langue	Tongue	*Tête de veau*	Calf's head in jelly
Lapin, lapereau	Rabbit, young rabbit	*Toro*	Bull meat
Lard, lardons	Bacon, diced bacon	*Tortue*	Turtle
Lièvre	Hare	*Tournedos*	Thick slices of fillet
Marcassin	Young wild boar	*Travers de porc*	Spare ribs
Merguez	Spicy, red sausage	*Tripes*	Tripe
Mouton	Mutton	*Veau*	Veal
Museau de veau	Muzzle of veal	*Venaison*	Venison
Oie	Goose		

Dishes and terms (meat and poultry)

Boeuf bourguignon	Beef stew with burgundy, onions and mushrooms	*Civet*	Game stew
		Confit	Meat preserve
Canard à l'orange	Roast duck with an orange-and-wine sauce	*Côte*	Chop, cutlet or rib
		Cou	Neck
Cassoulet	A casserole of beans and meat	*Cuisse*	Thigh-and-leg portion
		Épaule	Shoulder
Choucroute	Pickled cabbage with peppercorns, sausages, bacon and salami	*Médaillon*	Round piece
		Pavé	Thick slice
		En croûte	In pastry
Coq au vin	Chicken cooked until it falls off the bone with wine, onions and mushrooms	*Farci*	Stuffed
		Au feu de bois	Cooked over wood fire
		Au four	Baked
		Galantine	Cold dish of meat in aspic
Steak au poivre (vert/rouge)	Steak in a black (green/red) peppercorn sauce	*Garni*	With vegetables
		Gésier	Gizzard
		Grillé	Grilled
Steak tartare	Raw chopped beef usually accompanied by a raw egg yolk	*Jarret*	Knuckle
		Magret de canard	Duck breast slices
Blanquette, daube, estouffade, hochepôt, navarin and ragoût	All are types of stews	*Marmite*	Casserole
		Mijoté	Stewed
		Museau	Muzzle
Aile	Wing	*À la Périgordine*	In a truffle and foie gras sauce
Blanc	Breast or white meat		
Bordelaise	In a red wine, shallots and bone marrow sauce	*Persillade*	Cooked in parsley and oil
		Poêlée	Pan-fried, sauteed
À la boulangère	Baked with potatoes and onions	*Rillade*	Coarse pork-and-goose paté
À la bourgeoise	With carrots, onions, celery, bacon and braised lettuce	*Rôti*	Roast
		Sauté	Lightly cooked in butter
		Terrine	Solid loaf of finely puréed substance (duck liver, raspberry, etc)
À la broche	Spit-roasted		
Carré	Best end of neck, chop or cutlet		

Terms for steaks

Bleu	Almost raw	*Bien cuit*	Well done
Saignant	Rare	*Très bien cuit*	Very well cooked
A point	Medium	*Brochette*	Kebab

Garnishes and sauces

Beurre blanc	Sauce of white wine and shallots, with butter	*Mornay*	Cheese sauce
		Pays d'Auge	Cream and cider
Chasseur	White wine, mushrooms and shallots	*Piquante*	Gherkins or capers, vinegar and shallots
Diable	Strong mustard seasoning	*Provençale*	Tomatoes, garlic, olive oil and herbs
Forestière	With bacon and mushroom		
Fricassée	Rich, creamy sauce		

Vegetables (*Légumes*)

Algue	Seaweed	*rouges*	kidney
Artichaut	Artichoke	*blancs*	white
Asperges	Asparagus	*beurres*	butter
Avocat	Avocado	*Laitue*	Lettuce
Betterave	Beetroot	*Lentilles*	Lentils
Carotte	Carrot	*Maïs*	Corn
Céleri	Celery	*Navet*	Turnip
Champignons	Mushrooms; types include: de bois, de Paris, cèpes, chanterelles, girolles, grisets, mousserons	*Oignon*	Onion
		Oseille	Sorrel
		Panais	Parsnip
		Pâte	Pasta or pastry
Chicorée frisée	Curly chicory	*Petits pois*	Peas
Chou (rouge)	(Red) cabbage	*Pignons*	Pine nuts
Choufleur	Cauliflower	*Pissenlits*	Dandelion leaves
Citrouille	Pumpkin	*Poireau*	Leek
Concombre	Cucumber	*Pois chiche*	Chickpeas
Cornichon	Gherkin	*Pois mange-tout*	Snow peas
Cresson	Watercress	*Poivron (vert, rouge)*	Sweet pepper (green, red)
Échalotes	Shallots	*Pommes (de terre)*	Potatoes
Endive	Chicory	*Primeurs*	Spring greens
Épinards	Spinach	*Radis*	Radishes
Epis de maïs	Corn on the cob	*Riz*	Rice
Fenouil	Fennel	*Salade verte*	Green salad
Fèves	Broad beans	*Sarrasin/sarrazin*	Buckwheat
Flageolet	White beans	*Seigle*	Rye
Haricots	Beans	*Tomates*	Tomatoes
verts	string (French)	*Truffes*	Truffles

Herbs (*Herbes*) and Spices (*Épices*)

Ail	Garlic	*Marjolaine*	Marjoram
Anis	Aniseed	*Menthe*	Mint
Basilic	Basil	*Moutarde*	Mustard
Cannelle	Cinnamon	*Persil*	Parsley
Ciboulettes	Chives	*Piment*	Pimento
Estragon	Tarragon	*Pistou*	Ground basil, olive oil and garlic
Genièvre	Juniper	*Raifort*	Horseradish
Gingembre	Ginger	*Romarin*	Rosemary
Girofle	Clove	*Safran*	Saffron
Laurier	Bay leaf	*Serpolet*	Wild thyme

Some vegetable dishes and terms

Beignet	Fritter	*Ratatouille*	Mixture of aubergine, courgette, tomatoes, and garlic
Farci	Stuffed		
Gratin dauphinois	Potatoes baked in cream and garlic	*Rémoulade*	A mustard mayonnaise
		Salade niçoise	Salad of tomatoes, radishes, cucumber, hard-boiled eggs, anchovies, onion, artichokes, green peppers, beans, basil and garlic (rarely as comprehensive, even in Nice)
Gratiné	Browned with cheese or butter		
Jardinière	With mixed diced vegetables		
A la parisienne	Sautéed in butter (potatoes); with white wine sauce, and shallots		
Parmentier	With potatoes	*Sauté*	Lightly fried in butter
Pommes château, fondantes	Quartered potatoes sautéed in butter	*A la vapeur*	Steamed
		Je suis végétarien(ne).	I'm a vegetarian. Are there any non-meat dishes?
Pommes lyonnaise	Fried onions and potatoes	*Il y a quelques plats sans viande?*	

Fruits (*Fruits*) and Nuts (*Noix*)

Abricot	Apricot	*Myrtilles*	Blueberries
Amandes	Almonds	*Noisette*	Hazelnut
Ananas	Pineapple	*Noix*	Nuts
Banane	Banana	*Orange*	Orange
Brugnon, nectarine	Nectarine	*Pamplemousse*	Grapefruit
Cacahouète	Peanut	*Pastèque*	Watermelon
Cassis	Blackcurrants	*Pêche (blanche)*	(White) peach
Cérises	Cherries	*Pistache*	Pistachio
Citron	Lemon	*Poire*	Pear
Citron vert	Lime	*Pomme*	Apple
Citrouille	Pumpkin	*Prune*	Plum
Coing	Quince	*Pruneau*	Prune
Dattes	Dates	*Raisins*	Grapes
Figues	Figs	*Rhubarbe*	Rhubarb
Fraises	Strawberries		
Fraises de bois	Wild strawberries	**Terms:**	
Framboises	Raspberries	*Beignets*	Fritter
Grenade	Pomegranate	*Compôte de . . .*	Stewed . . .
Groseilles	Redcurrants or gooseberries	*Coulis*	Sauce
Marrons	Chestnuts	*Flambé*	Set aflame in alcohol
Melon	Melon	*Frappé*	Iced
Mirabelles	Greengages (type of plum)		

Desserts (*Desserts* or *Entremets*) and Pastries (*Pâtisserie*)

Bombe	An ice cream dessert made in a round or conical mould	*Crème pâtissière*	Thick pastry-filling made with eggs
Bonbons	Sweets	*Crêpes suzettes*	Thin pancakes with orange juice and liqueur
Brioche	Sweet, high yeast breakfast roll		
		Flan caramel	Caramelized pudding
Charlotte	Custard and fruit in lining of almond fingers	*Fromage blanc*	Cream cheese, more like strained yoghurt
Clafoutis	Fruit tart, usually with berries	*Gateaux*	Fruit pies, usually apple, peach or pear
Crème Chantilly	Vanilla-flavoured and sweetened whipped cream	*Glace*	Ice cream
Crème fraîche	Sour cream		

Continued overleaf

Desserts and Pastries contd.

Îles flottantes/	Soft meringues floating on	a nun
eufs à la neige	custard	*Yaourt, yogourt* Yoghurt
Madeleine	Small, shell-shaped sponge cake	**Terms:**
Marrons	Chestnut purée and cream on	*Barquette* Small boat-shaped flan
Mont Blanc	a rum-soaked sponge cake	*Bavarois* Refers to the mould, could
Palmiers	Caramelized puff pastries	be a mousse or custard
Parfait	Frozen mousse, sometimes ice cream	*Coupe* A serving of ice cream
		Crêpes Pancakes
Petit Suisse	A smooth mixture of cream and curds	*Gênoise* Rich sponge cake
		Sablé Shortbread biscuit
Petits fours	Bite-sized cakes or pastries	*Savarin* A filled, ring-shaped cake
Poires Belle Hélène	Pears and ice cream in	*Tarte* Tart
	chocolate sauce	*Tartelette* Small tart
Religieuse	Coffee or chocolate-coated	*Truffes* Truffles, the chocolate or
	choux pastry puffs,	liqueur variety
	supposedly in the shape of	

Cheese (*Fromage*)

There are over 400 types of French cheese, most of them named after their place of origin. *Chèvre* is goat's cheese, *brebis* is ewe's cheese. *Le plateau de fromages* is the cheeseboard, and bread, but not butter, is served with it. Some useful phrases: *une petite tranche de celui-ci* (a small piece of this one); *puis-je le gouter?* (may I taste it?)

Regional food

Catalonia:

Bouillinade	Fish stew flavoured with dry Banyuls wine
Perdreau à la Català	Partridge cooked with bitter oranges
Cargolade	Small grilled snails
Palombe	Pigeon
Bolet	Wood mushroom, often fried in olive oil, to accompany game dishes
Louillade	A stew of mixed vegetables and *charcuterie*, a popular winter dish in the Cerdagne
Bunyetes	Custard doughnuts
Rosquillas	Almond cake

Béarn:

Tourin	Onion, garlic and tomato soup
Cousinette	Mixed soup that often includes beet, sorrel or chicory
Garbure	A very thick soup using carrots, turnips, cabbage, parsley, and beans in poultry, lamb or pork stock
Poule au pot	Boiled chicken with vegetables
Tourtière	Puff pastry flavoured with

rum or plums soaked in Armagnac

Pays Basque:

Piperade	Usually omelette with peppers and tomatoes, served as a main dish but sometimes just the vegetables served as an accompaniment
Ttoro	Fish stew, usually with tuna
Chipirones / txiporomes	Small squid, either casseroled or stuffed and baked
Piballes	Baby eels
Tripotcha	Veal tripe cooked with spices
Loukinkas	Small garlic sausages
Jambon de Bayonne	Ham from Bayonne, eaten cold and thinly sliced
Gâteau Basque	Almond-custardy pie in a crumb crust, usually topped with cherry conserve
Touron	Marzipan garnished with pistachio nuts
Macarons	Macaroons, especially good from Saint-Jean-de-Luz
Mamia	Same as *cuajada* (see Spanish foods)

(sweetened) nectars such as apricot (*jus d'abricot*) and blackcurrant (*cassis*) still prevail. You can also get fresh orange and lemon juice (*orange/citron pressé*) at a price; otherwise it's just the standard fizzy canned stuff, such as Rio (based on blood-orange juice), or Fun Tea, essentially Lipton's peach- or lemon-flavoured iced tea. Rather better are **siropes** – concentrated pure-fruit essences dissolved in water, served at many mountain refuges and cafés. Bottles of **mineral water** (*eau minérale*) and spring water (*eau de source*) – either sparkling (*pétillante*) or still (*eau plate*) – abound, but there's not much wrong with the tap water (*l'eau du robinet*).

Coffee is invariably espresso, in small cups and very strong. *Un café* or *un express* is black; *un crème* is with milk; *un grand café* or *un grand crème* is a large cup. In the morning you can also ask for *un café au lait* – espresso in a large cup or bowl filled up with hot milk. *Un déca* is decaf, widely available but only as powdered in a sachet. Ordinary **tea** (*thé*) is Lipton's ninety percent of the time; to have it served with milk, ask for *un peu de lait frais* (a bit of fresh milk).

The most common varieties of **herbal teas** (*infusions* or *tisanes*) are *verveine* (verbena), *tilleul* (linden blossom), *menthe* (mint) and *camomille* (chamomile). *Chocolat chaud* – **hot chocolate** – unlike tea, lives up to the high standards of French food and drink and can be had in any café.

SPAIN

SPAIN

There are two ways to eat out in Spain: you can go to a *restaurante* or *comedor* (dining room) and have a full meal, or you can have a succession of *tapas* (small snacks) or *raciones* (larger ones) at one or more bars. Bars tend to work out pricier but a sometimes more interesting, allowing you to do the rounds and sample different local or house specialities.

BREAKFAST, SNACKS AND SANDWICHES

For **breakfast** you're best off in a bar or café, though some *hostales* and *fondas* will serve the "Continental" basics, and in Catalunya you may be offered the choice of a heartier **savoury breakfast** (*esmorzar de forquilla* in Catalan, *desayuno salado* in Castilian) – instead of coffee and pastry, you'll be given a spread of ham, salami, cheese and wine, sometimes with omelettes and sausages too, at roughly the same price.

The traditional Spanish breakfast is *churros con chocolate* – long tubular doughnuts (not for the weak of stomach) with thick drinking chocolate. But most places also serve *tostadas* (toasted rolls) with oil (*con aceite*) or butter and jam (*con mantequilla y mermelada*), or more substantial egg dishes (*huevos fritos* are fried eggs). *Tortilla* (potato omelette) also makes an excellent breakfast, perhaps along with *magdalenas* (little cupcakes).

LIVING OFF THE LAND

In season, **fresh produce** throughout the Pyrenees is both inexpensive and excellent. In Roussillon, for instance, crates of peaches, cherries, nectarines and, later in the year, apples, pears and kiwi fruit can be had for a song. You can buy local fresh eggs, honey and goat's cheese almost everywhere. Much fresh produce in Spain is disappointing, as most of the best-quality harvest is exported, but melons, olives, figs, plums and asparagus are reliable treats.

Pick-your-own is a possibility when you're on the road. Obviously nothing should be picked in national parks and nothing you know to be endangered. As a rule, selective picking is probably not too damaging. Hedgerow fruits and nuts – blackberries, rowanberries, raspberries, hazelnuts, chestnuts – can be taken as long as there aren't signs to the contrary. Ask permission where appropriate. If you know your wild mushrooms, the woods and fields provide delicious and plentiful harvesting in the early autumn – check what the locals are selecting. Common varieties include chanterelle (pale yellow and trumpet-shaped), *Lactarius deliciosus* (orange with ghastly green patches, but a pleasantly firm texture) and the large *cèp de Bordeaux*, the French favourite.

If you're trekking long distances, you'll have to rely on basic stocks; many refuges and mountain villages have very little in the way of victuals. Remember that food stores tend to close at lunchtime (noon–2pm in France; 2–4 or 5pm in Spain). Most mountain villages also have clean fountains, though if collecting from a stream check your map for upstream villages – they will almost certainly discharge everything into the watercourse.

Coffee and pastries (*pastas*) or doughnuts (*donuts*) are available at most cafés, too, though for a wider selection of cakes you should head for one of the many excellent *pastelerías* or *confiterías*. In larger towns, especially in Catalunya, there will often be a *panadería* or *croissantería* serving quite an array of appetizing (and healthier, whole-grain) baked goods besides the obvious bread, croissants and pizza.

Some bars specialize in **sandwiches** (*bocadillos*), and as they're usually outsize affairs in French bread, they'll do for breakfast or a light lunch. In a bar with *tapas* (see below), you can have most of what's on offer put in a sandwich, and you can often get them prepared (or buy the materials to do so) at grocery stores. Incidentally a *sandwich* is a toasted cheese and ham sandwich, usually on rather sad processed bread.

TAPAS

One of the advantages of eating in **bars** is that you can experiment. Many places have food laid out on the counter, so you can see what's available and order by pointing without necessarily knowing the names; others have blackboards (see the lists of snacks in the box on p.51). **Tapas** are small portions, three or four small chunks of fish or meat, or a dollop of salad, which traditionally used to be served up free with a drink. These days you have to pay for anything more than a few olives (where you do get free food now, it will often be called a *pincho*), but a single helping rarely costs more than 250–450ptas unless you're somewhere very flashy. In much of the Pyrenees, alas, *tapas* more often than not are apt to consist of just a cube of cheese or some tinned shellfish.

Raciones, literally "portions", are simply bigger plates of the same, and can be enough in themselves for a light meal; make sure you make it clear whether you want a *ración* or just a *tapa*. The more people you're with, of course, the better; half a dozen *tapas* or *pinchos* and three *raciones* can make a varied and quite filling meal for three or four people.

Tascas, **bodegas**, **cervecerías** and **tabernas** are all types of bar where you'll find *tapas* and *raciones*. Most of them have different sets of prices depending on whether you stand at the bar to eat (the basic charge) or sit at tables (up to 50 percent more expensive – and even more if you sit out on a terrace).

Wherever you have *tapas*, it is important to find out what is the local "**special**" and to order

it. Spaniards will commonly move from bar to bar, having just the one dish that they consider each bar does best. Other dishes, these days, can all too often be microwaved – not a good way to reheat fried squid.

MEALS AND RESTAURANTS

Once again, there's a multitude of distinctions. You can sit down and have a full meal in a *comedor*, a *cafetería*, a *restaurante* or a *marisquería* – all in addition to the more food-oriented bars.

Comedores are the places to seek out if your main criteria are price and quantity. Sometimes you will see them attached to a bar (often in a room behind), or as the dining room of a *pensión* or *hostal*, but as often as not they're virtually unmarked and discovered only if you pass an open door. You'll pay 1200–2000ptas for a **menú del día**, a complete meal of several courses, usually with wine; many *pensiones* and *hostales* offer only this, and no à la carte. At the upper end of this price range, you should expect four courses – a salad, then usually a soup, a main course and a dessert, and unlimited access to a soup tureen and wine bottle. You'll be gently pushed to take coffee after the *postre* or dessert, and it will almost always be charged extra.

Incidentally, the *comedores* of the **fancier hostales** share only the name with their humbler cousins; they can be very fancy indeed, with table linen, uniformed waiting staff and fare – and bills – to match. Incidentally, off the beaten tourist track, menus in Catalunya are often **in Catalan only** – thus the thorough translation list in the box.

Replacing *comedores* to some extent are **cafeterías**, which the local authorities now grade from one to three cups (the ratings, as with restaurants, seem to be based on facilities offered rather than the quality of the food). These can be good value, too, especially the self-service places, but their emphasis is on more northern European food, and the light snack-meals served tend to be dull. Food here often comes in the form of a **plato combinado** – literally a "combined plate" – which will be something like egg and chips or *calamares* and salad (or occasionally a weird combination like steak and a piece of fish), often with bread and a drink included. This will generally cost in the region of 700–1000ptas. *Cafeterías* often serve some kind of *menú del día* as well. You may prefer to get your *plato combinado* at a bar, which in small towns with no *comedores* may be the only way to eat inexpensively.

SPANISH FOOD AND DISHES

Basics

Pan	Bread	*Pimienta*	Pepper	*Miel*	Honey	*Cuchillo*	Knife
Mantequilla	Butter	*Sal*	Salt	*Botella*	Bottle	*Cuchara*	Spoon
Huevos	Eggs	*Azúcar*	Sugar	*Vaso*	Glass	*Mesa*	Table
Aceite	Oil	*Vinagre*	Vinegar	*Tenedor*	Fork	*La cuenta*	The bill

Typical Spanish snacks

The most usual **fillings for bocadillos** are *lomo* (loin of pork), *tortilla* and *calamares* (all of which may be served hot), *jamón* (*york* or, much better, *serrano*), *chorizo*, *salchichón* (and various other regional sausages – like the small, spicy Catalan *botifarras*), *queso* (cheese) and *atún* (probably canned). **Standard tapas and raciones** might include:

Aceitunas	Olives	*Habas*	Beans
Albondigas	Meatballs	*Habas con jamón*	Beans with ham
Anchoas	Anchovies	*Hígado*	Liver
Arroz a	Rice topped with fried	*Huevo cocido*	Hard-boiled egg
la cubana	egg and red sauce	*Jamón serrano*	Dried ham
Berberechos	Cockles	*Jamón york*	Ordinary ham
Boquerones	Fresh anchovies	*Mejillones*	Mussels
Calamares	Squid	*Navajas*	Razor clams
Callos	Tripe	*Patatas alli olli*	Potatoes in mayonnaise
Caracoles	Snails	*Patatas bravas*	Spicy potatoes
Carne en salsa	Meat in tomato sauce	*Pimientos*	Peppers
Champiñones	Mushrooms	*Pincho moruno*	Kebab
Chorizo	Spicy sausage	*Pulpo*	Octopus
Cocido	Stew	*Riñones al Jerez*	Kidneys in sherry
Empanadilla	Fish/meat turnover	*Salchichon*	Salami
Ensaladilla	Russian salad	*Sepia*	Cuttlefish
Escalibada	Aubergine/eggplant salad	*Tortilla española*	Potato omelette
Gambas	Shrimps	*Tortilla francesa*	Plain omelette

Soups (*Sopas*)

Sopa de mariscos	Seafood soup	*Gazpacho*	Cold tomato and
Caldo de gallina	Chicken soup		cucumber soup with
Sopa de pescado	Fish soup		garlic and other spices
Caldo verde or gallego	Thick cabbage-based	*Sopa de cocido*	Meat soup
	broth	*Sopa de pasta (fideos)*	Noodle soup
Caldillo	Clear fish soup		

Seafood (*Mariscos*)

Almejas	Clams		chicken
Calamares	Squid	*Chipirones*	Squid in ink
Centolla	Spider-crab	*en su tinta*	
Cigalas	King prawns	*Merluza/*	Hake/squid (or just about
Conchas finas	Large scallops	*calamares a*	anything else) fried in batter.
Gambas	Shrimps	*la romana*	
Langosta	Lobster	*Paella*	Classic Valencian dish with
Langostinos	Giant king prawns		saffron rice, chicken, seafood
Mejillones	Mussels		etc
Necora	Sea-crab	*Sepia*	Cuttlefish
Percebes	Goose-barnacles	*Vieiras*	Scallops
Pulpo	Octopus	*Zarzuela*	Seafood casserole
Arroz a la banda	Similar to paella but with no	*de mariscos*	

Fish (*Pescados*)

Anguila	Eel	*Chanquetes*	Whitebait	*Pez espada*	Swordfish
Angulas	Elvers (baby eel)	*Jurelas*	Similar to	*Rape*	Monkfish
Atún	Tuna		anchovies	*Raya*	Ray, skate
Bacalao	Cod (often salt)	*Lenguado*	Sole	*Salmonete*	Mullet
Bonito	Tuna	*Merluza*	Hake	*Sardinas*	Sardines
Boquerones	Anchovies (fresh)	*Mero*	Perch	*Trucha*	Trout

Meat (*Carne*) and Poultry (*Aves*)

Butifarra	Bratwurst	*Habas con jamón*	Ham and beans
Callos	Tripe	*Hígado*	Liver
Carne de vaca	Beef	*Lazón con grelos*	Trotter with turnips
Cerdo	Pork	*Lengua*	Tongue
Chuletas	Chops	*Lomo*	Loin (of pork)
Cochinillo	Suckling pig	*Pato*	Duck
Codorniz	Quail	*Pavo*	Turkey
Conejo	Rabbit	*Perdiz*	Partridge
Cordero	Lamb	*Pollo*	Chicken
Criadillas	Testicles	*Rebeco*	Chamois
Escalope/Milanesa	Breaded schnitzel	*Riñones*	Kidneys
Fabada asturiana	Hotpot with butter	*Solomillo*	Pork flank steak
	beans,black pudding, etc	*Ternera*	Veal

Vegetables (*Verduras y Legumes*)

Acielga	Chard	*Patatas (fritas)*	Potatoes (chips)
Alcachofas	Artichokes	*Pepino*	Cucumber
Arroz	Rice	*Pimientos (de piquillo)*	(Hot) peppers
Berenjena	Aubergine	*Puerros*	Leeks
Cardo, cardón	Cardoon stems	*Repollo*	Cabbage
Cebollas	Onions	*Tomate*	Tomatoes
Champiñones/Setas	Mushrooms	*Trigueros*	Green asparagus
Coliflor	Cauliflower	*Zanahoria*	Carrots
Espinacas	Spinach	*Arroz a la Cubana*	Rice with banana and
Garbanzos	Chickpeas		egg
Grelos	Turnips	*Pimientos rellenos*	Stuffed peppers
Guisantes	Peas	*Ensalada (mixta/verde)*	(Mixed/green) salad
Habas	Broad beans	*Menestra/*	Vegetable medley
Judías blancas	Haricot beans	*Panache de verduras*	
Judías verdes,	Green, red, black beans	*Pisto manchego*	Ratatouille
rojas, negras		*Verduras con patatas*	Boiled potatoes with
Lechuga	Lettuce		greens
Lentejas	Lentils		

Fruits (*Frutas*)

Albericoques	Apricots	*Fresas*	Strawberries	*Pavías*	Nectarines
Chirimoyas	Custard	*Higos*	Figs	*Peras*	Pears
	apples	*Limón*	Lemons	*Piña*	Pineapple
Cerezas	Cherries	*Manzanas*	Apples	*Plátanos*	Bananas
Ciruelas	Plums, prunes	*Melocotónes*	Peaches	*Sandía*	Watermelon
Datiles	Dates	*Melón*	Melon	*Toronja*	Grapefruit
Frambuesas	Raspberries	*Naranjas*	Oranges	*Uvas*	Grapes

Sweets (*Postres*)

Arroz con leche	Rice pudding	*Melocotón en almíbar*	Peaches in syrup
Crema catalana	Custard with a burnt crust	*Membrillo*	Quince paste
Cuajada	Cream-based dessert served with honey	*Nata*	Whipped cream
		Natillas	Custard
Flan	Creme caramel	*Requesón*	Whipped or beaten sweet-whey dessert
Helados	Ice cream		
		Yogur	Yogurt

Cheese

Cheeses (*quesos; formatge* in Catalan) are on the whole local, though you'll get the hard, salty *Queso manchego* everywhere. The best variety is *roncalés*, a sheep-milk product from the Valle de Roncal.

Some common terms

al ajillo	in garlic	*chilindrón*	tomato and pepper sauce served on poultry and meat
asado	roast		
a la Navarra	stuffed with ham		
a la parilla/plancha	grilled	*en salsa*	in (usually tomato) sauce
a la Romana/rebozado	fried in egg batter		
al horno	baked	*frito*	fried
alli olli	with mayonnaise	*guisado*	casserole
¡Bon Profit! (Catalan)/ ¡Buen provecho!! or ¡Aproveche! (Castilian)	bon appetit	*jarrete*	joint (of meat)
		rehogado	baked
		Soy vegeteriano.	I'm a vegetarian.
cazuela,	*cocido* stew	*Hay algo sin carne?*	Is there anything without meat?

Regional food

Catalunya: recipes and dishes

Pa amb tomaquet	Tomatoes and garlicky bread, usually taken as a late breakfast, though available all day
Esmorzar de forquilla	Breakfast of meats, cheese, omelette and perhaps wine
Samfaina	Ratatouille
Fideuà	Paella made with noodles, not rice
Amanida Català	Salad with salami
Escalivada	Baked or fried mixture of aubergines, tomatoes and peppers, often on toasted bread
Esqueixada	Salt cod and tomato salad
Epinacs a la Català	Spinach, pine nuts and raisins
Faves a la catalana	Catalan version of *Fabada*
Faves estofades	Pork and broad beans
Escudella	Thick soup based on ham or veal stock
Carn d'olla	Thick meat soup
Suquet de peix	Fish soup

Bacallá	Salt cod, served *a l'all* (with garlic) or *a l'all cremat* (creamed garlic)
Civet	Any rich game stew
Peus de porc	Pigs' feet
Confit de pato	Tender roast duck thigh/leg
Crema Català	Scorched-top custard
Menjar blanc	Almond pastry

Catalunya: basic ingredients and terms

Botifarra	Bratwurst-like sausage
Carn	Meat
Xai	Lamb
Vedella	Veal
Conill	Rabbit
Llebre	Hare
Pernil	Ham
Senglar	Boar
Pollastre	Chicken
Anxoves	Anchovies
Xipirons	Baby squid
Muslos	Mussels
Pebrot	Peppers
Pèsols	Peas

Continued overleaf

Mongets	White beans	Txipirones	Tiny squid cooked in
Suc	Fruit juice	en su tinto	their own ink
Truita	Omelette	Ajoarriero	Salted cod, often served
A la brasa	Grilled		with red peppers,
Graellada	Barbecued		tomatoes, garlic
		Angulas	Baby eels, often with garlic
Aragón:			and hot peppers
Boliches	Bean and sausage hot-pot	Idiazábal	A smoked cheese,
Migas	Fry-up of breadcrumbs,		identifiable by its yellow
	bacon and spices		rind
Serrano	Wind-dried raw ham, served	Merluza	Hake in sauce
	thinly sliced	a la Vasca	
Salmorej	Egg concoction like a potato	Ttoro	Mixed fish stew
	and rice omelette, eaten	Menestra de Tudela	Vegetable stew, using arti-
	with lots of garlic or an		chokes, beans, asparagus
	unusual poached-egg stew		and anything else in
Guirlache	Almond and toffee dessert		season
		Sopa cana	Christmas mix of milk,
Basque Country:			bread, cinnamon and
Calderete	Potato stew with sausage		turkey fat
Txistorra	A spicy sausage	Relleno	Stuffed lamb gut, like
Marmitako	Fish, potato, pepper and		Scotch haggis
	tomato stew	Txangarro	Spider crab

Moving up the scale, there are **restaurantes** (designated by one to five forks) and **marisquerías**, the latter specializing in fish and seafood. *Restaurantes* at the bottom of the scale are often not much different in price to *comedores*, and will also generally have *platos combinados* available. A fixed-price *cubierto*, *menú del día* or *menú de la casa* (all of which mean the same thing) is often better value, though: two or three courses plus wine and bread for 1000–1500ptas. Move above two forks, however, or find yourself in one of the fancier *marisquerías* (as opposed to a basic seafront fish-fry place), and prices can escalate rapidly.

In addition, in all but the most rock-bottom establishments it is customary to leave a small **tip**: the amount is up to you, though ten percent of the bill is quite sufficient. Service is normally included in a *menú del día*. The other thing to take account of in mid-range and top-end restaurants is the addition of **IVA**, a seven-percent sales tax on your bill. It should say on the menu (thus, *IVA no incluido*; in Catalan, *IVA no inclòs*) if you have to pay this. *Menús* usually include it, but not always; *a la carta* meals never do.

Spaniards generally eat very late, so most places serve food from around 1 until 4pm and from 8pm to midnight. Many restaurants **close on Sunday evening**.

DISHES

It's possible to make a few generalizations about Spanish food. If you like **fish and seafood**, you'll be in heaven in Spain as this forms the basis of a vast variety of *tapas* and is fresh and excellent even hundreds of kilometres from the sea. It's not cheap, so rarely forms part of the lowest priced *menús* (though you may get the most common fish – cod, often salted, hake or squid) but you really should make the most of what's on offer. Fish stews (*zarzuelas*) and rice-based *paellas* (which also contain meat, usually rabbit or chicken) are often memorable in seafood restaurants. *Paella* comes originally from Valencia, but you'll find versions of it all over the Pyrenees – regrettably much of it pre-packaged and microwaved.

Meat is most often grilled and served with a few fried potatoes and a couple of salad leaves, or cured or dried and served as a starter or in sandwiches. *Jamón serrano*, the Spanish version of Parma ham, is superb, though the best varieties, hailing from Extremadura and Andalucía, are extremely expensive.

Vegetables rarely amount to more than a few fries or boiled potatoes with the main dish (though you can often order a side dish, too). It's more usual to start your meal with a **salad**, or you may get hearty vegetable soups or a plate of boiled potatoes and greens as a starter. **Dessert** in the less expensive places is nearly always fresh fruit or *flan*, the Spanish *crème caramel*. There are also various varieties of *pudin* – rice pudding or assorted blancmange mixtures. Even in fancy restaurants you'll seldom find much better – stick to fruit and cheese, or make a separate foray to a *pastelería* (cake-shop). Worth a mention, if only for their grotesqueness, are certain **dessert oddities**: frozen citrus fruit (*limon* and *naranja*) stuffed with sherbet of the corresponding flavour; *músic* (nuts in muscatel); and various other decadent concoctions, mostly made by Camy and Menorquina, the two main factories. Indeed, if offered ice cream it's best to go up to the cold case and point to your choice; descriptions and ingredients are complicated, and the trade names not too informative. If you encounter a genuine *heladería* (ice cream parlour) that whips up its own, count your blessings.

VEGETARIANS AND VEGANS

Vegetarians have a fairly hard time of it in Spain: there's always something to eat, but you may get weary of eggs and omelettes (*tortilla francesa* is a plain omelette, *con champiñones* with mushrooms) offered in place of meat as a *segundo* on *menús* – and charged the same. In the larger Pyrenean foothill towns you'll find a few vegetarian restaurants and ethnic places which serve vegetable dishes. Otherwise, superb fresh produce is always available in the markets and shops; and cheese, fruit and eggs are available everywhere. In restaurants you're faced with the extra problem that pieces of meat – especially ham, which the Spanish don't seem to regard as real meat – are often added to vegetable dishes to "spice them up".

> The phrase to learn is *Soy vegetariano. Hay algo sin carne*? (I'm a vegetarian. Is there anything without meat?); you may have to add *y sin mariscos* (and without seafood) *y sin jamón* (and without ham) to be really safe.

If you're a **vegan**, you're either going have to be not too fussy or accept weight loss if you're away for any length of time. Some salads and vegetable dishes are strictly vegan, but they're few and far between. Fruit and nuts are widely available, though, nuts being sold by street vendors everywhere.

ALCOHOLIC DRINKS

Vino (wine), either *tinto* (red) – *ví negre* in Catalunya – *blanco* (white, *ví blanc* in Catalan) or *rosado/clarete* (rosé), is the invariable accompaniment to every meal and is, as a rule, extremely inexpensive. The most common bottled variety is Valdepeñas, a good standard wine from the central plains of New Castile; Rioja, from the area around Logroño, is better but a lot more expensive. Both are found all over the country. There are also scores of local wines – some of the best in Catalunya (Bach, Sangre de Toro) and Aragón (Somontano Viñas del Vero) – but you'll rarely be given any choice unless you're at a good restaurant.

Otherwise it's whatever comes out of the barrel, or the house-bottled special (ask for *caserío* or *de la casa*). This can be great, it can be lousy, but at least it will be distinctively local. In a bar, a small glass of wine will generally cost around 50–100ptas; in a restaurant, if wine is not included in the *menú*, prices start at around 400–450ptas a bottle. If it is included you'll usually get a whole bottle for two people, a *media botella* (a third to a half of a litre) for one. In Catalunya, **cavas** are the generic term for sparkling wines and champagnes trading in disguise; Freixenet will be familiar to Britons.

Cerveza, lager-type beer, is generally pretty good, though more expensive than wine. It comes in 300- to 330-ml bottles (*botellines*) or, for about the same price, on tap – a *caña* of draught beer is a small, 125-ml glass, a *caña doble* 250 ml. Many bartenders will assume you want a *doble*, so if you don't, say so. You get a *tubo* (tall narrow glass) or a *jarra* (squat stein); 500-ml measures are available as well. Locally brewed brands, such as Estrella Damm in Catalunya, tend to be more exciting than nationally available ones like Águila.

Equally refreshing, though often deceptively strong, is **sangría**, a wine-and-fruit punch which you'll come across at fiestas and in tourist bars; *tinto de verano* is basically the same red wine and soda or lemonade combination.

In mid-afternoon – or even at breakfast – many Spaniards take a *copa* of **liqueur** with their coffee. The best are *anís* (like Pernod) or *coñac*, excellent local brandy with a distinct vanilla flavour (try Magno, Soberano, or 103 to get an idea of the variety). In the Western Pyrenees, *pacharan* (often spelled *patxaran*) is a brandy made from rowanberries, not to be confused with the French wine Pacherenc.

Most **spirits** are ordered by brand name, since there are generally less expensive Spanish equivalents for standard imports. Larios Gin from Málaga, for instance, is about half the price of Gordon's Gin. Specify *nacional* to avoid getting an expensive foreign brand. Spirits can be very expensive at the trendier bars; however, wherever they are served, they tend to be staggeringly generous – the bar staff pouring from the bottle until you suggest they stop.

Mixed drinks are universally known as *Cuba Libre* or *Cubata*, though strictly speaking this is rum and Coke. Juice is *zumo*; orange, *naranja*; lemon, *limon*; tonic is *tónica*.

SOFT DRINKS AND HOT DRINKS

Try in particular *granizado* (fruit-syrup flavoured slush), the ubiquitous Bitter Kas (like a non-alcoholic Campari, very refreshing) or *horchata* (a milky drink made from tiger nuts or almonds) from one of the street stalls that spring up everywhere in summer. You can also get these drinks from *horchaterías* and from *heladerías* (ice cream parlours), or in Catalunya from the wonderful milk bars known as *granjas*. Although you can drink the **water** almost everywhere it usually tastes better out of a bottle – inexpensive *agua mineral* comes either sparkling (*con gas*) or still (*sin gas*).

Café (coffee) – served in cafés, *heladerías* and bars – is invariably espresso, slightly bitter and, unless you specify otherwise, served black (*café solo*). If you want it white ask for *café cortado* (small cup with a drop of milk) or *café con leche* (made with lots of hot milk). For a large cup ask for a *doble* or *grande*. Coffee is also frequently mixed with brandy or cognac, such concoctions being called *carajillo*.

Té (tea) is also available at most bars, although Spaniards usually drink it black. If you want milk it's safest to ask afterwards, since ordering *té con leche* might well get you a glass of warm milk with a teabag floating on top.

DRINKS AND BEVERAGES

ENGLISH	SPANISH		
		Tea	*Té*
		Drinking chocolate	*Chocolate*
Alcohol			
Beer	*Cerveza*	**Soft drinks**	
Wine	*Vino*	Water	*Agua*
Champagne	*Champan*	Mineral water	*Agua mineral*
		sparkling	*con gas*
Hot drinks		still	*sin gas*
Coffee	*Café*	Milk	*Leche*
Espresso coffee	*Café solo*	Juice	*Zumo*
Cappuccino coffee	*Café con leche*	Tiger-nut drink	*Horchata*
Decaff	*Descafeinado*	Non-alcoholic Campari	*Bitter Kas*

COMMUNICATIONS: POST, PHONES AND THE MEDIA

Both the French and Spanish postal and telecommunications systems work reasonably well, and with a smattering of secondary-school or university language study, you can derive enjoyment – or at least information – from the respective French and Spanish newspapers and magazines.

FRANCE

The French term for a **post office** is *La Poste*. Post offices are generally open 9am to noon and 2pm to 5pm, Monday to Saturday morning, though in the smaller villages lunch hours and closing times can vary. You can have letters sent to any post office; they should be addressed (preferably with the surname underlined and in capitals) **Poste Restante**, Poste Centrale, followed by the name of the town. To collect your mail you need a passport and there may be a small charge. Ask for all your names to be checked, as filing systems tend to be idiosyncratic.

For **sending** letters remember that you can buy **stamps** (*timbres*) with less queuing from tobacconists (*tabacs*). *Aérogrammes* are simplest; large letters or small packets are best sent at a main *poste*, where they'll probably be more conversant with overseas rates. Ordinary postcards and letters within the EU cost 3F, to North America 4.40F and to Australasia 5.20F. The postal service in the mountains is extremely efficient, though a little more relaxed than elsewhere in France. If there's snow blocking the road the post might not get collected, for instance, but delays

are on the whole no more common than down in the lowlands.

TELEPHONES

You can make **domestic and international phone calls** from any phone box (*cabine*) and can receive calls where there's a blue logo of a ringing bell – the number is usually on a metal plaque overhead. **Phone cards**, obtainable from PTT branches, train stations and some *tabacs*, have now mostly replaced coin phones; the cheapest cards cost 40.60F for 50 units or 97.50F for 100 units. In coin-only phone boxes, still found in cafés, bar basements and rural districts, put the money in first (0.5F, 1F, 2F, 5F, 10F pieces, minimum charge 1F) after lifting the receiver but before dialling; you can add more once you're connected.

For all calls within France, dial all ten digits of **the number**. Numbers beginning with ☎08.00 are toll-free; those beginning with ☎08.36 are premium rate. For international calls, dial ☎00, wait for a tone, and then dial the country code and subscriber number.

There are a growing number of Point Phone telephones in bars, restaurants, hotels and even shops. These tend to be expensive, as the tariff is set by the proprietor. The cheapest option – though these, like coin phones, are being phased out – is a post office *cabine*, where you don't use coins since a cashier keeps a tally of the bill. Even here, though, there's no meter – despite the French obsession with hi-tech – so it's worth checking the clerk's arithmetic as mistakes are made. You can avoid payment altogether with a **reverse-charge** or **collect call**, known in French as *téléphoner en PCV*. To do this for Britain through a UK operator, dial ☎00.00.44; for North America's AT&T operator, dial ☎00.00.11.

Cheap rates are in effect from midnight to 8am and 9.30pm to midnight Monday to Friday, from midnight to 8am and 2pm to midnight on Saturday, and all day Sunday. A cheap-rate call to the UK or the Irish Republic is about 3F/minute, to North America about 4F/minute and to Australasia nearly 8F/minute, but costs are dropping all the time as there's fierce competition from private carriers. Calling-cards, either pre-loaded or billed to a credit card, may work out cheaper, but you need to remember their free access number for

Speaking clock☎36.99

Mountain weather
Eastern Pyrenees ☎04.61.71.11.31 or 61.71.11.11 (24-hr recording)
Central Pyrenees ☎05.59.62.17.34 or 59.27.50.50 (24-hr recording)
Western Pyrenees ☎05.59.23.84.15 or 59.22.03.30 (24-hr recording)

Phoning abroad from France
to Australia: dial ☎00, wait for the international tone, then dial 61 + area code minus first 0 + number.
to Britain: dial ☎00, wait for the international tone, then dial 44 + area code minus first 0 + number.

to Ireland: dial ☎00, wait for the international tone, then dial 353 + area code minus first 0 + number.
to New Zealand: dial ☎00, wait for the international tone, then dial 64 + area code minus first 0 + number.
to North America: dial ☎00, wait for the international tone, then dial 1 + area code + number.

Phoning France
from Australia: dial ☎011 + 33 + nine-digit number (omitting first 0).
from Britain & Ireland: dial ☎00 + 33 + nine-digit number (omitting first 0).
from New Zealand: dial ☎0044 + 33 + nine-digit number (omitting first 0).
from North America: dial ☎011 + 33 + nine-digit number (omitting first 0).

France and your own account number when dialling – and the access numbers are often engaged.

THE MEDIA

A reasonable selection of **foreign newspapers** is on sale in selected resorts and larger towns such as Pau or Perpignan. Among **French national dailies**, *Le Monde* is the most intellectual, using a mainstream-style French that is easiest to understand, but austerely photo-less. *Libération* (*Libé* for short), is moderately left-wing, independent and colloquial, with good, selective, mostly feature coverage and colour format; it tends to sell out quickly. *L'Humanité* is the far-left, Communist-affiliated paper. Among the right-of-centre papers, *Le Figaro* is the most respected and readable.

Weeklies, in the *Time/Newsweek* mould, include left-leaning *Le Nouvel Observateur*, its conservative counterpart *L'Express* and the boringly centrist *L'Évenement de Jeudi*. **Satirical investigative journals** include the weekly *Canard Enchaîné*, while *Charlie-Hebdo* fits the mould of the UK *Private Eye*.

Nationwide **monthlies** include the young, trendy and cheap *Nova*, with excellent listings for cultural events, and *Actuel*, which is good for news analysis. The bi-monthly **Pyrénées** (widely available, 38F) is well worth a browse for destination features, news snippets and suggestions

for obscure trekking or touring routes; twice a year or so, there are *hors série* special issues (45F), devoted to distinct topics (eg the Basque country, Cathar castles, family day-walks).

If you've got a **radio**, you can catch the BBC World Service on 648kHz or 198kHz longwave from midnight to 5am, and Radio 4 during the day; BBC Radio 5 Live can be picked up on 693kHz. For radio news in French, there's the state-run France Inter (87.8FM), Europe 1 (104.7FM) or round-the-clock news on France Infos (105.5FM).

French **TV** has six channels, three public – F2, Arte and F3 – one subscription – Canal Plus, with some unencrypted programmes – and two commercial broadcasts – TF1 and M6. Arte is a joint Franco-German endeavour devoted to high-brow fare including opera, films and critics' panels. Canal Plus is the main movie channel (and funder of the French film industry), though F3 screens a fair selection of serious films, especially (undubbed) late Sunday night. The main news broadcasts are at 8.30pm on Arte, and at 8pm on F2 and TF1.

SPAIN

Post offices in Spain – marked *Correos* in Castilian, *Correus* in Catalan – are generally open Monday to Friday from 8am to noon and again from 5 to 7.30pm, though you will encounter differing schedules throughout the country, while big

SPAIN: USEFUL PHONE NUMBERS

Mountain weather
Central Pyrenees ☎976/23 43 36 or 23 09 01 (24-hr recording) or 56 91 06
Eastern Pyrenees ☎93/21 25 666 or ☎93/21 25 816
Western Pyrenees ☎943/27 40 30

Phoning abroad from Spain
to Australia: dial ☎07, wait for the international tone, then dial 61 + area code minus first 0 + number.
to Britain: dial ☎07, wait for the international tone, then dial 44 + area code minus first 0 + number.
to Ireland: dial ☎07, wait for the international tone, then dial 353 + area code minus first 0 + number.
to New Zealand: dial ☎07, wait for the international tone, then dial 64 + area code minus first 0 + number.

to North America: dial ☎07, wait for the international tone, then dial 1 + area code + number.

Phoning Spain
from Australia: dial ☎011 + 34 + area code less the 9 + number.
from Britain & Ireland: dial ☎00 + 34 + area code less the 9 + number.
from New Zealand: dial ☎0044 + 34 + area code less the 9 + number.
from North America: dial ☎011 + 34 + area code less the 9 + number.

Provincial area codes
Barcelona ☎93
Girona ☎972
Huesca ☎974
Lleida ☎973
Pamplona ☎948
San Sebastián ☎943
Mobile ☎908, 909

branches in large cities may have considerably longer hours. Except in the largest cities there's only one post office in each town.

You can have letters sent **poste restante** (*Lista de Correos*) to any Spanish post office: they should be addressed (preferably with the surname underlined and in capitals) to *Lista de Correos* followed by the name of the town and province. To collect, take along your passport and, if you're expecting mail, ask the clerk to check under all of your names – letters are often found filed under first or middle names.

Outbound mail is reasonably reliable, with letters or cards taking around five days to a week to the UK, a week to ten days to North America.

TELEPHONES

Spanish public **phone boxes** work well, though no number is posted so you can't phone them back. If you can't find one, many bars also have pay phones you can use. Boxes take both coins (5-, 25-, 50-, 100- or 250-peseta pieces, but only the lighter, post-1992 coins), or you can buy 1000-peseta or 2000-peseta **phonecards** at tobacconists, or use the most common **credit cards** (200pta minimum, but you'll have no trouble exceeding that on overseas calls). With credit cards, the swipe readers are rather temperamental; you'll know you've succeeded when the LCD display says "processing" in the local language. Spanish provincial (and some overseas) dialling codes are displayed in most cabins, as well as dialling – and credit card – instructions in English. The **ringing tone** is long, **engaged** is shorter and rapid; the standard Spanish response is *dígame* (speak to me).

For **international calls,** you can use any phone box marked *teléfono internacional,* or go to one of the dwindling number of public **Telefónica** offices, where you pay afterwards. International and domestic rates – among the highest in the EU at 8.93ptas per unit (about 70p a minute to the UK) – are slightly cheaper after 10pm, and after 2pm on Saturday and all day Sunday. If you're using a phone box to call abroad, you're best off using a phone card; failing that, insert at least 200ptas initially to ensure a connection, and make sure you have a good stock of 100-peseta pieces.

If you want to make a **reverse-charge** or **collect call** (*cobro revertido*), you'll have to go to a

ANDORRA
Andorra now has it's own phone code, ☎376.

Telefónica, where you can expect queues at cheap-rate times. Some hotels will arrange reverse-charge calls for you, but as with all phone calls from hotels you'll often be stung for an outrageous surcharge.

THE MEDIA

British newspapers and the *International Herald Tribune* are on sale during the summer season in most large foothill towns, particularly Girona, Pamplona and San Sebastián.

Of the **Spanish newspapers** the best are Madrid's *El País* and *El Mundo* and Barcelona's *La Vanguardia*, all of which are liberal in outlook and have good arts and foreign news coverage, including comprehensive regional "what's on" listings and supplements each Friday. *El País* is noted for exceptional (and independent) columnists such as Manuel Vázquez Montalban. Other national papers include *ABC*, solidly elitist with a hard moral line against divorce and abortion, and the centrist *Diario 16*.

The regional press is generally run by local magnates and is predominantly right-wing, though often supporting local autonomy movements. Nationalist press includes *Avui* in Catalunya, printed largely in Catalan, and the Basque papers *El Diario Vasco*, *Deia* and *Egin*, the last a supporter of ETA, and partly in Euskera.

Spain's most interesting **magazine** is *Ajo Blanco*, a monthly from Barcelona, providing a generally stimulating mix of politics, culture and style. The more arty and indulgent *El Europeo*, a massive quarterly publication from Madrid, can also be worth a browse. And of course, Spain is the home of chatty *Holá* – the parent of Britain's *Hello*.

If you can read Spanish, the Spanish travel magazine **Altaïr** (published in Barcelona) has a regular "Aire Libre" section on walking, biking or canyoning excursions to some of the more obscure corners of the country, as well as occasional main features – all well informed and good reading.

Even up in the mountains, you'll inadvertently catch more **TV** than you expect sitting in bars and restaurants; Spaniards are reckoned to be the continent's champion tube-heads in terms of annual hours per person in front of the box. Soaps – known as *culebrones* in Castilian – are a particular speciality, either South American *telenovas*, which take up most of the daytime programming, or well-travelled British or Australian exports. Sports fans are well catered for, with regular live coverage of **soccer** and basketball matches, mainly on Canal 5. In Catalunya, Channels 3 and 4 broadcast exclusively in Catalan.

If you have a **radio** which picks up short wave you can tune in to the BBC World Service, broadcasting in English for most of the day on frequencies between 12MHz (24m) and 4MHz (75m). The FM dial is often rewarding, particularly Catalunya's **classical station**, which can even be picked up in the high-altitude wilds of Cerdanya or Aigües Tortes.

OPENING HOURS AND PUBLIC HOLIDAYS

Almost everything in both France and Spain – shops, museums, churches, tourist offices, most banks – closes for a siesta of at least two hours in the hottest part of the day. There's a lot of variation but basic summer working hours are 9.30am to 1.30pm and 4.30 to 7.30pm in Spain, and 8am to noon or 1pm and 2 or 3pm to 6.30pm in France. In both countries certain shops do now stay open all day, and there is a move towards "normal" working hours. Nevertheless, you'll get far less aggravated if you accept that the early afternoon is best spent asleep, or in a bar, or both.

FRANCE

Food shops in France often don't re-open until halfway through the afternoon, closing between 7.30 and 8pm or just before the evening meal. So if you're intent on buying a picnic lunch, you'll need to do so before you're ready to think about eating. Sunday and Monday are the standard French **closing days**, though you'll always find at least one *boulangerie* (baker's) open. Street markets tend to operate in the mornings only.

Museums open between 9 and 10am, close for lunch at noon until 2pm or 3pm, with an afternoon shift only until 5pm or 6pm. Summer times may differ from winter times; if they do, both are indicated in the listings. **Summer hours** usually extend from mid-May or early June to mid-September, but sometimes they apply only during July and August, occasionally even from Palm Sunday to All Saints' Day. Don't forget closing days – usually Monday or Tuesday, sometimes both. Admission charges can be very off-putting, though most state-owned museums have one or two days of the week when they're free and you can get a big reduction at most places by showing a student card (or passport if you're under 26 or over 60).

Churches and cathedrals are almost always open all day, with charges only for the crypt, treasuries or cloister, and little fuss about how you're dressed. Where they are closed you may have to go during Mass to take a look, on Sunday morning or at other times which you'll see posted up on the door. In small towns and villages, how-

ever, getting the key is not difficult – ask anyone nearby or hunt out the priest, whose house is known as the *presbytère*.

FRENCH NATIONAL HOLIDAYS

There are thirteen French **national holidays** (*jours fériés*), when most shops and businesses, though not museums or restaurants, are closed. They are:
January 1 New Year's Day
Easter Sunday
Easter Monday
Ascension Day (forty days after Easter)
Pentecost (seventh Sunday after Easter, plus the Monday)
May 1 May Day/Labour Day
May 8 Victory in Europe Day
July 14 Bastille Day
August 15 Assumption of the Virgin Mary
November 1 All Saints' Day
December 25 Christmas Day

SPAIN

Most **museums** observe the siesta with a break between 1 and 4 in the afternoon. Their summer schedules are listed in the *Guide*; watch out for Sundays (most open mornings only) and Mondays (most close all day). Admission charges vary, but there's usually free entrance or a reduction if you show an ISIC or FIYTO card. Anywhere run by the Patrimonio Nacional, the national organization which preserves monuments, is free to EU citizens on Wednesday – take your passport to prove your nationality.

Getting into **churches** can present more of a problem. The really important ones, including most cathedrals, operate in much the same way as museums and almost always have some entry charge to see their most valued treasures and paintings, or their cloisters. Other churches, though, are usually kept locked, opening only for worship in the early morning and/or the evening (between around 6–9pm). So you'll either have to try at these times, or find someone with a key. This is time-consuming but rarely difficult, since a sacristan or custodian almost always lives nearby and most people will know where to direct you. You're expected to give a

SPANISH NATIONAL HOLIDAYS

January 1 New Year's Day
January 6 *Tres Reyes* (Three Kings; Epiphany)
Good Friday
Easter Sunday
Easter Monday
May 1 May Day/Labour Day
Corpus Christi (early or mid-June)
June 24 *Día de San Juan*, the king's name-saint
July 25 *Día de Santiago*

August 15 *Assunción de la Virgen*
(Assumption of the Virgin)
October 12 National Day
November 1 *Todos Santos* (All Saints' Day)
December 6 *Día de la Constitución*
December 8 *Día de la Concepción Inmaculada*
(Immaculate Conception)
December 25 Christmas Day

small tip, or donation. For all churches "decorous" dress is required, ie no shorts, bare shoulders, etc.

Public holidays can (and will) disrupt your plans at some stage. There are fourteen Spanish national holidays, listed in the box above, and scores of **local festivals** (different in every town and village, usually marking the local saint's day); any of them will mean that everything except bars (and *hostales*, etc) locks its doors.

In addition, **August** is Spain's own holiday month, when the big cities are semideserted, and many of the shops and restaurants, even museums, close. In contrast, it can prove nearly impossible to find a room in the more popular coastal and mountain resorts at these times; similarly, seats on planes, trains and buses at this time should be booked well in advance.

FESTIVALS

Especially in July and August, it's practically impossible not to stumble on some sort of festival during your stay: either a tourist-board-organized concert series, often in a wonderful medieval venue, or just a brass band and drinks in a pennant-hung village square. On both sides of the Pyrenees religion and folk history are the main launching platforms for a party, but apart from the occasional Mass to ensure everybody is spiritually insured, the festivities rarely dwell on solemn matters. Even pilgrimages are often celebrated with great gusto and, like many of the town and village celebrations, involve a colourful and photogenic procession. Festivals in major resorts tend to be more tourist-oriented, though, featuring music, art and theatre programmes.

The list of festivals is potentially endless, and although you'll find the major events detailed in features at the beginning of each chapter we can't pretend that it's exhaustive. Local tourist offices should have more information about what's going on in their area at any given time. Outsiders are always welcome at festivals, the one problem being that during any of the most popular you'll find it difficult and expensive to find a bed. If you're planning to coincide with a festival, try to reserve your accommodation well in advance.

FRANCE

Catholicism is still deeply engrained in the culture of the French Pyrenees; thus saints' days still bring people out in all their finery, ready to indulge before or after Mass has been said. Such occasions, along with the celebrations focused on wine and food production, are usually very genuine affairs intended for a local audience. Other festivals, based on historical events, folklore or literature, are more obviously money-spinners and forums for municipal prestige. Finally, there are the cultural seasons of the larger towns and resorts, centred on film, music or drama, which while enjoyable enough have few pretensions to religious significance.

Some **harvest** celebrations are highly public, with charges levied for sampling; others – in the smaller vineyards and cooperatives – are more a private celebration for the pickers and packers, though here again there are often open days for public tastings of previous years' produce. From early September the **Roussillon** wine region is particularly active, and later in the month there are *Fêtes des Pommes* all over the place (especially the **Têt valley**), with plenty of opportunity to sample and buy local produce from apple jelly to potent cider. An unusual variation on the harvest *fête* is the late October celebration of the pepper crop at **Espelette**, in the Western Pyrenees.

Easter Week is normally marked by special church services, processions and associated parties. One of the most striking is the *Procession de la Sanch* at **Perpignan**, where penitents parade around in red robes, tall pointed hats and masks reminiscent of Ku Klux Klan garb. Many small towns and villages have their own processions, often venerating an image from the parish church – a popular example is the *Procession de la Vierge* at **Font-Romeu** in September. A good example of the often more boisterous **folklore** festivals is the *Fête de l'Ours* at **Arles-sur-Tech** in February, which involves a lot of men chasing another lot of men dressed in bear costumes.

Most local carnivals are held in midsummer, and usually involve several days of eating, drinking and merry-making; as a rule, they do not prompt the increased hotel prices of some of the better-known events. Throughout the French Pyrenees, **Bastille Day** (July 14) is commemorated by marvellous firework displays. Innumerable other **historical events**, of varying degrees of impor-

tance, are celebrated all over the region. For instance, at Montségur in June there are *Son et Lumière* shows and fireworks commemorating the Cathars, while the next month at Foix there is a week-long festival celebrating the life of Gaston Fébus, including jousting and a medieval fair.

Sports events are great crowd-pullers, none more so than the **Tour de France** bike race, which visits the Pyrenees in July – even the police relax and enjoy themselves, loosening ties and accepting cool drinks. *Boules* tournaments and – in Basque areas – *pelota* championships are also guaranteed to stop normal business.

SPAIN

It's hard to beat the experience of arriving in some small Spanish village, expecting no more than a bed for the night, to discover the streets festooned with flags and streamers, a band playing in the plaza and the entire population out celebrating the local *fiesta*. Everywhere in the country, from the tiniest hamlet to the great cities, will take at least one day off a year to devote to partying. Usually it's the local saint's day, but there are celebrations, too, of harvests, of deliverance from the Moors, of safe return from the sea – any excuse will do. Although these take place throughout the year, it is often the obscure and unexpected event which proves to be most fun; there is always music, dancing, traditional costume and an immense spirit of enjoyment. The main event of most *fiestas* is a parade, either a solemn one behind a revered holy image, or a more light-hearted affair with fancy costumes and *gigantones*, grotesque giant carnival figures which trundle down the streets terrorizing children.

The most famous of all Spanish Pyrenean *fiestas* are the **San Fermines** at **Pamplona** (July 6–14), which attract thousands of visitors from all over the world. The main event is the **encierro** or running of the bulls, in which young men sprint through the streets in front of the terrified and aggressive animals – most of whom go to their deaths in the subsequent bullfights (see below). Many other towns and villages have similar festivities, with folk dancing, singing and a great deal of drinking, but these lesser events don't feature the inflated hotel and restaurant prices of Pamplona.

As in France, **harvest** time is also a big excuse for boozy celebrations, especially in the **Alt**

Empordà region. Many of the festivals in the Spanish Pyrenees are more conspicuously **religious** than on the French side, with more weight given to the procession of the revered holy image before the partying begins. Amongst better-known Catalan events are *Carnival* at various villages along the Noguera Pallaresa, the festival of *Sant Marc* at the shrine of Queralt on April 25 and – all over Catalunya – bonfires as the centrepiece of *Dia de Sant Joan* (June 21–24, variable) observances. The Corpus Christi *Festa de Patum* at **Berga** is the biggest late-spring bash in Catalunya, renowned for its high spirits and outrageous *gigantones*.

Folkloric and **rural** festivals are celebrated enthusiastically, often including demonstrations of dwindling skills in addition to the normal shenanigans: examples are the leather fair at Sort in January, Rialp's sheep-shearing contest in June and the traditional log-rafting at La Pobla de Segur on the first Sunday in July. An unusual **historical** event is the battle of the women, fought on the first Friday in May at **Jaca**, celebrating the role played by townswomen in a defeat of the Moorish enemy in 795.

Spain too has its succession of **local cultural programmes** in **July** and **August**, particularly at **San Sebastián**, interpolated with the two festivals of the **Virgin**: her ascension into heaven (*Assunción*) on August 14–15, and her birth on September 8.

SAINTS' DAYS

Note that saints' day festivals can **vary in date**, often being observed over the weekend closest to the dates given in our "Festivals" listings at the start of each chapter. In other cases the fun occurs on the **evening before** the date given, with only a Mass taking place on the morning concerned. Our listings often try to indicate this by giving a range of dates – the earlier you show up, the more likely the chance of coinciding with the actual party.

BULLFIGHTS

Bullfights are an integral part of many Pyrenean festivals, on both sides of the frontier; the larger foothill towns often stage a three- or four-day season during summer. **Los Toros**, as Spaniards refer to bullfighting, are big business. Each year an estimated 24,000 bulls are killed in Spain before a live audience of over thirty million, and many more on televison. The Interior Ministry estimates that 200,000 people are involved in some way in the Spanish industry, and the top performers, the **matadores**, have incomes on a par with the country's biggest pop stars. There is some opposition to the activity from Spanish animal-welfare groups, rather more from the French, but neither is widespread: if Spaniards tell you that bullfighting is controversial, they are probably referring to practices in the trade. In recent years, bullfighting critics (whom you will find on the arts pages of the newspapers) have been expressing their perennial outrage at the routine but illegal shaving of bulls' horns prior to the *corrida*. Bulls' horns are as sensitive as fingernails a few millimetres in, and raw horns deter the animal from charging; they affect the creature's gauging of distance, too, reducing the danger for the *matador* still further.

Notwithstanding such abuses (and there are plenty of others), *Los Toros* maintain their **aficionados**. Indeed, their numbers are on the rise, with the elaborate argot of the *corrida* attaining cult status among the young as the days of Franco's patronage of bullfighting are forgotten, and TV stations paying big money for major events. A surprising number of devotees are women and teenage girls – who have been known to shower heart-throb-handsome *matadores* with knickers and bras in the ring as tokens of appreciation. To more serious *aficionados* (a word that implies more knowledge and appreciation than the English "fan"), "the bulls" are a culture and a ritual in which the emphasis is on the way man and bull "perform" together, with art the issue rather than cruelty. If pressed on the slaughter of an animal, they generally fail to understand your point of view. Fighting bulls are, they will respond, bred for the industry; they live a reasonably pampered life before they are killed; and, if bullfights went, so too would the bulls.

In France, the resurgence of *Les Taureaux*, as it's called there, has been attended by fierce debate over whether *corridas* are really a traditional folkloric manifestation of the regions concerned – Languedoc-Rousillon and the Basque country, precisely those areas with a large population descended from Spanish immigrants settled there since the turn of the century. Thus advocates have been at pains to demonstrate evidence of bullfighting from before 1900; it now appears the spectacles will be allowed to proceed south of a line approximately joining Bayonne, Toulouse and Nîmes.

Whether you attend a *corrida*, obviously, is down to your own feelings and ethics. If you spend any time at all in the Pyrenees during the season (which runs March–Oct), you will encounter bullfights, at least on a bar TV, and that will as likely as not make up your mind. If you decide to go, try to see the biggest and most prestigious event available, where star performers are likely to despatch the bulls with "art" and a successful, "clean" kill. There are few sights worse than a *matador* making a prolonged and messy kill, while the audience whistles – unfortunately more likely in France, where there's not as yet significant homegrown talent in man or beast, and often second-rate bullfighters (and bulls) have to be imported. Established and popular **matadores** include Enrique Ponce, Cesar Rincón, Victor Mendes, Joselito, Litri, Paco Ojeda, Ortega Cano, José María Manzanares and Finito de Cordoba. Three new stars are El Cordobés, a young pretender of spectacular technique who claims to be his legendary namesake's illegitimate son; Jesulín de Ubrique, who in 1994 pioneered the idea of women-only audiences; and Cristina Sanchez, the first woman to make it into the top flight for many decades. The most exciting and skilful performances of all are by **mounted matadores**, or *rejoneadores*; this is the oldest form of *corrida*, developed in Andalucía during the seventeenth century.

THE CORRIDA

The *corrida* begins with a **procession**, to the accompaniment of a *paso doble* by the band. Leading the procession are two *algauziles* or "constables", on horseback and in traditional costume, followed by the three *matadores*, who will each fight two bulls, and their *cuadrillas*, their personal "team" comprising two mounted *picadores* and three *banderilleros*. At the back are the mule teams who will drag off the dead bulls.

Once the ring is empty, the *algauzil* opens the *toril* (the bulls' enclosure) and the first bull appears – a moment of great beauty – to be "tested" by the *matador* or his *banderilleros* using pink and gold capes. These preliminaries conducted (and they can be short, if the bull is ferocious), the **suerte de picar** ensues, in which the *picadores* ride out and take up position at opposite sides of the ring, while the bull is distracted by other

toreros. Once they are in place, the bull is made to charge one of the horses; the *picador* drives his short-pointed lance into the bull's neck, while it tries to toss his padded, blindfolded horse, thus tiring the bull's powerful neck and back muscles. This is repeated up to three times, until the horn sounds for the *picadores* to leave. For most neutral spectators, it is the least acceptable and most squalid stage of the *corrida*, and it is clearly not a pleasant experience for the horses, who have had their vocal cords cut out.

The next stage, the **suerte de banderillas**, involves the placing of three sets of *banderillas* (coloured sticks with barbed ends) into the bull's shoulders. Each of the three *banderilleros* delivers these in turn, attracting the bull's attention with the movement of his own body rather than a cape, and placing the *banderillas* whilst both he and the bull are running towards each other. He then runs to safety out of the bull's vision, sometimes with the assistance of his colleagues.

Once the *banderillas* have been placed, the **suerte de matar** begins, and the *matador* enters the ring alone, having exchanged his pink and gold cape for the red one. He (or she) salutes the president of the ring and then dedicates the bull either to an individual, to whom he gives his hat, or to the audience by placing his hat in the centre of the ring. It is in this part of the *corrida* that judgements are made and the performance is focused, as the *matador* displays his skills on the (by now exhausted) bull. He uses the movements of the cape to attract the bull, while his body remains still. If he does well, the band will start to play, while the crowd *olé* each pass. This stage lasts around ten minutes and ends with the kill. The *matador* attempts to get the bull into a position where he can drive a sword between its shoulders and through to the heart for a coup de grâce. In practice, he rarely succeeds, instead using a second sword, crossed at the end, to cut the bull's spinal cord; this causes instant death.

If the audience are impressed by the *matador*'s performance, they will wave their handkerchiefs and shout for an award to be made by the president. He can award one or both ears, and a tail – the better the display, the more pieces he gets – while if the *matador* has excelled himself, he will be carried out of the ring by the crowd, through the *puerta grande*, the main door, which is normally kept locked. The bull, too, may be applauded for its performance, as it is dragged out by the mule team.

If you want to know more about the international **opposition to bullfighting**, contact the World Society for the Protection of Animals, 2 Langley Lane, London SW8 1TJ ☎0171/793 0540; PO Box 190, Boston, MA 02130 ☎617/522-7000; PO Box 15, Toronto, Ontario, M5J 2HT ☎416/369-0044. Spain's Anti-Bullfight Committee (*Comité Antitaurino*) can be contacted by mail via: Apartado 3098, 50080 Zaragoza.

Tickets for *corridas* in Spain are 2000ptas and up – as much as 14,000ptas for the prime seats and prestigious fights. The cheapest seats are *gradas*, the highest rows at the back, from where you can see everything that happens without too much of the detail; the front rows are known as the *barreras*. Seats are also divided into *sol* (sun), *sombra* (shade) and *sol y sombra* (shaded after a while), though these distinctions have become less relevant as more and more bullfights start later in the day, at 6pm or 7pm, rather than the traditional 5pm. The *sombra* seats are more expensive, not so much for the spectators' comfort as the fact that most of the action takes place in the shade.

On the way in, you can rent **cushions** – two hours sitting on concrete is not much fun. Beer and soft drinks are sold inside.

TROUBLE, POLICE AND SEXUAL HARASSMENT

In general both sides of the Pyrenees are remarkably safe, with weather and terrain usually posing more potential threats than fellow holiday-makers. In the foothill towns and busy ski resorts, take normal precautions: keep your wallet in your front pocket and your handbag under your elbow, and you won't have much to worry about. If you should get attacked – only likely in the two or three largest cities described – hand over the money and start dialling the cancellation numbers for your travellers' cheques and credit cards.

FRANCE

All the comments about leaving cars unattended under "Spain", p.67, apply to France as well, with an extra need for vigilance in such larger towns as Perpignan, Pau or Bayonne. Foreign or rental number plates are easy to spot. Good insurance is the only answer, but even so do not tempt fate by leaving vehicles unlocked or valuables in plain sight, either of which may invalidate the best of policies.

OFFENCES

• If you have an **accident** while driving, you are required to fill in and sign a *constat à l'aimable* (jointly agreed statement); car insurers are supposed to give you this with a policy, though in practice few seem to have heard of it.

For non-criminal **driving violations** such as speeding or not wearing seat belts, the police will impose an on-the-spot fine; if you can't pay in cash or travellers' cheques, you and the vehicle may be locked up. You can be stopped anywhere in France and asked to produce ID – a far more likely proposition if you're black or Asian. If it happens, it's not worth being difficult or facetious.

• Should you be arrested on any charge, you have the right to contact your consulate or embassy. Although the police are not always as cooperative as they might be, it *is* their duty to assist you – likewise in the case of losing your passport or all your money.

• People caught smuggling or possessing **drugs**, even a few grammes of marijuana, are liable to find themselves in jail, and consulates will not be sympathetic. This is not to say that hard-drug consumption isn't a visible activity: there are scores of kids dealing in *poudre* (heroin) in the big French cities and the authorities are unable to do much about it. As a rule, people are no more nor less paranoid about marijuana busts than they are in the UK or USA.

POLICE

There are two main types of French police (popularly known as *les flics*): the **Police Nationale** and the **Gendarmeries Nationale**. For all practical purposes, they are indistinguishable; if you need to report a theft, or other incident, you can go to either.

A different proposition are the **CRS** (*Compagnies Républicaines de Sécurité*), a mobile force of heavies, sporadically dressed in green combat gear and armed with riot equipment, whose brutality in the May 1968 battles turned public opinion to the side of the students. But in the Pyrenees you may come across specialized **mountaineering sections** of the CRS; unlike their urban brethren, these are unfailingly helpful, friendly and approachable, providing rescue services and guidance.

SEXUAL AND RACIAL HARASSMENT

There's no need for women to feel any less safe in France than at home. Unlike further south in the Mediterranean, machismo is not overt, and young men don't, on the whole, feel honour-bound to pester any unaccompanied young female. In trains and on the trail alike, passers-by are prone to look you up and down and possibly make comment, but this is something women do as much as men.

Problems can arise, however, from misjudging situations without familiar linguistic and cultural clues. A "Bonjour" or "Bonsoir" on the street is almost always a pick-up line. If you so much as return the greeting, you let yourself in for a persistent monologue and a difficult brush-off job. On the other hand, it's not unusual to be offered a drink in a rural bar if you're on your own and not to be pestered even if you accept, so not every overture is necessarily a come-on.

You may, as a woman, be warned about "*les Arabes*" – routine French **racism**. If you are Arab, Asian or black, or just look like you might be, your chances of completely avoiding unpleasantness are slim. Empty hotels claiming to be full, police demanding your papers and abusive treatment from both immigration officials and ordinary people are depressingly commonplace. The clamp down on illegal immigration and much tougher public order laws have resulted in a significant increase in police stop-and-search operations, so carrying your passport at all times is a good idea.

SPAIN

While you're unlikely to encounter any trouble during the course of a normal visit to the Spanish Pyrenees, it's worth remembering that the Spanish police, polite enough in the usual course of events, can be extremely unpleasant if you get on the wrong side of them.

If you have a **car**, and especially if you're doing loop treks with the vehicle left at a trailhead, leave as little as possible in view, or indeed in the car at all. At the very least take the tape deck with you, or stash it out of sight. In the lonelier valleys organized gangs rifle parked cars, and they're not too picky about what they steal: tools, clothing, the registration papers in particular. The vehicles themselves are rarely stolen, if that's any consolation. **Cars with French numberplates** are more likely to be vandalized in the Spanish Basque country – this is usually ascribed to retaliation by ETA sympathizers for the French crackdown on their brethren. Rental vehicles, fortunately, are not conspicuously labelled as such.

Looking for hotel rooms, don't leave any bags unattended anywhere. This applies especially to buildings where the hotel or *hostal* is on the higher floors and you're tempted to leave baggage in the hallway or ground-floor lobby.

Catalunya now has a special tourist/consumer protection troubleshooting hotline: dial ☎900/30 03 03 (it's free), and an English-speaking operator will help you with misrepresented hotels, problems with air tickets, etc. It's designed more for package-tour patrons, but could be worth a try for other situations.

If your car or room is burgled, you need to **go to the police** to report it, not least because your insurance company will require a police report. Don't expect a great deal of concern if your loss is relatively small – and expect the process of completing forms and formalities to take ages. In the unlikely event that you're **mugged**, or otherwise threatened, *never* resist; hand over what's wanted and go straight to the police, who on these occasions will be more sympathetic.

OFFENCES

There are a few **offences** you might commit unwittingly that it's as well to be aware of.

• In theory you're supposed to carry some kind of **identification** at all times, and the police can stop you in the streets and demand it. In practice they're rarely bothered if you're clearly a (white) foreigner routinely trekking back and forth across the border ridge, but it's still a good idea to have passports or ID handy, since mountain refuges often require them as security against payment.

• **Nude bathing** or **unauthorized camping** are activities more likely to bring you into contact with officialdom, though a warning to cover up or move on is more likely than any real confrontation. In the Pyrenees, pitching a tent in any possible suitable place – except right in view of a *refugio* or in a national park – is the norm. **Topless** tanning is commonplace at all the trendier coastal resorts, but by Pyrenean streams and lakes, where attitudes are rather more traditional, you should take care not to upset local sensibilities.

• Spanish **drug laws** are in a somewhat ambiguous state at present. After the PSOE came to power in 1983, cannabis use (possession of up to 8g of hashish, *chocolate* in Castilian) was decriminalized. Subsequent pressures, and an influx of harder drugs, have changed that policy and – in theory at least – any drug use is now forbidden. You'll see signs in some bars saying "*porros no*" (no joints), which you should heed. However, the police are in practice little worried about personal use. Larger quantities (and any other drugs) are a very different matter.

• Should you be **arrested** you have the right to contact your **consulate**, and although they're notoriously reluctant to get involved they are required to assist you to some degree if you have your passport stolen or lose all your money. If you've been detained for a drugs offence, don't expect any sympathy or help from your consulate.

• If you have an **accident** while **driving**, try not to make a statement to anyone who doesn't speak English. Car rental agencies will provide you, in the glove box, with a bilingual statement to be filled in by both drivers if another car is involved. The SNTO in your home country can provide a list of the rules on the road in Spain.

THE POLICE

There are three basic types of Spanish **police**: the *Guardia Civil*, the *Policía Municipal* and the *Policía Nacional*, all of them armed.

The **Guardia Civil**, in green uniforms, are the most officious and the ones to avoid. Though their role has been drastically cut back since they operated as Franco's right hand – you'll see many of their abandoned barracks in the Pyrenees – they remain a reactionary force (it was a *Guardia Civil* colonel, Tejero, who held the Cortes hostage in the February 1981 failed coup).

If you do need the police – and above all if you're reporting a serious crime such as rape – always go to the more sympathetic **Policía Municipal**, who wear blue-and-white uniforms with red trim. In the countryside there may be only the *Guardia Civil*; though they're usually helpful, they are inclined to resent the suggestion that any crime exists on their turf and you may end up feeling as if you are the one who stands accused.

The brown-uniformed **Policía Nacional** are mainly seen in cities, armed with submachine guns and guarding key installations such as embassies, stations, post offices and their own barracks. They are also the force used to control crowds and demonstrations. In Euskadi there exists an additional autonomous Basque police force, distinguished by their red *boinas* or berets.

SEXUAL HARASSMENT

Spain's macho image has faded dramatically in the post-Franco years and these days there are relatively few parts of the country where foreign women, travelling alone, are likely to feel threatened, intimidated or noteworthy.

Inevitably, the **larger towns** – like any others in Europe – have their no-go areas, where street crime and especially drug-related hassles are on the rise, but there is little of the pestering and propositions that you have to contend with in, say, the larger Italian or Greek cities. The outdoor culture of *terrazas* (terrace bars) and the tendency of Spaniards to move around in large, mixed crowds, filling central bars, clubs and streets late into the night, help to make you feel less exposed. If you are in any doubt, there are always taxis – plentiful and reasonably priced.

Predictably, it is in **more isolated regions**, separated by less than a generation from desperate poverty (or still starkly poor), that most serious problems can occur. In some areas you can walk for hours without reaching an inhabited farm or house, and occasionally you still come upon shepherds working for nothing but the wine they take to their pastures. It's rare that this poses a threat – help and hospitality are much more the norm – but you are certainly more vulnerable. That said, **backcountry trekking** is becoming more popular in Spain as a whole and many women happily tramp the Pyrenees from one end to the other alone and without incident.

THE GREAT OUTDOORS

Although the high-rise resort apartments and wide pistes make skiing the most conspicuous outdoor pursuit of the Pyrenees, walking is a more widely practised Pyrenean recreation, and much of the range is crossed with well-maintained footpaths. In addition to these, the mountains and their coastal fringes offer a great range of variously energetic diversions, from gentle cross-country rides on horseback to the pulse-racing thrills of *parapente*.

WALKING

Not many people would argue with the proposition that the Pyrenees is the finest walking area in Europe. Unlike the Alps, where the high peaks are beyond the skills of the average person, any fit walker with a little determination can reach most of the major summits. All over the Pyrenees, paths and trails of varying length are marked out by local organizations, some of them private and some governmental. Many tourist offices will have details of shorter itineraries, and at least some information on the major walking routes.

LONG-DISTANCE WALKS

The principal **long-distance walks** are listed below; summaries of their routes are given where applicable throughout the *Guide*.

•**Haute Randonnée Pyrénéenne** (HRP) is the shortest and toughest traverse from Atlantic to Mediterranean, sticking close to the frontier, mainly in France but crossing into Spain when the terrain dictates. It's planned as a 45-day hike covering nearly 500km, staying in mountain refuges and unstaffed shelters. Not all of it is difficult but some sections do call for map-reading skills, a head for heights and the use of crampons and ice-axe early in the season. Often the HRP is not waymarked, but in places it merges with the well-marked GR10 – which can also make a good alternative to the hardest parts of the HRP. Georges Véron has written a detailed but now dated description – see "Books", in *Contexts*.

•**Grande Randonnée 10** (GR10) is a lower-level traverse, entirely in France, that puts about 300km on the distance. Most overnights can be spent in *gîtes d'étape*, huts or village accommodation, but there are sections where a tent or bivouac are necessary. The GR10 is marked in its entirety with red-and-white paint bars, and described in detail by the French Topoguide series, whose English-language translation – now out-of-print – is *Walking the Pyrenees* (see "Books", in *Contexts*); Alan Castle's *Pyrenean Trail: GR10* is an alternative.

•**Gran Recorrido 11** (GR11) is the Spanish equivalent of the GR10, a well-marked itinerary – again with red-and-white bars – which mostly uses well-established footpaths. Much of this route – which includes some of the wildest, most spectacular scenery in the Pyrenees, and a good compromise between the HRP and GR10 – is served by a mix of attended refuges and unstaffed huts, though again a tent or the willingness to bivouac is occasionally required. Thorough documentation of this *Senda Pirenaica*, as it's often called in Castilian, exists mainly in Spanish or Catalan, with the Catalunyan, Aragónese and Navarran alpine clubs each publishing a convenient paperback *topoguía* detailing the portion of the GR11 falling within their autonomous region. Alternatively, there's the mammoth, nonportable ring-binder edition combining all three regions, published jointly by Prames, FEDME and the Federación Aragonesa de Montaña – the loose pages are meant to be replaced periodically with updates. In English, there's only a single summary pocket guide, *Spanish Pyrenees – GR11* (see "Books" in *Contexts*).

•**GR12** shares much of the GR11's course within Navarra, but diverges at either edge of the region to trace the watershed between Navarra to the south and Gipuzkoa and Labourd on the north.

•**GR15**, the *Sendero Prepirenaico*, runs parallel to the GR11 at a much lower altitude, and can thus be followed when the higher elevations are inaccessible due to snow; in this guide it is described only at the southern fringe of the Ordesa region, and in the Valle de Gistau.

•**GR19** is a short trail confined to Alto Aragón, which crosses the GR15 and is most useful as a pleasant way between the Valle de Gistau and Ordesa.

•**GR36/GR4** is one of several major north–south traverses of the Pyrenees, from Albi in France to Montserrat in Spain, via Canigou and the Cerdagne/Cerdanya. GR36 is the French designation, GR4 the Spanish.

•**GR7** is the second major north–south traverse, reaching the Pyrenees in the Pays de Sault, curving through Andorra and into Spain as far as Barcelona. It is described in both a French *topoguide* and a Catalan-produced *topoguía*.

•**GR107**, from Montségur to the Sierra del Cadí, is also called the *Chemin des Bonshommes* or *Camí de les Bons Hommes*, and claims to follow the route of fleeing Cathars. A *topoguide/topoguía* should be available from 1998.

•**GR65**, the modern version of the medieval *Camino de Santiago/Chemin de Saint Jacques* pilgrimage route, crosses the Pyrenees from Saint-Jean-Pied-de-Port in the French Basque Country, via the Ibañeta pass and Roncesvalles to Pamplona and then on to Santiago de Compostela. The entire route is covered in detail by various guides, published by Cicerone Press or the confraternity of St James. The traditional Aragonese spur of the main route is now marked as the **GR65.3**, which enters Spain from the Vallée d'Aspe at the Somport pass, then descends to Jaca where it turns ninety degrees west, joining the GR65 southwest of Pamplona at Puenta la Reina. The Aragonese mountain club (FAM) describes this route in a *topoguía* available in English.

•**Le Sentier Cathare** is a partial traverse, linking all the sites from the Mediterranean to Foix that were significant to the Cathar religion. You pass through some fantastic scenery in Corbières and the Pays de Sault and visit great ruined fortresses such as Quéribus, Peyrepertuse, Puy-

laurens and Montségur. Well marked and well equipped with *gîtes d'étape*, it is described in French in *Le Sentier Cathare* by Louis Salavy and J.L. Sarret (Randonnées Pyrénéennes).

Mention must be made of **variants** (*variantes* in both French and Castilian), which are exactly what they sound like: alternative routings diverging briefly from the main GR, often of greater difficulty or providing necessary side links to villages just off the principal trail. Both the GR11 and GR10 have been substantially re-routed in spots during recent years, in response to requests from both walkers and farmers, who no longer wanted people traipsing through or past their land. Old sectors, if not altogether abandoned, tend to be demoted to *variante* status. One problem arising from the re-marking, or fresh plotting of **new trails**, is that the marking committee volunteers tend to do their work with little fanfare, leaving local villagers none the wiser; when asked, the locals will thus often deny that any path has been (re-)marked in their neighbourhood.

On both sides of the frontier there exist PR trails (**pequeño recorrido** in Castilian, **petit randonnée** in French), usually marked in yellow and white (in Spain), in yellow and red (France), or sometimes blue and yellow; these are itineraries designed to be completed within a day by persons with limited experience of high-mountain walking. Nonetheless, they are also of use to long-haul trekkers, often sparing you some fairly miserable road-tramping, and frequently sharing, or running parallel to, the course of a GR route. They are found in the greatest numbers around Benasque and Ansó/Hecho in Spain, and Ax-les-Thermes, Luchon or Cauterets in France, though any tourist board worth its salt seems to be devising these for every resort or valley. Locally produced guidelets describe most of them.

In the French Pyrenees, there are also more than a score of **local circuits** called *Tours*, lasting from three to seven days. These are all indicated on the more detailed maps published by Randonnées Pyrénéennes and some of the IGN ones, and most of them are also described in guidebooks from the same publisher. The best of these loops are summarized in the relevant chapters of this guide. On the Spanish side, you'll have to devise your own itineraries, using the Editorial Alpina maps and booklets, plus the other publications listed in *Contexts*.

WALKING SKILLS AND EQUIPMENT

Gauging the **distance** that can be covered in a day obviously depends on many variables, the most significant being level of fitness, type of terrain and load being carried. As rough estimates, most people can walk at about 4.5km per hour over flat country with a fairly light load, and climb at most 450m/1500ft per hour off-road; with a full (15- to 20-kilo) pack, they can climb 350m/1150ft per hour off-road. You should knock off 50m per hour from these climbing figures for bad trail surface or extraordinarily heavy loads, and always assume that going downhill is no quicker than ascending – if you love your knees, it won't be. If you're not used to it, 1000m of ascent in a single day, with a full pack, is pretty exhausting. You should reckon on **10km horizontally and 1000m of ascent as a sustainable daily average** at first. If you are reasonably fit you could doubtless manage 20km and/or 2000m of climb, but you probably won't feel much like walking the next day. As an idea of what really experienced individuals can achieve, the participants of the Cauterets-to-Vignemale race, involving 52km horizontally and 2700m of ascent, take between four and a half and eight hours.

Plenty of people attempt a Pyrenean traverse without having done any serious walking before. There's no reason why you shouldn't, but you must follow a few basic guidelines. As a rule of thumb you can carry a quarter of your own body weight comfortably in a **backpack**. A frame pack takes its load more easily but the soft pack is more versatile, closer fitting and with nothing to get caught on rocks when scrambling.

You shouldn't skimp on **boots**; if you're on the HRP or walking anywhere in winter you're going to need proper ones. Although serious mountain footwear weighs at least one kilo each side, you don't notice it so much when they're on your feet. High-tech, synthetic boots not only tend to be much hotter than old-fashioned leather ones, but fail to provide vital ankle support – as do trainers, which should never be worn on anything other than an hour-long, level stroll from car park to a nearby lake, without a full pack. As a compromise between flimsy trainers and rigid, expensive monsters intended to accommodate crampons, there are numerous all- or partly-leather designs with Vibram-type tread and some degree of stiffening around the ankle. In wetter regions where heat is not a big issue, as in the western Pyrenees, many walkers favour rubber boots, while in the warm, arid eastern Pyrenees canvas boots are popular,

Unless you're going up above 2500m or are camping in winter, there's no need for a specialist **tent**, though you should always pick one that's self-supporting and has a sewn-in groundsheet. The most up-to-date two-person tents can weigh in at less than four kilos, if optimistically rated in terms of capacity: two people will fit snugly, with no room for gear inside. Six or seven kilos is a more realistic allowance. Many long walks can be done without a tent, and hard cases can manage any of the traverses with a good poncho or cagoule and the use of caves, huts, refuges and *gîtes d'étape*. A big army-type poncho keeps you and your pack dry when you're on the trail, and at night you can roll it around your sleeping bag, or (with strips sewn on in strategic places) rig it as a canopy. It's not too comfortable, but many consider the saving on weight and bulk worthwhile.

As far as **clothing** is concerned, follow the **layer** principle. When you're ascending on a hot day you'll want only shorts and a T-shirt, but in colder conditions you'll need a long-sleeved shirt and trousers or breeches with long socks. There are all kinds of part-synthetic **pile** garments nowadays, warm and easy to wash. A pile top over a wool shirt, with long underwear as the lowest layer, should be as much warmth as you need. If it's raining, wear overtrousers and cagoule.

For the HRP or **winter** walking you're going to need **gaiters** to stop snow going down your boots, **crampons** (which fit only stiff mountain boots) and an ice-axe – plus the skill to use it effectively.

A good **sleeping bag** is essential. Down gives the best insulation relative to weight and bulk, but its efficiency falls drastically when it gets damp, which it's bound to do unless you have a proper tent, and a poncho to protect your pack from showers. An artificial filling is better, though much heavier and less compressible. Underneath either sort of bag you'll need a foam **mat** to protect it. Also get a sleeping-bag **liner** – cotton or thermal – which you can wash and dry easily en route, leaving the cleaning of your bag for back home.

Your personal gear will be complete with a **hat** (maybe two) for warmth and/or protection from the sun, **gloves**, **sunglasses** and **sunscreen**. For navigation a **compass** and **pocket altimeter** are both vital, together with the appropriate **maps**.

WATER AND FOOD

On a non-strenuous day the average person needs two litres of **water** from liquids and from food. Hiking you need at least **twice** that, and ski touring **three times** as much. In the mountains you can usually get fresh water along the way. Check your map for habitation upstream, as plenty of mountain villages still discharge untreated sewage into rivers; if there's nothing upstream a vigorous flow will be safe. If in doubt — ie if there are signs of livestock — add water **purification** tablets (available from all outdoor shops) or **boil** for four minutes.

On an easy walk you'll need forty calories per day per kilo of body weight — fifty for a tough hike and as much as sixty for ski touring. Fats provide most energy for weight, at around 7500 calories per kilo; dehydrated main-meal foods can give you 5000 calories per kilo; nuts and chocolate work out at around 4500 calories per kilo. Picking up supplies on the GR10, GR7 or GR65 is easy, as they're designed to pass through plenty of villages. On the HRP or the GR11 you'll probably have to make diversions. It is possible to pick wild food along the way — in season you'll find edible mushrooms plus things like wild spinach, wild strawberries, hazelnuts and herbs — but these have low caloric value and should be regarded only as supplements to the trekking diet.

For long trips in the wild you will need a **stove**. The best is the multi-fuel or MSR type, which is light, versatile, powerful — and expensive. Next best are the French-made Bleuet butane-cartridge stoves, as their fuel is clean, light and almost universally available, but they don't burn well at low temperatures or when the cartridge is running down. For the evening meal, packet soups, dried potatoes, couscous or thin pasta, supplemented with dry cheese or cured meat, are quick, high-calorie, light to carry and fuel-efficient. Although there's often little else suitable to buy in high villages, try to **avoid canned goods**, as they're not only heavy to carry but aggravate existing Pyrenean litter problems no matter where you dispose of them. For short excursions from civilization, a vacuum flask can carry enough hot water to rehydrate dried foods.

CLIMBING

Although the principal summits of the Pyrenees can be reached with only rudimentary climbing skills, the range has technical routes as demanding as any elsewhere. There are few places in the Pyrenees where you can't climb, but particularly good areas include **Aigües Tortes**, **Maladeta** and the entire **Ordesa** country in Spain, and **Haute-Garonne**, **Vallée d'Aure**, the **Cirque de Gavarnie** and the tops of the **Aspe** and **Ossau valleys** in France.

The traditional climbing grades 1 to 6 were long ago surpassed with the arrival of new techniques and equipment — routes at level 8 are now routinely tackled (especially on the Troubat cliffs near Montréjeau) and the rock gymnasts have been setting new parameters at level 9 throughout the early 1990s. Some climbers find artificial walls worthwhile. Indeed, the new French attitude — exemplified by the multicoloured tights and other high-fashion gear — is that the closer to an appreciative audience, the better. **Tarbes** has one of the biggest climbing walls, with routes up to 7b, but plenty of mountain villages are also now installing them, including **Luz-Saint-Sauveur**. Spain has recently inaugurated a climbing wall at its mountaineering school at **Benasque**, though it's intended for Spanish or select overseas guide candidates.

There are plenty of climbing courses on offer to summer visitors throughout the Pyrenees, most of them charging in the region of £40/$60 for four to six hours' tuition.

CAVING

The northern and southern foothills of the Pyrenees are largely Cretaceous or Jurassic **limestone**, and some of the high peaks are too, like Monte Perdido, Europe's highest limestone mountain. Although limestone is soluble, it's also non-porous, which means it dissolves only where the water can get in at cracks. Over millennia, this dissolving action produces vertical pot-holes and vast caverns. Thus, below the bizarrely eroded limestone around Pic d'Anie lurks the deepest cave system yet discovered in the Pyrenees, and one of the deepest in the world: the **Gouffre Pierre-Saint-Martin**. The Pyrenees also boasts the world's highest **ice caves** (caves hung with frozen waterfalls), on top of the Cirque de Gavarnie.

If you've never done any caving, are not in the least athletic, but would still like to experience it, there are several managed caves open to the public, such as **Grandes Canalettes** near Villefranche-de-Conflent or the **prehistoric** painted caves like **Niaux** and **Bédeilhac** in the Ariège. The next stage of difficulty would be a cave like **L'Aguzou** in the Aude, where small pre-booked, fully equipped parties are guided around an unilluminated system. Any normally fit person can go.

But if you're intent on caving as a sport, then you need to make arrangements through your own caving club or by signing up with a commercial school. It is possible to head off with your own gear if you know what you're doing, but many of the best caverns have now been locked, and only approved people can get the key. Rewarding areas include the karst country around **Pic d'Anie**, the entire **Ordesa/Cirque de Gavarnie/Monte Perdido** region, **the Comminges** and northern **Couserans**, the **Pays de Sault**, the **Ariège**, the **Aude**, the **Serra del Cadí**, the **Garrotxa** region and the **Têt** valley around Villefranche-de-Conflent.

SKIING

The comparatively gentle slopes of the Pyrenees are the perfect place to savour the delights of **ski mountaineering** and **cross-country** or **off-piste** skiing for the first time. Compared with the Alps, the risk of avalanche is much slighter, and the chance of falling into a crevasse or having a similar accident is minimal. There is no better way of getting real solitude than ski-traversing in the Pyrenees in winter. To learn, sign on with a guide in a resort like Barèges or Gavarnie, both spots giving access to marvellous itineraries ranging from one day to several. If you're already a mountain walker and a competent downhill skier, you're well on the way.

In terms of **piste skiing**, snow on prepared runs seldom approaches the ideal powder occasionally found in the Alps. As a general rule, resorts in the east of the range have these problems compounded by low precipitation and strong sun (also a problem on much of the Spanish side of the border), and by wind, which packs the snow hard. In the west there is a tendency to mist – a great snow-eater – and to rain brought in by the Atlantic weather systems.

Proximity to the Mediterranean means that snow is unreliable on the **eastern resorts** of **Vallter 2000** and **Núria** in Spain, and **Saint-Pierre-dels-Forcats**, **Eyne**, **Les Angles**, **Formigueres** and **Puyvalador** in France. For ski mountaineering and cross-country skiing, on the other hand, the higher reaches of the region are a delight, with little risk of either avalanche or exposure.

Pas de la Casa offers the most reliable snow in the **Andorra region**, but the development itself is a monstrosity. Best bet within Andorra is **Ordino-Arcalis**, set amongst magnificent high-mountain wilderness. Outside Andorra, Ax-les-Thermes has its own ski station of **Bonascre**, another blot on the landscape – but when you get up the lifts the scenery is sublime. In the French Cerdagne the most famous resort is **Font-Romeu,** though the best is **Porté-Puymorens**.

Spain has, for the time being, only four serious resorts relatively near Andorra, three of them overlooking the Spanish Cerdanya – **La Molina**, **Masella** and **Porte del Comte** – and the best, **Baqueira-Beret**, at the head of the Vall d'Aran. For **cross-country skiing** (*ski de fondo* in Castilian, *ski de fond* in French), the whole of the Cerdagne/Cerdanya and much of the Serra del Cadí are a playground of trails, during spring bathed in sunshine. **Ski-mountaineering** can be as easy or as tough as you want; the fearless can tackle the Ariège uplands, nicknamed the *Terre Courage.*

There are half a dozen ski resorts in **Alto Aragón**'s stretch of the Pyrenees and most of them – following the province's hosting of the 1982 University Winter Olympics – are well equipped, particularly **Candanchú**, **Astún** and **El Formigal**. When all is said and done, however, the **north slope** of the **central French Pyrenees** provides the most reliable conditions: **Barèges/La Mongie** comes first for its size. Other normally dependable destinations in this area include **Piau-Engaly**, **Cauterets** and **Gavarnie**.

Every significant resort in the Pyrenees is described in the *Guide*, with details of the height of the top lift and the number and type of pistes. The system for **grading pistes** is green for beginner, blue for easy, red for intermediate and black for difficult. These are not completely dependable ratings – black in one resort might be rated red in another – but it gives a fair idea. The most important thing is that a run should be long enough. Unlike in the Alps, **beginners** are well looked after – Gavarnie, for example, has a blue run from its top lift, as do several other resorts.

Package holidays are often the cheapest way of skiing – you may well find a British deal offering tuition, equipment hire, accommodation

AVALANCHE SAFETY

Ideally, anyone embarking on a long high-level traverse should learn the requisite safety skills on a course or from an experienced person, or read a specialist book on the subject. If you are undertaking a mountain walk early in the summer season, a winter climb or a ski tour, it is absolutely essential that you know the basics of avalanche safety.

Firstly, **always take local advice**: a shepherd or high-mountain guide will tell you which slopes avalanche regularly, which sometimes avalanche and which have never avalanched in living memory. Secondly, there are very few occasions when the crossing of a potential avalanche slope cannot be avoided; if there is even the remotest chance of avalanche, **don't do it**. Nobody is going to be impressed because, by good luck, you happened to cross a dangerous slope without mishap – certainly not the mountain rescue teams who might have had to risk their lives to dig you out (see below). Good route-finding is the key. **The safest routes** are along broad ridges, the bottoms of slopes beyond the estimated run-out zone of a possible avalanche, and areas with dense tree cover. Certain climatological conditions make avalanches more likely: heavy snowfall in the preceding 24 hours; a strong wind in the same period; and a rapid rise in temperature. In such conditions, **avoid** the following:

- gullies and bowls
- convex slopes showing signs of bulge or stress
- lee concave slopes and any slopes overhung by cornices
- slopes with an incline greater than 25 degrees

- south-facing slopes in strong sun with conditions above freezing
- canyons and gorges with dangerous slopes above
- sparsely treed or open slopes.

If you're forced to **cross a potential avalanche slope**, do so one at a time or spaced at 100-metre intervals if it's wide. Do up zippers, buttons and hoods, take your hands out of ski pole straps, release ski-retaining straps and tie a scarf around your mouth and nose. Some items of **safety equipment** are good investments if you'll be spending some time in open country – shovels, probes and rescue beacons or (second-best) avalanche cords for every member of the party. Read Tony Daffern's *Avalanche Safety for Skiers and Climbers* (published by Diadem in the UK).

If you're **caught in an avalanche**, you should jettison poles, skis and pack if there's time, and grab hold of a tree or rock, or swim or roll to the side of the avalanche path – and keep your mouth closed. If buried, try to hollow out a breathing space, relax and wait for rescue. Those spared the avalanche **should not go for help** unless it is not more than half an hour away and there is no way of freeing the victims quickly. Avalanche victims can soon suffocate, and it's therefore essential to begin excavation immediately.

If worst comes to worst, and you're near a staffed refuge, **mountain rescue squads** can be summoned from various spots on both sides of the range (see below). They should only be called on in real need, as these helicopter-equipped teams must be paid for and are extremely expensive.

MOUNTAIN RESCUE PHONE NUMBERS

SPAIN
Navarra ☎112
Aragón ☎062
Catalunya ☎085 (also for forest fires)
Roncal ☎948/89 32 48
Jaca ☎974/31 13 50
Stations also at Panticosa, Boltaña, Benasque and Viella.

ANDORRA ☎112

FRANCE
Western Pyrenees ☎112
Oloron-Sainte-Marie ☎05.59.39.86.22
Gavarnie valley ☎05.62.92.41.41
Luchon ☎05.61.79.28.36 or 05.61.79.83.79
Perpignan ☎04.68.61.79.20

and insurance at under £700 for two weeks. In such cases be sure to check the piste diagram in the resort brochure carefully – if a run ends below 1500m it's unlikely that you'll get snow all

the way down. Arranging matters on the spot, expect to pay around £80/$130 for a weekly pass and almost as much again for rental and insurance.

CYCLING

Cyclists shouldn't be daunted by the Pyrenees. You can find plenty of rolling hills and even some almost flat terrain – the Cerdanya/Cerdagne, for example. There are numerous recognized circuits on the French side and recommended routes are marked in yellow on the Randonnées Pyrénéennes maps. In the east there are relatively easy tours such as the Circuit des Aspres (85km) and Circuit des Donjons Cathares (105km); in the central zone the going gets tougher, but you can still find fairly undemanding routes through the Baronnies or in the Pays de Sault. On the other hand, if you want to emulate the heroics of the Tour de France riders, there are limitless opportunities, especially within a short radius of the Col de Tourmalet.

On the Spanish side you don't have the same extent of planned routes as in France – though more and more Spanish guides to bike-touring are being published – and the hotter weather discourages all but the hardiest from cycling inland, though you should find company as you get nearer to the sea, particularly on the Santiago de Compostela route.

If you're planning to cover long distances each day, a proper **touring bike** is the best machine, and you should always carry a basic kit of spanners, Allen keys, inner tube, lubricant and puncture repair set. Spare parts are not a problem on the French side, where many large villages will at least have a shop that can carry out temporary repairs, nor are they scarce on the Spanish side in Catalunya, or the more populated parts of Navarra and Gipuzkoa.

A **mountain bike** (abbreviated VTT or *Vélo Touts Terrains* in French, BTT or *Bici Todo Terreno* in Spanish) of course allows you to go hurtling around off-road, but whereas a touring bike's curled handlebars allow you to shift riding position occasionally, the straight bars of a mountain bike force you to stay in the same stance, which after a few hours becomes exhausting. Should you want to get off the tarmac, either plan on covering relatively short distances – if you're out of condition mountain-biking will feel scarcely easier than tour-biking over the same slope – lash your mountain bike to your car's roof-rack, or rent one when you get there – the latter is an option at plenty of resorts.

Rental rates on the Spanish side currently run to 1700–2300ptas per day, though the number of rental outlets – plus the quality of machines on offer – seems to be on the wane as more and more Spaniards are buying their own. Most French train stations also rent out bikes, though you'll find better maintained and more current models from specialist outlets. The best **maps** for cyclists are recommended in "Information and Maps" (see p.26).

If you want to make contact with cycling clubs ask at a **tourist office** or get hold of the *Randonnées dans les Pyrénées* information pack from Randonnées Pyrénéennes, listing all those on the French side.

HORSE-RIDING

As recently as the 1980s there were only a few riding stables in the Pyrenees but nowadays riding is available throughout the range, mostly in the foothills. The classic mount of the high mountains is the native Mérenguais breed – the Ariège is the place to ride these stocky horses, especially the village of **Mérens-les-Vals** south of Ax-les-Thermes. There's also a prominent stable at **L'Estanguet** in the Vallée d'Aspe. If you're only looking for a day or two's riding, you'll have plenty of opportunities as you tour around. A full day in the saddle should cost around 400F on the French side, slightly less on the Spanish side, where part-day rates of 2000ptas/hour are about standard.

RIVER SPORTS

The Pyrenees have plenty of rivers suitable for **canyoning**, **hydrospeed**, **canoeing** and **rafting**, especially in the east of the range and in Alto Aragón around Monte Perdido.

Canyoning basically involves jumping into a suitably smooth watercourse and letting it take you along, sometimes whooshing down waterfalls, sometimes abseiling down vertical drops, sometimes merely wading through near-freezing water. For the easier rivers you don't need any special abilities or equipment other than a wet suit and knowing how to swim, but tougher sections require helmets, inflatables, ropes and abseiling skills.

Obviously it can be dangerous, so unless you know what you're doing, it's best to go in a group led by a professional, who can give guidance and supply the gear. For more information about such guides, contact the headquarters of Compagnie des Pyrénées, 6 rue Eugéne-Tenot, 65000 Tarbes (☎05.62.93.03.30), or else Accompagnateurs en Montagne, 6 rue des Trois-Fours, 31400 Toulouse (☎05.61.55.01.98), who will put you in touch with leaders of groups into the Spanish and French canyons. One place to contact for details of canyoning trips in the **Garganta de Escuaín** is the Parque Nacional de Ordesa in Torla (☎974/48 62 12).

Hydrospeed is the same principle applied to really violent water: you cling to a sort of floating toboggan, wearing a brightly coloured buoyancy jacket, padding and an American football-style helmet. You look stupid, but once you get into the torrent you don't really care.

The Spanish **Noguera Pallaresa** is the great rafting and canoeing river of the whole range. Other major rivers where tuition and equipment are available include the **Têt**, **Aude**, **Ariège**, **Salat**, **Adour**, **Arros**, **Aure**, **Louron**, **Oloron**, **Gave de Pau**, **Ossau** and **Aspe**.

PARAPENTING

The relatively new sport of *parapente* is a blend of hang-gliding and parachuting, the wing-shaped *parapente* steering something like a hang-glider but having no rigid parts. You take off by running or skiing down a slope until you get enough lift; in 1000m of descent you might cover a distance of 4–6km. At first there were frequent accidents but improvements in design and teaching now make it relatively safe, if a bit expensive. You can get a single-flight "baptism" for about 250F/4000ptas, but a week's course can cost ten times as much and a full two-week course, taking you to a stage where you should be able to go off on your own, costs around 4500F/100,000ptas.

Major venues in the central Pyrenees include **Accous**, **Barèges**, **Saint-Lary**, **Val Louron**, **Luchon** and **Guzet-Neige** in France, and **Ager** and **Castejón de Sos** in Spain. Areas near the coast tend to be unsuitable because of the unpredictability of the winds.

DIRECTORY

FRANCE

ADDRESSES are written as: 18 bis rue Henri-Foucault 1er, which means an annexe or sub-premises of no.18 Henri-Foucault Street, on the first (*premier*) floor. Common abbreviations are pl for *place*, rte for *route*, av for *avenue* and bd for *boulevard*.

BEACHES are public property within five metres of the high-tide mark, so you can kick sand past private villas and land boats on islands but – under a different law – you can't camp on shorelines.

CHILDREN and babies are allowed in all bars and restaurants, most of which will offer children's menus or cook simpler food if you ask. Hotels charge by the room – there's a small supplement for an additional bed or cot – and family-run places will usually baby-sit while you go out. You'll have no difficulty finding disposable nappies (*couches à jeter*), baby foods and milk powders, though the latter two tend to be sweetened and/or very rich. The SNCF charges half-fare on trains and buses for kids aged four to twelve, nothing for under-fours. As far as entertainment goes, most local tourist offices detail specific children's activities (we've included some of the more exciting), and wherever you go there's generally a good reception.

CONTRACEPTIVES Condoms (*préservatifs*) have always been available at pharmacies, though contraception was only legalized in 1967. You can also get spermicidal cream and jelly (*dose contraceptive*), plus the suppositories (*ovules, suppositoires*) and (with a prescription) the pill (*la pillule*), a diaphragm or IUD (*le sterilet*).

DISABLED TRAVELLERS France has no special reputation for ease of access and facilities, but at least information is available. The tourist offices in most big towns have a free booklet *Touristes Quand Même!* covering accommodation, transport, accessibility of public places and particular aids such as buzzer signals on pedestrian crossings, ramps and trains adapted for wheelchairs.

ELECTRICITY is 220V out of double, round-pin wall sockets. Travellers from Britain or Australasia will therefore need three-to-two adaptors for appliances, and North Americans will additionally require a step-down transformer.

EQUIPMENT for skiing, climbing and other mountain activities is more expensive in France than in the USA, and about the same as in the UK, but the range is often wider – and you'll find some bargains in Andorran supermarkets.

FISHING You need to become a member of a fishing club to get rights – this is not difficult, any tourist office will give you a local address.

GAY AND LESBIAN LIFE France is more liberal than most other European countries on homosexuality. The legal age of consent is 15 and there are thriving gay communities in many of the towns in the south. Lesbian life is rather less upfront. Try to get hold of the country-wide gay guide to what's on, *Gai Pied Guide*.

LAUNDRIES have multiplied over the last few years but are still not the commonest sight along French main streets – have a look in the Yellow Pages under *Laveries Automatiques*. It's a good idea to carry travel soap or cold water washing liquid so that you can wash your own. If you're staying in hotels, keep quantities small as often it's expressly forbidden to wash clothes in rooms.

LEFT LUGGAGE There are various-sized lockers at all train stations and *consignes* for bigger items or longer periods.

SWIMMING POOLS are well signposted in most French Pyrenean towns and reasonably priced. Tourist offices have addresses.

TIME France is always one hour ahead of Britain since the institution of uniform EU Daylight Savings. For nearly all of the year, French time is six hours ahead of Eastern Standard Time, nine ahead of Pacific Standard Time.

TOILETS are usually to be found downstairs in bars, along with the phone, but they're often hole-in-the-ground squat-type, and paper is rare.

SPAIN

ADDRESSES are written as: c/Picasso 2, 4° izda. – which means Carrer or Calle Picasso no. 2, 4th floor, left- (*izquierda*) hand flat or office; dcha. (*derecha*) is right; cto. (*centro*) centre. Other confusions in Spanish addresses result from the different spellings, and sometimes words, used in Catalan, Aragonese and Basque – all of which are to some extent replacing their Castilian counterparts – and from the removal of Franco and other Falangist heroes from the main *avenidas* and *plazas*. On this latter front, Avenidas del Generalísimo have pretty much vanished all over the country (often changing to "Libertad" or "España"); so too are José Antonios, General Molas, Primo de Riveras, Falanges, and Caudillos. Note that a dwindling number of maps – including some official ones – haven't yet caught up; nor have a handful of right-wing-controlled towns. In some towns dual numbering systems are also in effect, and looking at the house plates it's difficult to tell which is the old and which the new scheme.

CHILDREN don't pose great travel problems. *Hostales*, *pensiones* and *restaurantes* generally welcome them and offer rooms with three or four beds; RENFE allows children under three to travel free on trains, with half price for those under seven; and some cities and resorts have special pamphlets on kids' attractions. As far as babies go, food seems to work out quite well (*hostales* often prepare food specially – or will let you use the kitchen to do so). If you're travelling in the winter, however, bear in mind that most Pyrenean *hostales* (as opposed to more expensive hotels) don't have any heating systems – and it can get cold. Disposable nappies and other standard needs are very widely available. Many *hostales* will be prepared to baby-sit, or at least to listen out for trouble. This is obviously more likely if you're staying in an old-fashioned family-run place than in the fancier hotels.

CONSULATES Closest UK consulates to the Pyrenees are in Bilbao and Barcelona; the US is represented only in Barcelona.

CONTRACEPTIVES Condoms no longer need to be smuggled into Spain – as during the Franco years. Along with the pill (prescription only), they're available from most *farmacías* and increasingly from vending machines in the trendier bars – AIDS (*SIDA*) has very definitely reached Spain.

ELECTRICITY The current in most of Spain is 220 volts AC (just occasionally it's still 110V): most European appliances should work as long as you have an adaptor for European-style two-pin plugs. North Americans will need this plus a step-down transformer.

FILM Movie-going remains a remarkably cheap and popular entertainment, with crowded cinemas in larger foothill and coastal towns. The majority of what's screened is the usual Hollywood fare poorly dubbed into Spanish, but in the cities you will find more exciting options and some films in their original language with subtitles. Look for *voz* or *versión original* (*subtitulada*), abbreviated "v.o.", in the listings; "v.e." means *versión español*.

FISHING Fortnightly permits are easily and cheaply obtained from any ICONA office – there's one in every big town (addresses from the local tourist office).

GAY AND LESBIAN LIFE Attitudes in the resorts are fairly relaxed, but the nearest thriving gay scene to the Pyrenees is in Barcelona. The age of consent is 18.

LAUNDRIES You'll find a few self-service launderettes (*lavanderías automáticas*) in medium-sized towns like Jaca, Pamplona or Olot, but otherwise they're absent – you normally have to leave your clothes for the full (and somewhat expensive) works. Remember that you're not allowed officially to leave laundry hanging out of windows over a street, though this law is increasingly ignored. A dry cleaner is a *tintorería*.

LUGGAGE At most important Spanish train stations, you'll find lockers large enough to hold most backpacks, plus a smaller bag, which cost about 200ptas a day. (Put the coin in to free the key.) These are not a viable alternative for long-term storage, however, as they're periodically emptied out by station staff. Bus terminals have manned *consignas* where you present a claim stub to get your gear back; the cost is about the same.

SWIMMING POOLS Most Spanish Pyrenean foothill towns – even quite small places – have a public swimming pool, or *piscina municipal* – a lifesaver in the summer and an excellent way to get the kinks out of muscles fatigued from trekking. Admission prices vary, but count on 400ptas; note that the water is almost never heated.

TIME Spain is one hour ahead of the UK all year now that Daylight Savings in the EU is uniform. Spain is six hours ahead of Eastern Standard Time and nine hours ahead of Pacific Standard Time, except for brief periods during April and October.

TOILETS Public ones are averagely clean but very rarely have any paper (best to carry your own). They're often squat-style. They are most commonly referred to and labelled *los servicios* (*servei* in Catalan), though signs may point you to *baños*, *aseos*, *retretes*, or *sanitarios*. Damas (Ladies) and Caballeros (Gentlemen) are the usual distinguishing signs for gender, though you may also see the confusing *Señoras* (Women) and *Señores* (Men).

PART TWO

THE

GUIDE

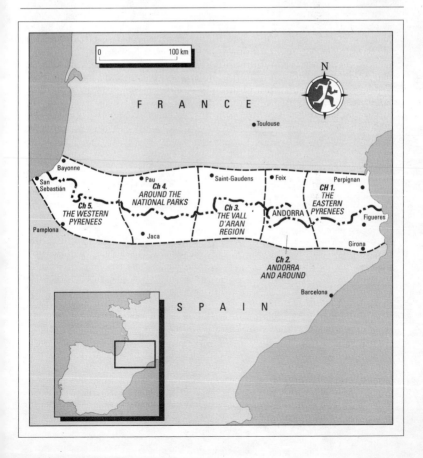

CHAPTER ONE

THE EASTERN PYRENEES

The **Eastern Pyrenees**, despite their comparatively modest height, are among the best-loved and most visited parts of the range. In part, this is due to ease of access – there are busy international airports at Perpignan in France and Girona in Spain – although visitors are also drawn by the ocean-tempered climate and sparkling scenery. The nearby Mediterranean intensifies the light, while the contrast in landscapes – between coastal wetlands and rainless scrub, or low-altitude deciduous groves and orchards and alpine forests – is immense. Given the terrain, there's a correspondingly wide variety of wildlife: waterfowl and upland birds of prey stipple the skies, while the land supports a surprising number of mammals, small and large, not yet eradicated by avid local hunters.

Running along the crest of the Albères section of the Pyrenees, the **border** is breached by just three road passes: the coastal **Col dels Balistres**, the **Col de Perthus** in the middle of the chain – supposedly used by Hannibal, and today the route of the main highway – and the **Col d'Ares** in the west. However, off-road vehicles and hikers can cross east of the Col de Perthus at the **Col de Banyuls**, which is rather isolated despite its close proximity to the resort-speckled Mediterranean. There are, of course, numerous other footpaths and tracks across the mountains, used by smugglers for centuries and by refugees escaping first north during the Spanish Civil War, then south in World War II.

For the **Catalan people** in both Spain and France, the national frontier is a fiction – even more so since European Community countries did away with Customs controls in 1993. Locals regularly cross back and forth on foot or by vehicle, as they always have done with their flocks and contraband. But while the Catalan language (*Català*) is the official language of Spanish Catalonia (*Catalunya*), it's no more than an option in the schools of Roussillon or French Catalonia; there is scarcely any interest in a politically unified, cross-border Catalan state, the universal presence of *els quatre barres* (the red-and-yellow Catalan pennant) notwithstanding. The whole of Catalonia was last under one ruler in the mid-seventeenth century, and the glories of the early medieval Catalan–Aragonese kingdoms are an even more distant memory.

Artificial though the border may be, it's convenient to consider the eastern Pyrenees as three distinct parts: the **French valleys**, flowing in every direction between the Cerdagne and the sea, from both the main Pyrenean crest and that of the Fenouillèdes; the **Mediterranean coast**, shared between the two parts of Catalonia; and the more uniformly south-facing **Spanish valleys**.

Perpignan is the only substantial town on the French side and the inevitable transport hub for the French valleys; most visitors head southwest up the parallel valleys of the **Tech** and **Têt**, where congenial towns like **Céret**, **Arles-sur-Tech**, **Prats-de-Molló** and **Prades** serve as handy forward bases. Monumental interest is lent by the medieval fortifications at **Mont-Louis** and **Villefranche-de-Conflent**, defending the Têt approaches to Perpignan, and by such compelling Romanesque foothill monasteries as the **Prieuré de Serrabone**, **Saint-Michel-de-Cuxa** and **Saint-Martin-du-Canigou**. The peak of **Canigou** itself, beacon and virtual logo of the region, offers several approaches and a variety of walking routes.

Because of the precipitous descent of the Pyrenean foothills, the Mediterranean coast is predominantly rocky, the shore road and rail line existing as corniche routes.

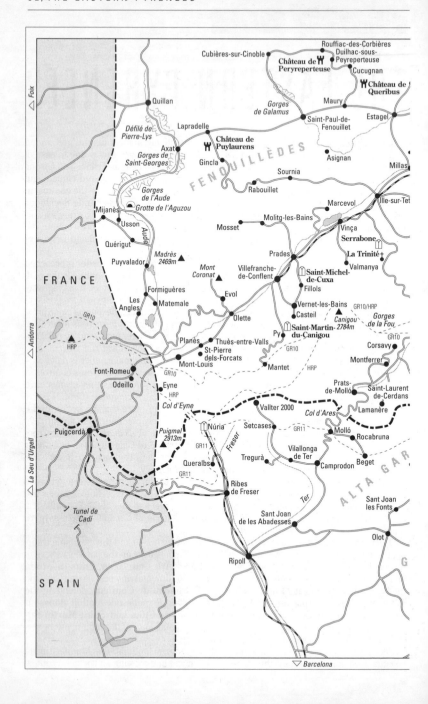

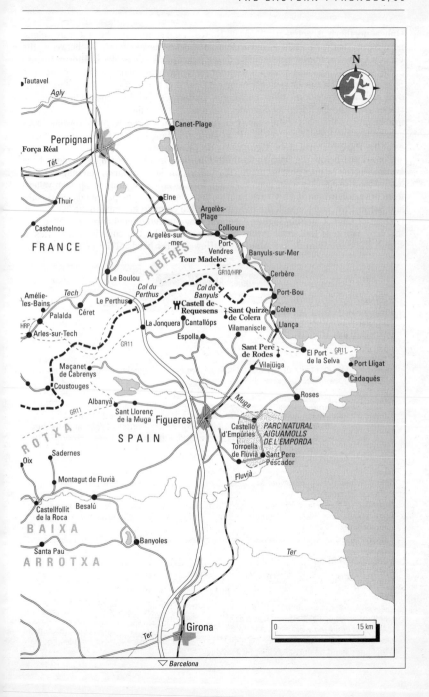

Only at northerly **Argelès-sur-Mer** and **Roses** in the south does the landscape relent, permitting sandy beaches – and extensive holiday development. In between, the French **Côte Vermeille** boasts half a dozen small port-resorts like **Collioure**, whose pretty surroundings first attracted summer patronage from artists a century ago. The Spanish **Costa Brava**, or rather the northern third of it abutting the Pyrenees, has its own artistic associations, most tangibly at **Cadaqués** and, just inland, at **Figueres**, respectively the backdrop for Salvador Dalí's adult- and childhood. There's more natural beauty on this part of the coast, too, ranging from the relatively uncrowded coves around low-key holiday centres like **Port Bou** and **Llançà**, to the bird-haunted marshes of the **Parc Natural dels Aiguamolls de l'Empordà**.

Poised just below the Spanish foothills, **Girona** – like Perpignan on its side of the border – is the staging-post for the nearby valleys; unlike Perpignan, you may well stay longer than planned in what is a charming, manageable city. Into the Spanish valleys from here, following the Fluvià river north, then west, takes you past medieval **Besalú** and **Santa Pau**, and through the volanic **Garrotxa** country, en route to the lively county town of **Olot**. Climbing higher, medieval religious monuments are integrated into the very fabric of the small towns, as demonstrated by the superb monasteries at **Ripoll** and **Sant Joan de les Abadesses**. However, the heads of the valleys seem less

FESTIVALS

JANUARY
First week Festival at Port Bou.
Nearest Sunday to 17 Procession of horses at Olot.
20–22 Annual festival at Llança.

FEBRUARY
Variable *Fête de l'Ours* at Arles-sur-Tech; *L'Encadanat*, three-day carnival at Prats-de-Molló; *Mascarade des Grégoires* at Amélie-les-Bains.

MARCH/APRIL
Easter Passion week processions at Besalú and Mieres; the red-and-black-robed *Procession de la Sanch* at Perpignan; *Procession Nocturne des Pénitents Noirs* at Arles-sur-Tech and Collioure; *Procession du Réssuscité* at Arles-sur-Tech and Céret; *Procession de l'Angelet* at Villefranche-de-Conflent.

MAY
Third week *Fires i Festes de la Santa Creu*, a week-long festival of processions and music at Figueres.
Monday of Pentecost Processions at L'Ermitage de St-Antoine in the Gorges de Galamus, L'Ermitage de Nôtre-Dame-de-Vie at Villefranche-de-Conflent and at Prieuré de Serrabonne.
Trinity Sunday *Fête de l'Ermitage de la Trinité*, near Boule d'Amont, including *sardanas*.
Variable *Fira de la Lana* (Wool Fair) the fourth Sunday after Easter at Ripoll.
Variable *Curso Internacional de Música* at Girona.

JUNE
23 *Fêtes des Feux* celebrated on various summits throughout Roussillon, including Canigou, and also at Perpignan and at Caudiés-de-Fenouillèdes.
24 *Dia de Sant Joan*, celebrated in some way in almost every town and village throughout Catalonia; for example, the "Dance of the Giants" takes place at Sant Joan les Fonts. Most shops and businesses close for two days.

urbanized than in France, with only **Camprodon** and **Núria** conspicuous as (pre-) alpine hill stations.

Most of the Eastern Pyrenees is served well by **public transport**. The international **train** line links Perpignan and Barcelona, running along the Côte Vermeille and the northern Costa Brava before turning inland to Figueres and Girona. There are also trains along the Têt valley; and from Barcelona to Ripoll and Ribes de Freser – with an extension from the latter to Núria along the incredible *cremallera* rack rail line (see p.164). **Buses** serve the Têt, Tech and Fenouillèdes regions, the resorts of the Côte Vermeille, parts of the Costa Brava and much of the Albères and Garrotxa, though – as ever – services tend to dwindle near the tops of the valleys on either side of the watershed.

THE FRENCH VALLEYS

Good international and local transport connections make **Perpignan**, 30km north of the frontier, the main gateway for the **French valleys** of the Eastern Pyrenees. Once the seat of a medieval kingdom that straddled the mountains, modern Perpignan is one of the most vital and multicultural cities of the Pyrenees, thanks to the influence of substantial

---

25 *Fête de la St Eloi*, the blessing of the mules at Amélie-les-Bains.
29 *Dia de Sant Pere* is another excuse for festivities all over Catalonia.

JULY
8-22 *Son et Lumière* at Caudies-de-Fenouillédes (and Aug 12–23).
10 *Sant Cristobal* in Olot, with traditional dances and processions.
Nearest weekend to 14 Taurine sports, *sardanas*, street bands in Céret.
25 *Festa de Sant Jaume* at Port Bou.
Variable *Sardanas* at Ripoll and Camprodon; *Salon des Arts* at Quillan.

JULY/AUGUST
Music festivals at Besalú, Cadaqués, Camprodon, Castellfollit de la Roca, Girona, Llança, Prades, Ripoll and Roses.

AUGUST
1–10 *Festa Major*, including the *Chasse à l'Ours*, at Saint-Laurent-de-Cerdans.
6 Annual festival at El Port de la Selva.
10–12 Annual festival at Castelló d'Empúries.
14–15 Festivals at Santa Pau, Ribes de Freser and Collioure (where there are fireworks on the water).
23–25 *Fête de St Louis* at Le Perthus.
29 *Fête Folklorique* at Banyuls-sur-Mer.

SEPTEMBER
First week Generalized festivities at Cadaqués.
7–8 Celebrations at Olot and Cadaqués, but most famously at Núria.
11 *La Diada*, National Day celebrations – with *sardanas* – all over Catalunya (Spain).
24 Annual festival at Besalú.
29 Annual festival at Colera.

OCTOBER
7 *Grand Fête Patronale* in Thuir and Amélie-les-Bains.
Last week *Fires de Sant Narcis* in Girona; also *Festa de Sant Martiriano* in Banyoles.

NOVEMBER
11 *Foire de la Saint-Martin* in Perpignan.

ACCOMMODATION PRICE CODES

Each place to stay in this book has been given a code which corresponds to one of the
following price categories.

① Under 2500ptas/under 100F   ② 2500–3500ptas/100–140F
③ 3500–5000ptas/140–200F   ④ 5000–7000ptas/200–260F
⑤ 7000–10,000ptas/260–340F   ⑥ 10,000ptas/340F and upwards

Category ① refers to the price *per person* of a bed; the other categories correspond to the
cheapest available double room in high season. For more details, see pp.34 & 37.

---

immigrant communities from Spain and North Africa and a growing university
population.

To approach the Pyrenees indirectly, head west out of Perpignan through the arid,
gorge- and-cave-slashed **Fenouillèdes**, a parallel range of hills in which the oldest
human remains in Europe have been found at **Tautavel**. Here you'll also find the easternmost of the **Cathar castles** (see p.94), linked to each other by long-distance paths.
More usual routes from Perpignan lie along the **Têt** and **Tech** valleys, respectively
northwest and southeast of the Canigou massif. **Prades**, famous for its summer music
festival held in the medieval monastery of Saint-Michel-de-Cuxa, serves effectively as
the "capital" of the Têt, whose other principal attractions are the fortified towns of **Villefranche-de-Conflent** and **Mont-Louis**, linked by the touristic **Train Jaune** – a narrow-gauge, electrically powered train service which spectacularly negotiates the river
valley. **Céret**, with its modern art collection, forms an attractive introduction to the
Tech watershed, while the spa town of **Amélie-les-Bains** and medieval **Arles-sur-
Tech** beckon up-valley.

On the tops, an ascent of **Canigou** is essential to any exploration of the Eastern Pyrenees. It's virtually the sacred mountain of Catalonia, and though it's far from being the
highest, the beauty of the approaches to the peak are impeccable as are the views to
Marseille and Andorra from the top.

Perpignan

PERPIGNAN, the capital of Roussillon or French Catalonia, is the most multinational
city in the Pyrenees. A substantial part of its population is descended from Spanish
Catalans who fled Franco's regime at its inception; there is a sizeable gypsy contingent;
some of the suburbs are settled by French Moroccans and Algerians who fled the independence upheavals of the 1950s and 1960s; while a run-down zone in the centre has
become the quarter for native Moroccans and Algerians who moved here in search of
a brighter economic future.

Perpignan's medieval walls were demolished early this century to allow for expansion, and replaced by wide boulevards. This, in fact, maintained the separation of the
city's older districts from the new, and it's still easy and enjoyable to get around the
compact medieval areas on foot. The overriding impression is favourable: the Mediterranean is perceptible to the east, the River Têt skirts the town to the north, while the
narrow River Basse threads through the centre, dispensing welcome greenery along
its banks. Between place de la Loge and place Rigaud, where the old streets are now a
maze of chic boutiques, you could be on the Left Bank in Paris.

However, between place Rigaud and place Cassanyes you enter a different country:
washing is strung high across narrow streets and people in *djellabas* greet one another with "*Ahlan wa sahlan*". Unfortunately, though, Perpignan is far from being a model

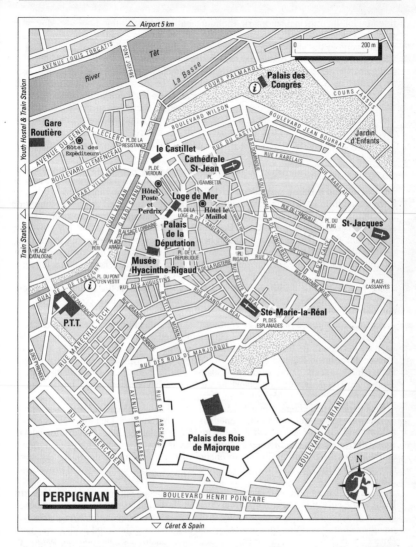

PERPIGNAN

of tolerance – Le Pen's *Front National* party has done well here at the polls, peddling a racist vision of white French nationals "swamped" by outsiders.

The City

The marble-paved **place de la Loge** has been the city's forum for eight hundred years, and now lies at the heart of the pedestrianized zone, graced with the most upscale shopping streets in Perpignan. However, the square itself is so small and narrow that you may not realize you've reached it until spotting the voluptuous statue of Venus by Aristide Maillol. Its principal landmark, the fourteenth-century Gothic **Loge de Mer,** was once the city's stock exchange and headquarters for maritime trade (symbolized by the weathervane in the shape of a medieval sailing ship); the ground floor has now been taken over by a fast-food restaurant, which sits incongruously with the lacy balustrades and gargoyles adorning the upper storeys. The adjoining building is the sixteenth-century **Hôtel de Ville** (with a second Maillol bronze, *La Méditerranée*, in the courtyard) and next door again is the fifteenth-century **Palais de la Deputation**, once home to the Roussillon parliament. The square long served as the scene of grisly executions, notably during a Catalan revolt of 1670 against recently imposed French rule. During World War II, place de la Loge's busy pavement cafés were the place to meet *passeurs*, the men – and sometimes women – who guided refugees across the Pyrenees into Spain.

To the north of place de la Loge rises the red-brick **Le Castillet**, the emblem of the city, built as a small fort in the fourteenth century and later used as a prison; the adjoining **Porte Notre-Dame** was added in 1478 by Louis XI as the main entrance to the town through its encircling walls (almost completely demolished at the beginning of this century). The whole building, with its massive nail-studded doors and spiral stone staircase, is now home to the **Casa Païral** (daily except Tues: summer 9.30am–7pm; winter 9am–6pm; 25F), a fascinating and beautifully designed museum of Catalan arts, crafts and traditional culture, with a great view from the roof of the town and distant mountains. The place de Verdun, on the south side of Le Castillet, is the setting for summer evening performances of the *sardana*, the solemn and passionate Catalan folk dance (see feature on p.136). Nearby, at 1 boulevard Wilson, is the battered but splendidly ornate **Cinema Castillet**, the oldest cinema in France, now converted into an eight-screen complex.

A couple of minutes' walk to the southeast of place de la Loge is the **place Rigaud**. The eponymous Hyacinthe Rigaud – commemorated by a statue in the square – was born in Perpignan in 1659 and went on to become court painter to Louis XIV. The **Musée Hyacinthe-Rigaud** at 16 rue de l'Ange, between place Arago and place des Poilus (daily except Tues: summer 9.30am–noon & 2.30–7pm; winter 9am–noon & 2–6pm; 25F), is dedicated to his work and that of early Catalan masters, but also has a collection of paintings by Maillol, Dufy, Picasso and others.

East of place de la Loge, along rue Saint-Jean and across place Gambetta, stands the **Cathédrale Saint-Jean**, commissioned in 1324 by Sancho, king of Mallorca (see below), and elevated to cathedral status in 1602, displacing Elne. Its exterior sports bands of river stones sandwiched by brick; inside is most interesting for its elaborate if dimly lit altarpieces and, in the south chapel (through a separate door), for the stark crucifix called the *Dévot Christ*, dating from the early fifteenth century and probably of Rhenish origin.

From the back of the cathedral, rue François Rabelais curves round to **place du Puig**, at the core of Perpignan's poorest quarter. Here, and around neighbouring **place Cassanyes**, the North African influence is at its greatest. Between the two squares, the medieval church of **Saint-Jacques** is the starting point for the Good Friday afternoon *Procession de la Sanch* (*sanch* means "blood" in Catalan), a sinister-looking parade of penitents in red or black hoods and robes, bearing images of Christ's Passion. Behind the church lie the secluded and quiet **Miranda Gardens**, laid out on part of the old city wall (Mon–Fri: summer 3–6.30pm; winter 2.30–5.30pm).

The Palais des Rois de Majorque
Perpignan's most famous sight, and the kernel around which it grew, is the massive **Palais des Rois de Majorque** (daily: June–Sept 10am–6pm; Oct–May 9am–5pm; closed Jan 1, May 1, Nov 1, Dec 25; 20F) on the southern fringe of the old city; the entrance is in rue des Archers, around fifteen minutes' walk from place de la Loge.

The history of Perpignan is more or less synonymous with that of the palace, originally built in the late thirteenth century as a residence for Jaume I of Mallorca, son of Jaume I of Aragón (The Conqueror), who drove the Saracens from Mallorca. At his death "The Conqueror" divided his kingdom between his two sons: to the elder, Pedro II, went the title of king of Aragón, but only a portion of the actual kingdom; the remainder, including Roussillon and Mallorca, went to the younger Jaume. The two branches of the family were immediately at each other's throats, and stayed that way until Roussillon and Aragón were reunited in the early fourteenth century by the more pacific Sancho. Having passed to the French, then back to the Spanish, Perpignan changed hands for the last time in 1642, a couple of years after France had occupied Roussillon in the wake of the revolt of the Catalans against Spanish rule; in September, after a siege that was at times commanded personally by Louis XIII and Cardinal Richelieu, Perpignan fell. Vauban, military engineer to Louis XIV, constructed the imposing outer walls in the fit of over-enthusiastic fortification that followed consolidation of French sovereignty accorded by the 1659 Treaty of the Pyrenees.

Perhaps the best aspects of the visit are the gypsy buskers in the tunnel entrance, and a view of Canigou from the gardens, which you can enter free of charge. Neither is a ticket needed for a look at the splendid **courtyard**, highlight of the palace, with its two storeys of dissimilar, now-Gothic, now-Moorish arches. The lower of the adjacent piggy-back **chapels** – one for the queen's worship, one for the king's – has elegant marble tracery on its porch. The interior apartments, though, with the exception of the majestic **great hall**, are barely furnished and less engaging.

Practicalities

The small **airport**, Aéroport International Perpignan-Rivesaltes (☎04.68.61.28.98), 6km north of town, handles daily flights to and from Paris, Montpellier, Lyon and Strasbourg, as well as services from London in summer. The airport **shuttle bus** (*la navette*; 28F) makes the twenty-minute trip up to eight times daily, stopping at both the bus station (see below) and train station; a **taxi** into the centre will cost around three times the bus fare.

Perpignan's **train station**, at the west end of av Général-de-Gaulle, was once dubbed "the centre of the world" by Salvador Dalí – hence the milestone atop an arch near the entrance which announces "Centre du Monde: 0.0km"; all **long-distance buses** stop outside the station. To get into the heart of the city from here, walk along the avenue, over place de Catalogne, and cross the River Basse at **place Arago**, close by the *quartier de piétonnes* (pedestrian zone) – a fifteen-minute walk. The other three key squares, **place de la Loge**, **place Rigaud** and **place Cassanyes** lie on a zigzag line eastwards, each five to ten minutes' walk from the next.

If you arrive by local bus or airport shuttle, you'll be dropped at the **gare routière**, just off av du Général-Leclerc near Pont Arago, a short distance northwest of place de la Résistance. For **city buses**, including frequent buses to Canet-Plage, the CTP kiosk in place Peri (near the *Palmarium* café) supplies information and tickets .

The **municipal tourist office** (summer Mon–Sat 9am–7pm, Sun 10am–noon & 2–5pm; winter Mon–Sat 9am–noon & 2–6pm; ☎04.68.66.30.30) is in the Palais des Congrès, the recently renovated white building at the end of the leafy Promenade des Platanes which runs parallel to boulevard Wilson. There's also a well-stocked **regional tourist office** (☎04.68.34.29.94; Mon–Sat 9am–12.30pm & 2–7pm) on the quai de Lattre-de-Tassigny, near the main **post office**. There are numerous **banks**, especially between quai Vauban and boulevard Clemenceau; you can also change money at the main post office, and at the *bureau de change* in the train station, near the buffet. If you need a **laundrette**, look no further than Laverie Foch at 23 rue Maréchal Foch (daily 7am–8pm).

Accommodation

For full **accommodation** lists, ask at the tourist office in the Palais des Congrès, or at the information bureau in the train station. Numerous quite reasonable **hotels** are strung along av Général-de-Gaulle, near the train station: the *Paris-Barcelone*, at no. 1 (☎04.68.34.42.60; ④), the *Terminus*, opposite at no. 2 (☎04.68.34.32.54; ③), and *Le Helder*, at no. 4 (☎04.68.34.38.05; ③), though slightly seedy, are all rated two-star. Cheapest on the avenue, but with particularly tacky decor, are *Le Berry*, at no. 6 (☎04.68.34.59.02; ②), and *L'Express*, no. 3 (☎04.68.34.89.96; ②). Other possibilities include the *Avenir* at 11 rue de l'Avenir, a quiet street off av Général-de-Gaulle (☎04.68.34.20.30; ③), or, if you're on a tight budget, *Hotel des Expéditeurs* at 19 av du Général-Leclerc (☎04.68.35.15.80; ②) – it's on a rather desolate stretch near the bus terminal, but has a good restaurant (see below). For a central but still reasonably priced place, try the friendly, long-established *Poste et Perdrix*, with balconied rooms near Le Castillet at 6 rue Fabriques-Nabot (☎04.68.34.42.53, fax 04.68.34.58.20; ④), or the smaller, quieter *Le Maillol* at 14 impasse des Cardeurs (☎04.68.51.10.20, fax 04.68.51.20.29; ④). Heading upmarket into three-star territory, the *Hotel de la Loge*, 1 rue Fabriques-Nabot (☎04.68.34.41.02, fax 04.68.34.25.13; ⑤), and the larger *Hotel Windsor*, 8 bd Wilson (☎04.68.51.18.65, fax 04.68.51.01.00; ⑤), are both recommended and very central.

The well-run **youth hostel** (☎04.68.34.63.32; closed 10am–6pm & Dec 20–Jan 20; ①) is between the train station and bus station in Parc de la Pépinière, behind the police station on av de Grande-Bretagne; it's clean and friendly but overlooks a noisy main road at the back. There are two reasonable **campsites**, both with a swimming pool, well signposted from the city centre: *Le Catalan* on route de Bompas north of town (☎04.68.63.16.92; open all year) and the smaller *La Garrigole*, west of town at 2 rue Maurice-Lévy (☎04.68.54.66.10; closed Dec).

Restaurants, cafés and markets

Don't dally when pondering **dinner**: most of Perpignan's restaurant shutters seem to roll down at 10pm sharp, though you can get served later at several brasseries which stay open till midnight, including the popular *Arago* and *Café Vienne* in the palm-shaded place Arago. Generally speaking, **av Général-de-Gaulle** is a good bet for reasonably priced meals: the best and most popular restaurant here is *Le Perroquet* (closed Wed Sept–Apr; menus from 62F), very close to the station on the north side of the street, with a good choice of Catalan specialities; *Chez Grand Mère*, across the way at no. 18 (closed Sun evening), offers good, reasonable Alsatian food. The restaurant in the *Hôtel des Expéditeurs* (closed Sat evening & Sun) offers excellent value, if tripe stew and other offal does not intimidate.

In **the centre**, try the delightful, long-established restaurant-brasserie *Can Marti* (known as "le Café Catalan"), just opposite Le Castillet in place de Verdun (closed Sun), with menus from 59F; or the atmospheric *Casa Sansa* in narrow rue Fabriques-Nadal, just off place de la Loge (closed Mon lunch & Sun). In quai Vauban, the attractive Art Deco *Brasserie le Vauban* at no. 29 (closed Sun) offers a special "cinema menu" comprising two courses, glass of wine and a cinema ticket for 125F (as does the less stylish *Pizzapapa*, at 4 place Arago, for 85F). Nearby, the *Espi* is the largest of several ice-cream parlours and teashops along quai Vauban.

South of the centre, at 10 rue Petite la Monnaie (closed Sun), *Tarteline* serves delicious homemade quiches and tarts, to eat in or take away. For a fix of Asian or North African food, head for the eastern side of the old town, particularly **rue Llucia**, where modest establishments serve up stir-frys and couscous/tagine dishes – you'll find food like this in very few other places along the Pyrenees.

Café life is centred on place de la Loge – call in at *Brasserie de la Loge* or *Grande Café de la Bourse* – and place de Verdun, where the *Grande Café de la Poste*, shaded by huge plane trees, is the best. *Café la Paix* in place Arago is another popular choice but best of all is the huge, airy *Palmarium*, on the opposite side overlooking the River Basse, a downbeat, self-service place, very popular with the locals, where you can linger for hours over a coffee.

The daily **markets** in place Rigaud and place de la République offer mainly fruit and vegetables, but the most colourful market takes place on Saturday and Sunday mornings in the tree-shaded place Cassanyes, with a mixture of French, Arab and African traders selling cheap clothes, crafts and all sorts of local produce. There's also a popular Sunday morning **flea market** out by the Palais des Expositions, on the north side of the River Têt.

The Fenouillèdes

Although the main crests of the Pyrenees rise to the southwest of Perpignan, some little-visited hills and ridges – the **Fenouillèdes** – lie 30–60km northwest of the city. This is a landscape of harsh, weirdly contorted limestone, scrubby vegetation and occasional fields of splintered schist on which grapevines somehow grow; only in the extreme west, under the rainier influence of the Aude, does the terrain become appreciably greener with full-sized forest.

Public transport into the region is limited to the single daily **bus service** along the Têt valley to Ille-sur-Têt, climbing northwest via the D2 to Montalba-le-Château, Sournia and

---

MOVING ON FROM PERPIGNAN

Perpignan serves as an important transport junction for the entire region. It's also easily the best place to rent transport if you haven't already done so. For **car rental**, contact Citer, 22 av Général-de-Gaulle (☎04.68.67.31.05), Europcar, 28 av Général-de-Gaulle (☎04.68.34.65.03), or Avis, 13 bd du Conflent (☎04.68.34.26.71); **bicycles** are available for rent at Cycles Mercier, 1 rue de Président-Doumer. Public transport options include the following services:

Buses
Several local bus companies (including Car Inter 66 and Car Verts du Roussillon) operate from the *gare routière*; the bus station's information office (daily 6.45am–7.15pm; ☎04.68.35.29.02) supplies timetables and can issue a **Tourist Pass** (150F) giving eight days' unlimited bus travel around the Pyrenees–Roussillon region (bring a passport-size photo). Regular services run south to Argelès and Collioure on the **Côte Vermeille**, where you can pick up the Interplages bus service in summer (linking all the coastal resorts from Le Barcarès in the north to Cerbère in the south). Along the **Tech valley** there are more or less two-hourly services along the D115 via Le Boulou, Céret, Amélie-les-Bains and Arles-sur-Tech; from Arles there are two connections daily to Saint-Laurent-de-Cerdans, and three daily to the valley's end at Prats-de-Molló. Along the **Têt valley**, there are half a dozen buses daily along the N116 as far as Villefranche-de-Conflent (where you can pick up the *Train Jaune*), with three continuing as far as Latour-de-Carol – one of which makes the detour to Font-Romeu. Four services a day (except Sun) ply the D612 to **Thuir**, while four buses daily (except Sun) run south along the N9 to the border at **Le Perthus**; from here, a Spanish minibus runs south to **Figueres**.

Trains
Trains run south from Perpignan station (☎04.68.51.93.39) to the coast at **Argelès-sur-Mer**, **Collioure** and onwards to the French–Spanish border at **Cerbère/Port-Bou**, where you change for trains to Figueres, Girona and Barcelona. Inland, the train service along the **Têt valley** ends at **Villefranche-de-Conflent** where you have to continue by the *Train Jaune* (see p.112), which terminates at Latour-de-Carol. Northwards, there are services to **Rivesaltes** and **Narbonne**, from where there are connections for Toulouse, Montpellier and Paris.

Rabouillet, in the heart of the region; or you can take the service that goes four times a day through Rivesaltes and Estagel to **Saint-Paul-de-Fenouillet**, two of them continuing most days of the week along the D117 to **Axat** and **Quillan** in the Aude valley.

Once in the range, there are two main walking routes to follow: the **Sentier Cathare**, which leads west into the Pays de Sault (see p.217), and the **Tour du Fenouillèdes**, a seven-day circuit that links the main sights of the region. Both occasionally share right-of-way with the **GR36**, and there are numerous variants of each which will become clear on consulting the appropriate IGN maps or *topoguides*.

Nôtre-Dame-de-Pène and Estagel

The bus journey from Perpignan to Saint-Paul-de-Fenouillet passes through **CASES-DE-PÈNE** (15km from Perpignan), near which is one of the strangest sites in Roussillon. Some 500m southwest of the village, a track climbs to **Nôtre-Dame-de-Pène**. A thirty-minute walk along it brings you to a grand staircase in the middle of nowhere, leading from bare

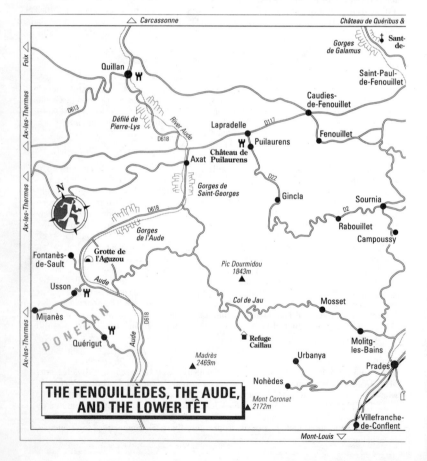

THE FENOUILLÈDES, THE AUDE, AND THE LOWER TÊT

rock to the white-painted facade of this seventeenth-century hermitage. There's no admittance to the public, but the walk is worth it for the views of the Agly river valley and the sea.

ESTAGEL, 7km further west from Cases-de-Pène, doesn't have much to recommend it other than the fact that it's well placed for exploring the area. Its sole sight is the statue in the main square celebrating François-Dominique Arago, the astronomer, physicist and politician after whom Perpignan's place Arago is named; he was born here in 1786. The *Nouvel Hôtel*, 9 bd Jean Jaurès (☎04.68.29.00.84; ②) is the place to stay; the municipal **campsite** is on av du Docteur Cortade, on the west side of town.

Tautavel

In 1971 archeologists working at the Caune de l'Arago, a cave near the village of **TAU-TAVEL**, 10km northeast of Estagel, discovered the front part of a skull that enabled them to determine the appearance of our pre-Neanderthal ancestors. An example of *Homo erectus* – an evolutionary midpoint between the African *Homo habilis* and mod-

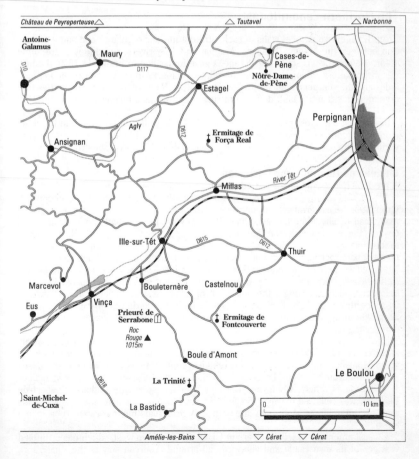

ern *Homo sapiens* – this particular male specimen would have been roaming the banks of the Verdouble around 450,000 years ago, a period from which scarcely any other human remains have been found in Europe.

The reconstructed skull, with its enormous cranial ridge and low eye sockets, is displayed in Tautavel's **Musée de la Préhistoire** (daily: Jan–March & Oct–Dec 10am–12.30pm & 2–6pm; April–June & Sept 10am–6pm; July & Aug 9am–9pm; 35F), centrepiece of a small but extremely moving exhibition. Cabinets and display panels show stone tools, animal bones and casts from the floor of the cave, and artists' impressions of the landscape and wildlife of the time. The cave itself (July & Aug daily 10am–noon & 12.30–5.30pm; visits in other seasons by arrangement with the museum) is situated in a low hill on the opposite side of the Verdouble valley; a telescope in the museum is trained on it. All the finds – some 250,000 objects – have been removed, but it's exciting to stand where primordial hunters dwelt half a million years ago.

A **bus** from Perpignan to Tautavel leaves at around 11am on schooldays only, changing at Estagel; total journey time is just under an hour.

The Northern Fenouillèdes

From Estagel two parallel walls of rock, striking in their regularity and sudden eruption between the Maury, Boulzane, Magnat and Agly rivers, run due west for some 40km. Before the Treaty of the Pyrenees gave Roussillon to France in 1659, the border with Spain ran along the northern wall, which marks the perimeter of the Fenouillèdes and the southern edge of the Corbières ridge. Ruins of the imposing **castles** that defended this frontier look down from ridges and peaks all along the winding D123 and D14 roads, to the northwest of Estagel. Amongst the various local rivers, the Agly – the largest and most permanent – has carved a magnificent **gorge** out of the limestone of the northerly ridge. All of these attractions are fairly accessible on foot from various points along the Perpignan–Saint-Paul-de-Fenouillet–Axat bus route.

Château de Quéribus and Cucugnan

A pre-1659 manuscript characterized the citadel of Carcassonne, one of the main strongholds of Catharism (see pp.218–19), as the "mother" castle, and the **Château de Quéribus**, the easternmost outrider, as one of her five "sons". To get there, turn off the main road or alight the bus at Maury, 10km beyond Estagel, and head up and north towards the pass known as the Grau de Maury, from where a steep, short side drive leads to the château – 6km, or about two hours' walking from Maury altogether. Visible on its turret of bare rock long before you reach it, the castle turns out to be much bigger than it looks, since much of the interior (May–Oct daily 10am–sunset; weekends only March, April, Nov & Dec; otherwise by arrangement only, but gate may be unlocked; 15F) is below ground level. Owing to the constraints of the site, a single stairway links all the various structures; highlight, in all senses, is the so-called **salle de palmier** in the polygonal keep, where the vaulted ceiling is supported by a graceful pillar sprouting a canopy of intersecting ribs.

Quéribus was constructed at the end of the tenth century, and belonged successively to the counts of Barcelona, the kings of Aragón and the counts of Fenouillèdes. After the fall of Montségur in 1244 it became the refuge of some of the last surviving Cathars (see p.221), an affront that King Louis IX decided to erase. His opportunity came in 1255 or 1256 (accounts differ), when the local lord who sponsored the Cathars, Chabert de Barbaira, was captured by royal forces and forced to cede this and other castles as his ransom. But unlike at Montségur, the Cathar garrison had time to escape, probably into Spain.

Closest amenities to Quéribus are in **CUCUGNAN**, 3km west, which has crumbled vestiges of its own castle and vineyards all around. You can stay at the *Auberge du*

Vigneron in the village centre (☎04.68.45.40.84, fax 04.68.45.03.00; ④), but you might prefer to eat at the *Auberge de Cucugnan* (reserve on ☎04.68.45.40.84), well signposted one street higher, where ample four-course menus start at about 100F (including house wine) and *cargolades* (Catalan barbecues) are a feature of the interior garden.

Château de Peyreperteuse and around

Another of the five "sons" of Carcassonne, the **Château de Peyreperteuse** (daily: Easter–June, Sept & Oct 9am–7pm; July 9am–9pm; Aug 9am–8pm), 4km west of Cucugnan, is the largest of the so-called Cathar castles. Its age and history of possession is nearly identical to that of Quéribus, with Paris assuming definitive control here by treaty with Aragon in 1258. Because the castle was garrisoned until 1789, the ruins are in good condition, and as at Quéribus you're pretty much allowed the run of the place, though special care is needed on the extremely slick steps of Saint-Louis to the west keep; access is banned altogether in stormy weather. You can approach from the village of Duilhac (see below) by a three-kilometre access road to the car park and ticket office on the south flank, via the *Sentier Cathare* to the same point, or within an hour along the G36 from Rouffiac (see below); the main entry with its barbican and ticket-checker is tucked into the north curtain wall. The setting of the castle, draped the length of a jagged ridge with sheer drops at most points, is its most impressive feature. No single architectural feature amongst various cisterns, chapels and towers claims attention, but from the highest **Chapelle San Jordi** there are sweeping views east to the Mediterranean and Perpignan, with Quéribus in between on its rock stalk.

Coiling picturesquely at the eastern foot of the castle ridge, the village of **DUILHAC** offers a shop and bakery for hikers, plus both a *gîte d'étape* (☎04.68.45.01.74; ①) in the centre and the comfortable, stone-clad *Auberge du Vieux Moulin* (☎04.68.45.02.17, fax 04.68.45.02.18; ④), with en-suite bathrooms, on the northerly through road. Its attached restaurant, next to the springs which once powered the mill of the name, has an undeniably appealing setting, but the menu is dull compared to fare on offer in Cucugnan or **ROUFFIAC DES CORBIÈRES**, the village 3km north. Here the *Auberge de Peyrepertuse* on the main through road (☎04.68.45.40.40; ④) serves hearty food and offers excellent en-suite rooms at the bottom of their price category. Otherwise there's a campsite, at the east end of the village, a tiny grocery installed in the filling station, and two or three weekly buses to Perpignan, either direct or via Saint-Paul-de-Fenouillet.

The Gorges de Galamus and Saint-Paul-de-Fenouillet

From Peyrepertuse the joint GR36 and *Sentier Cathare* head southwest, while from Rouffiac the D14 road curls in much the same direction to the **Gorges de Galamus**, a short but impressive limestone defile worn through the ridge by the River Agly. The D10, between Cubières-sur-Cinoble on the D14 and Saint-Paul-de-Fenouillet, is an occasionally perilous corniche road threading right through the gorge and offering alternative access. Most visitors get at the gorge near its downstream end, 3km out of Saint-Paul, where there's a fee car park and the start of a path to the impeccably sited **Ermitage de Saint-Antoine-de-Galamus**, about halfway down the east flank (daily 10am–6pm). Behind the modest facade of cold-drinks stand and souvenir shop, this proves to be a huge, sanctified grotto thrusting deep into the cliff; alas, there is no longer a functioning *gîte d'étape* here. The *ermitage* also has its own free (but small) car park further along the corniche road, at the top of entry steps tunnelled through the rock. For most, however, the gorge itself will be the most compelling attraction; a steep path, culminating in a rock ladder, drops from below the *ermitage* to pools in the river deep enough for swimming. This is also a popular canyoning venue, with wet-suited and helmeted parties entering the gorge from an easier point of access up at the Cubières end of the D10 – knots of parked cars mark the spot.

Hot and traffic-riven **SAINT-PAUL-DE-FENOUILLET**, despite proximity to these attractions, is no tourist mecca, having lost two of its four **hotels** in recent years. The survivors are *Le Chatelet*, on the main road (☎04.68.59.01.20; ③), and the more upmarket *Relais des Corbières* (☎04.68.59.23.89; ④), with an attached restaurant. At Saint-Paul, you can pick up onward buses to Auxat and Quillan.

Château de Puilaurens

Lapradelle, 18km west of Saint-Paul-de-Fenouillet, is the closest point on the D117 to the **Château de Puilaurens** (June–Sept daily 10am–6pm, 20F; Oct–May unrestricted access), another of Carcassonne's "sons", perched majestically on a 700-metre-high ridge. If you don't have your own transport, the castle is just under an hour away: 2km along the D22 to Puilaurens hamlet, then about a half-hour's climb up a marked path. With a car, there's a 1500-metre access road, not shown on IGN maps, beginning just south of the hamlet.

Built originally by the Visigoths, Puilaurens was enlarged not long before its indirect conquest by the anti-Cathar army in 1255 or 1256, which captured the Cathar champion Chabert de Barbaira and made the cession of all his local strongholds the condition of his release. You enter from the west, via a stepped maze of *chicanes* or staggered low walls; much of the interior is dilapidated, but be sure to catch the view east over piney hills from outside the southeast postern gate, and the point on the **western donjon** complex where you're allowed briefly on the curtain wall for a eyeful in the opposite direction. Nearby, on the parapet, are machicolations which apparently doubled as latrines, and the so-called **Tour de la Dame Blanche**, with rib vaulting and a *porte-voix* wormhole for communicating with different storeys of the tower.

If need be, you can **stay** in the village of **GINCLA**, 6km from the castle, at the *Hostellerie du Grand Duc* (☎04.68.20.55.02, fax 04.68.20.61.22; ④; closed in winter), with a rather laid-back, if well-regarded restaurant. In **LAPRADELLE**, the *Hotel Viaduc* – named after the disused rail viaduct opposite – has better food than promised from its appearance (menus from 62F) and could make an emergency stopover (☎04.58.20.53.01; ①).

Moving on from Lapradelle, you can take a bus westwards into the Aude valley at Axat; from there the same bus continues northwest to Quillan (see p.97), or you can pick up another bus (July to mid-Sept Mon, Wed & Fri) south to Quérigut (see p.99). Otherwise you could turn south into the central Fenouillèdes by hitching or driving along the twisty D22, then the D2, to Rabouillet, nearly 25km away (from where there's a bus service to Perpignan), or devote a few days to hiking the *Sentier Cathare* or the *Tour des Fenouillèdes*.

The Central Fenouillèdes

The heartland of the Fenouillèdes is relatively gentle walking country, where the pleasures of isolation are enhanced in spring (summer is far too hot to walk) by the pine-resinous aroma of the air. Rising from the east towards the Aude valley, it is nowhere very lofty – the highest point is 1843-metre **Pic Dourmidou** in the extreme west – but the rock has been eroded, baked and shattered into bizarre valleys, walls and pinnacles. The terrain is enlivened with occasional evergreen oaks, clumps of aromatic rosemary and – especially around the River Agly – even a few grapevines.

By public transport the only way into the Central Fenouillèdes is the infrequent bus service from Perpignan via Ille-sur-Têt (Wed & Sat 10.45am, Mon, Tues, Thurs & Fri 4.45pm). The terminus is **RABOUILLET**, 30km from Ille, but it's best to get off 8km earlier at **SOURNIA**, where there's a *gîte d'étape* and a **campsite** on the road out to Rabouillet, *Camping Municipal La Source* (☎04.68.97.72.44).

The Tour des Fenouillèdes

Sournia is also the hub of the region's walking trails, particularly the **Tour des Fenouillèdes**, which is intended as a full week's trek. The route heads southeast from Sournia to **MARCEVOL**, a hamlet near Arboussols, just above the dam in the Têt valley, with a *gîte d'étape* (☎04.68.96.21.85; ①). Next day you go north to **ANSIGNAN**, where there is a spectacular Roman aqueduct over the Agly and a series of dolmens some way to the west of the town; there's also a *gîte d'étape* (☎04.68.59.18.61; ①). From Ansignan, the *Tour* continues north via Saint-Paul-de-Fenouillet into the Gorges de Galamus (see p.95), after which it curves west and back southwards via Caudiès-de-Fenouillet (which has a hotel and shops) to **FENOUILLET** (*gîte d'étape*; ☎04.68.59.21.84 or 04.68.59.93.58; ①), a day's march from Sournia.

The Aude valley

The dramatic, short-lived **Aude** is one of the great rivers of the French Pyrenees, matched in the east of the range only by the Ariège. Rising on the east side of the Carlit Massif, it is restrained for a time by the dams of Matemale and Puyvalador, then loosed to hurtle through gorges to **Quillan**. Just upstream from the gorges, around **Quérigut**, sprawl vast forests of beech and pine interspersed with lush meadows – this is the **Donezan**, a scenic – but poor and neglected – corner of the Ariège. From Quillan, the Aude flows north across the plain to Carcassonne and into the sea between Narbonne and Beziers.

Quillan is linked to Perpignan by a regular **bus** service through Axat and Saint-Paul-de-Fenouillet, and to Carcassonne by both **train** and SNCF bus.

Quillan

Clustered on the west bank of the Aude about halfway along its course, **QUILLAN** makes a handy stopover on the way to the high Pyrenees. It's a half-heartedly industrialized place whose main attraction is the river itself, a sturdy torrent running right past the town. Canoeing and rafting are organized by the Centre de Séjour Sports Nature de la Forge (☎04.68.20.23.79, fax 04.68.20.13.64) at the south edge of town en route to Axat, which is also a **gîte d'étape** (①) and runs climbing and canyoning trips. The only monument of interest is the ruined **castle**, on the east bank of the Aude just across the Pont Vieux. Built on the site of a Visigothic fortress, it was burned by the Huguenots in 1575 and partly dismantled in the eighteenth century, but the remnants are still worth a scramble.

Train and bus **terminals** are both central, opposite the least expensive **hotel** in town – *Le Terminus*, at 45 bd Charles-de-Gaulle (☎04.68.20.05.72, fax 04.68.20.13.71; ②). Indeed all accommodation is on this same, noisy street, which doubles as the D117; you won't get much more peace and quiet, but you will get more comfort for scarcely more money at the *Cartier*, no. 31 (☎04.68.20.05.14; ③) or the *Canal* at no. 36 (☎04.68.20.08.62; ③). All have attached **restaurants**, though the *Canal*'s shuts Sunday. *La Sapinette* at 21 rue René-Delpech, off bd Jean Bourrel, is the closest **campsite**. The **tourist office** occupies a prominent kiosk beside the station (summer Mon–Sat 8am–noon & 2–7pm, Sun 9am–noon), and can help with Grotte de l'Aguzou reservations (see p.98) among other things.

South from Quillan: gorges and caves

The road **south from Quillan** is a fabulous approach to the eastern peaks of the Pyrenees. Coursing down from the Capcir plateau, the Aude has cut successively through granite, gneiss and schist, and finally soft limestone, carving spectacular cave systems and ever deeper gorges as it goes. Public transport is limited to just a thrice-weekly summer **bus** service to Quérigut, 44km south of Quillan.

Défilé de Pierre-Lys and Axat

Gorge country begins almost immediately after you leave Quillan heading south, with rock overhangs blasted as necessary to allow passage. The narrowest bit is the **Défilé de Pierre-Lys**, 8km to the south, where climbers can usually be seen swinging above the road. Four kilometres beyond the *défilé*, there's a campsite, *Le Moulin du Pont d'Al-iès* (April–Nov; canteen), at the eponymous crossroads, the junction where the D117 highway peels off east towards the Fenouillèdes. Just adjacent, Sud Rafting (☎04.68.20.53.73) offers canyoning through the Gorges de Galamus and rafting or hydrospeed through the closer Aude gorges.

Continuing south 1km beyond the crossroads on the D618 brings you to **AXAT**, where an old bridge, under which rafters often put in, links the through-road district with the east-bank quarter. There's just one reasonable **hotel-restaurant** here, the *L'Ensoleille* (☎04.68.20.51.43; ③), opposite the cinema and the *Mairie*.

Grotte de l'Aguzou

If you have sufficient time to spend in this region, try to visit the **Grotte de l'Aguzou**, 15km southwest of Axat towards the upstream end of the Gorges de l'Aude. The guided tour of this magnificent complex is as close as a non-speleologist can get to the real thing (booking essential, usually several days' notice; contact Philippe Moreno, ☎04.68.20.45.38, or at the booth near the petrol pump 400m upstream from the cave). Equipped with overalls, helmet and lamp, groups of four to ten people are taken into the unlit cave system at 9am, to be conducted through the *grandes salles* of stalactites, stalagmites, columns and draperies, some of which are 20m high. Lunch (you bring your own) is taken 600m underground, and then it's on to the so-called "gardens of crystals" – some growing from the rock in long, thin needles, or like pine cones dusted by hoar frost, and others clear and convoluted like the accidents of a Venetian glass-blower.

If you're on foot, the best place to **stay** for an early start is the designated *camping sauvage* area by the river, 300m from the cave entrance. There's a *gîte d'étape* (☎04.68.20.37.07; ①) just over 3km west at **FONTANÈS-DE-SAULT**.

The Donezan

In the twelfth century the **Donezan** region and its then-capital **USSON** – in the southern neck of the Gorges de l'Aude – became a sort of forerunner to Andorra: separated from the rest of Ariège by the **Col de Pailhères** (2001m), it was granted special financial privileges on account of its inaccessibility. Today Usson, like the rest of this remote region of seven villages, houses barely enough people to function as a *canton*; the spa of Usson-les-Bains 1km downstream is boarded up and for sale, while the dry-stone walls around the fields are as dilapidated as the **Château** (July & Aug Mon–Thurs & Sat 3–7pm, Sun 10am–noon & 3–7pm; Sept Sat 3–7pm & Sun 10am–noon & 3–7pm; 10F), the first place of safety for the four Cathars who escaped the massacre at Montségur. At least as old as the eleventh century, the castle spent much of the period between the thirteenth and sixteenth centuries in the possession of the counts of Foix (see p.215), champions of the Cathars.

Just above Usson, 3km along the D25 to Ax-les-Thermes, **MIJANÈS** is an immensely attractive stone-built village, where you may **stay and eat** year-round at the simple but perfectly adequate *Relais de Pailhères* (☎04.68.20.45.76; ②), with good-sized, wood-floored rooms. This is the only such facility of any standard between Quillan and Quérigut, with people coming from some distance away to patronize it, so reservations are advisable at weekends. When there's good snow the nearby **ski** station opens – not a frequent occurrence, as the four drag-lifts rise to only 2060m.

These days, **QUÉRIGUT**, 7km south of Usson, is the capital of the region. It stands at the head of a slope of neglected terraces, notable only for the stump of the **Château de Donezan**, the last stronghold of the Cathar leadership, who held out here for eleven years after the fall of Montségur (see p.221). Quérigut makes a good walking base for jaunts southwest through the forest; **accommodation** is either at the *Hôtel du Donezan* (☎04.68.20.42.40, fax 04.68.20.47.06; ③), uphill from the church opposite the fountain (also with the only **restaurant**), or the **campsite**, *Le Bousquet*, down by the stream below the village. Usson and Quérigut can be reached on Monday, Wednesday and Friday afternoons by Petit Charles **bus** from Quillan, about an hour's ride in total.

The lower Têt

From Perpignan the **Têt valley** (also known as the Conflent), provides a fast if initially not very scenic route southwest into the Pyrenees. The upper Têt is covered on p.109; the most interesting parts of the **lower Têt** are to be found in the foothills to the north of the valley, and in the region of **Les Aspres** to the east. Nevertheless, there are some pleasant small towns along the N116 road: **Millas**, **Ille-sur-Têt** and **Prades**, the last-named the most attractive of the trio and one of the gateways to Canigou.

Buses from Perpignan serve the lower Têt along the N116 roughly every two hours, while **trains** run about six times a day, taking fifteen minutes to reach Millas, 25 minutes to Ille-sur-Têt and 45 minutes to Prades.

Upstream towards Prades

MILLAS, 17km west of Perpignan, was first settled in prehistoric times, developed under Roman rule and flourished during the Middle Ages. Unfortunately, the only vestige of this lengthy history is the fourteenth-century village church, with its intricately carved interior. Surrounded by orchards and market gardens, with windbreaks of cypress and poplar, Millas is a good place to buy fruit and vegetables, and that's about all that can be said for it.

It's a pleasant stroll out of town to the **Ermitage de Força Réal**, along the footpath which starts about 1500m along the road north to the Col de la Bataille. The hermitage is another 4km on, standing atop a low ridge next to the remains of a twelfth-century Aragonese fort. The fort has now been taken over as a radio relay station, and the hermitage serves as a café, with a huge stone terrace from which to enjoy the view. To the north you'll see the parched Fenouillèdes; to the south the equally arid Aspres; to the east the coastal plain; and to the west the steadily rising line of the Pyrenees, with the scrubby Mediterranean vegetation giving way to forests of pine.

Thuir and Castelnou

THUIR, 9km southeast of Millas down the D612, is the main producer of the red aperitif wine called **Byrrh** (pronounced "beer"), stored in what is claimed to be the biggest oak vat in the world. The free 45-minute visit to the winery, located at 6 bd Violet (☎04.68.53.05.42; July–Aug daily 10–11.45am & 2–6.45pm; April–June & Sept Mon–Sat 9–11.45am & 2.30–5.45pm; Oct same hours but closed Sat; Nov–March by appointment only), includes a tasting – it's rather like sweet vermouth. You can reach Thuir directly by **bus** from Perpignan (4 daily, except Sun), but to head on west to Ille-sur-Têt in the main valley you'll have to drive yourself or hitch. The direct way to Ille lies 13km along the D615 (via Corbère-les-Cabane), but it's more interesting to divert southwest first, via Castelnou, 4km from Thuir.

CASTELNOU itself is a lovely stone village with a tenth-century **château** above, restored after a 1981 fire and now a museum (June 15–Sept 15 daily 10am–8pm; March–June 15 & Sept 15–Oct daily 11am–7pm; Feb, Nov & Dec Mon & Wed–Fri noon–5pm, Sat & Sun 11am–6pm; Jan Sat & Sun 11am–6pm; 28F). Its exterior and the view from up top are more compelling than the empty rooms within. You might plan a meal in Castelnou at *L'Hostal*, which specializes in *escargots* (though you should pre-order on ☎04.68.53.42.42).

The route beyond the village curves through the exquisite low hills of the eastern Aspres, past the picturesque **Ermitage de Fontcouverte**, before dropping down to Ille-sur-Têt, a 25-kilometre journey.

Ille-sur-Têt, Vinça and Eus

Seven kilometres up-valley from Millas, the picturesque medieval quarter of **ILLE-SUR-TÊT** has streets so narrow you have to flatten yourself against the houses if a car comes by. The town's **Centre d'Art Sacré**, in the seventeenth-century Hospice d'Ille (July–Sept daily 10am–noon & 2–7pm; rest of the year Mon & Wed–Fri 10am–noon & 3–6pm, Sat & Sun 3–6pm; 15F), has changing exhibitions to show the rich variety of paintings, sculptures, wood carving and precious objects from churches in the region. More remarkable are the clay cliffs just across the River Têt on the road north towards Sournia, which the elements have eroded into extraordinary figures known as *Les Orgues*, or the *Demoiselles d'Ille* (daily: July–Sept 9.30am–7.30pm; April–June 10am–6pm; Oct–March 10am–11.45am & 2–5pm; 15F). Two kilometres south of Ille, at St Michel de Llotes, is the **Musée de l'Agriculture Catalane** (daily except Tues: June–Sept 10am–noon & 3–7pm; Oct–May 10am–noon & 2–6pm; 15F), an interesting collection of old farming implements and techniques, from beekeeping to winemaking. If you decide that Ille calls for an overnight **stay**, there are *chambres d'hôtes* in rue Pierre Forché – better than the noisy and uninviting *Hôtel de Midi* on the main av Pasteur (☎04.68.84.00.32; ②). In addition to being a stop on the Têt bus routes, Ille is also visited by the daily bus (not Sun) from Perpignan into the Fenouillèdes.

Eight kilometres upstream, beyond the fortified village of Bouleternère, lies **VINÇA**, a place with few attractions other than **eating** at *Al Cargole*, which features *cargolade* (a sort of mixed grill of snails, lamb and sausage), or *La Petite Auberge*, at 64 av Général de Gaulle, which specializes in trout and *canards gras*. The nearby reservoir provides good swimming, windsurfing and canoeing. If you'd like to have a go at canoeing, contact Base de Canoë-Kayak UDSIS (☎04.68.96.20.33) at **EUS**, the expensively renovated medieval village perched on the hillside on the north bank of the Têt, just beyond the reservoir. You can also pick up the **Tour des Fenouillèdes** here (see p.97), or for a briefer outing, beginning beside Eus's church, take the one-hour stroll north along an old mule path to the derelict hamlet of Comes.

Les Aspres

The gentle hills of **Les Aspres** are best entered by turning south at Bouleternère and continuing through the gorge of the River Boulès; however, there's no public transport. About 8km along, the steeply winding D84 road leads 4km west up to the most celebrated Romanesque monument in Roussillon, the **Prieuré de Serrabone** (daily except public holidays 10am–6pm; 10F), whose exterior blends with the surrounding rocky landscape. Walkers can get to it by following a ten-kilometre route that starts as a track just outside Bouleternère, and continues as a footpath under the ridge of Roque Rouge. The situation is impressive, and the surrounding flora is so lush and diverse that a *jardin botanique* has been created around the priory.

Small slabs of local schist cover most of the plain exterior, and only the short paired columns of the cloister gallery – topped by ornate and amazingly well-preserved capitals – anticipate the richness inside. Halfway along the nave, against the bare walls, stands a fastidiously decorated tribune of rose marble with motifs of flowers and animals mythical and real, symbolic of various aspects of the beliefs and history of the Christian Church. Excavated columns found here suggest that much of the original priory – founded in the twelfth century – was as elaborate as the tribune.

Continuing south for 5km along the D618 through the village of Boule d'Amont brings you to the chapel of **La Trinité**, just before the Col Xatard (752m); it's also attainable by a three-hour walk along a footpath from the priory. Superb ironwork adorns the outside of the door, and inside there's a *Christ en Majesté*, a figure of the same type as the *Majestat* at Beget (see p.155).

From Col Xatard, the D618 drops south to enter the Tech valley at Amélie-les-Bains, 20km away. An attractive option for drivers is to complete a loop back to the Têt valley at Vinça: the road goes through the tiny village of **LA BASTIDE**, which has a *gîte d'étape* (☎04.68.39.41.56; ①), and then takes in Valmanya and Baillestavy (see "The Canigou Massif", p.104).

Prades

PRADES, a giant of a town compared with the others in the Têt valley, has a spate of singular distinctions. Aside from its distinctive pink-marble masonry and pavements, and its status as the birthplace in 1915 of Thomas Merton, the American Catholic mystic, Prades also draws thousands of visitors each July and August for the music festival begun in 1950 by the Catalan cellist **Pablo Casals** (Pau Casals in Catalan; 1876–1973). An exile from Franco's Spain, Casals spent much of his life here, not just playing but also composing; his works include the oratorio *The Crib* and the popular *Song of the Birds*, after which he named his house. The **Casals museum** (summer Mon–Sat 9am–noon & 2–6pm; winter Mon–Fri 9am–noon & 2–5pm), in the same building as the municipal tourist office (see below), is currently restricted to one large room, filled with photographs and memorabilia, though plans are afoot to move museum and tourist office to larger premises.

The festival performances take place at the monastery of **Saint-Michel-de-Cuxa,** whose single square tower suddenly appears above a copse of poplars 3km south of the town, on the orchard-lined road to Taurinya. Founded by a ninth-century Benedictine community which had abandoned a flooded monastery on the Têt, Saint-Michel reached its peak in the eleventh century and then went into slow decline. In 1790 the foundation was closed, suffering vandalism during the Revolution, and by the early part of this century more bits and pieces of the monastery were being bought up from nearby villages and shipped to the Cloisters Museum in New York – like many other Romanesque fragments from the region. Restoration began in the 1950s, using original materials wherever possible, and it's now open to visit (May–Sept Mon–Sat 9.30am–noon & 2–6pm, Sun 2–6pm; Oct–April Mon–Sat 9.30am–noon & 2–5pm, Sun 2–5pm; closed feast days; 15F). Some of the arches now incorporated into the gallery abutting the church were recovered from buildings in Prades, whereas the far side is composed of modern materials, except for the carved capitals.

Back in Prades itself, the church of **Saint-Pierre**, in the main place de la République, contains a huge and sumptuous seventeenth-century retable, a masterpiece by the Catalan sculptor Josep Sunyer. Prades is in fact conspicuously Catalan in feel, hosting a summertime Catalan university (☎04.68.96.10.84) and having established the first Catalan-language primary school in France. On Tuesdays there is an excellent **market** in the square and surrounding streets.

Practicalities

The **train station** is at the southern edge of Prades, about ten minutes' walk from the centre; **buses** set you down on the RN116 (av Général de Gaulle), which is the main road through the centre of town. The **tourist office** (☎04.68.05.41.02, fax 04.68.05.21.79; summer Mon–Sat 9am–12.30pm & 2–7pm, Sun 9am–noon; winter Mon–Fri 9am–noon & 2–5.30pm), at 4 rue Victor-Hugo, is a mine of information about everything from *chambres d'hôtes* and changing money to walking trails, biking trails and climbing the Canigou. The **music festival office** is next door (☎04.68.96.33.07, fax 04.68.96.50.95). You can rent touring and mountain **bikes** at Cycles Cerda, 114 av Général de Gaulle, or Michel Flament, 8 rue Arago.

For cheap and reasonable **accommodation**, you can't beat the faded elegance of the white-painted, simply furnished *Hostalrich*, at 156 av Général de Gaulle (☎04.68.96.05.38; ③), still run by a family who were friends of Casals; its spacious restaurant, with a 70F menu, also offers the best value in town. The best alternative is *Les Glycines* at 129 av Général de Gaulle (☎04.68.96.51.65; ④), more expensive and rather more bourgeois but spotlessly clean and friendly. The beautifully sited and well-managed municipal **campsite** (☎04.68.96.29.83), in the valley just east of the town centre off chemin du Gaz, has eighteen well-equipped and reasonably priced chalets for rent by the week or weekend (up to five people), and a great view of Canigou; the nearby *plan d'eau* is stocked for trout fishing, with rods for hire (35F for up to 4 trout).

If you have a car, you could try **Molitg-les-Bains**, the spa which lies 7km away on the north bank of the river, for accommodation. It has plenty of one-star hotels, of which the best are *Hôtel Saint Joseph* (☎04.68.05.02.11; April–Oct; ③), which also has a good restaurant, and *L'Oasis* (☎04.68.05.00.92; all year; ③), both in the spa sector; or, fifteen minutes away in the village proper, check out the two-star *Col de Jau* (☎04.68.05.03.20; ④).

Eating out in Prades offers a slightly better choice than accommodation: apart from the reliable *Hostalrich* (see above), you could try *El Patio*, at 19 place de la République (closed Wed except school holidays), which serves both traditional and Andalusian-style food for about 120F per person, or *L'Hostal de Nougarols* at Codalet on the road to Saint-Michel-de-Cuxa (closed Tues evening & Wed), serving Catalan specialities at similar prices. Café life is centred on the place de la République, where the *Café de France* has a reputation for the best *plats du jour*.

West from Prades

The D14, through Molitg and beyond, is a quiet and beautiful way of travelling **west to the Aude valley**. The road climbs 5km to **MOSSET**, where you'll find the *Ferme-Auberge Mas Lluganas* (☎04.68.05.00.37; ③) with rustic accommodation in the farmhouse, or *chambres d'hôtes* in the nearby *La Forge* (②) and home-cooked meals using their own produce. It then goes over the **Col de Jau** (1504m) where a track leads 5km south to the **Refuge Caillau** (☎04.68.05.00.06), close to the route of the **Tour du Coronat**, a very easy four-day walking circuit in the forests and open hillsides around Mont Coronat. Northwest of the Col de Jau, the road drops 23km through forests of fir to join the Aude at the Gorges de Saint-Georges.

Villefranche-de-Conflent

Beyond Prades the Têt valley narrows dramatically, becoming a gorge 6km further on, where the high walls of **VILLEFRANCHE-DE-CONFLENT** almost block the way. As there's almost no construction outside the walls, externally at least the town looks much as it did three hundred years ago: an elongated, two-street place squeezed between the palisade just to the south and the river. Within the ramparts, though, it's something of a let-down; entering through the Porte de France, at the eastern end, or the opposite Porte d'Espagne, you'll be confronted by over-restored houses and shops selling the sort of stuff you regret buying as soon as you're home. The atmosphere of the past is strongest on the bank of the Têt, by the thirteenth-century **Saint-Pierre**; the best view is from the far side, from where the weathered red-tiled roofs and the tower of the twelfth-century church of **Saint-Jacques** peer over the ramparts. But more satisfying, perhaps, than any man-made constructions are the vast cave complexes (see below) which riddle the strata below and around the town.

Villefranche dates from 1092, when – the Moorish threat having receded – Guillaume Raymond, count of Cerdagne, granted the charter for the foundation of Villa Libéra, soon called Villafranca and finally Villefranche. His seat was at Corneilla, just up the valley of the Cady, and as the principal menace was now the count of Roussillon, the logical site for the stronghold was here, at the confluence of the Cady and the Têt. Some remnants from that period still stand, notably the **Tour d'en Solenell** on the little square known as the **Placette**. In 1654 Villefranche – then controlled by Spain – was besieged by Louis XIV's troops, and fell after eight days' fighting. After the Treaty of the Pyrenees confirmed their annexation of Roussillon, the French rebuilt the Spanish fortifications, according to plans drawn up by Vauban.

As you walk the **ramparts** (daily: June–Sept 10am–7pm; April & May 10am–12.30pm & 2–6.30pm; March & Oct–Dec 2–6pm; 20F), their vulnerability to attack from the surrounding heights is obvious – a defensive weakness that Vauban remedied by adding various bastions and building the upper château now known as **Fort Liberia** (daily: June–Sept 9am–7pm; Oct–May 10am–6pm; 30F). Reached by a 734-step underground staircase or a much gentler trail (or by minibus from outside Porte de France, near the Prades–Vernet road – look for signs for *Navette Liberia*), the château has seen more service as a prison than as a fortress, and during World War I it held German POWs.

The caves

The most celebrated incident in Villefranche's history was the 1674 revolt against French rule, which culminated in the betrayal of **Charles de Llar** and his co-conspirators by Llar's daughter Inès. The tale was turned into melodrama by Louis Bertrand in his novel *L'Infante*, first published in 1930 and still in print. Llar's hiding place was the **Cova Bastéra**, a cave with an exit inside the walls of the town.

A double ticket gains admission to the Cova Bastéra and the limestone formations of **Grottes les Canalettes** (summer 9am–7pm; guided visit 45min; 35F), 1km along the road south towards Vernet-les-Bains; the most spectacular caves, however, are the adjoining **Grottes des Grandes Canalettes** which require a separate ticket (mid-June to mid-Sept daily 10am–6pm; March to mid-June & mid-Sept to Nov daily 10am–noon & 2–5pm; Dec–Feb Sun 2–5pm; guided visit approx 1hr; 40F). Entry is via a 160-metre passageway, hollowed out by water over the past four hundred million years; the water dripping down the sides is now directed over moulds to create limestone images for sale at the shop. Beyond a door you then enter a succession of huge chambers (*Blanche, Balcon, Angkor, Dôme Rouge*) crammed with stalactites, stalagmites, pillars and tiny feathery formations. Beyond the *Dôme Rouge* lies the *Gouffre sans Fond* (The Bottomless Pit), stretching for several kilometres and the preserve of speleologists only. If you have some caving experience, you can see caves that have not been rigged up with coloured illumination by contacting the Spéléo Club de Villefranche-de-Conflent, in town at 18 rue Saint-Jacques (☎04.68.96.40.35).

Practicalities

Main-line **trains** from Perpignan terminate in Villefranche, at the SNCF station (☎04.68.96.56.62), 400m north of the town; for onward *Train Jaune* services (see below), simply change platforms. The **tourist office** (summer Mon–Sat 9am–7pm, Sun 9am–noon & 2–7pm; ☎04.68.96.22.96) is in place de l'Eglise; in addition to the usual services, it sells copies of Bertrand's *L'Infante*. One of the less outrageously priced **hotels** inside the walls is *Le Canigou*, place du Génie, inside Porte de France (☎04.68.96.12.19; ③), with its own café-restaurant. There are several more **restaurants and crêperies**, most interesting the *Calypso*, serving omnivorous and vegetarian food, in rue Saint-

Pierre, the alley leading down to the Pont Saint-Pierre (and to one of the sets of stairs leading up to Fort Liberia).

To continue along the Têt, you can catch the yellow-and-red tourist train known as the **Train Jaune** (late May to late Sept 6 daily; 4 daily otherwise; see box p.112), from Villefranche to Mont-Louis, Font-Romeu, Bourg-Madame and Latour-de-Carol. **Buses** run south to Vernet-les-Bains (Mon–Sat 7 daily, Sun 3 daily) from outside the train station or from the route Nationale stop just outside the town walls at Porte de France.

The Canigou Massif

Rising to a height of 2785m between the Tech and Têt valleys, **Canigou** (*Canigó* in Catalan) is the great landmark of Catalonia, visible across the Empordà plain from the beaches of the Costa Brava and across the Roussillon lowlands from the Côte Radieuse. However, Canigou is not the highest mountain in Catalonia, nor even in the immediate area: a little to the west there's a whole group of greater peaks, including Pic de Prats de Bassibès (2845m) and Pic du Géant (2882m). Although situated well inside France, it symbolizes a Catalan unity endorsed by the small Catalan flags and other patriotic paraphernalia festooned from its summit cross.

There are essentially only two ways of reaching the top of Canigou – via the **Chalet Cortalets** (2150m) on the northern slopes, or via the **Refuge Mariailles** (1718m) to the southwest. The various bases from which to approach these shelters are detailed below. Routes from the Tech valley to the south are longer and therefore not specifically recommended as ways of climbing Canigou – although you might use them to move from the Tech to the Têt, taking in Canigou along the way. If you're serious about exploring the massif – which is a partly protected natural reserve, good for several days' trekking – either the 1:50,000 "Canigou/Vallespir/Fenouillèdes" *carte de randonnée* published by IGN, or its 1:25,000 **map** (no. 2349ET "Massif du Canigou"), are mandatory investments, available at shops and souvenir stalls in most of the surrounding villages.

Northern approaches to Canigou

The northeasternmost route up Canigou is the quiet and impressively steep (but not difficult) approach from **Valmanya**. Northwest of that, there is a jeep track from near **Prades**, a scenic but busy alternative.

The Valmanya route
From Vinça in the Têt valley (see p.100) the D13 follows the River Lentilla south along the eastern flanks of Canigou, past Finestret (4km), your last chance of an *épicerie* for a while. From here the **GR36** cuts through the wooded slopes and fields of the valley, rejoining the road at **BAILLESTAVY** (12km from Vinça), where there is a twelve-berth *gîte d'étape* (☎04.68.05.82.03; ①). As the russet streaks on nearby rocks suggest, the Canigou massif is rich in iron ore; there's a mine above the village and traces of a first-century forge by the river.

The Resistance stronghold of **VALMANYA**, another 5km further by road or GR trail, was destroyed by the Germans on August 2, 1944 – some of the houses being reduced to rubble, others set ablaze. Despite rebuilding and the magnificent setting at 900m, there's a lingering sadness to the place; it has no hotel and just one seasonal bar. For the ascent of Canigou, it's best to **camp** wild beside the river just beyond the hamlet of Los Masos, 2km past Valmanya (don't confuse this with the Los Masos near Prades).

From Los Masos, the **GR36** climbs sharply through woods more used by isards than walkers, to the awesome drop at **Ras del Prat Cabrera** (1739m), where it joins the track from Villerach, near Prades, and more attractively the **GR10**, which traverses a bit higher via la Tartère to the *Chalet des Cortalets*. Alternatively you can head almost due south from Valmanya on a minor trail to pick up the GR10 at the forestry hut at **Estagnole**. You could just about make the return trip from Valmanya to Canigou's summit in a day but it's more manageable with a night at or near the refuge.

The Prades route

The gentlest ascent to *Chalet des Cortalets* is the one used by the jeep-taxis (roughly 150F per person) from Prades; booking offices in Prades include Amalric Sports Shop (☎04.68.96.26.47) and La Bohec (☎04.68.05.20.48). If you're driving yourself, take the D35 out of the south side of Prades to Villerach (8km; signposted as "Clara-Villerach"), from where a dirt track rises to the chalet 20km away – an hour's drive. (If you're on foot, there are much better hikers' approaches – for which read on.) This is a superb approach, often running close to the River Llech, each turn revealing a new arrangement of rock, water, sky and forest. An ordinary car can easily get as far as the ruined hut at Prat Cabrera (1650m), an hour's walk from the *Chalet des Cortalets*, and – with extra care and ideal conditions – all the way to Cortalets.

Northwestern approaches: Vernet-les-Bains and around

More direct footpaths from the northwestern side begin from Fillols and Casteil, both above Vernet-les-Bains, the closest town of any consequence to the massif. Seven buses a day come from Perpignan through Villefranche to **VERNET-LES-BAINS**, the most pleasant of the spas around Canigou, though it's still somewhat stuffy. English visitors like Rudyard Kipling made the place fashionable during the last century and a waterfall, 3km out of town on a well-marked track, is even called the **Cascade des Anglais**. Along with the thermal paraphernalia of plunge-pools and institutional adjoining therapy wings – first installed in 1377 – a range of more contemporary pastimes are now offered (mountain biking, canyoning, hydrospeed and caving), though the baths are still the focus of activity. Visitors intent on these and nothing else often overlook the old quarter's warren of alleys, capped by the ninth-century but much-restored double church of **Notre Dame del Puig/St Saturnin**, which incorporates remaining bits of a castle.

Vernet has a *gîte d'étape* in chemin St-Saturnin, on the left bank of the Cady next to the municipal pool (☎04.68.05.53.25; ①). One-star **hotels** include the old-fashioned *d'Angleterre*, 9 av de Burnay (☎04.68.05.50.58; ③), and the *Hôtel des Thermes*, 22 av des Thermes (☎04.68.05.50.06; ②); for more comfort try the *des Deux Lions*, 18 bd Clemenceau (☎04.68.05.55.42; ④) or the *Moderne*, 7 av des Thermes (☎04.68.05.52.17; ③). There are plenty of **campsites** too: the nearest are *Les Cerisiers* (☎04.68.05.60.38), on the same side of the river as the *gîte*, and *Dels Bosc*, 1km north on the Villefranche road (☎04.68.05.51.62). **Eating out**, you can easily spend a fortune in the elegant surroundings of *Le Cortal* (closed Mon and in Oct & Nov), up in the old quarter behind the church at rue de Château. Down in the modern town, best value of about five restaurants is *L'Escapade* on av des Thermes.

The **tourist office** is quite central, on place de la Mairie, near the corner of bd Lambert-Violet and rue du Canigou (mid-June to mid-Sept Mon–Sat 9am–12.30pm & 1–6pm, Sun 10am–noon; rest of year Mon–Fri 10am–noon & 2–5pm, Sat 10am–noon; ☎04.68.05.55.35). **Jeep-taxis** up Canigou (same price as from Prades) can be arranged just 50m from the *d'Angleterre*, or through Taurigna (☎04.68.05.54.39).

The Fillols routes

The standard **walking ascent** from Vernet is by the footpath that begins 1km northeast along the D27, towards the tiny village of **FILLOLS**. Climbing 1km within three hours to the **Refuge de Bonneaigue** (Bonaigua; 1741m), the path there joins the **GR10** to the *Chalet des Cortalets*, another two hours distant; the eight-person *Bonneaigue* hut is very primitive, and the adjacent spring often dries up.

For those with a **jeep** or a very sturdy car, there's a track that begins some 5km from Vernet, just past Fillols; this is the route used by the jeep-taxis from these two villages – you can book a place at the *Café de l'Union* in Fillols (☎04.68.05.63.06), as well as arrange a meal. The track rises gradually at first, past the *Les Sauterelles* **campsite** (☎04.68.05.63.72), and then with dramatic steepness in a series of tight hairpins to the large **Refuge de Balatg** (1610m), the derelict *Cabane des Cortalets* (1975m) and finally the chalet itself. This isn't as pretty a route as that from Prades – and the poorer surface makes it inadvisable for much-loved cars – but a more open topography on the north face of the massif produces awesome views.

Casteil – and Saint-Martin-du-Canigou

From Vernet-les-Bains the paved road leads 2500m south to **CASTEIL**, where you can eat and stay at either *Relais St Martin* (☎04.68.05.56.76; ③), or the more picturesque two-star *Molière* (☎04.68.05.50.97; ④), with a delightful summer restaurant in the apple orchard. There's also a *gîte d'étape* (☎04.68.05.51.30; ①) and a **campsite**, *Camping St-Martin*, with a swimming pool. If you're lucky, you'll coincide with one of the four daily buses from Perpignan, via Villefranche-de-Conflent (not Sun). Casteil is an appealing, quiet hamlet, one of the best bases for getting to grips with Canigou and the GR10, the latter less than an hour away up on the **Col de Jou**, accessible by a delightful short trail designated as "Itinéraire 1" which shortcuts the road. On the ridge just east stands the recently restored **Tour de Goa**, originally twelfth century, reached by another path from the *col* which eventually drops down to the spa at Vernet.

But you're more likely to have come to Casteil to visit the nearby monastery of **Saint-Martin-du-Canigou**, a ubiquitous sight on local book covers, postcards and posters. Access is only by a thirty-minute climb up the path, or jeep transport from Casteil along a steep, narrow road, which helps protect the place from the worst tour-bus excesses – as does its continuing use by an active religious community.

Built from tan stone and roofed with grey slates, the monastery ranks as one of the most gorgeous monuments in the Eastern Pyrenees, and the surrounding woods of sweet chestnut, beech and aspen form an unimprovable backdrop to the pinnacle of rock on which it stands. The foundation stone of the much-restored building was laid in 1001 by Count Guifred de Cerdagne, who retired with his second wife Elisabeth to the monastery in 1035; you can see their purported **sarcophagi** at the base of the tower. Severely damaged by an earthquake in the fifteenth century – the tower lost a storey, never replaced – and thoroughly pillaged after abandonment in 1782, Saint-Martin was restored in two phases (1902–32 and 1952–82), initially through the efforts of the bishop of Perpignan. The glory of the place resides in its **cloister capitals**, retrieved by the good cleric from a particularly wide diaspora.

The monastery is now occupied by an unusual mixed order of monks and nuns, called the "Beatitudes", with a sprinkling of lay workers. Ordinarily, visitors are allowed only on silent, **guided tours** (approximately on the hour: June–Sept daily at 10am, noon, 2pm, 3pm, 4pm, 5pm; Oct–May daily except Tues 10am & noon, 2.30pm, 3.30 & 4.30pm; 15F). The "Beatitudes" community sponsor extended retreats by individuals (write to the abbey at 66820 Casteil, or phone on ☎04.68.05.50.03), but your Christian beliefs had better be genuine – before 1988, the order styled itself as that of the "Lion of Judah and the Immolated Lamb".

Descending from the rear of the complex, you can take an alternative marked footpath for half an hour back to Casteil via the entrance to the **Gorges du Cady**, where the river falls 500m over a distance of 3km, making this a popular spot for canyoning.

Saint-Martin to Mariailles or Cortalets

At the rear of the monastery grounds another path leads up to a signposted viewpoint. You can continue on the path, an excruciatingly steep but shady, beautiful and well-marked route, for four hours to the **Col de Segalès** (2040m) on the GR10. Despite the grade, this provides the most direct all-trail access from the Vernet area to the staffed *Refuge Mariailles* (see p.108), another two hours of up-and-down trekking, south of the *col* by a roundabout route. The two-and-a-half-hour traverse north to the *Bonneaigue* shelter and then to *Cortalets* is quite scenic and a bit more direct, but again there is a fair bit of roller-coastering and a short stretch of track-walking. Many people prefer to do the Sant-Martin-to-Cortalets leg in reverse, as part of an east–west traverse of the massif, beginning from Valmanya or Batère (for which see p.120).

Cortalets to the summit

A *maquisard* hideout in the last war, and consequently heavily shelled by occupation forces, the restored **Chalet des Cortalets** (open May–Oct; other times emergency shelter only; ☎04.68.96.36.19) is now run by the Club Alpin Français. There are double **rooms** (②) as well as the beds in the **dormitories** (①), while **meals** in the bar-restaurant cost about 80F. The smaller shelter adjacent, with no bunk linen provided, costs half as much as the dorms. Be warned that the main lodge can get overcrowded, and the tracks bring up jeeps-full of revellers – as opposed to walkers – at weekends to picnic at the tables around the little lake, ten minutes' walk west of the refuge. **Tents** are tolerated on the lake shore, and next to another smaller pond closer to *Cortalets*.

The summit

The normal, well-marked approach **to the summit** goes past the larger lake, with its fine view up into the summit cirque, then climbs south along the ridge connecting with the **Pic Joffre**, which often teems with isards at sunset. It takes about ninety minutes and provides only a slight sense of exposure as you reach the wrought-iron summit cross and *table d'orientation*. Even though it's the process of getting to the top that makes Canigou so memorable – rather than the experience of standing on the peak – the views encompassing everything from Andorra to the sea are wonderful.

At midsummer (technically June 21 but in Catalonia observed on the eve of June 23–24 , the *Festa de Sant Joan*), the refuge and the peak are both spots to avoid or gravitate towards depending on your temperament: seemingly half the population of Barcelona descends for merrymaking and the kindling of the traditional bonfire which is then relayed to light numerous others in Catalan villages on both sides of the frontier. Even at other times there is often a patriotic Catalan or two prepared to bivouac the night beside the peak's highest cairn.

There is an alternative, less frequented and even more dramatic route, climbing south from the *Cortalets* chalet along the **Crête de Barbet** to the **Porteille de Valmanya** (2591m), a beautiful ridge walk that becomes nerve-wracking beyond the *porteille* – there the route drops along a narrow cleft, leaving you to clamber over boulders to the summit (2hr 30min total). The Pic Joffre and Barbet routes can, of course, be combined to make a circuit.

Southwestern approaches: the Rotja valley

To tackle ascents of Canigou **from the southwest**, take a bus from Prades or Villefranche (Mon–Sat 1–2 daily) along the **Rotja valley** to Sahorre, after which you'll have to hitch: there's a fair bit of traffic, so chances are good.

PY, 6km upstream, remains a traditional old mountain village – certainly compared to more-visited Casteil or Mantet (see below) – but even here there are plenty of houses for sale, and evidence of seasonal occupation. So far the only concessions to tourism are a horse-riding stable, one *gîte d'étape* (☎04.68.05.58.38; ①) and a combination café-restaurant-*épicerie* with a few rooms to rent.

The usual approach to Canigou from Py is to follow the **GR10** northeast to the **Col de Jou** (1125m) and then take the track (recently made suitable for saloon cars, somewhat shortcut by the onward GR path) to the large and comfortable **Refuge Mariailles** (1718m; ☎04.68.96.22.90 or 09.32.95.40), four hours on foot from Py. After a night's sleep at *Mariailles*, take the GR10 south then east into the forest, climbing to the **Col Vert** and then dropping down to the Cady valley. Shortly afterwards the footpath heads west, then north, roller-coasting to the *Chalet des Cortalets* – an attractive route covered on the preceding page.

The direct way to the **summit** from this side, though, is to continue east along the Cady valley, past the simple, unstaffed *Refuge Arago*. From there the route climbs more or less north to the **Porteille de Valmanya** (2591m), then along the line of the ridge (keep below it – the view over the other side is frightening) and up an easy gully to the summit.

Mantet

From Py the paved road climbs steeply southwest through uncountable hairpins, many of which can be bypassed by following the GR10 instead, though generally it's a dull, steep hike and you should accept any lifts offered. When you reach the **Col de Mantet** (1761m), three hours' walking from Py, a glorious wilderness is spread in front of you: the village of Mantet is invisible, clinging to the hill 200m below the *col*, while still further south spreads the beautiful Alemany valley, its eastern flank covered in pines. The furthest end of the valley, where the **Porteille de Mantet** (2419m) leads into Spain, is the preserve of isards; protected by *réserve naturelle* status for now, it is threatened by development courtesy of the local Caisse d'Epargne.

The inhabitants of **MANTET** (pronounced *Mantett*, in the Catalan fashion, not *Mantay*) were expelled by the Nazis towards the end of World War II, and it wasn't until the 1960s that it was resettled. It's since been expensively restored for holiday homes, and despite having only twenty or so permanent inhabitants, Mantet supports two **gîtes d'étape**: *Chez Richard* (also an *auberge*; ☎04.68.05.60.99; ①), and another run by the owner of the stable *La Cavale* (☎04.68.05.57.59; doubles ④, dorms ①). There are also two **hotels**, the *Bouf'tic* (☎04.68.05.51.76; ③), with the liveliest bar in the village, and *La Girada* (☎04.68.05.68.69; ③), specializing in adventure sports. In addition, rooms are available at the *El Tupi* restaurant (☎04.68.05.61.27; ②).

Walks around Mantet

From Mantet the most spectacular **route up Canigou** involves climbing through the woods southeast from the Col de Mantet to the **Pla Segala** (2200m), and then along the ridge to **Roc Colom**; there you can pick up the **HRP** and follow it along the line of rock teeth known as the *Esquerdes de Rotja* to **Collade des Roques Blanches** and then **Pla Guillem** (2277m), where there is a simple, unstaffed refuge. It's already a long day but if you still have daylight and strength, the *Refuge Mariailles* – a ninety-minute descent further – is a lot more congenial.

Canigou aside, this is a great walking and riding area. Especially worthwhile treks are south along the **Ressec valley** (east of the main Alemany valley) to the source of the Mantet stream (4hr), and along the **Caret valley** (west of the Alemany), with its groups of ruined stone cottages and shady riverside path. The **GR10** itself stays in the Alemany valley before climbing west over the **Col del Pal**

(2294m) into the **Carança gorge** (5hr from Mantet; staffed summer refuge about halfway along it). From here, if you don't stick with the GR10 until Mont-Louis, you can head north down the valley for Thuès (see p.110) or south into Spain at Núria (see p.163).

The upper Têt

The lower Têt finishes at Villefranche-de-Conflent, above which the shaggy flanks of the **upper Têt** close dramatically around the narrow-gauge *Train Jaune* rail line and N116 which forge their separate ways along the river until Mont-Louis, at the top of the Têt. En route there are a number of small villages, on the valley floor or perched just above, which make serviceable bases for excursions into the hills. Of these, the hot springs and no-nonsense **Carança gorge** near **Thuès**, and the **Mont Coronat** area north of **Olette**, are the most rewarding.

Many of the **abandoned villages** on either slope of the Têt valley, upper and lower, are squatted by raving hippies, mostly non-French. You can't help but notice these flamboyantly garbed individuals staffing market stalls in the lower-altitude centres, or stalking about the streets *épatant le bourgeoisie*. The French government declines to doing anything about them on behalf of the erstwhile inhabitants of those villages, since the hippies have been in residence for more than twenty continuous years and have thus acquired squatters' rights to the properties – which are, however, completely bereft of electricity or other municipal services.

Excursions around the valley

Most of the villages along the Têt valley are not in themselves worth leaving the train for, but they do give access to a number of marvellous hikes. Alighting at **SERDINYA**, for instance, you could hitch the 7km south to **ESCARO** (*gîte d'étape;* ☎04.68.97.01.47; ①) for the three-stage **Tour des Tres Esteles**; accommodation for the other overnight stops is available in Py and Mantet (see p.108).

At **OLETTE**, the next stop, you can stay comfortably at either *Casa Vostra* (☎04.68.97.02.67; ②) – featuring trout in its affordable restaurant – or at the adjacent *La Fontaine* (☎04.68.97.03.67; ⑤ half-board), both on the main street. Incidentally, Olette is also home to the only groceries stores until Mont-Louis. From Olette it's a two-hour hike northeast to **JUJOLS**, where you can start the four-stage **Tour du Coronat**, a waymarked trip around the **Mont Coronat** massif. One night can be spent at the *gîte d'étape* in Jujols (☎04.68.97.02.40; ①), and another at the *gîte* at Urbanya (☎04.68.96.29.92; ①) – both good value – but two nights will have to be spent out of doors.

An alternative from Olette is to hitch or walk the couple of kilometres north to **EVOL**, where the church of **Saint André** contains a splendid painted retable by the so-called Maître du Roussillon, dating from 1428. The massive ruined **Château**, just above the village on the pot-holed road to the Col de Portus, was built in 1260, at a time when security from potential Moorish raids was still considered necessary. At the *col* (1736m) you can join the *Tour du Coronat* or climb northwest to the lakes known as the **Gorg Estelat** and **Gorg Nègre**, situated at the foot of the gentle **Pic Madrès** (2470m). The lakes are served by the basic *Refuge de Nohèdes*, beyond which rises **Roc Nègre**, a tough but technically not difficult approach to the summit.

Between Olette and Evol the D4 peels off into the tranquil **Cabrils valley**, a longer but more attractive road to Mont-Louis and the Capcir than the Têt route. The going is fairly tough for cyclists – the **Col de la Llose** rises to almost 1800m – and chances of a lift aren't good, so it's probably best left to those with their own vehicle.

The Carança gorge area

A few minutes past Olette on the *Train Jaune* at **NYER** (*Camping La Catalane*; ☎04.68.97.07.63), the road south from the station to the village climbs on into the impressive Gorges de Nyer. You can eat in Nyer at *Castel Val*, installed, as the name implies, in a small château; the gourmet restaurant features trout and quail for 90–120F.

However, you're probably better off staying on the train until **THUÈS-CARANÇA**, four minutes above the small spa of Thuès-les-Bains and the gateway for the even more spectacular Gorges de Carança. The nearby village of Thuès-entre-Valls is home to a delightful **gîte-campsite**, *Mas de Bordes* (☎04.68.97.05.00, fax 04.68.97.11.51; ①), next to the church – follow signs up the path from the train stop or from the main road (N116). This restored farm is part of a 300-hectare property which includes its own outdoor hot springs, a remote log cabin and a meadow for pitching tents. The place is always mobbed during July and August, when you must ring ahead, but it's worth trying to fit it into your plans for a night or two. Good *table d'hôte* suppers are provided for about 80F, a blessing since the village itself is not up to much at all.

The **Gorges de Carança** is clearly signposted from the train station and from Thuès village, and more notices at its mouth (over which the *Train Jaune* clatters on a bridge)

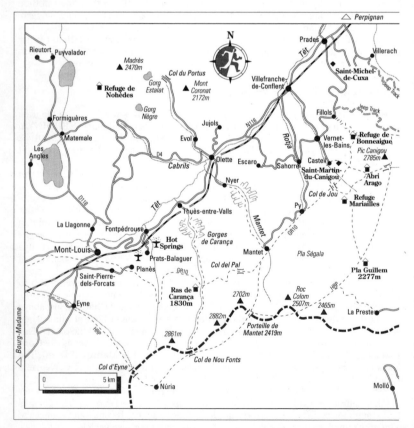

advise you of entry at your own risk. After a short walk from the car park, the path divides: the left-hand path (signposted for Roc Madrieu) climbs steeply up the wooded side of the valley, while the right-hand path (over a small bridge) follows the more spectacular corniche route; the two paths converge at the *pont des singes* (suspension bridge). The first ninety minutes of corniche walkway are the most amazing, poised over sheer four-hundred-metre drops – not for the vertigo-prone. Next are a series of nerve-wracking catwalks, ladders and wobbly metal suspension bridges, these last not advisable for heavily laden walkers.

Yet the overall climb towards the border is the gentlest around, so the canyon makes a popular outing: start off early to beat the crowds and the heat. Beyond the narrows, the route becomes a shady, streamside trail on the west bank; soon the countryside opens out, and you should reach **Ras de Carança** (1830m), with its summer-staffed refuge, in about three-and-a-half hours with a daypack, much more with a full rucksack. The twelve-bunk refuge offers very simple food, and there's plenty of camping space nearby. To reach the first of a series of lakes – the easternmost along the main Pyrenees crest – requires another ninety minutes, while the border at Col de Nou Fonts, opening towards Núria, is four hours distant and thus beyond the scope of a day-trip from Thuès.

THE UPPER TET, THE TECH
AND CANIGOU

THE TRAIN JAUNE

The best way to move up the Têt valley towards the Cerdagne is on the **Train Jaune**, once an essential local service, but now more of a fun ride – during summer some carriages are open-air. Built in the early twentieth century, the railway climbs for 63km from Villefranche (427m) up to Latour-de-Carol (1231m), where it connects with the Transpyrenean railway (Toulouse–Barcelona). Tourism saved the scenic narrow-gauge line from closure early in the 1970s, but a yearly repertory melodrama still features threats of funding cutbacks, counter-protests and a general air of future uncertainty. As it is, return tickets are valid for only 24 hours, with **fares** double those of French main-line services; as an example, Villefranche to Mont-Louis and back (the most popular stretch) will cost at least 96F.

In summer there's a minimum of five, usually six, **departures** a day in each direction; the first train of the day leaves Latour-de-Carol soon after 8am, and takes two and a half hours to reach Villefranche. Since most of the line is single track, there are often delays caused by long halts at Mont-Louis or Font-Romeu to allow the uphill train to pass, the first of these leaving Villefranche well before 8am. The train is scheduled to stop only at certain stations, designated in capital letters on the timetables and train maps; if you want to alight at one of the smaller, unstaffed stations (designated *arrêts facultatifs* on carriage placards) you have to notify the driver in advance, otherwise the train will chug on past. Similarly, to get on at such stations, you have to flag the train down.

For information on timetables and prices, contact the following stations: Villefranche-Vernet-Fuilla (☎04.68.96.56.62); Mont-Louis (☎04.68.96.56.65); Font-Romeu (☎04.68.96.56.66); Bourg-Madame (☎04.68.96.56.68); or Latour-de-Carol (☎04.68.04.80.62).

On to Planés

If you're a fan of hot springs, you can leave the train at **Fontpédrouse** station, the stop above Thuès-Carança, and follow the twisty road up towards the village of **PRATS-BALAGUER** on the south slope. From the second hairpin, you'll find a path that leads east and down to a trio of **thermal pools**, thus far unregimented. Alternatively, head for the large, beautifully renovated, open-air thermal baths at **SAINT-THOMAS-LES-BAINS** (☎04.68.97.03.13; daily 10am–8pm, July & Aug until 9pm; 18F), 3km from Fontpédrouse station, open all year round for a hot sulphurous dip and jacuzzi after skiing or hiking.

Just before Planès, the *Train Jaune* passes over the 150-metre-long **Pont Gisclard** suspension bridge, which carries the track 80m above the river; it was designed early this century by the mathematician and engineer Albert Gisclard, who was tragically killed by a runaway train on the very day of the official bridge trials in 1909. The peculiar triangular church at **PLANÈS** itself was once thought to be an adapted Moorish structure, but the bell-tower is typical of the Cerdagne, and the dome surrounded by three semicircular half-domed apses has close parallels throughout the region. Near Planès, there's a *gîte d'étape* (☎04.68.04.21.40; ①) at *La Cassagne* farm – to go directly there, get off the train at Planès station and follow the GR10 *variante* footpath northwards towards Mont-Louis for about twenty minutes.

Mont-Louis and around

The next *Train Jaune* station – **La Cabanasse** – serves the garrison town of **MONT-LOUIS**, at 1600m the highest town of the Têt, lying 14km southeast of the river's source, the Lac des Bouillouses. Known as the gateway to the Cerdagne, Mont-Louis (about ten minutes' walk up from the station) is the quintessential work of **Vauban**,

Louis XIV's military engineer, and has something of the ruthless chill of a missile silo. Vauban designed Mont-Louis for his royal client between 1679 and 1682, and reputedly selected the site not only on logistical grounds, but also because he was impressed by the longevity, the white teeth and the sparkling eyes of the villagers.

In contrast to the high, fragile walls of Villefranche, the moat-ringed **ramparts** of Mont-Louis are massive, built low to maximize their resistance to artillery fire. Also unlike Villefranche, even Vauban admitted that the finished product might signally fail in its intended function: throughout the eighteenth century hostile armies entered France through the Cerdagne along roads unguarded by the citadel. Though promoted as a resort, Mont-Louis is still essentially a military town, the French commandos occupying its citadel and training on the surrounding slopes. Apart from the walls, Mont-Louis' only other attraction is the world's first **solar oven** (*four solaire*), built in 1949 and now open for guided tours (daily: summer 10am–6.30pm, winter 10am–12.30pm & 2–6pm; 25F); the huge mirror for the *four* stands in the moat, just to the left of the main gate (Porte de France).

There is a **tourist office** in rue du Marché (mid-June to mid-Sept daily 10am–noon & 3–6pm; ☎04.68.04.21.97). The best-known hotel in Mont-Louis is the delightful *Lou Roubaillou* (☎04.68.04.23.26, fax 04.68.04.14.09; ④), near the barracks in rue des Ecoles Laïque, with a celebrated restaurant offering mushrooms, boar and duck among other local delicacies (menus 125F–195F). A good alternative is the attractively furnished *La Taverne*, in rue Victor Hugo (☎04.68.04.23.67, fax 04.68.04.13.35; ④), which has excellent-value menus (from 70F) and delicious pizzas from a wood-fired oven. The closest **campsite**, *Pla de Barres* (☎04.68.04.21.18; mid-June to mid-Sept), lies 3km west along the road towards Lac des Bouillouses; though a bit squalid in high summer when the uncollected rubbish accumulates, it is inexpensive and beautifully set under the pines by a stream.

Saint-Pierre dels Forcats and Eyne

The road from Mont-Louis to Planès passes through **SAINT-PIERRE-DELS-FOR-CATS**, which has the most easterly ski-lift system on the French side of the Pyrenees. Situated at the foot of **Cambre d'Aze** (2711m) – a huge lump of a mountain cleft by a quarry-like cirque – it has a top station of 2420m and fourteen north-facing pistes, but with the Mediterranean so close, the snow is unreliable. A single pass (see opposite) is issued for the nine stations of Cerdagne-Capcir, which means you can link with the ten pistes and seven lifts at nearby **EYNE** (the *Train Jaune* stop is Bolquère-Eyne).

The only **hotel** at Saint-Pierre is the rather overpriced *Le Moulin de Riu* (☎04.68.04.20.36, fax 04.68.04.20.25; ④). At Eyne, you can choose between two-star *Le Roc Blanc* (☎04.68.04.72.72; ③) and the *chambres d'hôtes* at *La Vallée* (☎04.68.84.81.64; ③). You can **eat** well at all three lodging establishments in Eyne, while half- or full-day horse-riding and botanical outings are available through *Le Licol Vert* (☎04.68.04.72.48).

Above Eyne to the southeast is the **Col d'Eyne** (or **Col de Núria**), the second most important bird migration route in the Pyrenees, after the Col Organbidexka in the Basque country; the autumn migration, from September to November, produces the greatest variety, including honey buzzards, kites and falcons, as well as the bee-eater and other rarities. A signposted path about 300m west of Eyne village, part of the HRP, runs up to the *col* through the forested river valley, which is blessed with a peculiar microclimate and therefore boasts a wealth of flowers and herbs in its meadows. After four hours the HRP attains the *col*, dropping down to Núria in Spain on the far side (see p.163) before looping back up to the Col de Nou Fonts at the head of the Carança valley.

The Capcir

Between the upper Têt valley and the gorges of the upper Aude spreads the sedimentary plateau called the **Capcir**. Bare and extremely flat in the centre – traits accentuated by the large artificial lakes of Matemale and Puyvalador – it is cradled by densely wooded slopes that sweep up to Pic Madrès and the Carlit Massif, with only the **ski-resort** pistes interrupting the trees. One of the harshest winter climates in southern France makes this excellent cross-country ski terrain, while summer promises wonderful, easy walking, with several refuges or *gîtes d'étape*, plus hotels in three of its eight villages. In July and August, and during ski season, all the main Capcir villages and resorts are served by a twice-daily taxi-bus, which departs from the Mont-Louis/La Cabanasse rail station.

Capcir ski resorts

All of the Capcir **ski resorts** lie on, or just off, the D118 road served by the taxi-bus. Nearest to Mont-Louis, **LES ANGLES** is also the area's largest, with 40km of pistes – half of them red, with the top run at 2100m. Chalets predominate rather than high-rises, but the old village has still been almost completely swamped. **Accommodation** is in five hotels and about twenty *résidences*, least expensive being *Le Coq d'Or* hotel, place du Coq d'Or (☎04.68.04.42.17; ③). The Bureau Montagne (☎04.68.04.34.30) is a multi-disciplinary sports outfitter for summertime activities such as horse-riding, mountain-biking and canyoning.

FORMIGUÈRES, 6km further north, is far more attractive with its shops (some selling outdoor gear), cafés and creperies giving it the feel of a county town. Its church of Sainte-Marie features an unusual triangular facade culminating in the belfry; inside is a masterful, seventeenth-century *majestat* or clothed figure of Christ, typical of the Catalan regions. The pistes here total just 20km, with no really tough runs, but a good-value seasonal pass is available through the local tourist office (see below). Moreover, standing at the heart of 100km of marked trails, Formiguères is the perfect place to start your **cross-country skiing** career; this sort of skiing requires no lessons – experience teaches you how to avoid falling over – and equipment rental can cost less than half downhill piste rates.

On the southeast corner of the church square there's a helpful **tourist office** (summer daily 9am–noon & 2–6pm; ☎04.68.04.47.35) which, among other things, rents keys for the municipal tennis courts. Horse-riding is offered through Balade a Cheval, 1km out on the Les Angles road (☎04.68.04.48.44). Formiguères has two **hotels**: the one-star *Picheyre* behind the church (☎04.68.04.40.07; ③; closed May) and the fancier *Auberge de la Tutte*, on the road out of town by the junction for Les Angles (☎04.68.04.40.21; ④). There's a *gîte d'étape* in an old barn, with a few doubles and meals offered, at Espousouille (☎04.68.04.45.37; ①), a kilometre or so up through the trees by footpath – but 6km by road. The **restaurant** in the *Picheyre* is resolutely old-fashioned, good value at 75F (no à la carte) but dull of menu, like lunching at your gran's and with a clientele to match.

If that doesn't suit, the *Auberge de la Belle Aude* in **MATEMALE,** a deceptively large village tucked in a hollow by the Aude 4km south, has more comfortable accommodation and richer, rather more creative menus starting at 95F (☎04.68.04.40.11, fax 04.68.04.39.89; ④); they've even managed to squeeze in a tiny pool under a conservatory for rare *Capcinoise* hot days. More serious outdoor pursuits here include mountain biking through Fugues VTT (☎04.68.04.42.06), down by the Matemale reservoir, as well as watersports.

The ski station at **PUYVALADOR**, at the north end of the Capcir plateau, is 5km west of its namesake reservoir and village (which has no amenities). It was created in 1982, with 20km of pistes, and has a top station of 2380m. The only tourist facilities at this end of the plateau, outside the ski station, are at **RIEUTORT**, 2km west of Puyvalador village. Here Vagabond'ane (☎04.68.04.41.22) on the main square rents mules and organizes donkey safaris on request; in winter snowshoeing is offered instead. Some fifty paces above the square you can feast on trout and crayfish straight from a tank at the excellent *Al Cortal* (open supper only during ski season; lunch and dinner in summer; weekends only otherwise), with slightly pricey four-course menus for 140F.

Hiking: La Tour du Capcir

The Capcir woodlands are eminently suitable hiking territory, well within the capabilities of a novice walker. The Randonnées Pyrénéennes organization issues maps and booklets about **La Tour du Capcir**, a four-day circuit (easy to pick up at Espousouille, Puyvalador or Matemale) that runs along both sides of the valley as well as taking in **Pic Madrès** (2469m) to the east. You can make use of the *gîtes d'étape* at Espousouille, the hotel at Matemale plus the staffed refuges at Bouillouses (see p.205) and Camporells, with one night either camping out or staying in the unstaffed *Refuge de Nohèdes*, a little to the southeast of Madrès summit. The *Refuge de Camporells* (☎04.68.04.49.86), by the cluster of eponymous lakes on the western leg of the *tour*, is wonderfully set in an area rich in wildlife, and is also partly accessible by the chair lift which operates even in summer at Formiguères (45-min walk from the top of the lift to the refuge).

The portion of the route between Camporells and Bouillouses passes close to the **Carlit Massif**, so you could improve the circuit with an ascent of the peak (add a day); alternatively you could hike on westwards to follow part of the *Tour du Carlit*, emerging at Porté-Puymorens (see "The Carlit Massif", p.204) or in the Ariège valley (see p.206). Moving **eastwards** out of the Capcir, you could link up with the *Tour du Coronat* after the Madrès ascent (see "The upper Têt", p.109).

The Tech valley and the Albères

The **Tech valley** (or Vallespir) is the southernmost in France, and its exceptional sunshine (300 days a year) and relatively low rainfall nurture a flora that includes oranges, cacti and bougainvillaea – as well as dense forest on the higher, wetter slopes. Proximity to the border made the Tech a tense place during the last war, when it was a major escape route from occupied France. The easiest mid-elevation pass into Spain, the **Col d'Ares**, was so heavily patrolled that the *passeurs* had to use more remote routes along the main **Albères** ridge, whose enduring loneliness still appeals to casual walkers. Escapers making contact at **Céret** or **Le Boulou** would be led out over one of two *cols*, either Lly (south of Céret) or Llosa. From **Amélie-les-Bains** – today a busy spa – there was a tough ascent over the 1450-metre Roc de France. From **Arles-sur-Tech**, further up the valley, the way led to **Saint-Laurent-de-Cerdans** and **Coustouges**, then either over Col des Massanes or along the Riou Majou into Alta Garrotxa. From the tiny spa of **La Preste** and the small walled town of **Prats-de-Molló**, refugees fled along the ancient paths of the *contrabandiers*, through the Col del Pal or the Collade de Prats. The solitude of this central part of the Albères – which extends from Saint-Laurent-de-Cerdans and Coustouges in the west to the Mediterranean at Banyuls-sur-Mer – is broken only on the east side of the Tech at **Le Perthus**, little better than a border shopping town and truck-stop.

Today, there is little in the way of frontier formalities and crossing from France into Spain is easy. Besides the crossing at Le Perthus, the D115 road up the Tech valley slips into Spain at the Col d'Ares, a scenic and almost equally popular route.

From Le Boulou to the border

LE BOULOU, a traffic-clogged little town situated just off the autoroute 20km south of Perpignan (12 buses daily), is the **cork** capital of France. At the beginning of the century there were 140 square kilometres under cork oak cultivation in this area, planted as a substitute for grapevines destroyed by phylloxera. Cultivated primarily to produce stoppers for the champagne industry, the plantations shrank to around 50 square kilometres in the face of competition from less expensive Portuguese cork, but a recent revival has been spurred by chronic local brush fires, as cork oak is very flame-resistant and therefore a better bet than more combustible crops; you can find out more at the **Musée de Liège** in Maureillas, 5km south of Le Boulou (mid-June to mid-Sept daily 10.30am–noon & 3.30–7pm; rest of year daily except Tues 2–5pm; 15F).

At least eight **buses** a day continue on from Le Boulou along the Tech valley to Céret and Arles-sur-Tech, and four buses a day (except Sun) to the border at Le Perthus, and back; it's also a possible changing-point for buses east to the Côte Vermeille at Argelès-sur-Mer (Cars Verts du Roussillon, 1 daily, via Saint-Genis-des-Fontaines and Sorède).

A few minutes' ride south of Le Boulou, just beyond Bains du Boulou, stands the remarkable chapel of **Saint-Martin-de-Fenollar** (mid-June to mid-Sept daily 10.30am–noon & 3.30–7pm; rest of year daily except Tues 2–5pm; 15F), signposted to the west of the N9. Its twelfth-century frescoes are the best Romanesque wall paintings in Roussillon, and their clarity and simplicity of line may well have been influential on Picasso, who sometimes stayed in nearby Céret.

A stretch of the old, non-toll N9 follows the line of the Roman Via Domitia, and there's evidence of the antiquity of the route 4km south of Saint-Martin, where a pair of ruined Roman forts cap the steep outcrops flanking the road. The one to the west, known as the **Château des Maures**, can be reached only by fording a stream. The other one requires a thirty-minute climb up the D71B from **L'ÉCLUSE** – a village whose name is derived from the Latin *clausura*, indicating the closure or control point on a road. The crumbling structure will fascinate none but ardent classicists, but the adjacent church of Saint-Nazaire contains frescoes reminiscent of those at Saint-Martin, and possibly by the same painter (key available from the *Mairie* in L'Écluse).

Le Perthus and the frontier

On the night of February 5, 1939, a column of twenty thousand Spanish Republicans arrived at the border post of **LE PERTHUS** (El Pertus or Els Límits, in Spain), 4km beyond L'Écluse, to seek sanctuary in France. Nowadays a consumer army descends here every day, disgorging from coaches to spend their money on foodstuffs, booze and perfume that is in fact not much cheaper than in Spain. If you're on a GR10 traverse and looking for a place to **stay**, your only choice is *Chez Grand-Mère* at the summit of the main road (☎04.68.83.60.96; ③).

In Roman times the Via Domitia crossed the Albères 2km to the west at the **Col de Panissars**, which is probably the way that Hannibal came in 218 BC. When Pompey returned victorious from Spain a century and a half later, he ordered a triumphal monument to be built at the *col*, and the excavated base of this edifice is now visible through a cordon of barbed wire. On a nearby mound, overlooking Panissars and Le Perthus, rises the **Fort de Bellegarde** (☎04.68.83.60.15; July–Sept daily 10.30am–12.30pm & 2.30–6.30pm; rest of the year, phone for details; 15F). Built in the sixteenth century and later reinforced by Vauban, it comprises two rows of dilapidated buildings and the deepest well in Europe (63m) within an enclosure of mighty walls, and gives superb views south into Spain and north across Roussillon. Both fort and monumental base are reached by taking the signposted road westwards out of Le Perthus, from near the high point of the main road. After fifteen minutes you're among cork oaks, as the tarmac curves behind a hill and the noise of cash registers fades away; the fort is about fifteen minutes further, while the monument is five minutes beyond that.

If you want to move on **into Spain** on foot you could simply pick your way from Col de Panissars down through the scrub, but it's so close to the road that anyone crossing here might arouse suspicion of cannabis smuggling – it's better to return to Le Perthus and take the minibus to Figueres (3 daily Mon–Sat, 2 on Sun), or hitch. Both the **GR10** and the **HRP**, here combined, pass through Le Perthus/Panissars on their east–west route along the summits of the Albères.

Banyuls-sur-Mer, on the Côte Vermeille (see p.128), lies two easy days' walking east of Le Perthus along the recently rerouted GR10, split by a night at the simple *Refuge de la Tagnarède*, just beyond **Pic Néulos**. You may prefer, at least for lunch, the *Chalet de l'Albère* (☎04.68.83.62.20; ①), three hours distant at the **Col de l'Ouillat**. This clean, 60-person *gîte d'étape* has a good **restaurant**, and is accessible in considerably less time by the D71 secondary road from Le Perthus through Saint-Jean and Saint-Martin hamlets. Heading westwards on the GR10/HRP, the nearest *gîte* is at **LAS ILLAS** (☎04.68.83.23.93; ①), just under half a day away but the only spot to divide the long stage to Arles-sur-Tech.

Céret

The cherry orchards of **CÉRET** are the basis of its prosperity, yielding around 4000 tonnes of fruit towards the end of April. It's a friendly and bustling town, with a shady *vieille ville* of narrow and winding streets that open onto small squares like **place des Neuf-Jets**, named after the fountain at its centre. Of the medieval fortifications, only parts of the two medieval gates remain, though many houses are incorporated integrally into the walls themselves.

According to legend the single-arched **Pont du Diable** – one of three bridges that span the Tech at Céret – was built by the Devil in 1321 in return for the soul of the first Céretian to cross. The engineer who made the bargain duly sent a cat over first, but the trick backfired as none of the locals would then risk the Devil's vengeance by using the bridge themselves. Other sights include the **war memorial** by Aristide Maillol and the **monument** to the composer Déodat de Séverac by the Catalan sculptor Manolo (who was the first artist to settle here), in av Clemenceau, just around the corner from bd Maréchal Joffre, up at the edge of the old quarter.

In summer Céret holds *sardanas* and *corridas* (see p.118), but what brings most visitors here is the **Musée d'Art Moderne** at 8 bd Maréchal Joffre (July–Sept daily 10am–7pm; Oct–June daily except Tues 10am–6pm; 35F). Established largely through the efforts of the artist Pierre Brune, who arrived here in 1916 when the town was already something of a creative colony, the collection evokes splendidly the milieu of the *Fauves*, Cubists and Surrealists, and the building has recently been expanded and renovated by architects Jaume Freixa and Philippe Pous. Much of the collection was donated by the artists who came to stay in the town: the extensive Picasso section includes a fine series of ceramic bowls depicting bullfights, plus a sketch of a local *sardana*, which he gave to the local branch of the Communist Party, which in turn donated it to the museum. There are a couple of quickly thrown-off Dalís, a pair of typical Chagalls, and some pieces by Matisse and Maillol, but the best come from Juan Gris and lesser-known artists represented by their major works – such as Pignon's nudes.

Practicalities

The easiest way of reaching Céret is by **bus** from Perpignan (12 daily, first 8am, last 8pm), which stops about 250m north of the *vieille ville* at the bottom of av Clemenceau; most buses continue along the Tech to Arles, and three or four go right to the head of the valley at Prats-de-Molló.

The **tourist office** (☎04.68.87.00.53) is at the top of av Clemenceau, on the corner of bd Maréchal Joffre. If you need to **rent a car**, try Rey Autocar (☎04.68.87.10.70) in bd Maréchal Joffre. The most central **accommodation** is provided by the characterful one-star *Vidal*, housed in the old bishop's palace, off place Soutine (☎04.68.87.00.85; ③). Opposite stands the two-star *Arcades* (☎04.68.87.12.30; ④), and you might also try the *Pyrénées* on rue de la République (☎04.68.87.11.02; ③). All these places have a variety of rooms available, with and without bath. There are several local **campsites**, two of them on route de Maureillas: *Les Cerisiers* (☎04.68.87.00.08) and *Les Deux Rivières*.

When it's time to **eat out**, you should perhaps forgo the hotel kitchens in favour of the good bistro-*crêperie*, *Le Pied dans le Plat* (closed Sun), and an adjacent pizzeria, both on place des Neuf-Jets, with outdoor seating. Social life at the *Grand Café* in bd Maréchal Joffre is perhaps not what it was when the "bande Picasso" hung out there, but it's still a good place to sit outside with a glass of wine and a plate of *frites*; there are more **cafés** around the corner by the Porte de France. Saturdays see a morning farmers' **market** on place Pablo-Picasso and av d'Espagne, the street stalls groaning with local produce.

Festivals

Céret is very Catalan – extending to such details as bilingual street-signs – and the **arena** in the north of the town holds regular bullfights and *sardanas*. To get to the arena, go down rue Joseph Parayre until you reach rue des Arènes on your right. The biggest local bash takes place in July, over the weekend closest to Bastille Day, when the street on the perimeter of the old town fills with booths selling sausages, seafood and drink; after dark, *coblas* give place to more riotous conventional dancing bands. There's also a Pamplona-style **running of bulls**, but of doubtful authenticity: half a dozen horsemen surround each beast, which has a good 10cm lopped off each horn. So, not much sport in this, or in the *corrida* (bullfight) that follows; moreover, seats are expensive at 160–400F.

Every August the **Festival International de la Sardane** provides a more generally appealing spectacle at the arena, the seats crowded and the ring packed with concentric circles of dancers.

Amélie-les-Bains and Palalda

The next stop, 8km up the valley, is the spa town of **AMÉLIE-LES-BAINS**, which tends to attract the elderly and rheumatic. Unless you are taking a cure (*balneothera-pie, drainage lymphatique* or other such dire treatments), there's nothing much to see or do here. Attempts have been made to inject a bit of youth interest by promoting mountain biking, horse-riding and hiking, but without much success. Nor is it worth pausing to see the claimed tourist attractions of the much-restored Roman baths and the Gorges du Mondony, poor relation of the nearby Gorges de la Fou (see below), while Fort les Bains (part of Vauban's defences), perched high above the town, is not open to visit. Two kilometres downstream, on the opposite bank, is the sister-town of **PALALDA**, whose medieval centre might delay you a little longer. Afterwards it's a choice between moving along the valley, striking north into the Aspres foothills between the Tech and the Têt (see "The lower Têt", p.99) or picking up the GR10 west into Canigou.

It's unlikely you'll want to stay in either place, but Amélie does have a glut of **accommodation**. The **tourist office**, near the bus stop on quai du 8 Mai (between the river and place de la République), can help you track it down. There's plenty of choice along the av du Vallespir, running through the centre of town, including the attractive one-star *La Chaumière* at no. 2 (☎04.68.39.05.35; ②), and the two-star *La Pergola* at no. 60, with a choice between rooms and studios (☎04.68.39.05.71, fax 04.68.39.81.15; ③); alternatively try the kitsch but friendly one-star *Jeanne d'Arc* (☎04.68.87.96.96; ③) in place de la République, which overlooks the river on one side. The municipal **campsite** is by the river, just off av Beau Soleil, the main road into town; *Camping du Gaou* is nearby, on the south side of the road.

For **eating out**, try the attractive *Au Poivre Vert* in place de la République, which offers Catalan specialities (closed Mon; menus 76F–130F); for an extra treat, head for the excellent patisserie and teashop *Pi-Roue*, at 6 av du Vallespir.

Arles-sur-Tech

ARLES-SUR-TECH, 4km further along the valley, is quieter and more atmospheric than Amélie, with a medieval quarter focused on the **abbey of Sainte-Marie**. The first abbey, built late in the eighth century, was soon destroyed by Viking raiders and the present church (daily 8am–noon & 2–6pm) was consecrated in 1046 and modified again two centuries later. The abbey's most renowned feature is the tranquil **cloister** (daily 9am–8pm), an elegant addition from the end of the thirteenth century, with pointed double-columned arches surrounding an attractive garden of box and cypress.

Arles is a close-knit community with an award-winning folk-dance group and rugby team; it is most famous, however, for its February **fête de l'Ours**, a pagan holdover claimed to be among the oldest observances in Europe. Traditionally, bears were said to interrupt their hibernation at the February new moon, terrorizing the villagers, who hit on the ploy of luring the boldest animal with a local girl, before chaining the bear and then shaving it. There being a contemporary shortage of bears, these days a young man is dressed in a bear skin, hunted down by the crowds, captured and stripped, after which a communal meal is served.

The **tourist office** (☎04.68.39.11.99; June–Sept Mon–Sat 10am–noon & 2–5.30pm; Oct & May 2–5pm), in rue Barjou at the top of the town, has suggestions for walks and trails around Arles, plus a map for 25F (the GR10, which passes through the town, is not well signposted locally); it also stocks a list of *chambres d'hôtes*, invaluable in hotel-poor Arles. The choice of **hotels** lies between the friendly but spartan *Le Commerce*, 1 rue Jean-Vilar (☎04.68.39.11.75; ②), by the upper main junction close to the tourist office, and the more comfortable two-star *Les Glycines*, 7 rue du Jeu-de-Paume (☎04.68.39.10.09, fax 04.68.3.83.02; ③; closed Nov–Jan), which also has the best **restaurant** in town, with a shaded terrace and Catalan specialities (menus 105F–165F). The alternatives for eating out are *La Treille* (☎04.68.39.89.59; Sept–May closed Mon) at the beginning of bd Riuferrer, with a pleasant vine-shaded terrace (70F menu); the grill-bar at the Musée Jean Cordomi (March–Dec 10am–10pm), opposite the *Mairie*; or the *Bar Central*, opposite *Le Commerce*, for a very reasonable omelette-and-*frites*. For homemade patés and takeaway savoury dishes, there's an exceptional *charcuterie*: Frères Coll, at 7 rue Jean-Vilar.

Among **campsites**, the scenic *Riuferrer* (☎04.68.39.11.06; open all year), is on the west side of town, near the mouth of the Freixe stream; *Le Vallespir* (☎04.68.39.90.00) lies on the road to Amélie-les-Bains; or there's the naturist camp *Le Ventous* (☎04.68.87.83.38; June–Sept) on the road to Prats-de-Mollo.

The Gorges de la Fou

A couple of kilometres up the main valley road from Arles are the **Gorges de la Fou** (☎04.68.39.16.21; Easter–end Oct 10am–6pm, closed during bad weather; 25F), one of the great – if touristy – spectacles of the Eastern Pyrenees. You need at least an hour to cover the 1500m of metal walkway to the end and back, squeezing between 200-metre-high walls, so close together that they have trapped falling rocks. In places, water erosion has made the walls as smooth as plaster, and the force of the torrent during storms in 1988 was sufficient to sweep part of the walk away. If you don't think you'll make it to the Gorges de Kakouetta in the French Basque country (see p.401), these are a more than respectable consolation prize. However, if the weather looks doubtful, phone to check that the gorge is open before visiting.

Walking out of Arles: to the Albères or Canigou

The GR10 climbs **southeast** from the town through the Arles forest to Montalba (no facilities), at the head of the Mondony gorge, and onto the summit ridge of the Albères, just below Roc de France (1450m). Indeed there's little habitation between Arles and the *gîte* at Las Illas (see "Le Perthus and the frontier", p.116), a long day's trek away.

Heading **northwest**, the **Arles-to-Cortalets** approach could be done in a single day, given an early enough start, but it's an arduous walk, beyond the capabilities of most walkers. From Arles, it's wisest to forego the first, unsightly section of the GR10 itself in favour of the blue-dot-waymarked path labelled "Dolmen 1hr 30min", which takes off from the road towards the campsite, just above the town pool. You can break the trek five hours along at the *gîte d'étape* (☎04.68.39.12.01; April–Oct; ①) taking up the old miners' hostel at **BATÈRE**, which has a good bistro. The iron-works themselves are evident as an ugly scar resulting from open-cast extraction between the twelfth and seventeenth centuries; some galleries are still worked today. If you're in a group, you're advised to save yourself some rather tedious trekking altogether by taking a **taxi** up to the *gîte*, along the paved D43 sideroad, which begins just beyond Arles. After 7km you'll pass the stone-built village of **CORSAVY** (7km), with its Romanesque chapel of Saint-Martin-de-Corsavy and three places to eat.

North of the mine and *gîte* the road turns to track, climbing on past the ruined **Tour de Batère** before dropping down to the road for Valmanya (see "The Canigou Massif", p.104).

Alpine Canigou truly begins just west of the *gîte* at the **Col de le Cirère** (1730m), beyond which unfurls the section of corniche trail dubbed the **Balcon du Canigou** for its sweeping views northeast. Two hours beyond Batère, the eight-bunk forestry hut at **Estagnole** has a good spring and an adjacent terrace suitable for camping; it's also easily reached from Valmanya, visible below, in less time. The *Chalet des Cortalets* (p.107) is still a good four-and-a-half hours away along the GR10.

The upper Tech

Accessible both along the D44 from Corsavy, and the D54 from the main valley floor, **MONTFERRER**, 6km from Arles by the shortest route, is – with its ruined castle and Romanesque church – one of the most attractive settlements in the upper Tech. Set amongst dense forest and crags, with sweeping views east to the opposite side of the valley, it enjoys its status as the truffle capital of Roussillon – the village can also muster a good **campsite** with a swimming pool.

Some 7km beyond Arles-sur-Tech, the D3 sideroad ascends south from the main D115 through forests of sweet chestnut to the village of **SAINT-LAURENT-DE-CERDANS** (9km from the junction). Three buses a day serve the village from Perpignan (2 on Sun). During World War II the local clergy oversaw the passage of refugees either southwest towards Mont Nègre, crossing the frontier by the Col des Massanes (1126m), or up to Coustouges for the Riou Majou trail. Nowadays, marked footpaths – variants of the HRP – run east and west along the border from both Saint-Laurent and Coustouges.

Passeurs normally asked their clients to wear espadrilles, which are quieter than ordinary shoes and – some claim – better suited to rock climbing. Saint-Laurent was once a major producer of *bigatanes*, the special Catalan espadrille that has a double rope sole and ankle-laces. You can see how espadrilles were made, and discover other rural crafts

such as weaving and beekeeping, in the local history museum, **Musée d'Arts et Traditions Populaire** (May–Sept 10am–noon & 3–6pm; 10F), near the tourist office on
the main road through town. Beside the Laurent stream are a pair of **campsites** (one
just before you enter the village and another just beyond it), while the nearest **hotel** is
the very comfortable but pricey *Domaine de Falgos*, converted from an old barn about
5km from Saint-Laurent in the direction of Coustouges (☎04.68.39.51.42, fax
04.68.39.52.30; ⑤; closed Jan).

From Saint-Laurent the road climbs 5km further east to the tiny hamlet of **COUS-
TOUGES** (1 bus daily Mon–Sat), from where the spine of the Albères rises north-
eastwards to the highest point of the chain at **Roc de France** (1450m). The large
church, built in unusual pink sandstone and granite, and with a richly carved portal,
would have also served the villages over the present frontier at the time of its construction in the twelfth century. There's just one **pension** here, the *Famille Barn-
abas* (☎04.68.39.51.04; ②).

Returning by road to the Tech valley, you can cut off along the D64, from which
a short detour brings you to Serralongue, which has a **campsite**. An alternative is
to take the high-level *variante* footpath west from Coustouges, which leads to the
delightfully secluded **LAMANÈRE**, the most southerly village in France; path and
track continue from here to the frontier at Col d'Ares, or the paved D44 descends
north to the main valley.

Prats-de-Molló

From Arles, the D115 climbs 19km to the medieval city of **PRATS-DE-MOLLÓ**. The
present road follows the path of a former railway (the old station houses can be seen
along the way), since the old road, with houses and bridges, was washed away in the
disastrous floods of October 1940.

In the seventeenth century, when the Treaty of the Pyrenees subjected this area
to the outrageous tax policies of Louis XIV, Prats-de-Molló and a number of other
towns and villages revolted against the French Crown. Living at the far end of what
was then a densely wooded valley, the rebels probably felt themselves invulnerable
when they murdered the king's tax collectors. And indeed they held off two battalions before the forces of Maréchal de Noailles made a surprise attack over the western flanks of Canigou to put down the insurrection. **Fort Lagarde** (April–Nov daily
10am–1pm; 15F), which dominates the town from above, was built in 1680 under the
direction of Vauban, as much to subdue the local population as to keep the Spanish
at bay; the town walls, raised on fourteenth-century foundations, are another Vauban
relic from this period. To climb up to the fort (about 25min), head for Porte de la
Fabrique, then either follow the footpath which winds up the hill from behind the
church or take the 170-metre covered walk leading steeply upwards to a square
tower, followed by a dark 100-metre underground tunnel (the entrance to the covered walk is in a ruined building to the right of the cemetery entrance). The fort
itself has been beautifully restored, and there are superb views all round from the
ramparts. An extra attraction here is the **Visite-Spectacle** on summer afternoons,
when horsemen dressed as cavaliers recreate eighteenth-century cavalry training,
with trick riding, sword fights and the firing of muskets and cannons (daily except
Sat: July & Aug 2.30pm & 4pm; June & Sept 3.30pm; 30F).

With Canigou at its back and the River Tech in front, picturesque Prats-de-Molló
has now become a tourist attraction but is still surprisingly unspoilt – particularly
the old *ville haute* within the city wall, with its steep, cobbled streets and ancient fortified church. In summer, the pedestrianized streets buzz with activity; the rest of
the year the hotels are locked up, and the locals pass the time at *boules* under the
plane trees of El Firal, the huge square outside the walls, where markets and fairs
have been held since 1308.

The **tourist office** in place le Firal (☎04.68.39.70.83; July & Aug daily 9am–7pm; April–June, Sept & Oct Mon–Sat 9am–noon & 2–6pm; Nov–March Mon–Fri 9am–noon & 2–6pm) has a wealth of information, including maps and advice for walking in the Haut-Vallespir. The only one-star **hotel** is the chintzy *Ausseil*, place Joseph Trinxeria (☎04.68.39.70.36; ③); among two-star hotels, both the family-oriented *Le Relais*, 3 place Joseph Trinxeria (☎04.68.39.71.30; ③), and the friendly *Bellevue* overlooking place le Firal (☎04.68.39.70.24; ③; closed Nov–Mar), serve reasonable **meals**, *Le Relais* at tables outside in the square. There's plenty of local **camping**, too: *St Martin* and *La Verneda*, beside the Tech, just before the town on the main road from Arles; the *Can Nadal* about 1km along the road towards La Preste, and another on the road to Col d'Ares.

Onward routes: into Spain

Transport from Prats-de-Molló is a problem: there are three or four **buses** a day back down the Tech, but none on **into Spain**. From Prats the road climbs 14km to the Span-ish border at **Col d'Ares**, dropping on the other side to Camprodon (see p.160). Rough-ly halfway to the border, just beyond the Col de la Seille on the left, you'll find the *Ferme-Auberge La Coste d'Adalt* (☎04.68.39.74.40; ③), a working farm with spotless rooms and good food, near the terminus of the path and track coming west from Lamanère. Four kilometres along the path towards Lamanère is a *gîte d'étape* at Ermitage Notre Dame du Coral (☎04.68.39.75.00; bed only ①, half-pension ③).

The easiest of the former escape trails is the one to the **Collade de Prats** (1596m) from the south side of the Tech, a short way along the N115. The route passes the ruined **Tour de Mir**, one of the series of signal towers built by Jaume of Mallorca in the late thirteenth century, like the Tour Madeloc above Banyuls-sur-Mer (see p.128); allow three hours to the pass (and two-plus back if you're not continuing into Spain).

From the nearby spa of **LA PRESTE** (8km west) there was a higher and more dif-ficult route through the **Coll del Pal** (2319m) over towards Setcases, between Pic de Costabona (2465m) and the smoothly rounded Roc Colom (2507m), on whose eastern flanks the Tech has its source. A good base for walking in the area above La Preste is the small refuge of *Chalet las Conques* (☎04.68.39.76.52; daily May–Oct; for group book-ings out of season phone ☎04.68.39.23.49; ①).

Canigou from the south

Another possibility at Prats-de-Molló is to ascend Canigou from the south and descend on the Têt side. Take the road to La Preste (1130m) and then the track up to the **Collade des Roques Blanches**, at the end of the long ridge of tooth-like rocks known as the **Esquerdes de Rotja**. From there you turn east to **Pla Guillem** (2277m) – where there's a simple refuge – and then continue to *Refuge Mariailles*. Alternatively, at the *collade*, you can veer westwards, either along the Esquerdes or on a forest track, towards Mantet. For a complete description of Pla Guillem, Mari-ailles and Mantet, see p.108, and consult the maps recommended in the introduction to "The Canigou Massif".

THE MEDITERRANEAN COAST

The Pyrenees meet the sea with a magnificent abruptness. Approaching from the north, **Argelès-sur-Mer** marks the point at which the flat strands of the Côte Radieuse give way to the rocky coves and scented foothills of the Albères, the most easterly limb of the Pyrenean range. The colourful clash of land and water has long attracted artists to this coast, most notably the group of early twentieth-century French painters known as the *Fauves* (Wild Beasts), because of their vividly emotional use of colour and form, who passed their summers at **Collioure**, immediately south of Argelès.

Continuing south, the corniche road traces an ever more tortuous line along the **Côte Vermeille** to the easternmost point of the French Pyrenees, where the mountains plummet into the Mediterranean at **Cap Cerbère**. Here the sea floor drops precipitously to a depth of 40m, creating a habitat that has been protected since 1974 by the *réserve marine* between **Banyuls-sur-Mer** and **Cerbère**. Once the most elegant resort of the Côte Vermeille, Banyuls was the home of Aristide Maillol, sculptor of robust nymphs; it also marks one end of the **GR10** and the **HRP** walking trails, which both run across to the Atlantic coast, 400km away.

Beyond the border at **Port Bou**, the orderly vineyards of France give way to the more dishevelled terraces of the **Costa Brava**, whose vineyards were ravaged last century by phylloxera. Yet some wine is still produced in this region, such as Garnatxa from **El Port de la Selva**, a town where fishing remains a major industry and the coastline remains fairly unknown to outsiders. The major local sight is the pre-Romanesque monastery of **Sant Pere de Rodes**, in the hills above El Port de la Selva.

At the **Cap de Creus** peninsula the Spanish Pyrenees reach the sea, as does Spain's own trans-Pyrenean footpath, the **GR11**. The rugged landscape continues around the cape to **Cadaqués** and **Port Lligat**, both pregnant with the memory of Surrealist artist Salvador Dalí, who lived here for decades. **Roses**, southernmost resort of Cap de Creus, brashly mimics the Côte d'Azur with its palm-lined promenade and pavement cafés; inland, the county town of **Figueres** is most remarkable for its Museu Dalí.

Public transport is generally more than adequate, with frequent buses and trains between Perpignan and every resort of the Côte Vermeille, strung along the N114. On the Spanish side trains and buses are nearly as good as long as you stick to the main C252 between Figueres and the frontier and the C260 linking Figueres to Roses, but connections around the Cap de Creus can be problematic.

The Côte Vermeille

When the *Fauves* discovered the **Côte Vermeille**, which extends southeast from Argelès-sur-Mer to the Spanish border, they found natural inspiration for their revolutionary use of colour: the warm-toned cliffs almost justify the title "vermilion", the sea is turquoise and, as Matisse wrote, "no sky is more blue than that at Collioure". The beauty of this stretch of coastline has inevitably been exploited, but cut up into the hills at the back of the resorts and you'll often be on your own: particularly enticing is the Balcon du Côte Vermeille path, out of Argèles-sur-Mer, and the panoramic trail past Tour Madeloc, south of Collioure.

Elne

Standing on a hill just 6km from the sea, on the main bus route between Perpignan and Argelès, the ancient fortified town of **ELNE** was once the capital of Roussillon. The new bypass and giant modern roundabout, to the east of the town, are jammed solid every summer weekend with beach-bound traffic but the old town, inside the sixteenth-century ramparts, is eerily quiet after dark. Elne has one great attraction worth visiting, the partly Romanesque cathedral and cloister of **Sainte-Eulalie** (June–Sept daily 9.30am–6.45pm; April, May & Oct daily 9.30am–noon & 2–5.45pm; Nov–March daily except Tues 10am–noon & 2–4.45pm; closed Dec 25, Jan 1, May 1; 20F), the seat of the Roussillon bishopric until Perpignan took over in 1602. The exterior sports a coarse pebbledash, often seen in this region's larger buildings, but the dark triple-aisled interior and the seven Gothic chapels are altogether more aloof and holy. The **cloister**,

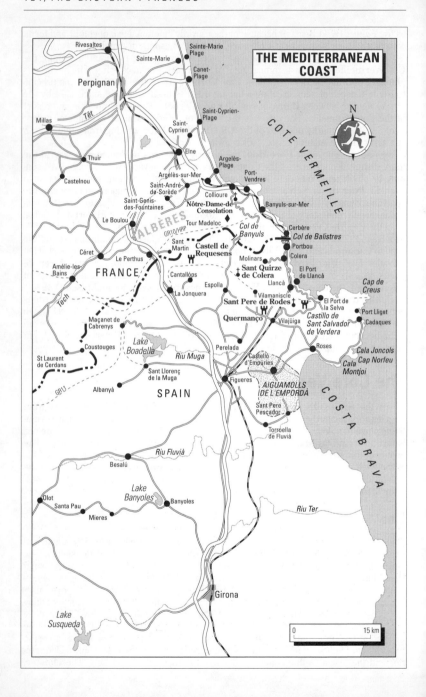

built from Céret marble, is the high spot: one intact side of twelfth-century Romanesque pillars and capitals, immaculately carved with motifs such as foliage, lions, goats and biblical figures, is complemented on the other three sides by fourteenth-century Gothic work that has been made to harmonize perfectly. A small museum in the twelfth-century Saint-Laurent chapel is mainly given over to exhibits found in the excavations of Roman villas around Elne. Opposite the cathedral, at 3 rue Balaguer, is the **Musée Terrus** (July–Sept daily 10am–7pm; April–June & Oct daily 10am–12.30pm & 2–6pm; rest of year daily except Tues 10am–noon & 2–5pm; 10F), dedicated to the landscape painter Etienne Terrus (1857–1922), a contemporary of the *Fauves* and friend of Maillol (whose bust of Terrus stands on the Plateau des Garaffes, nearby); the *salon de thé*, on the first floor, has a panoramic view.

Practicalities

The **train station**, on the main line from Perpignan to the Côte Vermeille, lies about ten minutes' walk west of the old town; **buses** stop at the parking place in the centre of the old town, near the cathedral. The **tourist office** is at 2 rue du Docteur Bolte (July & Aug Mon–Sat 9.30am–noon & 2–6pm, Sun 9.30am–noon; June & Sept Mon–Fri 9.30am–noon & 2–5pm, Sat 9.30am–noon; rest of the year Mon–Fri 10am–noon & 2–4pm; ☎04.68.22.05.07), between the **post office** and *Hôtel de Ville*. Of the three **hotels**, the modest *Cara Sol*, in bd Illibéris on the edge of the old town (☎04.68.22.10.42; ③), offers by far the best value and the best situation, with great views from the front rooms over the Tech valley, the Albères and Canigou. More upmarket is the two-star *Le Weekend*, 31 av Paul Reig (☎04.68.22.06.68; ④), just off centre on the Argelès road, with a celebrated garden **restaurant** (menus 90F–120F); less well situated is *Le Carrefour*, 1 av Paul Reig (☎04.68.22.06.08; ③), on a small but busy crossroads. There are two municipal **campsites** (June–end Sept): *Les Padraguets* (☎04.68.22.21.59) on the Argelès road and *Al Mouly* (☎04.68.22.08.46) on bd d'Archimède, in the direction of St-Cyprien.

Argelès-sur-Mer

More properly belonging to the Côte Radieuse than to the Côte Vermeille, **ARGELÈS-SUR-MER** has the last wide, sandy beach until Roses, well into Spain. At the end of the Spanish Civil War thousands of refugees lived in camps here, their numbers including the Republican poet Antonio Machado, who failed to survive the first harsh winter. Not surprisingly, given camp conditions, nearly ten thousand of the inmates volunteered to serve in the French army upon the 1939 outbreak of hostilities.

Nowadays, more than any other resort on this section of coast, this is a mass-tourist town, wooing its visitors with holiday essentials like mini-golf, gambling tables and beauty contests. This is also where the **Balcon de la Côte Vermeille** begins, a tough 25-kilometre walk to Banyuls, just feasible in a single long day. Set mostly on high ground with wide views over the coastline and its villages, it also gives glimpses south into the lonely landscape of Spain's Alt Empordà.

The town itself is divided in two: the old **Argelès-Ville**, a little inland, and the new **Argelès-Plage**, which receives an annual inundation of up to three hundred thousand French, Belgian, Dutch and English visitors. Plage Nord and Plage des Pins are of the smooth, sandy and potentially windblown variety, whereas **Le Racou** – the first bay of the Côte Vermeille – is more intimate and offers a taste of mountain coastline. The only cultural attraction is the old town's **Casa Catalana de les Albères**, in place des Castellans (☎04.68.81.42.74), a small museum of local art and traditions, mostly agricultural tools and implements (June–Sept Mon–Fri 9am–noon & 3–6pm, Sat 9am–noon; 10F).

Practicalities

The **train station** is a few minutes' walk west of the centre of the old town, while **buses** stop opposite the *Hôtel de Ville*. An hourly bus service (10F) runs in summer between the station, the old town and the beach (Plage-Nord). There is a summer **tourist office** in the old town (July & Aug Mon–Sat 9.30am–12.30pm & 2.30–6.30pm; ☎04.68.95.81.55), by the *Hôtel de Ville* on allée Ferdinand-Buisson; Argelès-Plage has its own office (summer daily 8.30am–8pm; out of season Mon–Fri 9am–noon & 2–6pm, Sat 9am–noon; ☎04.68.81.15.85), in place de l'Europe, on the corner of av des Platanes and av des Mimosas.

Rooms can be difficult to find in midsummer, especially for a short stay. If you're looking for a hotel in Argelès-Ville, try the long-established one-star *Le Soubirana*, 58 route Nationale (☎04.68.81.01.44; ③), or the two-star *Clair Logis*, 78 route de Collioure (☎04.68.81.03.27; ③). Among dozens of hotels in Argelès-Plage, the two-star *Les Mimosas*, 51 av des Mimosas (☎04.68.81.14.77; ④), and *Le Solarium*, 9 av du Vallespir (☎04.68.81.10.74; ④), are reasonably priced and well situated. At Le Racou, try *La Galion*, av Principale (☎04.68.81.08.64; ④). There should never be a problem finding a spot for your tent, as there are more than fifty **campsites** in the neighbourhood: *Calanque de l'Ouille* (☎04.68.81.12.79; April–Sept) and *Mini Camping* (☎04.68.81.08.72; April–Sept) are two desirable seafront establishments in the direction of Collioure.

Southwest: Saint-André and Saint-Genis

The Cars Verts du Roussillon **bus** service from Argelès-sur-Mer runs southwest along the D618 road through the Albères foothills to Le Boulou, right by the highway on the northern flank of the Albères range.

Some of the buses call at **SAINT-ANDRÉ-DE-SORÈDE**, 5km away, some at **SAINT-GENIS-DES-FONTAINES**, a similar distance beyond, and some at both. Most of the **Benedictine** abbey at Saint-Génis, founded in the ninth century, has disappeared (the cloister to the Philadelphia Museum), but the two-metre lintel over the doorway of the church, dating from 1020, is one of the earliest examples of Romanesque sculpture in France (May–Oct Mon–Fri 10am–noon & 2–6pm, Sat & Sun 9am–noon & 2–6pm; Nov–April daily 9.30am–noon & 2–5pm; 10F). The similar lintel at Saint-André – showing Christ surrounded by angels and apostles – is probably a slightly later copy, though the contemporary church that it adorns is in better condition than Saint-Genis.

Collioure

A short bus or train ride down the coast from Argelès-sur-Mer is **COLLIOURE**, a true Côte Vermeille town, which to a certain extent still banks on its maritime and artistic past. Established as a trading port by the Phoenicians and ancient Greeks, Collioure was later occupied by the Romans (who stayed for five centuries), the Visigoths and Arabs. Altogether, the place has been the focus of nearly a dozen territorial squabbles, including four invasions by the French and two by the Spanish. The sixteenth-century **Fort St Elme** overlooking the town from the south (now privately owned), and the seventeenth-century **Fort Miradou** to the north (still used by the military), are reminders of this turbulent past.

In the early 1900s, invaders of a different sort came, saw and stayed. The group of painters – including Matisse and Derain – known as **Les Fauves** made Collioure their summer base. Some of their original work adorns the bar at *Les Templiers* (see below), but for a comprehensive showing you must visit the art museum in Céret (see p.117); you can also follow the *Chemin du Fauvisme* around the town, a trail of twenty reproductions of paintings by Matisse and Derain placed on the sites at which they were painted (map available from the tourist office). Among other personalities drawn to the town, the poet Antonio Machado arrived with his family in January 1939, but died of pneumonia fifteen days later; after an appeal initiated by Pablo Casals, André Malraux and Albert Camus, he was reburied in a tomb in Collioure's cemetery in l956. A Picasso poster, *Hommage à Antonio Machado*, is on display in Collioure's **Musée d'Art Moderne** (July & Aug daily 10am–noon & 2–6pm; rest of year closed Tues; 12F), housed in the beautiful Villa Pams on the edge of the town in route de Port-Vendres, with a small permanent collection and temporary exhibitions by artists associated with the region.

The artistic tradition of Collioure survives today, albeit with less distinction; Collioure is tame and middle class, and none of the art is wild. The forest of easels that occupies the promenade in summer produces mainly tourist souvenirs, but there are also a few serious commercial galleries and, if you're inclined to try your own hand, plenty of studios for rent. Many of these are in the old quarter of the town, the **Mouré**, whose steep, narrow streets are lined by pastel-tinted houses and assorted shops and cafés. Lateen-rigged fishing boats might be moored in the **harbour** itself, or drawn up on the palm-lined beach; those no longer used by fishermen are now beautifully restored and sailed as pleasure vessels by their new owners. The working fleet – distinguished by bow-lamps – brings in the local catch of anchovies (cured in salt, an ancient technique for which Collioure is famous) and sardines (grilled fresh).

Château-Royal (daily: June–Sept 10am–6pm; Oct–May 9am–5pm; closed May 1, Nov 1, Dec 25, Jan 1; 20F), the imposing fortress which dominates the harbour, was founded by the Templars in the twelfth century, rebuilt and used as a summer residence by the kings of Mallorca and Aragón two hundred years later, and modernized by Vauban after the Treaty of the Pyrenees. The impressive ramparts and some of the well-restored rooms provide terrific settings for seasonal exhibitions of sculptures and paintings, and displays relating to local subjects like quilting and cork production, with great views over the harbour, town and vine-covered hills beyond; the beautiful courtyard at the heart of the castle is used for summer concerts.

At the opposite end of the harbour, the **Église Notre-Dame-des-Anges** was erected in the seventeenth century, replacing the ancient Sainte-Marie, razed on the orders of Vauban. The distinctive round bell-tower – once doubling as the lighthouse – onto which it was grafted has been damaged many times by storm and war: the base dates from the thirteenth century, the middle from the fourteenth to seventeenth centuries, and the bell-chamber from the nineteenth. It's worth taking a look inside the church (daily 8am–noon & 2–5.30pm) to see the magnificent gilt retable, carved and painted in three tiers, by the seventeenth-century Catalan sculptor Joseph Sunyer. Beyond the church, the tiny **Chapelle-St-Vincent** stands above the sea on a rocky peninsula, with the south-facing St Vincent beach on one side and the Plage Nord on the other.

Practicalities

Collioure's **train station** is less than ten minutes' walk west of the centre, along av Aristide Maillol; **buses** stop at the central car park, off av Général de Gaulle. The very helpful **tourist office** is just behind the harbour in place du 18 Juin (☎04.68.82.15.47; July & Aug Mon–Sat 9am–8pm, Sun 10am–noon & 3–6pm; June & Sept Mon–Sat 9am–noon & 2–7pm; rest of year Mon–Sat 9am–noon & 2–6pm), with information on everything from accommodation and eating out to walking tours, diving and sailing schools, and cruises around the bay. For **eating out**, there's a great choice of very reasonable creperies, sandwich bars and pizza-pasta places around the old Mouré quarter, but it's worth the premium to sit at a table on the fashionable rue Camille Pelletan, by the harbour, to watch the world go by – the most atmospheric is *Les Templiers*, a café-bar well known to the *Fauves*, and now filled with drawings and paintings donated by Matisse,

Maillol, Picasso and Dufy, among many other artists. **Markets** (Wed & Sun morning) are held in place du Général Leclerc.

The quieter Plage Boutigue, southeast of the harbour, has some desirable seaview **hotels** including the attractively furnished *Le Boramar* (☎04.68.82.07.06; closed Nov–April; ④) and the nearby, year-round *Triton*, 1 rue Jean-Bart (☎04.68.98.39.39, fax 04.68.82.11.32; ③). The most unusual accommodation is *Hostellerie des Templiers*, 12 quai de l'Amirauté (☎04.68.98.31.10, fax 04.68.98.01.24; ⑤), in which the individually decorated rooms, staircases and dining rooms are filled with original artworks; reservations here are essential. There's some low-cost accommodation as well, though it's difficult to find in high season. One-star hotels include *Bona Casa* on the busy av de la République (☎04.68.82.06.62; ③), with a fish restaurant attached (menus from 59F). There are three summer-only **campsites** to the north of the town, near the coast: the *Criques de Porteils* (☎04.68.81.12.73), on the Argelès road; *Les Amandiers* (☎04.68.81.14.69), in the sheltered bay known as L'Ouille; and, the best of the bunch, *La Girelle*, plage d'Ouille (☎04.68.81.25.56).

Walks south from Collioure

For an easy walk out of Collioure, take rue de la République from the harbour, cross the main road and follow signs for **Nôtre-Dame-de-Consolation**, reached by track, then path, within ninety minutes. This is an old hermitage, now in ruins but much loved locally for its barbecue and *boules* area; strangely for such an out-of-the-way place, there's also a *chambre d'hôtes* here (☎04.68.82.17.66; ③). If you're really serious about hiking and happy to progress south, continue on the trail to **Tour Madeloc** on the crest of a ridge (650m), descending on Banyuls-sur-Mer after about six hours; the last section uses the long-distance GR10 and HRP footpaths. The tower, also accessible by road from Banyuls, was built by Jaume I of Mallorca at the end of the thirteenth century as one of a chain of such signal stations.

Port-Vendres

The next settlement southeast, **PORT-VENDRES** (a 5min bus or train ride from Collioure), is marred by the busy main road, but for a genuine, unsophisticated fishing port, this is your best (indeed only) choice on the Côte Vermeille – though you probably won't want to stay longer than it takes to have a look around the port and tuck into a fish lunch, or to watch the fish auctions which take place at the far end of the port every weekday evening (usually 5–7pm). A huge fish-processing factory dominates one side of the harbour, while sardine-, and tuna-fishing boats are moored under the Maillol-designed war memorial opposite, with nets and other paraphernalia piled along the harbour wall. Salt has taken its toll on Maillol's work, and the uncharacteristically draped figures have lost limbs, noses and various other features.

To the Romans the town was *Portus Veneris* (Port of Venus), a place of strategic trading importance. By the Middle Ages its significance was diminishing in direct relation to the rising star of neighbouring Collioure, but by the eighteenth century it had recovered somewhat through the business of shipping Roussillon wines. In 1830 it became the primary port for dispatching soldiers and supplies to the French colony in Algeria, a link that lasted for more than a century.

Banyuls-sur-Mer to the frontier

As the road crosses the Col du Père Carnère and drops down towards the Plage des Elmes, the once-elegant wine town of **BANYULS-SUR-MER** comes into view, with dry-stone walls and orderly rows of vines stretching into the hills behind it. You could keep going for days on free samplings of the **Banyuls** dessert wine, which the French tend to drink as an aperitif. Try a guided tour of one of the larger cellars, such as the Cellier des Templiers in route du Mas-Reig (April–Oct daily 9am–7pm; rest of year Mon–Sat 9am–noon & 2–6pm).

Less fashionable than Collioure, Banyuls is still a lively and popular seaside resort. It's marred by the busy road which runs along the seafront, and the wide, stony main beach is less attractive than some of the smaller bays to the north and south, but the whole town comes alive in the evenings when everyone gets together to promenade along the seafront, play *boules* or eat out at one of the many beach cafés and seafood restaurants.

Don't leave Banyuls without visiting the **Laboratoire Arago**, the large white building overlooking the port. Run by the marine biology and land ecology department of the Sorbonne, its **aquarium** (daily: July & Aug 9am–noon & 2–10pm; rest of year 9am–noon & 2–6.30pm; 22F) comprises over forty tanks of fascinating local specimens, including seahorses, bright red starfish and wicked-looking eels, and is supplemented by a comprehensive display of local birds. The coastal waters of this area, rich in marine life due to the Pyrenees' steep underwater descent, were the first *réserve marine* to be declared in France, indeed throughout the Mediterranean; more than 530 species of invertebrates have been identified within the zone. Those with the requisite qualifications can **dive** within the reserve area by contacting Plongez Rederis Club, operating from the port (☎04.68.88.31.66 or 04.68.92.02.01).

Practicalities

The **train station** lies at the very western edge of town, while **buses** stop on the coastal boulevard. The **tourist office** is on the seafront, opposite the *Mairie* (☎04.68.88.31.58; July & Aug daily 9am–12.30pm & 2.30–7pm; rest of year closed Sun). Recommended one-star **hotels**, open all year, include the quaint and unpretentious *Hôtel Canal*, 9 rue Dugommier (☎04.68.88.00.75; ③), the slightly smarter *Le Manoir*, 20 rue du Maréchal-Joffre (☎04.68.88.32.98; ③), and its near neighbour *Sant Sebastien* (☎04.68.88.34.90; ④), all in the quieter back streets. For a reasonably priced hotel on the seafront, try *La Pergola*, 5 ave du Fontaulé (☎04.68.88.02.10; ④), near the port, where most rooms have a balcony and seaview; they also have a good restaurant (menus from 85F). **Camping** is at the *Camping du Stade*, rue Jean Boin (☎04.68.88.31.70), or the cheaper *Camping Municipal La Pinede* nearby, on route du Mas-Reig (☎04.68.88.32.13).

Banyuls has a good choice of **restaurants** specializing in fresh seafood. The most expensive, with starched tablecloths and live lobster tanks – among which *Le Sardinal*, 4 bis place Paul Reig, is reckoned the best – are lined up opposite the seafront, but there are several less expensive choices: the best is *Les Canadells*, just off the main boulevard at 4 av du Général de Gaulle, with excellent menus (from 78F) and specialities including *zarzuela*. *Chez Rosa*, 22 rue St Pierre (closed Sun), offers set lunches at reasonable prices and the nearby *Crêperie St Pierre* is good value, too; *Chez Rosa* also has a branch at 19 rue Jean Bart.

Walks from Banyuls: Maillol's tomb and Col de Banyuls

The four-kilometre hike from Banyuls to **Maillol's tomb** and house makes a pleasant excursion up into the vine-clad Albères. Walk the length of avenue Général-de-Gaulle, past the PTT, until you pass under a bridge. Shortly afterwards, where the road curves around to the right, take the left-hand road, following the line of a river: signs from here point the way to the "Musée et Tombeau de Maillol". The round trip takes about two-and-a-half hours.

Keen hikers could continue to the **Col de Banyuls** (2hr) and into Spain (consult the Randonnées Pyrénéennes 1:50,000 "Roussillon" map, or the Editorial Alpina 1:80,000 "Cadaqués" map); the dirt track has no Customs post on it. In 1793 the *col* was the scene of a brave but doomed stand by a small French force, which held back the Spanish long enough for their army to regroup; this was also the route followed by many refugees from the Spanish Civil War and from Nazism. Once over the pass you can walk to Espolla or follow the GR11 to Llança via Sant Quirze de Colera (see "North of Figueres", p.138). Either of these options requires a fairly long day.

Cerbère

The Côte Vermeille comes to an end at **CERBÈRE**. The harbour is quite pretty and the mountain backdrop is impressive, but the beach is negligible. Depending on the service, train passengers have to change either here or on the Spanish side of the border at much nicer Port Bou (see opposite), where the rail line changes track size. In Cerbère, you can **stay and eat** at *La Dorade* on the harbour (☎04.68.88.41.93; ④) or tent down at the palm- and cactus-fringed *Camping del Sorell* (☎04.68.88.41.64; June–Sept).

The Costa Brava

The **Costa Brava** extends for some 200km from the border to just north of Barcelona, a realm synonymous with the first – and arguably the worst – stirrings of post-World War II package tourism. Yet despite the commercialized tower-block fleshpots, it is still possible to encounter stretches of relatively unsullied shoreline, graced by the dramatic cliffs, pine-fringed coves and beaches which helped prompt all the development in the first place. This is far more likely in the northerly reaches of the Costa Brava, near the Mediterranean terminus of the Spanish GR11 at Cap de Creus, and accordingly coverage here is restricted to the smaller, more human-scale resorts north of the Golfo de Roses, where tired hill-walkers will most appreciate the chance of a few days by the sea.

One thing you'll notice upon crossing the border at the **Col dels Balistres** is an abrupt change from the tidy viniculture of the French hillsides to the shaggier Spanish slopes. The effects of the phylloxera plague last century, as devastating here as on the French side, were compounded by a killing frost in 1956 which finished off commercial olive production; and there have been continual brush- and forest-fires ever since, whose only beneficial result is the production of honey flavoured by the aromatic heather, lavender and myrtle which colonise the ashes.

Such deterioration of the agricultural economy has of course been accelerated by migration to Barcelona and further afield, and by the exponential growth of tourism. The most northerly resorts of the *costa* – **Port Bou**, **Colera**, **Llançà** and **El Port de**

ARISTIDE MAILLOL

Sculptor **Aristide Maillol** (1861–1944), the local boy made good, returned to Banyuls-sur-Mer after forty years away to concentrate on the fleshy nude sculptures that made him famous. He is buried at his farm, **La Baillaurie** (for directions, see "Walks from Banyuls" below), the tomb topped by his *La Pensée*. The farm has now been restored and opened as a museum (daily except Tues: May–Sept 10am–noon & 4–7pm; Oct, Nov & Jan–Apr 10am–noon & 2–5pm; closed public holidays; 20F), a commemoration inspired by Dina Vierny, Maillol's last model; you can see the rooms where he lived and worked, with a display of over thirty bronze statues and photographs. The sculptor's major piece in Banyuls proper is the half-relief war memorial on the **Ile Grosse**, the islet at the end of the jetty; there's also a sculpture in the garden of the *Mairie* (access via the back gate from av Général-de-Gaulle) and another, *La Jeune Fille*, on the raised promenade above the harbour. The artist's birthplace, now a Catalan crafts shop, is at 6 rue du Puig del Mas.

la Selva – are still very much for Catalans and passing French motorists, with little of the international development that has created the blight further down the coast. In season, **Cadaqués** is more cosmopolitan and, thanks to Dalí, has a self-consciously arty feel. Large-scale holiday developments start at **Roses**, where the terrain becomes easier for building. You'll never find complete tranquillity nearby in summer, but if you're willing to walk a bit you can still discover some near-empty beaches on the fire-ravaged **Cap de Creus** peninsula, as well as some compelling inland sites, like the Benedictine monastery of **Sant Pere de Rodes** or the wildlife reserve at **Aiguamolls de l'Empordà**.

Port Bou

PORT BOU, just 3km below the Spanish border, is the most northerly settlement of the Costa Brava. The village is built around a bay formed in the foothills of the Albères, surrounded by the sort of scenery that moved the Spanish poet Fernando Agulló to bestow the epithet *brava* (rugged) on what was then known simply as the *Costa de Llevant* (East Coast). Besides the main stony beach, still used by fishermen, small coves flank the harbour on either side, accessible by paths threading over the rocks.

Port Bou's small claim to fame is as a terminus of the Barcelona rail line, but it once had a reputation as a smugglers' haven. Today it has become a surprisingly (for a border post) popular resort, whose clientele come for the sake of the clean, attractive pebble bays nearby. If you'd like to **stay**, one-star *hostales* include the basic *Juventus*, Avda de Barcelona 3 (☎972/39 02 41; ②); the preferable *Plaza*, c/Mercat 15 (☎972/39 00 24; ②); the pricier, sea-view *Bahia*, c/de Cervera 1 (☎972/39 01 96; ③); or the *Costa Brava* at c/de Cervera 20 (☎972/39 03 86; ③); the latter two offer en-suite facilities. Further information is available from the friendly **tourist office**, on Passeig de la Sardana (summer daily 9am–8pm; ☎972/39 02 84).

On the same *passeig*, *L'Ancora* offers an excellent **seafood** paella and large tankards of beer; just inland at c/Mendez Nuñez 1, the courtyard of the *Hotel Comodoro* is a good venue for regional dishes.

Colera and Llançà

Some 10km from the frontier, **COLERA** – signposted as "Sant Miquel", its official name – is the first halt for slow trains on the Port Bou–Barcelona run. The town is split in two by the rail line: one part standing back from the large pebbly beach just off the main coast road, the other right on the shore. The situation is pretty, the village less so, but as it's used mainly by Spanish holidaymakers, Colera has stayed relatively quiet. The most comfortable **accommodation** is at the *Hostal Gambina* on the harbour front (☎972/38 90 14; ⑤); for somewhere cheaper, but still adequate, try the *Garbet* guesthouse at the beach of that name (☎972/38 90 01; ③). **Camping** is available at the *Garbet* (April–Oct), with a beach café nearby, or at *Camping Sant Miquel*, near the main road (☎972/38 90 18; April–Sept). For eating out, **restaurants** on the inland Plaça Pi i Margall tend to be more reasonable than waterfront ones.

For a real hike you could walk 12km west up the Molinars valley to the ruined eponymous settlement around the twelfth-century church of **Sant Miquel de Colera**, which now stands as semi-restored testimony to the fears and hardships of the coastal populations who fled inland from pirates. From here you could swing back to the coast again via the GR11 to **LLANÇÀ**, also set back from its port to avoid the perils of piracy. The place has a reputation for breeding rugged fishermen, on account of its exposed north-facing harbour, but the chief emphasis is on family tourism.

The main town, once prosperous thanks to its marble industry, does not now have a great deal to commend it, except for its attractive café-ringed **Plaça Major**, where the remains of a Gothic-cum-Romanesque bell-tower starkly contrast with the huge and plain eighteenth-century parish church on the opposite corner. While the road down to the sea is lined with fairly tacky development, the port itself is still the genuine article, with a coarse sandy **beach**. About half an hour's walk north of the town is the superior beach of **Capras**, part of a well-wooded nature reserve.

Up in Llançà's old town you'll find a number of inexpensive **habitacions and hostals,** such as *Casa Narra*, Castellá 7 (☎972/38 01 78; ③), while *Hostal Miramar*, Passeig Maritim 7 (☎972/38 01 32; ③), is a reasonable place to stay on the harbour. There are two **campsites**, signposted on the way in from the station: *L'Ombra* (☎972/38 03 35; open all year) and the smaller *Camping Llançà* (☎972/38 04 85; mid-June to Aug). The **tourist office** is in Avda d'Europa (June–Sept daily 9.30am–9pm; ☎972/38 08 55), the road into town. Recommended **restaurants** include *La Brasa*, Plaça de Catalunya 6 (closed Dec–Feb), specializing in grilled meat, and a seafood restaurant, *Can Manel*, Plaça del Port 5 (closed Thurs in winter).

El Port de la Selva and inland

From Llançà, it's 8km along the coast road (a few daily buses) to **El Port de la Selva**; hikers can get there indirectly via the **GR11**, which climbs up through vineyards and aromatic scrub to the monastery of **Sant Pere de Rodes** before dropping down to the sea again.

El Port de la Selva

Sitting on the eastern side of a large bay formed by the promontory of Cap de Creus, **EL PORT DE LA SELVA** is again a locals' resort, not especially picturesque but a good base for cove-walking. Fishing constitutes the lifeblood of the village: unless the *tramontana* is blowing, the boats venture forth most days to set their *bous* (nets pulled between two boats) or *teranyines* (long nets pulled by a single vessel).

Accommodation choices are limited: the *Fonda Sol y Sombra*, c/Non 8 (☎972/38 70 60; ③), is reasonable, though half-board is mandatory, while the *Hotel Porto Cristo*, c/Major 59 (☎972/38 70 62; ⑥), is more affordable out of season when the prices drop. Somewhere in between falls *Hostal L'Arola* (☎972/38 70 05; ④), right on the beach by the turning to Selva de la Mar, and near one of the two **campsites** – *Camping L'Arola*, towards Llançà (☎972/38 70 05; May–Sept), and *Port de la Selva*, towards Cadaqués (☎972/38 72 87; June–Sept).

Sant Pere de Rodes

Just below the 670-metre-high summit of Roda, stands the extraordinary Benedictine monastery of **Sant Pere de Rodes** (daily except Tues: June–Sept 10am–7pm; Oct–May 10am–1pm & 3–5pm; 400ptas). It's 6km up the road from El Port (paved until Selva de la Mar, 2km along); less by the GR11, which cuts across the hairpins. Set on the seaward side of the mountain with views of a magnificent stretch of coast from Colera to El Port, this is one of the most romantic ruins in all of Catalonia. The square Romanesque tower is floorless, the roofs are collapsed or overgrown and the barrel-vaulted nave with its eleventh-century columns is delectably dark and dank. Restoration began recently, not all of it sympathetic, and there is talk of fabricating new capitals for the cloister.

According to legend, Sant Pere was founded to enshrine the head and right arm of Saint Paul, after Pope Boniface IV had dispatched a trio of monks from Rome to find a place for the relics that would be safe from the threatening armies of Babylon and Persia. The monks eventually put in at the port of Armen Rodes (now El Port de la Selva), where they temporarily hid the holy remnants. Unable then to remember the exact hiding place, they supposedly built the monastery rather than return to the wrath of the pope. More realistically, the monastery is believed to have been built on the site of an ancient temple of Venus that appears on maps drawn by Ptolemy in the second century – a theory supported by the discovery of pagan sculpture in the vicinity.

The first documented reference to Sant Pere dates from 879, but it must have existed much earlier. By the late tenth century it was the most powerful monastery in the region, and commanded vast financial resources. But by the late thirteenth century the monks were being condemned for spending time in the fleshpots of Selva de la Mar, and the foundation went into relentless decline, spurred further by chronic disputes with local feudal lords. By 1789 the last discredited monks had departed and the buildings were left to plunderers and the weather.

From the monastery a path climbs to the top of the mountain and the severely ruined **Castillo de Sant Salvador de Verdera**, another contender for the original site of the temple of Venus. Built as a watchtower, it encompasses views south across the bay of Roses and the drained marshlands of the Empordà plain. Following the paved road away from the monastery brings you to the pre-Romanesque church of **Santa Elena**, as dilapidated as Sant Pere once was.

Dolmens – and Vilajuïga

A possible continuation from Sant Pere is along the eight-kilometre road to Vilajuïga, a village on the Barcelona–Port Bou train line and connected by bus to Cadaqués, Roses and Figueres. Small signs along the way indicate the path to **dolmens** dating from around five thousand years ago. Particularly impressive is a sequence of tombs off to the left of the road, some 3.5km from the monastery. Detouring to see them actually cuts out a long stretch of asphalt, bringing you to the road a couple of kilometres from the village.

VILAJUÏGA itself boasts the ruined Visigothic castle of **Quermançó** just north and an ancient synagogue – on the Plaça Margineda – that now serves as a church. Getting to the castle involves a ten-minute walk across the fields followed by a scramble up a steep outcrop, the rocks of which blend into the crumbling walls. If you want to **stay**, there's just the *Hostal Xavi* on the main road near the train station (☎972/53 00 03; ③).

Cadaqués and Port Lligat

A bijou resort of small, pebbly coves and traditional white-painted houses with designer interiors, **CADAQUÉS** was put on the map by its most notorious son, Surrealist painter Salvador Dalí, who lived with his wife Gala in nearby Port Lligat. Bohemian it may have been, hedonistic it may still be, but post-"discovery" Cadaqués no longer gets the sort of hippie crowd that once flocked here in the 1960s and 1970s.

The extravagantly large church – conspicuous whether you approach by sea or down the single, convoluted road – is a landmark that has guided generations of seafarers past the rocks and reefs at the harbour entrance. It might have been better off less visible: the village suffered numerous pirate raids, one of the worst being at the hands of the Ottoman "admiral" Barbarossa, who in 1543 sacked the town and burned the original church. The present edifice was built in the seventeenth century and has a remarkable Baroque altarpiece carved by Pedro Costa.

Close to the church, the **Museu d'Art Municipal** on c/Monturiol (April–Oct Mon–Sat 11am–1pm & 4–8.30pm, Sun 11am–1pm; 150ptas) features local artists dealing with local themes, juxtaposing almost every modern style. The **Museu Perrot-Moore** in c/Vigilant 1 (Easter–Dec daily 10.30am–1.30pm & 4.30–8.30pm; 500ptas) now contains only Dalí prints plus a few Picassos, other works having been dispersed to various museums worldwide.

Practicalities

Buses (several a day from Roses, one a day from El Port de la Selva) arrive at c/Sant Vicens, on the edge of town, from where it's less than ten minutes' walk to the beachside Plaça Frederic Rahola. The main **tourist office** is in the centre of town at c/des Cotxe 2 (June–Sept Mon–Sat 10am–2pm & 4–9pm, Sun 10am–1pm; Oct–May Mon–Sat 10.30am–1pm & 4–8pm; ☎972/25 83 15); this, or the town plan posted at the bus stop, will indicate all **accommodation** possibilities, which dwindle to nil at peak season. Least expensive rooms are at one of three *fondas* scattered about town: *Cala d'Or* (☎972/25 81 49; ③); *Veli* (☎972/25 84 70; ③), the best situated, below the church at Plaça de Església 5; and *Encarna* (☎972/25 80 19; ③). Moving one notch up, *Hostal Marina*, c/Frederic Rahola 2 (☎972/25 81 99; ④), and *Hostal Cristina*, c/la Riera 3 (☎972/25 81 38; ④), are both closer to the water and have pricier rooms with bath and off-season discounts. For **camping** – plus some cabins (③) – there's the noisy *Camping Cadaqués* (☎972/25 81 26; April–Sept), 1km along the road to Port Lligat.

The harbourside esplanade is chock-a-block with fairly indistinguishable pizzerias and **restaurants**. Three that stand out are *El Pescador* on Riba Nemesi Llorens – off on the right as you face the water, good for *menus del dia* (1500ptas) and paella; *La Galiota*, at c/Narciso Monturiol 9, serving fancy seafood (Oct–May open weekends only); and *Don Quijote* at Avda. Caritat Serinyana 6, the main road running inland from the square to the bus terminal.

Port Lligat

There's no public transport to **PORT LLIGAT**, but there is a choice of cross-country routes for walkers. As the road north from Cadaqués descends and deteriorates, the landscape opens out on a scene of hotels and well-spaced homes – including the whitewashed **Casa Dalí**. Bought as a tiny fisherman's cottage in 1929 and gradually extended, the house is instantly recognizable by the Dalí giant-egg trademark. From March 15 to the end of September the house is open to visitors by appointment (☎972/25 80 63; maximum of 8 people at a time; 1200ptas); even when it's not open, Dalí-lovers may still think the pilgrimage worth it, and the scenery is terrific.

Roses

Five or six buses a day run from Cadaqués west to **ROSES** along a steep, winding road through umbrella pine forest and terraced hillsides; it can also be reached by a very rough, twenty-kilometre track starting at the southern end of Cadaqués, by the *Rocamar* hotel. The town is easily accessible, too, from Figueres, with frequent bus connections throughout the day. This area has been inhabited since at least 3000 BC, as shown by the dolmens hereabouts. Greeks from Asia Minor established the trading port of Rhoda here in about 1000 BC, and by the eleventh century AD the town had effectively supplanted nearby Castelló d'Empúries, by then silting up. In 1543, Carlos I of Spain built the now-ruined, star-shaped fortress of **La Ciudadela**, dismantled by the French during the Peninsular War.

Roses is big for these parts, and getting larger every year. Four kilometres of beach on the wide sweep of the **Golfo de Roses** have been emphatically discovered by the package-holiday industry, while the Narbonne–Barcelona highway has boosted the resort's development; the massive new development of Empuriabrava (sandwiched between the two halves of the Aiguamolls nature reserve) boasts itself "the biggest residential marina in the world". Outside the high season, Roses has a palm-fringed elegance of sorts, but by August it has gone to pieces, the tone set more by the water park on the outskirts. The beach is good, though, and the setting photogenic.

Practicalities

Buses arrive right outside the post office, and on the seafront promenade there's a **tourist office** – whose aid will have to be enlisted if you show up in mid-season without an **accommodation** reservation. At slower times you might sample *Hostal Creus*, c/Palmerola 10 (☎972/25 63 71; ③), *Hostal Rom*, c/Trinitat 35 (☎972/25 65 81; ③), and *Hostal Sant Jordi*, Playa del Rastrell (☎972/25 62 50; ④). There are also several huge **campsites** on the road between Roses and Figueres. Recommendations for **eating out** seem pointless, given Roses' full-blown status as a resort, with a predictable rash of cafés and restaurants, not to mention supermarkets, discos and "English breakfasts". One exception lies 5km out at Playa Almadraba, where the *Almadraba Park* offers pricey gourmet cookery (mid-April to mid-Oct; 4000ptas per person).

Parc Natural dels Aiguamolls de l'Empordà

Inland and mainly to the south of Roses extends the **Parc Natural dels Aiguamolls de l'Empordà**, an important wetland reserve created by the Catalan government in 1983 to save what remained of the Empordà marshland, which once covered the entire plain here. The park (daily dawn–dusk; free admission) is especially interesting in spring and autumn when the *tramontana* blows, grounding the migrating birds.

It's cut in half by the Roses–Figueres road, along which run numerous daily **buses** of the SARFA company (which manages most buses on the Costa Brava). To reach the heart of the park, get off the bus at Castelló d'Empúries (15min) and take the turning south in the direction of Sant Pere Pescador. After walking about 4km, you'll see a sign on the left pointing the way to the **visitors' centre** at El Cortalet (daily: June–Sept 9.30am–2pm & 4.30–7pm; Oct–May 9.30am–2pm & 3.30–6pm; ☎972/45 42 22), where you can rent binoculars and see an exhibition on the birds of the area and migrant species. Alternatively, take the twice daily Roses–Girona bus (via Sant Pere Pescador), which stops near the Aiguamolls visitors' centre; buses en route from Figueres (see below) to Palafrugell also stop at Sant Pere Pescador, about 3km south of the centre.

Numerous **trails and viewing hides** have been set up in the reserve, many of them within yards of the beaches of the bay of Roses. You'll almost certainly see marsh harriers and various waterfowl, and might spot bee-eaters, kingfishers and the rare glossy ibis. A lesser-known hide stands 5km from Castelló d'Empúries, on the road to Palau-Saverdera; you have to walk or hitch, watching out for the tiny signpost by an electricity pylon on the left.

Bases: Castelló d'Empúries, Sant Pere and Torroella

Eight kilometres west of Roses, **CASTELLÓ D'EMPÚRIES**, with its tiny medieval quarter astride the Riu Muga, makes much the best base for extended tours of the park. Good **accommodation** choices include the *Hostal Ca L'Anton* (☎972/25 05 09; ③), near the bus stop; *Fonda Cal Avi*, c/Muralla 23 (☎972/25 05 07; ②), the best budget option; and the well-sited *Hostal Canet* (☎972/25 03 40; ④), at Plaça Joc de la Pilota 2. All these establishments serve food, and while pricier than you'd expect for their categories, it's worth the extra to enjoy the narrow alleys, church and fine bridge in peace and quiet once the day-trippers have departed.

By contrast, **SANT PERE PESCADOR**, 8km to the south, is not nearly as appealing, though despite this the village is surprisingly developed, with a half-dozen places to **stay** – such as the one-star *El Molí*, Ctra. de la Platge 36 (☎972/52 00 69; ④). Within the park itself there's only the expensive **campsite** of *Nautic Almata* (☎972/45 44 77), lying between the two villages. Better than either might be the hamlet of **TORROELLA DE FLUVIÀ**, 4km southwest of Sant Pere, where *El Sugué* (☎972/55 00 67; ④) is a country house restored as an inn for up to 23 guests, with both cooking facilities and regional meals on offer. It's open all year round.

Figueres and around

FIGUERES is the capital of Alt Empordà county – the upper part of the massive alluvial plain formed by the rivers Muga and Fluvià – but its sole claim on most tourists, excepting its role as transport hub, is that **Salvador Dalí** (1904–89) was born here, began his career here and died here. Yet if you linger after touring the museum devoted to his work, you'll discover a pleasant town with a lively central *rambla* and adequate food and lodging.

From Figueres, most travellers head either to the coast or the high Pyrenees, ignoring the corner of the Albères immediately to the north of the town. From **Maçanet de Cabrenys** in the west to **Espolla** in the east stretches a virtually unknown region of semi-ruined villages hidden among resin-scented hills, dotted with occasional vineyards, olive groves and shady cork plantations.

The Town

Figueres' **Teatre-Museu Dalí** (July–Sept daily 9am–8pm, plus night visits, 10pm–12.30am: phone ☎972/51 19 76 for dates; Oct–June Tues–Sun 10.30am–5.15pm; 1000ptas), in Plaça Gala i Salvador Dalí, is the most visited museum in Spain after the Prado, but it's more a theatrical fantasy than a conventional art collection – appropriately, since the building was once the town theatre, which was the venue for Dalí's first exhibition of paintings in 1919 (when he was 14) but was destroyed at the end of the Spanish Civil War. You can't miss it: one outside wall is painted terracotta pink, decorated with yellow blobs and topped with giant eggs and a large glass dome. Every part of the burnt-out theatre, from the central courtyard and stage to the crypt, foyer and staircases, has been transformed by Dalí's unique designs and artworks: you view the face of Mae West constructed as a living room with a shiny red sofa as the lips, use telescopes and coin-op machines to see paintings and constructions move and change, and gaze at totem poles of TV sets and car tyres. Although many of Dalí's paintings and sculptures (and some by other artists) are on display, this is not a collection of Dalí's "greatest hits"; nonetheless, the assembly beggars description and is not to be missed.

After suffering severe burns in a 1984 fire, Dalí moved into the Torre Galatea, the tower adjacent to the museum. Controversy surrounded his final years, with some observers believing that he didn't so much choose to live as a recluse as find himself imprisoned by his three guardians, who controlled all his artistic and financial dealings. It is known, for instance, that Dalí signed blank canvases and sheets of paper; this has inevitably raised doubts concerning the authenticity of many of his later works.

The nearby **Museu de l'Empordà** at Rambla 1 (July–Sept Tues–Sat 11am–1pm & 4–9pm, Sun & public holidays 5–9pm; Oct–June Tues–Sat 11am–1pm & 3.30–7pm, Sun & public holidays 11am–2pm; 300ptas, or free with a Dalí museum ticket), a serious collection of paintings by regional artists and works borrowed from the Prado in Madrid, remains largely unvisited. Figueres also has a toy museum, the **Museu dels Joguets** (closed for repairs at the time of writing; ☎972/50 45 85), housed in a beautiful but crumbling old hotel in the Rambla, above *Cafe Emporium*. The only other sight is the huge seventeenth-century **Castell de Sant Ferran** to the northwest of town, the last bastion of the Republicans for a week in February 1939 after the fall of Barcelona. It's still in use by the military but the five-kilometre perimeter of star-shaped walls makes a good walk.

Practicalities

The **train station** lies directly east of the centre, in Plaça Estació; the **bus station**, opposite, has left-luggage lockers (300ptas a day), and information and tickets for local and international buses. The focal point of the town – the Rambla – is reached from the stations by walking west along c/Sant Llàtzer and then turning right along c/Nou. To find the central **tourist office**, at Plaça del Sol (☎972/50 31 55; June–Sept Mon–Sat 9am–9pm; Oct–May Mon–Fri 9am–7pm, Sat 9am–2pm), leave the Rambla by its southwest corner along c/Lasauca.

The least expensive **accommodation** in Figueres, though perfectly acceptable, is *Pensió Bartis*, c/Mendez Nunyez 2 (☎972/50 14 73; ①), near the bus and train stations. Moving up in price, roughly halfway between the central tourist office and the Museu Dalí, there's the friendly *Pensió Venta del Toro* on c/Pep Ventura (☎972/51 05 10; ②), while east of the museum, the *Bar Brindis* has *habitacions* at c/de la Muralla 12 (☎972/50 00 04; ②). For a very reasonable *hostal* right in the centre of town, try *Hostal L'Espanya* (☎972/50 08 69; ③) at c/Jonquera 26, very close to the Museu Dalí, or the cheaper but less attractive *Pensió Isabel II*, c/Isabel II 16 (☎972/50 47 35; ③). There's a good **youth hostel** (☎972/50 12 13; open all year except Sept; ①), at c/Anicet Pages 2, off Plaça del Sol, immediately behind the tourist office. **Camping** is about 2km out on the main road north, at the rather neglected and overpriced *Pous* (☎972/50 00 14).

A gaggle of tourist **restaurants** cram the narrow streets around the Dalí museum, particularly along c/Jonquera; they offer low-price menus of variable quality but usually charge extra for wine, water and coffee, which can double the bill. For excellent value, try the *Bar Brindis* (see above), a small down-to-earth bar-restaurant with hearty home cooking; plenty of locals come here for the 900ptas lunch menu, which includes bread, water and coffee. Far more stylish, and still reasonably priced, is *L'Agora* in the old casino building, on the corner of c/Ample and c/Peralada, a spacious, modern bar-restaurant with excellent menus (1350–2700ptas) including Catalan specialities. If money's no object, head for the *Hotel Duran*, c/Lasauca 5, where they serve generous regional dishes with a modern touch. The Rambla has several popular pavement **cafés**, though the cafés in Plaça Ajuntament, near the Dalí museum, are quieter and less cramped; look out, too, for good-value sandwich-and-*tapas* bars, such as the *Cosmos* in c/Peralada.

Moving on, frequent **trains** run north to the border and south to Barcelona. There are fairly regular SARFA **bus** services to Roses and Cadaqués, and less frequent services to Palafrugell and Girona; two smaller bus companies provide weekday services into the Albères, including La Jonquera, Espolla and Maçanet.

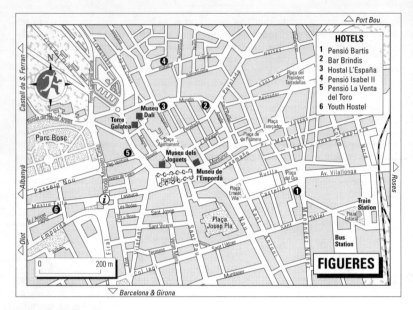

HOTELS

1 Pensió Bartis
2 Bar Brindis
3 Hostal L'España
4 Pensió Isabel II
5 Pensió La Venta del Toro
6 Youth Hostel

FIGUERES

North of Figueres

During World War II the region **north of Figueres** was so deserted that there were no Guardia Civil stationed between the Castell de Requesens and Port Bou, which made the eastern Albères a favoured escape route from France. A few foreigners – mainly Dutch and German – have moved in to convert the crumbling farms; otherwise the twentieth century seems far away.

The Maçanet region

An enjoyable excursion from Figueres involves taking the noon bus to **SANT LLORENÇ DE LA MUGA**, about 15km northwest of the town, near the shore of the Boadella reservoir. From Sant Llorenç a track crosses the hills to **MAÇANET DE CABRENYS**, looking down on the wetland fringes of the lake's west side – a haven for herons. The principal sight of Maçanet is the **Menhir O Pedra Dreta**, dating from around 3000 BC and standing 2m high on the western fringe of the village, just beyond Mas Pitxo. After spending the night at one of three **hostals** here – the *Cal Ratero*, c/de les Dòmines 6 (also known as *Hostal Oliveros*; ☎972/54 40 68; ③), is good – you can return to Figueres by one of the two daily buses. The bus goes through **DARNIUS**, a little to the north of which there's another menhir of the same name; should you want to explore the area, there's **accommodation** at the *Hostal Darnius*, Ctra. de Maçanet 41 (☎972/53 51 17; ③).

The Espolla region

The environs of Espolla, northeast of Figueres and served by just one daily bus from Figueres, is even more fruitful for prehistorians, with at least ten known sites in the immediate area. Easiest to find is the **Dolmen de la Cabana Arqueta**, dating from around 2500 BC; from Espolla take the Sant Climent road, and at the rising bend 1km beyond the village take the farm track to the right – the dolmen is ten minutes' walk on. The most important, however, is **Dolmen del Barranc**, the only carved tomb yet found in the area: it lies 3km from the village off the track leading north to the Col de Banyuls (see p.129).

ESPOLLA itself is a typical Alt Empordà village, its shuttered houses crammed in a labyrinth of streets that buzz each year with the flurry of the grape harvest. The only **accommodation** here is the friendly, family-run *La Manela*, Plaça del Carmé 7 (☎972/56 30 65; ③), which also serves good, inexpensive meals. There's also the more upscale *Can Calau* **restaurant** on the edge of the village.

Walking routes north

If you continue along the Col de Banyuls path to the goat-overrun farmstead of Jaça de l'Home, and then turn right onto the waymarked GR11, you can reach the ruined, tenth-century monastery of **Sant Quirze de Colera** in around four hours: it's startlingly impressive in its wilderness location. From here, bear southeast to the village of **VILAMANISCLE**, where you can spend the night (ask for private rooms or camp), and pick up the Figueres-bound bus early in the morning. The walk from the monastery to the coast at Colera or Llançà will take about five hours more.

Alternatively, from Espolla it's possible to walk northwest for a very long day to the **Col du Perthus** via Cantallóps, where there are more dolmens – enquire locally before setting out, though, as the route goes through army territory, and shooting is common on weekdays. **CANTALLÓPS** is also the start of a well-marked path to the **Castell de Requesens**, an easy walk that becomes increasingly worthwhile as the views over Alt Empordà grow ever wider and the castle looms ahead. Standing amidst marvellous cork forest, the dilapidated castle is usually closed, but keys can be obtained at the nearby farm.

THE SPANISH VALLEYS

The higher valleys on the Spanish side of the Eastern Pyrenees don't really begin until well away from the Mediterranean coast. The easiest access to the mountains lies through **Girona**, 40km south of Figueres, an ancient capital with ample cultural appeal; it also has Catalunya's largest airport outside Barcelona, handling year-round charter flights from Britain. From Girona, the most attractive route is to head northwest through lakeside **Banyoles** to the exquisite medieval town of **Besalú**, then west into the heart of the volcanic **Garrotxa** region, centred on the town of **Olot**. Continuing in the same direction brings you to **Ripoll** and its famous monastery, or to **Sant Joan de les Abadesses**, with another monastic cathedral. Just northeast of here, **Camprodon** is the first town truly enclosed by the foothills, but for a more dramatic introduction to the Spanish Catalan Pyrenees, the upper **Freser valley** awaits just north of Ripoll, with its popular narrow-gauge train and grandiose shrine at **Núria**.

Public transport connections from Girona towards the hills are excellent, with numerous daily bus departures as far as Olot, via Banyoles and Besalú; a few services continue on to Ripoll. Heading northeast from Girona, there are frequent train services towards Figueres and the northerly Costa Brava resorts.

Girona

The obvious way-station on any eastern approach to the Spanish Pyrenees is **GIRONA** (formerly Gerona), which sits on a fortified hill above the occasionally stagnant but carp-clogged Riu Onyar, just before it joins the Ter. Like Perpignan – the equivalent gateway city on the French side – it has a distinctly Arab flavour, but in this instance the influence dates from the Moorish conquest, retained in the architecture and narrow streets of its old quarter. Full of historical and cultural interest, it's a fine place to relax before or after tackling the mountains, and one where you're likely to spend more time than planned. At least two nights are recommended: although the place now gets plenty of attention from passing French motorists and day-tripping tour groups from nearby Costa Brava resorts, calm returns to the old town after dark, when Girona's abiding character reasserts itself.

The City

The "City of a Thousand Sieges", Girona has been fought over in almost every century since it was the Roman fortress of Gerunda on the Via Augusta. In the eighth century it suffered seven sieges and became the seat of an earldom within Charlemagne's empire. The Moors stayed for over two hundred years, a fact apparent in the web of narrow central lanes, and there was also a continuous Jewish presence through six centuries. By the eighteenth century Girona had been besieged on 21 occasions, and in the next century it earned itself the nickname "Immortal" by surviving five attacks, of which the longest was a seven-month assault by the French. Each occupier left a mark on the architecture of the town, and connoisseurs can identify a succession of styles in various buildings from Roman Classicism to *Modernistame*. The overall impression, though, is of an overwhelmingly beautiful medieval city, amplified by its river setting and adorned by multi-storeyed pastel houses leaning over the banks.

Arrival and information

Girona's **airport**, 13km south of the city, is used mainly by Costa Brava package charters whose clientele are taken to their resorts by special buses; accordingly there's no airport bus, so you'll have to take a taxi into town. The **train station** is at Plaça d'Espanya, southwest of the centre; the **bus station** – also serving international arrivals – is at the rear of the same building. Both are a mere twenty-minute walk from the old quarter, where you'll probably spend most of your time.

The central **tourist office** (Mon–Fri 8am–8pm, Sat 8am–2pm & 4–8pm; July & Aug also Sun 9am–2pm; ☎972/22 65 75) is at Rambla de la Llibertat 1, the tree-lined promenade one block behind the river, with a satellite branch inside the train station (Mon–Sat 9am–2pm); both offices have English-speaking staff and stock useful maps and brochures, accommodation lists and local transport timetables. If you can read (or at least decode) Catalan, there are two **listings pamphlets** usually left lying around bars and restaurants: the monthly *La Lluna*, and the weekly *Cartellera* (out Thurs).

Accommodation

There are nearly a dozen reasonable **fondas and hostals** in Girona, on both sides of the river, so with few exceptions (indicated below) you shouldn't need to book ahead, except perhaps at the height of summer. Although there are a few places near the train and bus station, given a reasonable arrival time and light luggage, you should make for the old quarter. The nearest **campsite** is 8km south at Fornells de la Selva (☎972/47 61 17; year-round), with excellent amenities and an English-speaking proprietor, though you might prefer to camp at livelier Banyoles, half an hour northwest (see p.146).

Alberg de Joventut, c/dels Ciutadans 9, near the Plaça del Vi (☎972/21 80 03 or 20 15 54). Girona's youth hostel has a central old-town location and smart modern facilities, including laundry, TV and video. However, it's hardly better value than the cheaper of the pensions, and if you're over 25 it's actually more expensive. Reception open 8–11am and 6–10pm; breakfast included in price, supper available. ①–②.

Fonda Barnet, c/Santa Clara 16 (☎972/20 00 33). Cheapest digs in town – crumbling bath-less rooms, unrated by the tourism authorities – but an unbeatable riverside location near the Pont de Pedra. Look for the ground-floor *comedor* (see "Eating and drinking", below). ②.

Pensió Bellmirall, c/Bellmirall 3 (☎972/20 40 09). An attractive choice, close to the cathedral, nicely done up with stone walls, artefacts and paintings. Only seven rooms of varying sizes, which need to be reserved. Price includes breakfast. ④–⑤.

Pensió Gerunda, c/de Barcelona 34 (☎972/20 30 39). Just in front of the train station, on the main through road, this makes a reasonable en-suite fallback for late arrivals. ③.

Pensió Lladó, c/de la Barca 31 (☎972/21 09 98). Basic and slightly dubious, but handy for many monuments and museums. ②.

Hotel Peninsular, c/Nou 3 (☎972/20 38 00). Well-located, if bland, hotel just across the Pont de Pedra from the old town, with a choice between shared and en-suite bathrooms. ③–④.

Hostal Reyma, Pujada del Rei Martí 15 (☎972/20 02 28). Girona's best budget choice, close to many attractions and – handy if you're driving – parking spaces; reservations suggested. Singles and balconied rooms available, with a choice between shared and en-suite bathrooms. ③–④.

Pensió Viladomat, c/de Ciutadans 5 (☎972/20 31 76). Clean, white interiors, with plenty of cell-like singles, in this central building; no en-suites. ③.

The City

Although most of the modern city sprawls southwest of the Riu Onyar, all points of interest are concentrated in the compact medieval quarter, or **Casc Antic**, spilling down the north hillside to the east bank. As it only takes a half-hour or so to walk from end to end, this fascinating zone of parapeted walls, stepped streets and secluded courtyards is easy to explore thoroughly. Recent restoration and inevitable gentrification have not yet managed to completely banish the everyday life of local shops and bars. Girona is also home to a small university, its student contingent serving as a welcome corrective to chi-chi galleries and exclusive shops, which reflect the fact that Girona and its province have the highest per capita income in Spain.

The Catedral and the Museu d'Art

Balanced on a steep slope and reached by a majestic Baroque staircase, the **Catedral** (summer daily 10am–6pm; closed afternoons in winter), is the focus of the *Casc Antic* and, with its emphasis on width and height, the outstanding example of "Catalan Gothic". There has been a place of worship here since a temple was built in Roman times, and a Moorish mosque stood on the site before the foundation of the cathedral in 1038. Most of the building dates from the fifteenth century, though parts are four hundred years older, notably the five-storey **Torre de Carlemany** and the Romanesque **cloisters** with their exquisite sculpted capitals.

The main **facade**, remodelled in the eighteenth century, writhes with exuberant ornamentation: figures, coats-of-arms, and Saints Peter and Paul flanking the door. Inside, the cathedral is awesome: no aisles, just a single **nave** with a span of 22m, the widest Gothic vault in the world. Contemporary sceptics deemed the proposed design unsafe, and the vault was only raised after an appeal by the architect, Guillermo Bofill, to an independent panel of architects. The walls rise to stained-glass windows, the only thing interrupting the sweep of space being an enormous organ installed last century.

Admittance to the cloisters is by the same ticket that gets you into the **Museu Capitular** (Tues–Sat 10am–2pm & 4–7pm, Sun 10am–2pm; 400ptas), a small but first-rate collection of religious art that includes a copy of Beatus's *Commentary on the Apocalypse* made in 975 by Mozarabic miniaturists, and a magnificent tapestry of *The Creation* dating from around 1100, the finest surviving specimen of Romanesque textile, depicting in strong colours the seasons and elements of the earth.

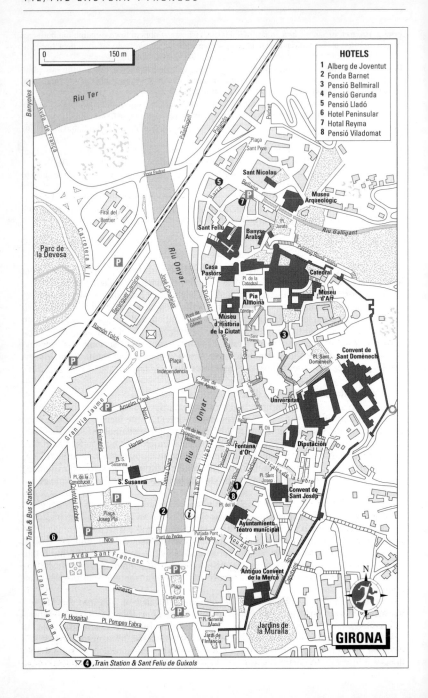

0   150 m

HOTELS

1 Alberg de Joventut
2 Fonda Barnet
3 Pensió Bellmirall
4 Pensió Gerunda
5 Pensió Lladó
6 Hotel Peninsular
7 Hotal Reyma
8 Pensió Viladomat

Riu Ter

Banyoles

Avda. de França

Parc de
la Devesa

Firal del
Bestier

Carretera N.II

P

Berenguer Carrec

José Canalejas

Ramón Folch

Riu Onyar

Pont Barcat

Pedret

Pedret

Plaça
Sant Pere

Sant Nicolau

Bellaire

Barca

Museu
Arqueològic

Sant Feliu

Banys
Àrabs

Riu Galligant

Pl.
Jurats

Passeig Reina Joana

Casa
Pastórs

Pl. de la
Catedral

Catedral

Córdona

Pia
Almoina

Museu
d'Art

Museu
d'Història
de la Ciutat

Pont de
Manuel Gómez

Força

Pl. Sant
Llorenç

Pl. Sant
Domènech

Convent de
Sant Dòmenech

Plaça
Independencia

Pont de
Sant Agustí

Universitat

Gran Via Jaume I

Anselm Clavé

F. Eiximenis

Pont de les
Pescateries
Velles

Pl. Oli

Fontana
d'Or

Diputación

P

Hortes

Pl. S.
Susanna

Santa Clara

Riu Onyar

Rambla Llibertat

Les Escales de la Llebre

Train & Bus Stations

Pl. de la
Constitució

S. Susanna

P

Plaça
Josep Pla

P

Ciutadans

Pl. Sant
Josep

Convent de
Sant Josep

Nou

Avda Sant Francesc

Gran Via Jaume I

Ginesta

Pont de Pedra

Pl. del Vi

Putjada Pont
de Pedra

Ayuntamiento,
Teatro municipal

Nou de Teatre

Pl. Hospital

Pl. Pompeu Fabra

Plaça
Catalunya

P

Antiguo Convent
de la Mercè

Calabuig

Pl. General
Marvà

Jardi de
l'Infància

Jardins de
la Muralla

N

GIRONA

Girona's **Museu d'Art** (summer Tues–Sat 10am–7pm, Sun 10am–2pm; winter Tues–Sat 10am–6pm, Sun 10am–2pm; 200ptas), in the well-restored episcopal palace next door, has galleries arranged chronologically as you climb through five floors. Early wings highlight Romanesque art, particularly rare manuscripts and impressive *Majestats* (wooden images of Christ garbed in a tunic), before progressing through Renaissance works to the collection of nineteenth- and twentieth-century Catalan art on the top two floors. Noteworthy here is a selection of pieces by the so-called "Olot School" (better represented in the Olot museum, for which see p.150), depictions of the French siege and some entertaining pieces of *Modernista* sculpture in the highest hall.

Sant Feliu and around

One of Girona's best-known landmarks is the tower of **Sant Feliu**, best viewed as you descend the cathedral steps. Shortened by a lightning strike in 1581 and never repaired, the slim belfry tops a hemmed-in church that happily combines Romanesque, Gothic and Baroque styles. Massive restoration works are under way at present, as well as some "urban clearance" on the river side of the church.

The narrow streets north of Sant Feliu towards the river, especially **c/de la Barca**, are a bit frowsier than the norm for Girona, with their bare bars and corner groceries. This was in fact once a rather tame red-light district, but the area has been cleaned up, with many premises bricked up and hung with "for sale" signs. Doubtless this little warren will soon receive the sort of attention lately visited on c/de la Barca's southern continuations, c/Calderers and c/Ballesteries, now lined with lively bars and exclusive shops.

The Banys Arabs

Very near the cathedral, reached by going through the twin-towered **Portal de Sobreportas**, and then turning right, stand the so-called **Banys Arabs** or "Arab Baths" (summer Tues–Sat 10am–7pm, Sun 10am–2pm; winter Tues–Sun 10am–2pm; 100ptas), probably built by Moorish craftsmen during the thirteenth century, some two hundred years after the Moorish occupation of Girona had ended. The finest of their type in Spain apart from those at Granada, they have the usual under-floor heating system and the Roman-derived layout of three principal rooms. The *apodyterium* or changing room is the most interesting, despite the insertion of some unfortunate modern art; there are niches for one's clothes and a stone bench for relaxation after bathing, while the room is unusually lit by a central vaulted skylight supported on an octagon of columns.

The Museu Arqueològic and the city walls

From the Banys Arabs it's a short downhill stroll, over the usually dry Riu Galligant, to the **Museu Provincial Arqueològic** (Tues–Sat 10am–1pm & 4.30–7pm, Sun 10am–1pm; 200ptas), housed in the former church of Sant Pere Galligants. The church itself contains Roman artefacts, while the fine **cloisters** shelter medieval relics, including nearly a dozen inscribed stones from the former Jewish cemetery. The Romanesque architecture is perhaps the most memorable feature of a visit, reinforced by the inclusion of a full-size replica of the west rose window in the transept. Extensive galleries above the cloisters methodically outline the region's history from Paleolithic to Roman times, but unless you read Catalan or Spanish you'll get little out of these exhibits.

Near the museum you can investigate the nearby Passeig Arqueològic, with steps through landscaped grounds leading up onto the **city walls**, from where there are fine views over Girona and the Ter valley. Once onto the ramparts, walkways lead completely around their perimeter, with an intermediate bail-out behind the Sant Domènech convent before the final descent to Plaça Catalunya, at the south end of the old town.

The Call

Heading back south instead of north through the Portal de Sobreportas, c/de la Força leads past the **Call**, reached via the intersecting c/Sant Llorenç and considered the best-preserved Jewish quarter in western Europe. A **Jewish community** was well established in Girona from at least the ninth century – probably earlier – with an initial settlement near the cathedral shifting up to c/de la Força. With a population of almost a thousand at its peak, the new quarter became known as the *Call*, forming a semi-autonomous town within Girona, under royal protection in exchange for payment of a tribute. However, Jews here suffered systematic and escalating persecution from the eleventh century onwards, conditions only improving temporarily under Alfons II and Alfons III of Aragón. In 1391 a mob stormed the *Call* and killed forty of its residents, after which the neighbourhood became a restrictive ghetto like those of northern Europe until the expulsion of the Jews from Spain a century later.

For an idea of the layout of this sector of tall narrow houses and maze-like interconnecting passages, visit the **Centre Bonastruc Ça Porta** (June–Oct Mon–Sat 10am–9pm, Sun 10am–2pm; Nov–May Tues–Sun 10am–2pm; 200ptas), signposted as "Call Jueu" at the top of c/Sant Llorenç. Opened to the public in 1975, this multilevel complex of rooms, stairways and a courtyard was the site of the synagogue, the kosher slaughterhouse and community baths. Excavations are ongoing, with nearby alleys sealed off pending investigations; at the main site there's an information and ticket office, as well as temporary exhibitions in the lower levels.

The Museu d'Historia de la Ciutat

Not part of the *Call* proper but housed in the eighteenth-century convent of Sant Antoni just across c/de la Força, the **Museu d'Historia de la Ciutat** (Tues–Sat 10am–2pm & 5–7pm, Sun 10am–2pm; 100ptas) completes Girona's complement of museums, and despite being labelled only in Catalan, is likely to prove the most rewarding – certainly the most eclectic – one. A portion of the convent's cemetery is visible on the right as you enter, with niches for the (vanished) deceased. The entire ground floor is given over to the development of local industry and technology, with an antique dealer's bonanza, salvaged from around the province, of ancient phones, printing presses, dynamos and even an arc-lamp cine projector. The first floor covers the evolution of the *sardana*, the history of broadcasting in Catalunya – complete with some magnificent old radio sets – and Roman Gerunda, featuring a rather crude mosaic from a villa on the surrounding plain. On the top floor is a modern art exhibition, including a few works by Dalí and Miró.

Eating and drinking

Girona's chic **restaurants** are grouped along and just off c/de la Força, while outdoor daytime **cafés** cluster on and around the riverside Rambla de la Llibertat, and on the parallel Plaça del Vi. **Bars** are more scattered, though some of interest are along c/Ballesteries and its various continuations.

Restaurants

Fonda Barnet, c/Santa Clara 16. The *comedor* of this hotel is the cheapest in Girona, and the food's better than the spartan surroundings would suggest.

El Barri Veil, c/Cort-Reial 17. Cheap and cheerful competition for *Los Jara* (see below).

Boira, Plaça de la Independencia 17. The best food on the square, with 1200-pta (lunch only) and 2000-pta menus. Outdoor seating, or upstairs in the river-view salon; there's also a street-level bar with river windows that's good for breakfast.

Can Lluis, c/dels Alemanys 3. Pizzas, pasta and salads, just around the corner from *Pensió Bellmirall*. Supper only; closed Mon.

Los Jara, c/de la Força 4. Ample 1100-pta menus served in the stone-walled room behind the bar, though the quality and service don't always match the quantity.

La Penyora, c/Nou del Teatre 3. Catalan *nouvelle cuisine* in suitably minimalist surroundings; achingly slow service (count on two hours for supper), painfully high bills. Only really worth it at lunchtime, when there's a reasonable *menú*. Closed Tues.

El Pou de la Call, c/de la Força 14. Good meals in pleasant surroundings right next to the *Call*; 1750-pta menu, otherwise count on about 3000ptas per head.

Bars and cafés

Antiga, Plaça del Vi 8. A nice line in cakes, puddings, *orxata* and other sweet delights at this marble-table spot.

L'Arcada, Rambla de la Llibertat 38. Bar-café tucked under the arcades, with an old-fashioned interior and pleasant outdoor tables.

El Cul de la Lleona, c/Calderers 8. A trendy café, with outside seating by an old fountain and limited lunch *menú*.

Inèdit, c/Figuerola 12 in the new town. Lively bar with acoustic concerts Wed, taped rock at weekends.

Café Le Bistrot, Pujada de Sant Domènech. Snacks, crepes and drinks until late, either outside on the steps below the church, or inside in cool, stylish, tiled-floor surroundings.

La Plaçeta, c/Carreras-Peralta 7 (a widening in c/de la Força). Loud, crowded music pub with tables outside.

Silent Block, c/Palafrugell 20, Pedret district. Currently the cool techno and Brit-pop bar; happy hours Thurs–Sat 11pm–1am.

Cafeteria Sol, Plaça del Vi. No-nonsense bar that's good for breakfast under the arcade.

Tapa't, c/Cort-Reial 1. An outstanding *tapas* bar with generous portions, where you can assemble a small meal for about 1000ptas.

La Terra, c/Ballesteries 23. The main student hangout, open until late: a wonderfully cavernous bar, with tiles everywhere and river-view windows.

Listings

Airport ☎972/18 66 00 for flight information.

Banks and exchange There's an exchange bureau in the train station, and you'll find several banks with ATMs on Rambla de la Llibertat.

Books and maps Ulysus, c/Ballesteries 29, is a travel-book specialist with lots of guides to Catalunya, as well as all Editorial Alpina and many SGE and IGN maps.

Buses Teisa (☎972/20 02 75) runs services northeast through the Garrotxa to Olot.

Car rental and driving Most agencies are found on c/de Barcelona, near the train station. If you break down, contact Reial Automobil Club de Catalunya, c/de Barcelona 30 (☎972/20 08 68).

Emergencies Creu Roja (☎972/22 22 22).

Hospitals Dr Josep Trueta, Avda. França 60 (☎972/20 27 00); at night go instead to the Institut de la Salut (☎972/20 00 08).

Newspapers English-language papers are available at the train station and along Rambla de la Llibertat.

Police Policia Municipal at c/Bacià 4 (☎972/20 45 26).

Taxis The most convenient ranks are at Plaça de Independencia, Pont de Pedra (old town) and the train station.

Train information RENFE ☎972/20 70 93.

The Fluvià valley and the Garrotxa

To the northwest of Girona lies the beautiful Garrotxa region, bisected by the Río Fluvià, which for much of its course is more or less paralleled by the main C150 road up towards Andorra. Lush and humid, the landscape of the Garrotxa fosters an extraordinary diffuse light, which can make this old-fashioned rural area nostalgically resemble an early photograph.

South of the Fluvià extends the volcanic **Baixa Garrotxa**, where ten thousand years of erosion have moulded dormant cinder cones into rounded and fertile hills. The northern part, the **Alta Garrotxa**, is an area of deserted farms set amid low chunky mountains, the highest of which – the 1558-metre Puig de Comanegra – straddles the frontier.

Any route traced straight through the area will miss something special. The easiest option on public transport is to take the regular bus from Girona along the C150, which is often spectacular, especially as it approaches resolutely medieval **Besalú**, or **Castellfollit de la Roca**, whose houses peer over a sheer basalt cliff. But along this road you see little of backcountry Garrotxa. A more rewarding approach with your own vehicle is the tiny C524 from **Banyoles** to **Olot**, capital of the Garrotxa region, via **Santa Pau** (a much less frequent bus route). Here, there's some easy, scenic walking in the **Parc Natural de la Zona Volcanica**, set aside to protect the best of the Garrotxa's landscapes, including remnants of the great beech wood known as **La Fageda d'en Jordà**.

Banyoles

The Pyrenees are only on the horizon at **BANYOLES**, just 17km north of Girona, but it's a moderately pleasant place to pass a few hours, or the night, on the way to Besalú or Santa Pau. What makes Banyoles special, however, is the **Estany** (lake), 64m at its deepest point just offshore from the football stadium. Although under state protection since l951, it's no longer the wilderness it once was: cruises, rowing boats and pedaloes are on offer, and private waterside gazebos, lakeside hotels and restaurants have transformed the lake, a process completed by its hosting of the 1992 Olympic rowing events. Landlubbers can have an enjoyable picnic on the shore, throwing any leftovers to the famous giant carp. The eight-kilometre walking circuit of the lake passes through the tiny hamlet of **Porqueres**, whose barrel-vaulted church of **Santa Maria** was consecrated in 1182 and has unusual capitals with plant and animal designs.

Back in town, the arcaded **Plaça Major**, studded with plane trees, has hosted a Wednesday market since the eleventh century. From here, signs point the way northeast to the nearby **Museu Arqueològic Comarcal** (July & Aug Tues–Sat 11am–1.30pm & 4–6.30pm, Sun 10.30am–2pm; Sept–June Tues–Sun 10.30am–1.30pm & 4–6.30pm; 500ptas). Installed in a fourteenth-century almshouse on Plaça de la Font, the collection used to contain the famous jawbone of a pre-Neanderthal man found in the nearby Serinya caves, but nowadays you have to make do with a replica; authentic specimens include Paleolithic tools and bison, elephant and lion bones, all found locally. The **Museu Darder d'Historia Natural**, in nearby Plaça dels Estudis (same hours, same admission ticket), has a useful display of local flora and fauna. Further northeast of the two museums stands the originally ninth-century Benedictine **Monestir de Sant Esteve**, easily the most imposing structure in the old quarter and the kernel around which the town later grew. It's generally closed to the public, who miss seeing a sumptuous fifteenth-century *retablo* (altarpiece) by Joan Antigo, and an eighteenth-century cloister. Between the monastery and the museums stands the **Llotja del Tint**, the medieval dye market.

Practicalities

All **buses** stop on Passeig de la Industria, with the ticket office nearby at the intersection with c/Alvarez de Castro. The Plaça Major lies two minutes' walk northeast from here, while the **tourist office** is in the opposite direction at Passeig de la Industria 25 (Mon–Fri 10am–3pm & 5–7pm, Sat 10am–1pm; June & Aug also open Sat afternoon & Sun; ☎972/57 55 73). The Centre Excursionista de Banyoles at c/del Puig 6, near Sant Esteve (Mon, Wed & Fri 7–9pm), has a range of maps and information available for local **treks and hikes**.

With Girona so near, there's little point in staying in Banyoles, where most **accommodation** is overpriced anyway. An exception is the immaculate *Fonda Comas*, c/del Canal 19 (☎972/57 01 27; ③), west of Plaça dels Estudis, a modern but unobtrusive building built around a courtyard, with its own restaurant. **Camping** by the lake takes better advantage of the town's setting; there are four sites, including the large *El Llac* (☎972/57 03 05), on the way to Porqueres, just below and before the church.

There are a limited number of places to **eat** in the old quarter, but enough perhaps to make Banyoles a feasible lunch stop. *Fonda Comas* offers a good 1200-peseta *menu* (wine and IVA extra), while *La Parra*, on the Carrer de la Rambla side of Plaça de les Rodes in the northwest of the old town, has a proper lunch *comedor* beside the bar. *Les Olles* at Plaça dels Estudis 6 – essentially a bar serving a bit of food at outdoor seats – is a distinct third choice. Eating at the several hotel restaurants overlooking the lake is more expensive, though the *Mirallac* at Passeig Darder 50 won't break the bank as long as you eat meat rather than fish. Best venue for a coffee or evening **drink** are the various bars and cafés under the arcades around Plaça Major.

Besalú

From the road, the imposing twelfth-century fortified bridge by the confluence of the Fluvià and Capellada rivers is the only sign that there is anything remarkable about **BESALÚ**, 14km from Banyoles. But pass under the portcullis in the bridge's central gatehouse and you'll enter a medieval settlement that arguably provides the most interesting half-day outing from Girona. Steep narrow streets, sunbaked squares and dark arcaded shops bear silent witness to an illustrious history out of proportion to its current humble status. Besalú was an important town before the medieval period – Roman, Visigothic, Frankish and Moorish despots came and went – but all the surviving monuments date from the eleventh century and after, when it briefly became the seat of a small, independent principality.

Christian rather than Moorish intolerance drove the Jews out of Besalú, and their **Miqvé** (ritual bath house) was later turned into a dye works. Originally attached to a synagogue, the *Miqvé* (key from tourist office; 50ptas per person) hides inconspicuously down by the river, at the end of signposted Baixada de Mikwè, underneath the bridge-viewing platform. It proves to be a high, single-vaulted chamber, with steps leading down into the former plunge-pool.

Continuing in the same direction, you'll reach the porticoed **Plaça Llibertat**, enveloped by medieval buildings such as the thirteenth-century Casa de la Vila, now home to the *Ajuntament* and the tourist office. The weekly **market** takes place here on Tuesday, under the arches. Majestically arcaded c/Tallaferro leads uphill to the ruined shell of Santa Maria (no admission), which for just two years (1018–1020) was designated cathedral of the bishopric of Besalú; political union with Barcelona meant the end of its short-lived episcopal independence.

Further west, you'll emerge onto a vast, fan-shaped square, the Prat de Sant Pere, dominated by the twelfth-century Benedictine monastery church of **Sant Pere**. The barrel-vaulted interior is impressive enough, with a fine colonnaded ambulatory preserving some carved column capitals, but the church's most eye-catching feature is the arched Gothic window of the main facade, flanked by a pair of grotesque stone lions; it's best admired from a pair of cafés immediately opposite. Also on the square is the **Casa Cornellà**, a rare example of Romanesque domestic architecture which houses a museum of antique household and agricultural implements.

Working your way up towards the main road brings you to **Sant Vicenç**, whose east entrance arches are decorated with mythical monsters; it, too, has a Gothic window, high up on its southwest facade, while the little landscaped square around it, Plaça Sant Vicenç, is far more intimate than Prat de Sant Pere.

Practicalities

Buses stop on the main road, from where it's a short walk south to the central Plaça de la Llibertat. The **tourist office** here (daily 10am–2pm & 4–7pm; ☎972/59 12 40) keeps the usual stock of brochures, as well as keys to locked monuments, and can help sort out vacancies in the surrounding area when accommodation in Besalú itself is full (often the case in summer).

If you can manage it, **staying** is recommended, since Besalú's character changes completely for the better once the daily quota of trippers has departed. Of the three accommodation outfits, the pin-neat, en-suite *Fonda Venència* at c/Major 8 (☎972/59 12 57; ③) is the quietest and best value; *Residència Marià*, Plaça Llibertat 4 (☎972/59 01 06; ④) is a more atmospheric, rambling old building; while *Fonda Siqués* (☎972/59 01 10; ③), at Avda. Lluis Companys 6, just east of the bus stop on the main through highway, is the noisiest of the three. The most reasonable **food** is at *Can Quei*, Plaça Sant Vicenç 4, with well-selected menus at 1100ptas and 1700ptas served in the smart *comedor*, while *Fonda Siqués* has a 2500-pta menu which includes coffee, water and wine, but not VAT. If money's no object, you can burn it to the tune of 4000ptas at *Pont Vell*, c/Pont Vell 28, which has tables more or less under the bridge. At Plaça Llibertat 14, the lively bar-restaurant *Curia Reial* (closed Tues and Jan), housed in a fine old building, falls somewhere in between, with attractive outdoor seating overlooking the river.

Castellfollit de la Roca

CASTELLFOLLIT DE LA ROCA, 14km west of Besalú, promises great things as it perches atop a sixty-metre precipice overlooking the Riu Fluvià, with the church crowded by houses onto the very rim of the cliff. Arrival is most impressive by night, when spotlights play on the natural basalt columns. But as the road curls around and up, Castellfollit proves to be a disappointment, with a traffic-plagued main street whose tightly packed rows of grubby brown buildings give no hint of the extraordinary palisade. You might leave your bus or car, however, to sample the view over the edge of the cliff: head south from the prominent clocktower to the church and the banistered viewing platform behind. On the through road, 100m downhill from the clocktower, Castellfollit's **Museum of Sausages** (Mon–Sat 9.30am–1.30pm & 4–8pm, Sun 9.30am–2pm & 4.30–8pm), run by the Sala family to celebrate a century and a half in the skin-stuffing business, is almost certainly unique, as claimed. Pungent with the smell of sausages, it's mainly an excuse to sell them (counter on the premises); the exhibits consist mostly of antique production machinery.

There's absolutely no need to **stay** the night, but if you get stuck, try the two-star *Pensió Cala Paula*, next to the clocktower at Plaça de Sant Roc 3 (☎972/29 40 15; ③), which has a decent and popular ground-floor bar-restaurant.

Olot

Unlike Castellfollit, **OLOT** – capital of the Garrotxa region – is far more rewarding than initial impressions of its sprawling, anonymous outskirts would suggest. Follow any of the narrow lanes north into the *barri antic* from the through road, and the scene quickly changes to one of intimate squares, elegant shops, a pleasant *rambla* and convivial bars. Except for the church of Sant Esteve with its landmark belfry just behind the *rambla*, most of the centre consists of eighteenth- and nineteenth-century buildings, a consequence of devastating fifteenth-century earthquakes which levelled the medieval town. Olot is poised between three (dormant) volcanic cones easily acessible without long treks or drives; the bare-topped **Montsacopa volcano**, in particular, is worth the walk, with its summit chapel of Sant Francesc affording good views. Moreover, frequent bus connections and a decent choice of food and lodging make Olot the best base for touring the Garrotxa.

The town's enduring prosperity is based on its crafts tradition. A religious-images business was established here in 1880 and remained a major industry until the 1950s. Cotton-milling also flourished during the late eighteenth century, alongside workshops printing the textiles with coloured patterns; the latter were instrumental in the formation of the *Escola Pública de Dibuix* (Public School of Drawing) in 1783. Joaquim Vayreda i Vila (1843–94), one founder of the **Olot School** of painters which included Josep Berga i Boix and Modest Urgell, was a pupil at the drawing school, but an 1871 trip to Paris brought him under the spell of Millet's rural painting, and presumably exposed him to the Impressionists. From these influences, and the strange Garrotxa scenery, sprang the distinctive style of the Olot artists.

Arrival and information

Olot is easily accessible by **bus**: from Barcelona and Girona through Banyoles and Besalú, direct from Figueres, from Ripoll and Sant Joan de les Abadesses, and from Banyoles via Mieres and Santa Pau. The helpful county **tourist office** (Mon–Fri 9am–2pm & 3–7pm, Sat 10am–1pm & 5–7pm, Sun 11am–2pm) is right opposite the bus station on c/Bisbe Lorenzana; there's also a municipally funded information office at no. 33 of the street's westerly continuation, c/Mulleras (Mon–Fri 9am–1pm & 4–7pm, Sat 10am–1pm & 5–7pm), in the central market building. One or the other should stock all-important schematic maps of the designated walking routes through the Garrotxa. Next to the whimsical Teatre Principal on Passeig d'en Blay, the very irregularly open Centro Excursionista de Olot is another potential source of information on hiking and the great outdoors. At the southeast end of the same *passeig*, on the ground floor of a *Modernista* building, the Drac **bookstore** keeps commercial maps and guides (in Spanish) for the area.

Accommodation

There are several reasonable, central **lodgings**, as well as a less convenient **youth hostel**. Closest **campsites** are the riverside *Les Tries* (☎972/26 24 05), 2km east of town on the main Girona road – shady and offering discounted tickets to the swimming pool next door – and *La Fageda* (☎972/27 12 39), 4km out on the minor road to Santa Pau.

Alberg Torre Malagrida, Passeig de Barcelona 15 (☎972/26 42 00). Olot's youth hostel lies southwest of the centre, in an apartment block overlooking the river, about halfway to the Casal dels Volcans. Reception hours are 8–10am and 1pm–midnight; closed Sept, and Sun and Mon in winter. ①.

Hostal La Garrotxa, Plaça de Mora 3, 2nd floor (☎972/26 98 07). Good location, near the museum and restaurants; doubles sharing bathrooms only. ②.

Pensió Narmar, c/Sant Roc 1, on the corner of Plaça Major (☎972/26 98 07). Clean, modern rooms, including a few cheaper singles with sinks. ③.

Hostal Sant Bernat, Ctra. de les Feixes s/n (☎972/26 19 19). A bit out-of-the-way towards the northeastern end of the town, but quiet, excellent value and very friendly, offering singles, doubles and triples. Most rooms – expansion is planned – have bath, heating and TV, and its secure garage makes it the best choice if you have a car or bike. ②.

Hostal Stop, c/Sant Pere Màrtir 29, just west of the old quarter (☎972/26 10 48). Decrepit-looking from the outside, but acceptable, large rooms, with showers down the hall. ②.

The Town

Some of the best work produced by the Olot School can be seen in the **Museu Comarcal de la Garrotxa** (daily except Tues & Sun 11am–2pm & 4–7pm; 200pta, same ticket admits to Casal dels Volcans), installed in a converted eighteenth-century hospital at c/Hospici 8. Of the works in the collection, Joaquim Vayreda's *Les Falgueres* is typical in its rendering of the Garrotxa light, but by no means all the collection's pieces are landscapes. Ramon Casas' famous *La Càrrega*, for example, long thought to depict the violent suppression of a 1902 Barcelona demonstration but actually painted in 1899, bears the mark of Goya's great protest paintings, while the "Paris Cigarettes" poster series were locals' entries for a contest sponsored by an Argentine manufacturer. Sculpture is also strongly represented, notably in the work of Miquel Blay i Fabrega and Josep Clarà i Ayals; other pieces by this pair can be seen around town in the eponymous Plaça Clarà and Passeig d'en Blay.

There are also extensive exhibits devoted to rural and town crafts. Besides the saints' images from religious workshops, the secular figures of Ramon Amadeu are outstandingly vivid, fluid and, on occasion, humorous. Olot's specialization in textiles meant, among other activities, a large number of turn-of-the-century workshops for production of *barretinas* or *gores* – the typical Catalan men's cap.

A well-signposted half-hour walk from the centre brings you to the landscaped **Jardí Botànic**, where – especially if you read Catalan or Castilian – you'll learn a lot about the Garrotxa volcanic region from the displays, photographs, diagrams and rock samples in the **Casal dels Volcans** (daily except Tues: July–Sept 10am–2pm & 5–7pm; Oct–June 10am–2pm & 4–6pm; same ticket as Museu Comarcal), housed within the gardens. The building also houses an information centre on activities throughout the Garrotxa.

Eating, drinking and nightlife

People line up outside for the down-to-earth Catalan **food** at *Can Guix*, c/Mulleras 3 (closed Sun), where you can stuff yourself for a little over 1000ptas, and the local wine comes by the *porrón*. If you're in need of an antidote to *lomo* and fries, head for Olot's **vegetarian** restaurant, *La Plaça dels Gegants* at Plaça Major, with mostly vegan dishes both à la carte or on a menu; it also has a small retail section of organic and special-diet products. There's also an excellent, good-value restaurant-patisserie across the square at the *Pensió Narmar*, with an 1100-peseta menu. Don't turn your nose up at the institutional decor of *La Garrotxa* self-service restaurant, near the museum at c/Serra i Ginesta 14, open daily with a changing list of specials (950-pta menu served Mon–Fri, à la carte weekends). It's not expensive for what you get: 1700pta or so, if you go a la carte, for a lot of decent food. On Plaça Móra, *Font de l'Angel* is a snackbar-café with garden seating and inexpensive menus, closed on Sunday after characteristically lively Saturday nights, while *Bar-Restaurant Ramón* at Plaça Clarà 11 offers mid-priced Catalan dishes, as well as an economical menu; its seating under the arcade makes a good vantage point if you just want a drink. *Set al Gust*, Passeig d'en Blay 49, is a smartly appointed pizzeria offering unconventional toppings such as *bacalao* (cod); a pizza with local wine runs to about 1600ptas per head.

More than a dozen **bars and cafés** between the bullring and Plaça Carmé at the eastern end of the *barri antic* cater to most tastes. Aside from some obvious ones on the *passeig*, two to pick out are the arty, genteel *Cocodrilo* on c/Sant Roc, and the more raucous *Komix Bar*, c/Sant Ferriol 36, near Plaça Clarà. There are even two **cinemas**, the classy Colom on the Paseig d'en Blay and the Nuria near Plaça Carmé. Most concerts and other events in the **summer festival** take place in Plaça del Mig, behind the museum.

The Baixa Garrotxa Volcanic Zone

In 1985 the Catalan parliament decreed that much of the **Baixa Garrotxa**, a vast area extending southeast of Olot, would become the **Parc Natural de la Zona Volcanica de la Garrotxa**. This designation means less than one might think. The volcanic cones themselves, and the **Fageda d'en Jordà** beech wood lying between the cones and Olot, gained some necessary protection, but cinder-quarrying (for building materials) and large-scale rubbish dumping had already spoiled some of the proposed park.

The Baixa Garrotxa is not a zone of belching steam and boiling mud. It's been nearly twelve thousand years since the last eruption, during which time the ash and lava have weathered into a fertile soil whose luxuriant vegetation – including extensive fields of corn, beans and various grains – masks the contours of the dormant volcanoes. There are thirty cones in all, the largest of them around 160m above the level of their surroundings, and 1500m in diameter. Evergreen oak (*Quercus mediterraneo-montanum*) is the predominant tree, followed by various deciduous oaks and beeches – making this excellent territory for the acorn-eating wild boar. Genets, beech martens and wildcats are more elusive native mammals, as are three types of shrew, oak dormouse and even the occasional otter. Woodpeckers, owls and **birds** of prey such as the goshawk or short-toed eagle are similarly hard to see on a casual visit. There are a claimed 143 other bird species to spot, however, and lizards abound. At lizard-eye level, some 1500 types of **small flora** have been documented, including several endemics found nowhere else in the world.

Santa Pau

The central village of the volcanic zone, medieval **SANTA PAU**, 9km southeast of Olot, presents to the outside world a defensive perimeter of continuous and almost windowless house walls. Slightly less discovered than Besalú, it's even more atmospheric, though verging on the twee. At the very least, it's a mandatory meal stop, and would be a good base for exploring the park's ever-increasing network of signposted paths and tracks. Without your own vehicle, it's a three-to-four-hour trail-walk from Olot (a route covered below), or you can catch one of the twice-daily **buses** on the Olot–Mieres–Banyoles route.

Santa Pau's outer archways open onto dark, ancient buildings, many of them sympathetically converted into business premises and homes. At the core of the village is the thirteenth-century **Firal dels Bous** (also known as Plaça Major), with its pair of archway shops, the Can Vayreda information centre (summer Mon–Sat 10.30am–2pm & 4.30–7pm, Sun 10.30am–2pm), and Romanesque church of **Santa Maria** (which is rarely open). In the adjacent **Plaçeta dels Balls**, overlooked by the three-storeyed tower of the Balls family, you'll find pricey but tasty **meals** at *Cal Sastre*. **Accommodation** is also available here (☎972/68 04 21; ④), but the place is small enough (just 7 bedrooms) that both eating and sleeping can be difficult during peak season without advance notice. Two kilometres up the road towards Olot, at the foot of the Volcà Santa Margarida (see below), *Mas Collelldemunt* (☎972/19 50 26; ④) is an excellent *casa de pagès*, where breakfast is included in the room price, run by the only officially certified guide for the park; another kilometre back towards Olot is *Lava* (☎972/68 03 58; open all year), a large, well-positioned **campsite** in the shadow of two cones.

A loop walk

An excellent way to get acquainted with the Baixa Garrotxa is to take a **loop walk** out of Olot, which almost completely avoids paved roads and can easily be completed by any reasonably fit person in a single day. Note that this route does not exactly correspond to any of the numbered and signposted itineraries – often just point-to-point – prepared by the park authorities, but combines the virtues of several.

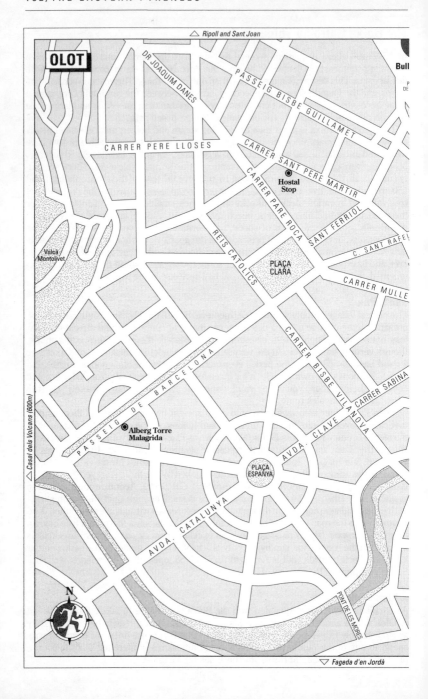

△ Ripoll and Sant Joan

OLOT

Bull

DR JOAQUIM DANES

PASSEIG BISBE GUILLAMET

CARRER PERE LLOSES

CARRER SANT PERE MARTIR

CARRER PARE ROCA

**Hostal
Stop**

SANT FERRIOL

Volcà
Montolivet

REIS CATOLICS

C. SANT RAFEL

**PLAÇA
CLARA**

CARRER MULLE

CARRER BISBE VILANOVA

CARRER SABINA

PASSEIG DE BARCELONA

△ Casal dels Volcans (600m)

AVDA. CLAVE

**Alberg Torre
Malagrida**

**PLAÇA
ESPANYA**

AVDA. CATALUNYA

PONT DE LES MORES

N

▽ Fageda d'en Jordà

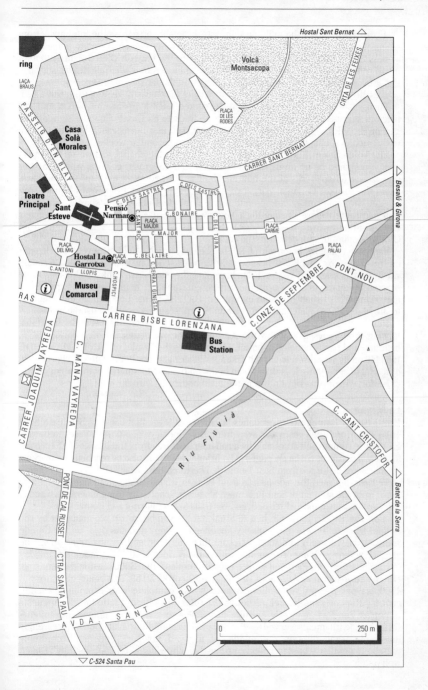

Volcà
Montsacopa

ring

LAÇA
BRAUS

PLAÇA
DE LES
RODES

CRTA DE LES FEIXES

CARRER SANT BERNAT

△ Besalú & Girona

Casa
Solà
Morales

PASSEIG D'EN BLAY

Teatre
Principal

Sant
Esteve

Pensió
Narmar

C. DELS SASTRES

C. DELS SASTRES

C. BONAIRE

C. DEL TURA

PLAÇA
CARME

PLAÇA
DEL MIG

PLAÇA
MAJOR

C. SANT ROC

C. MAJOR

PLAÇA
PALAU

PONT NOU

Hostal La
Garrotxa

PLAÇA
MORA

C. BELLAIRE

C. SERRA I GINESTA

C. ANTONI LLOPIS

(i)

RAS

Museu
Comarcal

C. HOSPICI

CARRER BISBE LORENZANA

(i)

C. ONZE DE SEPTEMBRE

Bus
Station

CARRER JOAQUIM VAYREDA

C. MANA VAYREDA

Riu Fluvià

C. SANT CRISTOFOR

△ Batet de la Serra

PONT DE CAL RUSSET

CTRA SANTA PAU

CTRA SANTA PAU

AVDA. SANT JORDI

0   250 m

▽ C-524 Santa Pau

From Olot, follow the multiple signposts directing you across the Riu Fluvià, from where it's an hour south along surfaced country lanes – equally suited to horse-riding or mountain-biking (as is most of this circuit) – to the **Fageda d'en Jordà**. Although much reduced, this beech forest is still a treat in the autumn when the leaves are turning; it takes about half an hour more to emerge on the far side of the spooky, maze-like groves, deserted except for the tourist *carruatges* (horsecarts) visiting from Santa Pau.

Turn left when you meet the helpfully marked **GR2** long-distance trail, then right twice in succession when you encounter the track to Sa Cot. Follow the signposts to stay on the GR2, which soon becomes a proper path as it heads east for thirty minutes to the medieval chapel of **Sant Miquel de Sa Cot**, a popular weekend picnic spot.

The **Volcà Santa Margarida** is visible just behind the chapel, and within forty minutes you should be up on its rim and then down in its grassy caldera, where another tiny *ermita* (chapel) sits at the bottom; allow at least an extra hour for this side trip. From the turn-off to Santa Margarida – just fifteen minutes from Sant Miquel – you resume the main route, and descend to the **Font de Can Roure**, source of the only water en route, before skirting Roca Negra with its disused quarry and entering Santa Pau: 45 minutes from the shoulder of Santa Margarida, and some three hours from Olot (not counting the detour to the caldera).

Rather than follow the onward GR2 (see below), which would inconveniently lengthen the circuit for dayhikers, bear west at **Can Mascou** and approach **Volcà Croscat** via the *Lava* campsite (see p.151). You skirt the northeast flank of Croscat, badly scarred by quarrying, and from the campsite it's another hour, along a progressively narrowing track – unsignposted except for "BATET" painted on hunting-zone signs – to the high (720m) plateau of **Batet de la Serra**, scattered with handsome farms.

Here you meet a marked path-and-track coming west from the Serra de Sant Julià, turning west yourself to follow the road briefly before taking the well-marked *camí*, beautiful and partly cobbled in basalt, which passes the hamlet of **SANTA MARIA DE BATET** on its way down to Olot. It takes just under another hour of downhill progress, or a total of something less than seven hours on the day, to emerge at the top of c/Sant Cristòfor, which runs right down to the main boulevard through Olot.

La Miana

From Santa Pau the GR2 continues briefly north towards the scenic **Serra de Sant Julià del Mont**, then veers east away from park itinerary no. 6 down a valley to Besalú. East of the summit and accessible by a half-hour spur trail from the hamlet of El Torn are a group of excellent **cases de pagès** at **La Miana**, which can also be reached by a marked, six-kilometre dirt track from Sant Jaume de Llierca on the Besalú–Olot road. The proprietors have indicated the side path in from El Torn, and soon intend to signpost the way down from the summit of Sant Julià, itself already reachable by using itineraries 6 and 8. They have also signposted onward, non-GR trails to Sant Ferriol and Besalú (3hr).

Can Jou (☎972/19 02 63; bed & breakfast ②, half-board ③), co-managed by the helpful Michael Peters, has capacity for fifteen persons and sits right on the Coll de Jou with views south and west. Michael, his wife Rosi and assistants also run the area's best horse-riding programme, with half-day rides around the mountain, full-day excursions to Santa Pau, and longer trips on request. Just 300m east is the amazing, Dutch-run *Rectoria de la Miana* (☎972/19 01 90 or 22 30 59; half-board obligatory at 4500ptas per person), a medieval manor house complete with crumbling twelfth-century Romanesque chapel. Although the room-to-bathroom ratio for fifteen guests is not as good as at mostly en-suite *Can Jou*, every room is unique and antique-furnished, with meals served in the arcaded ground-floor hall. Both places enjoy incredible tranquillity in the middle of forested nowhere and are accordingly massively popular – best to reserve rather than showing up on spec, as they've been well publicized.

If you strike unlucky, there's one more *casa de pagès* in the area: *El Turrós* (☎972/68 73 50; ③ half-board), some 4km north down the dirt track towards Sant Jaume de Llierca, and then another very rough kilometre down a steep drive. This rambling country manor has a maximum capacity of fourteen in four rooms and is particularly good for families, though it's not nearly so convenient for walkers as *Can Jou* or *Rectoria de la Miana*.

The Alta Garrotxa

The **Alta Garrotxa** stretches north from the main Besalú–Olot road as far as the frontier summits. For speleologists, the region is almost inexhaustible, with more than a hundred catalogued **caves**, and for walkers or mountain-bikers it's a rewarding area as well, especially in spring or autumn when the highest Pyrenees are inaccessible. Whichever of the following routes you go for – all begin outside Castellfollit de la Roca – the Editorial Alpina "Garrotxa" map is a useful, though far from infallible, aid.

North to France

It's around 7km from Castellfollit up the **Llierca valley** (served by a minor paved road) via Montagut de Fluvià to Sadernes. Between Montagut and Sadernes there's a **campsite**, the only overnighting facility in the area. From Sadernes you continue first on dirt track, and later by a gradually ascending trail to the Ermita de Sant Aniol de Aguja, a landmark chapel astride the GR11. The much-used **Col des Massanes** (1126m) can be reached by continuing northeast on the footpath from the refuge, spending the next night at Coustouges or Saint-Laurent-de-Cerdans (see "The upper Tech", pp.120–121).

Northwest to El Ripollès: Oix, Beget and Rocabruna

Staying in Spain, a more interesting route heads **northwest** into the Ripoll region, which is covered in the next section. Take the paved road 9km northwest to **OIX**, which dominates a bowl-shaped, intensely cultivated valley. The attractive village, surrounded by huge barns, boasts the Romanesque church of Sant Llorenç and a Roman bridge, as well as a pair of **restaurants**; there's no accommodation, however, except for two **campsites** 1km west, on opposite sides of the valley: *Els Alous*, in a plantation of trees, and *Masia Can Vila*, on the grounds of an old farm. Both have swimming pools and the latter a restaurant.

To continue, leave the village passing under the "castle" (a fortified manor house), ignoring private roads, and then bear left at the signposted fork 500m outside Oix. This wide, comfortable dirt road leads northwest 12km, via the high hamlet of Sant Miquel de Pera, to the showcase village of **BEGET** (510m), restored by lowlanders as a weekend retreat but no less attractive for that. Two slender bridges link three neighbourhoods separated by the confluence of two streams, and the graceful twelfth-century church of **Sant Cristòfor**, standing at the entrance to the village, is celebrated for its particularly solemn and serene *Majestat*. All but a dozen or so of these Catalan wooden images of a fully dressed Christ were destroyed in 1936; this example, perhaps as old as the church itself, is one of the very few that can be seen as intended (keys available from the souvenir shop at no. 15 when the church is closed). Beget has two decent **restaurants**, both with **accommodation**: *Can Joanic*, by the church (☎972/74 12 41; ③), which has rooms with shared bathrooms above a fair-value restaurant with a riverside terrace, and *El Forn* (☎972/74 12 30; ③) near the top of the village, also with shared bathrooms and commanding views. The GR11 passes through here, and now that the inn *La Farga*, 3km east, has shut down (despite its continued appearance in local literature), these are the only places to stay on this stretch of the trail.

Some 5km west on either the GR11 or the now-paved road, **ROCABRUNA** and its ruined castle stand on the watershed dividing the Garrotxa from El Ripollès, the county

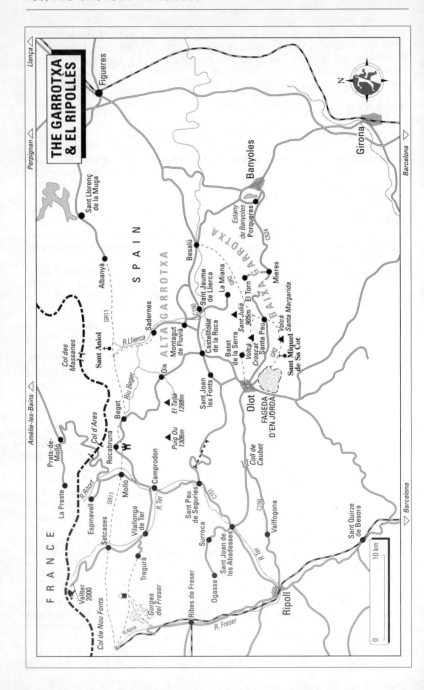

THE GARROTXA & EL RIPOLLÈS

of Ripoll. There are two small **restaurants** serving the needs of trekkers, mountain bikers and car tourists (there's no bus up this way), but since the *Casa de Pagès Etxalde* shut down there's no place to stay. From here it's 7km down to the Camprodon–Molló road.

El Ripollès

Moving towards Cerdanya and Andorra along the main roads from the Costa Brava, you begin to feel among high mountains in the *comarque* (county) of **El Ripollès**. The C150 climbs west from Olot through densely tree-clad foothills to the Coll de Caubet, where a vista of receding peaks opens up, then drops to the county town of **Ripoll**, along the scenic Vallfogona valley. Motorists, and the occasional bus, can also use the C153 from Olot to Sant Pau de Seguries, a route shortened some twenty minutes by tunnels under the Coll de Capsacosta. By train the approach is different, entering the *comarque* from the south via Sant Quirze de Besora.

From Ripoll an important "Romanesque Route" of beautiful churches and monasteries – most notably at **Sant Joan de les Abadesses** and **Camprodon** – can be followed northeast towards the high ridges. Above Camprodon, isolated valleys lead up to the frontier and road crossing at the Col d'Ares/Aras (1513m); winter sport enthusiasts can patronize the ski station of **Vallter 2000**.

Due north of Ripoll, road and rail climb to **Ribes de Freser** and then west out of the *comarque* at the Collada de Toses. From Ribes, there's the option of riding the dramatic, narrow-gauge *cremallera* railway up the gorge to **Queralbs** and **Núria**, the sanctuary and ski station below the summit of 2910-metre **Puigmal**. Walkers can link the valleys of Ter and Núria by hiking between Setcases and Queralbs, along the marvellous **Riu Freser** trail.

Ripoll is the hub of **public transport**, with trains continuing north to Puigcerdà and the French border, while the most regular bus lines head east to Olot and northeast to Sant Joan and Camprodon.

Ripoll

RIPOLL occupies so prominent a place in Catalunya's history that it's impossible not to be initially disappointed by this rather shabby place, buzzed by traffic and divided by the manifestly polluted Riu Ter. But just ten minutes' walk from the southeast corner of town – where trains and buses stop – is a small, relatively peaceful old quarter, with one of the most remarkable monuments in the Catalan Pyrenees, the Monestir de Santa Maria, founded in 888 to spur Christian resettlement of the surrounding valleys following the expulsion of the Moors.

The chief monastic centre of medieval Catalunya, Ripoll later became a major producer of weapons, a development foreshadowed by the career of the monastery's founder, **Guifré el Pilós** (Wilfred the Hairy). He was the archetypal "fighting Christian", first of the powerful counts of Barcelona who, in the mid-ninth century, ruled not only that city, but also the counties of Cerdagne, Urgell and Osona, and ultimately Girona and Besalú as well. He was killed in 898, struck by a Moorish chief's lance during a raid.

The Town

Following an 1835 fire, the Benedictine **Monestir de Santa Maria** lay in ruins; today's barrel-vaulted nave (daily 8am–1pm & 3–8pm) is a copy of the original structure erected over Guifré's tomb by Abbot Oliba in the early eleventh century. (Oliba and his twelfth-century successors created an important library here and – in contrast with Guifré – were instrumental in the preservation of Moorish scholarship.) The magnifi-

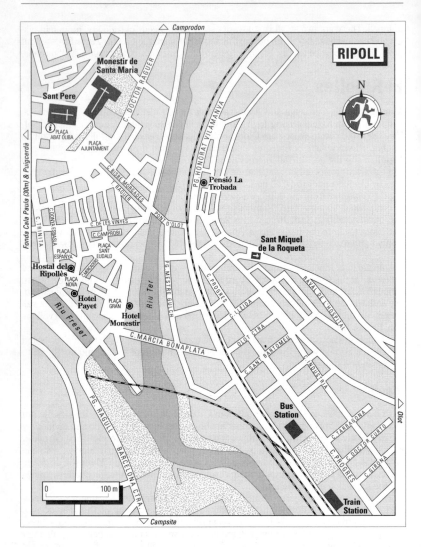

cent Romanesque **west portal**, however, survived the fire, and is now protected by a glass conservatory against the elements. Erected in the twelfth century, and now the main entrance, the portal squirms with carvings of religious and astrological subjects: the Apocalypse (across the top), the Book of Kings (to the left), Exodus (to the right), scenes from the lives of David, St Peter and St Paul (at the bottom), and the months of the year (around the inner side of the pillars).

The double-columned **cloisters** (June–Aug daily 10am–1pm & 3–7pm; Sept–May Tues–Sun 10am–1pm & 3–7pm; 100ptas), far less damaged in the succession of earthquakes, sackings and fires visited on the monastery, are particularly beautiful. The

capitals, dating from the twelfth-century Romanesque "Golden Age", portray monks and nuns, beasts mundane and mythical, plus secular characters of the period. They completely overshadow the nominal **Museu Lapidari** here, which displays assorted stonework, sarcophagi and funerary art along the walls.

Adjacent to the monastery stands the fourteenth-century church of **Sant Pere**, part of which houses the **Museu dels Pireneus** (Tues–Sun: late June–late Sept 9.30am–7pm; late Sept–late June 9.30am–1pm & 3.30–6pm; 300ptas), with a diverse collection of folk, craft and archeological exhibits, particularly relating to the seventeenth-century local arms and metal-smelting industry. You're only likely to get into the church itself if it serves as a venue for Ripoll's music **festival**, staged on successive weekends during July and August.

Besides the monastery and museum there's little to detain you, though it's worth climbing around the back of Sant Pere to a **terrace** from where you can overlook Santa Maria. A nearby bar has tables here, too, certainly the nicest seats in town. Down in the modern district, two *Modernista* specimens may claim your attention: the spouting stone flourishes of **Can Bonada**, c/del Progés 14, on the way to the bus and train stations, and the tiny church of **Sant Miquel de la Roqueta** (1912), a couple of blocks up the hill, looking like a pixie's house with a witch's cap on top.

Practicalities

The **train and bus stations** are within sight of each other, just a ten-minute walk from the heart of town, over the Pont d'Olot. On Plaça d'Abat Oliba, the **tourist office** (Mon–Sat 10am–1pm & 5–7pm, Sun 10am–1pm; ☎972/70 23 51) stands near the Museu dels Pireneus, under the sundial. No English is spoken, but the office has plenty of maps, pamphlets and local transport timetables.

Accommodation choices, all in or near the old town, are generally overpriced, noisy and uninspiring; that, and the limited choice of restaurants, makes it highly advisable to stay in Sant Joan de les Abadesses or Ribes de Freser, and make a flying visit. Least expensive is the *Fonda Cala Paula*, Plaça de l'Abat Arnulf 6 (☎972/70 00 11; ②), thirty seconds' walk to the left of the tourist office as you face it. It's basic (all rooms without plumbing), but clean and friendly; the doubles and triples are better than the cell-like, windowless singles. Next niche up is occupied by the *Hotel Payet* (☎972/70 02 50; ③), at Plaça Nova 2 – a rambling old place, with some dreadful singles, largish doubles with and without bath, and an all-pervading mustiness. For more comfort try *Hotel Monestir*, Plaça Gran 4 (☎972/70 41 33; ④), or *Hostal Del Ripollès*, across from the *Payet* (☎972/70 02 15; ④). *Pensió La Trobada*, Passeig Honorat Vilamanyà 4 (☎972/71 43 53; ⑤), across the river, is the most overpriced of the bunch and a desperation option only. There's also a **campsite**, the *Solana de Ter* (☎972/70 10 62; open all year), 2km south of town on the Barcelona road.

Eating and drinking options, too, are far from plentiful. *Restaurant Perla*, Plaça Gran 4, features rather expensive à la carte food, though *El Passeig*, across the Riu Freser at Passeig Ragull 10, is worth trying for lunch (supper served at weekends). These are the only full-service restaurants in the centre; for excellent *tapas* and crepes, head for *Bar El Punt* at Plaça Ajuntament 10, which has tables both outside and in the air-conditioned premises. *Bar Stop* also has relatively traffic-free outdoor tables at Plaça Tomàs Raguer 15, a block or two south of Plaça Ajuntament.

Sant Joan de les Abadesses

The small town of **SANT JOAN DE LES ABADESSES**, 11km northeast of Ripoll, owes its existence to the eponymous **monastery** (mid-June to mid-Sept daily 10am–2pm & 4–7pm; rest of year daily 11am–2pm & 4–6pm, except Nov to mid-March Mon–Fri 11am–2.30pm, Sat & Sun 11am–2pm & 4–6pm; 300ptas) founded in 887 by

Guifré el Pilós, apparently for the benefit of his daughter Emma, the first abbess. The present church, consecrated in 1150, is a single-nave structure of impressive austerity, built to a Latin-cross plan with five apses, and housing a curious thirteenth-century wooden sculpture, the *Santíssim Misteri*, in its main chapel. This moving work, depicting Christ's deposition, retains on His forehead "a piece of Holy Bread . . . preserved untouched for seven hundred years", according to the monastery's literature. Admission to the monastery also includes entry to the Gothic **cloisters** and the **Museu del Monestir**, whose well-presented exhibits include ornate chalices, curiosities such as a crucifix in rock crystal, and a fine series of late medieval altarpieces.

Other than the monastery, there are few specific sights in Sant Joan, but the old quarter boasts a fair-sized grid of ancient houses along streets almost shorter than their names, all leading to a small but appealingly arcaded **Plaça Major**. The slender twelfth-century **bridge** down in the well-tilled valley was only restored in 1976, after being destroyed in fierce fighting of February 1939, during the final Republican retreat of the Civil War. Having strolled around and scared the pigeons from the abandoned shell of **Sant Pol** church in the centre, you've pretty much exhausted the potential of the town.

Practicalities

Buses arrive at a shelter behind the monastery, just around the corner from the main *rambla*, Passeig Comte Guifré, where the **tourist office** occupies no. 5 (Mon–Sat 11am–1pm & 5–7pm, Sun 11am–1pm; ☎972/72 05 99).

You may well want to stay, given the frequent bus links in each direction; in any case, Sant Joan makes a far more pleasant base than Ripoll. Pick of the **accommodation** is the *Hostal Ter*, overlooking both the new and old bridges from c/Vista Alegra 2 (☎972/72 00 05; ③), family run and also a good source of decent meals. In the new district, near the bus stop, *Hostal Casa Nati* at c/Pere Rovira 3 (☎972/72 01 14; ②) has large rooms (without bath); while *Hostal Can Janpere*, c/del Mestre Josep Andreu 3 (☎972/72 00 77; ③), is more expensive, some rooms with en-suite facilities. *Habitacions Mateu* is almost next door on the corner, at c/Mossèn Masdèu 10 (☎972/72 01 86; ②), but it's fairly unprepossessing.

Better than any of these, if you have a car, is the *Casa de Pagès Mas Mitjavila*, 11km northwest of Sant Joan at the hamlet of **OGASSA** (☎972/19 80 68 or 72 20 20; ④). From the north side of the new bridge, follow the asphalt road 4km to Surroca village, and then continue the remaining distance on a cement driveway. With the adjacent tenth-century church of Sant Martí de Ogassa, *Mas Mitjavila* was once a dependency of the monastery of Sant Joan, and enjoys a superb eyrie-like setting 1300m up, overlooking the valleys of Ripoll. Ready meals and farm produce are both available, as are easy hikes in the surrounding mountains.

All of the in-town lodgings have reasonable attached **restaurants**, with economical *menús* offered at *Casa Nati* and *Can Janpere*. Otherwise you can sit outside at the pleasant cafés on the *rambla*, one of which (*Cafeteria La Rambla*) does a *menú* and *platos combinados*.

Camprodon

Approaching from points south, the first place with the character of a real mountain town is **CAMPRODON** (950m), a fact exploited last century by the Catalan gentry who arrived by a (now defunct) rail line to spend summer in the hills. The town, 14km from Sant Joan, still retains the prosperous air of those times, with shops full of leather goods, outdoor gear, cheese and sausages. Ornate villas front a *rambla* clogged with towering trees, and other townhouses are occasionally embellished with *Modernista* flourishes.

Like Ripoll, Camprodon straddles the confluence of two rivers, here the Ter and the Ritort, and is knit together by little bridges. The principal one, the sixteenth-century **Pont Nou**, still has a defensive tower. From here you can follow the narrow main street, c/València, to the restored Romanesque monastic church of **Sant Pere** (consecrated in 904, not to be confused with the larger parish church), near the northeast end of town. There is also a small castle overhead, but no apparent way up.

Camprodon was the birthplace of the composer **Isaac Albéniz** (1860–1909), a fact which neither the town nor the region makes much of – probably because there is little distinctively Catalan in the music he produced during his wanderings through Spain. (His most celebrated work, for piano or guitar, is entitled *Iberia*.)

Practicalities

Buses from Ripoll stop at the TEISA depot, well south of the main Plaça d'Espanya, where you'll find the **tourist office** (July–Sept Mon–Sat 10am–1.30pm & 4.30–8pm, Sun 10am–2pm; limited hours otherwise; ☎972/74 00 10) in the *Ajuntament* building.

Accommodation tends to be slightly expensive, given the town's role as a minor ski resort, with advance reservations advisable throughout the year. Working up the price ladder, on c/Josep Morera there's *Can Ganasi* at no. 9 (☎972/74 01 34; ③) and *Hostal Sayola* at no. 4 (☎972/74 01 42; ③), both also having rather more expensive rooms with bath. *Hostal Sant Roc* (☎972/74 01 19; ③) and the *Hotel La Placeta* (☎972/70 15 20; ③) line Plaça del Carmé, east of c/Josep Morera and the first square you reach as you come into town. The elegance of the dead-central *Hotel Güell*, Plaça d'Espanya 8 (☎972/74 00 11; ④), justifies a mild splurge. Some 3km up the road to Molló there's a **campsite**, *Els Solans* (☎972/74 00 12), not brilliant and geared mostly for caravans.

Can Ganasi's **restaurant** offers several different menus plus local dishes, while *Hotel La Placeta* also has an attached diner (dinner only). Otherwise *Bar-Restaurant Nuria*, at Plaça d'Espanya 11, is a characterful place and features a good-value lunch menu (à la carte only at night). Local specialities include **pinyes**, extremely rich and dense pine-nut sweets, which you can find on sale at bakeries throughout the town.

Beyond Camprodon: the Ter and Ritort valleys

Beyond Camprodon you're increasingly dependent on your own transport and ultimately your own legs. The majority of people who venture this way are either hikers, or skiers driving northwest up the **Ter valley** to the lifts of Vallter 2000, with comparatively little traffic moving northeast up the **Ritort** that isn't ultimately headed for France.

The first settlement that might tempt you to stop is the rather ordinary **VILAL-LONGA DE TER**, 5km from Camprodon, with two simple *habitacions*: *Cal Mestre* at c/del Pau (☎972/74 04 07; ③) and *Sunyer i Blanco* at c/Canigó 7 (☎972/13 00 11; ④), as well as a fancy all-year **campsite**, *Conca de Ter* (☎972/74 06 29), pitched at caravanners. Two or three times daily, a **bus** from Camprodon passes through here on its way to Setcases (see below).

You can bear left 1km past Vilallonga for **TREGURÀ**, 4km from the main road; perched on a sunny hillside at 1400m, with sweeping views east over the valley, the upper part of the double village has a church dating from about 980, plus two places to **stay**: *Fonda Rigà* (☎972/13 60 00; ③), also with a **restaurant**, and *Hotel El Serrat* (☎972/13 60 19; ④).

From Tregurà, it's possible to hike west in a day to Queralbs, where you can pick up the rack-and-pinion railway down to Ribes or up to Núria. This route provides a lower-altitude, far more scenic alternative to the GR11, which crosses the Ter valley much higher up. The lower path climbs towards Puig Castell (2125m) and then through the Coll dels Tres Pics (2hr) to the dilapidated, unstaffed *Refugi Coma de Vaca* (4hr) at the top of the **Gorges del Freser**. From just before the refuge, on the south bank of the Freser, a distinct and beautiful trail drops westwards through a stunning gorge to Queralbs (7hr). Another path connects Coma de Vaca with the *Refugí Vall de Ter* (open July–Sept and weekends all year) on the slopes of Vallter. In summer, hikers can also follow the ski-mountaineering itineraries described on p.164.

Setcases and Vallter 2000

Back in the Ter valley, **SETCASES**, 6km northwest of Vilallonga, has been almost completely gentrified from its former decrepitude. Once an important agricultural village, it was almost totally abandoned until the nearby ski station began to attract hoteliers and second-home owners. The ski trade ensures that beds and food are pricey, with some unfriendly, not to say grasping attitudes on the part of some proprietors – a shame, as Setcases straddles the GR11, a half-day's march west from Molló (see below). If you need to stay, the most affordable **accommodation** sits all in a row on the riverbank road: the *Hostal Ter* (☎972/713 60 96; ⑤), the *Can Tiranda* (☎972/13 60 52; ④) and finally *Can Jepet* (☎972/13 61 04; ③).

Situated at the head of the valley, below the frontier summit of Pic de la Dona (2702m), **VALLTER 2000** is the most easterly ski resort of the Pyrenees. It doesn't have a reliable snow record, but if you're in the area and the snow is good it's worthwhile for the range of pistes laid out in its glacial bowl – three green runs, three blue, five red and four black.

Ski mountaineers can work their way **westwards** to Núria, either via the 2826-metre Pic de la Vaca (about 10hr) or above the Riu Freser (8hr), a route that's more advisable in windy conditions. To go **eastwards** via the 2507-metre-high (but gently rounded) Roc Colom to the French *Refuge Mariailles* (see p.108) is not technically difficult, but the distance of 25km means it's for hard cases only – and a pre-dawn start is necessary. The *Refuge Jean Dasilva* in the Rotja valley provides a bailing-out point from the Collade des Roques Blanches, about two-thirds of the way along – allow about an hour to drop down to the hut from the pass. Less ambitious off-piste skiers can traverse from the top lift of Vallter **northwards** to the Portella de Mantet (2415m), and then drop down to the French village of Mantet (p.108): you'll need about three hours to get there, twice that to get back again next day.

Along the Ritort

From Camprodon, the road up to **Col d'Ares** (1513m) and into France (via the Col d'Ares/Prats-de-Molló border crossing) initially follows the fairly treeless **Ritort valley**. The slight attraction of **MOLLÓ**, 8km from Camprodon, is the Romanesque church of Santa Cecília, with its four-storey bell-tower. It has a pair of **hotel-restaurants**: *Can Calitxto* in the village (☎972/74 03 86; ④), with plush, balconied rooms and half-board rates available, and the *François* (☎972/74 03 88; ④), less inspiringly sited down on the through road. One daily **bus** (not Sun) makes the trip up here from Camprodon. Your final chance of **food** and a **place to stay** before the border is the hamlet of **ESPINAVELL**, where the new *Fonda Les Planes* (☎972/74 13 74; ③) awaits.

The upper Freser valley

From Ripoll, the Freser valley rises to Ribes de Freser (912m) and then climbs steeply to Queralbs, where it swings eastwards through a gorge of awesome beauty. Just above Queralbs, to the north, the Riu Núria has scoured out a second gorge, beyond which lie the ski station and valley sanctuary of Núria itself (1967m), the usual point of access to Puigmal (2913m) and other frontier peaks.

Ribes de Freser

Generally bypassed in the rush up to Núria, dull but unobjectionable **RIBES DE FRESER** offers little to the traveller except **hotels** – more plentiful and better value than anything in Ripoll – and, out of season, its integrity as a real town. Local shops sell sacks of grain, seeds, oils and other agricultural and domestic paraphernalia, and there's a lively weekly market.

You won't neccessarily want (or need) to see any of this. Regular **trains** on the Barcelona–Puigcerdà line serve Ribes in either direction. Get off at "Ribes de Freser-RENFE" for the ten-minute walk into town, or just cross the platform to "Ribes-Enllaç" and take the *cremallera* train (see box on p.164), which makes a stop in the centre of town (Ribes-Vila) to pick up more passengers before heading on up into the mountains.

If the idea of **staying** appeals, pick of the bunch is *Mas Ventaiola*, a *casa de pagès* 1km from the centre, past the cemetery on the Pardinas road (☎972/72 79 48; ③), with meals available. Otherwise, in the town itself, very close to the *cremallera* station, *Hotel Caçadors-Fanet*, c/Balandrau 24 (☎972/72 70 06; ④), or the *Hostal Traces* around the corner at c/de N. S. de Gràcia 3 (☎972/72 71 37; ③) are the quietest choices; the *Fonda Vilalta*, c/de Cerdanyà 6, a steep car-less lane (☎972/72 70 95; ③), is another possibility. Noisily situated on the main through road, by the river bridge, *Hotel San Antoni* (☎972/72 70 18; ④), has rather plain rooms for the price, but does serve huge portions of boarding-house food. If you're still stuck, there's a helpful **tourist office** on Plaça de l'Ajuntament (Tues–Sat 10am–2pm & 5–8pm, Sun 11am–1pm) by the much-restored church.

Queralbs

The only intermediate stop on the *cremallera*, **QUERALBS** (1220m) is an attractive stone-built village, sympathetically renovated and suffering from the attentions of too many tourists only in peak season. Near the highest point, beside the GR11 which passes through here, is the tenth-century church of **Sant Jaume**, sporting a fine colonnaded porch. Reasonable en-suite **accommodation** is provided by the co-run *Fonda Sierco/Hostal L'Avet*, on the main street 70m in from the car park (☎972/72 73 77; ④, half-board at 4800ptas per person mandatory in summer). The *hostal* rooms are small but wood-trimmed, with a cosy lounge on the ground floor, and the refurbished *fonda* units are directly over the restaurant *Ca La Mary*, which has all keys. Other **restaurants** here include the recommended *Can Constans*, 200m above the village on the Fontalba road, and the more expensive *Restaurant de la Plaça*, on the main square.

Núria

Beyond Queralbs, the *cremallera* hauls itself up the precipitous valley to **NÚRIA**, twenty minutes further on. Once the train passes the entrance to the Gorges del Freser, seen tantalizingly to the right, and enters the Gorges de Núria the views are dramatic and your exposure sometimes terrifying – the impact enhanced by a sequence of tunnels.

Once through a final tunnel, you emerge into a south-facing bowl, with a small, dam-augmented lake at the bottom and – at the far end – the hideously monolithic, coffee-coloured **Santuario de Nuestra Senyora de Núria**, founded in the eleventh century on the spot where an image of the Virgin was miraculously found. Patroness of local shepherds, the Virgin of Núria is also believed to bestow fertility on female pilgrims, and many Catalan girls – presumably the result of successful supernatural intervention – are named after her.

The sanctuary building combines a dull church, tourist office (which posts weather reports), bar, restaurants, ski centre and **hotel** all in one. Rates at the *Hotel Vall de Núria* (☎972/73 20 00; ⑥) vary widely by season – June, July and September are mid-range – and its **restaurant**, open for lunch and supper, offers some cheap *menús*.

THE CREMALLERA RAILWAY

The **Cremallera** ("Zipper" in Catalan) railway, built in 1931, is the last rack-and-pinion line operating in Catalunya, a miniature – though rather more daring – version of the *Train Jaune* just over the border. After a leisurely start through the lower valley, the tiny, three-car train lurches up into the mountains on its third rail, following the river between great crags before starting to climb high above both river and forests. Occasionally it slows down, leaving you poised between a sheer drop into the valley and an equally precipitous rock-face soaring overhead.

Services **depart** Ribes-Enllaç daily in summer (mid-July to mid-Sept) and in winter, hourly from 9.15am to 7.15pm (except 2.15pm); there's an additional, final departure at 8.50pm Fridays and Saturdays, plus an extra train daily at 10.15am whenever the ski station is functioning. Trains pass through Ribes-Vila, where there's a weather report posted, eight minutes later. In spring and early summer, there are reduced departures – 9.15 & 11.15am, 1.15, 3.15 & 5.15pm. The **journey time** up or down is 45 minutes; return **tickets** to Núria from Ribes cost around 2200ptas (one-ways available at about 60 percent of prevailing price). Children's tickets are half-price, but rail passes of any kind are not valid.

The only indoor budget lodging is the **youth hostel** *Pic de L'Àliga* (☎972/73 20 48; ①), marvellously poised at the top of the cable-car line (free ride up with train ticket). **Camping** is permitted only at a designated site behind the sanctuary complex.

Besides the hotel, **eating** options include *La Cabana dels Pastors*, a separate building behind the complex offering expensive bistro fare at lunchtime only; the *Bar Finestrelles*, downstairs in the sanctuary building, offering typical bar snacks; and, best value of all, the lunchtime-only *Autoservei* self-service restaurant in the west wing, where you can eat reasonably well for between 1600–2000 pesetas. Above *Bar Finestrelles*, a shop, La Botica, sells souvenir-type food, though it's not a really serious option for stocking up to go trekking.

Activities laid on in the valley include an archery range, horse-riding programme (high summer only) and boating on the lake.

Skiing and winter mountaineering

The **skiing** at Núria is usually more reliable than at Vallter 2000, but the lift system is very limited and the top station is only at 2262m, so it's best for beginners and weak intermediates. There are two green runs, two blue, four red and one black.

Off-piste, the summits of **Pic/Puig de Finestrelles** (2829m) and **Puigmal** (2913m) are fairly easy to conquer. Finestrelles is more or less northwest of the sanctuary, reached by following the valley and then bearing away a little to the west before curving back towards the top. The approach to Puigmal begins in the same way but soon turns southwest along the route known as the **Coma de l'Embut**; at the rain gauge swing southeast for the Collada de l'Embut and, once through, make straight for the summit. Each ascent takes three to five hours, depending on conditions and skill; crampons may be required. It's possible to take in both peaks as a full day's outing, passing between them along the frontier ridge.

Ascending northeast of Núria to the Col de Nou Fonts you can continue to the **Carança lakes** in France, returning the same day, or continue east to Vallter 2000, a full day away. Many of these routes are detailed on the Editorial Alpina 1:25,000 "Puigmal-Núria" map and accompanying booklet.

Walking

Walkers in summer can follow the same routes, with slight variations that are clear from the trodden paths; for example, summer walks east along the **GR11**, which follows the high frontier ridge – a risky stretch in poor visibility – end up in Setcases rather than Vallter 2000. Hikes northeast are especially recommended; once over the Col de Nou Fonts (visited by the GR11) you have a choice betweeen the various itineraries described under "The Carança gorge area" on p.110.

A return **to Queralbs on foot** along the river gorge is perhaps the most popular hike out of Núria. The GR11 threads the gorge on a high-quality, well-marked path, but you'll still need good, over-the-ankle shoes and a water bottle (there are a few potable torrents and springs en route). You'll need two to two-and-a-half hours descending, depending on load and stops, three to three-and-a-half hours going up. The trail generally adopts the opposite side of the gorge to the _cremallera_ tracks, giving you the opportunity to watch the little train at work; the valley begins to open out below Sallent del Sastre, and after crossing back to the west bank for good at the Pont de Cremal, you'll see the Freser gorge yawning to the east.

A more challenging, six-hour descent, traced more or less correctly on the "Catalunya Valle de Núria" tourist brochure, gives you the best of both gorges. Start by initially climbing southeast along the east bank of Núria gorge, beginning under the cable-car lines. This soon swings east and drops into the Gorges del Freser, where the precipices are unforgettable, but fairly safe. When you finally get level with the Riu Freser at the _Refugi Coma de Vaca_, cross the stream and take the path that leads back along the Freser to Queralbs.

travel details

French trains
Perpignan to: Cerbère (at least 14 daily; 50min); Prades (6 daily; 45min); Villefranche-de-Conflent (6 daily; 52min).
Quillan to: Carcassonne (3 daily Mon–Sat, 4 on Sun & holidays; 1hr). _NB Most of these services are on SNCF buses._
Villefranche-de-Conflent to: Latour-de-Carol (6 daily in summer; 3hr).

Spanish trains
Figueres to: Barcelona (19 daily; 1hr 45min); Colera (5 daily; 25min); Girona (20 daily; 45min); Port Bou (10 daily; 35min).
Girona to: Barcelona (20 daily; 1hr 20min); Figueres (19 daily; 35min); Llançà (10 daily; 1hr); Port Bou (17 daily; 1hr 15min).
Ribes de Freser to: Núria (10–11 daily in summer; 45min); Queralbs (10–11 daily; 25min).
Ripoll to: Barcelona (12 daily; 1hr 45min–2hr); Puigcerdà (6 daily; 1hr 20min; 3 continue to the first French station, Latour-de-Carol).

French buses
Collioure to: Port-Vendres (11 daily; 5min).
Ille-sur-Têt to: Rabouillet (1 daily; 30min).
La Cabanasse/Mont-Louis to: Puyvalador via Les Angles, Matemale and Formiguères (2 daily in summer and ski season at 10.35am and 6pm,

returns mid-afternoon and dawn; 50min; contact SARL Asparre on %04.68.04.40.20 to confirm).
Perpignan to: Arles-sur-Tech (8 daily; 1hr 15min); Axat (2 daily; 1hr 40min); Banyuls-sur-Mer (5 daily; 1hr 10min); Céret (12 daily; 45min); Collioure (5 daily; 45min); Estagel (5 daily; 30min); Latour-de-Carol (3 daily; 2hr); Le Boulou (12 daily; 30min); Le Perthus (5 daily; 45min); Mont-Louis (3 daily; 1hr 30min); Prades (7 daily; 1hr); Prats-de-Molló (5 daily; 1hr 45min); Saint-Laurent-de-Cerdans (3 daily; 1hr 45min); Saint-Paul-de-Fenouillet (4 daily Mon–Sat, 2 on Sun; 1hr); Tautavel (1–2 daily Mon–Fri; 30min); Thuir (4 daily; 15min); Villefranche-de-Conflent (7 daily; 1hr 15min).
Quillan to: Carcassonne (4 daily; 1hr 15min); Comus (2 daily; 1hr 5min); Foix via Lavelanet (2 daily; 3hr); Perpignan, via Axat and Saint-Paul-de-Fenouillet (2 daily; 1hr 30min); Quérigut (3 weekly in summer).
Villefranche-de-Conflent to: Casteil (4 daily; 15min); Sahorre (1–2 daily Mon–Sat; 15min); Vernet-les-Bains (7 daily; 10min).

Spanish buses
Figueres to: Barcelona (3–8 daily; 1hr 30min); Cadaqués (4 daily; 1hr 15min); Castelló d'Empúries (every 30min; 15min); Espolla (1 daily; 35min); Girona (3–8 daily; 1hr); Llançà (5 daily Mon–Fri; 20min); Maçanet de Cabrenys (1–2

daily; 1hr); Olot (2–3 daily; 1hr 30min); Roses (every 30min; 40min); Vilajuïga (1 daily; 50min).

Girona to: Banyoles (13 daily Mon–Sat, 4 on Sun; 30min); Barcelona (6–9 daily Mon–Sat, 3 on Sun; 1hr); Figueres (6–10 daily Mon–Sat, 4 on Sun; 50min); Olot via Besalú (7 daily Mon–Sat, 3 on Sun; 1hr 15min).

Olot to: Barcelona (3–4 daily; 2hr 15min); Besalú (7–8 daily Mon–Sat, 1 on Sun; 30min); Camprodon (1–2 daily; 45min); Figueres (2–3 daily; 1hr 15min); Girona (9 daily Mon–Sat, 5 on Sun; 1hr 15min); Ripoll (4–5 daily; 50min–1hr 10min); Santa Pau (Wed & Sat only; 15min); Sant Joan de les Abadesses (2–3 daily; 50min).

Ripoll to: Camprodon (6–8 daily; 45min); Guardiola de Berguedà (1 daily Mon–Fri at 5.25pm; 2hr); La Pobla de Lillet (1 daily Mon–Fri at 5.25pm; 1hr 45min); Olot (3–5 daily; 50min–1hr 10min); Sant Joan de les Abadesses (6–8 daily; 20min).

CHAPTER TWO

ANDORRA AND AROUND

Approaching from the Mediterranean, you begin to see permanently snow-tipped mountains appear around the principality of Andorra, set in a part of the range containing true wilderness and almost every kind of Pyrenean landscape. On the Spanish side, the best appetizer for the high peaks on your way to Andorra is the **Parc Natural del Cadí-Moixeró**, featuring that most distinctive Spanish Catalan peak, the cloven **Pedraforca**. In 1916 Picasso came to Gòsol, at the foot of the mountain, in search of fresh inspiration, and most of what he found still exists: unspoilt, strangely coloured scenery, golden eagles soaring overhead and herds of isards. The growth of summer holiday communities has been the biggest change in what was once a region of dwindling agricultural villages, but the Cadí remains virtually free of ski development and is still good for spring or autumn hiking and mountain-biking country.

La Seu d'Urgell, capital of the Spanish **Alt Urgell** region, just northwest of the Cadí, is one of the two main gateways to Andorra, and pivotal to its history. La Seu's bishops shared control of the principality with the nobility of Foix, in an almost unique feudal power-sharing arrangement that endured, more or less peacefully, for over seven centuries, until Andorra voted for full independence in 1993. There are just two ways of entering **Andorra** itself by road: along the Valira valley from La Seu d'Urgell, or from the Col de Puymorens in France. At each frontier, and for a considerable distance beyond, duty-free megastores peddling cut-rate consumer durables line streets congested with shoppers' cars. But much of the territory of Andorra remains thus untrammelled by development, and on foot or skis you can traverse the principality without touching asphalt or seeing a single shop, experiencing Andorra as it was until the 1950s.

Like Catalonia, the mountain-ringed plateau of **Cerdanya**, southeast of Andorra, was partitioned by the Treaty of the Pyrenees, a division that left **Llívia** as an island of Spanish territory surrounded by the **Cerdagne**, as the French called their part of this formerly unified territory. **Puigcerdà** on the Spanish side, once capital of the entire district, is now a kilometre or so from the border at Bourg-Madame, to the north of which – behind the mega-resort of **Font-Romeu** – rises the **Carlit Massif**, the most easterly high-alpine region in the Pyrenees.

The **Ariège valley**, north of Andorra, is an excellent choice if you have time for only one other region near the principality. The caves around **Tarascon** include the world's most stunning publicly accessible prehistoric paintings at **Niaux**, and a magnificent forest of stalactites and stalagmites at **Lombrives**, the largest open cave in Europe. The steep slopes and cathedral-like outcrops of this deep valley are so unspoiled that the upland border of Haute Ariège and Andorra is one of just three Pyrenean habitats for

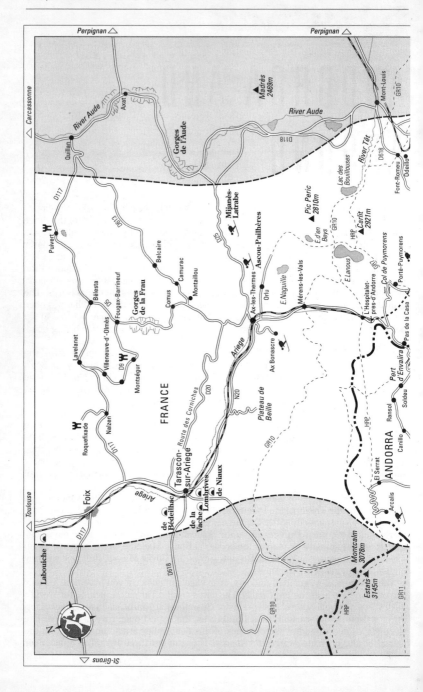

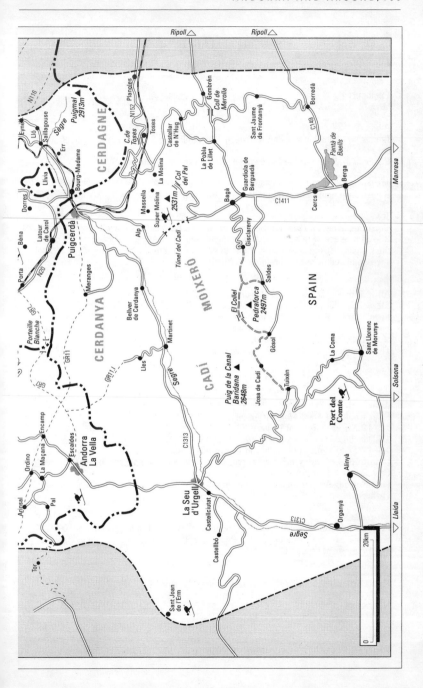

FESTIVALS

JANUARY
17 *Festa de Sant Antoni* in Sant Llorenç de Morunys.

FEBRUARY
Variable Carnival week at La Molina.

APRIL
Easter week Easter Monday, festival at Talló; following Sunday, *Pascuilla* celebrations at Llívia.
25 *Festa de Sant Marc* in Puigcerdà and at the shrine of Queralt.

MAY
8 Festival at Sant Miquel d'Engolasters (Andorra).

JUNE
Corpus Christi *La Patum* in Berga – the biggest bash in Catalunya.
23–24 The eve of *Día de Sant Joan*, which is one of the most important saint's days in the Cerdanya/Cerdagne, marks the start of summer. Fireworks at Montségur and solstice events on or near Pedraforca on the night of June 23.

JULY
All month *Son et Lumière* at Puivert.
All weekends, and into August Music festival at Sant Llorenç de Morunys.
First Sunday Annual festival in Puigcerdà.
Second week Week-long *Les Journées Mediévales de Gaston Fébus*, a medieval market at Foix. Country fair at Lavelanet.
Third weekend *Festa Major* at Canillo (Andorra).
25–27 *Fiesta Major* at Sant Julià de Lòria (Andorra); also at Sant Jaume de Frontanyà and Bellver de Cerdana.

AUGUST
All month *Son et Lumière* at Puivert.
First weekend *Festa Major* at Andorra la Vella.
12/13 *Son et Lumière* at Puivert.
15 Dancing at Gòsol; festival at Font-Romeu.
15–17 *Festa Major* at Encamp and La Maçana (Andorra).
Penultimate Sunday *Festa del Llac* at Puigcerdà; international sheep-dog trials at Castellar de N'hug.
Last Sunday Annual fair at La Seu d'Urgell.
Variable Medieval fair at Ax-les-Thermes.

SEPTEMBER
First and second week *Fête* at Foix, with fireworks and torchlit procession.
8 Fiesta at Meritxell (Andorra); *Procession de la Vierge* from Font-Romeu to Odeillo.
16/17 Fiesta at Ordino (Andorra) .

OCTOBER
Third Sunday Fair of *La Guinguette* at Bourg-Madame.

NOVEMBER
1 *Sant Ermengol* celebrations in La Seu d'Urgell.

December
24 *La Faia-Faia* torchlit procession at Bagà.

the brown bear, in imminent danger of local extinction. For walkers, **Ax-les-Thermes**
makes the most attractive place to stay, with the entire length of the Ariège accessible
by train, and a trio of long-distance footpaths – the **HRP**, **GR10** or **GR7**– within easy
reach.

North of the Ariège lies the isolated **Pays de Sault**, an area inseparable from the
tragic history of Catharism, a religion persecuted virtually out of existence by the kings
of France and the Catholic Church. At **Montségur** in 1244, the last leading figures of
the Cathar sect were besieged by a combined crusade of pope and Paris, a campaign
that ended with the mass execution of more than two hundred members of this community of "pure ones".

Public transport in the region is scarce except on routes in the main north–south
valleys. Buses from the south run up the corridor from Lleida to La Seu d'Urgell and
Andorra, and from Berga to Puigcerdà; while the last surviving trans-Pyrenean rail
line links Ripoll, Puigcerdà, Ax-les-Thermes and Foix, with a change of trains at the
border station of Latour-de-Carol. Exceptional east–west bus services include one
between La Seu and Puigcerdà, and another between Quillan and Foix, crossing the
Pays de Sault.

THE CADÍ-MOIXERÓ PARK
AND AROUND

A little to the west of Ripoll, virtually following the line of the road between **La Pobla
de Lillet** and **Castellar de N'Hug**, runs the eastern boundary of the **Parc Natural
del Cadí-Moixeró**, an area of more than 400 square kilometres that extends north to
Alt Urgell and the Cerdanya and west almost as far as the Riu Segre. Too steep for modern agriculture and largely unsuitable for downhill ski development, the greater part of
the Cadí-Moixeró Massif – essentially a giant block of limestone extending from Ripoll
to Adraén in the west – is perfect for hiking and climbing. The area's highest mountain,
Puig de la Canal Baridana, and the whole **Serra del Cadí** range are completely
unexploited, and even the much-visited peak of **Pedraforca** bears only slight marks of
development (though many farms and villas in the surrounding villages are seasonally
occupied by holidaymaking outsiders). The boundaries of the actual park are inconspicuously posted with black-on-white "parc natural" signs; as a general rule, the park
limits begin just outside most of the towns and villages described – there are no
entrance booths or other means of controlling access.

Although the designation *parc natural* does not necessarily entail a great degree of
wildlife protection, the Cadí-Moixeró now shelters Spain's largest herd of chamois
(*isard* in Catalan), restrictions on hunting having led to the growth of their numbers
from a few score to nearly a thousand. Red and roe deer were hunted out, however, and

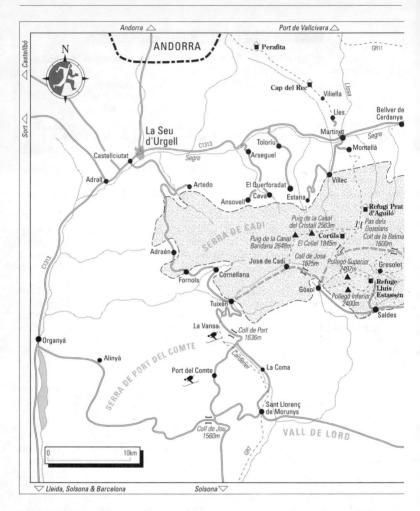

have only recently been reintroduced. Capercaillie breed here, as do the golden eagle and the black woodpecker, symbol of the park. For botanists, a big attraction is the green-petalled *Xatardia scabra*, endemic to the eastern Pyrenees and common on scree slopes in the park. Also widespread are *Gentiana alpina,* the deep-blue southern gentian; the violet-flowered Ice Age survivor *Ramonda myconi*; and *Rhododendron ferrugineum*. The lower slopes are heavily forested with dense stands of pine and silver fir.

The main C1411 from the south – used by buses from Barcelona and Manresa to **Berga** – cuts the park into two unequal portions: the Cadí watershed and half the Moixeró lie to the west of the **Túnel del Cadí**, where the C1411 disappears under the range to emerge near Puigcerdà; the rest of the Moixeró, including Castellar de N'Hug and the ski resorts of **La Molina** and **Masella**, lie to the east.

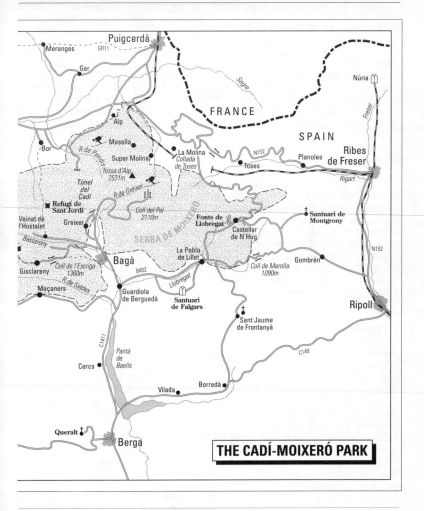

THE CADÍ-MOIXERÓ PARK

Approaches from Ripoll

From Ripoll (p.157), two routes pass the easterly fringes of the *parc natural*: the northerly N152, relatively well served by public transport, passing two popular ski resorts; and the southerly B402 road towards the C1411, skimming the edge of the Moixeró region and seeing just one bus a day (though there are more from Berga).

The northerly ski resorts

The more **northerly** of the routes west from Ripoll ascends the valley of the Riu Rigart from Ribes de Freser: the train line to Puigcerdà sticks to the bottom of the valley, while the N152 road takes a higher course, allowing a look south over the Serra Montgrony.

PLANOLES, 7km from Ribes in the valley bottom, makes a good base with its plenitude of affordable **accommodation**. Of the three *cases de pagès*, *Mas Cal Sadurní* (☎972/73 61 35; ③), close to the train station on the way to Navà hamlet, and *Can Gasparó* (☎972/73 60 82; ③), 2km out of the village on the same road, stand out. If these are both full, try the third, *Cal Mestre* (☎972/73 61 63; ③), in the hamlet of Fornells, between Planoles and Toses. There are also no fewer than three youth hostels in and around Planoles, but they're generally booked out by Spanish student groups.

Road and train then enter Cerdanya at the **Collada de Toses** (1800m) – the railway by tunnel – with its excellent views west, the bare rolling mountains of the Montgrony range relieved by swathes of deep green forest.

The broad meadows of Tossa d'Alp form the pistes of **LA MOLINA/SUPER MOLINA** and **MASELLA**, adjacent ski resorts strung out along the north-facing slopes. By Spanish Pyrenean standards the skiing is impressive, both resorts having lifts almost to the top of the 2531-metre-high peak. La Molina/Super Molina has 137 snow cannons and 29 pistes: 8 green, 7 blue, 10 red and 4 black; Masella's 42 pistes are classified as 7 green, 12 blue, 17 red and 6 black. In summer both become upmarket holiday camps for organized activities such as riding, archery and mountain-biking. **Accommodation** prices are generally high: *Maina,* c/Afores (☎972/89 20 76; ④), *La Molina* (☎972/89 20 42; ⑤) and *Els Quatre Vents,* c/Afores (☎972/89 20 97; ⑤) are probably the best-value *hostals* up by the slopes, with some other possibilities in the village of **ALP**, a few kilometres west, between the rail line and the C1411: *Pensió La Tossa* (☎972/89 00 08; ④) and *Hostal Roca* (☎972/89 00 11; ④).

La Pobla de Lillet and around

The **southerly route** from Ripoll aims right at the heart of the Cadí-Moixeró region. Beginning just north of Ripoll, at Campdevanol, this minor road crosses the Riu Freser and heads west 9km to the foothill village of Gombrén. If you miss the single weekday 5.25pm bus along this stretch from Ripoll, hitchhiking may be productive. About 3km beyond Gombrén, a paved road on the right leads north to the **Santuari de Montgrony**, worth the six-kilometre detour for the secluded setting. Although the resident priest and his cook can no longer accommodate visitors, there's a restaurant with *habitacions* adjacent. The track to the left just before the sanctuary leads to a simple, modern **refuge** equipped with a fireplace and running water outside, making this a popular picnic spot in season. With your own transport you can continue another 10km from the *santuari* (12km from the B402 junction) to Castellar de N'Hug (see below), an easier drive than the way up from La Pobla de Lillet.

The main road west continues to the **Coll de Merolla** (1090m) – with some weird rock formations to the southwest and some excruciating curves to either side of the pass – and then drops to **LA POBLA DE LILLET**, 28km from Ripoll. Here two ancient bridges arch over the infant Llobregat river, but there's little else to see besides a pair of minor Romanesque churches – ruined, monastic Santa Maria and the curious circular Sant Miquel – both 1500m east of town, and currently undergoing restoration. **Accommodation** and **dining** are restricted to the central *Hostal Pericas*, c/Furrioles Altes 3 (☎972/823 61 62; ④), though the food is only average, and the service excruciatingly slow. There's also a small, sporadically open **tourist office** by the smaller of the bridges.

Fonts de Llobregat and Castellar de N'Hug

From La Pobla there's a steady eleven-kilometre ascent towards Castellar de N'Hug and, since you can leave the road only for a short section at the beginning and at the end, you miss little by hitching – or waiting for the Monday-to-Saturday evening **bus** up from Berga via La Pobla. Three kilometres out of La Pobla on the left, stands a disused cement factory, a flamboyant *Modernista* building designed by Rafael Guastavino in 1901; it looks lie a stack of cave dwellings, now eerily empty, with the turreted *xalet* for the bosses crumbling off to one side.

Approaching Castellar, you'll come to the **Fonts de Llobregat**, source of the river that divides Spanish Catalonia in two, entering the sea at Barcelona. Numerous jets of water burst from the rock of a densely wooded ravine, the most powerful ones forming a broad, photogenic waterfall. Every year hundreds of Catalans come here as if on a pilgrimage – summer droughts cause many of Catalonia's rivers to dwindle to nothing, so there's great pride in any durable water source, and this one has never stopped in living memory, even during the driest year. Coming uphill, the main access is by a signposted side turning at about Km8, leading past the giant *Hostal Les Fonts* to a parking lot and old water mill, a few minutes' walk from the cascades. You can also get here via a fifteen-minute stepped path from the bottom of Castellar de N'Hug (see below).

Heaped up against the rise of the Serra de Montgrony, **CASTELLAR DE N'HUG** makes a good base for the Moixeró section of the park; curiously, high seasons here are September and October, when people come mushroom-hunting in the surrounding forests, and the skiing season of January and February. There's a fair amount of inexpensive **accommodation**: first choices are the friendly *Hostal La Muntanya* (☎93/825 70 65; ③) at Plaça Major 4, with excellent, copious suppers and rooms spread over two premises, and the *Fonda Fanxicó* (☎93/825 70 15; ④) across the way, which also does meals. One to avoid is the unwelcoming, overpriced *Pere Miquel*, while the *Fonda Armengou* near the church now only does meals, despite its name. For slightly more luxury, there's the *Hostal Alt Llobregat* (☎93/825 70 74; ④), at the southeast edge of the village on the road down towards the Santuari de Montgrony.

North from Castellar, the paved road continues over the range to La Molina and the Collada de Toses via the **Coll de la Creueta**; there are paths in this direction as well, but they're not marked, and it's best to ask advice in the village for the five-hour walks to Toses or Planoles, and to equip yourself with the Editorial Alpina map *Montgrony/Fonts de Llobregat*.

Serra de Catllaràs

Southwest of La Pobla de Lillet rises the **Serra de Catllaràs**, claimed to be the only Spanish habitat of edelweiss (*flor de neu* in Catalan, a common local business name). If you haven't got a four-wheel-drive vehicle, you can use the GR4.2 which skims the range on its way west to Guardiola de Berguedà; the obvious staging point is the rather hideous **Santuari de Falgars**, where the pilgrims' *hospedaría* houses – and feeds – all comers (☎93/744 10 95; ①) in spare but clean quarters.

Sant Jaume de Frontanyà and beyond

The eleventh-century church at **SANT JAUME DE FRONTANYÀ**, unquestionably the finest Romanesque church in the region, lies 11km southeast of La Pobla, accessible by a newly paved road not yet shown on commercial or tourist office maps; the turning south from the B402, 2km east of La Pobla, is well marked, with only the first kilometre down to the river currently still unmade.

Built in the shape of a Latin cross with three apses, this Augustinian foundation has an engaging setting at the foot of a naturally terraced cliff. The twelve-sided squinch-supported lantern was unique in Catalunya until the restoration of the monastery at Ripoll. Inside (either of the two restaurants keeps a set of keys – see below) the church is chill and bare, echoing and evocative in its emptiness.

The surrounding hamlet, all of a dozen stone houses, offers two characterful **restaurants**, *Sant Jaume* and *Fonda Cal Marxandó*, the latter with inexpensive **rooms** (☎93/823 90 02; ③) above its good-value, beam-ceilinged *menjador*.

From Sant Jaume the road continues 9km south to nondescript **BORREDÀ** on the C149, where small lumber mills on the outskirts slowly process the lush surrounding forest. If you get stuck here – possible, as there's just one morning bus daily to Berga – there's only the *Baix Pirineu* **restaurant** on the main street, with rooms suitable for emergencies, and a few bars. Otherwise, from Borredà it's another 21km southwest to Berga, passing the **Pantà de Baells**, a reservoir on the Llobregat, where at low water local boaters claim you can see the cupola and crumbled walls of a submerged monastic church.

Berga and around

From the south, the major public transport approach to the Cadí park is the twice-daily bus from Barcelona to **BERGA**, where the Pyrenees seem suddenly to rear up with startling abruptness. The town itself is fairly dull, but it does have a ruined castle, a well-preserved medieval core and – as capital of Berguedà *comarque* – onward connections to higher settlements in the county, provided by the ATSA bus company at the top of Passeig de la Pau.

There's just one other reason to come to Berga, and that's at Corpus Christi when the town hosts the **Festa de la Patum**, one of the most famous of Catalunya's festivals. For three days, huge figures of giants and dwarves process to hornpipe music along streets packed with red-hatted Catalans intent on a good time. A dragon attacks onlookers in the course of a symbolic battle between good and evil, firecrackers blazing from its mouth, while the climax comes on the Saturday night, with a dance performed by masked men covered in grass.

Not surprisingly, **accommodation** is impossible to find during the festival unless you've booked weeks in advance; at other times you should have few problems. There are at least eight places to stay, most of them reasonably priced: try *Hotel Passasserras*, c/La Valldan (☎93/821 06 45; ④); *Habitacions Paseo*, Passeig de la Pau 12 (☎93/821 04 15; ③), run by the electrical appliance store below; or the very central *Hotel Queralt*, Plaça de la Creu 4 (☎93/821 06 11; ④). If you need assistance, the **tourist office** is at Plaça de Sant Pere 1 (Mon–Sat 9am–3pm; ☎93/821 03 04). The best **restaurant** in town is the *Sala* at Passeig de la Pau 27 (closed Sun dinner and Mon) – count on about 5000ptas each for full gourmet meals (with a rare place of honour for vegetables), less if you opt for the *menú*.

West of Berga: Sant Llorenç de Morunys

Although the scenic drive itself is magnificent, there's little other than the panoramic **chapel of Queralt** (4km northwest of Berga) to stop for along the 32km of winding road west to Sant Llorenç de Morunys, which skirts the very southern rim of the Pyrenean foothills. Just one **bus** a day covers this route.

The chief appeal of **SANT LLORENÇ DE MORUNYS** lies in its setting near the head of the lofty-sounding Vall de Lord, but the ancient city walls enclosing a defensive huddle of houses, and the steep, narrow streets leading to several portals, will reward a half-hour's stroll. The eleventh-century monastic **church** has a beguilingly odd interior, one of its two chapels being overwhelmed by Baroque gilt work, the altar by a huge fifteenth-century retable. Until restoration is completed you can't enter the cloisters with their plain-capitalled columns, but must be content with viewing them through a large window in the church.

Sant Llorenç has an adequate amount of **accommodation**, though none of it is in the old quarter, or particularly inexpensive. If travelling by public transport you should plan on spending the night, as the single daily bus from Berga arrives in the evening.

First choice would be the newly renovated *Hostal La Catalana*, Plaça del Dr. Ferran 1 (☎973/49 21 25; ④), or the refurbished *Hostal Piteus* immediately opposite on the through road (☎973/49 23 40; ④), which also has penthouse apartments. Unless both of these are full, there seems little reason to patronize the dreary-looking *Pensió Casa Joan*, on the road northwest out of town (☎973/49 20 55; ④). There's also a **campsite**, *El Morunys*, 2km north of town, just off the side road to La Pedra hamlet. In the old walled town, a decent independent **restaurant** is *Can Peratà*, on c/Santa Isabel, at the corner of c/San Nicolau.

Onwards from Sant Llorenç

In whichever direction you leave Sant Llorenç, the views are startling, though it's best to have a car or bike as there's no public transport. If you hitch, don't accept any partial rides, as traffic to the west especially is sparse.

To the **west** the road climbs 8km to the **Coll de Jou** (1560m) and then briefly along a corniche before dropping through a tunnelled gorge to join the C1313, 44km further along, in the Segre river valley near Organyà. Along this paved but one-lane road there's little but farming hamlets, each individual house seemingly signposted; the only substantial place en route is **ALINYÀ**, tucked into a Shangri-La-like valley with a trio of hamlets overhead: La Vall de Mig, L'Alzina, the highest, and Llobera, the lowest, 700m from the main road,with a *casa de pagès* if you get stranded.

A daily bus to Solsona runs along the crests to the **south**, with dizzying ravine views. Alternatively, the GR7 long-distance route goes there too, threading through the Riu Cardoner gorge and passing the Romanesque church at Olius with its magnificent crypt, before completing a long day at **Solsona**. This fine old walled town, rather larger but less spectacularly set than Sant Llorenç, offers inexpensive accommodation and transport connections towards Barcelona.

To the **north** of Sant Llorenç looms the ski resort of **PORT DEL COMTE**, reached either via the village of La Coma, 6km from Sant Llorenç near the sources of the Cardoner, or by a more direct road that climbs from the Coll de Jou. **Accommodation** in this beginners' centre is relatively expensive, and the nearest reasonable options are in **LA COMA**, 11km east and downhill; try the rather basic *Fonda Cal Nin* (☎973/49 23 54; ③), in the village centre by the church, or the fancier *Hotel Fonts del Cardoner* (☎973/49 23 77; ④), north of the village on the highway.

The **GR7** heads north from Sant Llorenç via La Coma to the 1636-metre **Coll de Port**, and then on to Tuixèn – a day's march – but the marked route is so often track or asphalt rather than path that, frankly, if you can arrange a ride along the paved road, do so. At Tuixèn (see p.180) you're at the very edge of the Cadí *parc natural*.

North of Berga: Guardiola de Berguedà and Bagà

The towns along the Llobregat and Greixer valleys **north of Berga** were once centres of a flourishing smuggling trade with Andorra, protected from law-enforcing pursuers by the barrier of the Serra del Cadí. Nowadays the Túnel del Cadí cuts under that mountainous screen, allowing passage for the C1411, and neither of the main towns en route – **Guardiola de Berguedà** and **Bagà** – retains any suggestion of illicit activity. They aren't particularly enticing either, though they each have accommodation options suitable for an emergency overnight en route to the Cadí.

Strung out grimly along the old course of the C1411 (a new bypass avoids the town), **GUARDIOLA DE BERGUEDÀ** is on the bus route from Berga to La Pobla de Lillet and only 1500m past the turning for Saldes and Gòsol (see below). Sole **accommodation** option is *Fonda Guardiola* (☎93/824 00 01; ③), on the main street at the south end of town, which also does meals. If you don't feel like waiting around for the daily 5.35pm bus to Saldes and Gòsol – note that it doesn't enter town, but turns at the junction 1500m south – the mailman stops at the *Bar L'Avellaner* at 11am on weekdays; provided you don't have too much luggage, he'll take you as far as Gòsol.

BAGÀ, 5km further north and the second town in the *comarque* after Berga, has more going for it in the form of a tiny old quarter, a park information office and **accommodation** options. Choose between *Hotel La Pineda*, c/Raval 50 (☎93/824 40 10; ④), at the eastern end of the main shopping street, and the *Fonda Ca L'Amagat* (☎93/824 40 32; ③), quietly placed in the heart of the old town. A **campsite**, the *Bastareny* (☎93/824 44 20; open all year), 1km west of town, caters mostly to caravans.

Continuing north through the five-kilometre **Túnel del Cadí** (no pedestrians or bicycles) brings you into the Cerdanya, for which see p.195. To the west of Bagà stretches the newly designated GR 107, "El Camí de les Bonnes Hommes", which begins in France and purports to be the route used by fleeing Cathars (see p.218); locally it links Bagà with Gòsol (see below) via Gisclareny.

The Serra del Cadí

The western part of the Cadí-Moixeró park– the karstic **Serra del Cadí** – offers equipped and experienced hikers three or four days' worth of trekking through wild, lonely areas. A number of tracks and paths cross the range, though the favourite excursion for most visitors remains the ascent of **Pedraforca**. As in other limestone massifs, finding fresh **water** can be problematic, and that – combined with intense summer heat at this relatively low altitude – means that the peak visitor seasons are May to June, and September. The Cadí supports three fairly well-placed, seasonally staffed **refuges**, accessible from a number of foothill villages which are served poorly or not at all by bus, so you may have to drive, hitch or walk to them from the larger towns downvalley. Extended explorations of this region imply possession of the Editorial Alpina 1:25,000 "Serra del Cadí/Pedraforca" and "Moixeró" **maps** and guide booklets.

From the Llobregat valley north of Berga there are two major ways west into the Cadí. **From Bagà**, a partly paved track follows the Riu Bastareny to the hamlet of Gisclareny. A much busier paved road begins 1500m south of **Guardiola de Berguedà** and leads to Gòsol, via Saldes.

From Bagà: via the Bastareny valley

The fourteen-kilometre vehicle route up the **Bastareny valley** begins at the campsite by the river on the west side of Bagà: from there the partly paved road crosses the river, passes through a tunnel, turns to track, and then climbs steeply through dense forest to naked white cliffs before emerging through the **Coll de l'Escriga** (1360m) onto the south side of the mountain. The views over the Saldes valley are superb, the river glinting far below, with range after range of mountains unfurling to the south.

GISCLARENY, 3km beyond the pass, is nothing more than a handful of spread-out farms (with a total population of 31) and two **campsites**, one of which – *Cal Tasconet* (☎908/69 98 79), 1500m west of the hamlet centre – also operates a **refuge** (①). Beyond Gisclareny, the track continues through **Coll de la Balma** (1600m), where it divides: left (southwest) means a sharp down-and-up to the village of Saldes (see opposite) via the lushly forested Gresolet valley; right (west) a more level if less interesting trajectory via El Collel. The former route takes about three hours, the latter at least five.

Usson château

Santa Maria monastery, Ripoll

Camprodon

Besiberri and Estany Negre, Aigües
Tortes National Park

The Núria Gorge

North flank of Serra del Cadí, Prat d'Aguilo

Andorra: Pas de la Casa

Montségur village and castle

St-Aventin church, Luchon area

La Seu de Urguell

Estany Llong, Aigües Tortes National Park

The twisty road up the Bastareny valley can be negotiated on mountain bike or by 4WD vehicle; if you're on foot, it might be better to skip it in favour of the direct Bagà–Gisclareny **path**, shown more or less correctly on the Editorial Alpina "Moixeró" map. From the *Cal Tasconet* refuge (where you'll need to confirm directions) a path drops down into the beeches and silver firs of Gresolet en route to Saldes, two hours shorter – assuming you don't lose the way – than the roundabout track option.

Traverses of the Moixeró

By staying with the Bastareny valley-bottom track rather than going through the tunnel noted on the previous page, you'll reach a cluster of farms at **VEINAT DE L'HOSTALET**, from where a good trail leads up to the staffed *Refugí de Sant Jordi* (1640m), four hours from Bagà. Once over the Coll de Pendis (1800m), just above the refuge, you have to dodge – and briefly use – an unsightly jeep track, but it's possible to devise a mostly trail-and-overland traverse of four hours more to Bor in the Segre valley, linked by paved road to Bellver de la Cerdanya. From the refuge you can also ridgewalk east along the Moixeró watershed all the way to Massella, a popular route in winter with nordic skiers.

From Guardiola: via the Saldes valley

The minor road from just south of **Guardiola to Saldes** and Gòsol is quite a spectacle, with steep drops into the Riera de Saldes on the early stretch, giving way to brilliant views of Pedraforca once beyond the hamlet of Maçaners (Massanés). Campsites and accommodation spaced at intervals along the road attract sufficient cars – mostly Catalan vacationers – in summer almost to guarantee a lift. The *El Berguedà* **campsite** is 3km from the turning off the main road; the *Repòs del Pedraforca* (☎93/825 80 44; open all year) appears 13km from the turning, with a pool and bungalows to rent; while at the "Km 15" marker, south of the road, the somewhat isolated *Fonda Cal General* (☎93/825 80 54; ④) makes a practical base if you have your own vehicle. It's as well to know that the municipality of Saldes has recently decided to clamp down on rough camping, so those tenting down are expected to patronize the sites listed.

Saldes

SALDES, a small village 18km from Guardiola, set dramatically at the foot of Pedraforca itself, is an ideal starting point for explorations of the peak. Here you'll find two stores with staple provisions suitable for trekking, plus two inexpensive **inns** where reservations are virtually mandatory in season: the *Fonda Carinyena* (☎93/825 80 25; ③) near the church, and the pricier *Cal Manuel* (☎93/825 80 41; ④), on Plaça Pedraforca (where cars park) serving meals. Better value than either of these, however, is *Cal Xic* (☎93/825 8081; ③), a **casa de pagès** 1500m west of the village in Cardina hamlet, at the start of the road up towards Pedraforca. Although it's a modern, somewhat sterile building, the simple, en-suite rooms are clean and cheerful, and asking for a *desayuno salado* gets you ham, sausages, cheese and a *porrón* to wash it all down, rather than the usual sickly continental breakfast.

Beyond Saldes the scenery changes abruptly, first to the black-stained rocks of a lignite mine, then into speckled, deeply eroded gold-and-red rock, and then back again to lush, extensive pasture and forest. Mining activities have destroyed the old trail between Saldes and Gòsol, leaving walkers no alternative but to hitch or trudge along the road.

Gòsol

The old stone village of **GÒSOL**, 10km beyond Saldes at 1430m elevation, is an altogether more substantial place, spilling appealingly off a castellated hill. Pablo Picasso came here from Paris during the summer of 1906 and stayed for several weeks in fairly primitive conditions, inspired to paint by the striking countryside; one of the streets off the Plaça Major is named after him. Well established by the ninth century, the original village now lies in ruins, a fifteen-minute walk above the present one; the twelfth-century castle commands sweeping views of the valley, as well as the less spectacular backside of Pedraforca.

Gòsol makes a good alternative base to Saldes for explorations of the entire Cadí; the GR107 goes through here, communicating with the saddle of El Collell to the north (see p.182). There are two **hostals**, both with decent attached restaurants: *Cal Francisco*, on the little roundabout as you come into town (☎973/37 00 75; ③), or the smaller, central *Can Triuet*, Plaça Major 4 (☎973/37 00 72; ③). There's also a **campsite** southwest of the village, reached by dirt road from beside Cal Francisco. A handful of **bars** and one other independent **restaurant** around the main *plaça* cater in part to the Barcelona-based summer-home dwellers. If you want to arrange a **taxi** ask in the gift shop or ring ☎973/37 00 65.

West of Gòsol: Josa de Cadí and Tuixèn

To skirt the Cadí by vehicle, keep on the sparsely travelled dirt track – just manageable in an ordinary car – west to Josa de Cadí. By way of two long hairpins it climbs into the **Coll de Josa** (1625m), 5km from Gosòl, where there are superb views north, with the summit of Cadí almost dead ahead; from here the track drops through Scots pine to the Riveru Josa.

JOSA DE CADÍ, 6km beyond the pass on a church-capped hill with one slope plunging to a ravine, is one of the most picturesquely set villages of Catalunya. Despite its remoteness it has become another second-home venue for urban Catalans, and the traditional dwellings with their windows outlined in chalky blue paint and their ancient wooden doors are fast disappearing, replaced by modern conversions. As yet there's neither bar nor accommodation here, for either of which you have to proceed another 8km southwest to **TUIXÈN (TUIXENT)** – by contrast one of the more touristically equipped of the Cadí villages, an attractive and relatively lively place set in a gently sloping basin. It has an unreliably open **park information office**, just off the main square that doubles as a car park; all **accommodation** lines c/Coll, the short street linking this parking area with the nominal Plaça Major. Best are the *casa de pagès Can Farragetes* (☎973/37 00 34; ②) at no. 7, which also rents **mountain bikes**, and the *Fonda Can Custodi*, on the corner with Plaça Major (☎973/37 00 33; ③) with the best **restaurant** hereabouts, featuring sustaining four-course *menús*. The closest official **campsite** lies 3km west. In winter the mountains southwest of Tuixèn offer excellent **cross-country skiing** at the *La Vansa* resort, with 25km of marked trails ranging between altitudes of 1600m and 2100m.

To the south, a tarmac road rises for a steep 8km to the Coll de Port with its bar-restaurant and the side road for *La Vansa*, continuing to Sant Llorenç de Morunys (30km). In the opposite direction another paved road threads through the villages of Cornellana (9km), Fornols (12km) – food and lodging available at both – and Adraén (19km), their houses largely renovated as summer homes. This northern route is nominally the GR7, which reaches La Seu d'Urgell after a good seven hours' walking. The path, as so often track surface or sliced up by the road, is not brilliant and you're best off driving, cycling or hitching this stretch from Tuixèn.

Walks and climbs on Pedraforca

Pedraforca is for Spanish Catalonia what Canigou is to Roussillon: the virtual symbol of the region, and accordingly much loved. The name means "stone pitchfork", supposedly the Devil's, and indeed from afar the mountain does look like an upended goat's hoof. The distinctive two-pronged summit – **Pollegó Superior** (2497m) and **Pollegó Inferior** (2400m) – is divided by a gentler saddle called the **Forcadura** (2350m); in medieval times, local witches' covens met here, and it's still a popular place to camp on the eve of 24 June, *El Dia de Sant Joan*. Some personality from the Catalan "alternative" world generally organizes some sort of after-dark, summer-solstice happening, either here or down in Saldes.

From behind *Cal Xic*, some 1500m west of Saldes, a partly paved road winds just under 5km to within fifteen minutes' walk of a mountaineers' refuge (the *Refugí Lluís Estassen*, see below), just above the car park and **Mirador de Gresolet**, which looks down into the Gresolet valley. From Saldes proper a more direct path shortcuts much of this road, but you still face a fair amount of asphalt-walking, so arrange a ride if possible. One kilometre before the *mirador* and the well-signposted final trailhead to the refuge, the path from Saldes passes a *zona de acampada libre* with water and tables provided. This impromptu **campsite** is not in fact "free", as somebody comes up from Saldes each morning and evening to collect a nominal charge – essentially a fine levied by the park authorities on Saldes village for allowing illegal camping – and move along those who have been camped here for more than three days.

At 1640m, the **Refugí Lluís Estassen** (☎908/31 53 12; ①), owned by the FEEC, has space for one hundred, and offers hot showers and evening meals for about 1700ptas. Although open all year, the peak seasons are spring and autumn, especially on weekends, when big-wall climbers come to tackle the sheer north face of Pedraforca.

The ascent

Despite appearances, a **walking ascent** of the peak is strenuous but not technically difficult. From the refuge you have a choice of a relatively dull but easy out-and-back approach from the southeast, or a more challenging and exciting loop over the mountain, beginning north of the summit. In either case a dawn start is advisable, or you'll be baked by the summer sun against the bare rock.

For the **simpler approach**, head south for forty minutes from the refuge fountain, along a narrow but well-trodden path through pine and box, to the base of the giant scree gully leading up to Forcadura. Turning sharply west up this, guided by a few red-and-yellow paint splodges, brings you to the saddle in just under two hours from the refuge, after a very slippery, mostly trailless climb. At Forcadura, you'll glimpse Gòsol to the west – and a gentler, distinct trail slithering up the **Canal de Gòsol** (*canal* meaning ravine in local parlance). From Forcadura it's another 25 minutes north up a reasonable, obvious trail to the top of Pollegó Superior, with its assorted Catalan flags, "mailbox" for dedications and the expected views. Return is by the same route, for a total outing of just under five hours.

The **more difficult** circuit route involves initial progress west from the *Refugí Lluís Estassen* along a trail shaded in the morning, and then a sharp climb up to the **Collada de Verdet** (2250m; 2hr), where you meet yet another path coming up from Gòsol via the **Canal de Verdet**. From this pass you turn south, then east, creeping along the very spine of Pedraforca towards Pollegó Superior; a rope and a partner are suggested if you're acrophobic, and it will soon be obvious why you can't use this section going downhill. You descend to Forcadura and return to the refuge as in the first itinerary, after a six-hour-plus day.

A south–north traverse of the Cadí

From the south, the peaks of the Cadí appear as a chain of rounded summits separated by shallow saddles, but seen from the north they form a wall of sheer, bare rock, in places dropping 500m. A one-to-two-day **traverse from south to north** takes in all aspects of the Cadí, coming down into the Cerdanya to intercept the Puigcerdà–La Seu d'Urgell road.

For traverses, Gòsol serves as a slightly better starting point than Saldes; from its centre, adopt the GR107, which soon dwindles to a path heading northeast through jagged rock teeth to the strategic pass known as **El Collell** (1845m; 2hr 15min), with fine views east over Gresolet and west towards Josa de Cadí. El Collell is also reachable in about an hour from the *Refugí Lluís Estassen*, a rather unexciting if shady track walk. No motorized vehicles are allowed on the mountain slopes north of the pass, though they may continue east.

Stay with the track coming up from the refuge as it curls east towards Gisclareny for another kilometre, and then take the zigzagging, obvious path on your left (north), leading towards the apparent ridge of the Cadí. The ascent to the **Pas dels Gosolans** (2410m; 3hr from El Collell) is not straightforward and takes longer than expected, owing to the up-and-down, limestone-dell topography and the necessity of clearing the minor Serra Pedragosa.

At the pass – essentially a slight notch in the watershed, well used by smugglers in years past – you're near the roof of the Cadí, with awesome views west along the crest and north across the Segre valley. Plainly visible below, the **Refugí Prat d'Aguiló** (2037m; always open; staffed with a ① fee charged in summer) is an hour's descent along a steep path negotiating a convenient spur. From the refuge and its spring you should arrange a ride along the 15km of track north via Montellà to Martinet, on the main Puigcerdà–La Seu d'Urgell road, roughly halfway between the two towns.

A more advanced **ridge-walking** option veers off west just before the Pas dels Gosolans: two conspicuous paths head towards the top of the Cortils canyon, where you'll find a rare spring and a former shepherds' cottage usable as a shelter. You should overnight here before completing a long day westwards cross-country along most of the Cadí summits, taking in **Puig de la Canal Baridana** (2648m), the highest of the range. Rather than descending the savagely steep namesake *canal*, it's better to back-track an hour to the **Puig de la Canal de Cristall** and use the more gentle ravine there, well provided with springs, to complete the day in the pretty village of **ESTANA** (no amenities but camping tolerated nearby). From there you're only 10km from the main Segre valley road; buses run along it between Puigcerdà and La Seu d'Urgell in each direction three times a day.

West of the Cadí: routes to Alt Urgell

Daily buses from Barcelona and Lleida, bound for La Seu d'Urgell, head into the *comarque* of **Alt Urgell** along the C1313 road, which threads through the impressive gorge of Tresponts as it follows the Riu Segre upstream. Exciting as the scenery is, only one spot – **ORGANYÀ** – might induce a brief stop en route. A small, round building (summer Mon–Sat 10am–2pm & 6–9pm, Sun 10am–2pm; winter Mon–Sat 11am–2pm & 5–7pm, Sun 11am–2pm) on the main road contains both the local **tourist office**, and what is possibly the oldest document in the Catalan language. Written in the twelfth century, the *Homilies d'Organyà* are annotations to some Latin sermons, discovered in a local presbytery at the beginning of this century and now displayed in back-lit glass cases. If you get stranded here – and Organyà isn't the most attractive town – there are two similar **hostals** on the bend of the road almost opposite: *La Cabana*, Avda. de Montana 2 (☎973/38 30 00; ③), and *Els Tres Ponts* (☎973/38 30 92; ③), both with affiliated **restaurants**.

La Seu d'Urgell and around

Even though it's the capital of Alt Urgell, **LA SEU D'URGELL**, beside the Riu Segre 23km upstream from Organyà, has for years been a rather sleepy place – there seems no point in trying to compete with nearby Andorra, the biggest knock-down bazaar in

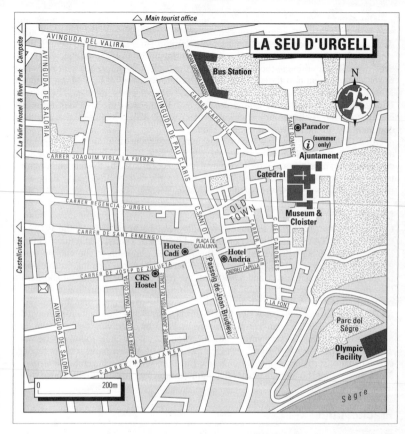

the Pyrenees. But since the 1992 Olympic canoeing competitions were held nearby, La Seu and its previously neglected medieval quarter have undergone a mild transformation: there are two or three fancy new hotels, as well as the purpose-built canoe facilities by the Segre, but as most new development has fallen outside the old quarter, you should still be able to enjoy a fairly relaxed stay before sampling the excesses of Andorra.

The Town

Named after the imposing cathedral (La Seu) at the end of c/Major, the town has always had a dual function as episcopal seat and commercial centre; there's still a street farmers' market each Tuesday and Saturday, attracting vendors from throughout the *comarca*. By 820 a bishopric already existed here, and all the parishes of Andorra belonged to the counts of Urgell, but in the wake of the Moorish retreat they headed south, and by the early twelfth century La Seu's bishops had acquired these possessions. Ambiguities of jurisdiction eventually led to a conflict between the bishops and the French nobility of Foix, settled by the 1278 Act of *Paréatge*, which allowed for joint control of the principality.

The original cathedral and city, on the hill where Castellciutat (see below) now stands, was destroyed in the eighth century by Moorish invaders. The present **Cathedral** was consecrated in 839 but completely rebuilt in 1175, and restored several times since. Nonetheless, it retains some graceful interior decoration and fine cloisters with droll capitals; admission to the latter is around the back of the church, where a 300-ptas ticket also gets you into the adjacent eleventh-century chapel of Sant Miquel and the Museu Diocesano; to see only the cloister and chapel costs 150ptas. The **Museu Diocesano** (Mon–Sat 10am–1pm & 4–7pm, Sun 10am–1pm) merits a visit for a brilliantly coloured tenth-century Mozarabic manuscript with miniatures, the *Beatus*, a commentary on the *Apocalypse* of Saint John.

Other than these few sights, time is most agreeably spent strolling the dark, cobbled and arcaded streets west of the cathedral, which is where you'll find many of La Seu's best bars and restaurants. A strong medieval feel is accentuated by the fine buildings lining c/dels Canonges (parallel to c/Major); the town's fourteenth-century stone corn measures still stand under the arcade on c/Major.

Castellciutat

Comprehensive panoramas of the Segre valley can be enjoyed from the village of **CASTELLCIUTAT**, just 1km west of town, and its nearby ruined castle (now a luxury hotel). Follow c/Sant Ermengol, cross the river and climb up to the village, which glories in the views that La Seu never gets. There's still some farming on the slopes below the tiny stone church, and a *pensió* on the road up to the village and another on the square (see "Accommodation" below), both make a nice retreat from La Seu. To continue your walk, follow a path around the base of the castle and cross the main road for the nearby Torre Solsona. A sign here reads "Danger" and the scanty remains of the old fortifications are indeed crumbling away, assisted by quarrying below – take care near the edges. You can vary your route to Castellciutat or back by following the walkways through the very pleasant, post-Olympic riverside **Valira** park, with its modern cloister made from pink stone; Dalí, Casals, Einstein, Winston Churchill and Groucho Marx are among the famous twentieth-century characters (mainly men) whose heads decorate the capitals.

Practicalities

The **bus station** is on c/Joan Garriga Massó, just north of the old town; local services include the twice-daily Alsina Graells buses to Puigcerdà, and much more frequent La Hispano-Andorrana departures to Andorra (for details of which, see p.188). The **tourist office** (Mon–Sat 10am–2pm & 5–8pm; ☎973/35 15 11) is in Avinguda de les Valls d'Andorra, the main road into town from the north; in July and August, there's also an information office behind the cathedral, near the *Ajuntament*, which supplies maps and hotel information.

Accommodation

In the wake of the Olympic facelift, not much decent **budget accommodation** remains in La Seu. The best bet is the *CRS* (*Centre Residencial i de Serveis*) at Sant Joan Bta. de la Salle 51 (☎973/35 38 16; ①), one of the Olympic hostels built in 1992 with individual, double or treble rooms and a swimming pool, very near the centre (you need YHA membership or student card). Otherwise there's *La Valira* **youth hostel** (☎973/35 38 97; closed Sept; ①), at the western end of c/Joaquim Viola la Fuerza, by the Valira park. The **campsite**, *En Valira* (☎973/35 10 35; open all year), is 300m northeast of the hostel, at Avda. del Valira 10.

Under the circumstances, you're probably better off at one of the **hotels** on the main road through town. Best placed of these is the *Andría*, Passeig Joan Brudieu 24

(☎973/35 03 00; ④), an elegantly faded establishment which probably offers the most value of the hotels if there are two of you. Less attractive, but friendly and adequate, is the *Cadí* (☎973/35 01 50; ③) in c/Josep de Zulueta, close to Plaça de Catalunya. Top-of-the-range places include the elegant *Parador* (converted from a former monastery), very near the cathedral at c/Sant Domènec 6 (☎973/35 20 00; ⑥), and the exclusive *El Castell* (☎973/35 07 04; ⑥), a four-star hotel, discreetly incorporated within the castle at Castellciutat. Or you might consider staying in the village of **Castellciutat** itself: the friendly, family-run *Pensió Fransol* in the central Plaça de l'Arbre (☎973/35 02 19; ③) is nicely positioned; alternatively, try the newer, more expensive *Hostal La Glorieta* (☎973/35 10 45, fax 35 42 61; ⑤), with a pool and restaurant, just above the river on the road up to the village.

Eating and drinking

Lively **tapas bars** are plentiful in La Seu's old town: try *Bar Lalin*, c/Major 24, or *Bodega Fabrega*, c/Major 81. For excellent-value **restaurant** meals, *Cal Pacho*, in a quiet corner on c/la Font (at the southern end of c/Major, then east), has a very Catalan menu, worth trying for lunch or dinner, though it's often fully booked.

Outside the old town there are plenty of choices, too. *Palace*, by the bus terminal at the corner of c/Joan Garriga Massó and the highway, has an all-you-can-eat buffet for 1200ptas; at no. 7 in the same street, *Les Tres Portes* offers a good-value three-course menu (1300ptas) in a quaint chalet-style house and garden. More centrally, the best place to eat budget Catalan food is the busy *Restaurant Canigó*, at c/Sant Ot 3 (at the north end of the *passeig*), which offers an array of *platos combinados* and an excellent *menu del dia* (including bread and wine) for 950ptas. East of the main *passeig*, *Bambola Pizzeria-Creperia*, c/Andreu Capella 4, serves – no surprises here – tasty and reasonable pizzas and crepes. The adjacent *Nazario* is a good if expensive *orxateria-gelateria* with outdoor seating. The *Hotel Andría* restaurant, nearby, is no great food bargain but its garden terrace makes a pleasant setting for a drink.

West of La Seu: Castellbó and Sant Joan de l'Erm

Four kilometres south of La Seu a road climbs west along the River Solanell, between cornfields and then over successively more scrubby rises, to the village of **CASTELLBÓ**, 14km from La Seu. This was the seat of Arnau de Castellbó, whose marriage to Arnalda de Caboet merged the Andorran fiefdoms of Caboet and Castellbó, which were then conveyed to France through the marriage of their daughter to the count of Foix. The only thing to see now is the thirteenth-century church of **Santa Maria**, an example of Romanesque-Gothic transitional style with its pointed arches and Romanesque ironwork. There's a **campsite**, with a shop, on the edge of the village.

Beyond Castellbó you can climb on to the *Refugí Pla de la Basseta* (☎973/35 13 43; ①; open all year) at **SANT JOAN DE L'ERM**, a superb cross-country **ski** resort with 150km of trails between 1600 and 2150m. Westward progress is on jeep and mountain-bike tracks; without your own transport, the best option is to hitch along the 47km road west from **ADRALL**, 7km south of La Seu, to Sort in the Noguera Pallaresa.

ANDORRA

After seven hundred years of feudalism, the twentieth century has finally forced itself upon **ANDORRA**, 450 square kilometres of mountainous land between France and Spain. A referendum held in March 1993 produced an overwhelming vote in favour of a democratic constitution, replacing a system in effect since 1278, when the Spanish bishops of La Seu d'Urgell and the French counts of Foix settled a long-standing quarrel by granting Andorra semi-autonomous status under joint sovereignty. In 1185 Arnalda d'Isarn de Caboet had married Arnau de Castellbó, thus combining the Andorran possessions that the two families had been granted by the bishops of La Seu. Their only daughter Ermensende later married Roger-Bernard II, count of Foix, who claimed sole rights to Andorra when Arnau died without male issue. The bishops of La Seu contested this, claiming that sovereignty reverted to them with the cession of the male line of Castellbó. The consequent strife between the bishops and the house of Foix was brought to an end in 1278 by the Act of *Paréatges*, which made La Seu d'Urgell and Foix *co-seigneurs* of Andorra. (Incidentally, the Act also forbade the building of castles in Andorra, which explains their absence here.)

Despite a certain devolution of powers – the counts' sovereignty passed successively to the French king and then the French president – the principality largely managed to maintain its independence over the centuries. The Spanish and French *co-seigneurs* appointed regents who took little interest in the day-to-day life of the principality. The country was run instead by the *Consell General de les Valls* (General Council of the Valleys), made up of appointed representatives from Andorra's seven valley communes, who ensured that the principality remained well out of the European mainstream – it even managed to maintain neutrality during the Spanish Civil War and World War II.

It was during these conflicts that Andorra began its meteoric economic rise, as locals first smuggled goods from France into Spain during the Civil War and, a few years later, goods from Spain into France under German occupation. After World War II, this trade was largely replaced by legitimate duty-free business in alcohol, tobacco and electronics, and by the huge demand for winter skiing. Much of the principality became little more than an unsightly, drive-in megastore, with the main road through the country clogged with French and Spanish visitors after cut-price hi-fi and electrical gear, mountain bikes, ski equipment, car parts and a tankful of discount petrol. Seasoned Spain-watcher John Hooper has called Andorra "a kind of cross between Shangri-La and Heathrow Duty-Free", while the Spanish daily broadsheet *El Pais* once dismissed it as a "high-altitude Kuwait".

Ironically, though, this tax-free status held the seeds of Andorra's belated conversion to democracy. Although the inhabitants enjoyed one of Europe's highest standards of living, twelve million visitors a year began to cause serious logistical problems: the country's infrastructure was sorely stretched, the valleys increasingly blighted by speculators' building sites, while the budget deficit grew alarmingly since little entrepreneurial wealth went towards the public sector. Spanish entry to the EC in 1986 only exacerbated the situation, diminishing the difference in price of imported goods between Spain and Andorra.

The 1993 referendum was an attempt to come to terms with the economic realities of twentieth-century Europe. Or rather, some of the economic realities, since none of the parties involved in the negotations and arguments seriously suggested that the solution would be to introduce direct taxation: there is still no income tax in Andorra, and barely any indirect taxes either. Instead, the idea is to transform Andorra into a kind of "offshore" banking centre, to rival the likes of Gibraltar, Lichtenstein and Luxembourg.

Following the referendum, the state's first **constitutional election** was held in December 1993. Only the ten thousand native Andorrans were entitled to vote (out of a total population of sixty thousand) and an eighty percent turnout gave Oscar Ribas Reig, outgoing head of the *Consell General*, the biggest share of the vote. His Agrupament Nacional Democratic took eight seats in the new 28-seat parliament and formed a coalition with other right-wing parties to usher in the new democratic era. For the first time, Andorran citizens (those born there, or who have lived there for over 20 years) can vote freely, and join trade unions or political parties, while their government now

L'Hospitaler △

FRANCE

Soulcem Dam
2878m
2903m Borda de Sordeny
Tristaina Lakes
Col de la Mine
El Serrat
Arcalis
Port de Rat 2540m
Llorts
Alt de Coma Pedrosa 2942m
P. de Baiau
Arinsal
Aigüesjuntes
Pal
La Maçana
Ordino

Coll de Fontargent
2913m
Cabana Sordy
Etang de Couart
Estanys de Juclar
Vall d'Incles
Ransol
Soldeu
Port d'Envalira
Pas de la Casa
Valira d'Ordino
Canillo
Valira del Orient
Santuari de Meritxell
Grau Roig
2825m

Latour-de-Carol ▷ Ax-les-Thermes ▷ Porta ▷

Port de Bouet ◁
Jeep track to Tor ◁

Pic dels Pessons 2865m
Encamp
ANDORRA
L'Illa
Porteille Blanche 2517m
2869m

Meranges ▷

N
2691m
ANDORRA LA VELLA
Escaldes-Engordany
S.Miquel
Sta. Coloma
Madriu Valley
Pla de l'Ingla
2898m
Perafita
Port de Perafita 2582m
Port de Vallcivera 2519m
Llosa
Cap del Rec
Viliella
SPAIN
Sant Julià de Lòria
2754m
Aranser
Lles

ANDORRA

0   5 km

▽ La Seu

has the right to run its own foreign policy and establish its own judicial system; Andorra has already been accepted as a full member of the United Nations, and as a member of the Council of Europe.

Given all this, it's useful to remember that as recently as thirty years ago Andorra was virtually cut off from the rest of the world – an archaic region which, romantically, happened also to be a separate country. There are still no planes and no trains, but for many visitors that is now the full extent of any attractive quaintness. It can take an hour in bumper-to-bumper traffic to drive the few kilometres from La Seu d'Urgell to Andorra la Vella, the main town; surprisingly, the main crop here, which you see on either side of the road and in every small available space throughout Andorra, is tobacco. Up in the valleys, large-scale ski resorts have already monopolized the most attractive corners of the state, with yet another planned for the beautiful Prat Primer upland. This sort of development – coupled with Andorra's historically lax regulations – scarcely benefits wildlife, already hard-pressed by helicopter- and 4WD-equipped gunmen who fire away with impunity during officially closed seasons and at protected species.

But it's nonetheless worth leaving the capital and main developments behind to see some of the scenery that attracted early visitors. Although the highest point (Alt de Coma Pedrosa on the western border) reaches just 2942m, there is wilderness in plenty here. Scots pine is endemic, and the mountain pine *Pinus mugo* thrives at altitudes up to 2200m, or even 2400m on south-facing slopes; moisture-craving silver fir grows on north-facing slopes between 1600 and 2000m. Wild boar, golden eagles and griffon vultures are native to the area, but bears might no longer be – the last confirmed sighting was in 1978.

Through Andorra by road

The main through road – jointly the CG1 from Spain to Andorra la Vella and the CG2 from the latter to the French border – plies 38km north, then east, through the main

ANDORRA PRACTICALITIES

Getting there
From Spain, there are two daily direct buses from Barcelona (4hr 30min), and regular services from La Seu d'Urgell which depart at 8am, 9.30am, 12.15pm, 2pm, 3.20pm, 6pm and 7.15pm, taking forty minutes to reach the capital of Andorra la Vella.

From France, a bus leaves L'Hospitalet at 7.40am and 6.15pm, arriving at Pas de la Casa half an hour later; from Pas de la Casa the onward bus journey to Andorra la Vella takes one hour ten minutes.

Even if you're **driving** you might as well leave the car behind and take the bus – in high season (summer or winter) the traffic is so bad that the bus isn't much slower, and parking in Andorra la Vella is an ordeal.

Leaving Andorra
Buses back to La Seu d'Urgell leave from Plaça Guillemó in Andorra la Vella, parallel to the main road. Departures are Monday to Saturday at 8am, 9am, 11.30am, 1.30pm, 4pm, 6pm and 8pm; Sun 9am, 11.30am, 1.30pm, 4pm and 8pm.

To France, La Hispano-Andorrana SL company (☎376/82 13 72 or 82 03 27) runs two buses a day from Andorra la Vella to Pas de la Casa (1hr 15min) and L'Hospitalet (2hr 15min), one leaving in the morning and one in the afternoon.

Getting around
Internal **bus services** are cheap and frequent on the following routes (between about 7.30am and 9pm): Andorra la Vella–Sant Julià de Lòria, Andorra la Vella–Encamp–Canillo, and Andorra la Vella–La Maçana–Ordino; buses leave from Plaça Guillemó. **Hiking** details are given in the text.

Customs
Inspections of goods upon leaving and entering are non-existent, but French, Spanish and Andorran police will board buses looking for faces that don't fit, and ask luggage bays to be opened, as a check against illegal immigrants.

Currency, phones and mail
Andorra has no money of its own, so both pesetas and French francs are accepted; prices in shops and restaurants are quoted in both currencies. There's also a shared postal system, with both a French and Spanish post office in Andorra la Vella. But Andorra does have its own phone code – ☎376 – applicable to the whole republic.

Population and language
The **population** of Andorra is around sixty-five thousand, of which about twelve thousand are native Andorrans – the rest are mainly French, Spanish or Portuguese, with a smattering of other nationalities. Catalan is the official **language**, but Spanish and, to a slightly lesser extent, French are widely understood.

valley draining Andorra. The CG3 heads northwest up the dead-end, and therefore quieter, Valira del Nord. Whichever way you go, and whether you travel by bus or your own car, it's likely to be a slow business – the hordes of shoppers and skiers are intent on getting from A to B, and rarely leave the traffic lines to go sightseeing.

Andorra la Vella

With its stone church of **Sant Esteve**, fast-flowing river and appealing setting amidst crags and green slopes, **ANDORRA LA VELLA**, the capital – 7km from the Spanish border – must once have been an attractive little town. The main street is now a seething mass of tourist restaurants (specializing in six-language menus), tacky discos and brightly lit shops crammed with everything from electricals, perfumes and watches to cars and kitchenware.

There's partial respite in the narrow streets of the old quarter, or *barri antic*, which lies on the heights above the River Valira, south of the main through road, Avda. Princep Benlloch. Besides the church, its sole monument is the **Casa de la Vall** in c/de la Vall (free guided tours Mon–Fri 10am–1pm & 3–7pm). Built in 1580 for the wealthy Busquet family, this solidly built stone house was purchased by the *Consell General* in 1702; it now houses the *Sala de Sessions* of Andorra's parliament and the chief courtroom (*Tribunal de Corts*). Between Sant Esteve and the town hall, Rambla Molines leads to the raised Plaça del Poble, laid out as a spacious pedestrian square with stone benches, sculptures, flower beds, fountains and a covered picnic place; there are cafés, WCs and telephones here too, and the tourist office (see below) is nearby. The church of **Santa Coloma**, over 1km west of the centre in the namesake suburb, merits a glance for the oddity of its round tower – virtually all Romanesque churches have square ones.

Practicalities

Buses leave passengers on Avda. Princep Benlloch, very near the church of Sant Esteve. There are about half a dozen public **car parks** scattered around town, should you bring your own vehicle – count on walking up to a kilometre from any space you happen to find.

Andorra la Vella's **tourist office**, on c/Dr. Vilanova (Mon–Sat 9am–1pm & 3–7pm; ☎376/82 02 14), east of the *barri antic*, has astonishingly complete lists of local accommodation, restaurants and bus timetables, and also sells a good topographical map of Andorra. It's the main information post for the entire principality, though smaller booths keep similar hours in every sizeable village.

There are several reasonable places if you decide to **stay**: the friendly, basic *Hostal del Sol*, at Plaça Guillemó 3 (☎376/82 37 01; ③); the slightly larger *Hotel Les Arcades* on the same square at no. 5 (☎376/82 13 55; ③); the rock-bottom *Residència Baró* at c/Puial 21, just up some steps from the main boulevard (☎376/82 14 84; ①); and, the only spot in the heart of the old quarter, *Hotel Racó d'en Joan*, c/de la Vall 22 (☎376/82 08 11; ③).

A better plan, perhaps, is to linger long enough for something to **eat** before retreating to more attractive surroundings; intense competition fosters low prices, and the town boasts some of the few ethnic restaurants in the Pyrenees. Best value in the *barri antic* is *Minim's*, tucked away in the tiny Placeta de la Consorcia (July–Sept daily 1–3.30pm & 8–11pm; rest of year closed Wed), a small, stylish place with hearty French cuisine (1250ptas/55F menu). Other fairly central and characterful places include *Pizzeria Primavera*, c/Dr Nequi 4, near the *barri antic*; *Restaurant Macary*, c/Mossén Tremosa 6, just northeast of the Plaça Princep Benlloch; and *Les Arcades* at Plaça Guillemó 5, for filling combo specials and a bargain 950-pta/40F menu. South of the centre, on the far side of the river, *El Viet Nam* – under an apartment building just off Avda. Tarragona – provides the only Asian food for valleys around.

Escaldes-Engordany

Andorra la Vella merges seamlessly with **ESCALDES-ENGORDANY**, in effect a northern suburb, its pavements still choked with visitors eager to buy something, or dunk themselves in the hot spa which has given the place its name. The ultramodern thermal baths of **Caldea**, opened in 1994 with their landmark glass pyramid, provide the very latest in hydrotherapy and beauty treatments with an outdoor and indoor lagoon, Indo-Roman baths and luxury treatment rooms (☎376/82 86 00; daily 10am–11pm; minimum 2200ptas/3hr). Cultural relief is provided by the work of Catalan sculptor Josep Viladomat i Maçanes, 140 of whose pieces are on display at **Salita Parc** in Avda. Parc de la Mola (Mon–Sat 5–9pm, Sun 11am–2pm & 5–9pm); his stylistic affinities lie with Miquel Blay and Josep Clarà of Olot (see p.150).

The church of **Sant Miquel d'Engolasters**, one of the most attractive Romanesque churches in the area, stands on a shelf to the south of Escaldes. The quick way is to take the road that climbs to the Engolasters reservoir, passing the church after 4km, but if you want to make a day of it, you can follow the **GR7** for two hours from the main street in Escaldes to just beyond the hamlet of Ramio, where you follow the marked footpath towards Encamp (see below) for another hour. Sant Miquel's frescoes, like those of many Andorran churches, have been appropriated by the Museu d'Art de Catalunya in Barcelona, but this eleventh-century chapel is still an evocative sight.

There's an abundance of **hotels** in Escaldes, though most are aimed firmly at the free-spending ski crowd. Exceptions include *Pont de la Tosca* at Avda. Miquel Mateu 6 (☎376/82 19 38; ③), *Astòria* at Avda. de les Escoles 16 (☎376/82 05 15; ③), *Residència Roca* at c/Engordany 3 (☎376/82 08 58; ③), and the slightly more expensive *Núria* at c/Santa Anna 11 (☎376/82 15 72; ③). The most reasonable **eating** is found at *Restaurant Bon Profit*, Avda. Carlemany 53, and *Pizzeria Roma*, on the same street at no. 95.

The Valira del Nord

For a bit of peace and quiet you can head up the **Valira del Nord** (also known as Valira d'Ordino) from Escaldes, but you'll have to wait until you get past La Maçana, 7km northwest, for it to begin. The left-hand fork here climbs 4km to the popular ski resort of **ARINSAL**, in winter served by three daily buses from Andorra la Vella. Its twelve lifts reach to around 2500m and serve 21 pistes: two green, eight blue, seven red and four black. The most reasonable **accommodation** here is provided by *Hotel Palanques* (☎376/83 50 07; ②) or the slightly larger *Naudi* (☎376/83 50 95; ②), both in Avda. Sant Antoni. Nearby **PAL** is a pretty, stone-built village with limited skiing; the fourteen lifts serve twenty short pistes: four green, three blue, twelve red and one black.

Back at La Maçana, the right fork leads to **ORDINO**, 3km on, a quiet, agreeable place whose handful of old stone edifices mingles with new chalets and apartment buildings. One of the seventeenth-century family houses in the middle of the village, with splendid carved wood furniture and patterned pebble floors, is now open as the **Museu-Casa d'Areny-Plandolit** (guided tours 9.30am–1.30pm & 3–6.30pm; 300ptas). The least expensive of several well-appointed **hotels** here is the small *Hotel/Restaurant Quim*, on the main square, opposite the church (☎376/83 50 13; ③). For delicious cakes and snacks, try the café-patisserie *1930*, opposite the museum; the bar-restaurant *Babi*, next door, has more substantial meals at reasonable prices. Mountain bikes are for hire outside the **tourist office** (☎376/83 69 63) on the main road, near the church, which also displays the daily weather forecast.

Beyond Ordino – served by frequent buses from the capital – the landscape begins to get more interesting, but even here tourism is perceptible in the forms of suspiciously fancy restaurants and numerous half-built hotels or apartments sprouting in former tobacco fields and pastures. At the head of the valley, 18km (and 3 daily bus departures) from Andorra la Vella, stands the village of **EL SERRAT**, graced by some tumbling waterfalls. Nearby **hotels** include the *Hotel Tristaina* (☎376/83 50 81; ③) and *Hotel dels Llacs* (☎376/83 51 31; ④), both in the village; and the *Hostal la Cortinada* (☎376/85 51 51; ③) in La Cortinada, or the *Hotel Vilaró* in Llorts (☎376/85 52 25; ③), both on the road up from Ordino. Just beyond Ordino, there's a riverside **campsite** at Ansalonga (☎376/85 03 74) and another further up the valley at Llorts (☎376/85 00 22).

From El Serrat the road climbs steeply to the new ski resort of **ORDINO-ARCALIS**, probably the most pleasant place to ski in Andorra. The main appeal of Arcalis resides in its high-mountain setting, overlooking the Tristaina lakes, which makes up for the limited pistes.

The Valira del Orient

It's around 33km from Escaldes to the French border at Pas de la Casa along the **Valira del Orient**, a route served as far as Soldeu by hourly buses from the capital. You're unlikely to be tempted to get off anywhere for casual touring, though with your own car or a ski holiday in mind there are several possibilities.

ENCAMP, 6km from Escaldes, is your first chance to stay somewhere tolerable beyond Escaldes. In the centre of town, among old stone houses and concrete highrise, the startlingly modern town hall stands out like a giant video screen. For a pleasant stroll, follow the riverside walkway on the west bank, to the unspoilt village of **Les Bons**, with its tiny twelfth-century Romanesque chapel of Sant Romà and the remains of a ruined castle standing above. Recommended **hotels** here include the *Pere d'Urg* (☎376/83 15 15; ②), on the riverside at the lower end of town, with a mainly young clientele; the friendly *Helena*, opposite the tourist office at Plaça dels Consell 11 (☎376/83 11 35; ③), run by a charming French couple; and the slightly more upmarket but excellent-value *Hotel Coray* (☎376/83 15 13, fax 83 18 06; ④), at the top of the town above the town hall, which is used by the Ramblers' Association as their base for walking holidays.

Some 3km past Encamp, a small road climbs south to the **Santuari de Meritxell**, the ugly shrine designed by Olympic architect Ricardo Bofill to replace a Romanesque building that burned down in 1972. The fire also destroyed the ancient carving known as *Our Lady of Meritxell*, described by Nina Epton as having "the barbaric appeal of a recently converted Christian with her long astonished face and enormous black Byzantine eyes". A replica stands in her place.

CANILLO, nearly 6km from Encamp, makes one of the best compromise bases in Andorra: well served by bus and fairly close to the shops of Andorra la Vella, but far enough away to retain some dignity and character. Beautifully situated at 1562m, among rocky cliffs and green slopes, it's an excellent centre for day hikes. On the eastern fringe of the town, the bell-tower of the Romanesque church of **Sant Joan de Caselles** is original, but the porch is a fifteenth-century addition. **Hotels** are concentrated around c/General, the main through road; the best options are the friendly *Casa Nostra* (☎376/85 10 23; ②), which has a pleasant bar and restaurant, and the smaller *Canigó* opposite (☎376/85 10 24; ③). The lovely tree-shaded *Camping Santa Creu* (☎376/85 14 62) is near the centre, on the opposite bank of the river.

SOLDEU, sprawling at the head of the valley 19km from the capital, won't win any beauty contests but does offer some tranquil **skiing**, with some beautiful runs through trees from near the 2560-metre summit of Tossa de la Llosada. A total of 22 lifts serve 60km of pistes: fifteen green, six blue, eight red and three black. Most **hotels** are in the through boulevard, best value among them being *Soldeu "Maistre"* (☎376/85 10 35; ②), *Bruxelles* (☎376/85 10 10; ③) and *Peretol d'Envalira* (☎376/85 12 64; ③). From just below Soldeu, a tiny road heads north up the lovely **Vall d'Incles valley**. There's an inexpensive though basic **campsite** at the far end, well placed for the HRP – allow an hour to walk there from the main road.

Pas de la Casa

Once over the **Port d'Envalira**, the road descends steeply down bald hillsides to the ghastly high-rise **PAS DE LA CASA**, a combination of duty-free bazaar and ski station. The best that can be said of it is that with a bottom station of 2100m and a top of 2800m, it can guarantee snow in all but the mildest winters. Its **skiing** is linked to that of Grau Roig (see below), a tiny place in the next valley, giving a total of 27 lifts serving 58km of pistes: ten green, twelve blue, fourteen red and four black. Among Pas de la Casa's pricey **hotels**, *Hotel Residència Casado*, close to the ski slopes at c/Catalunya 23 (☎376/85 52 19; ⑤), stands out as being helpful, clean and good value. Less expensive options, though further from the ski lifts, are *Hotel Olimpic*, c/des Abelletes 6 (☎376/85 53 22; ③), the small *Hotel l'Eidelweiss*, c/Major 20 (☎376/85 51 92; ③), *Hotel La Muntanya*, c/Catalunya 12 (☎376/85 53 18; ③) and *Hotel El Chat*, c/La Solana (☎376/85 53 61; ④).

Andorra on foot

You can make a **walking tour** of Andorra, hardly touching any of the towns and seeing its most appealing side, by following the ski circuit described in the box opposite. But if you just want to move onwards, the principal **traverse routes** are: the **GR7**, which skirts the southeastern mountains; the **GR11**, which traverses quickly between the Perafita area and Alt de Coma Pedrosa, via Encamp, Ordino, La Cortinada and Arinsal; and the **HRP**, which keeps to the northern fringes of the principality. Most of the alpine shelters en route are small and pretty basic. The best **maps** are the Randonnées Pyrénéennes 1:50,000 "Haute-Ariège-Andorre", or the Editorial Alpina 1:40,000 "Andorra"; the eastern half of Andorra is also shown on the IGN 1:50,000 "Cerdagne-Capcir" sheet, and the IGN 1:50,000 "Fontargente" map. The main tourist office in Andorra la Vella supplies a useful map showing the location and size of all the mountain huts and refuges.

Southeast from the Porteille Blanche: the GR7

Many walks into and around Andorra follow the old paths of the *paquetaires* (*paqueteros* in Spanish), the smugglers who carried heavy packets of Andorran tobacco and other contraband across the border, normally travelling at night to avoid detection. Porta (see p.203 for access details), at the top of the Carol valley in France, was one of the great smuggling villages of the Pyrenees, on account of its link with Andorra along the Campcardos valley, now the route of the **GR7**.

A three-hour climb up the valley from Porta brings you to the **Porteille Blanche** (Portella Blanca; 2517m), from where you can detour slightly north to **Pic Negre d'Envalira** (2825m), just south of the source of the Ariège. From the summit you look down into the valley of the Valira del Orient to the northwest; the fact that the three nations' borders meet here allowed any *paquetaire* encountering trouble to step quickly into France, Andorra or Spain. West of the pass the GR7 descends towards the ski station at **GRAU ROIG**, where the only accommodation is at the *Hotel Refugí* (☎376/85 55 56; ④–⑤).

Next day you continue via the **Cirque dels Pessons** into the **Gargantillar** lake region, where there is a refuge (always open) at **Estany l'Illa**. The next refuge – a more logical choice for an overnight – is at **Pla de l'Ingla**, at the head of the beautiful

A SKI CIRCUIT OF ANDORRA

A six-day **ski circuit** virtually traces the perimeter of Andorra, using refuges and village accommodation. Only experienced ski mountaineers should attempt it, and necessary equipment includes snow-saw, ice-axe and a four-season sleeping bag for the huts, some of which have no stove. The classic itinerary stays very close to the border ridge, at one point crossing for a short time into Spain – so passports are suggested, even for EU citizens who, technically, no longer need them to cross borders. The best **map** for the tour is the *Vals d'Andorre* 1:50,000 map, on sale at all local tourist offices.

Day One (5–6hr)
Drive, take a taxi or hitch to Aixirivall, in the mountains to the east of Sant Julià, and after crossing two bridges head northeast to the **Febrerrussa valley**, first climbing, then descending to the **Coma de Claror**. Pass **Etany de la Nou** and the **Perafita**, heading east to the **Collada de Maïana** and the valley of **Madriu**. Stay overnight in the *Refugi del Orris*.

Day Two (3–4hr)
Make for **Estany la Bova**, then the **Estany de l'Illa** reservoir. Climb northeast along the **Col des Isards** (2779m), descending by the **Circ dels Pessons** to the parking area of the **Grau Roig** ski station. If snow conditions are unfavourable, substitute the easier but longer descent via the **Collada de Montmalus**, which will add three hours to the day.

Day Three (5–6hr)
Head in the direction of **Port d'Envalira**, climb **Pic Maïa**, following the line of the ridge until **El Port Dret**. From here, keep north until **Pas de les Vasques** (2560m), descending to the **Incles valley** before going west through forest to pass through the **Collada del Clot Sort** (2458m). Descend to the plain of **Ransol**, following an easy track to Ransol village.

Day Four (8–9hr)
Make your way to **Fond de la Coma** and there head west for the **Col de la Mine** (2713m). Pass the *Refugi de Sorteny* and follow the track to the **Rialb bridge**. Climb up the **Rialb valley** to the *Refugi de Rialb*. After the **Montjo pass** the valley heads east; you'll negotiate easy slopes to reach the **Portella de Rialb**, from there descending to the **Castellar hut**.

Day Five (3–4hr)
Either follow the route to the **Port du Rat** or take the Arcalis chairlift to get to the **Coma del Forat**. Head south via the **Portella de Cataverdis** (2715m), descending steeply to the **Estany l'Angonella**. At the lake head southwest through the **Portella de Montmatell** (2649m), finally descending to the *Pla de l'Estany* refuge.

Day Six (4–5hr)
Head north from the refuge, then veer left to slip through the small *col* almost immediately above it. Go west to the cirque at the end of the valley, then climb southwest to the **Collada de Malhiverns** (2826m) through a steep corridor. Descend to the valley, looking out for a rocky spur at about 2400m. Here go south to the **Portella de Sanfons** (2577m), descending on the Spanish side in the direction of Port Vell. Pass right of Pic Negre until **Coll Petit**, coming down to the Port de Cabris road. Here you'll have to pole along until **Coll de la Botella**. From the *col* you can either follow the road to the parking area of Pal ski station or take the **Couloir de Cardemeller**, a steep route which gets you into Pal quicker but brings a serious risk of avalanches.

Madriu valley (2000m; always open). Here you can continue on the GR7 along the valley to Escaldes, or cut through the **Collada de la Maiana** to the west, reaching the Andorra la Vella–La Seu d'Urgell road near Santa Coloma.

West from the Ariège: the GR10/HRP

The routes **west** from the top of Ariège into the Incles valley are beautiful approaches to the best of Andorra's landscape. From the train station at **HOSPITALET-PRÈS-L'ANDORRE**, the **HRP** *variante* initially climbs the Sisca valley, then switches to the Baldarques, going past the **Étang de Pedourrès** to the **Étang de Couart**, where it joins a path from Mérens-les-Vals.

Coming from **MÉRENS-LES-VALS** itself, you can take the **GR10** westwards up the more inspiring **Mourgouillou valley**. After ninety minutes or so the GR climbs back to the right – go straight on, past the **Étang de Comte**, through the defile and over the chaos of boulders to link up with the HRP at the Étang de Couart. From the lake, amid bleak, rocky terrain, the HRP cuts between the twin **Estanys de Juclar** – just inside Andorra – and then down to the head of the **Vall d'Incles**, where you'll call it a day at the campsite there.

To avoid going down to Soldeu and the main road along the Valira del Orient, you should continue on the HRP to El Serrat, near the head of the Valira d'Ordino, and finally out into France via the **Port de l'Abeille**. There are three ways of accomplishing this, more or less parallel to each other.

The easiest route is the most southerly, climbing west from the head of the Incles valley, dropping down into the head of the **Ransol valley** and climbing out again into the **Col de la Mine**. The middle route passes the small *Refugí Cabana Sorda* (2000m; always open) on **Cabana Sorda** lake, then follows the frontier peaks to Col de la Mine. The hardest and wildest is the variant that goes north from Incles through the **Port de Fontargente** to the Fontargente lakes, then curves west to re-enter Andorra through the **Port de Soulanet**.

Whichever of the three options you choose, you can use the **Refugí Borda de Sorteny** (1969m; always open) towards the end of the trek, its thirty places making it one of the roomiest refuges in Andorra. From here it's a ten-minute walk to the end of the road coming up the 5km from El Serrat. Maniacs can manage the Incles–El Serrat hike in eight hours; everyone else takes two days.

West from the Cerdanya: the GR11

From the Spanish Cerdanya, the logical starting points are the villages of Meranges (see p.196) on the GR11 trail, and Llés (see p.196), near the boundary with Urgell *comarca*. The **GR11** from Meranges bears west across the Llosa valley, past the permanently open refuge of **Els Esparvers**, then through the **Port de Vallcivera** (2519m) into the Madriu valley. The route from Llés actually starts at the *refugí* 6km above, beyond the hamlet of Viliella. From here, **GR11 variant 1** heads northeast via the well-spaced *refugís* of Cap del Rec and La Pera before slipping over the **Port de Perafita** (2582m) and then down into the eponymous Andorran cirque, before rejoining the main GR11 near the bottom of the Madriu valley. Either of these routes occupies a fairly leisurely two days.

West out of Andorra: the GR11 and HRP

There are several trails **west out of Andorra** towards the Montcalm-Estats-massif on the Franco-Spanish border, of which the main ones are the HRP from near El Serrat, initially into France, and the easier GR11 from Arinsal directly to Spain.

The classic choice begins from the ski station of Ordino-Arcalis, from which a clear trail – part of the HRP – climbs the short distance to **Port de Rat** (2540m) on the French frontier. From there drop sharply to the track running south from the Soulcem dam, then climb equally steeply on the far side to the **Port de Bouet** (2520m) on the Spanish border. Descend on the path west until you meet a track at the **Pla de Bouet**, from where the *Refugi de Vall Ferrera* (open summer only) is a short distance north. Even with a lift to the trailhead at Ordino-Arcalis, it's a challenging day of about seven walking hours; if you have to hoof it from El Serrat, add two hours more.

The **GR11** from Arinsal doesn't involve so much roller-coastering – there's only one up-and-down – and is consequently simpler, though no less scenic. From Arinsal you climb west into the valley of **Aigüesjuntes**, in the very shadow of Alt de Coma Pedrosa, before negotiating the **Portella de Baiau** (2796m); the guarded *Refugi de Coma Pedrosa* (☎376/83 50 93; June–Sept; ①), with sixty places, food and hot showers, is five minutes' walk from Estany de les Truites. Once on the Spanish side, there's a lake and simple refuge at the head of the **Baiau valley**, along which the GR11 bears north to intersect briefly with the HRP some distance below the Port de Bouet.

CERDANYA/CERDAGNE

Ringed by mountains, the high, fertile upland of the **Cerdanya** (Catalan) or **Cerdagne** (French) – about one-fifth of the way along the Pyrenean watershed – has never quite been able to decide for itself whether it is French or Spanish. The 1659 Treaty of the Pyrenees imposed nominal allegiances, which rather arbitrarily divided a region that considered itself Catalan in language and culture. Yet development of overt French or Spanish national consciousness, and a hardening of the notoriously porous frontier, was a long time coming. French and Spanish didn't come into official use until the early nineteenth century, following the French Revolution, a border war of 1793–95 and the Napoleonic campaigns. A formal boundary was marked for the first time only after the supplementary Treaty of Bayonne in 1866.

Essentially the basin of a prehistoric lake, once the largest in the Pyrenees, the Cerdanya/Cerdagne's traditional isolation and lack of natural frontiers has lent it an ambiguous identity. It's also inextricably linked with the **Carlit Massif** to the north, which has provided wood, pasturage and water from the very earliest times, and is thus usually considered as part of the Cerdagne.

Because of its former military significance, good **roads** have long converged on the region. Mont-Louis, on the eastern fringe of the French Cerdagne, had a road – now the **N116** – in from Villefranche as early as the seventeenth century, while Napoleon ordered the construction of the original **N20** from the north, terminating at insignificant Bourg-Madame. Spanish development inevitably lagged behind, but this century the **C1313** – alias the **N260** – was paved from La Seu d'Urgell, west of the Spanish Cerdanya, as was the **C1411** from points south, both meeting at **Puigcerdà**, more or less at the geographical centre of the region.

Because of its gentle terrain, the Cerdanya/Cerdagne supported the first – and now last-surviving – trans-Pyrenean **rail line**, funnelling traffic between Barcelona and Toulouse via Puigcerdà and Latour-de-Carol. Threatened abolition of the service between Puigcerdà and Ripoll was only averted in 1985 by a massive Cerdan letter-writing campaign to Spanish premier Felipe Gonzalez, coupled with half-serious threats to request renegotiation of the Treaty of the Pyrenees and secession to France.

The Cerdanya

The name **Cerdanya** refers to the Spanish portion of the upper Segre valley (a high plateau which actually continues on the French side as far as Mont-Louis). To the north it is flanked by mountains rising to the Andorran frontier, dotted with tiny villages high above the road on outcrops and shoulders; on the southern side, the Cadí mountains form an impressive barrier. The frontier is at **Puigcerdà**, connected by a six-kilometre corridor of road to the territorial anomaly of **Llívia**, former capital of the region and now a Spanish enclave in French territory. The Cerdanya remains more rural and traditional than the French side, and has been a popular summer holiday area for wealthy Barcelonans since the last century.

Bellver de Cerdanya

Coming from La Seu along the C1313/N260, there's no compelling reason to get off the bus unless you intend to go hiking to the north or south. The main pretext for a lunch stop would be **BELLVER DE CERDANYA**, standing on a low hill on the left bank of the trout-laden Riu Segre, 18km west of Puigcerdà. With a ruined castle and its sprinkling of old balconied houses, it's a much-visited example of a typical mountain village, made doubly attractive by the Romanesque church of **Santa María de Talló**, a short stroll south of the town. Known locally as the "Cathedral of Cerdanya", this is a rather plain twelfth-century building, but has a few nice decorative touches in the nave and apse, and retains a wooden statue of the Virgin that's as old as the building itself.

The **tourist office** at Plaça Sant Roc 9 (July–Sept Mon–Fri 10am–1pm & 4–7pm, Sat & Sun 10am–1pm) can fill you in on **accommodation** details: the *Vianya*, c/Sant Roc 11 (☎973/51 00 44; ②), and the *Hostal Pendís*, Avda. Cerdanya 36 (☎973/51 04 79; ②), are the more modest outfits; *Hostal Mas Martí*, c/Martí de Bares (☎973/51 00 22; ③–④), and *Mesón Maties*, Crtra. Puigcerdà (☎973/51 00 39; ③–④) have slightly more expensive rooms, with and without bath. For **eating**, look no further than the dining room of the *Mas Marti* (daily late July to late Sept and holidays year-round), which mixes French and local cuisine for about 2500ptas per person.

Hiking north and south

From Ger, about halfway between Bellver and Puigcerdà, a narrow road leads 10km north to **MERANGES** past hayfields, hamlets and copses of silver birch and maple. Set at 1540m, at the front of a lake-filled basin at the foot of **Pic del Calm Colomer** and **Puig Pedros**, this summer-holiday village was once important to the smuggling trade. You can **stay** here at *Fonda Can Joan*, c/Central 5 (☎972/88 00 96; ③), before heading west on the GR11 towards Andorra as described above (see "West from the Cerdanya: the GR11", p.194).

Alighting from the bus at **MARTINET**, 8km west of Bellver, allows access to trailheads both south and north of the C1313/N260. The tracks from Estana village and the shelter at Prat d'Aguilo, in the Cadí foothills to the south, emerge here; the north face of the Cadí looks impregnable, but it's actually not that difficult to reverse the directions given on p.181. If you need to stay in Martinet, there are the **fondas** *Miravet*, c/Arenas 2 (☎973/51 50 16; ③), and *Plubinet*, c/Segre 13 (☎973/51 50 18; ③).

From here a paved road climbs steeply north 9km to **LLÉS** (pronounced "Yes"; 1471m), a good base for a popular nordic skiing centre 6km further on. There's stable accommodation in the *Fonda Cal'Abel* (☎973/51 50 48; ③), the *Domingo* (☎973/51 50 87; ③) or the *Pensió Mirador*, Plaça Sant Pere 4 (☎973/51 50 75; ④). The resort itself, exposed to the full glare of the sun, has 29km of marked pistes; in summer an eighty-bunk *refugí* (①) here remains open, renting out mountain bikes suitable for exploring the myriad local tracks. From the refuge you're well poised to enter Andorra on a two-day traverse via the Port de Perafita.

Puigcerdà

Although it was founded by King Alfonso I of Aragón in 1177 as a new capital for then-unified Cerdanya, **PUIGCERDÀ** retains no compelling medieval monuments, partly owing to heavy bombing during the Civil War. The church of Santa Maria itself no longer exists, a wartime casualty, but its forty-metre-high **bell-tower** still stands in the namesake *plaça*. The east end of town, down the pleasant, tree-lined Passeig Deu d'Abril, escaped more lightly; here, you can see medieval murals in the gloomy parish church of **Sant Domenèc**. Dwelling morbidly on the saint's martyrdom, surviving fragments show Dominic's head being cloven in two by a sabre – he's already been run through by a sword thrust – while another monk, still standing, has a bloody sword through his skull. The renovated thirteenth-century convent next door is now used as a local cultural and youth centre; work continues to restore what's left of the medieval cloisters behind.

The greatest attraction of the town, however, is its atmosphere – if you've just arrived from France, the attractive streets and squares, with their busy pavement cafés and well-stocked shops, present a marked contrast to moribund Bourg-Madame. Allow at least enough time for lunch, if not an overnight stop. French day-trippers certainly endorse this strategy, crowding out the bars and eateries all summer. The most enjoyable of the outdoor cafés crowd the merged *plaças* of Santa Maria and dels Herois; between drinks, you can explore the older quarter between Plaça de l'Ajuntament and Passeig Deu d'Abril, or amble up to the small recreational lake, five minutes' walk to the north.

Arrival and accommodation

Puigcerdà is on the main line from Barcelona to Latour-de-Carol (3 trains a day from Barcelona, 4 from Latour). From the **train station** (outside which buses stop) in Plaça de l'Estació, wearyingly steep steps lead ten minutes up to Plaça de l'Ajuntament in the heart of town, with reviving views far west over the Cerdanya. At the top of the steps, to the right, stands the new **Casa de la Vila**, a replacement for the Gothic original destroyed in the Civil War, with the **tourist office** alongside at c/Querol 1 (June–Aug daily 10am–8pm; Sept–May Tues–Sat 10am–1pm & 4–7pm, Sun 10am–2pm; ☎972/88 05 42), which dispenses useful brochures.

There's plenty of **accommodation** up in town, and no advantage whatsoever in staying at the obvious establishments near the train station. Best bet among the cheaper places is *Hostal La Muntanya*, c/Coronel Molera 1 (☎972/88 02 02; ③), close to Plaça Barcelona, and very reasonable for its price; the very central *Hostal Alfonso*, c/d'Espanya 5 (☎972/88 02 46; ②) is also cheap and friendly, but depressingly dingy. *Pensió Núria*, Plaça Cabrinetty 22 (☎972/88 17 56; ④), which overlooks a pretty square near the tourist office, is clean and neat, but you should book in advance to be sure of a place. For a mild splurge, there's none better than the *Hostal del Lago*, Avda. Dr. Puiguillém (☎972/88 10 00; ⑤), just off Plaça Barcelona towards the lake. One **campsite**, *Stel* (☎972/88 23 61; open all year), is 1km out of Puigcerdà on the road to Llívia, just before you cross into France; there's another, *Pirineus*, 3km out of town in the opposite direction, beyond the train station.

Eating and drinking

Passing French tourists are responsible for the relatively high prices in Puigcerdà, but there are still a number of reasonable places to **eat**. At the budget end of the scale, *Sant Remo* at c/Ramon Cosp 9, is a straightforward bar offering large menús at 900 and 1300ptas. *La Cantonada*, c/Major 48, beyond the bell-tower, has more attractive surroundings and a 900-ptas menú, while at *Cris Bar*, Passeig Deu d'Abril, the *tapas* are typically Catalan, and washed down with a strong, home-made red wine.

A bit more expensive (though not nearly so grand as it sounds) the *Montserrat* at the back of the *Hotel Alfonso*, at c/d'Espanya 5, offers fish and shellfish, including local trout. At the top of the same street, the busy *Bar-Restaurant Kennedy*, with outside seating on Plaça dels Herois, serves *tapas* at the bar and a good three-course menu for 1400ptas.

The other **bars** with outdoor seating on Plaça dels Herois and the adjoining Plaça de Santa Maria – *Miami* and *Sol i Sombra* – are usually busy, with the last-named doing a lucrative side-line in cured meat to take away. The *cervesseria* on Plaça Cabrinetty styles itself as an international beer specialist, and if you're so inclined you can sit outside, drinking your way around the world's breweries.

Llívia

The Spanish town of **LLÍVIA**, 6km from Puigcerdà but totally surrounded by French territory, is a curious place indeed, worth visiting not least so you can say you've been

BORDER CROSSING TO FRANCE

Just three **trains** daily cross the border, bearing northwest to Latour-de-Carol, six minutes away, where you change for Toulouse (4hr) and Paris (12hr). If you're **driving**, you enter France via the adjacent small town of Bourg-Madame (see p.202); it's also a simple matter to walk across to Bourg-Madame, 2km maximum from the centre of Puigcerdà. The frontier is open 24 hours, year round, and formal checks here are almost non-existent: the French don't bother much and the Spanish just want to see that you have a valid passport.

there. There are only a couple of **buses** daily from Puigcerdà (the Alsina Graells bus stops in front of the train station and in Plaça Barcelona), but the ninety-minute walk out isn't too strenous: bear left at the junction 1km outside town, just before the Bourg-Madame border post, and keep to the main road. From French territory, the turn-off to Llívia is completely unmarked; your only clues are the flyover carrying the access highway, flanked by a K-Supermarket and an inconspicuous slip road with its abandoned and vandalized customs post.

French history books claim that Llívia's anomalous position is the result of an oversight. According to the traditional version of events, in the exchanges that followed the Treaty of the Pyrenees the French delegates insisted on possession of the 33 Cerdan villages between the Ariège and newly acquired Roussillon. The Spanish agreed, and then pointed out that Llívia was technically a town rather than a village, and was thus excluded from the terms of the handover. Llívia had in fact been capital of the valley until the foundation of Puigcerdà, and Spain had every intention of retaining it at the negotiations, which were held in Llívia itself.

The Romans were perhaps the first to recognize the strategic value of the site, and named their settlement Julia Livia. The castle was destroyed on the orders of Louis XI in 1479, but there's still a strong medieval feel to the centre of town, not least in the fifteenth-century fortified **church** (June–Sept daily 10am–1pm & 3–7pm; Oct–May Tues–Sun 10am–1pm & 3–6pm), which boasts a curious nail-reinforced door and carved stone floor. Inside is a beautiful gilt altarpiece, delicately carved and painted with cherubs and scenes from the Nativity, and (in the middle side chapel on the left) an unadorned crucifix, the *Cristo de Transición,* a fine example of the Romanesque-Gothic transitional style. Since 1982, an increasingly popular music festival has been held in and around the church on August weekends.

Opposite the church, the unusual **Museu Municipal** (April–Sept Tues–Sat 10am–1pm & 3–7pm, Sun 10am–2pm; Oct–March Tues–Sat 10am–1pm & 3–6pm, Sun 10am–2pm; 150ptas) contains the interior of the oldest pharmacy in Europe, functioning in Llívia from 1594 until 1918. Displays accordingly emphasize apothecarial pots and hand-painted boxes of herbs, as well as local Bronze Age relics, old maps and even the bell mechanism from the church. The entry ticket also gets you into the fifteenth-century **Tour Bernat de So**, adjoining the church and home to the sporadically functioning **tourist office** (☎972/89 60 11). The rest of the town is nowhere near as atmospheric as this medieval kernel, though the square kilometres of ski chalets are at least faced in local stone and wood.

Practicalities

Most visitors just stay long enough for a **meal** – not a bad idea given the limited choice of accommodation. In the main Plaça Major, there's the attractive *Can Ventura* restaurant (☎972/89 61 78; closed Mon eve & Tues), with its flower-filled balconies on an eighteenth-century building, whose simple cuisine with the freshest ingredients weighs in at a mildly extravagant 3500ptas each. *Fonda-Restaurant Can Marcelli,* visible just up the street, has a pleasant dining room above the bar serving a 1500-pta *menú*. Still further up the street, *Can Francesc* at c/Forns 7 has the least expensive food in town – not bad for all that – with courtyard dining in summer. For sandwiches and snacks, there's a friendly corner café-bar and a *charcuterie* on the main square.

The few places to **stay** tend to fill quickly and you'll need a reservation during much of the year. The small *Can Marcelli* (☎972/89 63 94; ③) has reasonable rooms – ask at the bar – or there's the similarly priced *Fonda Mercé* (☎972/89 60 40; ③), at c/d'Estavar 31, down c/Raval from the main square and on the left at the end. There seems little point in staying at the pair of much more expensive hotels on the busy main road below the old quarter – you'll do much better for the money in Puigcerdà.

The Cerdagne

The **Cerdagne** is the sunniest area in the French Pyrenees, the ripe colours of summer grain and hay on its treeless, rolling hills reinforcing this impression. It is bracketed in the west by **Bourg-Madame**, virtually contiguous with Spanish Puigcerdà, and in the east by Mont-Louis at the head of the Têt valley, the plateau's usual point of entry on the French side. To the southeast rises **Puigmal**, one source of the River Sègre, while the northwestern flank is formed by the mountains of the **Carlit Massif**, which provides the pistes for the overrated ski station of **Font-Romeu** and offers excellent walks.

The *Train Jaune* (see p.112 for details) continues from Mont-Louis as far as **Latour-de-Carol**, from where regular train services run north into the Ariège under the **Col de Puymorens**. The road, which once snaked over the pass, now passes through the new Tunnel de Puymorens, opened in 1995.

Font-Romeu and around

Sprawling at the foot of Roc de la Calme, at the southeast corner of the Carlit Massif, **FONT-ROMEU** (the *Train Jaune* station is Odeillo/Via) is one of the most famous ski resorts in the Pyrenees. Ski brochures make much of its *Cité Préolympique*, without revealing that its main purpose was altitude training for the 1968 Mexico summer games. What's more, its top station is a mere 2200m, the maximum vertical descent is just 450m, and out of thirty pistes only five are challenging to the good skier and only a handful are north-facing (thus holding good long-term snow). It does, however, have 256 snow-cannons (the most in Europe), and extensive cross-country skiing. Adjacent Superbolquére, better known as **PYRENÉES 2000**, is no higher than Font-Romeu and of an ugliness exceeded only by other purpose-built French winter resorts.

In summer Font-Romeu keeps its holidaymakers occupied with an Olympic-sized swimming pool and the usual assortment of sporting facilities. Year round there's plenty of nightlife, with several clubs and discos, and a casino. If that's what you want from your ski resort, Font-Romeu fits the bill perfectly, but if you're looking for a place with a mountain soul, give it a wide berth.

The Ermitage

Font-Romeu's name is Catalan for "pilgrim's spring" – the legend of the town's foundation tells of a cowherd uncovering a buried figure of the Virgin and a source of clear water, having been led to the spot by a bull. Just a stroll from the main town, off av Emmanuel Brousse, the Virgin has been installed in the barracks-like **Ermitage**, a seventeenth-century enlargement of the original fourteenth-century shrine. The Catalan artist Josep Sunyer sculpted the retable in 1707, and five years later created a sumptuous "bedroom" for the Virgin, known as the *camaril*.

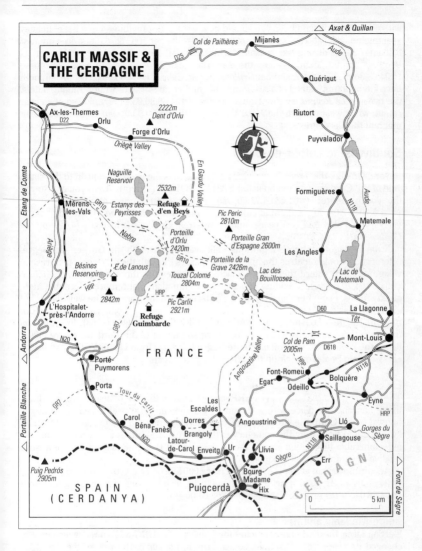

CARLIT MASSIF & THE CERDAGNE

On September 8 the Virgin is taken down the hill to **ODEILLO**, returning on Trinity Sunday. Odeillo has the only other "sight" of the immediate area – the **Four Solaire**, or solar power station (daily 10am–12.30pm & 1.30–5.30pm, until 6.30pm July & Aug; closed Nov 15–30; 25F). It no longer functions as a generator, but rather as a museum and PR exercise, with occasional full-moon-powered demonstrations on summer evenings.

Practicalities

From the **train station** it's a fairly steep two-kilometre walk north to Font-Romeu, passing Odeillo about halfway. **Accommodation** in Font-Romeu tends to be expensive, but with eighteen thousand beds you should be able to find something. For a list of holiday apartments ask at the **tourist office** (daily: 9am–noon & 4–6pm in summer; 8.30am–7.30pm during ski season; ☎04.68.30.02.74) near the top of av Emmanuel Brousse. In the central area, the *L'Homme des Neiges*, av Emmanuel Brousse (☎04.68.30.07.76; ③–④), and *Les Grillons*, rue de Cabrils (☎04.68.30.03.38; ③–④), both have kitchenettes instead of a restaurant; the higher rates are for winter. Among hotels, the two-star *Le Regina*, av Emmanuel Brousse (☎04.68.30.03.81; ④), is also open year round, while west of town the *Hôtel Y Sem Bé* (☎04.68.30.00.54; ④) enjoys views over much of the Cerdagne.

Southwest to Latour-de-Carol

Beyond Odeillo, the *Train Jaune* winds its way across the wide open plain to the south side of the Cerdagne, to depopulated **SAILLAGOUSE** (1302m) where you can stay at the **youth hostel** (☎04.68.04.71.69; ①), or the *Hôtel Planes*, place de Cerdagne (☎04.68.04.72.08; ④), and **eat** at either the *Planes* or the *Christiana*. At the edge of the village you'll also find two year-round **campsites**, *Le Sègre* (☎04.68.04.74.72) and *Le Cerdan* (☎04.68.04.70.46).

From Saillagouse there's a glorious walk available through the **Gorges du Sègre**. After a couple of kilometres the hiking route passes through the extremely picturesque village of **LLÓ**, where there are no facilities besides the three-star *Auberge Atalaya* (☎04.68.04.70.04; ⑤), providing expensive accommodation and more affordable high-quality meals. From here an easy track climbs through the gorge to the well-placed but extremely basic *Refuge de la Culasse*, after which the track becomes a path to the **Col de Finestrelles** (2604m), above Núria in Spanish Catalonia (see p.163). From the *col* there are three attractive choices: drop back southwest to the **Font de Sègre**, 400m below the 2795-metre summit of **Pic de Sègre** (it's a day from Lló to the *font* and back); carry on into Spain; or pick up the **HRP** along the crests.

Err

The next *Train Jaune* stop serves **ERR**, a tiny village at the foot of heavily wooded Puigmal – and another place with a "found Virgin" legend. The twelfth-century effigy is housed in the **Chapelle de la Vierge**, considerably enlarged in the eighteenth century. Separated from it by the cemetery is the church of **Saint-Genis**, which an almost indecipherable inscription says is the burial place of Bishop Radulf of Urgell, a close relative of Guifré el Pilos of Ripoll.

Accommodation at Err is in its *gîte d'étape* (☎04.68.04.74.20; ①) or the *Hôtel Imberm* (☎04.68.04.71.21; ③). For a quick start to a hike you can call **taxis** here (☎04.68.04.70.18) or in Saillagouse (☎04.68.04.00.46).

Bourg-Madame and Hix

Skirting Llívia, the *Train Jaune* reaches the frontier at **BOURG-MADAME**, which in 1815 changed its name from Les Guinguettes d'Hix in honour of the wife of the duc d'Angoulême, bearer of the title "Madame Royale". It had grown from insignificance to a major bazaar over the course of the eighteenth century, both as a smuggler's entrepôt and legitimate competitor to Puigcerdà. But since the renaming it hasn't amounted to much, and insofar as EC unification is proceeding, Bourg-Madame is visibly depressed and fading, its vitality sapped by its more favoured neighbour. There are no **hotels** cheaper than the two-star *Celisol*, though you've a choice of three **campsites**, all open year round: *Le Sègre* on route de Toulouse (☎04.68.04.65.87), the *Caravaneige Mas Piques* (☎04.68.04.62.11) and a basic place 4km north, between the Llívia side road and the village of Ur. Simple **meals** are available at *Snack Bar Le Catalan*, on the train station's access road.

Just to the east, **HIX**, now virtually part of Bourg-Madame, was the summer home of the counts of Cerdagne; its eleventh-century chapel, considered one of the oldest Romanesque structures in the area, has a delicacy which only such early examples display.

Latour-de-Carol/Enveitg

From Bourg-Madame, Puigcerdà is plainly visible on its hill and it's quicker (and cheaper) to get off the *Train Jaune* here and walk across the frontier. If you stay on board, the end of the line comes fifteen minutes further on, at the *Gare Internationale* of **LATOUR-DE-CAROL/ENVEITG**, the interchange for trains south towards Barcelona and north towards Toulouse. Four well-spaced daily trains (currently 8.13am, 11.07am, 1.21pm and 6.59pm) cross the border **into Spain**.

The train station lies between the two villages, though it's actually much closer (700m) to Enveitg, the larger place – though neither is overwhelmingly bigger than the vast railyards of the international exchange itself. Because this is the main road between Spain and the Ariège, some very tacky **hotels** can get away with charging too much. It's best to stay at Enveitg's *Hôtel Transpyrénéen* (☎04.68.04.81.05; ④), between the Enveitg village centre and the station. You **camp** at either the riverside *Municipal de l'Oratory* in Latour-de-Carol (☎04.68.04.83.70) or the more expensive *Caravaneige Le Robinson* in Enveitg (☎04.68.04.80.38).

Northwest to the Col de Puymorens

The long debate over whether or not to put a road tunnel under **Col de Puymorens** (1920m), high in the mountains northwest of Latour, was finally swung in favour by the imminence of the single European market. The new tunnel was completed in 1995 and the road – like the railway – now disappears under the *col* to reappear in the Ariège (cars 37F one way, 45F return).

Porta

On the way up to the pass you'll see the much-photographed but seldom-visited towers at Carol, all that's left of a castle built to defend the Cerdagne from Foix. Near the top of the climb, 13km from Latour, the village of **PORTA** has a sporadically functioning *gîte d'étape* (☎04.68.04.83.92; ①), *La Pastorale*, which serves the **GR7**. If it's closed, there's only the *Hôtel Pujols* (☎04.68.04.82.26; ③), whose restaurant at least is surly and overpriced – it's best to **eat** at *Auberge la Cajole*. All of these amenities are on the main road, not in the pretty old quarter slightly uphill. Hikers need to come supplied, as there's no store.

Porté-Puymorens

The nearby ski station above the village of **PORTÉ-PUYMORENS** – locally referred to as Porté, and thus easily confused with Porta – is probably the best the French Catalan Pyrenees has to offer. For although the Col de Puymorens marks the shift from the arid Cerdagne to the damp Ariège, a lot of snow often falls on the Cerdan side and stays there, protected from the worst of the wind. Porté-Puymorens has 40km of pistes and eight lifts, with a top station at 2430m. The village itself also has a nice valley setting, off the main highway, and horse-riding facilities to its credit.

Developers have big plans for **hotels** here; for the moment, there's just the *Hôtel Restaurant du Col* (☎04.68.04.82.06; ③) down in the village, plus two others including the *Michette*, which sells maps. The valley-bottom **campsite** – *La Forêt* (☎04.68.04.82.20) – is open all year, but you'd have to be a polar bear to stay in winter.

Overall, Porté has a bit more going for it than Porta; the **GR7** east into the Carlit Massif is easy to find at the far end of the village. The path presents the gentlest grade into the Carlit, but it is also the most spoiled western approach, what with overhead cable-cars, various damworks and the general dullness of the topography. For an alternate trailhead for Carlit, you might consider L'Hospitalet (for the HRP) or Mérens-le-Vals (for the GR10), both slightly north on the Latour–Toulouse rail line (see "The upper Ariège" p.206).

The Carlit Massif

The granite ridges of the lake-spangled **Carlit Massif** occupy a compact area just north of the Cerdanya/Cerdagne, the last truly alpine region of the Pyrenees – east of here, Canigou notwithstanding, only foothills undulate on the horizon. Being easy of access, these mountains are popular, and the lakes – even where not dammed – are sometimes a little overly manicured, but there is still ample scope for several days of trekking or scrambling. The massif's upland marshes have been disrupted by the French power corporation's dams which manipulate water levels, most notably at Lac des Bouillouses and several other reservoirs, but nonetheless some relatively unspoiled corners remain.

The ascent of **Pic Carlit** (2921m) is within the capabilities of any reasonably fit person, especially from Lac des Bouillouses on its eastern slopes. Three major walking routes – the **HRP**, the north–south **GR7** and the trans-Pyrenean **GR10** – as well as marked secondary trails cross the massif, while segments of the GR7 and GR10 comprise sections of the less demanding **Tour du Carlit**. For all of these explorations you'll want the IGN 1:50,000 *Carte de Randonnées no. 7*, "Cerdagne-Capcir"; the IGN 1:25,000 no. 2249 ET is also well worth having.

Traverses and alpine loops

The three western **trailhead villages** are Mérens-les-Vals (p.207), L'Hospitalet-près-l'Andorre (p.206) and Porté (p.203). All of the suggested routes converge near the centre of the range, close to the focal Porteille d'Orlu.

From Porté, the GR7 leaves the village at the first hairpin, climbing gradually east and then north towards the grey concrete wall of the **Lanous** dam, four hours out of Porté – not a particularly aesthetic trip. Just beyond, at the entrance to the Fourats valley, the decrepit, three-person *Refuge de la Guimbarde*, overlooking the reservoir, is only useful in dire emergencies; most people prefer either to camp on the turf below, or to get an early enough start out of Porté to finish the day at a more exciting spot. The GR7 continues northeast for another ninety minutes above the lakeshore, initially quite steeply, before joining the GR10 which cuts roughly east–west across the top of the lake from the easy pass of Porteille de la Grave.

From Mérens-les-Vals, the GR10 climbs sharply up the **Nabre valley** to reach the new, staffed refuge at the **Bésines** reservoir in something over five hours; the HRP **from L'Hospitalet-près-l'Andorre** gets to the same place in roughly half the time. As you proceed east from Bésines towards the GR10/GR7 intersection, there are no more refuges, only a limited number of **campsites** at the north end of Lanous.

From Lanous, the climb up the south grade of the **Porteille d'Orlu** is deceptively easy, but once up top the Carlit reveals its other, uncompromising nature in the view north: granite spires, giant boulder falls and drifting cloud. It's vital to keep west here for the grassy route skirting the **Étang de Feury**, thus avoiding the deadly rocks; at Feury a nameless variant heads west via the **Porteille de Madides** (2.5km) to shortcut the GR10, joining the latter at Courals de la Présasse and allowing rapid descent to Mérens-les-Vals.

Even if the mist doesn't close in, you'll still need about three hours to descend northeast from the Porteille d'Orlu along the often poorly marked GR7 to **Étang d'en Beys**

(1980m), a natural lake surrounded by scree, pasture and clumps of rhododendron. Here the useful, sixty-person **refuge** managed by the Orlu municipality (☎05.61.64.24.24; ①) is strategically located below the intersection of several traverse routes.

From the lake it's about two hours down to the end of the road tracing the **Oriège valley**, three hours coming uphill, but it's strongly suggested that you elect some other way to finish a traverse or circuit. Particularly if you have left a vehicle at Lac des Bouillouses (see below), which lies one day's reasonable march distant via the Porteille de la Grave, you can return an alternative way: some twenty minutes below the lake, you part company with the GR7 and adopt a cairned and paint-splodged (but unnamed) route which curls around through the **Porteille Gran d'Espagne** (2600m), before descending through a lake-speckled valley enclosed by 2810-metre **Pic Péric** to Bouillouses, all within six hours.

If you're going to finish a traverse in the Oriège valley (see p.210), you might reduce the amount of road-tramping involved by following yet another anonymous but marked route up to the easy **Couillade de Beys** (2345m), then descend past the easterly **Peyrisse** lake to the **Noguille reservoir**, finally dropping by track to the Forges d'Orlu in about five hours.

Climbing the peak

If you're merely intent on bagging the summit of Pic Carlit, a quick approach can be made from Mont-Louis **on the east** side, up the very narrow but paved D60 road. On a fine summer day, expect hundreds of cars at the **Lac des Bouillouses** parking area 13km along, with an even greater number of trippers milling about – unspoilt it isn't, and with family groups crammed four to a vehicle, you've little chance of hitching a lift. For purist hikers who don't mind a long slog, the **GR10** out of Bolquère climbs gently through woods to the **Col del Pam** (2005m), where it links with the HRP coming from Font-Romeu, both continuing past ski lifts and pistes to Lac des Bouillouses (5hr from either town).

To serve the hordes, there's plenty of **accommodation** and **food** at the Bouillouses lake, actually a huge reservoir dating from early this century. The CAF-run *Refuge des Bouillouses* (formerly *Combaleran*; ☎04.68.04.20.76; dorm beds ①, doubles ③), the cheapest option, stands east of the dam wall at just under 2000m. Tucked inconspicuously behind this is the smallish, privately managed *Auberge du Carlit* (☎04.68.04.22.23; ④), with menus hovering around the 100-franc mark. Just above the west end of the dam at 2050m altitude looms the gigantic *Refuge Le Bones Hores* (☎04.68.04.24.22, fax 04.68.04.13.63; dorm beds ①, doubles with obligatory half-board ⑥), popular with families.

From next to *Le Bones Hores*, where a placard informs fishermen which lakes are legally open, you get on the **HRP**, whose course is scantily waymarked with faded paint splodges but deeply grooved into the terrain and sometimes cairned. You arc up gently through the woods, between **Étang Noir** and **Étang Vive**, reached twenty minutes along; the next natural lake, **Dougues**, is a mere 45 minutes above the dam, and thus a hugely popular outing. However the crowds do thin somewhat as you press on past the necklace of smaller lakes – Casteilla, Trébens and Soubirans – under the shadow of **Touzal Colomé** (2804m), and finally up the ridge that leads to the summit from the east. This is a superb climb, with the tarns glinting in the sun, the grass green in June but usually a faded ochre by August, and the scree-strewn pyramid of Carlit overhead. There and back from Lac des Bouillouses is at most six-and-a-half hours, an easy day's walk in good conditions – though rather ominously there are green sheds by most of the lakes, for sheltering from foul weather which is often not long in appearing. If – as so many do – you just want to take in the lakes, it's only a three-hour round-trip from the dam to the highest one, Soubirans, at 2320m.

From the west, the ascent of Carlit is a little more difficult, a good four hours one way starting in the vicinity of the derelict *Refuge de la Guimbarde*, close to the Lanous dam (see above). Again using HRP cairns and blazes, follow the **Fourats valley** east to its tiny lake and then either keep going straight to the summit, or – if that looks too formidable – bear away towards the *col* on the south and approach the summit more or less along the line of the ridge, dropping a little way down the eastern slope when the ridge gets too narrow.

The Tour du Carlit

The **Tour du Carlit**, aimed at hikers of medium experience, is meant to take three days, much of it through lower-altitude zones and on tracks. If you're coming by regular train, the easiest places to pick up the circuit are at Porta or Porté-Puymorens. If you're on the *Train Jaune*, get off at Béna-Fanès, the stop before Latour-de-Carol, and try to hitch a lift the 6km up to Béna.

From Porta you've a short initial day's walking southeast over the pessimistically named Col de l'Homme Mort (2300m) to **BÉNA**, a delightful hamlet with an equally wonderful *gîte d'étape* (☎04.68.04.81.64; ①) housed in a restored *mas* or Catalan farmhouse. You could lengthen the day if desired by pressing along the track east, via the hamlets of Fanès and Brangoly, to the attractive and well-positioned village of **DORRES**, which offers the characterful *Hotel-Restaurant Marty* (☎04.68.30.07.52; ④) and a public hot spring (daily 8am–9pm, later in summer) for bathing. Whatever you do, the second day out is less enchanting as you skirt the spa of Les Escaldes to thread north through the **Angoustrine valley** on dirt track, before linking up with the GR10 at Lac des Bouilloses. The third day's walking follows the GR10 west over the gentle **Porteille de la Grave** (2426m), alongside the infant River Têt, to intersect the GR7; you then reverse the directions given above under "Traverses and alpine loops" (p.204) for a descent to Porté.

THE ARIÈGE AND THE PAYS DE SAULT

From the residents' point of view, the **Ariège valley** – draining north from the Col du Puymorens – is one of the most depressed areas of France, with low income levels, high unemployment and an ageing population. Unsurprisingly, perhaps, it has long been a stronghold for nonconformists and antiroyalists, and, in more recent times, the political left, the latter movement inspired as much by resentment of Parisian neglect as by espoused Marxist views. Yet for visitors the Ariège is a favourite corner of the Pyrenees, the experience of its natural attractions, such as the **Oriège** tributary valley and the bear-sheltering forests west of the river, enhanced by the prehistoric painted caves around **Tarascon**. On the main valley floor, the resorts of **Mérens-les-Vals** and **Ax-les-Thermes** are serviceable bases for excursions into the surrounding mountains, including the severe fastness of Carlit. Further downriver, the showcase town of **Foix** is almost in the flatlands, but affords access to the gorge-furrowed, Cathar-haunted **Pays de Sault**, an eerie tableland extending between the Ariège and the Aude valley to the east. Here, the Cathars began the local tradition of rebellion against centralizing Church and State almost eight centuries ago, antecedents which the modern *Ariègeois* acknowledge with pride.

The upper Ariège

The train line into the valley from the Cerdagne tunnels underneath the Col de Puymorens to emerge at **L'HOSPITALET-PRÈS-L'ANDORRE**, whose sole interest – in the absence of any monumental or natural attraction – is as a route convergence: the

HRP goes through here, as do buses to and from Andorra, and trains south into the Cerdagne and north to Toulouse. There are two one-star **hotels** – the *Puymorens* (☎05.61.64.23.03; ③) and *Le Sisca* (☎05.61.64.23.02; ③), plus a campsite. Heading into the Carlit Massif, the **HRP** gets you quickly to grips with the mountains, offering the shortest approach from the west as it climbs unusually gently to the dam and pair of refuges at Bésines, where you link up with the GR10.

Mérens-les-Vals

The reputation of **MÉRENS-LES-VALS**, 10km further north, rests on the stocky frame of the **Mérenguais horse**, a breed which – partly on the strength of the Niaux cave paintings (see p.212) – is considered the closest thing in western Europe to the wild horse of prehistory. Nowadays there are more specimens outside the mountains of Mérens than in them, but the village remains a place of pilgrimage for horse lovers. Mérens itself, though, is unexceptional, one part clustered on the main road, the other spread out on the slopes to the east around a Romanesque church. The village straddles the GR10, which accounts for the attractively restored **gîte d'étape** in the upper village (☎05.61.64.32.50, fax 05.61.64.02.75; ①), a congenial place to base yourself for a few days's walking, serving excellent food – luckily enough, since there are no other hotels or restaurants open in the town at present, though there is a **campsite** just off the main road, near the river.

Walking from Mérens

Mérens makes a good base for **walks**, short or long. A popular one-day circuit involves following the GR10, and then a local path, southwest up the Mourgouillou valley (where Mérenguais horses still graze) to the **Étang de Couart**, and then dropping back down to the train station at L'Hospitalet by using the HRP. Heading **southeast**, the GR10 offers a more appealing, if more strenuous introduction to the Carlit range than the GR7 out of Porté or the HRP from L'Hospitalet, but be warned that both French and translated *topoguides* sketch the route on the wrong bank of the River Nabre.

Ax-les-Thermes and around

Eight kilometres beyond Mérens, at the confluence of the Ariège, Oriège and Lauze rivers, stands **AX-LES-THERMES**. It's an unobjectionable spa resort with little specifically to see – owing to numerous disastrous fires in centuries past – other than a lively Monday market along the river promenade, but it makes the most convenient centre for skiing or walking in the Ariège. **Hikes** can be routed in circuits, permitting use of the town as a base, and several **ski resorts**, both downhill and nordic, are scattered in all directions within a convenient distance.

Ax itself dates back to at least Roman times, the commercial exploitation of its hot springs to the thirteenth century. The smell of sulphur that early twentieth-century travellers complained about has gone, but the ambience of a spa remains. Four *thermes* still exist, all of them part of the central *Hôtel Royal Thermal*. In total there are more than forty sources, producing a total volume of water in excess of 600,000 litres per day, at temperatures hotter than 70°C in a few cases. If you'd like to experience the waters without paying, you can indulge in the local custom of foot-dangling in the **Bassin des Ladres**, an open bath beside the central place du Breilh, which is the only surviving portion of a thirteenth-century hospital for Crusaders.

Practicalities

The **train station** is on the northwest side of town, just off the main av Delcassé. You'll pass two-star **hotels** as you walk into the centre, first *Le France* (☎05.61.64.20.30; ③)

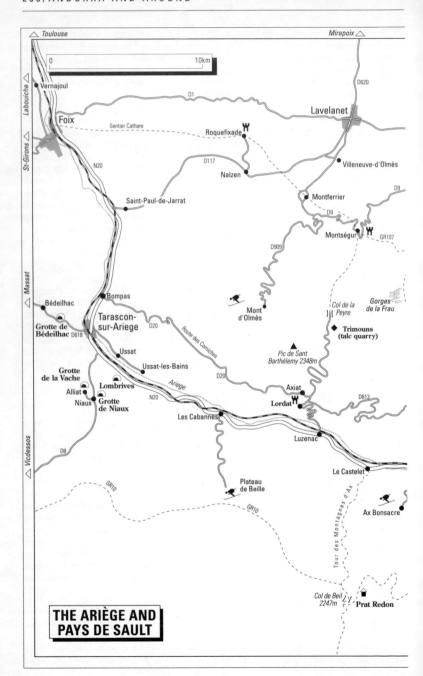

THE ARIÈGE AND
PAYS DE SAULT

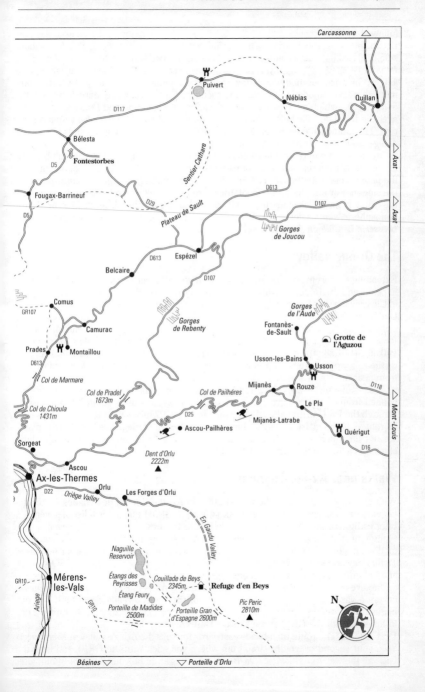

followed by *Les Pyrénées* (☎05.61.64.21.01; ③), before arriving at the central place du Breilh, home to the **tourist office** (Mon–Sat 8am–noon & 2–6pm, Sun 9am–noon; ☎05.61.64.20.64) and another old-fashioned two-star hotel, the *La Paix* (☎05.61.64.22.61; ②). Nearby, at Ax Sports (owned by an Englishman), you can replace any lost or worn-out mountaineering and ski gear. Other convenient, quiet and recommendable accommodation includes the friendly *La Terrasse*, 7 rue Marcaillou (☎05.61. 64.20.33; ③), which attracts many skiers and has a restaurant; and *Pension Barat-Aliot* near the Hôtel de Ville below place du Marché(☎05.61.64.22.01; ②), also with a restaurant. The municipal **campsite**, *Malazéou* (☎05.61.64.22.21; open all year), is beside the Ariège, 500m from the train station.

Other than the hotel dining rooms and restaurants, **eating** prospects aren't brilliant in Ax – thus the preponderance of half-board offers at the hotels. Exceptions include the pizzeria opposite the *Hôtel de France* on the main road, and the *Terminus Bar* near the station. For **snacks** on the hoof, there are numerous cheap *boulangeries* and over-the-counter pizza places in rue de l'Horloge, leading off the place du Marché. More atmospheric venues for a **drink** are the old *Grand Café*, beside *Les Pyrénées*, and *Brasserie Le Club* on place Roussel.

The Oriège valley

Extending east from Ax, the damp, leafy **Oriège valley** allows access to both the Carlit peaks and the **Réserve Nationale d'Orlu**, created south of the road in 1975 to benefit a growing herd of isards as well as roe deer, golden eagles and lammergeiers. Under the shadow of the distinctive Dent d'Orlu, beloved of technical climbers, the D22 road heads up the valley to **ORLU**, where there's camping at the *Municipal* (☎05.61.64.30.09) and a popular *gîte d'étape* aimed at walkers, the *Relais Montagnard* (☎05.61.64.61.88; ①). A path from **Les Forges d'Orlu** (a place, not a village) further up the valley permits a link-up with the *Tour des Montagnes d'Ax* (see below), via a climb from near the power station to the dam at **Naguille**.

At a popular picnic area some 12km from Ax, the asphalt ends and all private cars are banned from further progress along a jeep track which climbs south into the *réserve* through the **En Gaudu valley**, before meeting the GR7 below the Étang d'en Beys with its refuge. If you insist on approaching the Carlit via the Oriège, it's well worth splashing out for a taxi to the picnic grounds: the walk in is tedious and steep, with little chance of a lift in either direction.

Walks near Ax-les-Thermes

With an office next door to the tourist office in Ax, the Bureau des Guides et Accompagnateurs Montagne des Vallées d Ax (☎05.61.64.31.51) maintains a list of seventeen brief **walks** around the town, ranging in length from twenty minutes to seven hours, though most of these prove rather short and over-generously timed; it also keeps information on all the mountain huts and refuges, climbing courses and weather forecasts. To fill a day properly, take the suggested itinerary to the attractive village of **SORGEAT** and link this hike with other sections.

The five-day, four-night **Tour des Montagnes d'Ax** is most recommended, since it covers a variety of terrain, including parts of the Carlit already described. You can begin at **Le Castelet**, on the main road 5km northwest of Ax, climbing south for a day to hook up with the GR10 at the **Col de Beil** (2247m); the closest crude shelter is at **Prat Redon**. The route then heads eastwards to cross the Ariège valley at Mérens-les-Vals, your second overnight stop, from where you stick with the GR10, and later the GR7, all the way to the *Refuge d'en Beys* – the refuge will be your third night out, after

---

SKIING AROUND AX-LES-THERMES

The nearest ski station to Ax is **AX-BONASCRE**, 8km south up the D820; in winter there are ski-bus services from the town. Bonascre itself is a hideous knot of black-clad high-rises, but once you get into the *télécabine* and up to the **Plateau du Saquet**, it's a different matter. The snow record is good, there are 55km of pistes (some over 3km long) and the top lift is at 2305m – all this and the beautiful Andorra frontier peaks as a backdrop.

Three valleys west of Bonascre, the **Plateau de Beille** is also a likely area for cross-country skiing. The 55km of pistes range from 1–20km, at an altitude of just under 2000m – which should ensure adequate snow. The plateau is reached by the *Route Forestière* from the village of Les Cabannes, 15km down the main N20 road.

To the north of Ax there's good cross-country skiing to be had around the **Col de Chioula** (1431m), while 13km east of Ax, **ASCOU-PAILHÈRES** has 10km of downhill runs and a top station of 2020m. It's a pretty drive up, and though the station has just one black piste, it is quite challenging.

---

a very long day unless you use the Porteille de Madides shortcut, or you could insert an extra overnight stay at Bésines. From the refuge, you've a shorter day up to the gentle **Couillade de Beys** (2345m), then past the easterly Étang des Peyrisses and the Naguille dam before the descent to the floor of the Oriège valley.

The Route des Corniches

A scenic alternative to the N20 road along the floor of the Ariège valley is the **Route des Corniches**, between Ascou and Bompas, which you can access from Ax by taking the serpentine D613 (the Belcaire road) up past Ascou. About halfway along you pass the village of **AXIAT**, which has an appealing Romanesque church and lies a short way south of the extremely unappealing **talc quarry** at **Trimouns**.

This huge, ghastly scar produces around 300,000 tons of talc per season, eight percent of the world total; so far about ten million tons have gone, leaving fourteen million – over thirty years' work – to be scoured out of the earth. The workers are mainly Spanish, Portuguese and Moroccan, who supplement their earnings by selling semiprecious stones to tourists (regular tours of the quarry June–Sept). It was by the trail over the Col de la Peyre, just above the quarry, that the four Cathars from Montségur made their escape; apparently for aesthetic reasons, this path has not been included in the recently designated GR 107.

Just below Axiat stands the castle of **LORDAT**. Although it escaped dismantling during the sixteenth-century Wars of Religion – "too big" came back the report to future king, Henri de Navarre – the castle is now comprehensively ruined, but worth a look all the same. The church above has a distinctive squat, square bell-tower, with a double layer of arches on each face. The corniche comes back to the base of the valley at Bompas, 3km north of Tarascon on the road to Foix.

Tarascon-sur-Ariège

A small, utilitarian mining and metallurgy centre where traffic roars past on the bypass highway, **TARASCON-SUR-ARIÈGE** has nothing about it to suggest that this is the heart of one of the most fascinating areas in Europe. Any account of the emergence of the human species must include the caves around Tarascon, which taken as a group constitute an unequalled display of **prehistoric painting and artefacts**. There are four main sites, all accessible in a single day if you have your own transport.

Yet the town itself is more rewarding than first impressions imply, and worth an hour's stroll. From the east bank of the Ariège, where riverside cafés provide pleasant vantage points, a narrow pedestrian lane leads up, past craft shops and even narrower alleys, to the old quarter. Here the church of St-Michel presides over a partly arcaded square, and various surviving bits of the medieval walls, razed in 1632, crop up here and there: the **Tour Saint-Michel**, and the **Porte d'Espagne** with a fountain inside. From the gate, the short hike past walled orchards up to the **Tour du Castella**, now a clock-tower, is worthwhile for the views over the five valleys which converge here.

Practicalities

Buses and trains call frequently from nearby Ax-les-Thermes and Foix, on the line from Toulouse to La-Tour; the **train station** is on the left bank of the Ariège, in the northern half of town. The **tourist office** (summer daily 9am–7pm; rest of year Mon–Sat 9am–1pm & 2–6pm; ☎05.61.05.94.94) is inside the multipurpose hall known as the Espace François Mitterand, on av. des Pyrénées in the centre. Quietest and most attractive of the **hotels** is the *Confort* on the riverside quai Armand-Sylvestre (☎05.61.05.61.90; ③), with some rooms facing a courtyard where ice cream and light snacks are served. For more comfort, with the quieter rooms facing the river, try the *Hostellerie de la Poste*, 200m north on the main through road (☎05.61.05.60.41, fax 05.61.5.70.59; ③). If these are full, your third choice will be the somewhat noisy *La Bellevue*, between the two at 7 place Jean-Jaurès (☎05.61.05.60.45; ③). There are two **campsites**: *La Bernière*, near the junction of the road to Bédeilhac, and the municipal *Pré Lombard*, upstream from town on the right bank. All of the hotels have attached **restaurants**, with the best food and service at *Hostellerie de la Poste,* which offers a reasonably priced Gascon *menu* featuring *auzinat*, a rich hot-pot of cabbage, potato, sausage, game and other goodies.

The caves

Painted **prehistoric caves** have been discovered along the northwest coast of Spain, in the Dordogne and in the Pyrenees, of which unquestionably the finest is the **Grotte de Niaux**, 2km southwest of Tarascon. The high concentration of caves in the Ariège is due mostly to the limestone which constitutes the hillsides here, such strata being ideally suited to the millennial work of seeping water necessary for cavern-creation. What served as shelters – and, arguably, as places of worship – for early humans later came in handy as hideouts for religious dissidents during the Christian era.

Grotte de Niaux

Such rivals as Lascaux in the Dordogne and Altamira in Spain are now closed or very nearly so, but the only restriction on access to the **Grotte de Niaux** is the mandatory reservation (call ☎05.61.05.88.37) for places in the guided twenty-person groups that are the only mode of admisssion (daily: July–early Sept 8.30–11.30am & 1.30–5.15pm; early Sept to end Sept 10–11.30am & 1.30–5.15pm; Oct–June visits at 11am, 3pm & 4.30pm; 60F).

The contemporary entrance to Niaux is a tunnel created in 1968 near the low and narrow natural opening under an enormous rock overhang. Using torches for illumination, you penetrate 900m (from a total 4km of galleries) to see just some of the famous black outlines of horse and bison, minimally shaded yet capturing every nuance. Analysis has established that these drawings, and those of the ibex and stag in the recess further back, were produced around 10,800 BC with a "crayon" made of bison fat and manganese oxide. A line of footprints left by the artists can be seen in a part of the cave that was opened up in 1970, while their primitive form of writing is represented by the dots and bunches of lines on the wall of the main cavity.

NIAUX village itself, between the cave and Tarascon, has a small, private **Musée Paysan** (daily: April–Sept 9am–8pm; Oct–March 10am–noon & 2–6pm), which displays a splendid collection of tools, furnishings, archival photos and impedimenta illustrating the vanished traditions of the Ariège. Exhibits also explain local Pyrenean architecture, with its use of *lauzes* (stone slabs), *ardoise* (slate) and occasionally *chaume* (thatch) for roofing. About halfway between Niaux and Tarascon, keep your eye peeled also for the picturesque remains of a medieval smelting works by the riverside.

Grotte de la Vache

The **Grotte de la Vache** at Alliat is well worth the couple of kilometres' journey across the valley from Niaux (July & Aug daily 10am–5.30pm; Easter–June & Sept daily except Tues 2.30–4pm; other times by ringing ☎05.61.05.95.06; 42F); a path, beginning some 150m before the Niaux museum, slightly shortcuts the road. Excavations over two decades sifted through the detritus of ten thousand years of habitation, beginning between 15,000 and 12,500 BC and ending in the Bronze Age. Around thirty thousand fragments of flint tools were unearthed here and over six thousand complete tools, mainly for engraving in rock; some pieces are displayed in the cave.

Grotte de Bédeilhac

To reach the **Grotte de Bédeilhac** (July & Aug Mon–Sat 10am–5.30pm; Easter–June & Sept, plus school holidays, daily except Tues, guided visits at 2.30 & 4pm, Sun 2.30, 3.15 & 4pm; Oct to mid-Nov Sun only, guided visits at 2.30, 3.15 & 4pm; other times by arrangement on ☎05.61.05.95.06; 42F) above the eponymous village, you have to return to Tarascon and cover 5km along the D618 towards Saurat. This cave, a hollow in the ridge of Soudour, contains examples of every known technique of Paleolithic art, including polychrome painting (now faded to monochrome). The imposing entrance yawns 35m wide by 20m high, making it easy to understand how the Germans managed to adapt the cavern as an aircraft hangar during World War II. Although the art within is not as immediately powerful as at Niaux, diversity compensates: low reliefs in mud, paintings of bison, deer and ibex, and stalagmites used to model figures.

In the village below, **beds** are provided by the *Relais d' Étape* (☎05.61.05.15.56; ①) and **meals** by the adjacent *Auberge de la Grotte*, on the through road next to the *Mairie* and the post office.

Lombrives and Fontanet

The **Grotte de Lombrives** (July & Aug daily 10am–7pm; June & Sept daily tours at 10am, 10.45am & 2–5.30pm; Easter–May & Oct–early Nov, weekends & holidays tours at 10am, 10.45am & 2.30pm, plus May Mon–Fri 2–5.30pm; or by appointment, ☎05.61.05.98.40), 3km south of Tarascon along the N20, near Ussat-les-Bains, could only disappoint if you've already seen Niaux, Vache and Soudour. The access by underground train gives it something of an amusement-park atmosphere – as do the nocturnal *spéctacles* regularly staged here in July and August – but the stalagmite formations are superb, and the sheer size of the complex is impressive. It is, in fact, the largest cavern in the EU open to tourists, and would take five days' walking to see it in its entirety. For groups of eight or more, you can arrange for three- or five-hour walk-throughs by ringing the number given.

Lombrives was inhabited around 4000 BC, but all the material found here now rests in museums such as that at Foix. Its later history is embellished by legends of the last Cathars walled up inside in 1328, and of 250 soldiers subsequently disappearing without trace, the victims of cave-dwelling bandits. For a more serious visit, you can book

CAVE ART

The **painted caves** of the Pyrenees are known to have been created by nomadic and seminomadic communities of *Homo sapiens* during the Late Paleolithic period, between 10,000 and 35,000 years ago. Almost everything else about them is conjecture.

The big historical names in the evaluation of cave art are the French prehistorians and authors **Abbé Breuil** (1877–1961), **André Leroi-Gourhan** (1911–86) and the latter's colleague **Annette Laming-Emperaire**. Abbé Breuil began his career working on the caves of the Dordogne, but dedicated years of study to the western and central Pyrenees, arriving at the theory that cave art served a **magical function**, to ensure "that the game should be plentiful, that it should increase and that sufficient should be killed". The frequency with which ibex, wild boar, reindeer and bison appear on the walls makes this notion attractive, but there are objections to it, the most obvious being that the animal remains found in the caves show that the species depicted were not the main food supply. Moreover, although some of the animals are marked by symbols that might be arrows, over ninety percent of them are not. And finally, the Late Paleolithic period seems to have been a time of plenty, when hunters would have needed no magical assistance.

Leroi-Gourhan's and Laming-Emperaire's main contention is that cave art was arranged in a **specific layout**, much like the decorative schemes of frescoed Christian churches. From examination of 865 subjects in 62 caves they noted, for example, that hands were depicted only at the entrance to caves or in the centre, and that mammoths and bison were confined to the centre. More controversially, they went on to suggest that the arrangement had a sexual polarity, with bison symbolizing the female element, and horses the male. Some people have raised the objection that the weak illumination available to the cavedwellers – grease and a wick perhaps, or wooden torches – would not have allowed them to see the cave decorations as a unity. A problem is also posed by the way successive outlines were superimposed to the extent that they became indecipherable, even though suitable areas of blank rock were available to either side. Nevertheless, most experts agree that there is some sort of pattern: bison and horses, for example, are thirty times more likely to occur in the central area than are deer, a statistic impossible to dismiss as coincidence.

The most cogent refutation of the above theories was published in late 1996 as *Les Chamanes de la Prehistoire* (Editions Seuil) by Jean Clottes, a French prehistorian and cave-art expert, and David Lewis-Williams, a South African archeologist specializing in the art and beliefs of the Kalahari Bushmen, one of the last surviving hunter-gatherer societies with strong parallels to European Paleolithic culture. They propose that many of the images may have been executed by **shamans** in a trance or other altered state, and that "the paintings and engravings do not represent real animals that are hunted for food in an actual landscape; rather they are visions drawn from the subterranean world of spirits because of their supernatural powers and ability to help the shamans."

The caves will doubtless continue to stimulate speculation. From the accumulation of rubbish on the cave floors – sometimes nearly 4m deep – and from the apparent stylistic development of the paintings, it would seem that habitation in these caves was quite stable, and it is possible that painting was the responsibility of one person within the community. Furthermore, the similarities between decorative work in caves hundreds of kilometres apart would seem to indicate that there was interaction between groups all along the range.

A great many decorated caves of the Pyrenees are closed to the general public, an essential precaution if they are to be preserved; application through a caving organization might gain access to some of these. The most spectacular examples, though, are open to all. After the Tarascon group, the major Pyrenean cave is **Gargas**, with its vast array of hand prints in red and black, many with apparently mutilated fingers (p.283).

Whatever the uncertainties about its significance and the ways in which it was made, Pyrenean cave art offers an extraordinary aesthetic experience, marvellously conjuring shape and movement from the most basic natural materials, and even, in places, exploiting the very contours of the rock. Niaux itself contains an excellent example of such artistic opportunism: one of the bison carved on the clay floor is formed around holes caused by dripping water, which now function as an eye and wound marks.

on one of the *Visites longue durées caractère spéléologique*, which are run from June to September (same phone number as above).

Qualified cavers can also get permission to visit nearby **Fontanet**, on the north side of the Ariège beyond the village of Ussat. The small but comprehensive inventory includes a polychrome bison, a female figure and human faces.

Labouiche

Some 3km northwest of Foix (see below) – take the Vernajoul road from the town centre – lies the subterranean **river-cavern of Labouiche** (daily mid-April to mid-Nov 9am–5.30pm; usually a 15-minute wait; 42F), claimed to be the longest such navigable cave in the EU. It appears never to have been humanly inhabited, and indeed winter water levels are such as to completely block access. The same amusement-park atmosphere prevails as at Lombrives: boatloads of a dozen persons each travel for 75 minutes in opposite directions along the 1500m of galleries open to the public. Entry is either via the natural entrance, or an artificial one bored at the upstream end, on either side of the well-signposted ticket office – you're told which to assemble by. Highlights are the waterfall at the upstream end of the river and a small chamber full of formations below the artificial entry; these and other oddities along the way are described by the guides who do their best to keep up a witty patter while hauling on the ceiling-mounted cables which are the mode of propulsion.

Foix

FOIX, 16km downstream from Tarascon, is the smallest departmental capital in France – in this case, of the Ariège – and the most agreeable base in the valley if you don't mind catching a train or bus to get into the mountains. A non-industrial livelihood based on bureaucracy and tourism means a well-preserved old town of narrow alleys in the triangle between the Ariège and the Arget rivers, where a few of the overhanging houses date from the fourteenth to sixteenth centuries; especially attractive are place Pyrène and place Saint-Vincent with their fountains, though many junctions in the old town sport some sort of water-quirk. All lanes seem to lead eventually to the conspicuously large church of **Saint-Volusien** in the north of the old town, originally Romanesque but almost completely reconstructed after being razed during the Wars of Religion. Its eponymous square, along with the Halles des Grains just off cours Gabriel-Fauré, hosts lively Wednesday and Friday **markets**: produce and plants at place Saint-Volusien, meat, cheese, savouries and pastries at the metal-roofed *halles*, on other days a prime drinking venue.

Presiding over everything is the grey hilltop **castle**, not so much a single fortification as three magnificent, dissimilar towers from different eras, and dramatic when viewed from any angle. From 1012 the castle on this site was the seat of the counts of Foix, whose association with the Cathar faith led to its being besieged four times by Simon de Montfort, who failed to break the fort's resistance. Count Roger-Bernard II – known as *Le Grand* – was a determined opponent of the anti-Cathar crusade, but perhaps made his most lasting contribution to history by marrying Ermensende of Castellbó early in the thirteenth century, thereby linking the fortunes of Foix and Andorra. Although the dynasty ended illustriously with Henri III of Foix-Béarn and Navarre, who annexed what had become a Pyrenean mini-state to the Crown on becoming Henri IV of France, the biggest name in Foix is that of the fair-haired knight whose features can be seen on postcards all over town – Gaston III, known as Gaston Fébus (see feature on p.216).

The best aspect of a castle visit (daily: July & Aug 9.30am–6.30pm; June & Sept 9.45am–noon & 2–6.30pm; Oct–May 10.30am–noon & 2–6pm; 25F) is the opportunity

---

GASTON FÉBUS

Sooner or later in the Central Pyrenees, you'll come across the name **Gaston Fébus**, count of Foix and viscount of Béarn. He was born in 1331 and died sixty years later, but it is difficult to disentangle the events of the intervening years from the myths – often self-promoted – that sprung up around him. The troubadour poets acknowledged him as a friend and doubtless embellished his deeds in their lyrics, and Jean Froissart – chronicler of the Hundred Years' War – was invited by Fébus to document and popularize his life. Gaston was a poet himself and the author of a book on hunting, but his most lasting literary creation was his own name, *Fébus*: derived from the Occitan for sun, it celebrated his long, golden hair. Although an autocratic ruler, who abolished the legislative assemblies of his lands in order to strengthen his grip on them, he cultivated a reputation as a fair-minded and dauntless soldier, intending always to lead his men into battle with the cry *Fébus avan* (Fébus at the front).

His ambition was to create an autonomous kingdom of the Pyrenees, adding by conquest the regions of Bigorre and Soule to the inherited lands of Nébouzan (around Saint-Gaudens), Béarn and Foix. Politically this was made impossible by the continuing Hundred Years' War, which divided the loyalties of his subjects: in the west lived people used to an English master – in particular the Black Prince, who was in direct control between 1362 and 1371 – while to the east lay Languedoc, subject to France. In addition, feuding between the leading families of the area kept him occupied; one of his most significant victories came in 1362, when he crushed his arch-enemies, the Armagnacs. In time he lost the appetite to pursue his grand plan, by most accounts after 1380, when it seems Fébus killed his only son on discovering the son's role in a plot to assassinate him.

Thereafter Fébus dedicated himself to campaigning for a strong, united France, pledging that his lands should be inherited by the Crown of France and not by any of the local families with whom he had fought for most of his life. Yet this was not to happen until 1589, with the accession to the Parisian throne of Henri III of Foix-Béarn and Navarre, a descendant of Fébus' fierce rivals, the d'Albrets.

---

to clamber up worn stairs in the southern and central towers for startling views up the valley. The interior houses the rather listless **Musée d'Ariège** (guided visits only, within hours stated), four rooms whose exhibits range from prehistoric to medieval times.

Practicalities

The **train station** sits on the right bank of the Ariège; most **buses** stop on the central cours Gabriel-Fauré, near the Resistance monument. In addition to the mainline train and bus services between Toulouse and the Spanish frontier at Latour-de-Carol, there's a daily **bus** service (not Sun) east via Lavelanet to Quillan on the Aude, and four buses daily west to Saint-Girons in the Couserans. The **tourist office** at 45 cours Gabriel-Fauré (July & Aug Mon–Sat 9am–7pm, Sun 10am–12.30pm & 3–6pm; rest of year Mon–Sat 9am–noon & 2–6pm; ☎05.61.65.12.12) can be reached from the train station by walking south along the east bank of the Ariège and then crossing the Pont-Neuf.

Most **accommodation** is found in the old town, on the west bank of the Ariège, though little of it is inspiring. If you have the means, the quietest and most comfortable option is the three-star *Hôtel Lons* on 6 place Duthil, near the Pont Vieux (☎05.61.65.52.44, fax 05.61.02.68.18; ⑤). *La Barbacane*, 1 av de Lerida (☎05.61.65.50.44; ④), and *L'Echauguette*, rue Paul Laffont (☎05.61.2.88.88; ③), occupy the next rank down, though both suffer from traffic noise. The *Eychenne*, 11 rue Nöel-Peyrevidal (☎05.61.65.00.04; ②) is the only real cheapie, with decent enough rooms but a nocturnally lively bar on the ground floor; across the street at no. 16, the *Auberge Léo Lagrange*

(☎05.61.65.09.04; ①) fills the youth hostel niche. The municipal **campsite**, *Lac de Labarre* (May–Oct; ☎05.61.65.11.58), is on the N20 towards Toulouse.

The best area for **eating** is rue de la Faurie, the old blacksmiths' bazaar, where the best of several establishments is *Des 4 Saisons* at no. 11, serving until 10.30pm. They have an interesting gimmick: the *pierrade* or hot ceramic square, brought to your table, on which you cook fish and meat pieces yourself; they also do a wide range of crepes. *Le Jeu de L'Oie* nearby at no. 17 is also worth trying for more traditional fare, while *Auberge Miranda* at 36 rue Labistour (the continuation of Faurie) is an old-fashioned bar with *plats de jour*. Food at *L'Henri IV* on place Pyrène is nothing extraordinary, but the outdoor seating is a good way to take in the square and the castle; the nearby *Le Petit Creux* at rue Lazéma 9 has a limited but well-executed menu which guarantees sidewalk-table crowds at lunchtime.

The Pays de Sault

If you haven't got a car or a bike, the magnificent **Pays de Sault** – the upland area bounded by the Aude, the Ariège and the main road from Quillan to Foix – can be crossed in a few days on foot, making occasional use of the sporadic public transport. A network of **walking itineraries** – the Tour du Pays de Sault, the Tour du Massif de Tabe, the Piémont and the GR107, plus forestry tracks – provide various ways of exploring. The most popular route is the **Sentier Cathare**, which begins at Foix and arrives at Montségur in two stages via Roquefixade (see p.222), then continues to the Mediterranean; it's easy walking much of the year (avoid mid-winter and mid-summer), with strategically placed accommodation in *gîtes d'étape*.

Regular **bus services** cross the Pays de Sault: one links the train station in Quillan with the one in Foix, via **Puivert** and **Lavelanet**, 10km north of Montségur; the other runs from Quillan via Belcaire and Camurac to **Comus**, 12km southeast, from where Montségur can be reached through the Gorges de la Frau. Because departures are slightly more frequent from the east, the two routes described below approach the area from Quillan.

Much of the Pays de Sault is a spacious agricultural plateau, but it contains more vertiginous terrain, too. At the southeast edge, the dramatic D107 road from Axat to Axles-Thermes runs through the **Rebenty** and **Joucou** gorges and over the **Col du Pradel** (1673m), a tough but wonderful cycling route; further west beyond the heart of the Sault looms the clifftop castle of **Montségur**, the greatest stronghold of the Cathars.

The vast highlands themselves are composed primarily of limestone, and thus riddled with caves and ravines like the spectacular **Gorges de la Frau**. Above ground, its agriculture seems to have changed little since Cathar times; pesticides have yet to infiltrate the region's ecosystem, so the silhouettes of birds of prey are seldom out of the sky.

Neither of the region's downhill **ski stations** is worth much effort. The Monts d'Olmes resort, southwest of Montségur, is crowned with a seedy apartment development, while the one at Camurac comprises a "village" of decaying chalets – and both have impossibly low top-lifts of only 1940m.

There is good **cross-country skiing** on the plateau, however, with a small rental and tuition operation at **Comus** and especially good terrain at the **Col de Marmare**.

Puivert

Although it's just twenty minutes out of Quillan by vehicle, the countryside around **PUIVERT** feels quite different, a vast upland planted with corn and sunflowers,

---

THE CATHARS

The origins of Cathar belief seem to lie in **Manicheism**, a doctrine founded on the concept of the material world as an invasion of the world of Light by the powers of Darkness. This first found practical expression in Europe among the Bogomils of the Balkan peninsula, who – following years of persecution – converted to Islam under the Ottomans. By the twelfth century a modified version of this principle had taken hold in the south of France, especially in the area of Albi – hence the alternative name of **Albigeois** (or Albigenses) for the Cathars.

According to Cathar thinking, the creator of the material world was the Devil, and Christ was incarnated as a messenger from the world of Light, with whom souls could be united and found released into immortality. Cathar belief posed a number of problems for the Church of Rome. Firstly, Cathars denied the doctrine of the Virgin Birth, and insisted that the Catholic faithful, in worshipping any Creator, were in fact worshipping the Devil. They were necessarily **antimaterialists** and thus had no need for sumptuous buildings or institutions. They were initially **pacifists**, and condemned the Crusades, one of the methods used to increase papal and aristocratic fortunes. The austere spirituality of their leaders – the *parfaits* and *parfaites* (lay adherents were known simply as *bons hommes* and *bonnes femmes*) – was a constant rebuke to the dissolute clergy of the Church. And on top of all this, their conviction that they were exempt from feudal vows of allegiance made them politically dangerous.

Shortly after his election in 1198, **Pope Innocent III** called for a crusade against the Cathars and found ready support in Paris from Philippe Auguste, who was intent on taking over Languedoc. Ranged against this formidable combination were the *seigneurs* of Languedoc, who had been in constant territorial competition with the bishops of the region, and many of whose subjects had become adherents of Catharism.

The first target was **Raymond VI of Toulouse**, excommunicated by the pope in 1207 for his tacit approval of Catharism. The following year Raymond succeeded in persuading the papal legate to have the excommunication lifted, but on the day after agreement was reached the legate was murdered, providing his enemies with a pretext for military action.

In 1209 an army led by the archbishop of Narbonne and new legate, **Arnaud Amaury**, invaded Languedoc, with a heavy contingent of English mercenaries in its ranks. Béziers was besieged and its entire population – a figure put by some authorities at twenty thousand – was massacred for refusing to surrender a score or so Cathars in their midst. When asked how the Catholic citizens were to be distinguished from the heretics, Amaury replied: "Kill them all, God will recognize His own." After more protracted resistance, Carcassonne fell, eventually to be handed over – as Béziers had been – to the professional English crusader, **Simon de Montfort**, Count of Leicester. Not content with his gains, de Montfort renewed hostilities with Raymond VI, forcing him and his son to flee to the English court of King John, the elder Raymond's brother-in-law. When the two Raymonds returned from exile, they resumed battle with de Montfort at Toulouse, which their arch-foe was besieging – a campaign that cost him his life in June 1218.

---

buzzed by amateur pilots using the small airport near the middle. The village itself offers all amenities, including a **gîte d'étape** on the main highway above the marionette workshop (☎04.68.20.80.69; dorm beds ①, doubles ③), with a quieter rear terrace, and the **restaurant** *Dame Blanche*. Less than a kilometre south of the village is a small lake – more of a large pond – with a **campsite** and swimming area (daily except Mon), a welcome sight whether you've been cycling, driving or hiking.

The **château**, standing alone like a child's cardboard cut-out atop a gently rounded hill a kilometre or so east of the village, fell to the anti-Cathar crusade in 1210. More a place of culture than of arms, it was closely associated with the **troubadour** poets, whose preoccupation with themes of romance might seem incompatible with the

Their success was fairly short-lived; although the younger Raymond, who succeeded his father in 1222, managed to regain lost territory and reorganize the Cathar communities therein, a new scorched-earth campaign unleashed in 1226 brought him to his knees by 1229. Led naked by a cord around his neck, Raymond VII had to submit to public flagellation, the razing of the walls of Toulouse, the loss of his possessions beyond the Rhône and the marriage of his only daughter to the younger brother of the Parisian king Louis IX.

In 1233, the papacy authorized the creation of the infamous **Inquisition**, to be supervised by Dominican and Franciscan monks. The Dominican order itself had been founded in 1206 by Domingo de Guzmán, later known to the world as **Saint Dominic**, who came specially from Castille to the Cathar heartland to counter the growing heresy. Leaving violent coercion to others, his preferred strategies were strenuous disputations with Cathar theologians, imitation of their austere habits and the founding of a convent at Prouille to receive Cathar women who recanted their beliefs.

The fate of the Cathars was sealed when, in 1242, a group of sixty from Montségur, led by **Pierre-Roger de Mirepoix**, went to Avignonet and assassinated the eleven chief inquisitors. The retaliatory asault on Montségur, by a force of almost ten thousand men, began in May 1243, and continued through the winter – the first time in the Cathar crusades that the fighting was not suspended when the weather turned. In March 1244, de Mirepoix, despairing of relief, agreed terms: the two hundred non-Cathar soldiers within the citadel would be allowed to go, but after fifteen days' truce the Cathars themselves were to abjure their faith or submit to whatever fate their tormenters devised for them. On the night of March 15, in contravention of the terms, four Cathars climbed down the cliffs, escaped over the Col de la Peyre and recovered the Cathar "treasure" from a cave where it had been hidden at Christmas; what happened to it is a mystery, giving rise to legends – especially in German sources – identifying the treasure as the Holy Grail, and the Cathars themselves as the Knights of the Round Table. The next day Montségur surrendered, and the 225 surviving Cathar civilians who refused to abjure their beliefs were burned on a mass pyre, those who could not walk being thrown on with their stretchers.

In effect, Catharism ceased to exist as a significant force in France after the holocaust at Montségur, though two of the four escapees later appeared in Lombardy with proceeds from the "treasure" which went to support a refugee Cathar community established there. Quéribus and Puylaurens – the final Cathar fortifications in Roussillon – came under royal control between 1255 and 1258. When Raymond VII's daughter died childless in 1271, all of Languedoc passed to the French Crown. From then on, Catharism persisted mainly as an underground network, with safe houses and escape routes extending across the mountains into Spanish Aragón and Catalunya. The last significant figure in Cathar history, Guilhem Bélibaste, was executed in 1321, having been caught returning from Spain to proselytize, and the last Lombard *bons hommes* were rooted out by the Inquisition in 1412.

asceticism of the Cathars. What united them was the Occitan language, then spoken all across southern France. For the troubadours the *langue d'Oc* was simply the natural language of poetry and love; for the Cathars it expressed their defiance of Paris. Little remains of the pre-1210 structure; most of what's visible (daily: April–Sept 8am–7pm; rest of year 10am–5pm; 25F) dates from the fourteenth century. Visits concentrate on the various floors of the donjon, with stairs all the way to the roof; the chapel features vigil seats at the north and south windows, a wall font and ceiling ribvaulting culminating in a keystone embossed with images of the Virgin and Saint George. The highest chamber is dubbed the "musicians' room" after its eight *culs-de-lamps* or torch sockets at the termini of more rib-vaulting, each sculpted in the form of a figure playing a different period instrument.

Northern approaches to Montségur

From Puivert the road heads west over the Col de Teil, the divide between the Aude and the Ariège, and also the Pyrenean watershed: east of it, rivers flow to the Mediterranean, while on the west they empty in the Atlantic. You can walk from Puivert to Montségur along the **Sentier Cathare**, a long but not difficult day of some 25km, mostly through dense fir forests.

Bélesta and Fougax-Barrineuf

A better place to begin the walk, however, is 11km west at **BÉLESTA**, the next stop on the bus route. It's a far more manageable village than Lavelanet (see below), and if you get stranded there's **accommodation** at the somewhat pricey *Le Troubador*, on the through road (☎05.61.01.60.57; ③), a cheaper no-name *Café-Hotel* diagonally across from the *Mairie* on the main square (②) and **camping** on the east side of the village at *Le Val d'Amour* (June–Sept). Attractions begin almost immediately on the way south: some 1500m out of Bélesta, the route to Montségur passes **Fontesorbes**, an artesian spring (*source intermittente*) under a rock overhang that in summer spurts water for six-minute periods evenly separated by 32-minute pauses (in winter the water flows continuously). From the *source* you can continue directly to Montségur by walking along various marked GRs (3hr), hitching 13km along the D5 and then the D9, or taking a longer detour via the Gorges de la Frau, 8km south (see below).

The most direct approaches pass through the double village of **FOUGAX-BAR-RINEUF**, 2km southwest, which offers a fine **restaurant**, *Les Cinque Fours*, occupying an old bone-comb factory (formerly an important local industry, established by Protestants betwen the sixteenth and eighteenth centuries). The portions aren't huge, but neither are they *minceur*, and the 85F menu is quite adequate as a four-course lunch.

Lavelanet and Villeneuve-d'Olmès

LAVELANET, 8km west of Bélesta, has little to offer other than its onward bus connections, its **tourist office** (☎05.61.01.22.20) on the central *rond point* and the clean, modern *Camping de Lavelanet* (April–Sept; ☎05.61.01.55.54) southwest of the centre. There's no excuse for getting stuck here, and if you do such **hotels** as the *Lafayette* (☎05.61.01.46.25; ③) and the *Parc* (☎05.61.68.10.29; ④), both on the road out to Bélesta, and the *Espagne*, on the road to Foix (☎05.61.01.00.78; ④), are hardly enticing. The next bus stop, **VILLENEUVE-D'OLMÈS**, has *chambres d'hôtes* available at 3 av du 11 Novembre (☎05.61.01.17.91; ③) and is a bit closer to the castle.

The southern approach to Montségur via Comus

From Monday to Friday there are two late-afternoon buses daily from Quillan to Comus. If you've read Emmanuel Le Roy Ladurie's *Montaillou* you may want to get off at Camurac, 3km short of Comus, and walk the rest of the way via Montaillou village, subject of the book and a detour which takes about two hours. **CAMURAC** is actually much closer to Ax-les-Thermes (see p.207) and can offer **accommodation** at the *Auberge du Pays de Sault* (☎04.68.20.32.09; ②) as well as *Camping les Sapins*.

MONTAILLOU subscribed to the Cathar heresy long after the fall of Montségur, until the Inquisition, directed by the bishop of Pamiers, set to work here during the 1320s. The records compiled by the inquisitors were so precise that Le Roy Ladurie has been able to recreate every aspect of the villagers' lives from them, from the minutiae of domestic economics to the details of their sexual habits; it's a fascinating book, essential for understanding the local past. Fewer than twenty people live here permanently now, all of them descendants of the Cathars, as you can see by comparing their surnames with those on the headstones in the ancient graveyard.

COMUS isn't a lot bigger than Montaillou, but does have an excellent **gîte d'étape** (☎04.68.20.33.69; ①) attached to the Centre École Pleine Nature, which specializes in **caving**, the limestone hereabouts being peppered with two hundred known caves. Montségur is 13km away, through the **Gorges de la Frau**. From Comus take the recently designated GR107, formerly the GR7B, which drops down as a mule track between fields to a wide gorge that suddenly becomes a defile, where thousand-metre cliffs admit the sun only during the early afternoon. When the gorge widens again, you meet the dead-end of the D5 coming south from Bélesta and Fougax-Barrineuf. There are two ways of continuing to Montségur: either along the Sentier Cathare westwards, wrapped in tree-shade alongside a stream (turn off at the first farm, 45min along the D5), or a bridle trail beginning about an hour along the tarmac, offering higher, more open ground. Either way, walking time from Comus is four hours.

Montségur

The ruined castle of **MONTSÉGUR** lives up to the promise of its distant view, its plain stone walls poised emphatically above the straggling, namesake village on a 1207-metre-high *pog* (from the Occitan *puèg*, or "mountain"). The original fortifications were built by Guillaume "Short-Nose", duke of Aquitaine, but between 1204 and 1232 it was reconstructed as a bastion of the Cathars under the direction of Guilhabert de Castres, leader of the sect. Drastically eroded into naked vertical faces and gullies, the *pog* would have been a formidable defence. Only on the western side is it possible to walk up to the summit (about 30min), through what is now called the *prat dels cremats*, where the surviving Cathars were burned to death after the castle fell (a stone memorial pays tribute to them); the gist of the story is explained in the feature on pp.218–19.

The beauty of **the site** (daily: April 10am–5pm; May–Sept 9am–7pm; Oct & Nov 10am–5pm; 20F, or 25F including admission to the museum) is what hits you first, since the original walls were reduced by half after the siege, and all internal structures are gone except the simple keep, now open to the sky. Then you begin to wonder how that last Cathar community of five hundred people could have held out so long in so small an area. Even given that some lived in now-vanished houses at the foot of the walls on the north and west faces, there was a garrison of two hundred to be accommodated, together with the *faydits* – local aristocrats dispossessed by the crusade against Catharism. What's left of the castle takes no more than a few minutes – rather disappointingly, you're no longer allowed to climb up on the walls, merely to traverse the keep to visit the west donjon – but it isn't so much what you see at Montségur that makes the trip unforgettable, as what your imagination can re-create from its remnants.

Down in the village, 1km below, a one-room **archeological museum** (April, Oct & Nov 11am–4pm; May–Sept 10am–1pm & 2–7pm; 10F) displays artefacts excavated since the 1950s from the original village up beside the walls, from both pre- and post-Cathar periods – mostly food bones, personal effects, tools and surviving fragments of houses.

Practicalities

Despite its small size, tourist numbers at Montségur village have prompted a **tourist office** (July–Sept daily 10am–1pm & 2–6pm; ☎05.61.03.03.03), of most use for information on the precise route of the GR107; a *topoguide* is due to be published in 1998, which they will hopefully stock. If you'd like to stay the night – and the beautiful scenery certainly encourages the notion – there are three **hotels**: the old-fashioned *Couquet* (☎05.61.01.10.28; ③), a rambling country pension of wood-furnished rooms with washbasins; the adjacent, en-suite *Costes* (☎05.61.01.10.24; ④) just uphill; and *Le Bufadou*, at the lower entrance to the village (☎05.61.01.98.99; ④). All have attached, nourishing and reasonably priced **restaurants**: the *Couquet* represents great value with four large home-made courses for well under 100F; the *Costes* is fancier, featuring game and *Ariègeois* specialities for well over that figure, while *Le Bufadou* offers a three-course vegetarian menu for under 100F. The *Costes* manages the nearby **gîte d'étape** (①), while the closest **campsite** (tents only) is the *Point Acceuil Jeunes* (☎05.61.01.10.27), at the lower end of the village on the Bélesta side.

Villeneuve d'Olmès or Comus are the obvious places to pick up a **bus to move on** from Montségur. From Villeneuve, buses go west to Foix at 9.40am and 6pm, and east to Quillan at 2.15pm – and there's an additional 6.55am service to Quillan from Lavelanet, 4km north of Villeneuve. From Comus, buses leave for Quillan at 6.40am and 11.25am, Monday to Friday.

Roquefixade

Approximately 8km west of Lavelanet, the village of Nalzen is the best point along the D117 for access to **ROQUEFIXADE**, westernmost of the Cathar castles and last stop on the *Sentier Cathare* before Foix. A two-kilometre side road leads up to the eponymous village, rebuilt after the Cathar crusades as a *bastide*. From the high end of the village it's a twenty-minute climb to the castle (unenclosed, free), which takes its name (originally *roca fissada*) from the vast natural fissures augmenting its defences. Perched at the west end of a long ridge, it's bigger than it appears from below but utterly ruinous; your main reward is the view over the valley below with its clustered villages, and south (weather permitting) to the high Pyrenean ridge.

A *gîte d'étape* (☎05.61.03.01.36; ①) stands by the base of the path up to the castle, and their outdoor seating is a good place for a drink after the climb; however, they only have twelve places, so let them know in good time if you wish to **stay**. Alternative accommodation if they're full is the *Relais des Pogs* (☎05.61.01.14.50; ②).

travel details

FRANCE

Trains

Foix to: Ax-les-Thermes (6–7 daily; 45min); L'Hospitalet-près-l'Andorre (4 daily; 1hr 10min–1hr 30min); Tarascon-sur-Ariège (6–7 daily; 20min); Toulouse (11 daily; 1hr–1hr 15min). *NB. Often SNCF buses substitute for, or supplement, trains in the Ariège valley, especially above Tarascon.*

Latour-de-Carol to: Ax-les-Thermes (5 daily; 55min); Bourg-Madame (5 daily; 15min); Foix (4 daily; 1hr 30min–1hr 40min); L'Hospitalet-près-l'Andorre (5 daily; 25min); Mont-Louis (5 daily; 1hr 20min); Puigcerdà (4 daily; 7min); Tarascon-sur-Ariège (4 daily; 1hr 15min–1hr 25min); Toulouse (4 daily; 2hr 30min–2hr 45min); Villefranche-de-Conflent (4 daily; 2hr 25min–2hr 55min).

Buses

Ax-les-Thermes to: Foix (6 daily Mon–Fri, 4 Sat, 2 Sun; 1hr); Pas de la Casa (2 daily; 45min); Tarascon-sur-Ariège (same frequencies; 30min).

Comus to: Quillan (2 daily Mon–Fri; 1hr 5min).

Foix to: Lavelanet (Mon–Sat 2 daily at 11.30am & 2.35pm, except Wed in school term 1 daily at 2.35pm; 35min); Quillan (Mon–Sat 1 daily at 2.35pm; 2hr); St-Girons (4 daily; 45min).

L'Hospitalet-près-l'Andorre (SNCF bus) to: Andorra la Vella (2 daily; 1hr 30min–1hr 40min); Pas de la Casa (2 daily; 25–30min).

Latour-de-Carol to: Font-Romeu (4 daily, 2 only on the return journey; 50min).

Lavelanet to: Quillan (Mon–Sat 2 daily at 6.55am & 3.05pm; 1hr); Toulouse (6 daily Mon–Sat, 2 Sun; 2hr 30min).

Villeneuve-d'Olmès to: Foix (2 daily at 9.40am & 6pm; 40min).

SPAIN

Trains

Puigcerdà to: Barcelona (6 daily; 3hr 15min); Latour-de-Carol (3 daily; 7min); Ripoll (6 daily; 1hr 15min).

Buses

Berga to: Barcelona (4–5 daily; 2hr); Borredà (1 daily Mon–Sat at 1–2pm, returns 7.30–8.30am; 30min); Castèllar de N'Hug (1 daily Mon–Sat at 6pm, returns next morning; 1hr 20min); Gòsol via Saldes (1 daily at 5.35pm, returns next morning; 1hr); La Pobla de Lillet (2–4 daily; 1hr); Ripoll (1 daily at 7.15am, returns at 12.30pm; 1hr 20min); Sant Llorenç de Morunys (1 daily Mon–Fri at 5.30pm, returns next morning; 1hr).

Puigcerdà to: Llivia (2 daily; 10min); La Seu d'Urgell (2 daily at 7.30am & 2.45pm; 1hr).

La Seu d'Urgell to: Andorra la Vella (6–7 daily; 30min); Barcelona (2 daily; 3hr 30min); Lleida (2 daily; 2hr 30min); Puigcerdà (2 daily at 12.30pm & 7pm; 1hr).

ANDORRA

Domestic buses

Andorra la Vella to: Arinsal (3 daily; 30min); El Serrat (2 daily; 30min); Encamp (every 20min 7am–9.30pm; 15min); Ordino (every 30min 7am–9pm; 20min); Pas de la Casa (2 daily; 1hr 30min); Soldeu (hourly 9am–8pm; 45min).

Long-distance buses

Andorra la Vella to: Ax-les-Thermes (2 daily; 2hr 15min–2hr 30min); Barcelona (2 daily; 4hr); L'Hospitalet-près-l'Andorre (2 daily; 1hr 30min); La Seu d'Urgell (7 daily Mon–Sat, 5 Sun; 40min); Latour-de-Carol (2 daily; 2hr 15min–2hr 30min); Porté-Puymorens (2 daily; 2hr 30min).

CHAPTER THREE

THE VALL D'ARAN REGION

The **Vall d'Aran** is something of a curiosity: isolated from Spain and opening towards France, the frontier here is thrust so far northwards that both sources of the Garonne, one of southern France's major rivers, lie in Spanish territory. Due to its relatively easy accessibility from both Spain and France, the Vall d'Aran makes an obvious jumping-off point into the surrounding mountains, and – although overdeveloped in spots for skiers and summer weekenders from Toulouse and Barcelona – the Aran region itself is not lacking in interest.

Apart from anything else, it's a pervasive, long-standing misconception that the Pyrenees consist of two separate mountain chains which overlap for some 70km at the Vall d'Aran. The definitive geomorphological map of the range, produced in 1973 by the French company Elf-Aquitaine, effectively debunks this: the watershed is merely distorted here, so that an important spur off the main ridge which would ordinarily point south–north is deflected east–west instead, lending the illusion of separate peak lines. In fact, only some low hills to the west, in the Basque country, are tectonically separate from the main body of the Pyrenees.

Between Aran and Andorra to the east, the easternmost of the Pyrenean "three-thousanders", **Montcalm** and **Estats**, rear up over remote valleys on either side of the border, which constitute approaches scarcely visited except for the banks of the mighty **Noguera Pallaresa**, one of the great Pyrenean rivers which drains from just east of Aran south to Lleida. South of Aran, and also accessible from the Noguera Pallaresa valley, spreads the only national park in Catalunya, the **Parc Nacional d'Aigües Tortes i Estany de Sant Maurici**, a 15,000-hectare wonderland of crags, tarns and dense forest which delights hikers, alpine skiers and naturalists.

Maladeta – the great massif southwest of Aran, in Alto Aragón – was erroneously translated from the Aragonese *Mala Eta* as "The Accursed" by early French climbers, rather than as "The Highest Point", a misinterpretation that had much to do with the terrifying glaciers which used to dominate this part of the range. Such was the fear induced by their crevasses that the first successful ascent of **Aneto** – at 3404m, the roof of the Pyrenees – was not made until 1842, by a long and convoluted route that avoided the ice. Owing, perhaps, to global warming, today's glaciers are scant vestiges of those that once covered the peaks, and modern maps and equipment further reduce this terrain's power to intimidate.

Immediately west of Maladeta looms the comparatively unsung massif of **Posets**, second highest in the Pyrenees and equally beloved by alpine aficionados. Together these two great mountains form a vast region far easier seen and crossed on foot or skis than by vehicle, so it comes as a welcome surprise to find the populous, comfortable town of **Benasque**, mountaineering capital of eastern Aragón, at the bottom of the Ésera valley separating the two mountains. There's no other appreciable settlement until you reach the villages of the **Valle de Gistau**, on Poset's western flank.

If Spain has the region's most spectacular high-mountain scenery, France boasts the finest man-made attractions. Two thousand years of settlement have left their traces at **Saint-Bertrand-de-Comminges**, on the Garonne, and there's a similar air of antiquity at **Saint-Lizier**, originally founded by the Romans. Further back, the people of the prehistoric Magdalenian culture (15,000–8000 BC) left drawings and sculptures in several caves, including **Mas d'Azil**, between Foix and Saint-Girons, and mysterious, "mutilated" hand outlines at the **Grotte de Gargas** near Saint-Bertrand. Depopulation is severe all over this French region, but particularly in the backward Pay de Couserans region, unfolding south from Saint-Girons to the Vall d'Aran. Here, because of scant contact with the outside world, traditional customs, costumes and occupations persisted until the start of this century.

Often the only signs of development on either side of the frontier are eyesore **hydro-electric schemes** which have proliferated in almost every canyon. Neither the sites – often still littered with construction debris – nor the procession of pylons marching away from them were conceived with much consideration for aesthetics, wildlife preservation or for the wishes of the admittedly dwindling number of human locals.

Public transport is fairly sketchy on the French side, though things tend to improve during the ski season. In Spain, bus services are hardly more frequent, again a consequence of rural depopulation. **Trains** from the south stop at Lleida (with onward, tourist-group departures up to La Pobla de Segur), while in the north there is a foothill rail (or rail-bus) service only on the spur line from Montréjeau to Bagnères-de-Luchon. By contrast the busy main highway between Montréjeau and La Pobla, threading the entire length of Aran and passing close to Aigües Tortes, sees a relative abundance of **buses**, as does the road which heads south from Viella, capital of Aran, for Lleida. Away from this central hub, Benasque in the west has adequate bus services, as does much of the Couserans, with all connections through its regional capital of Saint-Girons.

THE MONTCALM-ESTATS
MASSIF AND AROUND

The joint massif of French **Montcalm** (3077m) and border-straddling **Estats** (3143m) – the latter the highest mountain in Catalonia – is so remote from human settlement that a few bears and lynx are believed to still live somewhere below the summits. Tucked into a fold of land where the Spanish and French borders meet the westernmost corner of Andorra, this is one of the least-known areas of the Pyrenees – and one of the least accessible. Public transport on either the French or Spanish sides runs no closer than about 20km distant, from which point it's a good day's walk to the flanks of the mountain.

There are three usual ways into the massif or its foothills: by road from the **Vicdessos valley**, in the Ariège; by track, then trail, from the Spanish valleys of Cardós and Ferrera,

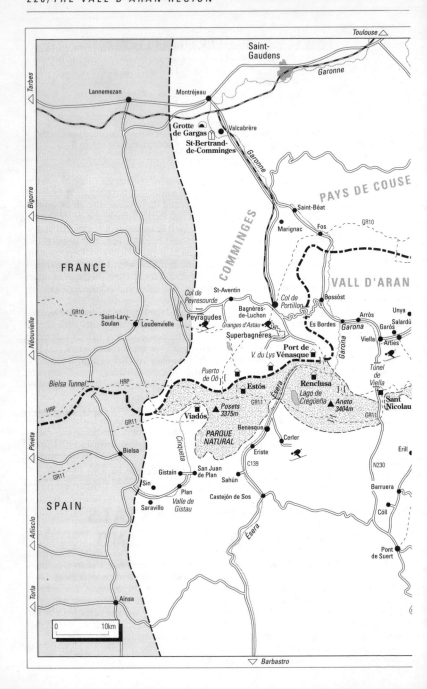

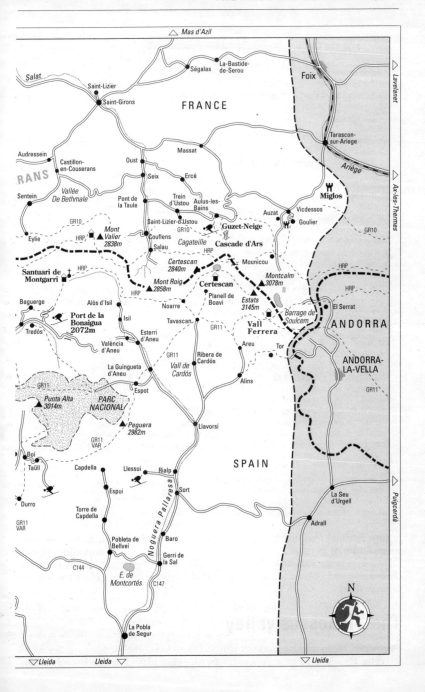

FESTIVALS

JANUARY
7 *Festa Major de Sant Julià* at La Guingueta d'Àneu and Espui.
16 Festival at Gerri de la Sal.
20 Festival at El Pont de Suert.
24 Leather fair at Sort.

FEBRUARY
Variable Shrove Tuesday at Sort, Rialp, Esterri d'Àneu and Pobleta de Bellveí.
12 *Festa Major de Santa Eulàlia* at Erill la Vall.
14 *Festa Major de Sant Valentí* at Boí.

MARCH/APRIL
Easter Particularly lively festivities at Alins and La Pobla de Segur.
Sunday after Easter *Fira de la Pasqüeta* at Esterri d'Àneu.
28 April Spring fair at Sort.

MAY
3 *Festa de la Santa Creu* at Salardú.
6 Festival at Llavorsí.
First Sunday Festival at Arròs.
First and last Sunday Festival at Gerri de la Sal.

JUNE
Whit Sunday Festival at Mare de Déu de les Ares.
Whit Monday Festival at Arròs.
12 Wool fair at Rialp; sheep-shearing at Llessuí.
14 *Romeria de Sant Quirç* at Taüll.
16 *Romeria de Sant Quirç* at Durro.
Third Sunday Festival at Es Bordes.
23 *Feux de la Saint Jean* at Bagnères-de-Luchon.
23–24 Festivals at Arties, Lés, Boí and Saint-Lizier.
28–29 *Festa de Sants Pau i Pere* at Alins and Tor.
30 *Ball de Benás* in honour of San Marcial at Benasque.
Variable *Festival du Chant Pyrénéen* at Bagnères-de-Luchon.
Late June *Raiers*, old-time log-raft festival, at Sort, continues into early July.

JULY
First Sunday *Raiers* at La Pobla de Segur.
First two weeks Classical music festival at Saint-Lizier.
2 Festival at Santuari de Montgarri.
10 *Festa Major de Sant Cristòfol* at Erill la Vall.

in turn reached from the larger **Noguera Pallaresa** downstream; or by footpath **from Andorra** (a route already covered on pp.194–5). The two **summits** are connected by a ridge walk that crosses the border; to the west a particularly beautiful, challenging and isolated section of the HRP zigzags for two days along the frontier towards Aran.

The Vicdessos valley

Steep-sided, damp-smelling and lined with deciduous forest, the **Vicdessos valley** is typical of the Haute-Ariège – a sunless, uncomfortable place to live in winter. But it does have

19–20 *Festa Major* at La Guingueta d'Àneu.
24 Festival at Llavorsí.
24–25 *Festa de Sant Jaume* at La Pobla de Segur and Arties.
31 Festival at Gerri de la Sal.
Third or fourth weekend *Festa Major dels Rosers* at Taüll; torchlight procession Fri pm, live bands Sat pm, folk dancing Sun noon.
Mid-July to mid-August Music festival at Saint-Lizier. **End July to August** Music festival at Saint-Bertrand-de-Comminges.
All month International Canoe Rally on the Noguera Pallaresa.

August
Early part of the month Music festival at Saint-Lizier.
First Sunday *La Pujada* Catalan–Occitan solidarity festival at the Port de Salau.
1–3 *Festa Major de Sant Feliu* and canoe racing at Sort; *Festa Major* at Barruera.
3 *Festa de Sant Esteve* in Tredòs.
15 Canoe racing at Rialp.
Second weekend *Festa Major* at El Pont de Suert.
10 *Festa Major de Sant Martí* at Torre de Capdella.
15–16 Festivals at several Baixaran villages, including Bossòst.
Third Sunday Flower festival at Bagnères-de-Luchon.
27 *Festa de Sant Llisser* at Alòs d'Isil.
Fourth Sunday *Festa Major* at Capdella.

September
7–9 Birth of the Virgin observances at Sort, Esterri d'Àneu, Ribera de Cardós, Barruera, Durro, Cóll, Viella and Es Bordes.
22 *Festa Major* at Ermita de Sant Maurici.
Weekend closest to 26 *Festa Major de Sants Cosme i Damià* at Tredòs.
Last Sunday *Festa de Sant Miquel* at Llessuí.

October
8 Fair at Viella.
20 Annual festival at Bossost.

November
7–9 Grand Autumn Fair at Sort.
23 *Festa de Sant Climent* at Taüll.
30 *Festa de Sant Andreu* at Salardú.

December
9 *Festa de Santa Llogaia* at Espot.
24 Festival at La Guingueta d'Àneu.

some intrinsic interest – specifically castles at **Miglos** and **Montréal de Sos** – aside from being the most convenient French corridor to Montcalm.

There are occasional (weekdays in term time, every Friday and alternate Mondays otherwise) late afternoon buses from Foix and Tarascon-sur-Ariège up the valley as far as Auzat, which leaves you just 7km short of the *gîte d'étape* at Mounicou, the usual Montcalm base camp.

Miglos and around

Your first stop heading up the valley along the D8 might be the ruined fourteenth-century château of **Miglos**, perched atop a rocky outcrop above the valley, a couple of kilometres upstream from Niaux. The medieval locals, resenting taxation by its owner Guillaume Arnaud d'Arnave, petitioned Gaston Fébus who obliged them by substituting his own taxes; the château was later razed by Richelieu, though the towers – best seen from the northerly approach road – remain intact. You can stay at nearby **JUNAC** (2km downhill on the valley floor) in *chambres d'hôtes* run by a Dutch couple (☎05.61.05.89.88; ③).

If you have your own transport you could detour down the dead-end D24 to **SIGUER**, where the three-storey, brick-and-timber **Maison des Comptes de Foix** just off the square (closed for restoration) is a splendid Renaissance hunting lodge used by Gaston Fébus, and **LERCOUL**, a tiny hamlet clinging to the top of a near-vertical cliff. The GR10 passes through both villages as it comes west from Mérens-les-Vals, then continues over the Col de Lercoul to the tiny ski station of Goulier-Neige and the village of **GOULIER**, above Vicdessos. This can offer two **gîte d'étapes**: *Relais de L'Endron* (☎05.61.03.80.70; ①) and the larger *Al Cantou* (☎05.61.64.81.84; ①).

Vicdessos and Auzat

VICDESSOS, 9km beyond Capoulet, and its close neighbour **AUZAT** are the most southerly outposts of civilization in the valley. Important foundry centres in decades past, neither has much to recommend it now, though Auzat is pleasant enough, with a little stream coursing through between rows of plane trees.

At the nearby Templar château of **Montreál de Sos** a medieval mural of the Holy Lance and Grail was discovered in 1890; these days, it's almost invisible. The ruins stand on a mound above the tiny hamlet of Olbier, reached by a footpath from the east bank of the river just past Auzat, or by a track beginning halfway along the road connecting Vicdessos and Goulier. The Templars were responsible for many pilgrims' hospices in the Pyrenees, but became too rich for the liking of the Catholic Church and its allies, who in 1307 accused them of corruption, heresy and sexual depravity, tortured their leaders and finally burnt them to death. The view from the ruins is fabulous, marred only by the aluminium works at Auzat, the last remaining significant source of local employment. In the Middle Ages the inhabitants of Vicdessos had the right to work in the now-exhausted iron mine at nearby Rancié and to sell whatever they extracted to one of the numerous forges hereabouts.

Practicalities

Local **hotels** are limited to the one-star *Hivert* in Vicdessos (☎05.61.64.88.17; ③), on the through road, and the *Hôtel Denjean-La Bonne Auberge* (☎05.61.64.88.36; ③) at the east entrance to Auzat. More attractive are the *chambres d'hotes*, *Les Marmousets*, offered by the Pittoni family (☎05/61.64.81.62; ④) in Vicdessos, either in the main house or in two independent chalets. Both hotels have attached **restaurants**, though the *Denjean*'s is overpriced and mediocre. Each village also boasts a **campsite**: the large *La Bexanelle* (☎05.61.64.82.22) at Vicdessos and *La Verniere* at Auzat (☎05.61.64.84.46). The **Maison du Pays** in Auzat (July & Aug daily 8am–noon & 2–6pm; Sept–June Mon–Fri 8am–noon & 2–6pm; ☎05.61.64.87.53) is quite helpful – as well they might be, with relatively few passing tourists to lavish attention on. There's also an **Office du Tourisme** in Vicdessos (☎05/61.64.82.59). Organized local activities are still limited, but you can ride horses with the Centre Equestre at Ournac, 2km south of Auzat (☎05.61.64.84.66), or make like a bird with a *parapente* school, Les Aigles du Montcalm (☎05.61.03.80.36, answering machine; early May–early Oct).

The ascent of Montcalm

Around 7km south of Auzat and 1km past the village of Marc, you reach the *gîte d'étape* at minuscule **MOUNICOU** (☎05.61.64.87.66; ①), situated on both the GR10 and a northerly variant of the HRP. An uninterrupted **ascent of Montcalm** from the *gîte* is long and hard, but the only way to divide it into stages is to stay overnight in a tent or some badly maintained unstaffed refuges along the way. Allowing for stops, it takes around twelve hours to the summit and back, or to move on to the *Refugí de Vall Ferrera* (see p.234) in Spain – and early in the season you'll need crampons. At all times, the requisite IGN 1:25,000 **map** is TOP 25 2148 OT "Montcalm-Estats".

From Marc, follow the side road west towards L'Artigue for about half an hour; a clear track then goes off south at the semiderelict *Refuge de Montcalm*, ending just short of the tiny pastoral hovels at Orrys de Pujol, from where it's another half-hour to the head of the **Pla de Subra**.

From here, Montcalm looks formidable, its summit looming more than 1000m overhead, the bare rock sunless above the grass and trees. The easy going is all behind you now. Over scree and rock – with one very steep section – you scramble first to a wide shelf known as the **Tables de Montcalm**, a sort of gangway rising southwards; before the end you start clambering up rocks to the right, finally gaining a relatively easy shoulder leading to the summit. The walk along the ridge up to Estats can be done in about forty minutes more. To descend, either retrace your steps or reverse the instructions from the Vall Ferrera (see "Approach to Estats from Llavorsí", p.234).

Trekking west of Mounicou

A short distance west of the Mounicou *gîte d'étape*, the HRP and the GR10 go their separate ways. The **GR10** runs through Marc and up onto the hillsides above the west bank of the River Vicdessos to the hamlet of Hérout. There it bears northwest, climbing very steeply to the dammed lakes of Escales and Bassiès and then up again to Étang d'Alate, from which you descend to the **Port de Saleix** (1794m) and then west through forest to Aulus-les-Bains (p.278) – a total of about eight hours' walking. You can break the sector at the *Refuge des Etangs de Bassiès* (☎05.61.61.89.98; staffed June–Sept; 50 places; 15-place section always open; ①), above the higher, smaller lake.

Beyond Marc, the more circuitous **HRP** route goes through L'Artigue, from where it climbs west-southwest to the **Port de l'Artigue** (2480m; 5hr) on the Spanish frontier. After this the general line is northwest, but for the rest of the day good compass work is essential. From the pass you drop down to a marshy tarn in the Spanish Aguiló valley, skirting it to the north and climbing steeply westwards along the stream to the lower of the two lakes known as **Estanys d'Aguiló** (*Guiló* on some French maps). From these you continue northwest to the **Port de Colatx/Port de Couillac** (2416m). The first day's goal, the **Étang de la Hillette** (1800m), is now two hours below, magnificently situated above the Cirque de Cagateille (10–12hr from Mounicou). Noncampers can stay in the *Cabane de la Hillette* (15 places) or the *Vieille Cabane de la Hillette* (4 places), until a staffed refuge is built here.

After this, the HRP recrosses into Spain via the **Port de Marterat/Materet** (2217m), exiting quickly through the Ruhos/Crusous pass (2300m), a difficult meander along the frontier, devoid of cairns, which precedes a steady descent to Salau (9hr from Hillette). If you or the weather are not up to this, it's better to opt for the beautiful half-day ramble from Hillette down the **Cirque de Cagateille** (see p.277 for more details on this), through the woods and along the Cors stream, reaching the D38 and the GR10 at Saint-Lizier-d'Ustou. The downstream hamlet of **TREIN D'USTOU**, 3km away in the Ustou valley, has a fifteen-place *gîte d'étape/auberge* (☎61.96.52.43; ①)05.61.96.52.43; ①), as well as the more comfortable *Hotel Restaurant L'Auberge des Ormeaux* (☎05.61.96.53.22, fax 05.61.66.84.19; ④), the most reliable place to eat in the valley. Next day you can catch the bus to Saint-Girons.

Up the Noguera Pallaresa

The **Noguera Pallaresa**, the most powerful river in the Spanish Pyrenees, was once used to float logs from the upper valley to the sawmills at **La Pobla de Segur**, a job now done by truck. Nowadays, this is the Pyrenean river every rafter wants to tackle, but if you have less specialized enthusiasms, the valley – beautiful and dramatic though it can be – is primarily a way of getting to the mountains to either side, or arriving in the Vall d'Aran. To ascend Estats and Montcalm, you leave the Noguera Pallaresa at **Llavorsí**, heading northeast along the valleys of **Çardós** and **Ferrera**; for Aran, the busier C142 road continues northwest, via the **Vall d'Àneu**, up to the seasonally open **Port de Bonaigua**.

Access from the east

Access to the valley is easiest through La Pobla de Segur, which has public transport connections in every direction except eastwards. Coming into the Noguera Pallaresa **from the east** involves either driving or hitching along the 46-kilometre road from Adrall (near La Seu d'Urgell) to Sort, or taking one of a number of mountain-biking or walking routes. The track from Sant Joan de l'Erm, beyond Castellbó (west of La Seu), drops into the Noguera Pallaresa between Rialp and Llavorsí, north of Sort. There's also a track from Ars, just outside Andorra's extreme southwest corner, coming down to Tirvia near Llavorsí. From inside Andorra there's the track – passable to jeeps – from Pal over the Coll de la Botella, descending into Spain at Tor, at the head of the Tor valley; from there you move into the Vall Ferrera valley at Alins and finally into the Cardós valley, not far from Llavorsí. Yet another possibility is to use the **HRP variant** from El Serrat in the northwest corner of Andorra to Tavascan.

La Pobla de Segur

LA POBLA DE SEGUR is a lively enough town if you want to break your journey, but frankly most people only come here for onward connections. As well as buses further north along the Noguera Pallaresa, local services also journey west to El Pont de Suert, Boí and Capdella for jumping off into the Aigües Tortes region, and through the Túnel de Viella to the Vall d'Aran.

La Pobla is served by a daily Alsina Graells **bus** from Barcelona (departs 7.30am from Plaça de la Universitat, labelled *Pont de Rei*, from June to mid-Nov), and by several daily **trains** from Lleida which terminate here. The bus from Barcelona continues up the Noguera Pallaresa through Sort and Llavorsí, passing the side road for the Cardós and Ferrera valleys, and within 7km of Espot, a major entry point to the Aigües Tortes national park (see p.250). Arriving from Lleida, morning train and bus services should dovetail well with the onward bus up the Noguera Pallaresa at 11.40am; there's another at 6.30pm.

Trains arrive in the new town, from where you walk up the road, cross the bridge and head along the main street towards the terminals of the various **bus** companies: Alsina Graells, for Noguera Pallaresa services, is at the beginning of the onward road to Sort, on the west side of the street. Should you need to **stay**, there are two *fondas* in the centre: *Roy*, Avda. de la Font (☎973/68 00 31; ③), and *Torrentet*, at Plaça Pedrera 5 (☎973/68 03 52; ③).

Gerri de la Sal and around

From La Pobla de Segur the C147 road threads through the red and steel-grey rocks of the **Desfiladero de Collegats**, an impressive gorge hewn by the Noguera Pallaresa through three-hundred-metre-high cliffs. Unfortunately, since a new tunnel was blasted through much of the defile, drivers see little of the spectacular valley, though the narrow, abandoned old road is still open to cyclists and pedestrians.

As the canyon opens out, you emerge at the rickety village of **GERRI DE LA SAL** – "de la Sal" because of the local salt-making industry. You'll see surviving salt pans by the riverside as you pass, but more obvious is the Benedictine monastery of **Santa Maria**, originally founded in 807. The present twelfth-century structure, with its huge and dilapidated bell-wall, faces the village on the far side of a beautiful old bridge; the church interior (200ptas) is a three-aisled basilica whose soaring barrel vaulting is upheld by four fluted columns; a few recent frescoes are of limited interest. Opening hours are erratic – try hunting for the warden at the little drinks café – but it's worth a look even from the outside, where an arched hay-loft runs along the south side of the building.

If you have a vehicle this is a fine place for a short break, but it's inconvenient for anyone on public transport. In Gerri itself there's a restaurant and a bar, and some rather dubious-looking *habitacions* signposted on the river side of the through highway. More **accommodation** is found 3km north at the tiny village of **BARO**, where there are rooms at the *Bar Mariano* (☎973/68 05 50; ②). There's also a **campsite**, the *Pallars Sobirà* (☎973/66 20 30; open all year), and a supermarket.

West to Pobleta de Bellveí: Estany de Montcortès

The very minor road from Gerri de la Sal to Pobleta de Bellveí, 17km west, makes a pristine and tranquil run through rolling uplands speckled with picturesque villages. It's ideal for mountain-biking or those with their own motor vehicle, but don't hitch or walk it: there's little traffic and the initial climb up to Peramea is punishing and unshaded. This road, incidentally, is wrongly shown on the Firestone map – it does go through, and it's paved all the way. From Bretui, 10km along, you've fine views into the gorge of Cortscastells, a tributary of Collegats, but high point of the route, figuratively and literally (1021m), is the idyllic little **Estany de Montcortès**, just west of the eponymous village. Though reed-fringed, this attractive karstic lake is warm and has a sharp drop-off to thirty-metre depths, so there's no bottom muck to contend with. Several wooden jetties allow access to the deep water, and a swim is just the thing if you're cycling or motoring by. Beyond here is the sharp, featureless descent to Pobleta de Bellveí in the Vall Fosca (see p.251).

NOGUERA PALLARESA WATER SPORTS

Rafting season on the Noguera Pallaresa lasts from April until the end of August. The original rafts – used for the journey downstream to the sawmills of La Pobla de Segur – were logs lashed together ten-wide, controlled by a long, stern-mounted oar. (These perilous vessels are commemorated by raft races at Pobla on the first Sunday in July, as well as at the valley festival.) Today's water-sport versions are reinforced inflatables, up to six-and-a-half metres long, and weighing around 100 kilos. If you sign on for a trip you'll share the boat with as many as a dozen others, all togged out in crash helmets, buoyancy jackets, lightweight paddles and – if it's early in the season – wet suits. The person who actually knows what they are doing sits at the rear, wielding a pair of long oars. The passengers spread around the sides, feet wedged into stirrups. At the very least you're in for a soaking and about as much excitement as any well-balanced person would want. But it can be more dangerous – people do fall out and boats do sometimes capsize. If you get pitched in, the advice is to "go with the flow", feet first, and wait until you drift past an easy place to get ashore.

The 12km or so below Llavorsí is the most challenging section of the river and apart from rafting you can also try your hand at canoeing and the relatively new sport of hydrospeed. Best described as tobogganing on water, hydrospeed requires an outfit of day-glo helmet, flotation jacket, knee pads and wet suit; once encased in this kit, you launch yourself into waterfalls and whirlpools clutching a streamlined plastic float. It's great fun, but can be dangerous, despite the armour.

Typical **prices** in the valley for the various activities are about 4500ptas for a two-hour rafting trip, 3500ptas for an hour's canoeing, and 5800ptas for a seven-kilometre beginner's session of hydrospeed.

Sort to Llavorsí

SORT, 30km north of La Pobla, has an attractive old centre of tall, narrow houses, now hemmed in by apartment buildings. The main reason for this rapid development is that Sort and neighbouring villages have suddenly found themselves among the premier river-running spots in Europe. After the spring thaw the area swarms with kayakers, canoeists and rafters, mostly foreign and encumbered with hi-tech gear. And every year during late June/early July, the communities of the valley stage the festival of the *Raiers* (Rafters), re-enacting the exploits of the old-time timber pilots who could still put the slick new daredevils to shame.

Because of the upmarket sports clientele it attracts, Sort has priced itself out of any casual trade, and in any case it's not a place to linger unless you're here for the action (which can be exhilarating; see the feature on p.233). Its main street is almost exclusively devoted to rafting and adventure shops, and there's nowhere inexpensive to stay or eat, though there is a **tourist office** (summer Mon–Fri 9am–2pm & 5–9pm, Sat 10am–1pm & 5–8pm) on the main street. The bus stops at an obvious shelter on Plaça Catalina Albert, at the north end of town where the two through roads join up. **RIALP**, 3km north, is a marginally more appealing mix of old houses and new boutiques; the bus stop/ticket office here is the bar under the *Hotel Victor*.

Around 16km to the west of Sort and Rialp there's skiing at **LLESSUÍ**, an attractive old stone village – now expanded – on the denuded slopes of **Tossal de Serradet**. A place to come for a weekend rather than a full holiday, it has a fair chance of snow from the 1950-metre mid-station, which gives access to short runs of all standards.

Llavorsí

Probably the most attractive place to stay along this stretch is **LLAVORSÍ**, 10km above Rialp. Despite extensive renovation, a rash of new bar/restaurants and rafting outfitters on the main road, and a mammoth power substation across the way, this tight huddle of stone-built houses and slate roofs at the confluence of the Noguera Pallaresa and the Cardós rivers still retains much of its character. There's a good riverside **campsite** 1km north of town (with a bar and swimming pool), plus any number of **hostals** catering for the new trade. You should reserve in advance in rafting season; try the *Hostal Lamoga* (☎973/62 20 06; May–Sept only; ④), with a good *menú*, and the quieter *Hostal de Rey*, adjacent on the riverfront (☎973/62 20 11; ④); or the *Hostal Noguera* (☎973/62 20 12; ③), on the opposite bank, whose restaurant has river-view seating and a reasonable if rather limited *menú*. Some 500m south of Llavorsí, on the west bank of the river opposite a road tunnel, the bizarrely named Yeti Emotions (☎973/62 22 01, fax 62 22 60) is one of the better-established local **adventure outfitters**, offering rafting, canyoning, hydrospeed, mountain-biking and horse-riding.

Approach to Estats from Llavorsí

From Llavorsí, the initially paved road up to the *Refugí de Vall Ferrera* – base for the ascent of Estats and Montcalm – is almost a full day's slog through an underpopulated area of pastures and hayfields, the latter scythed in July; hitch or get a taxi if you're vehicle-less. The first part of the route follows the Cardós valley (see below) from Llavorsí; after a little over 4km, you turn off east along the **Vall Ferrera** towards **ALINS** – 13.5km from Llavorsí – where there's a choice of **accommodation**: the modern *Hotel Salòria* (☎973/62 43 41; ④), with slightly cheaper beds in the co-managed *Fonda Llesuy* (③) across the street, and the *Hostal Muntanya* (☎973/62 44 11; ③). Another 5km beyond along the main valley lies the tiny village of **ÀREU**, the last settlement before Estats, and on the GR11: it has a small shop, a pleasant, tent-oriented campsite with a pool, the *Pica d'Estats* (☎973/62 90 47; open July to mid-Sept), and **accommodation** at the rambling *Hostal Vall Ferrera* (☎973/62 90 57; ④); they also have the main village restaurant, with half-board available, though the management can be somewhat grasping. Àreu also has ample, less expensive lodging in the *casa de pagès* scheme, such as *Casa Xicot* (☎973/62 43 48; ③) and *Casa Gabatxò* (☎973/62 43 22; ③), both of which offer half-board.

The route up the mountain continues, first via dirt track and then, 3.5km above Àreu, along the marked east-bank trail #17, "Camí Vell del Port de Boet-Pla de Boet", routed in common with the GR11, to just below the **Refugí de Vall Ferrera** (open and staffed May–Sept), nearly four hours from Àreu.

Next day, allow about five hours to get up to **Estats**. Strike north into the Sottlo valley and past the lakes of Sottlo and Estats, then up into the Port de Sottlo (2894m); from here a short ridge walk leads to the summit. Another ridge leads 45 minutes northeast to **Montcalm**, from where you can either backtrack or link up with the route from L'Artigue in France.

Onward routes from the refuge

East of the *Vall Ferrera* refuge, the HRP variant and GR11 lead into Andorra by different sets of passes – described on p.195; the GR11 is easier, not exceeding 2517m elevation en route, at the small unstaffed refuge of Baiau just before the frontier. **Northwards, then westwards**, you can make the traverse to Tavascan (12hr – see below) initially via the Sotllo lake, where you should bear west over the 2618-metre Coll de Barborte to the **Baborte** lake (5hr; unlocked refuge adjacent) and **Planell de Boavi** (10hr), a beautiful but over-subscribed wilderness camping area among birches and firs.

The Vall de Cardós and beyond

If you stay with the road up the generally broader and more touristically developed Vall de Cardós instead of taking the right turn into the Vall Ferrera, you'll pass through **RIBERA DE CARDÓS** (10km from Llavorsí), a sizable and attractive village with a twelfth-century, squat-belfried church and the two-star **hostal** *Sol i Neu* (☎973/62 31 37; ③), by the river at the south entry to the village. An adventure centre opposite the hotel offers mountain-biking excursions and horse-riding. There's also **camping** at the caravan-oriented, riverside *La Borda del Pubill* (☎973/62 30 88; mid-June to mid-Sept), with a pool and tennis courts, and *Del Cardós* (☎973/66 30 12; April–Sept), with similar amenities, north of the village. There are also horse-riding and trekking outfitters at Ribera, as well as a giant sawmill to inject a bit of industrial reality into the picture.

The road continues past other steeple-crowned hamlets (Ainet de Cardós has another campsite) surrounded by hayfields to **TAVASCAN**, 20km from Llavorsí, whose single high street is a solid mass of hotels. This recent gentrification is owed largely to a **nordic ski station**, *Pleta de Prat* (info booth ☎973/63 30 46), 11km northwest past Noarre hamlet. The two fanciest **hotels** are *Marxant* (☎973/62 31 51, fax 62 30 39; ③) and the *Llacs del Cardós* (☎973/62 31 78, fax 62 31 26; ④), with extensive common areas, but there's also the *Casa Pagès Feliu* (☎973/62 31 63; ③), the last grocery store before the wilderness, and a **campsite**, *Bordes de Graus*, 5km up towards the ski centre.

Trekking and walking out of Vall de Cardós

If you're traversing east to west (or vice versa) along the **HRP** (see below), there are good arguments for skipping Tavascan altogether: it's an expensive spot, and you'd have to lose and regain a lot of altitude to get there. The GR11, however, is routed through Tavascan, and for the less committed forms the basis of a half-day **loop-walk**, locally marked as "Ruta 14", taking in the highlights of the upper valley. Beginning next to the Hotel Marxant, this route heads south to the villages of Aineto and Lleret on the GR11; crosses to the east bank of the valley at Lladorre; and then climbs up to Boldí Jussà and Boldí Sobirà to rejoin the GR11 for a northerly descent to Tavascan.

Above Tavascan there's a choice of other tracks: the more easterly, towards Planell de Boavi, for the direct route to Pic de Certescan (2853m); the other, northwesterly option, beyond the power station, connects at Noarre with the HRP towards the Vall d'Aran. Both routes lead to delightful wildernesses of long valleys and tarn-spangled cirques up against the border; to a certain extent they can be combined, as the HRP passes the base of Pic de Certescan.

For the **Certescan area**, take a turn-off at the dam 6km beyond Tavascan on the rough track towards Boavi, at first traversing and then climbing fairly steeply up the Sierra Marinera past the western shore of the superb **Estany de Naorte**, with the summit of Estats just visible above the low, rounded hills and sparse pines of the opposite bank. About an hour later – or three-and-a-half from Tavascan – you reach the **Llac de Certescan**, the largest lake in these parts, and star of many a postcard. (If you have a 4WD, you can drive to within half an hour of the lake on a jeep track contouring initially far below Naorte.) At its south end stands the *Refugí de Certescan* (2240m; staffed mid-June to mid-Sept, with 40 places; 20-place section always open; ☎973/62 13 89; ①), with hot showers, meals and cooking facilities; from here the **Pic de Certescan** is an easy and enjoyable half-day round-trip ascent.

Since the refuge is also virtually astride the **HRP** it's possible to follow this west for six hours to the hamlet of **NOARRE** (no facilities), but it's a tough section with lots of cross-country route-finding, only feasible in good conditions. From Noarre – accessible directly from Tavascan in two hours by the alternative track – or from the next wilderness campsite another hour upstream at **Pleta de l'Arenal**, you can continue west to Salardú in Aran. This involves two or three days' walking on the HRP or one of its variants, the quickest being to head due west for Alòs d'Isil, about ten hours away via a necklace of tarns at the base of 2864-metre **Mont Roig**.

Alternatively, the Cardós valley is linked with both the Vall Ferrera and the Vall d'Àneu (see below) by the somewhat easier though less dramatic **GR11**, which passes right through Tavascan. From just above Àreu in the Vall Ferrera the route cuts over Monattarenyo ridge via the Coll de Tudela to Tavascan, then bears sharply southwest over another 2500-metre spur to La Guingueta d'Àneu. Either sector makes for an easy walking day.

The Vall d'Àneu

From Llavorsí the bus continues along the Noguera Pallaresa, past the turning for Espot (see "The Aigües Tortes-Sant Maurici region", p.246) and the placid, artificial lake of Pantà de la Torrasa, to **LA GUINGUETA D'ÀNEU** at the head of the reservoir. This is the first of three villages incorporating the name of the local valley, **Vall d'Àneu**, and it consists mostly of a small cluster of roadside **accommodation**; the best options are either the budget *Hostal Orteu* (☎973/62 60 86; ③), whose bar seems to be the local hangout, or the top-end *Hotel Poldo* (☎973/62 60 80, fax 62 63 85; ⑤, half-board only). The *Poldo* has the more exciting restaurant, with outdoor seating and spit-grilled meats. There's also a decent **campsite** opposite the reservoir.

Esterri d'Àneu

ESTERRI D'ÀNEU, 4km further beyond the lake, has been transformed virtually overnight from somnolent farming community to chic resort. Parts of town still form as graceful an ensemble as you'll see in the Catalan Pyrenees – the few huddled houses between the road and the river, an arched bridge and slender-towered Sant Vicenç church – but the new apartment buildings and fancy hotels to the south are another matter. Nonetheless, there are far worse places to stop overnight; among **accommodation** choices, best value is the delightful *Fonda Agustí* (π973/62 60 34; ③), quietly set behind the church in Plaça de l'Església, which serves enormous **meals** for well under 2000ptas in its old-fashioned *comedor*. *Hostal Costa* at c/Major 14 (π973/62 60 61; ④) is plusher but you should ask for the second of their two premises to ensure nocturnal calm. The closest **campsite**, *La Presalla* (π973/62 60 31; April–Sept), is 1km south of the village. For local water sports, contact Verd'Àneu on c/Major 12 (π973/62 64 02). From late November to May, the village is also the end of the line for the bus from Barcelona, the pass to the west being snowbound all winter.

The Vall d'Isil

From the centre of Esterri d'Àneu, you can bear north along a narrow but paved road up the **Vall d'Isil**, its atmospheric villages little visited and half-abandoned. The highlight, 11km along just before **ISIL**, is the engaging Romanesque church of Sant Joan, with its fine south portal, two Gothic windows retaining some tracery, its apse just about in the river, and pairs of strange carved figures studding the roofline. The village itself can offer the *Refugi Casa Sastrés* (π973/62 63 20; 52 places; ①), by the river, a welcome sight if you've trekked west from Noarre or east from the Mongarri (Montgarry) valley (see p.243). It's an attractive nineteenth-century building, with beamed-ceiling diner, though the *smallest* room is six beds. If you require more privacy, there are a few *cases de pagès* locally, such as *Casa Fuster* (π973/62 61 96; ③). **ALÓS**, at the end of the paved route, has no facilities, but the *Bonabé* **nordic ski centre** lies just 4km north along a dirt road.

València d'Àneu and the Port de la Bonaigua

Three kilometres further up the main road, **VALÈNCIA D'ÀNEU**, with its traditional stone houses and small Romanesque church of Sant Andreu, has been far less disrupted by development than Esterri d'Àneu. Best choice for **accommodation** here is the exceptionally good-value *Hotel La Morera* (π973/62 61 24; ④), with enormous balconied rooms, a valley-side pool and wonderful breakfasts; runners-up are the *habitacions* above the recommended **restaurant** *La Bonaigua* (π973/62 61 10; ④; closed early Jan to Easter & mid-Oct to Nov), which features local game and trout on its affordable menus.

Beyond València, the road quits the Noguera Pallaresa as it climbs above the quilt of green and brown fields around Esterri; the Riu de la Bonaigua takes over as the roadside stream, lined by forests of silver birch, pine and fir. The views get ever more impressive as you approach the treeline, above which is perched the combination **restaurant-bar** of *Mare de Déu de les Ares*, next to the eponymous *ermita*. There's a good, varied lunch menu for under 2000ptas, but the place shuts by 7pm; the inn here has closed and the nearest accommodation is the alpine refuge at Mataró (see p.244). Two hairpins above the *ermita*, you'll notice the trailhead for the path up into the Gerber and Mataró valleys – in season parked cars mark the spot. Near the top of the bleak **Port de la Bonaigua** (2072m; closed in winter), snow patches persist year round, half-wild horses graze and you get simultaneous panoramas of the valleys you've just left and the Vall d'Aran to come.

THE VALL D'ARAN

Though undeniably on the French side of the Pyrenean watershed, the **Vall d'Aran** has long been under Spanish sovereignty. This oddity seems even more pronounced when you consider that Andorra, while opening towards Spain, was long semi-autonomous (and recently opted for independence), and that the Cerdanya/Cerdagne, despite a lack of pronounced natural demarcations, is divided between the two countries.

Cut off from the outside world for centuries, the Vall d'Aran has evolved its own language – **Aranés** – based on Gascon plus elements of Catalan and Basque, and which is only spoken (and written) in the valley. Its name, however, is not Aranés but pure Basque, and "Vall" is technically redundant: *aran* means "valley". (From here westwards, Basque place-names are commonly encountered, tide-markers of the former and greater extent of a people now restricted to the west end of the range.) The Aranese spelling of local place-names is increasingly used on local signs, and so given in parentheses in the following accounts.

Aran has strong historical links to both France and Spain, and was a source of conflict as long ago as 1192, when it passed from the counts of Comminges to the kings of Aragón. In 1808 Napoleon announced he was annexing it, sending 2500 French troops from nearby Bagnères. Only a thousand reached the Vall d'Aran, the rest having deserted, but this remnant nonetheless briefly expelled the Spanish. A stronghold of Republicanism during the Spanish Civil War and – relatively safe behind passes snowed up half the year – a refuge for the defeated afterwards, the valley was reinvaded by Franco's Nationalists in 1944. The isolation of Aran was finally relieved by the boring of the **Túnel de Viella** in 1958, allowing the N232 road to link the valley directly with the provincial capital of Lleida.

You'll occasionally still hear the Vall d'Aran described as one of the most remote corners of the Pyrenees, but especially since Franco's passing life in the valley has changed beyond recognition. Your first clues are the ranks of high-tension electricity pylons from Llavorsí over the Port de la Bonaigua, and more of the same through the dense forest of the Coll du Portillon in the west; heavy traffic through the Túnel de Viella towards the valley capital of Viella is another indication of modern development. Scythe-wielding hay-reapers of past summers have been replaced by Massey-Ferguson balers, the hayfields themselves overlooked by holiday chalets built for city folk, which have sprouted at the edge of every village. Although most new buildings adhere to the vernacular, stone-built style, an increasing number of restaurants and sports shops, plus a single main through road clogged with French trippers in summer and winter, have combined to make the Vall d'Aran one of the more overrated and expensive corners of the Spanish Pyrenees.

That said, if you leave the main route in favour of side valleys like the Ruda or the Unyola, you can recapture something of the region as it was thirty years ago. But even here, don't expect superlative wilderness walking: Aran is best viewed as a comfortable

---

THE SOURCES OF THE GARONA/GARONNE

The river draining the Vall d'Aran begins life as the **Garona**, then once in France becomes the **Garonne**, swinging northeast through Saint-Gaudens and Toulouse and then northwest to the Atlantic at Bordeaux. The river has two commonly accepted sources: the Ruda stream at the east end of the valley, fed by the Saboredo lakes, and the Joeu, in the west beyond Viella, up against the French frontier.

Contrary to what was believed until 1931, the **Joeu** doesn't rise in Aran at all, but in the Maladeta-Aneto Massif, to the southwest, on the opposite side of the watershed from the Vall d'Aran. In that year, the French speleologist Norbert Casteret (see p.281) proved that the Joeu was a resurgence by emptying 55 kilos of dye into the **Forau de Aiguallut/Trou du Toro**, the sinkhole for the Aneto glacier's meltwater. In Casteret's own words: "Next day, the Garonne revealed its secret. For twenty-seven hours a million cubic yards of bright green water poured down the Vall d'Aran and for over fifty miles into France."

overnight stop on Pyrenean traverses, rather than a target in its own right. The fact that the best-selling local guide is for mountain-biking, not hiking, is a frank admission of the valley's limitations on foot.

Aran's legendary greenness derives not from any extraordinary rainfall but from the streams that drain into it, mostly from lakes in the Aigües Tortes country to the south. When the weather *is* wet, there's a good chance of seeing black-and-yellow fire salamanders moving slowly on the damp tracks and paths; before and after the rain, equally brilliant butterflies, for which the valley is famous, flutter about.

Nautaran

Nautaran, or "High Valley", is the more scenic eastern portion of the region, and a good start- or end-point for walks in the Aigües Tortes park. Salardú is the largest of a cluster of villages well set near the top of the valley, most of them within walking distance of each other. From almost any elevated point in Nautaran you'll be treated to full-frontal views of snowy Maladeta, hovering like a ghost to the west.

Baqueira-Beret

The road descent west from Port de la Bonaigua is adventurous, to say the least – and often plain terrifying as you contemplate the choice between the long drop on one side and the sheer rock wall on the other. Coming down, the first place you encounter is the purpose-built apartment resort of **BAQUEIRA-BERET**, a mammoth skiing development much frequented by French tourists, and by no less than the Spanish royal family. This resort acts as the primary engine of change in the region, and the surrounding land has all been subdivided into lots awaiting sale. Baqueira offers serious, west-facing runs off **Cap de Baqueira**, with views from the chairlift south to Saburedo and Aigües Tortes. The top runs occupy open bowls above the trees; the total is 22 lifts (highest 2500m) and 43 pistes – three green, sixteen blue, nineteen red and five black. It's considered one of the best such resorts on the Spanish side, and packages for it are sold in the UK through Ski Miquel Holidays (see p.5 in *Basics*).

Salardú

SALARDÚ, a few kilometres further west, is in effect the capital of Nautaran and the most logical base for explorations: large enough to offer a reasonable choice of accommodation and food, but small enough to feel pleasantly remote (except in August or peak ski season). With steeply pitched roofs clustered around the church, it retains some traditional character, but even here the clock in the octagonal fifteenth-century belfry tolls the hours with an electronic tone instead of a bell (programmed to fall silent between midnight and 7am).

The principal attraction of staying is the opportunity to visit the surrounding villages, all – like Salardú – centred on beautiful **Romanesque churches**. Salardú's is the roomy, thirteenth-century **Sant Andreu**, set in its own pleasant grounds. The doors are usually open, allowing you to see the *Sant Crist de Salardú*, a detailed wooden crucifix contemporary with the church. Sturdy Nautaranese **houses** are traditionally built of stone, with slate roofs, and there's surprisingly little to distinguish a four-hundred-year-old home from a four-year-old one. Many display dates on the lintels – not of the same vintage as the churches but respectable enough, with some going back as far as the sixteenth century.

Practicalities

The **bus** from Barcelona gets in at around 2pm, setting you down near a wood-hut **tourist office** (Mon–Fri 10.30am–1.30pm & 4.30–8pm, Sat 10am–1pm & 4–7pm, Sun 10am–1pm), just off the main road at the turning for Bagergue. The single **bank** has normal opening hours all year, plus an autoteller.

Even at the height of the summer you should be able to find a **bed** (though not necessarily a room) easily enough in Salardú. Try the wood-decor rooms, with or without bathrooms above the *Bar Montanha*, c/Major 8 (☎973/64 41 08; ②–③), or the *Residència Aiguamòg* at c/Sant Andreu 12 (☎973/64 54 96; ④) – though both fill quickly, summer or winter. Accommodation aimed specifically at hikers includes the *Refugí Rosti*, Plaça Major 1 (☎973/64 53 08, fax 64 58 14; July to mid-Sept; dorm ①, rooms ③), in a rambling, three-hundred-year-old building, and the *Xalet-Refugí Juli Soler i Santaló*, run by the Centre Excursionista Catalunya (☎973/64 50 16; dorm ①, 4-bed rooms ②, half-board available), in c/del Port, 200m east of the tourist office, next to the municipal pool. In addition to these, five more expensive *hostals* and hotels advertise themselves conspicuously; one of the best of these, on the quiet cul-de-sac Plaça dera Pica, is the two-star *Hotel Deth Païs* (☎973/64 58 36, fax 64 45 00; ④).

Most of the places to stay in Salardú serve good-value **meals**; those at the *Refugí Juli Soler i Santaló* are particularly large and tasty, for 1200 to 1300 pesetas. Reasonable alternatives are scarce, since the handful of independent restaurants are rather overpriced, though there's a smart pizzeria on the main street. While the restaurant at the *Refugí Rosti* is decent enough, its main appeal is the nicest **bar** in town, *Delicatesen*.

Villages around Salardú

UNYA (Unha), 700m up the hill into the Unyola valley, has a church of the same age as that in Salardú, though you're more likely to want to climb up to eat at one of the half-dozen **restaurants**, the most popular and reasonable being *Es de Don Joan Carmela* and the *Casa Restaurante Perez* – which also has **accommodation** at *Casa Benito* (☎973/64 57 52; ③).

BAGERGUE, 2km higher up the road (or along a path beginning in Garòs) and spared the view of Baqueira by the rounded contours of Roc de Macia, boasts yet another medieval church. Though the most countrified of the local settlements, it too can muster three chi-chi **restaurants**, a giant ski chalet complex and a recommended place to **stay**, the *Residencia Seixes* (☎973/64 54 06; ④).

Across the river from Salardú, and about twenty minutes' walk upstream along the signposted *camí reiau*, **TREDÒS** – once the prettiest of the Nautaran villages – has had its old core overwhelmed by a rash of new ski chalets. It has at least one inexpensive place to **stay** – *Casa Eriva* (☎973/64 50 59; ②) – and the usual twelfth-century church, one of whose murals was removed to the Cloisters Museum in New York. If money's no object, there are two plush places to part with it locally: the *Parador de Tredòs* on the road to Baquiera Beret (☎973/64 40 14, fax 64 43 00; ⑥), which often has one-week all-in ski packages, and the *Banhs de Tredòs* (☎973/25 30 03; ⑥), 8km up the Aiguamotx valley to the south, recently reopened as a quasi-New-Age spa with alternative treatments and gourmet cuisine. Back near *Casa Eriva*, the *Restaurante Saburedo* is very good, cheap and popular at lunch especially, when you can have a three-course **meal** for well under 2000 pesetas a including their own vintage wine.

Arties and Garòs

The next valley community of any size, **ARTIES**, 3km west of Salardú, is little different to what's gone before, though it's dominated by the extraordinary fortified church of **Santa María**, with a ninth-century font, a twelfth-century Templar belfry base and fortification walls from the late fourteenth century. The village is otherwise known for its hot springs, but these have been shut for years. However, the *camí* leading west past them cuts out 3km of the busy main highway, rejoining it at the river bridge below Garòs – a boon if you're cycling.

There's **accommodation** in Arties, too, which takes up the overflow from Salardú. Good choices include the comfortable and central *Residencia Hotel Besiberri* at Deth Fort 4 (☎973/64 08 29; ⑤), overlooking the Valarties stream and the mountains, and the *Casa Portola* nearby at c/Major 21 (☎973/64 08 28; ③), with a wonderful wood-and-tiled-interior, bathtubs and tasteful rooms. There's a well-appointed **campsite**, *Era Yerla d'Arties* (☎973/64 16 02; closed mid-Sept to Nov) with a heated pool, just below the village on the main road to Viella. *Casa Irene* at c/Major 4 is acknowledged as one of the best, and most expensive, **restaurants** in Aran. For the rest of us *Montagut*, up on the main highway, is excellent, with attentive service and menus from 1200 to 3000 pesetas; the mid-priced one gives you the best from the à la carte list of local specialities such as *sopa de ajo* and duck.

The village of **GARÒS**, 3km west, is the lowest of Nautaran, completely ringed with new, stone-built holiday cottages. Yet its old core, focused on the twelfth-to-fourteenth-century church of San Julian, retains some charm, and offers two more places to **stay**: *Hotel Plaça Garòs* (☎973/64 17 74; ④), with a pricey ground-floor bar and restaurant, and the nearby *Casa Amiell* (☎973/64 02 65; ③).

Mijaran and Baixaran

From Nautaran you continue west into **Mijaran** (Mid-Valley), whose major town is **Viella**, capital of the region, served by two long-distance bus routes: one – during snow-free seasons only – from Barcelona, and the other from Lleida via El Pont de Suert, a spectacular journey in its final stages, culminating in the six-kilometre **Túnel de Viella**. The latter route sees you emerge near the southwest corner of Aran, with Viella visible far below. North of here the road (and onward buses) make for the French border just 28km away, through **Baixaran**, the lower part of the valley.

Viella

In truth, the ride towards **VIELLA** (Vielha) from either direction is more attractive than the town itself, and there's little reason to stay if you can make a bus connection onwards. A sort of mini-Andorra (though with few of Andorra's bargains), Viella has become intensely developed and smartened up since 1990, a trend aggravated by the French patrons of the numerous supermarkets, boutiques and restaurants. If you have time to kill, pop into the parish church of **Sant Miquèu**, right in the centre on the east bank of the Riu Nere; its twelfth-century wooden bust, the *Cristo de Mijaran* – probably part of a *Descent from the Cross* – is reckoned the finest specimen of Romanesque art in this part of the Pyrenees. The **Museu deth Val** (Mon–Sat 10am–1pm & 5–8pm, Sun 10am–1pm; 200ptas), at c/Major 26, west of the church and across the river, is also worth a look for its coverage of Aranese history and folklore.

Viella provides most of the accommodation and *après ski* life for the ski resort of **LA TUCA**, just to the south. The snow record of the whole valley is generally good, with its proximity to the highest mountains in the range, but even so La Tuca's top-lift elevation of under 2200m sometimes causes problems.

Practicalities

Buses stop next to the telephone office, on the roundabout at the west edge of town – information and **tickets** are available from inside the booth. The **tourist office**, offering maps and accommodation lists (daily summer Mon–Sat 10am–2pm & 4.30–7.30pm), is at c/Sarriulera 6 near the **post office**, just off the church square.

As you might expect, there's no shortage of **accommodation** in Viella, but most of it is for the ski business, with little of outstanding value. Coming from the church, you'll find the best of the inexpensive places by turning left along the main street and then right down the lane just across the bridge. Just off to the left, at Plaça Sant Orenç 3, there's the *Hostal El Ciervo* (☎973/64 01 65; ③); the often full *Pensió Puig*, c/Camí Reiau 4 (☎973/64 00 31; ②); or the tiny *Pension Casa Vicenta* across the way at no. 3 (☎973/64 08 19; ③). On the opposite side of the through road, above the museum, *Pensió Monge* at Des Clòses 7 (no sign; ☎973/64 02 46; ②) is also good value.

Least expensive and most central of Viella's **restaurants**, *Et Hurat* at Passeig dera Llibertat 14, is a supper-only crêperie (closed Tues, & closed late June and Nov). *Casa Turnay* (closed May, June, Oct & Nov), in the hamlet of Escunhau 2km east, offers traditional Aranese cuisine, which features game, fish and ornate vegetable dishes. If you're really impecunious, about the best you can do is to order one of the *menús* at the *Et Curné* bar on Passeig dera Llibertat 7, or at the *Bar Vidal*, c/Major 6a.

Baixaran

You can continue from Viella by bus, car or bike through **ARRÒS** (6km) and **ES BORDES** (Era Bordeta; 9km). There are two **campsites** at Arròs – the *Artigane* (☎973/64 01 89; June–Sept) up by the road and *Verneda* (☎973/64 10 24; June-Sept) closer to the river – plus some **cases de pagès**, including *Casa Guillamon* (☎973/64 03 34; ②) and *Casa Cucay* (☎973/64 11 67; ②).

The focus of **Baixaran** is the large village of **BOSSÒST**, 18km from Viella, where the houses are strung out along the main road and both sides of the curving Garona, alternating with tacky shops. Its twelfth-century **Romanesque** church has a carved tympanum and three apses with the typical raised brickwork known as Lombard banding. This being the direct N230 road between France and the Viella tunnel, accommodation is pricey, but then there's no real reason to stop: it's only 10km to the **French border** at Pont de Rei (Pont deth Rei in Aranés, but either way it's a place-name only, with no habitation); 13km to the first French village on the GR 10, Fos; and 20km to the first significant French town, Saint-Béat.

An alternative road out of Bossòst into France is the C141 from just south of the village, climbing through dense woods to the unguarded French frontier at **Coll du Portillon**, and then descending sharply to Bagnères-de-Luchon.

Walking or biking from the Vall d'Aran

Numerous tracks and rather fewer footpaths make it possible to walk and mountain-bike from the valley in virtually every direction. Editorial Alpina publishes a 1:40,000 "Vall d'Aran" **map** of the whole area, but if you are going to stray beyond you'll need various adjacent 1:25,000 sheets as well: "Montgarri/Mont Valier" and "Pica d'Estats/Mont Roig" if you're going east; "Sant Maurici" plus "Vall de Boí" for the whole of Aigües Tortes to the south; "La Ribagorça" together with "Maladeta/Aneto" if you're bound for points west. The French IGN Randonnées Pyrénéennes 1:50,000 series covers the Vall d'Aran plus the territory to the north – either the "Couserans/Cap d'Aran" (no. 6) if you want to head northeast, or "Luchon" (no. 7) going northwest.

East to Montgarri and Vall d'Isil

An easy excursion takes you **east** along the sources of the Noguera Pallaresa, which flows initially northeast before curling around to head south. Make an early start **from Salardú** up the road towards Bagergue, and after 500m cut off onto a wide path that connects with the track running between Bagergue and Baqueira; if you're cycling rather than walking, you'll have to pick up the track in Bagergue. In either case, after just under an hour you join the tarmac road from Baqueira into the Noguera Pallaresa valley – keep on it, past the first trickle of the river, until the dirt track resumes about an hour later.

You're now on the broad **Pla de Beret**, with just grass and cows in the foreground, and a tangle of frontier peaks in the far distance. Four to five walking hours (15km) out of Salardú – half that time on a bike – you come to the twelfth-century **Santuari de Montgarri**, next to which is the *Refugí Amics de Montgarri* (1657m; ☎973/64 50 64; 30 places; ①), catering for traversers in summer and nordic skiers in winter. Although it might sound boring to walk on track, it's an attractive route – though popular in summer – with some sweeping views from the plateau, especially beyond Montgarri.

If you're making a day walk you should retrace your steps; otherwise stay at the refuge or keep going the same distance again, to Alòs d'Isil, and thence to Isil (see p.237) with its refuge. At Alòs, you're ten hours' very tough walk – no bikes – from Noarre, using cairned cross-country sections of the HRP more than paths, across wild and sometimes storm-lashed ridges leading off from Mont Roig. Most people will opt for a paved-road descent for the 12km to Esterri d'Àneu.

North towards France

To head **into France** from the upper Noguera Pallaresa means following an HRP *variante* northeast from Montgarri or Alòs through the Port de Salau, or a less used route over the Col de la Pale to the *Refuge des Estagnous* (see p.279), on the west side of **Mont Valier** (2838m). Neither is easy – more for long-haul trekking than biking.

It's also possible to get into France at a more westerly point using the initially dreary, shadeless, rutted track up the **Unyola valley** from Bagergue, passable in its lower reaches by tough jeeps and mountain-cyclists. Beyond some abandoned mines, both landscape and trail improve before reaching **Estany de Liat** (4–5hr). Here you can link with another section of the HRP, climbing due north from the lake through the **Portillo d'Albi** (2457m) on the frontier, an hour's stiff climb past the tiny Estany d'Albi.

Once through the pass you drop down over scree towards another lake, confusingly known as the Étang d'Albe; from here you head north onto the ridge behind, and follow it northeast until the **Col de la Serre d'Araing**, where you pick up the GR10. After that, simply follow the GR down to the northeast corner of the **Étang d'Araing** reservoir, under the bare pyramid of **Pic de Crabère** (2630m), where there is a **refuge**. This is ten to twelve hours from Salardú and thus provides a welcome respite (see p.280 for full details).

The Étang d'Araing reservoir is about three hours on foot from Eylie, the roadhead to Sentein and Saint-Girons, and lies on the *Tour de Biros*; the famous Gouffre Martel and Grotte de la Cigalère are both nearby.

South to Aigües Tortes

South of Nautaran, two lengths of tarmac and a pair of tracks then trails, a track-then-trail, and a narrow path run towards the beautiful Aigües Tortes region; only the latter two approaches provide enticing walking, and are described first.

Via Saboredo

The approach to Saboredo begins on the south side of the river at Tredòs before curling past the edge of Baqueira to run along the west bank of the **Riu de Ruda**. Although you can see and hear traffic to the east descending from Bonaigua, and power lines arc overhead, closer to hand there's little other than wide green pasture until you catch sight of the **Circ de Saboredo** and the jumble of busted granite peaks along the north edge of the Aigües Tortes park. Three hours from Salardú the track dwindles to path, changing banks of the Ruda, and you ascend into the heart of the cirque beyond a succession of tiny lakes, to the recently refurbished **Refugí de Saboredo** at 2310m (4hr 30min from Salardú; 18 places; staffed late Feb to early April & mid-June to Sept; ☎973/25 30 15 for reservations). There's no other facility for another three hours, walking through the easy **Port de Ratera** (2530m) to the **Refugí-Xalet d'Amitges** (2380m; 80 places; staffed most of March & mid-June to early Oct; reservations ☎973/25 00 07), inside the park by Estany Gran.

Via Gerber

A quicker, though more challenging way of getting to the Amitges refuge takes off from two road-curves 1.5km above *Mare de Déu de les Ares*, the chapel/restaurant 4km southeast of the Port de la Bonaigua. Take the obvious footpath, initially under high-tension cables, south along the **Vall Gerber** to **Estany Gerber**, and then to one of several lakes in the region known as Estany Llong – this one is tiny – with its simple metal refuge of *Mataró* (2460m; 3hr 30min; 16 places; always open). Continue south into the park proper, negotiating the **Coll d'Amitges** (2740m), between Tuc de Saboredo and Pic d'Amitges, before descending steeply to the Amitges refuge. This will be problematic after a snowy winter, necessitating crampons and ice-axe on the north flank, and probably an early start from the main highway trailhead – count on four hours beyond Mataró.

By using the easier Col de Gerber (2582m) above *Refugí Mataró*, you attain the Circ de Saboredo with its dozen lakes and staffed refuge within five-and-a-half hours of leaving the trailhead, and are thus poised to complete a magnificent and popular **one-day circuit** combining the two approaches detailed above. The main trick, descending the track along the Ruda stream, is to adopt a path heading steeply up right just before the route changes to the true left bank; this ascending trail will bring you back to the trailhead below Bonaigua for a total on the day of eight to nine hours – and thirty-seven lakes or tarns en route, some without names.

Via Aiguamotx

From Tredòs, a partly paved road ascends steeply up the attractive **Vall d'Aiguamotx** (Aiguamoth) towards the exquisite **Circ de Colomers**; walking the steep road is, however, neither attractive nor exquisite, so arrange a ride if at all possible. In winter the Centre d'Esqui Nordic Nautaran operates a reserve of marked pistes about 4km above Tredòs. The potholed tarmac finishes after about 8km (2hr on foot) near the luxury *Banhs de Tredòs* hotel, leaving another ninety minutes on dirt track, then path (no cycling) to the **Refugí de Colomers** (2100m; 40 places; staffed late Feb to early April, mid-June to mid-Sept, early Dec; reservations ☎973/64 05 92 or 25 30 08).

The refuge sits on a dam, but there are literally dozens of natural lakes and tarns in the cirque, set among stands of black pine. An adequate sketch map of two day-hikes – a two-hour circuit waymarked in red and yellow, and a four-hour loop blazed in red – is available from the management. Full-pack treks from Colomers include the five-hour hike south, then west via the **Port de Colomers** (2591m) to the popular *Refugí Ventosa i Calvell* (see p.255 for details). Alternatively, four hours' walk west along the joint HRP/GR11.18 takes you via the easier **Port de Caldes** and the **Port de Collcrestada** (both *c.* 2500m) to the *Refugí de la Restanca* (see below). En route you skirt the foot of **Montarto d'Aran** (sometimes *Montardo*; 2830m) – an easy ascent with fabulous views over Aran.

Via Valarties

The **Refugí de la Restanca** (2010m; 80 places; staffed early Jan, late Feb, weekends in March & April plus Easter week, mid-June to late Sept; ☎908/03 65 59 for reservations) can be reached directly from Arties via a road threading up the **Valarties**. However, there's little chance of hitching this, and the way up on foot, dotted by day-trippers' parked cars and illicit tents, is even less inspiring than the Aiguamotx slog, though shorter. After 5km, tarmac yields to dirt, from where there are another 3km to the road's end at the bottom of a short, sharp climb to the refuge, relocated from its former position by the Restanca dam to the eastern shore of the reservoir.

West to Maladeta

The *Restanca* refuge also permits the quickest access from the Aran to the **Maladeta** massif, via the refuges and camping spots near the south end of the Túnel de Viella. You have the choice from Estany de la Restanca of the long and difficult HRP – around **Estany de Mar** and **Estany Tort de Rius** (7hr) – or the GR11, which makes an easy, direct and well-marked traverse past **Estany de Rius** (5hr). The HRP is recommended if you're an experienced, lightly laden trekker, since Mar is one of the area's most savagely impressive lakes: a small, bare island hunkers in the middle, with a chaos of huge grey boulders on the shoreline, and the peak of Besiberri Nord looming to the south.

The HRP and GR11 rejoin momentarily at the **Refugí Sant Nicolau** (aka *Boca Sur Tunel de Vielha*, or *Er Ospitau de Vielha*), rebuilt on the site of a medieval pilgrims' hospice (☎973/69 70 52; ① dorm, ③ doubles). Though virtually on the main highway, it's the only amenity for miles around, and a welcome sight. Reasonable meals are provided (not Mon in winter), though there's no shop for reprovisioning. If you don't stay at the refuge, you may be interested in the unrestricted and sometimes squalid free **campsite**, 1500m south along the well-blazed GR11.

Approaches from the Noguera Ribagorçana

The Noguera Ribagorçana has its source near the tunnel, and crossing it you forsake Catalunya for Aragón – and face a choice of three approaches to (and past) Maladeta itself.

The **HRP** takes the classic route west via the Mulleres valley and the **Coll de Mulleres** (2928m) – a gruelling but spectacular traverse, which can be split by overnighting at the simple *Refugí Mulleres* (2360m; 12 places; unstaffed, always open), by some tarns just below the pass. The **Cap de Tòro**, a fifteen-minute scramble up the north side of the saddle, gives a magnificent view over Maladeta's northeast glacier – where one branch of the Garona rises – and into the Joeu valley, where the infant river emerges after its 4km underground.

The **GR11** continues south from the *ICONA* campsite/shelter to the head of the **Basserca (Senet) reservoir**, where it crosses the road and dips into the mouth of the **Salenques valley**, keeping to the south (true right) bank. Fairly well marked at first, the route divides about an hour along.

The inconspicuous right-hand option crosses the stream and then labours through rhododendron-cloaked boulders prior to an exhausting slither through scree and snow to the **Coll de Salenques** (2810m); camping is possible two-thirds of the way up. But it's an easier gradient down the other side to the **Plan de Aiguallut**, one of the best wild campsites in the Pyrenees, also easily accessible from the Coll de Mulleres.

The waymarked, left-hand bearing is the **official GR11**, which threads through the lake-speckled **Vall d'Anglòs** and then over the easy **Collado de Vallhiverna** (Vallibierna; 2730m), affording spectacular views of Maladeta's southwest face. Passing more lakes on the descent, the GR11 meets the track coming up the **Vallhiverna valley**, following this down to Benasque – again a long day out of Noguera Ribagorçana, best broken with a night out on either side of the pass. There's an unstaffed refuge at about 2200m, beside the easterly Ibón de Anglòs, if it looks like you'll get benighted before the highest pass.

Approach via the Joeu valley

The easiest approach to Aragón and the Maladeta region starts from Es Bordes, 9km west of Viella on the main road, from where you walk (or taxi) south down the **Joeu valley** as far as the **Pla de l'Artiga** (8km; 1410m; simple unstaffed refuge) and the resurgence of the waters from the Forau de Aiguallut. From here a path climbs west to the **Port de la Picada** (2470m; 3hr from the Pla), through which you descend gently to choose from a range of options: following the Ésera valley in front of you downstream; crossing its head to the Plan de Aiguallut; or slipping over the nearby Port de Venasque towards Bagnères-de-Luchon. All of these destinations are covered in detail later in this chapter.

THE AIGÜES TORTES-SANT MAURICI REGION

Water is the salient feature of the **Parc Nacional d'Aigües Tortes i Estany de Sant Maurici**, whether as flashing streams and waterfalls, myriad lakes reflecting harsh granite peaks, or reed-fringed upland marshes. And on almost half the days of the year rain or snow falls on these mountains, some of which reach to 3000m. On the other hand, the name *Aigües Tortes* – meaning "Twisted Waters" – has lately become something of a bad joke, since many local streams have been diverted through pipes, and numerous lakes (Sant Maurici among them) intermittently become mud-bowls.

The park – bounded by the Vall d'Aran, the Noguera Pallaresa and the Noguera Ribagorçana – was established in 1955 at the same time as the hydroelectric schemes began, no conflict being apparent to the Francoist government. Under the rules laid down by the International Union for the Conservation of Nature and Natural Resources, no hydroelectric exploitation is permitted in such a reserve, but as this is still Catalunya's only full-fledged national park, the authorities proudly brandish the title despite a continuing lack of international recognition. The arrogance of the bureaucrats of the era can be judged from this sentence in a 1970s' pamphlet published by the Instituto Nacional Para la Conservación de la Naturaleza (ICONA): "Some changes have occurred recently with the construction of hydroelectrical installations which the country needs, and Nature has had to pay her tribute to man, The King."

But don't let such a history put you off: attitudes are slowly changing. The park's western area increased considerably during 1986 through the cession of lands by the Boí municipality, and again in 1996 when a huge area north of Caldes de Boí was incorporated, though further expansion will be less likely given the spiralling costs of compensating the power corporation and other private landowners. It's easy to steer clear of the dams, and recommended **walking routes** keep to the wilder corners as far as possible. In terms of difficulty, there is something for everyone, ranging from the simple middle-altitude track-jaunt crossing the park from east to west, to gruelling climbs

PARK RULES AND PRACTICALITIES

Park entry
Entry to the park is free, and unrestricted for hikers, but private cars are completely prohibited except for local shepherds with special permits. Ordinarily the only means of vehicle access is via the reasonably priced jeep-taxis, on which passage is arranged at the park information offices in Boí and Espot.

Accommodation
Accommodation inside the park is limited to five **mountain refuges**, which are staffed from mid-June to the end of September, and at certain other times during the spring nordic skiing season. There are five more refuges in equally impressive alpine areas just outside the park boundaries. Each refuge has a kitchen, telephone and bunks for your sleeping bag; FEEC-managed places allow you to cook your own food inside, CEC-managed ones do not. **Camping wild** in the park is officially forbidden, and technically restricted in a 25,000-hectare peripheral "protection zone" of varying width – where you're supposed to secure a permit from the nearest village – but as long as you pitch your tent well away from refuges and paths nobody will bother you. There are managed campsites close to Caldes de Boí and Taüll in the west, and at Espot to the east. All the approach villages have *cases de pagès*, *hostals* and hotels.

Maps and guides
For extended explorations, you'll want current editions of the Editorial Alpina 1:25,000 "Sant Maurici" and "Montardo/Vall de Boí" **maps**; these are easily available in all of the peripheral villages except Capdella. The best regional **guide** is the Editorial Everest volume, *El Parque Nacional de Aigües Tortes y Lago San Mauricio*, comprehensive but not yet available in English.

Weather and route conditions
Be aware of, and prepared for, bad **weather**, which, as everywhere in the Pyrenees, can arrive rapidly and without warning. Local climatic patterns in recent years have alternated between daily rain showers throughout July and August, or prolonged drought, with a general trend towards warmer, drier summers. Many **passes**, even those mapped with a bona fide trail over them, will be difficult or worse after a harsh winter owing to snowpack. If you're going to do an unusual traverse, tell the warden of the refuge you'll be leaving, who should be able to give current route pointers and, if there's any cause for concern, phone ahead to your destination to give an estimated time of arrival – and perhaps make you a reservation.

Skiing
In winter, the park is excellent for cross-country and high-mountain **skiing**, though there are no marked routes. There are two downhill resorts on the fringes of the park: Boí-Taüll in the west and Super Espot to the east.

over jagged passes requiring snow equipment, by way of several popular trekkers' traverses using the GR11 or its variants.

Flora and fauna

The most common **trees** in Aigües Tortes-Sant Maurici are fir and Scotch pine, along with silver birch and beech, especially on north-facing slopes. There's also an abundance of **flowers** in spring and early summer, with blooms present until August above 2000m.

Perhaps the most curious animal of this region is the long-nosed, mole-sized **desman**, which lives in holes along the stream banks, feeding on aquatic insects: its timidity and

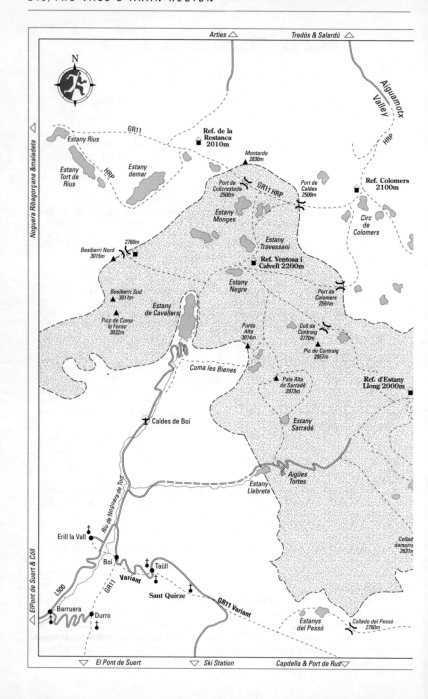

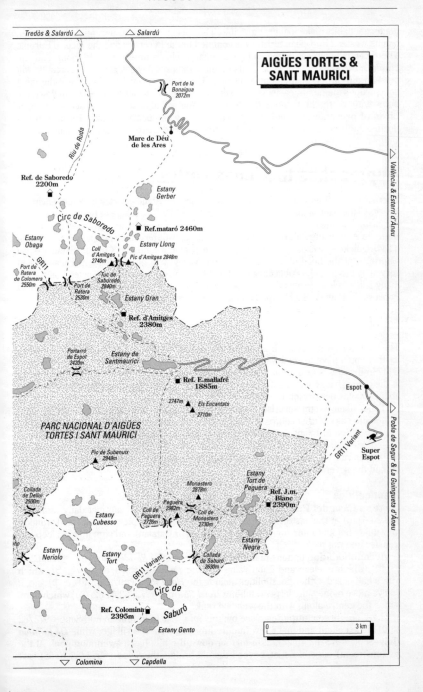

AIGÜES TORTES & SANT MAURICI

Tredòs & Salardú △   △ Salardú

Port de la Bonaigua 2072m

Mare de Déu de les Ares

Riu de Ruda

Ref. de Saboredo 2200m

Estany Gerber

Circ de Saboredo

Ref.mataró 2460m

Estany Obaga

Estany Llong

Coll d'Amitges 2740m   Pic d'Amitges 2848m

Port de Ratera de Colomers 2550m

Tuc de Saboredo 2840m

Port de Ratera 2530m

Estany Gran

Ref. d'Amitges 2380m

Portarró de Espot 2420m

Estany de Santmaurici

Ref. E.mallafré 1885m

Espot

2747m   Els Encantats 2710m

PARC NACIONAL D'AIGÜES TORTES I SANT MAURICI

Pic de Subenuix 2949m

GR11 Variant

Super Espot

Collada de Dellui 2500m

Monastero 2878m

Estany Tort de Peguera

Ref. J.m. Blanc 2390m

Peguera 2982m

Coll de Peguera 2726m   Coll de Monastero 2730m

Estany Cubesso

Estany Negre

Estany Neriolo

Estany Tort

GR11 Variant

Collada de Saburó 2630m

Circ de

Ref. Colomina 2395m   Saburó

Estany Gento

0 ⟞——————⟝ 3 km

▽ Colomina   ▽ Capdella

△ València & Esterri d'Àneu

▷ Pobla de Segur & La Guingueta d'Àneu

nocturnal habits make it almost invisible. The species is highly susceptible to pollution, and its western European territory is confined to the Pyrenees and the Picos d'Europa. The **otter** falls almost in the same category of elusiveness, the **wild boar** and the **capercaillie** somewhat less so. Outside the spring display-season the capercaillie will be seen only when flushed out by chance. **Chamoix** (*isards* in Catalan) are the most conspicuous mammals, easily seen in winter when harsh weather drives them downhill, but staying on the high summits in summer. You will almost certainly see spectacular **birds of prey**, however: **golden eagles** soaring with open-V wings; **griffon vultures** floating high above like huge tasselled scarves; and **kestrels** hovering, tails fanned, wings pumping to maintain altitude.

Approaches to Aigües Tortes

There are four chief **bases** from which to explore the Aigües Tortes park and environs. Access to the Sant Maurici and Monestero areas is from the village of **Espot**, just beyond the eastern fringe of the park and within 7km of the La Pobla de Segur–Vall d'Aran bus route. In Aran itself, **Salardú** makes a good base, with possible approaches covered on p.244. Quickest access to the high, remote peaks around the Circ de Saburó is via **Capdella**, at the head of the Vall Fosca, one valley west of the Noguera Pallaresa and served by bus from La Pobla de Segur. Finally, for the western Aigües Tortes zone, or the many lakes below Besiberri peak, the usual entry is from **Boí**, served by bus from La Pobla via El Pont de Suert – the latter also on a bus route from Viella.

Espot

The main disadvantage of an approach through **ESPOT** (1430m) is the high probability that you'll have to road-walk the very steep 7km up from the turning on the main C147 highway where the Barcelona–Viella bus drops you. If there's a **jeep-taxi** waiting at the turn-off, take it and save your legs for later – it leaves when full, and should cost about 500ptas per person for the short run up to the village.

Espot itself is still surprisingly unspoiled, though teetering on the edge of mass exploitation as a tourist centre. It's split into two distinct sections: across the ancient La Capella bridge in Espot Solau (south-facing Espot), where visitors less often venture, the cobbled streets are still reassuringly splattered with goat shit; but even in the tourist district of Espot Obago (north-facing Espot), hay spills out of barns tucked behind the several hotels.

Practicalities

There's a **Casa del Parc Nacional** (park information office; summer daily 9am–1pm & 3.30–7pm) at the eastern edge of Espot, where you can pick up maps and wonderful wildlife books (unfortunately only in Spanish or Catalan) and sign up for a jeep-taxi transfer into the park.

Accommodation options in the village start with the *Residència Felip* (☎973/62 40 93; ③), which is clean and good value or *Casa Palmira* (☎973/62 40 72; ③), which offers half-board. Other possibilities include the *Hotel Roya* (☎973/62 40 40; ③) and, if you've more money, the large, rambling *Hotel Saurat* (☎973/62 41 62; ④), which dominates the centre along with the jeep-taxi rank.

There are three **campsites** close by: the *Sol i Neu* (mid-June to mid-Sept; ☎973/62 40 01) is excellent and just a few hundred metres from the village, while *De la Mola* (July–Sept; ☎973/62 40 24), 2km further down the hill, has a swimming pool. At the far (upstream) edge of Espot, beyond the old bridge, the *Solau* (☎973/62 40 68) isn't a wonderful campsite, but it also rents out rooms with self-catering facilities at *Casa Peretó* (③), a good fallback if the village itself is full.

As for **eating**, you pay for the fact that you're in a tourist mill, miles from anywhere – there are no especially economical *menús del dia*. Most of the bars serve sandwiches and *platos combinados*; the *L'Isard* is welcoming and as fair value as you'll find here. There are two well-stocked **supermarkets** and another shop selling maps, camping-gas cartridges and the like. Other entertainment comes in the form of a public pool and a clutch of pubs.

Into the park

In the middle of the village, the tarmac divides. The left-hand turning brings you in 2km to the tiny tatty ski station of **Super Espot**. Straight ahead, to the west, is the road into the park: it's 3km to the official boundary and 7km to the end of the tarmac at **Estany de Sant Maurici**. The jeep-taxis carry eight people, departing when full, and at about 500ptas a head it's an eminently reasonable way to cut out some fairly dull road-tramping.

If you don't want any part of either track-trudging or jeep-riding, a wonderful trail leads southwest from Espot Obago in just under four hours to the **Refugí Josep Maria Blanc** (2390m; 40 places; open Easter & mid-June to late Sept; reservations ☎973/25 01 08), just inside the park boundary on **Estany Tort de Peguera**. You can continue from here to the Colomina shelter, over the 2630-metre **Collada de Saburó**, in as much time again; the entire way from Espot is a well-travelled, lake-flecked route, marked as a variant of the GR11.

Capdella

The bus ride from Pobla de Segur (Mon–Sat at 5.30pm) along the narrow and sparsely inhabited Vall Fosca terminates in the lower of the two parts of **CAPDELLA** (30km from Pobla), based around the local power works. The two places to **stay** are the modern *Hostal Monseny* (☎973/66 30 79; ③) and, 800m above, the elegant *Hostal Leo* (☎973/66 31 57; ③), originally built to host power company staff. Since there's no shop or restaurant apart from the *hostals*, good meals on half-board basis are provided at both.

From Capdella it's a half-day trek, past the ugly Sallente dam, to the wonderful **Refugí Colomina** (2395m; staffed early Feb, mid-March to mid-April & mid-June to Sept; part always open; ☎973/25 20 00), an old wooden chalet ceded to mountaineers by the electricity industry and set among the high-mountain lakes of the **Circ de Saburó** on the southern perimeter of the park. You can cut out much of the hike by taking the **cable car** (the *teleféric*) from the back of the Sallente dam to within 45 minutes' walk of the refuge (departures July–Sept only, 9am & 3pm; 525ptas one way, 900ptas return).

El Pont de Suert

The route into the southwestern area of Aigües Tortes begins at **EL PONT DE SUERT**, a small town 41km northwest of La Pobla de Segur; currently, there's a 2pm La Oscense bus from La Pobla de Segur, as well as services from Viella (2 daily) and from Lleida. The buses all stop on the main road, opposite the unmissably hideous church.

El Pont de Suert is pleasant enough if you have to spend the night before catching next morning's bus north to Boí. The old town, a small maze of arcaded streets, compensates amply for the rather grim buildings lining the through highway. There are several outdoor **cafés and bars** doing sandwiches and *platos combinados*, while you can stock up in the supermarkets and bakeries for the days ahead. You'll find the least expensive **accommodation** at *Habitacions Gállego* (☎973/69 02 42; ②), opposite the bus stop. There are more comfortable *hostals* on two interconnecting squares in the old town: *Can Mestre* at Plaça Major 8 (☎973/69 03 06; ④), and the *Hostal Cotori* at Plaça Mercadal 8 (☎973/69 00 96; ③), both with river-view *comedors*.

North towards Boí

From El Pont de Suert, a bus (June to mid-Sept 1 daily, currently at 11.15am) runs **north up the Noguera de Tor valley** towards Caldes de Boí, passing the side turnings for several villages on the way. It's an area crammed with **Romanesque churches**, dating from a time when the valleys were both more populous and wealthier than at any time since. As a happy result, these churches have never been rebuilt, and rank as the finest such specimens in Catalunya. All were constructed with astonishing detail and elegance from hand-split chunks of local stone, topped by slates. The only disappointments are that most of their frescoes are reproductions, the originals having long since been whisked away to the Museu d'Art de Catalunya in Barcelona, and that many are open only for Mass, or guided tours offered by the local tourist office.

Cóll and Barruera

After about 8km along the valley floor, the twelfth-century **Santa Maria** appears on the hillside to the left at **CÓLL** (3km off the main road); the ironwork on the door is particularly fine, but you're in for a long walk afterwards if you get off a bus to see it. **BARRUERA**, 4km further on and much larger, has several places to **stay**, the best value being the *Casa Coll* (☎973/69 40 05 or contact Besiberri Sports on the main road; ③), an echoing old mansion near the top of c/Major in the old town. The hygienic rooms are on the top floor, with a self-catering kitchen available on the ground floor. Alternatives are the *Hotel Farre d'Avall* (☎973/69 40 29; ④), in the village centre, or (in desperation) the *Noray* (☎973/69 40 21; June–Sept only; ③), right on the main road. Barruera also boasts the main **tourist office** for the entire valley (Mon–Fri 10am–2pm & 4–7pm, Sat 10am–1pm & 4–6pm; ☎973/69 40 00), right opposite the *Camping Boneta*, cramped with caravans (☎973/69 60 86; April–Sept). Also near here is Barruera's Romanesque church, the riverside Sant Feliu, with its engaging portal and creaking fourteenth-century interior.

Durro and Erill La Vall

Another fine Romanesque specimen stands in the small village of **DURRO**, 3km away by road on the hillside to the east. **Santa Maria de la Nativitat** has the valley's most massive bell-tower, its brickwork in the raised Lombard style contrasting with crude masonry and the stark southern portal. In the village, certainly the most untouched of the valley settlements, you can stay at the new *casa de pagès Can Marques* and eat at the *Restaurant Xoquín*; it's not such an impractical staging post as it might seem, since the village lies astride a GR11 variant linking El Pont de Suert with Boí and Taüll. Coming from Boí (see below), the well-signposted path starts just over the little bridge behind the old district, climbs 45 minutes to a shrine on a saddle, and then drops, in another fifteen minutes, to Durro. Beginning in Durro, you can make a brief excursion to the twelfth-century *ermita* of Sant Quirze, prominent on the ridge opposite, or take a longer day-hike to the Estany de Durro in the hills to the east.

Further on, just before the turn-off for Boí, a one-kilometre side road leads west to **ERILL LA VALL**, whose twelfth-century church of **Santa Eulàlia** sports an unusual arcaded porch, and a six-storey belfry which rivals Sant Climent's in Taüll (see p.254). In high season it's a relatively quiet base, more likely to have a vacancy than either Boí or Taüll. In ascending order of price, **accommodation** includes the simple but homely *Casa Pernallé* (☎973/69 60 49; ②), just before the entrance to the village, with kitchen facilities but no en-suite bathrooms; *Hostal La Plaça* (☎973/69 60 26, fax 69 61 28; ④), right opposite the belfry, with comfortable rooms including family suites, and a decent *comedor*, and the nearby *Hostal L'Aüt* (☎973/69 60 48, fax 69 61 26; ⑤), a bit overpriced but with a varied and economical **restaurant**. Erill is also home to the local mountain-guiding centre, Guíes de Muntanya de la Vall de Boí (☎973/69 61 07), housed in *Bar La Granja*, which organizes trekking, canyoning and rock-climbing expeditions. To start less demanding outings – for example the Boí-to-Durro walk noted above – a useful path links Erill and Boí within half an hour.

Boí

BOÍ stands 1km above the main road, which continues up to Caldes de Boí (see p.254); buses usually take you up into the centre. On arrival, the village may prove something of an anticlimax: a minuscule medieval core swamped by a mess of car parks, modern buildings, old houses defaced with new brick repairs, overpriced accommodation, and – in common with almost every village in the Tor valley – somewhat more worthwhile adventure-travel outfits offering guided hikes, mountain-bike tours and special-interest safaris. Even the twelfth-century church of **Sant Joan** has been extensively renovated, the only original parts being the squat belfry and part of the apse; the interior mural (again a copy) shows the stoning of St Stephen.

Practicalities

Although Boí is not the most prepossessing of local villages, you may want or need to **stay** at the beginning of or conclusion to a visit to the park. Despite being out of the way, one good choice is the *Hostal Pascual*, down by the junction and bridge, equidistant from Erill (☎973/69 60 14; ②), with helpful owners and a decent *menú* in the dining room. In the village itself, *Hostal Beneria* (☎973/69 60 30; ④), *Hostal Fondevila* (☎973/69 60 11; ④) and *Pensió Pey* (☎973/69 60 36; ④) are more expensive for roughly the same facilities. Less pricey are the clean modern **rooms** (②) just through the stone archway in the old quarter – look for the *habitacions* sign – and a number of *casa de pagès* places (②); for vacancies at these, call ☎973/69 60 49.

Eating out, you'll not do better than at the *Casa Higinio*, 200m up the road to Taüll, above the village centre. Its wood-fired range produces excellent grilled meat dishes, or try the fine *escudella* (minestrone soup) and trout. A big meal accompanied by the local wine will come to just under 2000ptas, but there's no *carta* advising you of this, so don't order separate items needlessly – and budget plenty of time for the often glacially slow service. None of the other diners attached to the various central *hostals* are anywhere near as good value, though the *Pey* offers a menu for 1600ptas, served on its popular terrace overlooking the main Plaça del Treio.

The **Casa del Parc Nacional** (summer daily 9am–1pm & 3.30–7pm; ☎973/69 61 89) is on the main square, and you can buy maps there at a slight markup, or book passage into the park on a jeep-taxi (see below). The **bank** behind the supermarket has an ATM.

Into the park

It's 3.5km from Boí to the national park entrance, above the La Farga car park, and another 3.5km to the scenic waterfalls of Aigües Tortes, tumbling from their eponymous water-meadows to feed the reedy Estany Llebreta, where half-wild horses gambol. A final kilometre above the falls – passed closely by both road and trail #5 (see below) – there's yet another park information booth (July–Sept daily 9.30am–2pm & 4–7pm), next to which is a map-placard with many suggested **day-hikes**, complete with more or less accurate elapsed times. The most popular stroll, about an hour one-way with a day-pack, leads east from the information post to Estany Llong.

Jeep-taxis from Boí's village square make the trip as far as the booth; as in Espot, this costs a flat rate of 500ptas one-way, 1000ptas round-trip. Vehicles wait to depart until they're full; last downhill return from Aigües Tortes is at 7pm in mid-summer. The closest you can get to the park boundary in your **own vehicle** is the car park at La Farga, or another, smaller one 1.5km east right at the boundary. If you leave your car at either, and arrange for a jeep-taxi to meet you and take you further uphill, at day's end you can follow marked trail #5 from the info booth ("Aparcament") which shortcuts the road by a good 45 minutes.

Alternatively, you can flag down the one midday bus from the junction of the Boí side road up to the large and expensive spa complex of **CALDES DE BOÍ**, 57km upstream. Between it and the conspicuously high dam at the south end of Estany de Cavallers there's a free camping area, but more interestingly the dam itself marks the trailhead for walks towards the beautiful natural lakes northwest of the park, just below Besiberri and Montarto peaks.

Taüll

The character of **TAÜLL** – 3km above Boí by road or 2km along a moderately steep, forty-minute section of the GR11 variant – has been altered considerably by the ski resort of Boí-Taüll, established on the mountainside a few kilometres to the southeast. A new lift is planned to reach 2800m, which will make it the highest in the Pyrenees and improve what is already one of the best ski centres in the range. There's an enormously hideous holiday complex 1500m beyond the village, en route to the ski station, and even in summer Taüll is a target for tour coaches and family cars seeking out panoramic picnic spots. But once away from the peripheral ski chalets, the village centre retains considerable character, and is certainly preferable to Boí as a long-term base.

Moreover, two of the best local Romanesque churches stand in the village. Of the pair, consecrated on successive days in 1123, **Sant Climent de Taüll** (10.30am–2pm & 4–8pm; 100ptas) is the more immediately impressive by virtue of its famous six-storey belfry and original triple apse. The stark interior, pressed into service as an impromptu museum of religious artefacts, also retains copies of vivid murals showing Christ, saints and apostles, plus scenes from the New Testament and the Apocalypse. Your admission ticket entitles you to climb the rickety wooden steps to the top of the bell-tower for sweeping views through the delicately arched windows.

At the heart of the village, **Santa Maria** is very similar in design, though its belfry has only four storeys; after a millennium of subsidence, there's not one right angle remaining in the building, with the tower in particular at an engaging list. Admission is by the same ticket as for Sant Climent, and it's supposedly open the same hours, but since Santa Maria is also the parish church it may in fact be open longer or shorter hours. The mural (a reproduction), more soberly coloured in reddish brown and blue, shows the Virgin and Child.

Practicalities

Accommodation options, mostly under the *case de pagès* programme, include the *Pensió La Coma* (☎973/69 60 25; ③) at the village entrance, or *Casa Planominguero* (☎973/69 01 17; ③), well located in the upper part of the village, with its own parking (a problem here). *Ca de Corral* (☎973/69 60 04 or 69 60 28; ②), run by the *Bar Mallador* (see below), is a renovated old house well situated in the lower part of the village. Other inexpensive rooms without en-suite facilities are either at the friendly *Casa Llovet*, Plaça Franch 5 (☎973/69 60 32; ②), or *Casa Chep* (☎973/69 60 54; ②), just below Plaça Santa Maria. A **campsite** (☎973/69 60 82), also offering bungalows, spreads attractively on the slope below Sant Climent.

La Coma's **restaurant** is justly popular for its local menu (wild boar and quail) and good service; *El Caliu*, at the top of Taüll in a new apartment building, is also reasonable, though tending towards *cuisine minceur* in its portions. Just outside Sant Climent,

Mallador is an appealing **garden-bar** run by nice people with good taste in music (closed May to mid-June & Oct to mid-Nov). It's the only place in the village that serves any sort of made-to-order breakfast (not on the menu); somewhat pricey gourmet main meals are also on offer here.

Walking in Aigües Tortes

Initial stretches of trail or track into Aigües Tortes are detailed in the preceding sections "Approaches to Aigües Tortes" and "South to Aigües Tortes". Moving deeper into the region, the clearly signposted **GR11** long-distance path skims the northern margins of the park, linking Espot with the Túnel de Viella; a **variant** connects Espot and the Tor valley. There are also numerous waymarked (but unnumbered) **linking paths** which permit an infinity of circuits and traverses taking in the best of the park and peripheral zone. Less exciting, and sometimes overly subscribed because of its ease, is the east–west **track** crossing the park from Estany de Sant Maurici to the information post near the springs of Aigües Tortes.

If you want any degree of solitude and wilderness, stick to the more difficult **south–north trails**, which run perpendicular to most hiker traffic. Off the more trammelled routes, map and compass are essential – it's easy to get lost amongst the two hundred-plus lakes and the granite whalebacks dividing them, especially when it's all wrapped in cloud.

Traverses

Starting from the *Refugí Colomina* (see "Capdella", p.251) there are three good traverses of the park in addition to the one to or from Espot via the *Refugí Josep Maria Blanc* (see p.251).

North to Refugí Ernest Mallafré via Monastero valley
Heading north through the often snow-clogged, always steep **Coll de Peguera** (2726m) and down the beautiful **Monastero valley**, it's a full day to the **Refugí Ernest Mallafré**, near the dam and roadhead at Sant Maurici (36 places; ☎973/25 01 05; open most of March & mid-June to mid-Oct). Next day you could leave the park via the gentle **Port de Ratera de Colomers**, finishing this less strenuous leg at the *Refugí de Colomers*, from where you're well poised to continue along the routes described on p.244.

Northwest to Refugís d'Estany Llong, Ventosa i Calvell and Restanca
More adventurously, you can head northwest from *Refugí Colomina* through the easy trekkers' passes **Collada de Dellui** (c. 2500m) or **Collada de Morrano** (2631m) to the **Refugí d' Estany Llong** (2000m; 36 places; currently not operating, but try ☎973/69 62 84), sited by the lake of that name. If it's still shut, the nearby, unstaffed *Refugí Centraleta* (8 bunks, fireplace) will be your home for the night. The Dellui route descends, with a slight detour past the scenic tarns of Corticelles/Cortiselles.

On the following day, you climb 3.5hr to the cirque-bound Estany de Contraig, with two very sharp grades on route. This lies just below the **Coll de Contraix** (2770m) another hour along, with stunning views but requiring snow equipment after a heavy winter. From here you can drop down, along the horrid north side (self-arrest device always required), to the very popular **Refugí Ventosa i Calvell** (2200m; 70 places; open most of March & mid-June to late Oct; reservations mandatory ☎973/29 70 90), 2hr 15min away just beside **Estany Negre**, where again you're near the heart of a lake-rich glacial basin. From here, you can take an easy half-day to the *Refugí de la Restanca* (p.245), just beyond the recently extended park boundary, and happily spend any remaining daylight on various day-hikes around the refuge.

West to Boí

Finally, again beginning from *Colomina*, it is possible to head due west through absolutely deserted country along the GR11 variant **to Boí**, a long, nine-hour day via one of two passes. The easy **Port de Rus** carries both the variant and the old spa patrons' *camí* from Capdella, but it's more exciting to maintain altitude by the park boundary, via a series of lakes and the inconspicuous **Collado del Pessó** (2760m), testing your cross-country skills.

Sant Maurici to Aigües Tortes

If you're not fully committed to alpine trekking, stick to the broad *camí* **between Sant Maurici and Aigües Tortes**; it's the remaining part of the old donkey track which once linked Boí with Espot, and happily not negotiable even for a jeep. This fifteen-kilometre stretch can be walked in seven to eight hours, but you won't be alone and most of the time you'll be looking up at the peaks rather than down from them. The exceptional moments come on either side of the **Portarró d'Espot** (2420m), from where you could detour to either side for some moderate ridge-touring. It's best to take a jeep-taxi at one or both ends of the traverse, otherwise the distance doubles.

You can of course eke out the journey by staying at either the *Refugí Ernest Mallafré* or *Refugí-Xalet d'Amitges* on the Espot side, or (providing it has reopened) at the *Estany Llong* refuge west of the Portarró d'Espot. Jeep-taxis also serve the *Amitges* refuge, just off the GR11 on the way to the two Ratera passes.

Peak ascents

The subject of countless posters, postcards, window-stickers and T-shirts, the double-pinnacle profile of **Els Encantats** is effectively the logo of the park. In local mythology, the *Encantats* – "Enchanted Ones" – are two Espot shepherds turned to stone by a priest for sneaking out of Mass to go hunting. Like the Agulles d'Amitges near the *Amitges* refuge, they're a favourite with technical climbers, but experienced mountain walkers equipped with a rope can reach the top of **Grand Encantat** (2747m) in about five hours from the *Ernest Mallafré* refuge, via the gully separating the twin summits.

The second highest peak inside the park, **Pala Alta de Sarradé** (Serrader on some maps; 2973m), is actually a far easier proposition, reached from Boí by the track to the park entrance and then via Estany Sarradé and a gully to the summit – use of a jeep-taxi cuts the one-way time from five hours to three and a half. Its near neighbour and top park summit, **Punta Alta** (3014m), is usually climbed from the vicinity of the Cavallers dam, via a path up the vale and tarns of **Coma les Bienes** and then scrambling. From either of these peaks you can carry on to the *Ventosa i Calvell* refuge.

Nor does the third-highest park summit, **Pic de Peguera** (2982m), present any problems for hikers if tackled from the Coll de Monastero, half an hour to the east; the coll is less than two hours from the *Josep Maria Blanc* hut and three from *Ernest Mallafré*. From the *coll* a cairned route leads southwest to the top in 45 minutes.

MALADETA AND POSETS

The trough-like **Ésera valley** runs through the heart of the Pyrenees' supreme high mountain wilderness, with Aneto peak (3404m) crowning the **Maladeta** massif to the east, and **Posets** (3375m) looming to the west. Both of these ranges have at last garnered

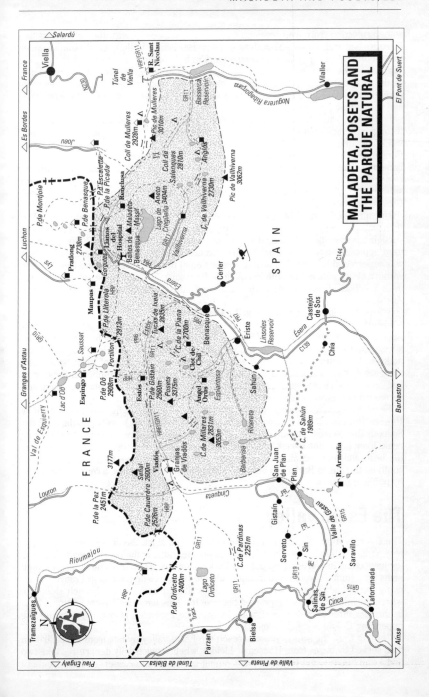

MALADETA, POSETS AND
THE PARQUE NATURAL

some protection from overdevelopment and over-popularity, with the creation of the **Parque Natural Posets-Maladeta** in 1996. **Benasque** is the pivotal point, a small valley-bottom town that lives for alpine tourism but has managed to retain some rural Aragonese character, not least in a vigorous recent campaign to promote renewed use of the regional language. Aragonese renditions of place-names are given below in parentheses following the Spanish, since, increasingly, this is what you will see on maps and road signs.

In tandem with the resurgence of regional feeling, efforts have been mounted throughout traditionally backward Alto Aragón to improve the quality of tourist services and information – especially trail guides and mapping – to match those of Catalunya. The mountain Aragonese feel, with some justice, that the Catalans have benefited disproportionately from the proceeds of tourism, besides tampering with the regional history and linguistics. Local advocates point out that Catalunya was long subsumed within the kingdom of Aragón, and claim that even the yellow-and-red Catalan flag is merely an adaptation of the original, horizontal Aragonese version.

Unconquered until 1842, **Aneto** long remained the preserve of mountaineers rather than walkers, not so much because of any technical difficulty – although it does have vertiginous moments in the final stage – but on account of its inaccessibility. The standard approach used to be from France through the Portillón de Benasque, but that was superseded in the 1970s with the extension of the C139 road beyond Benasque to within a short walk of both the Portillón de Benasque, just northwest, and the *Refugio de la Renclusa* (directly south of the road's end), the standard base for the conquest of Aneto.

The most momentous day seen at the **Portillón de Benasque/Port de Vénasque** – historic route across the watershed for travellers both legitimate and illicit – was April 1, 1938, when thousands of Spanish Republicans fled this way from a Nationalist advance that had cut them off in the Ésera cul-de-sac. Many of their colleagues didn't make it, being trapped by a snowstorm next day, and the luck of many successful refugees did not last long. At the end of World War II, a large number of those who had crossed in 1938 assumed the time had also come to end Francoism in Spain, and recrossed to their deaths.

Finishing second seldom impresses, which is perhaps why few tourists know **Posets**. But the sculpted massif with its paradisical valleys is hugely popular with the Spanish themselves, boasting more staffed refuges than any other major Pyrenean peak. Even if you don't want to bag the 3375-metre summit, a traverse or half-circuit is the best, and most scenic passage west – otherwise you have to detour way to the south on the bus to Barbastro before heading up the Cinca valley, a route not covered by public transport.

The Ésera valley

The **Ésera valley** remains a dead end for cars, and since the area's inclusion in the new *parque natural* further restrictions on private traffic at the remote head of the valley have come into effect (see below). Park status has apparently ended long-mooted plans for a tunnel through the frontier ridge to Bagnères-de-Luchon in France, which many locals had agitated for since the 1980s. It's an issue on the French side, too, where the inhabitants feel aggrieved because the Alps have had 300km of tunnel built in the last three decades, as against 8km in the Pyrenees (17km if you count the impending Col du Somport project).

Coming from the **south** you can reach the Ésera valley by bus from Barbastro (in turn served by buses from Huesca or Lleida), whence twice-daily departures take two and a half hours to get to Benasque. Coming from El Pont de Suert and the Noguera

Ribagorçana valley to the **east**, along the lonely, 41-kilometre C144 road to Castejón de Sos, you're dependent on your own motor vehicle or bicycle; hitching this route can be very slow.

Castejón de Sos, Sahún and Eriste

The C144 meets the Ésera at **CASTEJÓN DE SOS** (Castilló de Sos), 14km south of Benasque, and – if you've come up from Barbastro – the first place you'll see with much mountain character. The unique local topography has made it a mecca for **parapentists**, with two international competitions here annually. If you want to **stay**, there are a few moderately priced *hostales*, including the en-suite *Plaza* at Plaza El Pilar 2 (☎974/55 30 50; ④), the simpler *Pirineos*, Avda. El Ral 38 (☎974/55 32 51; ③), and the recently improved *Miranda* at El Ral 68 (☎974/55 32 22; ③). There are also a number of dorm-style *albergues* locally, mostly affiliated with *parapente* schools – *Pajaro Loco* at El Ral 48 (☎974/55 30 03; ②), *Liri* (☎974/55 33 50; ①) in the eponymous hamlet 2km north and *El Run* (☎974/55 35 50; ①), 1km southwest – as well as a **campsite** 1.5km north of town, *Alto Esera* (☎974/55 34 56; May–Sept).

If you have your own vehicle, the unspoilt hillside village of **SAHÚN**, 7km up the valley on the west slope, makes a far more atmospheric base, especially in high season. There are just two places to **stay** here, both gems: *Hostal Casa Lacreu* on the Plaza Mayor (☎974/55 13 35; ④), a recently restored manor house with spotless en-suite rooms, an arcaded bar and cheery, good-value *comedor*, and *Casa Falisia* right opposite (not staffed, reservations mandatory on ☎974/55 13 40; ③). Prime excursions here are the all-day hikes along locally marked *caminos* 9 and 10: the former north past the deconsecrated Guayente monastery (now a private educational foundation), then west along the Aigüeta valley to the Ibón (Lake) de la Ribereta; the latter south, then west along the Arroyo Llisat stream to the scattered *ibones* of Barbarisa. Both are designed for moderately fit individuals, and get a fraction of the patronage of the more "classic" walks up-valley (see below).

ERISTE (Grist), 3km further north and just 4km shy of Benasque, is less immediately appealing than Sahún, especially the modern district abutting the main road. Access to Posets via the Eriste valley makes it a good emergency base if Benasque is full, and Eriste is a low-key **water-sports** centre (Grist-Kayak, at the jetty or ☎974/55 10 92) thanks to its position near the Linsoles reservoir. There are three not terribly inspiring *hostales* with attached restaurants on the main highway – including *Pirineos* (☎974/55 13 07; ④) – but by far the best place to **stay**, at the southwest corner of the old quarter, is the very kind and homely *Casa Roy* (☎974/55 13 92; ②–④), which has rooms with en-suite or shared bathrooms and offers meals.

Benasque and Cerler

Surrounded by hayfields in a wide part of the Ésera valley, **BENASQUE** (Benás) strikes most people as an agreeable place, combining modern amenities – shunted wisely off to one side – with old stone houses, some of them built as summer homes for the Aragonese nobility in the seventeenth century. The town was once a seat of the counts of Ribagorça, who provided it with a castle and perimeter walls, both razed during the Napoleonic wars. The remaining old quarter, with its thirteenth-century church of **San Marcial** and the fifteenth-century **Torre Juste** to enliven the skyline, is still homogenous, atmospheric and large enough to get lost in.

Despite murmurings of despoliation, modern Benasque and its ski annexe above nearby Cerler are nothing like as obtrusive as the new developments in the Vall d'Aran – and before or after the rigours of Aneto or Posets, you'll welcome the chance to indulge in a little luxury. Benasque seems to attract a younger, less staid clientele than Aran – mostly well-heeled Barcelonan yuppies intent on a good time – and consequently has plenty of nightlife as well.

Arrival and information

Buses from Barbastro stop on the main Avda de los Tilos, a little south of the compact old quarter. The **Turismo** (daily 9am–2pm and 5–8pm; ☎974/55 12 89) is found at the southeast corner of the old town, dispensing pamphlets on local walks as well as publicity for local activities outfits. More stimulating, perhaps, will be the **Centro de Visitantes** (visitors' centre) for the *parque*, 500m south of the bus stop on the Anciles road (mid-June to mid-Sept daily 10am–2pm & 4–8pm; rest of year weekends & holidays same hours, except autumn & winter 10am–2pm & 3–6pm), which documents the extent, geology and traditional livelihoods of the park territory. There are several **banks** with ATMs in Benasque – the only ones you'll see for some distance, trekking east or west – and a **laundrette**, Ardilla, on the bypass road east of the Torre Juste.

Accommodation

Budget **accommodation** clusters at the entrance to the old town: try the basic *Fonda Barrabés*, c/Mayor 5 (☎974/55 16 54; ②), run by and for outdoor types, or the superior rooms above *Restaurante Bardanca*, c/Las Plazas 6 (☎974/55 13 60; ②), or those at the quieter *Casa Gabás*, c/El Castillo 17 (☎974/55 12 75; ③), which has self-catering units as well. Slightly run down and beset by disco noise, the *Hostal Salvaguardia* at c/San Marcial 3 (☎974/55 10 39; ③) is a last resort despite its prime position by the church. Moving up the scale, the best choices are the well-kept *Hotel Avenida* at Avda. de los Tilos 3 (☎974/55 11 26, fax 55 15 15; ⑤), a long-standing mountaineers' hangout, and the *Aragüells* at no. 1 on the same street (☎974/55 16 19, fax 55 16 64; ⑤). Otherwise the Valero Llanas family seems to control a fair percentage of lodging in town, spread over five hotels and *hostales*; start by asking at the conspicuous *Hotel Aneto*, just south of the C139 skirting town (☎974/55 10 61, fax 55 15 09; ④), where they may refer you to the nearby, co-managed *Hostal Valero* (same phone; ④) or the *Hotel El Pilar* (☎974/55 12 63; ④). The closest authorized **campsites** are three somewhat basic ones beginning 4km upstream along the Ésera valley, conveniently near the junction with the GR11: *Aneto*, *Chuise* and *Ixeia*. The former freelance sites further up at the boundaries of the *parque natural* have been phased out, and rough camping anywhere near the valley floor is highly frowned upon.

Eating and drinking

Eating out presents no problems. Competition has driven prices down, so that 1000–1500-peseta *menús* abound at the *Barrabés*, *Bardanca* and *Salvaguardia*, where people queue for cheap but sustaining stews and such at the handful of tables. On the ring road, *La Parilla* is popular with families for the sake of its good-value *menús* and à la carte grills, while *Sayó* on c/Mayor also has economical fare. For trendier dining, try the decent pizzeria on c/Los Huertos, near the old town's south entry, or *Les Arkades*, a combination creperie and pricier full-on restaurant south of the church. You can cobble together **breakfast** at *Granja Flor de Nieve* at c/Major 17, and **drink** at *Pepe & Company*, c/Mayor, or *Disco Ñaka*, near the church.

Activities and equipment

Everything in Benasque revolves around the great outdoors, as is evident from the number of people strolling about in brightly coloured Goretex outfits. Two rival **guiding centres**, Casa de la Montaña, Avda. de Los Tilos, and Compañia de Guías Valle de Benasque (☎974/55 13 36), organize trekking, technical climbing and rafting expeditions, including both nearby summits in five days. More sedately, you can **horse-ride** with La Cuadra Verde in Anciles, 1.5km south; rates start from 2000ptas for two hours. Of several **mountaineering equipment shops**, most conspicuous and one of the biggest in Spain, if not Europe, is Galleria Barrabés, near the corner of the C139 and Avda. de los Tilos: four floors of outdoor gear, with a café on the third floor and a soft-goods annexe across the road. Do, however, visit Deportes Aigualluts on Avda. de los Tilos before deciding where to replace worn-out trekking items, and also Libreria Rodolfoto across from Deportes Aigualluts, which has Benasque's best stock of **maps and guidebooks**.

Most useful of the books on sale is *Senderos de Pequeño Recorrido: Valle de Benasque*, issued by the Aragonese mountain club together with an invaluable map, and worthwhile even if you don't read Spanish. If you're unsure about tackling high-mountain walks, then the various local yellow-and-white-blazed *pequeño recorrido* (PR) **short-haul paths** are an ideal introduction. The PR itineraries, routed to avoid roads as much as possible, lead to surrounding villages and also to all three local refuges. The tourist office's free single-sheet leaflets "El Placer de Caminar" and "El Placer de Caminar y Pedalear" contain descriptions (in Spanish) and a crude sketch map, and will get you off to a good enough start, provided you have a proper map.

Cerler

CERLER (Sarllé), a small dependency of Benasque reached by a six-kilometre access road or the one-hour PR-1 path, ranks as the highest (1505m) village in Aragón. It's an attractive enough, if rather depopulated place which only comes alive in winter under the influence of the adjacent **ski resort** – whose fourteen lifts have been extended to nearly 2700m, after Taüll the highest in the range. Among the thirty runs, mostly red-rated, are two blacks, nine blues and six greens. Reasonable **accommodation** that's likely to be open in the summer season as well as ski time includes *Pension Casa Cornel*, c/El Obispo 11 (☎974/55 11 02; ④), and the non-en-suite *Casa Llorgodo*, c/La Fuente (☎974/55 10 67; ②). **Horse-riding** is offered by Casa Paulo in the upper quarter (☎974/55 10 92).

Into the Parque Natural Posets-Maladeta from Benasque

Benasque offers the only road access to the recently inaugurated **Parque Natural Posets-Maladeta**, which extends from the Noguera Ribagorçana in the east to the Valle de Gistau on the west; the lowest reaches of the Ésera valley are not included up to the *Baños de Benasque*, an old spa or *balneario* 10km from Benasque(see below). **Private vehicle traffic** into the park is restricted between July 10 and August 31. The track east into the Vallhiverna valley, 6km above Benasque, is closed to entry from 8am to 8pm, and the barrier is lifted for cars exiting only from 10 to 11am and again from 3 to 6pm. Some 11.5km north of Benasque, the C139 splits; the right-hand option leads after 1500m to a parking lot at **El Vado**, beyond which passage is again forbidden between 8am and 8pm on the dates specified, though exit is always allowed. Guards tend the barriers to make sure the rules are followed; the only exceptions made are for those continuing about 500m from El Vado to the parking lot of the Hospital de Benasque (see below). In summer (July 10–Aug 31), there's a **bus** service (250ptas round trip) provided from El Vado to La Besurta, road's end and site of another car park for the *Refugio de la Renclusa* and the Forau de Aiguallut. At other times of the year, the car-less wanting a jump-start to excursions might use two rival **alpine taxi** services both confusingly named Autotaxi Benasque: ☎908/93 04 50 for a 4WD Land Rover, or ☎974/55 11 57 for a VW transporter.

The Baños de Benasque and Llanos del Hospital

The **Baños de Benasque**, part of the Valero **hotel** empire (☎974/34 40 00, fax 34 42 49; ④; mid-June to early Oct), has tried to make itself more of a contemporary spa with a full hydrocure and massage programme. The premises, however, remain resolutely old-fashioned, with a rather funky plunge pool (32°C; 400ptas) downstairs and a popular bar above it, whose terrace tables are at a premium on fair days.

The derelict old pilgrims' hospice of **Hospital de Benasque**, a Templar foundation of the twelfth century, was acquired by an activities group in 1994 and revamped and enlarged to wide acclaim as the **Llanos del Hospital** (☎974/55 20 12, fax 55 10 52, mobile ☎908/53 60 53). It offers pricey **lodging** in three formats: alpine *refugio* with nine-bunk dorms (①), *albergue* with five- or six-bunk dorms, en-suite bathrooms and linen provided (② per person), or *hostal* (double rooms ⑤); it's also the focus of a popular nordic skiing centre, whose routes extend up-valley to La Besurta. On the ground floor are a convivial **bar** and a highly regarded **restaurant**, with *menús* at three price scales and lots of regional dishes (eg, *recau*, a chickpea-and-greens hotpot) available à la carte.

The best and most popular summer excursion near *Llanos del Hospital* is the easy **half-day hike** to two small tarns and one sizable lake to the north, the largest bodies of water on the Spanish side of the frontier ridge hereabouts. The least complicated trailhead, with parking available year-round, is that at the abrupt end of the left-hand fork in the C139, below the El Vado car park. The path, not shown accurately on the Alpina "Maladeta" map, climbs more or less due north to cross the Torrente de Gorgutes, then veers briefly east to skim above the two well-hidden **Ibones de la Montañeta**, the smaller of which is shallow and warm enough to swim in. The route then curls west to reach the **Lago de Gorgutes**, behind which is 2367-metre **Puerto de la Glera**, an easy pedestrian route into France. Not counting stops, it's two-and-a-half-hour round trip from the trailhead.

Maladeta climbs and walks

Despite its forbidding appearance from a distance, the **Maladeta Massif** offers scope, not only for alpine climbing, but for day-hikes, traverses and circuits of differing levels of difficulty. The main drawback of walking around Maladeta is the presence of just one staffed refuge, sited to be of more use to peak-baggers than long-distance trekkers; for any other extended forays you'd do well to have a **tent**. The appropriate Editorial Alpina 1:25,000 **map** is "Maladeta/Aneto"; the map of the same scale supplied with the *Senderos de Pequeño Recorrido* booklet unhappily crops half the mountain. To get a head-start up the mountain, see above for details of access from Benasque.

The ascent of Aneto

The **ascent of Aneto** begins at the **Refugio de la Renclusa** (2140m; 105 places; staffed Easter, at weekends Easter to mid-June, daily end-June to Sept, emergency shelter open in winter; reservations ☎974/55 11 26; ①), located well north of the summit close to the border. The final stop of the summertime bus service from El Vado at the La Besurta parking area lies 45 minutes' hike below *Renclusa*. If you prefer or need to walk the whole distance, a forestry track runs most of the way along the east bank of the Ésera, with more path short-cuts on the opposite bank once past the *Llanos del Hospital* – the entire way marked as the four-and-a-half-hour **PR-4**.

Unless you're incredibly fit and experienced, plan for a full day to the summit and back, including the necessary stops, and assuming a start before sunrise. Walking equipment must include **crampons**, **ice-axe** and a **rope**. For a winter ascent on **skis**, follow the walking instructions below; it's a 1480-metre climb, possible in about ten hours.

Routes – and their history

There are two basic routes on the northeast face, which can be combined to make a circuit. The standard itinerary heads south from the refuge, climbing steeply towards the pass known as **Portillón Inferior** (2745m); before the top, bear away southwest to the next pass along, **Portillón Superior** (2900m), which you should reach in about three hours.

Now you have your first good view of Aneto ahead, with the secondary peak of **Maladeta** (3308m) to your right. The guide Pierre Barrau – who with Frédéric Parrot made the first recorded ascent of Maladeta on September 29, 1817 – was killed when, unroped, he fell into a crevasse on the Maladeta glacier in 1824, and it was probably his death that postponed the conquest of Aneto for almost another twenty years. His body emerged from the ice 117 years later.

On the far side of Portillón Superior a gully descends to a saddle beyond which ice fields lead to the Aneto glacier. During the summer months, a "path" will have been worn across it, a little whiter than the grit-stained glacier to each side. Normally it should be perfectly safe but if there is any doubt, rope up. You now cover 2500m south-southeast to the **Collado de Coronas** (3198m; 4hr 30min from the refuge), where – in a notch in the crest below – a summertime lake forms once in every five years or so, a brilliant blue on a sunny day.

Climb east beyond the *collado*, possibly with crampons and ice-axe, to the broad jumble of rocks known as the **Puente de Mahoma**. This, negotiated on all fours, represents 50m of sheer terror for the inexperienced, especially if iced up (in Islam, "Mohammed's rope" is the bridge over Hell to Paradise). On the other side of the "bridge" the **Aneto summit** (3404m) is staked by a large cross and what looks like a small rocket, but turns out to be a Virgin and Child on a metal pedestal. Savour your triumph, but don't linger, especially if clouds begin accumulating – climbers staying into the mid-afternoon have been killed by lightning.

The first men to stand here, on July 20, 1842, were the Russian, Platon de Tchihatcheff, the French count, Albert de Franqueville, and their guides, Bernard Ursule, Pierre Redonet, Jean Argarot and Pierre Sanio. However, they did not use the route described, but avoided the formidable main northerly glacier by skirting most of the crest in an anticlockwise direction and coming up the smaller Coronas glacier on the south side of the ridge. Today, these pioneers would probably opt for the classical modern route – Aneto's glaciers, like all those in the Pyrenees, have shrunk forty to fifty percent since last century.

To make a **circuit**, descend to Collado de Coronas and then bear right on another, easterly path across the glacier leading to the Plan de Aiguallut (below) and the **Forau de Aiguallut/Trou du Toro**, a pit of grey, splintered rock into which cascading waters of the Aneto glacier disappear before re-emerging in the Joeu valley. From beside a green shed-refuge, upstream from the sinkhole, an initially very faint path leads directly west back to the *Refugio de la Renclusa*.

Walks around Maladeta

If you don't want to stay at the *Renclusa* shelter, or if it's full, wilderness **camping** at the Plan de Aiguallut is highly recommended – though don't be surprised to find tents banned or restricted here in the near future. The *plan* is your destination coming westwards from the Noguera Ribagorçana over either the Coll de Salenques or the Coll de Mulleres – approaches detailed in "West to Maladeta" on p.245. By using **Plan de Aiguallut (Aigualluts)** as a base, you're also well positioned for a few days of rewarding and not too strenuous **day-hikes**; by happy coincidence there are four relatively gentle passes on the crests to the northeast, and the paths through them can be combined into circuits. Otherwise, starting **from Benasque**, two other targets for day-hikes are slightly beyond the scope of the local PR excursions in length and effort.

Itineraries around Plan d'Aiguallut

The way up from Plan de Aiguallut towards the Coll de Mulleres along the **Valleta de la Escaleta** brings you to the **Coll de Tòro** (2235m) and, shortly after, the **Coll dels Aranesos** (2455m), both of which overlook lakes and sharp but scenic descents – largely cross-country – to the Pla de l'Artiga in the Vall d'Aran. You can return to the Aragonese side of the crest via a well-trodden trail up the Pomèro valley, leading to the **Port de la Picada** (2740m), where half-wild horses can often be seen grazing, and where the boundaries of Aragón, Catalunya and France meet.

The **Portillón de Benasque/Port de Vénasque** (2448m), the age-old route to Luchon in France, is the next pass west of Picada, an easy three hours' walk by well-trodden paths from either *Refugio de la Renclusa* or Plan de Aiguallut. Even if you're not bound for France, this notch in the ridge makes a worthwhile goal for the opportunity it gives to visit **Pico de Salvaguarda/Sauvegarde** (2738m), 45 minutes' walk west of the pass. The views in all directions from the summit are among the best in the entire Pyrenees, especially south over Maladeta, a giant reef of dark rock striped by patches of snow and ice. Less than an hour north, on the shore of a large lake, is the friendly *Refuge de Vénasque*, well placed for a lunch stop (see p.287 for details).

Itineraries from Benasque

The first, longer hike from Benasque is the steep trek up to **Lago de Cregüeña** (2630m), third largest lake in the Pyrenees, trapped in a deep cirque southwest of Maladeta. To get there, turn off the PR-4 route at the fountain and waterfall of **San Ferrer** (San Farré), about ninety minutes above Benasque; the path up the Cregüeña is distinct and cairned. Allow nine hours out and back. (Although it's optimistically depicted on tourist office handouts, the route over the 2930-metre pass to the southeast into the Valle de Vallhiverna (see below) is a tough exercise for the properly equipped only, out of bounds for most casual hikers.)

About half an hour before San Ferrer, at the **Puente de Vallhiverna** by the Paso Nuevo reservoir, you can also leave the PR-4 to explore the **Vallhiverna valley** (Ballibierna) by following the eastbound GR11 – unfortunately forced onto jeep track here, though there's little traffic in high season when access is limited. At **Puente de Coronas**, two-and-a-half hours from the Ésera near the top of this idyllic tributary, you'll find a permanently open, fourteen-person **refuge** for use if you're making a traverse rather than day-hiking; camping is theoretically forbidden here.

From Puente de Coronas, you can either tackle Aneto via the cirque and glacier of Coronas – the final approach of the 1842 pioneers – or, more likely, continue east **along the GR11** into the Anglòs (Angliós) valley on the Noguera Ribagorçana side, via the lakes and Coll de Vallhiverna (2720m). It's a very long day to the *Refugí Sant Nicolau* at the Viella tunnel mouth, but there is an unstaffed refuge at the easterly Anglòs lakes two hours below the pass, and emergency camping – whatever its official status – is unlikely to be remarked on in this remote, rugged country.

Posets climbs and walks

From Aneto, the magnificent dark granite mass of **Posets** (3375m), topped by an almost complete circle of low schist ridges, looks like some kind of giant's fort. From the west it seems even more formidable, rising up as a huge free-standing lump, deeply etched by gullies and false trails. An ascent requires ice-axe, crampons and rope, and perhaps a helmet to guard against falling rocks near the summit.

For day-hikers and long-haul trekkers alike, Posets is perhaps more user-friendly than Maladeta, with no fewer than three well-sited, staffed refuges, a host of places to camp – though you don't really need to – and options for circuits and traverses of varying length. From Benasque there are two main approaches for either climbs or traverses; you're likely to exit the region via the Valle de Gistau on the west, well poised for hikes further into Aragón. The recommended **map** is Editorial Alpina 1:25,000 "Posets"; if you intend walking in or out via the *Viadós* refuge and the Valle de Gistau in the west, take the "Bachimala" sheet too. At a pinch, the map supplied with *Senderos de Pequeño Recorrido* will do for less rigorous walks, giving the same coverage as the Editorial Alpina production.

The approach from Estós

More pastorally attractive and unspoilt than the Ésera, the **Estós valley** curls around Posets to the northeast; although the track through its lower reaches is driveable, all private cars are banned except for the jeep belonging to the warden of the modern three-storey *Refugio de Estós* (1890m; 185 places; self-catering kitchen; staffed all year; ☎974/55 14 83; ①).

To reach valley and refuge, follow the PR-5 path from Benasque, then a bit of the PR-4, to the medieval **Cuera (San Jaime) bridge** 45 minutes above town, following which you switch to the GR11 as it heads northwest over the bridge. After another hour or so, the PR-6 peels off from the GR11 track and adopts the opposite bank of the valley stream – though the track is by no means objectionable – rejoining it shortly before the *Estós* refuge. Whatever route you take, count on four hours total from Benasque to the shelter, considered one of the more luxurious in the Pyrenees.

The ascent of the peak
The *Estós* refuge marks the start of the easier and more popular six-hour **ascent of Posets**, whether on foot or on skis. Drop down to the bridge, cross it and follow the path along the stream's right (south) bank. After a couple of kilometres leave the main valley on the path climbing into the Coma de la Paúl, leading to the **Glaciar de la Paúl**, beyond which you reach the **Collado de la Paúl** (3062m). Once on the south side of this, cross the **Glaciar de Posets** – normally by a clearly trodden path – to the east face of the summit. A scramble up a narrow gully brings you to the top, known locally as **Lardana**.

The approach from Eriste

The much less frequented **Eriste valley** forges into the alpine heart of Posets from the southeast; near the top stands the *Refugio Ángel Orús (Forcau)*, the alternative base camp for the attempt of Posets (2100m; 30 places; staffed Easter & July–Sept; part always open; ☎974/34 40 44; ①). To get there, use the PR-7 path from Benasque to Eriste village (p.259), and then the PR-11 route up the narrow, wild canyon, cloaked in foothill vegetation thanks to a mild microclimate. After an hour or so, mostly on track, you come to the bridge and waterfalls of **Espiantosa**, from where it's another two hours' trail-walk to the refuge – or nearly four hours in total from Benasque. If *Refugio Ángel Orús* is full you can **camp** an hour to the north, in or around the simple *Cabana de Llardana*.

From Espiantosa you could also take a signposted path northeast to the unstaffed *Refugio Clot de Chil* (2000m; 16 places; always open), well placed for climbing the pointy-headed **Tucas de Ixeia** (2835m), star of many a Benasque postcard – and also a favourite launch pad for *parapentistas*.

From the *Ángel Orús* refuge, the best approach to the summit lies along the **Llardaneta valley** (between the refuge and the *Cabana de Llardana*), up the **Canal Fonda** between the outcrops of Tuca Alta and Diente de Llardana at the end of the *canal*, and then straight up for the summit – a total of five hours one-way (nine hours return).

Skiing on Posets

A winter ascent of Posets on **skis** is a tougher proposition than Aneto, longer and with more difficulties towards the summit. The easiest way involves repeating the summer walking route from the *Estós* refuge, described previously. When you reach the Collado de la Paúl, only continue to the summit if the conditions are ideal. The exhilarating ski descent to the *Estós* refuge from the *collado* is your reward for trying in any case.

Alternatively, you could make an alpine tour (but carrying a heavier load) by skirting the Glaciar de Posets from the pass, instead dropping a little south of east into the Valle de los Ibóns (see below), to the **Lago de las Alforjas** (2250m) – another gorgeous and fairly easy descent. From the lake you have an easy ski south to the *Ángel Orús* refuge (open weekends only in winter); next day, you move down the Eriste valley to Eriste village and the main C139 road.

All ski possibilities are detailed in Spanish in the booklet accompanying the Editorial Alpina "Posets" map; if you prefer reading French, a ski traverse is described in Pierre Merlin's *Guide des Raids à Ski*.

Traverses and circuits

The following **traverses and partial circuits** can of course be combined into a giant loop around the massif, so that with three or four days at your disposal you trek through all the best that Posets has to offer. Outside of peak season – when resources are always strained – you can save pack weight by dispensing with food and tent, relying on the well-spaced refuges.

Traverse via Batisielles

A superb traverse from the vicinity of the *Ángel Orús* refuge to the Estós valley starts by entering the **Valle de los Ibóns** northeast of Llardaneta and then, just below the Lago de las Alforjas, ascending east to the **Collado de la Piana** (2700m). On the other side, the sparsely cairned, cross-country route descends more sharply into the **Valle de Perramó**, with the lake of the same name huddled at the base of the Tucas de Ixeia. From there the route swings north again to the Escarpinosa lake, where a clearly trodden path begins down to the meadows of **Batisielles** – a wonderful place to camp, which you may have to do since it's six to seven hours' trekking from *Ángel Orús* to here. Without a tent, you should press on for another ninety minutes, through meadow and woods, to the *Estós* refuge.

The Posets half-circuit

The most popular Posets activity for non-climbers is the **half-circuit** of the massif which follows the GR11 west, skirting the mountain's north and west flanks. From the *Estós* refuge you continue along the valley, climbing to the **Puerto de Gistaín** (*Chistau* in Aragonese; 2560m; 2hr 15min), before descending on the other side to the head of the **Cinqueta de Añes Cruces**. As you amble down this progressively more hospitable valley, you're treated to increasingly impressive views of the mountain's forbidding west flank before arriving at bucolic **Granjas de Viadós**, a dozen or so scattered barns amongst hayfields tended in summer and one of the most beautiful spots in the Spanish Pyrenees. You can do the entire walk in five to six hours, with plenty of daylight left over for the worthwhile hop up to **Señal de Viadós** (2600m), a hill giving the best possible look east to Posets and west over the Cinqueta valley.

Viadós – and back to Benasque

At Granjas de Viadós, the **Refugio de Viadós** (*Biadors*; 1760m; open Easter and weekends to June 25, thereafter continuously to Sept 25; 40 places; ☎974/50 60 82 summer,

50 07 27 winter; ①) is privately operated by Joaquin Cazcarra and family; if you have the "Bachimala" Alpina map with you, get him to autograph it – he was partly responsible for it. In some measure because the refuge is road-accessible, meals and bunks are less expensive than the Pyrenean norm. The Cazcarra family also runs a **campsite**, *El Forcallo* (same phone numbers), nearby at 1580m elevation; thus free camping in the meadow beside the refuge may no longer be allowed.

It's possible – and recommended – to loop **back to Benasque** by one of two demanding but non-technical routes, which cut through the Posets crest admired by so many from Granjas de Viadós. You'll need extra water on this stretch, some rope at one point, and crampons and an axe after a heavy winter. From the *Refugio de Viadós*, you descend by path to the river and then, once across, up a trail through the **Valle de Millares** (Bal de Millás) to the eponymous lake. Above Millares, the narrow trail fizzles out, and only a few cairns guide you over the rock-girt **Collado de Millares** (2831m), three and a half hours along. More cross-country work through a moonscape of tortured granite is involved in the descent southeast to **Lago Alto**. Beyond this you turn east-northeast through the Brecha de Llantia – where the rope might come in handy – and then between the spires of Llantia and Forcau, down the Valle de Forcau, to reach *Refugio Ángel Orús* – a challenging day of seven walking hours.

Alternatively, you can shun the Millares lake in favour of another pass (2860m) between 3007-metre La Forqueta and 3010-metre Diente Royo, which gives onto **Lago Llardaneta** and the eponymous valley which drains down to the refuge. This route is slightly easier and shorter than the preceding one, and won't require any rope work.

Onwards from Posets

From Posets your trekking options consist of heading north **into France** via several passes of varying difficulty in the border ridge, or continuing west and south deeper **into Aragón**.

Into France

If you're walking north from Posets into France, two fairly difficult but spectacular routes lead to the popular **Lac d'Oô** on the GR10 (see p.288). From the *Estós* refuge, ascend due north up the **Valle de Gías**, past its three tarns, and into France via the **Puerto d'Oô** (pronounced "oh"; 2908m); it's a wearisome four hours up, much of it through a forbidding boulder-field, with no real path in the screes for quite a distance to either side of the pass. From here it's another three (easier) hours' trekking down to the Espingo refuge and lake, via the **Lac du Port** (also known on French maps as the *Lac Glacé* after its permanent ice floes) and Lac Saussat.

Alternatively, bear eastwards away from the Gías trail about a third of the way up, through the **Collada de Molseret** (2520m) and then to the frontier pass of **Portillón d'Oô** (2913m; 4hr 30min). The *portillón* is guarded by permanent ice and might require crampons, but the seasonally staffed refuge at **Lac du Portillon** (on the HRP) lies only an hour beyond. *Espingo*, the next refuge, is another two hours down-valley via the **Lac Saussat**; the Lac de Oô, an hour below *Espingo*, lies nearly three hours down-valley, a favourite picnic spot, not far above the roadhead at **Granges d'Astau**. All these spots are covered in detail under "Walks from Luchon", at the end of this chapter.

Two easier ways into France depart from the *Refugio de Viadós*: either up the Cinqueta (River-valley) de la Pez to the **Puerto de la Pez** (2451m), giving onto the Louron valley, or through the even easier **Puerto de Ordiceto** (2400m) north of the eponymous lake, from where a variant of the HRP leads down to the roadhead and hospice in the Rioumajou valley. But you get what you pay for in effort expended – neither route can compare to the Oô itineraries. Slightly more exciting is a third itinerary, again starting along Cinqueta de la Pez but then veering west up to the **Puerto d'a Madera** (2560m); on the far side of this you descend along the Couarère stream to the main Rioumajou drainage. All of these routes take a full day's walk to reach the next permanent habitation or suitable camping spot.

Into Aragón

From the *Refugio de Viadós*, the main trekking alternatives west and south into Aragón involve following the GR11 or the GR19 Spanish long-distance trails; both begin with a sharp descent to the valley of the **Cinqueta** (Zinqueta) stream.

The GR11 stays with the vehicle track until turning right onto another track at **La Sargueta**, which shortly reaches a junction. Heading up and right puts you on the main GR11 branch to **Lago Ordiceto** (Urdiceto; 2369m) – popular with picnickers despite its unsightly dam – from where a jeep track descends 11km to the main road, 5km north of Bielsa. It's best to come here only as a day-walk from *Viadós*, or to enter the French Rioumajou valley.

From the ruined **Opital de Chistén**, twenty minutes south of La Sargueta, a reasonable *camino* leads two hours up to the shallow **Collada de Pardinas** (2251m), but thereafter it's mostly cross-country for four more hours to Bielsa, with minimal waymarking as a GR11 *variante* – but this is in fact the old, middle-altitude shepherd's route from Viadós to the Cinca (Zinca) valley.

The GR19 forest track spares you about an hour of trudging down the main track along the Cinqueta, but it's not brilliant and if you can, you should arrange a lift along the main road, either 11km down to the turning for Gistaín or the full 14km to Plan, "capital" of the valley described below.

The Valle de Gistau

Little known except among Spaniards, for whom it is famous as a repository of Aragonese culture and language, the **Valle de Gistau** (Chistau, Xistau), essentially the lower reaches of the Cinqueta valley, makes a worthwhile rest-stop if you're trekking between Posets and the Ordesa region. Tourism has come late to the area – only after other, more immediately spectacular regions became saturated – but facilities are multiplying, and indeed the oldest Spanish alpine refuge of Armeña lies less than a day's hike south, between two celebrated lakes.

The valley itself remains famous for a joint lonelyhearts ad placed in the national press during 1985 by its preponderance of bachelors, one of the more bizarre consequences of Aragonese rural depopulation. Remaining mountain women were (and still are) unwilling to marry those not inclined to move down to the more prosperous towns. The bachelors threw a three-day *fiesta* to welcome the applicants, a surprising number of whom ended up marrying and settling down here.

By car, Gistau can be reached from the east, starting at **Chía** in the Ésera valley, via a 25-kilometre, signposted forest track over the 1989-metre Collado de Sahún. It's dirt surface, and first-gear driving most of the way, but the countryside's superb with views northwest to numerous frontier peaks. The more common approach from the west is along the paved side road beginning at **Salinas de Sin**, home to a very keen and well-stocked **tourist office** (mid-June to mid-Sept daily except Thurs 9am–7pm; ☎974/50 40 89, fax 50 60 01), a roadside booth serving the entire valley. Beyond the turnings for Saravillo and Sin (see below), the road threads through a series of dramatic tunnels bored through the rock downstream from the local dam.

Valley villages

A trio of villages, linked by a mesh of PR trails on the Benasque model, nestles at the head of the valley, and between them offer most of the area's tourist facilities. Boasting a couple of hundred inhabitants, **PLAN** has shops and the valley's only proper **hotel**, the one-star *Mediodia* (☎974/50 60 06; ④), as well as the Guías de la Bal de Chistau (☎974/50 61 78), offering the usual range of caving, climbing, canyoning and trekking activities. **SAN JUAN DE PLAN** (San Chuan), 2km upstream, is smaller still, but sports a **hostel**, the *Albergue El Molin* (☎974/50 62 44, fax 50 62 08; ①). Particularly well perched on the north flank of the valley, **GISTAÍN** (Chistén) can offer filling **meals** and **rooms** at the popular *Fonda Casa Elvira* (☎974/50 69 78; ①) by the church – but the village itself presents a disappointing profile, a hotchpotch of half-timbered and modern brick walls, its roofs made of both asbestos and traditional slate. That said, it's still a vital mountain settlement where rural pursuits remain dominant over tourism.

Simple, inexpensive **casas rurales**, largely the brainchild of one Josefina Loste de Mur, are the norm for accommodation – and half-board **meals** – in the entire area, and tend to be taken up for a week at a time by Spaniards. Still, you should try Josefina's *Pension Casa la Plaza* (☎974/50 60 52; ②), with pricier en-suite rooms, or the non-en-suite *Casa Sánches* (☎974/50 60 50; ②) or *Casa Zuera* (☎974/50 60 40; ②), all in San Juan de Plan; *Casa Mur* (☎974/50 61 23; ①) and *Casa Ruche* (☎974/50 60 72; ②) in Plan; or the friendly Carolina Bruned's *Casa Zuera* (☎974/50 60 38; ①) and the larger, relatively fancy *Casa Fontamil* (☎974/50 61 92; ②–③), with en-suite or shared bathrooms and some loft rooms, in Gistaín. If you draw a blank with all these possibilities, there are at least twice as many more *habitaciones* in the villages concerned – ask around or let yourself be referred.

West to the Cinca valley

There's no bus service to or from the Valle de Gistau; heading west, rather than hitch the 12km to the main road at Salinas de Sin, it's preferable to use either the onward **GR19** track-and-trail from Gistaín, or the wilder **GR15** along the valley's south slope, which can be picked up easily from Plan.

The GR19 leads high along the north flank of the valley through the quiet villages of **SERVETO** (Serbeto; 1hr 30min) – from where there's a scenic PR down to the valley floor – and **SIN** (2hr), where there's an *albergue* popular with school groups (☎974/50 62 12; ①). If you continue west from Sin, the GR19 – now mostly a handsome trail through densely forested territory – leads in two hours to **SALINAS DE SIN** in the Cinca valley, an insignificant place aside from its aforementioned tourist booth; the only accommodation, *Hotel Mesón de Salinas* (☎974/50 40 01; ③), is often full. From Salinas you'll still have to road-walk on to either Bielsa (7km north) or Lafortunada (5km south). For coverage of these places, see p.357 and p.361.

If you have no transport awaiting you on the main highway, it's best, at Sin, to descend via another PR itinerary to **SARAVILLO** (Sarabillo), near the mouth of the valley. This can offer a large **campsite**, *Los Vives* (☎974/50 61 71; June–Sept), and **habitaciones** at *Restaurante Pallaruelo* (☎974/50 62 73; ②), as well as horse-riding at Entremon. Saravillo is also on the GR15 trail, which heads west, then south in two pleasant hours to Lafortunada, the initial stretch on track but path thereafter.

The best trekking option – and one which incorporates the most popular short excursion in the valley – involves joining the **GR15** from Plan, in the vicinity of the area's two natural lakes. At the municipal *piscina* across the river from town, take the dirt track heading west uphill; after about half an hour, adopt a signposted *camino* heading very steeply south into evocatively shaped mountains, to arrive after 2hr 30min at the postcard-worthy **Ibón de Plan** (Basa de la Mora), ensconced in its own cirque. From this lake, the GR15 heads west to Saravillo within two hours, downhill once past the crude forest hut at Labasar. Alternatively, from Basa de la Mora the GR15 effects another two-hour traverse, via two moderate passes, southeast to the unguarded *Refugio de Armeña* (1835m; 25 bunks; open year-round), near the **Ibón de Armeña**.

THE COUSERANS AND THE COMMINGES

North of the Vall d'Aran, beyond the frontier, sprawls a neglected corner of France, an isolated realm slashed by a purported total of eighteen valleys large and small, tilting in every direction. Except in its southeastern corner, where the old spa of **Aulus-les-Bains** sees some entrepreneurial activity, the **Couserans** is an eerily remote landscape of unkempt pastures, abandoned terraces and ruined barns. Most of the local mines – producing aluminium, tungsten, lead, zinc and, above all, iron – have been worked out, and the small farms bankrupted by competition from mechanized plains agriculture. The population has halved during the past century, yet unemployment remains high. Traditionally marginal – and no longer viable – livelihoods included gold-panning, itinerant peddling and acting as wet-nurses for city families. Nowadays the main rural products are hay, cheese and honey, the latter two on sale everywhere.

Saint-Girons, 44km west of Foix and capital of the Couserans, is not particularly interesting in itself, but you come here for the sake of the adjacent charming old town of **Saint-Lizier**, and for the bus services which make it the hub for all local exploration. Well north of the bus route from Foix to Saint-Girons, **Mas d'Azil** is one of the great prehistoric caves of the Pyrenees, giving its name to a whole epoch – the Azilian.

Heading southwards into the "empty quarter" extending towards the border and the Vall d'Aran, furrowed by the River Salat, there are bus connections from Saint-Girons to Aulus-les-Bains via **Seix**, an important canoeing centre, and via Castillon-en-Couserans to Sentein, near the roadhead for the local portion of the GR10. The **Vallée de Bethmale**, between Seix and Castillon, is one of the big names in Pyrenean folklore, its distinctive costume (now rarely displayed) popularized by a number of writers. What you see here instead are Toulousains come to stay in their holiday homes, and walkers bound for **Mont Valier** – an easy, beautiful and popular ascent.

Just to the west, straddling the Garonne, is the marginally more prosperous **Comminges** region. Since 1790, it has fallen into a different administrative *département* (Haute-Garonne), yet the Couserans has always had more in common with it – both areas being Catholic and Gascon-speaking – than with historically Protestant and Languedoc-speaking Ariège, its neighbour in the same modern *département*-of-convenience. All along the southern part of Couserans west from Aulus and on into the Comminges – the most mountainous part of Haute-Garonne – there are relatively few tourist facilities and not many man-made "sights". This changes abruptly once you encounter the relatively busy road and rail line between **Saint-Gaudens**, functional capital of the Comminges, and **Bagnères-de-Luchon**, an old-fashioned spa now revelling in a new identity as a ski resort and hikers' centre. Southwest of Saint-Gaudens, the magnificent cathedral at **Saint-Bertrand-de-Comminges** vies for your attention with the **Grotte de Gargas**, whose tracings of truncated prehistoric hands still generate speculation.

Saint-Girons

Well-connected, though relatively sleepy **SAINT-GIRONS** will possibly be your first taste of the Couserans. It's a pleasant enough town straddling the River Salat, with two sets of rapids by the old bridge, best known (in France, at least) for its cigarette-paper industry, but has little specifically to see other than nearby Saint-Lizier.

Buses, including those from Foix, Aulus-les-Bains and Boussens, arrive at the **place des Capots** on the left (west) bank. Orient yourself by facing east on the sixteenth-century **Pont-Vieux** over the River Salat: walking straight ahead onto the right bank leads into the old commercial centre, with the tourist office, the *Maison de Couserans* (daily except Sun: July & Aug 9.30am–6.30pm; Sept–June 9am–noon & 2–6pm; ☎05.61.96.26.60), a few paces left along the river, on place Alphonse-Sentein. On the right (south), the **place des Poilus** is ringed by elegantly faded period pieces – including two hotels (see below) and the *Grand Café de l'Union*. Next to the square, along the river, a gravelled promenade of plane trees, the **Champ de Mars**, hosts a general market on the second and fourth Mondays of the month, and a regular produce market every Saturday morning.

Practicalities

If you need **to stay**, choose from among the *Hôtel de l'Union* on rue du Champ de Mars, corner Place de Poilus (☎05.61.66.09.12, fax 05.61.04.81.73; ③), the *Grand Hôtel de France* at Place de Poilus 4 (☎05.61.66.00.23, fax 05.61.04.84.85; ②), with an acceptable restaurant, and the more modern and comfortable *La Clairière*, at the edge of town on the road to Seix (☎05.61.66.66.66, fax 05.61.66.70.72; ④), with a pool and arguably the best restaurant in Saint-Girons. Indeed, **eating** prospects apart from the hotels are rather undistinguished; there are a few rather dreary places in the west bank quarter, as well as the *Bar Galopin*, a good spot for a **drink**, with outdoor seats opposite the rapids. Alternatively, there's a **campsite** at the Centre de Loisirs du Parc de Paletès (☎05.61.66.06.79), 2km out along av des Évadés, with an excellent affiliated terrace restaurant, *La Table de l'Ours*. If you want to cycle out to Mas d'Azil, **bike rental** is available from Cycles Brunet, rue Joseph Pujol, five minutes' walk west from Saint-Girons' church.

Saint-Lizier

SAINT-LIZIER is only a five-minute journey north of Saint-Girons by bus from the defunct train station on the D117 road, but you may as well walk the 2km instead and make a circuit, returning via the walled medieval village of Montjoie (3km away by a minor road), with its fortified church. From there, back to Saint-Girons, it's 45 minutes' walk.

An important centre of Christianity since the sixth century, when it traded the Roman name of *Austria* for that of its first proselytizing bishop, Saint-Lizier is impressive even from a distance, with its turreted **episcopal Palace** at the top of the hill, and cascades of red-tiled roofs all the way down to the river. Once you get inside the stone walls – built on the fourth-century Gallo-Roman foundations – it's even better, with atmospheric cobbled streets and tiny arcaded alleys flanked by half-timbered houses. As a showcase period-piece, Saint-Lizier seems devoid of most conventional tourist facilities, which gives it a curiously lifeless air, especially between mid-September and mid-June.

The main **Cathédrale de Saint-Lizier** (closed noon–2pm) sports an octagonal keep-like tower in lieu of a dome, as well as twelfth-century frescoes faded almost to invisibility. The highlight is the Romanesque cloister, from the same period as the frescoes, with the usual array of unique, sculpted capitals, though these have suffered in recent years and can't compare in quality to those at Ripoll (see p.158) or San Juan de la Peña (see p.380). A second cathedral, **Nôtre-Dame-de-Sède**, within the grounds of the bishop's palace, is shut indefinitely for renovation, though the palace itself is also home to the **Musée Départmentale de l'Ariège** on the first floor (May–Sept daily 10am–12.30pm & 2–6/6.30pm; Oct–April weekends & holidays 2–5.30pm; 25F), which contains a permanent ethnographic collection devoted to the Vallée du Bethmale, not really worth the admission fee.

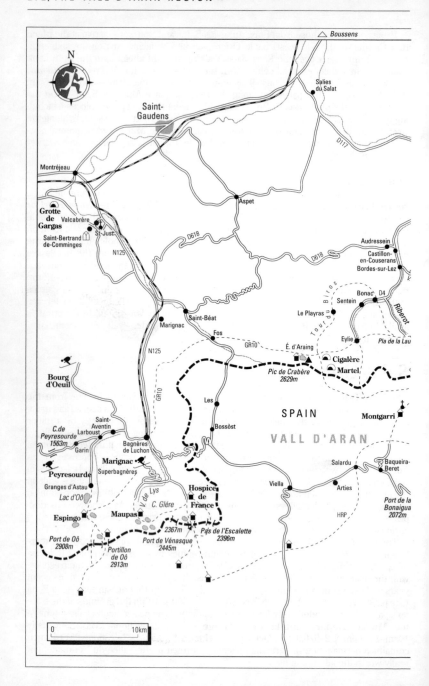

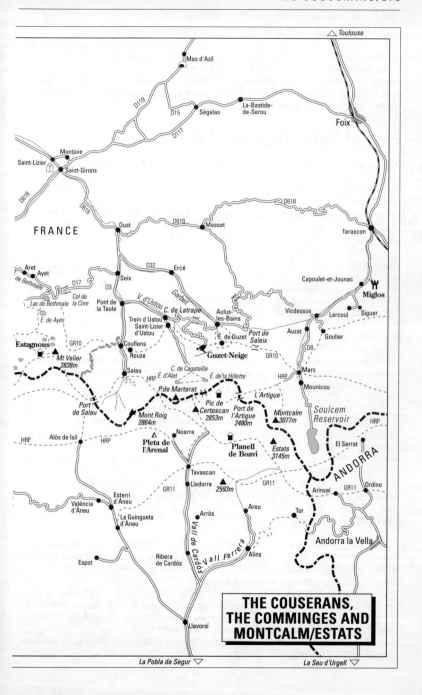

△ Toulouse

Mas d'Azil

D119

D15   Ségalas   La-Bastide-de-Serou

D117   Foix

Montjoie

Saint-Lizier   Saint-Girons

D618

D618   Oust   D618   Massat   Tarascon

FRANCE

Aret

Ayet

de Bethmale   D17

Col de   D32   Ercé

Lac de Bethmale   la Core

É. de Ayés   Pont de   V. d'Ustou

la Taule   Capoulet-et-Jounac

D3   Seix   Garbet   Miglos

Estagnous   GR10   Trein d'Ustou   C. de Latrape   Vicdessos   Lercoul   Siguer

Saint-Lizier   Aulus-   Auzat   Goulier

Mt Valier   d'Ustou   les-Bains

2838m   Couflens   É. de Guzet   Port de

Rouze   Saleix   GR10   D8

Guzet-Neige

Salau   É. d'Alet   HRP   Marc

HRP   C. de Cagateille   É. de la Hillette   Mounicou

P. de Marterat   L'Artigue

Port   Pic de   Port de   Soulcem

de Salau   Mont Roig   Certescan   l'Artigue   Montcalm   Reservoir

2864m   2853m   2480m   3077m   HRP

HRP   Alòs de Isil   HRP   Noarre   El Serrat

Pleta de   Planell   Estats

l'Arenal   de Boavi   3145m

València   Esterri   Tavascan   GR11   Arinsal   Ordino

d'Aneu   d'Aneu   Lladorre   2593m   Areu   GR11   ANDORRA

La Guingueta   GR11   Tor

d'Aneu   Arròs

Vall de Cardós   Vall Ferrera   Andorra la Vella

Espot   Ribera   Alins

de Cardós

THE COUSERANS,
THE COMMINGES AND
MONTCALM/ESTATS

Llavorsí

La Pobla de Segur ▽   La Seu d'Urgell ▽

The helpful **tourist office** by the lower cathedral (May–Oct Mon–Sat 10am–noon & 2–6pm, Sun 2–6pm; Oct–May Sat & Sun 2–6pm; ☎05.61.96.77.77) can direct bona fide religious pilgrims to a **hostel**; Saint-Lizier was and is a minor stop on the Santiago de Compostela route. On rue des Nobles a **cultural centre** hosts expositions and musical events, while the lower cathedral with its excellent acoustics is also used as a performance centre during the summer **music festival** (information on ☎05.61.66.67.89), which runs from early to mid-August.

East of Saint-Girons: Mas d'Azil

Public transport to the fabulous **Mas d'Azil cave** is poor, except from Toulouse which offers a direct bus service; the four daily buses between Foix and Saint-Girons along the D117 leave you with a fair walk or hitch for the final distance. Alternatively, you could either sign up for a group **tour**, or **rent a bike** in either Foix or Saint-Girons, the latter linked to the cave by a 25-kilometre direct road, the D119. The closest bus stop on the D117 is Ségalas, from where it's a twelve-kilometre up-and-down walk along the pretty D15, past the ruined hilltop château of Saint Barthélémy.

The cave

As you approach the Mas d'Azil cave along the Arize, the river – and the modern D119 road – suddenly disappear together through an awesome 65-metre-high opening and into the half-kilometre cavern it has carved over the millennia. The **caves** on the right bank (June–Sept daily 10am–noon & 2–6pm; April & May Mon–Sat 2–6pm, Sun 10am–noon & 2–6pm; Oct & Nov Sun 2–6pm; rest of the year by appointment, ☎05.61.69.97.22; 30F) can only be seen on a 45-minute guided tour, which shows you the various finds from 30,000 to 8000 BC, taking in the **Salle Mandment** – with its mammoth and bear bones – and the **Salle du Temple**, used as a Christian chapel in the third century and as a sanctuary for Cathars and Protestants in more recent times.

Exhibited in glass cases on site, the **prehistoric finds** include needles, antler harpoons and other tools, engraved bones and decorated stones; also on display is a reproduction of a superb sculpted head of a neighing horse. Edouard Piette, who discovered these pieces in 1887, went on to play a major role in the controversy over the Altamira caves in Spain, which were opened up two years after Mas d'Azil. Many establishment prehistorians dismissed Altamira as a forgery, on account of the sophistication of its paintings; Piette, with his knowledge of the artistry of these specimens, argued successfully for Altamira's authenticity.

The village and museum

In the centre of the village of **MAS D'AZIL**, 1km beyond the caves, the **Musée de la Préhistoire** (daily: mid-June to Sept 10am–1pm & 2–7pm; rest of year 2–6pm; 20F) has more engravings and tools, including the so-called *faon aux oiseaux* (fawn with birds), a carved antler possibly used as a spear-thrower.

The village itself began life in the late thirteenth century as a **bastide**, one of those fortified settlements, all built to a similar grid plan, which were deliberately scattered across southwestern France in the period when Paris first began consolidating its power. Inevitably some of these strongholds went over to the Cathar – and later Huguenot – cause; Mas d'Azil in particular successfully resisted a five-week siege by a fourteen-thousand-strong Catholic army in 1625.

If you were thinking of making a night of it – and Mas d'Azil village isn't bad, if a little slow – there are two **hotels** here, the basic *Commenge* (☎05.61.69.90.29; ③) and the two-star *Gardel* (☎05.61.69.90.05; ③) on the main square, the latter with a decent restaurant. Another popular **eating** option, out of the centre in St-Ferréol district, is *Le Jardin de Cadettou* (closed Mon all day, Wed & Sun evening, Sat lunchtime), specializing in various *confits* (roasts). There's also the riverside *Camping Castagnès* (☎05.61.69.79.70; mid-June to mid-Sept), 1.5km from the centre on the road towards Pamiers.

South of Saint-Girons: the "Empty Quarter"

Every day except Sunday there are several buses **south from Saint-Girons** into the so-called "**empty quarter**", between the town and the Spanish frontier: two going southeast to Seix, Couflens and Aulus-les-Bains (daily during the ski season), and one or two southwest to Castillon-en-Couserans and Sentein. These routes can be used as entry and exit modes for traverses along the **GR10**, which passes through Aulus, Couflens, Seix and Eylie, south of Sentein, the latter two villages also close to the **Tour du Biros**. This skims the flanks of **Mont Valier**, a much-loved target of climbers, served by both the GR10 and the HRP, as well as a staffed refuge. Between Seix and Aulus, you can detour south at Trein d'Ustou to take in the **Cirque de Cagateille**, second largest in the range after the Cirque de Gavarnie (see p.327), but with a fraction of the crowds. All of these places, if a bit depressed and depopulated, have tourist facilities and some monumental interest in the form of ancient churches or rickety houses. About a quarter of the houses are for sale at any given moment, though demand from *Toulousains* has ensured that properties aren't particularly cheap any longer.

Seix and Oust

The county town of the lower Salat valley, **SEIX** appears as a congenial jumble of old, galleried houses strewn by the river, culminating in a vine-draped fifteenth-century castle, now closed up and decrepit. The seventeenth-century riverside church possesses a particularly elaborate *clocher-mur*, illuminated by night, while the old market hall a few paces north sees lively use on the first and third Thursdays of the month. Amongst the shops, cafés and bakeries on the west bank are two retailers for hiking maps and outdoor gear. This is also the region's main **canoeing and kayaking** centre, with Label Bleu, 2km south upriver at Base de Moulin (☎05.61.66.89.31), the principal operator.

There's a **tourist office** in a small booth on the Place Champ de Mars on the east bank (summer daily 9am–1pm & 3–7pm; ☎05.61.96.52), which sells hiking guides and maps, and keeps transportation timetables to hand; buses to and from Saint-Girons stop virtually adjacent. Of the two **hotels**, also on this side of the river, the *Mont-Valier* on the Ustou road (☎05.61.66.83.68; ③) has some river-view rooms but its restaurant isn't up to much; the *Auberge du Haut-Salat* around the corner at Place de l'Alée (☎05.61.66.88.03; ③) is a far better bet for **eating**, with gourmet menus starting at under 100F – the 125F one will pretty much give you the run of the à la carte list.

If necessary, **OUST**, 2km north back towards Saint-Girons, can also serve as a base, with much the best **hotel** this side of Aulus, in the same family for five generations: *Hostellerie de la Poste* (☎05.61.66.86.33; ③; closed Oct–April), with a pool garden and a well-regarded restaurant. However the village itself, despite its position at the junction of roads and the rivers Salat and Garbet, is dead compared to Seix, and turns its back on the Garbet bounding it to the north. Two local **campsites**, however, do take advantage of the riverbanks: *Les Quatre Saisons* (June–Sept), on the D32 towards Aulus, and *La Côte* (mid-May to Sept) between Oust and Seix.

The Vallée de Bethmale

Seix is also the easterly point of enty – via the D17 over the Col de la Core, or the GR10 – to the **Vallée de Bethmale**, celebrated by folklorists in the past for its vivid, almost Balkan female costumes, and gold-nailed wooden *sabots* (clogs) for both sexes. These have long vanished except for their appearance on a few feast days, like that on August 15; what remains is an exceptionally beautiful valley, even by Pyrenean standards, and exceptional depopulation even for the Couserans norm. On the heights there's little specifically to see other than an extraordinary number of abandoned *granges* or **barns**, traditionally used to store hay but increasingly restored as summer quarters by lowlanders. A little west of the Col de la Core, on both D17 and GR10, the tranquil, green **Lac de Bethmale**, ringed by beech trees, is a popular picnic or fishing spot.

Down in the valley bottom, which drains from the *col* northwest towards Bordes-sur-Lez in the Vallée du Biros (see over), huddle half a dozen half-empty hamlets. Of the two highest, both graced by homogeneous eighteenth-century architecture, **AYET** offers a friendly, twelve-bunk *gîte d'étape* (☎05.61.96.81.71; open all year; ①), where places must be reserved in summer. If you're vehicle-less, you can also at this point adopt a marked, non-GR trail up to the lake. Just downhill, **ARET** has the last **sabot-making workshop** in the valley, open all year for purchases. The curvy-pointed clogs were traditionally exchanged as tokens of betrothal between the newly engaged.

Excursion to the Étang d'Ayès

The Lac de Bethmale marks the start of the most popular excursion from the valley, to the **Étang d'Ayès**, an ideal sampler of the mountains hereabouts if you're not committed to full-pack treks. If you're without a car, than you'll have to hike the whole distance along the GR10 (2hr 30min one way). With a car, though, you can cut out much of the climb by driving fifteen minutes along the *piste forestière* marked "Mont Ner/Noir" up to a barred gate and a car park. Here a yellow-waymarked path – the old GR10, prior to re-routing – toils up to the Col d'Auédole and junction with the new GR10 within forty minutes. Turn right (southeast), continuing another twenty minutes along the GR10 to reach the sizeable glacial tarn, just above treeline at 1694m, hemmed in by crags on the south but marvellously open to the north. With such ease of access, Étang d'Ayès is understandably a popular picnic and camping spot, and just about swimmable on a hot day. The return route is the same, as is the elapsed time, owing to a killer grade just above the parking area.

The upper Salat

Upstream and south from Seix, the D3 follows the Salat almost to its source, passing en route a few hamlets which make tranquil bases and start-points for forays along the GR10 or HRP. **PONT DE LA TAULE**, where the D8 veers off up the Vallée d'Ustou (see opposite) 4km south of Seix, is the last spot on the Salat with public transport, and can offer the welcoming **hotel-restaurant** *Auberge des Deux Rivières* (☎ & fax 05.61.66.83.57; closed Nov), where 115F spent at their river-terrace restaurant will net you regional treats. Of the rooms, the modern under-loft en-suite units (③) are far preferable to the creaky first-floor ones (②).

COUFLENS, 5km up the still-paved but drastically narrowed D3, is a deceptively substantial place lining the river, hemmed in by shaggy hillsides. There's no longer a shop here, and all tourist facilities for this halt on the GR10 are slightly out of town: *Camping Les Bouriès* 1.5km west, or the recommendable **gîte d'étape** (☎05.61.66.95.45; ①) 1km east at Rouze, which doubles as a cheese farm run by the Assémet family.

The highest village and end of the line for most traffic, another 5km on, **SALAU** proves even bigger, with more amenities – including an all-important shop – on the single high street. Here the **hotel-restaurant** *Auberge des Myrtilles* (☎05.61.66.82.58; ②; closed Nov, restaurant closed Tues) is an utter bargain, most of the rooms having a shower; they also operate a riverside café between meal hours. If they're full or your finances won't stretch even that far, there's the *Centre de Montagne* (☎05.61.66.83.02; ①), a municipally run *gîte* a few paces downhill. The HRP skims just above the village, heading west for the ruined frontier hospice at **Port de Salau**, site of a big solidarity festival (*La Pujada*) between Occitans and Catalans on the first Sunday in August.

The Vallée d'Ustou and the Cirque de Cagateille

From Pont de la Taule, the D8 heads southeast up the sunnier and more generously proportioned **Vallé d'Ustou**, gateway to the Cirque de Cagateille. Much the biggest places en route are Trein d'Ustou (see p.231), and **SAINT-LIZIER D'USTOU**, 1km south astride the GR10, served by a *Camping Municipal*, with sixty places and a pool.

Some 7.5km above Trein d'Ustou, the road ends above the last farms, at a 1000-metre-high car park and trailheads for the **Étang d'Alet** (3hr one-way, 1900m) and the underrated, forest-girt **Cirque de Cagateille** (40min to its base at 1120m). The Cagateille path continues to lobular **Étang de la Hillette** (2hr 45min, 1800m), tucked away into a hanging glacial valley above the cirque; a proposed staffed refuge will probably be built here in coming years. Rather than crossing the frontier to Certescans at the 2416-metre **Port de Couillac**, you can make a satisfying circuit by continuing west to Alet and thence down to the car park, all on locally marked and maintained paths. It's a seven- to eight-hour walking day, harder and thus less frequented than the nearby Cascade d'Ars loop (see p.278). If you've arrived without the proper maps, a placard at the car park details all walking possibilities.

THE BEAR TRAINERS

The villages of Oust, Ercé and Aulus-les-Bains were formerly renowned for their bear-trainers who, driven by poverty, toured the lowlands with their performing beasts. In the 1950s the writer Nina Epton interviewed Jean Doumenc, last of the Pyrenean bear-trainers: " 'The best performing bears . . . came from Hungary. We used to go down to the port of Marseilles and buy them there. Our bears could never stand up so straight as they could. They were inclined to be bow-legged and clumsy-looking.'

When I asked Monsieur Doumenc about the coloured postcards in the bazaar, he chuckled. 'I guess he must have made a packet, that fellow who photographed us in 1899 – yes, that's a photograph of me and my father with the last two bears we ever raised from around these parts. One of them died when it was three years old, but the other one, its twin, lived to a ripe old age. It was my father's last and favourite pet. He took great pains over its training and when it was fully grown they travelled together through every valley in the Pyrenees. In fact, they were never really happy unless they were on the road. The bear followed my father like a dog. But the old man was getting old and his rheumatism was bad. It didn't help, either, to have to sleep out under the stars. . . . Well, one day, we got a telegram at home, sent by a doctor in Pau . . . and the telegram read – "OLD MAN ILL STOP COME AND FETCH BEAST." That meant that I had to go to Pau to collect the bear and then walk all the way back again to Oust with it, while my father stayed in hospital at Pau. It looked so fierce, that bear, nobody would go near it when Father wasn't about. That was my father's last trip and my last trek over the mountains with a bear!' "

Aulus-les-Bains

The spa of **AULUS-LES-BAINS**, thirty minutes by bus southeast of Seix along the Vallée d'Ustou and over the Col de Latrape, has one of the most stunning locations in the Pyrenees, near the head of the narrow Vallée de Garbet. (If you're driving or cycling, it's far easier to arrive along the D32 threading the latter valley, via Ercé.) Dense forests and dramatic peaks rise steeply on either side, while at the end of the valley, rock walls channel water into numerous lakes and, a little to the west, into the River Ars with its waterfalls.

Aulus is a sleepy, faded place with little to do other than enjoy the scenery – though new apartments dwarfing the original houses suggest that someone has big plans. This being a spa town, **hotels** tend to be a little pricey; the least expensive place is the helpful *gîte d'étape La Presbytère* (☎05.61.96.02.21; 15 places; open all year; ①), 150m downhill from the church. Otherwise, try the *Hôtel de France* (☎05.61.96.00.90, fax ☎05.61 96 03 29; ③; closed mid-Oct to mid-Dec) at the downstream end of the main street passing the *termal*, with in-room showers for the price. The **restaurant** here is a classic example of a dying breed, with its set *menu de jour* for well under 100F (no à la carte, wine extra), served amidst wooden pillars, live dogs and a stuffed bestiary; after four hearty courses, they'll have to wheel you out in a barrow. The more comfortable, antique-furnished *Hôtel La Terrasse* (☎05.61.96.00.98; ④; closed Oct–May), just upstream from the baths, has a correspondingly fancier gourmet restaurant, with seating on the river-view terrace. If you want to feel that you're staying in a mountain village rather than a spa, then the two-star *Hotel Les Oussaillès* on the main shopping street (☎05.61.96.03.68, fax 05.61.96.03.70; ④) is the place, its rooms with TV, phones and full plumbing. The downstairs restaurant, less generous in terms of portion size but perhaps more elegant than the other hotels, is devoted equally to *ariègoise* specialities and vegetarian plates. **Camping** is at *Le Couledous* (☎61.96.02.26; open all year), 500m west between the road to Ercé and the river.

If you'd like to see some of the surrounding area, the **tourist office** (daily: July & Aug 10am–1pm & 2–7pm; Sept–June 10am–noon & 2–6pm; ☎05.61.96.01.79) in allées des Thermes rents out bikes between June and September, and can also provide information on canoeing, *parapente* or horse-riding – the latter offered, too, by the Centre Équestre Centaurus (☎05.61.96.02.02) on the river. The ornate glass-and-wood, centrally placed **thermal baths** themselves are just the thing to banish trekkers' aches and pains (mid-May to mid-Oct Mon–Sat 8.30am–noon & 3–7pm, Sun 9am–noon & 3–7pm). At busy times, only the afternoon hours may be available for clientele who aren't taking a cure; in an effort to update its image, the spa offers a wide variety of fitness, yoga and massage programmes.

The Cascade d'Ars and Étang de Guzet

South of Aulus-les-Bains, the famous Cascade d'Ars and the Étang de Guzet are favourite walking destinations, and can easily be combined for a five-hour loop. The anticlockwise circuit described makes getting lost much less likely. Start at the road curve above town, where a sign indicates a non-GR trail for Plan de Souliou and the Étang de Guzet. It's a one-hour climb up through beeches to the junction with the GR10, just past the bracken-covered *plan*, a clearing affording great views of the ridges surrounding Aulus. You've another half-hour, with firs now on a par with the beeches, to the **Étang de Guzet** at 1425m, an idyllic, clear pool just west of and below the GR10 · via clear side trails. Most of the climb is over now, as the trail proceeds another hour, as a corniche route, along the hillside to the meadow and bridge – the **Passerelle d'Ars** (1485m) just above the falls. Over the next half an hour the path curls around and under the famous **Cascade d'Ars**, with the best views just before the trail disappears into the forest again. The cascades plunge over 110m in three stages, the top one long and slender; during the spring melt there is reportedly just a single, long drop. From the vicinity of the falls it's another ninety minutes back to Aulus, following the river, mostly on the left bank, mostly on path, which can get muddy near the bottom of the grade. Cross the **Pont de la Mouline** over the Garbet, turn left, then left again when you meet the asphalt, and you're at the edge of town.

Guzet-Neige

It's worth the half-hour wintertime bus journey from Aulus-les-Bains to **GUZET-NEIGE** just for the view. Located on a high shoulder 800m above Aulus, it looks down on the town, northwest along the River Garbet and south over the frontier peaks. The ski-season bus climbs first into the **Col de Latrape** – at 1111m almost always too low for the single drag-lift to operate – then to the lift station at 1340m, and finally up to the resort itself.

Unfortunately the development – a collection of shed-like chalets plus a couple of large hotels – isn't up to the setting. The top lift is only 2061m, hence the 45 snow-cannons. As with so many other Pyrenean resorts, don't book a two-week holiday in advance, but if you're in the area and the snow is good, you'll have an enjoyable few days. The chalets can be reserved by calling ☎05.61.02.30.80.

Mont Valier and around

Pyramidal **Mont Valier** (2838m), the most famous mountain of the Couserans, was long mistaken for the highest peak in the Pyrenees; it's named after a fifth-century bishop of the Couserans, Valerius, who – crucifix in hand – supposedly made the first recorded ascent. Effectively the beacon and mascot of the valleys that it protects, it conceals no fewer than five lakes in its folds and even a tiny glacier on the north face.

Approaches: Castillon and Audreissen

Mont Valier is accessible along both the GR10 and the HRP, the former skirting it to the east, north and west, the latter skimming along its south flank. If you're not following either of these, take a bus from Saint-Girons towards Sentein, along the Vallée du Biros, drained by the River Lez. Some 12km along you'll pass through the old village of **CASTILLON-EN-COUSERANS**, its houses topped by the fortified chapel which is all that Cardinal Richelieu left standing of the château. Castillon is the location of the regional **tourist office** (summer Mon–Sat 9.30am–12.30pm & 2.30–6.30pm, Sun 9.30am–12.30pm; ☎05.61.96.72.64), housed in the disused train station, and hosts a Tuesday street market. Best of a half-dozen **places to eat** is *Le Cléquérec* at the north end of the through road, with its pricier gourmet menu offering kidneys and frog legs; service is very laid-back, and it functions as a creperie between meal hours.

All told, however, it's best to halt 1km north at **AUDRESSEIN**, which boasts the engaging fifteenth-century **church of Notre-Dame de Tramesaygues**, built at the confluence of the Lez and the Bourgane and venue for a lively September 8 festival. The village also offers an excellent place to **stay and eat**: *L'Auberge d'Audressein* (☎05.61.96.11.80; ③), a former forge house at the crossroads. You'll need fluent French to translate the restaurant menu, but rest assured it's all delicious – reputedly the best in the Couserans – and well priced at 115F and 149F for the *menus*. Rooms are plain but adequate, almost all with shower and sink, plus views of either the mountains or the river.

The Refuge des Estagnous

Most passengers will let the bus take them another 4km from Castillon to the **Riberot valley** turning, on the left. There's a good chance of a lift along the 8km of tarmac up the Riberot to the parking area and junction with the GR10 at **Pla de la Lau** (927m). From here it's four hours' hiking, past the famous **Cascade de Nerech** about halfway along, to the **Refuge des Estagnous** (2240m; 50 places; staffed continually July to mid-Sept, weather permitting June & Oct; part always open; ☎05.61.96.76.22; ①).

After the exertion of getting to Estagnous, the summit is just a couple of hours away next morning, so you can leave most of your gear at the refuge; walk southeast on the clear path to **Col du Faustin** (2643m) and then northeast on the path to the **summit**. The views facing south are terrific – Montcalm and Estats on your left, the Vall d'Aran and Aigües Tortes in the middle, the Maladeta massif to your right. If you're tempted by what you see, you can trek across the border to the headwaters of the Noguera Pallaresa.

The other standard day-walks from the refuge are to the lakes **Etang Rond** and **Etang Long**, just southwest of Mont Valier, or north over the Col de Pécouch on the shoulder of Valier to follow the longer *Circuit de Trois Lacs*, the lakes in question being **Cruzou**, **Arouech** and **Milouga**. A link trail from the circuit heads north to the GR10, an interesting variant for returning to the car park.

The Tour du Biros

The popular **Tour du Biros** will occupy between four and five days and is marked on the IGN Randonnées Pyrénéennes 1:50,000 "Couserans – Cap d'Aran" map.

From the *Estagnous* refuge you can pick up the *Tour* by redescending towards Pla de la Lau in the Riberot valley, and adopting the GR10 going west. After three hours' steep climbing followed by an hour's equally severe descent into the Besset forest, you're on the *Tour*, waymarked in red-and-yellow stripes and for a time accompanying the GR10. There's a well-sited twenty-bunk *gîte d'étape* (☎05.61.96.14.00; ①) at the former mining hamlet of **EYLIE**, another four to five hours ahead, at the very top of the Vallée de Biros. If you've reached Eylie by car, you'll finally feel you're in the mountains, with barns and rivulets clinging to the steep slopes all around. As a major trailhead, it has ample signposting to various points of hiking interest.

Next day the joint *Tour*/GR10 climbs past the old lead and zinc mines at Bentaillou, and close by the caves of Gouffre Martel and Cigalère, the latter discovered by Norbert Casteret (see feature opposite). Four hours from Eylie you reach **Étang d'Araing**, with the **Pic de Crabère** (2629m) reflected in its waters and the *Refuge de l'Étang d'Araing* beside it (1950m; 58 places; staffed continuously mid-June to mid-Sept, weekends only May to mid-June & mid-Sept to Oct; part always open; ☎05.61.96.73.73; ①). The remainder of the day can be spent scaling Crabère, a three-hour round-trip affair.

The *Tour* now diverges from the GR10, swinging back northeast on a relatively easy half-day through beech forests to the abandoned hamlet of **LE PLAYRAS**, where there is, however, a *gîte d'étape* (☎05.61.96.77.14; ①). You can carry on from there, along the north flank of the valley, to complete a fairly long walking day at **BONAC** on the valley floor. Here, the *Relais Montagnard de Bonac*, next to the church, serves as a *gîte d'étape* (☎05.61.66.75.57; ①), offering good meals, often including the local trout.

The main village in these parts, and end of the bus line from Saint-Girons, lies 2km west of Bonac at **SENTEIN**, which features on its central square a curious fortified fifteenth-century church with three towers (originally there were four) and some surviving interior frescoes. It also has an all-important shop, a **tourist office** (summer Mon–Sat 10am–noon & 3–7pm, Sun 11am–1pm & 5–7pm; ☎05.61.96.10.90), a **campsite** (*La Grange*) and the rather unprepossesing modern **hotel**, *Le Crabère* (☎05.61.96.70.92; ③), on the through road.

The final, less frequented leg of the *Tour* heads south from Bonac along the east flank of the Orle valley to meet the GR10 again at Besset (unstaffed refuge sleeping five) within six hours. If you want to follow the GR10 west from the Étang d'Araing, it's a six-hour sector to **FOS**, a rather moribund village on the main road between Viella (in Spain) and Saint-Béat. There's a *gîte d'étape* here, *Le Moulin* (☎05.61.79.44.51; ①), and a shop, but no public transportation in any direction.

Along the Garonne: into the Comminges

The **Comminges** is an ancient feudal county which – never possessing the prestige or power of neighbouring Foix or Bigorre – was absorbed into a unifying France as early as 1454. Haute-Garonne, the modern successor *département* that approximates the traditional boundaries, is drained by the **Garonne** and its tributary the Pique. The quickest way from the Couserans into the valley of the Garonne is the bus ride (several daily) from Saint-Girons to **Boussens**, from where more than a dozen daily trains run fifteen minutes west along the river to **Saint-Gaudens**, the first town of any size. This is mostly of interest as the functional transport hub for visiting the area's great, adjacent attractions, **Saint-Bertrand-de-Comminges** and the **Grotte de Gargas**.

Saint-Gaudens to Valcabrère

Although capital of the Comminges, **SAINT-GAUDENS** is essentially a way-station rather than a place to linger, its commercial and industrial character epitomized by a lively Thursday market – and a cellulose plant, spewing thick yellowish smoke. However, the **Musée du Comminges** (Mon–Sat 9am–noon & 2–6pm), in the place Mas-St-Pierre by the church, could merit a call for its prehistoric finds, Gallo-Roman ceramics and local history display. Also on this square is one of the town's most pleasant **hotels**, the *Esplanade* (☎05.61.89.15.90; ④); nearly as central, and of similar calibre,

---

NORBERT CASTERET

Norbert Casteret (1897–1987), who lived 4km outside Saint-Gaudens, was almost unique in that he was a professional speleologist, earning his living from his books and from survey work for hydroelectric companies. His first big coup came in 1922 with the penetration of **Montespan**, a cave on the south bank of the Garonne halfway between Saint-Gaudens and Salies. Casteret's account captures the moments of discovery:

"We entered a gallery which I had neglected to explore on the former occasion, and stopped in amazement before the statue of a bear modelled in clay. Farther on lay more of these figures: two felines walking in file, and some horses. Next day we came upon some curious tracks; the cave had undoubtedly been used as a shelter or hiding-place by prehistoric people. We were the first men to enter that chamber since the cave-folk dwelt there several thousand years ago. On the muddy floor there were imprints of their naked feet, and also some stone weapons. The walls had been ornamented with the aid of sharpened flints, and we gazed in wonder upon the fauna of far distant ages: mammoth, reindeer, horses, bison, chamois . . .The clay figures of Montespan . . . date from the beginning of the Magdalenian era, say about 20,000 years ago, and are therefore the oldest known statues in the world."

In 1926, with his wife Elisabeth, Casteret discovered the **Grotte Casteret** on Mont Perdu/Monte Perdido, the highest known ice cave in the world. Four years later came the discovery of animal engravings at Labastide, west of Saint-Gaudens in the Baronnies. The following year Castaret's dye test – described on p.238 – proved that the Garonne sprang in part from the Aneto glacier, and he also explored the Grotte de la Cigalère, south of Saint-Gaudens. In 1952, as part of a team plumbing the depths of Gouffre Pierre Saint-Martin in the western Pyrenees, Casteret broke his own cavern-descent mark set two decades previously, at the 303-metre-deep Gouffre Martel near Cigalère. This record of cave exploration in the Pyrenees has no equal, and it's unlikely that anyone will ever surpass his tally of "firsts" in these mountains.

Note: Montespan, Labastide, Cigalère and Pierre Saint-Martin are accessible only to experienced speleologists. For an account of the Grotte Casteret, see p.329.

is the two-star *Pedussaut*, 9 av de Boulogne (☎05.61.89.15.70; ④). The **tourist office** is at 2 rue Thiers (☎05.61.94.77.61). A meal stop in Saint-Gaudens seems more likely than an overnight, in which case either the **restaurant** attached to the *Pedussaut*, or the meat-only *Restaurant de l'Abattoir*, on bd Leconte-de-Lisle, beyond the *gare* opposite the slaughterhouse, can oblige.

Valcabrère

En route to Luchon, you pass the village of **VALCABRÈRE**, with its rough stone barns and open lofts for hay-drying; to get there without your own transport, take the train from Saint-Gaudens to Montréjeau, transfer to the SNCF bus service (usually 4 daily) headed south for Luchon and get off after 6km at Labroquère, 500m northeast of Valcabrère, just before the road crosses the Garonne. Standing among cypresses to the south of Valcabrère, you'll find the jewel-box-like eleventh-century Romanesque church of **Saint-Just** (July–Sept daily 9am–7pm; March–June & Oct–Dec Sat & Sun 2–6pm; 10F). Saint-Just was built largely of stone from the Roman city of Lugdunum Conventarum (see below), founded here by Pompey in 72 BC. Once through the elegantly sculpted north portal, there's ample evidence of recycled masonry: marble in the altar floor, an inscription dated 347 AD on the wall of the nave and several round columns augmenting the six massive stone piers upholding the nave. Between the altar and the triple apse ending in a semicircular pattern of ten recessed arches looms a carved Gothic free-standing shrine, with a sarcophagus which presumably once contained the saint's relics. Not surprisingly given the soaring vaulted ceiling, the acoustics are splendid, and Saint-Just is a major music venue for the summer *Festival du Comminges*.

A little further on, protruding above the grass on each side of the crossroads, are the excavated foundations of **Lugdunum Conventarum** (currently closed for excavations), once a town of sixty thousand and thus one of the most important in Roman Aquitaine. According to the Jewish historian Josephus, Herod Antipas – who ordered the execution of John the Baptist and to whom Pontius Pilate sent Christ – was exiled here with his wife Herodias around 39 AD. The town, at its height during the first and second centuries AD, persisted well into the Christian era despite destructive raids by Vandals and Burgundians in the fifth and sixth centuries respectively.

Elaborating on the Roman theme, Valcabrère boasts a posh **restaurant**, *Le Lugdunum* (closed Tues in off-season), where for 165F and up you can sample recipes purported to be those of the very Caesars themselves.

Saint-Bertrand-de-Comminges

This part of the French Pyrenees boasts few monuments, but at **SAINT-BERTRAND-DE-COMMINGES** stands one of the finest in the range – a magnificent cathedral reflecting three distinct eras of architecture. To reach this village from Saint-Gaudens without your own transport, follow the directions for Valcabrère outlined above as far as Labroquère, then take the turning west for Saint-Bertrand; it's then a pleasant half-hour walk between fields of grain and hay, with the poplar-lined river on your right and the grey, fortress-like cathedral of Saint-Bertrand commanding the plain from the knoll ahead. Cars are no longer allowed in the village itself between 10am and 7pm, but a *navette* (minibus shuttle) operates from the parking area below, sparing you all of a ten-minute walk up.

The Roman city stretched up the hill to where Saint-Bertrand now stands. The lower part was destroyed by the Vandals in 409 AD, and the more defensible walled upper part – where a Christian church had meanwhile been built – was wrecked in 585 by

King Gontran of Burgundy. For five centuries the site lay deserted, until the Gascon aristocrat Bertrand de l'Isle – made bishop of Comminges in 1073 and canonized in 1218 – began to rebuild.

The village and cathedral

The handsome walled and gated village of Saint-Bertrand-de-Comminges, with many of its half-timbered-and-brick houses dating from the fifteenth and sixteenth centuries, clusters tightly around the **Cathedral** (April–Sept daily 9am–noon & 2–7pm; Oct –March Mon–Sat 9am–noon & 2–6pm, Sun 9–10.30am & 2–6pm; admission to cloister and choir 17F). Dedicated not to St Bertrand as one might expect, but to the Virgin Mary, its white-veined facade and ponderous buttressing are vaguely menacing, but a Romanesque **cloister** with engagingly carved capitals looks south towards the foothills, while the aisleless **interior** forms a showcase of decorative art from three great periods. Bertrand's Romanesque church was enlarged during the late thirteenth century in the Gothic style by the future Clement V (first of the Avignon popes), and the interior was finally remodelled in the Renaissance style by another bishop, Jean de Mauléon, in the sixteenth century. In the ambulatory, a fifteenth-century shrine depicts scenes from Bertrand's life, with the church and village visible in the background of the top right panel; the saint's marble tomb, still venerated by pilgrims, is here too. The small area reserved for the laity at the west end has a richly carved oak organ, a pulpit and a spiral stair, but the cathedral's real treasure is the central **choir**, built by *Toulousain* journeymen and installed over the course of a decade or so after 1523.

The elaborately carved choir **stalls** – 66 in all – are a feast of virtuosity, mingling piety, irony and malicious satire, each one the work of a different journeyman. In the misericords and partitions separating them, the ingenuity and humour of their creators is best seen; each of the gangways dividing the sections of misericords has a representation of a cardinal sin on top of the end partition. By the middle gangway on the south side, for example, Envy is represented by two monks, faces contorted with hate, fighting over the abbot's baton of office, pushing against each other foot to foot in a furious tug-of-war. The armrest on the left of the rood-screen entrance depicts the abbot birching a monk, while the bishop's throne has a particularly lovely back panel in marquetry depicting St Bertrand and St John.

Practicalities

Across the small square in front of the cathedral, the *Hôtel du Comminges* (☎05.61.88.31.43, fax 05.61.94.98.22; ③; closed Dec, Jan and weekdays Nov–March) makes for a fine, old-fashioned overnight and has a reasonable **restaurant** (April–Sept). Otherwise there's more updated *Hôtel L'Oppidum* (☎05.61.88.33.50; ④; closed late Nov–late Jan except for Christmas), north of (behind) the cathedral, which also has a restaurant. The nearest **campsite** – shady, well laid out and with a few chalets to rent – is *Es Pibous* (☎05.61.88.31.42; March–Sept), north of the road to Saint-Just, with *La Vieille Auberge* across the road serving good, if basic **meals**. In July and August the cathedral and Saint-Just in Valcabrère host the musical **Festival du Comminges** (information from the festival office on the cathedral square: daily 10.30am–12.30pm & 3–7pm; or phone ☎05.61.88.32.00 in summer, ☎05.61.95.81.25 the rest of the year).

Grotte de Gargas

Easily accessible from Saint-Bertrand, the **Grotte de Gargas** (guided tours only; daily: July & Aug 10–11.30am & 2–6pm; Easter–June & Sept to mid-Oct 2.30–5pm; mid-Oct to

Easter 2.30–4pm; 25F; ☎05.62.39.72.07) merits a visit for its hand prints, a form of decoration that makes the presence of their prehistoric creators seem almost immediate.

If you're walking, from the mound of Saint-Bertrand drop down onto the road again, turn left (northwestwards) and keep going for another 6km – the view back to the cathedral before the last concealing bend is its finest angle; with so much tourist traffic there's an excellent chance of a lift. You can also walk direct from the station at Montréjeau, heading about 4km southwest via Mazères de Neste.

Although it also has engravings and finger tracings of mammoths, horses, bison and deer, what makes the Gargas cave special are its **hand outlines**, many of them with apparently half-amputated fingers. Castillo in Spanish Cantabria is the only other place where hand images have been found in large numbers, and the Castillo cavern has only fifty of them, as against 231 here – though only a fraction are available for viewing.

How you respond to the hands depends on whether or not you regard them as genuine outlines – perhaps created by spraying red and black pigment from a reed – or as free drawings. If they are true outlines, then the hands that were placed on the cave walls some 20,000 to 25,000 years ago were probably either ritually mutilated, or destroyed by leprosy or frostbite. But another theory has a persuasive adherent in the French prehistorian André Leroi-Gourhan: he has proposed that the hands represent a code such as that used today by South African Bushmen for silent communication when hunting.

The upper Comminges

Upstream from Valcabrère and Saint-Bertrand extends the upper portion of the Comminges. **Bagnères-de-Luchon** – universally referred to as **Luchon** for short – is a versatile resort at the end of all public transport lines, a staging post for numerous classic walking itineraries and less rewarding ski runs. There's also a notable collection of Romanesque churches in the vicinity.

Bagnères-de-Luchon

Along with Gavarnie, the spa resort of **BAGNÈRES-DE-LUCHON** – 13km south of Marignac on the River Pique – has long been one of the lodestars of Pyrenean exploration. Modern Luchon re-entered history during the eighteenth century, when Jacques Barrau and Baron Antoine d'Étigny revived the thermal baths built by the Roman emperor Tiberius. Showing a flair for advertising well ahead of their time, they persuaded Louis Richelieu, governor of Gascony in 1755 and great-nephew of Cardinal Richelieu, to give the *thermes* his endorsement – and the fashionable set from Paris duly descended for the waters and the salons. After the peak-bagging expeditions of Ramond de Carbonnières in the late eighteenth and early nineteenth century, Luchon became a base of choice for serious climbers and also attracted numerous Romantic literati.

East of **allée d'Étigny**, the main thoroughfare, Luchon's glory days have left a huge neighbourhood of sumptuous villas, which go some way towards justifying the town's self-bestowed title as the "Queen of the Pyrenees". Yet if you venture west of the commercial district, the narrow lanes off the place Rouy with their vernacular houses suggest the mountain village this once was. Roughly halfway along the French side of the range, it's the largest and arguably most sophisticated Pyrenean resort, and much the most elegant place this side of Biarritz. There's little of the usual spa-town fustiness, and Luchon has successfully reinvented itself as a versatile resort, attracting all social classes and age groups. Because of the peculiar local topography, the valley here is one of the major French centres for *parapente* and light aviation. At the end of the day everyone gathers at the boisterous pavement cafés under the linden trees along allée d'Étigny, looking up from newspapers, drinks and heated debate to watch airplanes and *parapentes* floating high in the still of sundown.

The Town

Adjacent to the tourist office at 18 allée d'Étigny, Luchon's dusty **museum** (Mon–Sat 9am–noon & 2–6pm, group tour only) has the air of a mad professor's personal collection: moth-eaten stuffed birds and animals in glass cases; faded and sometimes signed photographs of famous visitors like Victor Hugo, Bismarck or Marshal Foch; models of the Pyrenees and a room devoted to the pioneer climbers. Nineteenth-century statues add a few grace notes to the streets and squares of Luchon: there's a concentration of them in the **Parc de Quinconces** (around the *thermes*) and in the **Parc du Casino**, where Coutheilai's Rodinesque *Baiser à la Source* provides the town's most pleasing image.

The nineteenth-century **thermal baths** (dips for those who haven't been medically referred daily 4–8pm; 30F) are once again fashionable, augmented since 1973 by the **Vaporium**, a natural cave sauna.

Practicalities

From the **train station** on av de Toulouse (where **buses** also stop), the way south into town is across the River One and down av Maréchal-Foch, which leads into allée d'Étigny. The **tourist office**, at 18 allée d'Étigny (July & Aug daily 9am–7pm; Sept & Oct daily 9am–1pm & 2–7pm; mid-Dec to March daily 8.30am–7pm; rest of year Mon–Fri 9am–12.30pm & 2–6pm; ☎05.61.79.21.21), is adjacent to the premises of the Bureau des Guides – the people to see if you want to sign on for organized walks or climbs.

There's plenty of **accommodation** in Luchon, and you don't even have to leave the allée d'Étigny for it (though the best deal is in nearby Montauban, detailed below) – the *Bellevue* (☎05.61.79.01.65; ⑤) and *Central* (☎05.61.79.03.15; ③) are both obvious, if not especially economical choices. If it's too noisy here – the cafés at street level bustle until late – you can find better value in the quieter streets to either side; possibilities include *Hôtel des Deux Nations* at 5 rue Victor-Hugo (☎05.61.79.01.71; ③), with a good attached restaurant; the *Céleste*, 32 rue Lamartine (☎05.61.74.64.84; ③), with heating and off-street parking; and the one-stars, *Pension Hotel Le Chalet*, on pedestrianized rue Gambetta at no. 21 (☎05.61.79.04.54; ③), and *Des Neiges*, 27 rue Victor Hugo (☎05.61.79.02; ③), the latter particularly basic, though acceptable. If you're staying for a week or more, note that the tourist office maintains a noticeboard of apartments and rooms to rent.

There are ten **campsites** in the vicinity, including three adjacent ones on av de Vénasque, the continuation of cours de Quinconces. The least cramped, however, is *Camping La Lanette*, 1.5km east over the Pique (down rue Lamartine) near the village of **Montauban-de-Luchon**.

Montauban also boasts an outstanding lodging deal, above the church, in *Le Jardin des Cascades* (☎05.61.79.83.09; ③–④; closed mid-Oct to April), which has rooms with shared or en-suite bathrooms and is backed by a wild, hilly garden nurtured by the falls of the name (5F admission for non-customers). Moreover the creative gourmet food, valley views and service at its shaded terrace **restaurant** are remarkably good (around 210F per person; reservations mandatory). A similar distance south of Luchon on the D125, the slightly less expensive *L'Auberge de Castel-Vielh* (closed weekdays Nov–April) serves more countrified fare in another converted old house. Back in Luchon, *La Crémaillère* at 30 allée d'Étigny does excellent crepes and buckwheat-flour *galettes* that will do for a light lunch. *Le Clos du Silène* (supper only), 19 cours des Quinconces in a grand villa almost opposite the baths, is another good choice for a light but elegant meal, well priced at about 45F per plate or in various *formules* including a

---

CLIMBING FROM LUCHON IN THE NINETEENTH CENTURY

Charles Packe – barrister, amateur scientist and explorer in the great Victorian tradition – published his famous *Guide to the Pyrenees* in 1862. The book contains this summary of Luchon, his base when climbing Maladeta, and gives an evocative picture of the style of the times:

"Of horses and guides there is an ample supply at Luchon at reasonable charges. Tariffs are fixed at the bathing establishments and at the principal hotels, with the prices for the different courses and by the day. If the excursion is made on horseback, the guide is indispensable to look to the horses; but if the tourist is sufficiently hale and hearty to trust to his own feet, there is scarcely an excursion from Luchon, with the exception of the ascent of the Maladeta, requiring other guide than a good local map and compass . . .

Throughout the chain, and especially on the Spanish side, there is a great deficiency of hotel accommodation on the mountains, so that a sleeping bag is almost an indispensable part of his kit to anyone who would see and thoroughly enjoy the grander parts of the Pyrenees . . . More may be seen in the mountains in four or five days camping out than in three weeks of hotel life with an occasional excursion. Besides the bag, a tin saucepan with a lid, a frying pan and a few spoons ought to be taken. Fresh meat may be provided for two days' consumption; but a good supply of fat bacon stowed in tin boxes is the most useful form of animal food. It always contributes to the meal, whether eaten as rashers or used for frying fish or making soup. This, with bread and wine, tea, coffee, chocolate, sugar, salt and pepper is all that is absolutely necessary, though other little extras will, of course, be added. An extra short, two pairs of socks, towel, pair of espadrilles and perhaps a light overcoat is all that should be taken in the way of clothing. All the eatables should as far as possible be packed in tin boxes, as otherwise the contents . . . are often turned out in a most deplorable plight, especially after a wet night. Each man engaged as porter ought to carry 15 kilogrammes."

---

dessert. For heartier, emphatically non-vegetarian eating, *Le Pailhet* at 12 av du Maréchal-Foch towards the *gare* (closed Mon off-season), serves game, duck and regional offal specialities such as *pétéram* (sheep tripe) and *pistache* (a particularly rich *cassoulet*) in portions fit to fell an ox; count on 120F a head, with drink.

Local activities

Across the Pique, which flows through the heart of town, you'll find the **swimming pool** (daily July & Aug 11am–6pm) and **tennis courts**. The Centre Équestre (☎05.61.79.06.64) on the north side of the River One provide **horse-riding** possibilities, while **kayaks** can be rented at Base d'Antignac (☎05.61.79.19.20), 3km north at Antignac, which also gives lessons and organizes **rafting** expeditions. You can get **airborne** on either a biplane or a glider at Aéroclub de Luchon (☎05.61.79.19.64) or learn to parapente from certified instructors at either Odysée (☎05.61.79.89.89), in Moustajon 3km south of Luchon, or Soaring, 14 rue Sylvie (☎05.61.79.29.23). If you're not sure what you want to do, Virgule 7 at 4 place du Comminges, off av du Maréchal Foch, offers a bit of everything, including **mountain-bike rental**. For the utterly sedentary, the **télécabine** is the easy way up the 2666m to Superbagnères (see p.288), with some superb views en route (April daily 1.30–5pm; May, June & Sept to mid-Oct Sat & Sun 1.30–5pm; July & Aug daily 9.45am–12.15pm & 1.30–6pm; 38F return, 22F one-way).

Walks from Luchon

There's enough walking **around Luchon** to keep you occupied for an entire holiday, mostly amongst the frontier peaks and over the border in the Maladeta and Posets massifs. The tourist office sells a booklet of recommended short walks, which is fine as far as it goes – but since waymarking sometimes leaves a bit to be desired, a good IGN map is an essential supplementary purchase.

Southeast towards Maladeta from Hospice de France

If you're at all intrigued by the history of Pyrenean exploration then you should make the classic approach from Luchon to **Maladeta**, or at least do the stretch between **Hospice de France** (1386m) and the **Port de Vénasque** (2445m) on the frontier. The roadhead for Port de Vénasque is 11km south of Luchon – if you're car-less, walk or book an excursion at the Bureau des Guides in Luchon. There's ample parking beside the abandoned hospice, ensconced in a wooded hollow by the Knights of St John during the fourteenth century, and due to be refurbished in 1998 or 1999. Meanwhile camping is tolerated in the meadows nearby.

The way up to the pass – appearing U-shaped against the sky at first sight but culminating in a narrow passage when you actually get to it – lies firstly through a steep stream valley, the grade not deterring a steady procession of dogs and five-year-olds en route. Some two hours along (2hr 30min with a full backpack) you reach the four clear, turquoise tarns known alternatively as the **Boums du Port** or **Lacs de Boum**, brimming with trout and the occasional hardy human swimmer. Beside the highest and largest lake stands the CAF *Refuge de Vénasque* (2249m; June–Oct 15; 15 places; ☎05.61.79.26.46; ①), whose genial wardens serve excellent four-course lunches (including homemade dessert) to all comers, until late in the afternoon, as well as supper to overnighters. Suitably fortified, you can now tackle the thirty-to-forty-minute trail-climb to the pass (3hr total to the Port de Vénasque from the Hospice de France), where the entire crestline of Maladeta is literally in your face. If you're continuing that way, the just-visible *Renclusa* refuge is another two and a half hours away along well-trodden paths, while the *Llanos del Hospital* refuge-restaurant is just over half as far away, on the floor of the Ésera valley (see p.262).

Otherwise you can complete a satisfying circuit by taking the distinct trail labelled as "23" to the left and east, a minute beyond the Port de Vénasque, leading in Spanish territory within 45 minutes to the **Puerto de la Picada** (2480m). Beyond this you descend gradually for about twenty minutes to the peak and pass of Espelette, with half-wild horses often grazing nearby. You can slip north through the frontier again via the "23" trail through the **Pas d'Escalette**, but staying close to the border until drawing even with the **Pas de Montjoie**, from where you descend through the woods of the Frêche valley back to the Hospice de France; this completes a seven-hour walking circuit.

Alternatively, you can abbreviate the day to six hours by plunging down to the **Étangs de Fréche**, the higher one visible from the cement cairn on the frontier ridge a few moments west of the Pas d'Escalette. This route is cairned though initially there's no path; it's half an hour down to the top tarn at 2200m, and another twenty minutes to the lower, banana-shaped lake (2100m). Here the maintained "24" trail kicks in, taking you back to the Hospice de France within ninety minutes more, passing riotous growths of wildflowers on bare slopes near the lakes, with the final stretch through beech and fir.

South of Luchon: the Vallée du Lys and Cirque de la Glère

The **Vallée du Lys**, south of Luchon, provides another corridor to serious walking, the road up it terminating after 10km under the **Cascade d'Enfer**, a spectacular waterfall squeezed out between two walls of rock in the **Cirque du Lys**. The unstaffed *Pratlong* refuge (1921m), around three hours from the roadhead, is rather small – better to keep going for an hour to the more serious *Refuge Maupas* (2450m; 40 places; staffed May–Sept; part always open; ☎05.61.79.16.07; ①). From there you can either visit some pristine lakes nearby to the southeast, or make a loop back to

Luchon via the **Cirque de la Glère**. From the cirque a path climbs southwest to the **Col de la Glère** (2367m), giving access to Spain at the Gorgutes lake (see p.262).

Southwest to Posets

For **Posets** you take the GR10 steeply south from Luchon up through the Sahage woods to Superbagnères (3hr; see below), then west five hours to the *Refuge Espingo* (1967m; 60 places; staffed May–Oct; ☎05.61.79.20.01; ①), situated just south of the GR10, above its namesake lake (see below).

As an alternative you could get a lift or drive to **Granges d'Astau** (1139m), where there is a bar and a *gîte d'étape* (☎05.61.79.35.63; ①), plus the parking area for **Lac d'Oô**. From the roadhead a crowded section of the GR10, initially on broad track, climbs in an hour to the dammed lake (1504m), where the privately run *Refuge Chez Tintin* (May–Oct; snacks for passers-by; ☎05.61.79.12.29; ①) perches beyond the west end of the dam, its shoreline tables enjoying views of the superb 300-metre waterfall at the far side of the lake, and Hounts Secs peak to the east. The onward, well-engineered path skims the east shore as it mounts to the Col d'Espingo, where the GR10 bears northeast towards Luchon but most hikers press on to the *Espingo* refuge just below the pass, exactly an hour above Oô. The hut here overlooks the beautiful, undammed **Lac d'Espingo**, and the frontier ridge; however, there's no snack bar or drinks service for casual passers-by.

Power lines, and most day-trippers with their toddlers and poodles in tow, tend to stop here; beyond lies serious high-mountain country. From the vicinity of the refuge, the path continues south past **Lac Saussat**, whose shores prove extremely popular for camping in season. A short way above, there's a choice of possible routes into Spain, both partly visible from Saussat: directly via the **Port d'Oô** (*Puerto de Oô* in Spanish), or by a more easterly route via the **Lac du Portillon**. The path for the latter option, like much of the Oô–Espingo section, is paved with stone slabs, relics of the construction of the Portillon dam in the 1930s.

The *Refuge du Portillon*, an ex-construction workers' hut at the foot of the dam (2hr from Espingo; 2571m; 25 places; staffed June 15–Sept 15; ①), lies on the HRP, with either the *Llanos del Hospital* hospice or the *Refugio de la Renclusa* on Maladeta a full day's trekking east through the **Col de Litérole/Collado de Lliterola** (3049m). On a sunny summer's day the lake appears cobalt blue against the surrounding grey rock and scree, occasional patches of shoreline grass dotted with saxifrage and gentian. From here the route to the *Estós* refuge in the Ésera valley slips south through the **Portillon d'Oô**, high above the lake, and then southwest – at first over permanent ice – to join with the path descending from the Port d'Oô/Puerto d'Oô. Count on four to five hard-slogging hours, albeit downhill, from either pass to *Estós*.

Skiing around Luchon

Despite relative proximity to the highest mountain in the Pyrenees, Luchon's own ski resort of **SUPERBAGNÈRES** (17km away; regular ski-bus in season) is too low, situated on a shoulder at around 1800m, with half the runs going downwards from there. To get to the higher runs you have to descend and then ascend again, taking two long chairlifts, and even then you only reach 2260m. When snow is plentiful there are a couple of good long reds and one long black run. The *Grand Hôtel*, a mighty edifice in the Swiss fashion, was here half a century before the apartments and ski lifts were built around it. Cable cars of the *télécabine* run in summer to top, used by *parapentists* as a launch-pad. **BOURG D'OUEIL**, 15km northwest of Luchon at the head of the Oueil valley, is also attractive enough, but with a top lift at only 1600m it's not a serious contender.

The best chance of snow is at the double resort of **LES AGUDES** and **PEYRE-SOURDE** (*Peyragudes* in tourist-board-speak), which straddles the Col de Peyresourde 14km west of Luchon. Although the top is still only 2400m in elevation, the east-, west- and north-facing slopes on each side of the spine stretching south from the *col* serve as snow-traps. The development is fairly ugly but the skiing is serious, with seventeen lifts and forty pistes: four green, twenty-one blue, twelve red and three black.

West to the Col de Peyresourde

Along the direct road west from Luchon over the **Col de Peyresourde** (1563m) you can only hitch or drive – there's no bus. Along the way, three churches are worth more than a cursory look. The most famous is the twelfth-century **Saint-Aventin**, perched with its namesake village on an incredibly steep slope some 5km out of Luchon. Its two Romanesque towers were immaculately renovated in the nineteenth century, and a good deal of **relief decoration** remains on the exterior. Above the south door, the carved tympanum shows Christ in Majesty, borne heavenward in his mandorla by angels; on the right is an excellent *Virgin and Child*. The column capitals flanking the door are finely worked as well, depicting the *Washing of the Feet* (left), as well as a bear; the hermit Aventin was the local patron of bears, who would approach him, Androcles-style, to have thorns removed from their paws. To the right, Aventin is beheaded by the Moors (in 813), and further along on the wall a bullock paws at the ground to reveal the saint's buried body. Inside (key-keeper in the house with grey door), there are more carvings near his tomb showing Aventin helping a bear, and carrying his detached head around, as well as some twelfth-century frescoes.

Two kilometres further on, the church of **LARBOUST** has a series of fifteenth-century frescoes portraying episodes from the Old and New Testaments in particular, Adam sleeping through the Creation of Woman, and a lurid *Last Judgement* in sombre shades of ochre and red, rediscovered and a bit over-restored in the nineteenth century. Unfortunately this church is generally locked (enquire at the Luchon tourist office). After another 2km, the squat and barn-like **Saint-Pé-de-la-Moraine** just west of the village of Garin is a rarity, a pre-Romanesque edifice from the ninth century, cobbled together from Roman masonry.

If you need somewhere to **stay**, try the two-star *Hotel L'Esquérade* in the Castillon district of Larboust, 1km past Saint-Aventin (☎05.61.79.19.64, fax 05.61.79.26.29; ④; closed Oct–April). It has an excellent restaurant featuring game, and offers weekend or five-day activity packages or *forfaits* (kayaking, horse-riding, *parapente*) in conjunction with a local outfitter.

Col de Peyresourde

The **Col de Peyresourde**, hemmed in by steep slopes 5km west of Garin, is often part of the **Tour de France** route, generally the midpoint of a long day of masochistic climbs. If you're in the area on the date the pack passes through and you want a good view, be sure to get a place on the roadside a few hours before the expected time of arrival – by the time the leaders come over the pass, the crowds will be twenty deep. The most ardent devotees of the *Tour* position themselves under the banner marking the crest of the *col*, armed with sheafs of newspapers – not to fill in the wait for the cyclists, but to give them assistance. As the riders appear, the newspapers are held out so that the cyclists can take them and tuck them under their shirts – providing essential insulation from the freezing descent, on which the bikes reach speeds of around 100km per hour. (For more on the *Tour*, see the feature on pp.312–313).

travel details

Trains

Bagnères-de-Luchon to: Montréjeau (4–5 daily; 45min).

La Pobla de Segur to: Lleida (4 daily; 2hr 30min).

Montréjeau to: Bagnères-de-Luchon (3–4 daily; 45min); Boussens (15 daily; 25min); Lourdes (10 daily; 50min); Pau (10 daily; 1hr 35min); Saint-Gaudens (10 daily; 10min); Tarbes (10 daily; 35min); Toulouse (10 daily; 1hr 15min).

Spanish buses

Benasque to: Barbastro (2 daily; 2hr 30min), with connections to Huesca (2 daily; 50min) and Lleida (2 daily; 1hr 20min).

La Pobla de Segur to: Barcelona (2 daily; 3hr 30min); Capdella (Mon–Sat 1 daily, in the afternoon; 1hr); Esterri de Àneu (Mon–Sat 1 daily, at 6pm; 1hr 10min); Lleida (Mon–Sat 1 daily, at 6.30am; 2hr); El Pont de Suert (1 daily, at 9.30am; 1hr 20min); Viella via Bonaigua (1 daily June–end Oct, at 9.30am; 3hr 30min).

El Pont de Suert to: Boí (1 daily, at 11.15am, returns 2pm; 30min).

Viella to: Barruera (Mon–Sat 1 daily, at 1pm; 1hr 15min); French border (Mon–Fri 4 daily; 45min); Lleida via Túnel de Viella (2 daily year-round, at 5.30am & 1.30pm; 5hr 45min); La Pobla de Segur via Salardú and Bonaigua (1 daily, June to mid-Nov, at 11am; 3hr 15min); El Pont de Suert (2 daily, same times as Lleida service; 50min); Tredòs (Mon–Fri 4 daily, 2 on weekends; 20min).

French buses

Auzat to: Tarascon-sur-Ariège (Mon–Fri in school term, 1 daily at dawn, plus year-round at noon Fri & alternate Mon; 30min).

Bagnères-de-Luchon to: Montréjeau (4 daily; 50min); Saint-Gaudens (1 daily; 1hr 15min); Toulouse (1 daily; 3hr 30min).

Saint-Girons to: Aulus-les-Bains (Mon–Fri 2 daily, 1 on Sat; 1hr 15min); Boussens (Mon–Sat 3 daily, 2 on Sun; 45min); Foix (4 daily; 1hr); Seix (Mon–Sat 3–4 daily between noon & 7pm; 20min); Sentein (1–2 daily; 1hr).

CHAPTER FOUR

AROUND THE NATIONAL PARKS

The allure of the Pyrenees' two largest national parks – the French Parc National des Pyrénées and the Spanish Parque Nacional de Ordesa y Monte Perdido – cannot be matched by any other part of the range. These contain the landscapes that inspired the wealthy gentleman-explorers who pioneered numerous Pyrenean ascents from the late eighteenth century onwards, and it was here that many Romantic poets and painters came to brood. While the exaltation that Ramond de Carbonnières felt standing on the summit of Monte Perdido in 1802 was partly due to his mistaken belief that this was the highest point of the range, he had already explored Aneto – the true high point – without feeling the same delight. So great was the devotion of the eccentric Count Henry Russell that he had caves cut near the summit of Vignemale, highest point of the French Pyrenees, from which he and his guests could watch the changing colours on the frontier peaks. Nobody can walk through the Brèche de Roland, the natural gateway through the wall-like Cirque de Gavarnie, without being profoundly impressed: in one direction you look down over the mighty rock faces of Gavarnie, in the other you gaze out towards the thousand-metre-high walls of the Ordesa canyon.

The standard approaches to the Gavarnie area **from the north** are along the **Gave de Pau**, the river valley named for Pau, the elegant, relatively cosmopolitan capital of the *département* of Pyrénées-Atlantiques. Every summer afternoon, tour buses tear along the narrow roads to the cirque, many of them carrying pilgrims from the Marian cult centre of **Lourdes**, upstream from Pau. Less immediately stunning areas such as the **Baronnies**, in the foothills to the north of the high peaks, are spared this seasonal influx, and depopulation and unemployment are typical of the whole region.

On the other side of the border, in Alto Aragón, this trend is even more pronounced, depopulation having been accelerated by the effects of the Spanish Civil War and subsequent Francoist policies. **From the south**, heading up either the **Ara** or **Cinca** river valleys towards the Parque Nacional de Ordesa, you'll encounter the highest proportion of abandoned villages in rural Spain; only where tourism can guarantee a living – as at **Torla**, gateway to the park, or **Ainsa** and **Bielsa**, on a main route to France – are there signs of life. The one sizeable town of any real interest, thanks to its position on the Santiago de Compostela pilgrimage route, is **Jaca** in the Aragón valley, whose appeal is bolstered by the nearby monastery of **San Juan de la Peña**.

In the two parks, which adjoin each other, you are virtually certain to see Europe's rarest bird of prey, the **lammergeier**, while **griffon vultures**, **golden eagles**, **isards** and **marmots**, reintroduced in 1948, are also fairly easy to spot. A few lynx and brown bear still survive, but the chances of encountering them are very slim.

At present the high mountains are relatively undisturbed by human intervention. There are no cross-border roads between the **Bielsa** tunnel in the east – connecting the

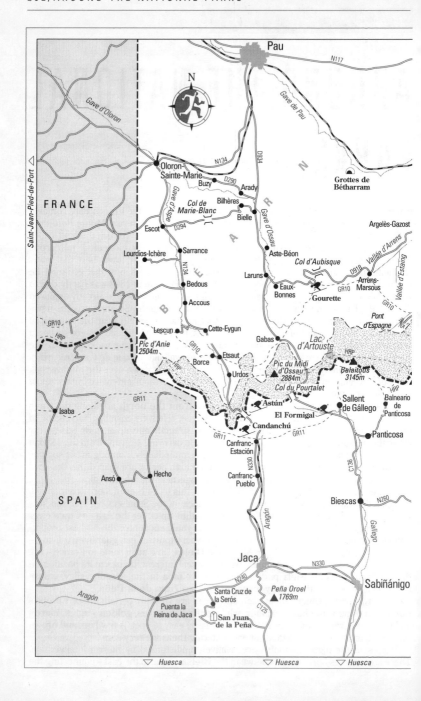

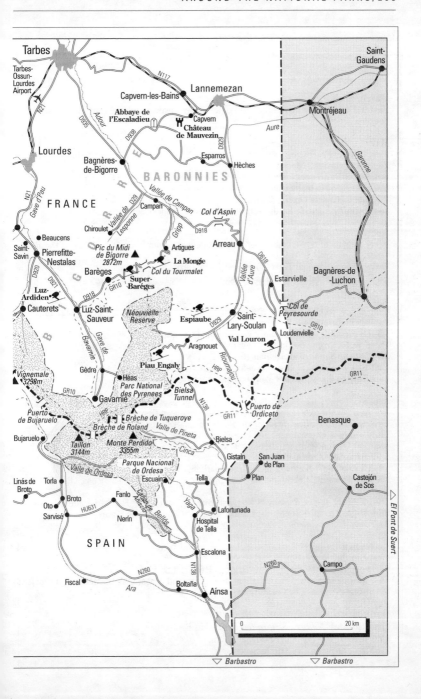

FESTIVALS

FEBRUARY
Variable Carnival at Panticosa and Bielsa.

March/April
Easter Good Friday marks the start of a ten-day Festival of Sacred Art and Music, in Lourdes.

MAY
First Friday Processions and folkloric events in Jaca commemorate the battle of Las Tiendas against the Moors, and celebrate the courage of the town's women.
Sunday of Pentecost Pilgrimage of San Indalecio, at San Juan de la Peña. Celebrations for Santa Elena in many villages of the Valle de Tena.
25 *Fiesta de Santa Orosia*, at Jaca.
Last Sunday *Romería* for the *Virgen de la Cueva*, Peña Oroel (near Jaca).

JUNE
Early Regatta of tree-trunks – *not* lashed together – from Laspuña to Ainsa on the Río Cinca.
Variable International Travel Film Festival in Tarbes.
13 Celebrations for Santa Elena, Biescas.

JULY
Last three weeks *Pirineos Sur* at Salent de Gallego, one of the best world music festivals in Europe.
15–18 *Fiesta de Nuestra Señora de Carmen* at Canfranc.
Third week Cirque de Gavarnie Festival, with the staging of a classic play.
25 *Fiesta de Santiago* at Sabiñánigo.
Last two weeks to first two weeks August Theatre, dance and music at Pau.
Late July to early August World music festival at Aínsa.

AUGUST
4 *Virgen Blanca* observances at Candanchú.
First weekend *Festival de la Montagne*, Luz-Saint-Sauveur.
Early August International Folklore Festival of the Pyrenees in Jaca (odd-numbered years) or Oloron (even-numbered years).
5 Fiesta at Sallent de Gállego.
14–15 *Fiestas del Barrio* in Jaca; street markets and parties.
15 and around Celebrations for the *Virgen de la Asunción* at Panticosa, Oto, Bielsa, Héas and Laruns.
14–17 *Fiesta de San Roque y la Virgen* at Biescas, with a "Big Heads" parade.
Mid-August to mid-September Music festival at Bagnères-de-Bigorre.
31 *Fiesta de San Ramón* at Buesa.

SEPTEMBER
First Sunday Procession at Sarrance.
8 Observance of the Birth of the Virgin at Héas and Sarvisé.
14 *Fiesta de la Santa Cruz* at Sallent de Gállego and Ainsa; also *La Morisma*, a mock Moors-and-Christians battle, at Ainsa.

OCTOBER
First Sunday *Nuestra Señora del Rosario* in Broto.
12 *Fiesta de la Virgen del Pilar*, at Sabiñánigo and Torla.
20 *Fiesta* at Santa Cruz de la Serós.

ACCOMMODATION PRICE CODES

Each place to stay in this book has been given a code which corresponds to one of the following price categories.

   ① Under 2500ptas/under 100F   ② 2500–3500ptas/100–140F
   ③ 3500–5000ptas/140–200F   ④ 5000–7000ptas/200–260F
   ⑤ 7000–10,000ptas/260–340F   ⑥ 10,000ptas/340F and upwards

Category ① refers to the price *per person* of a bed; the other categories correspond to the **cheapest available double room in high season**. For more details, see pp.34 & 37.

Vallée d'Aure in France with the **Cinca** valley in Spain – and the **Ossau** and **Aspe** valleys in the west. But the integrity of the terrain is now threatened on several fronts: by plans for new roads and tunnels, by pressure to allow ski lifts in the parks themselves (both the French and Spanish have built resorts at a dozen places along the edges of their park), and – on the Spanish side – by new hydroelectric schemes. On the plus side, the Parque Nacional de Ordesa was expanded in the early 1990s to include the equally spectacular **Cañon de Añisclo** and the head of the glacial **Valle de Pineta**.

THE NORTHERN APPROACHES

The French **Parc National des Pyrénées** (PNP, or just the *parc national*) was a long time coming, meeting such strong local resistance to its establishment in 1967 that it is limited for most of its length to a thin ribbon along the border. It has real girth only around **Pic du Midi d'Ossau**, between **Cauterets** and **Vignemale**, and where it adjoins the **Réserve Naturelle de Néouvielle**; in places – for example, near the Col du Somport – it's as little as 1500m across.

The traditional independence of and competition between 87 different mountain *communes* here in the Central Pyrenees was a large part of the problem. Already by medieval times the mountains were effectively carved up between local families, the Catholic Church and a few autonomous valley communities, all grouped together into two huge feudal counties: **Béarn**, created in 820 and not swallowed by the French Crown until 1589, and **Bigorre**, which kept out of Parisian clutches until 1607. Following the unification of France, and the subsequent French Revolution, everything was administratively rearranged into *commissions syndicales*, *syndicats de communes* and *copropriétaires*. However, rivalry between these bodies created a situation nearly as complicated as that prevailing in the feudal era. During the years leading up to 1967, the *communes* – and local hunting clubs – fiercely resisted any abrogation of their privileges regarding the montane environment, privileges that were often guaranteed by ancient charters and treaties.

Given such a background, the creation of a national park was inevitably time-consuming, with the compromise result limited in its objectives, and pleasing no one entirely. The park is too easy for vehicles to reach, and is not big enough; the paltry number of bears, which the park is supposed to protect, live almost entirely outside its boundaries. Indeed, the plight of the bears is a convenient stick used by critics to beat park administrators, who retort that they have their hands more than full with the task of protecting other, less high-profile species – as well as having to accommodate rural livelihoods near the park and repair the damage caused by tourism.

From the visitor's point of view, the most obvious effects of the park's establishment are a system of **trails** amounting to over 400km, including – but not limited to – the GR and HRP routes, and a number of staffed **refuges**, either taken over from the French

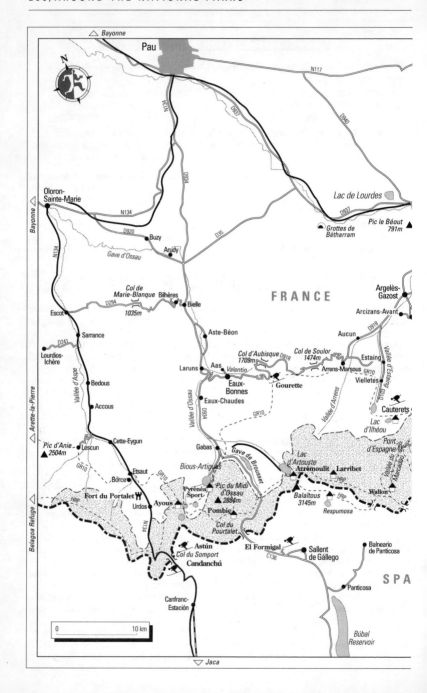

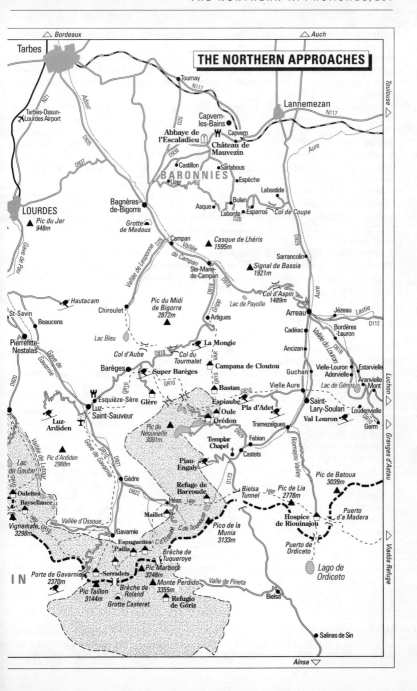

THE NORTHERN APPROACHES

alpine club or built from scratch. The paths are marked by red or green lettering on yellow **signs**, though the walking times quoted are usually overestimated by between a quarter and a third. Park **boundaries** are marked by red-and-white signs with an izard's head in silhouette; within these limits there is not supposed to be any permanent habitation or obtrusive man-made structures other than alpine refuges, and camping is severely restricted.

The four main north–south valleys on the northern side of the watershed give fast access to the mountains from the major centres of Lannemezan, Tarbes, Pau and Oloron-Sainte-Marie respectively. From **Lannemezan** there are buses down the **Vallée d'Aure**, past the almost deserted **Baronnies** region, through the valley capital of **Arreau** and on towards the last French settlement of **Aragnouet**, from where there is spectacular, if demanding trekking into either the wildlife reserve of the **Néouvielle Massif** or the magnificent and unspoilt **Cirque de Troumouse**.

From **Tarbes** there are buses to **Bagnères-de-Bigorre** and the rural **Vallée de Campan**, with onward connections to the winter-sports village of **La Mongie**. Tarbes is also connected by bus and train to **Lourdes**; however, it is far preferable to continue by bus through Lourdes to **Gavarnie**, or to the ski stations/spas of **Barèges** and **Cauterets**.

From elegant **Pau**, in the northwest of this region, there are reliable direct buses up the wild **Vallée d'Ossau** as far as **Laruns** (less dependably beyond), while trains and buses call at the river-junction town of **Oloron-Sainte-Marie** on the way up to **Urdos** – and on into Spain – via the **Vallée d'Aspe**.

The Vallée d'Aure

The **Vallée d'Aure** extends from just south of Lannemezan up to Aragnouet, the last significant habitation before the Bielsa tunnel and the frontier. It's an attractive route to follow on the D929, especially from the county-town of Arreau and beyond, where a dozen stone-built villages cling to the steep, green banks of the valley.

Two of the premier ski resorts in the Pyrenees – Espiaube and Piau-Engaly – are found southwest of Arreau. The **Réserve Naturelle de Néouvielle**, immediately above the ski stations and south of Pic du Midi du Bigorre and the Col du Tourmalet, offers superb hiking around (or over) the celebrated **Pic de Néouvielle** (3092m) and up one of the easiest three-thousanders, **Turon de Néouvielle** (3035m). The eastern end of the Parc National des Pyrénées, up against the border, is a tougher proposition but with its own rewards, including a high-mountain approach to the **Cirque de Troumouse**, numbered among the most beautiful spots in the range.

The bus ride along the Vallée d'Aure towards the *parc national* begins at Lannemezan train station, a major stop on the Pau–Tarbes–Toulouse line. Although the journey provides a sort of geography lesson on glaciation and montane agriculture – grazing on denuded south-facing slopes, firs on the north-facing hillsides – there's little to justify leaving your bus or car until Arreau, except for the Romanesque **church of Saint-Ebons**, built to a Greek-cross plan in the village of Sarrancolin, 19km from Lannemezan. Inside you can see the gilded and enamelled copper casket for the saint's relics, and carved choir stalls with typically grotesque faces.

Arreau

ARREAU, 27km from Lannemezan, sits at the confluence of the Louron, Lastie and Aure rivers, a strategic position that first made it capital of the ancient Comté d'Aure under the kings of Aragón, and later the heart of the Pays de Quatre Vallées, which was finally absorbed by France in 1475. A neat little village, its tone is set by the medieval **market** building (market day Thursday), the half-timbered houses with their *fleur-de-lys* motifs and flower-boxes (especially the Maison des Lys opposite), and the shops selling *Gâteau à la Broche*, the spit-cooked cake that is the speciality of this *département*. The cosiness of it all is enhanced by an almost rainless microclimate, the result of the shelter of Pic l'Arbizon in the southwest. On the opposite side of the river from the market, the **Chapelle Saint-Exupère** by the *Poste* merits a look for its flamboyant Gothic nave and eroded Romanesque portal. The town's Château des Nestes now houses both the **tourist office** (summer Mon–Sat 9.30am–noon & 2–7pm, Sun 9.30am–noon; ☎05.62.98.63.15) and a **museum** of Pyrenean life (same hours; 10F). If your appetite is whetted for more of the same, the small village of Jézeau, 3km east, can also offer a similarly ancient church surrounded by fine vernacular houses.

Arreau makes an agreeable touring base; places to **stay** are the central *Hôtel de l'Arbizon* (☎05.62.98.64.35; ④), simple but clean, with some of its six rooms having river views, or the much fancier, quieter *Hôtel d'Angleterre* (☎05.62.98.63.30, fax 05.62.98.69.66; ⑤; closed Nov & Dec), off the south end of the main street, which has a peaceful rear garden and private parking. Both hotels have good **restaurants**, the *De l'Arbizon*'s with two decent menus under 100F and river-esplanade seating; otherwise there's only a riverside crêperie opposite the church. The municipal **campsite** (☎05.62.98.65.56; closed Oct) lies just south of the village, or there's the nearby *Camping Le Refuge* (☎05.62.98.63.34; year-round).

Southeast of Arreau: the Vallée du Louron

The main excursion from Arreau leads into the **Vallée du Louron**, which can also be reached by road from the Col de Peyresourde, or on foot along the GR10 (see below). There's no bus up the valley, which means making your way along the D618 road towards Bagnères-de-Luchon, or picking up the *Tour de la Vallée d'Aure* footpath at the hamlet of Lançon, 2km above Arreau on the D618.

The local **tourist office** (summer Mon–Sat 9am–noon & 2–6pm; ☎05.62.98.64.12), which runs tours to most of the **painted churches** further up the valley, is at Bordères-Louron, another 2km above Lançon, but there's little to see here aside from a Sunday morning riverside market. The notable concentration of frescoed churches here is owed to the discovery of the New World, and consequent new markets for the wool-weavers of the valley; the wealth so generated funded a widespread sixteenth-century mural campaign inside far older churches, part and parcel of the Counter-Reformation.

The first – and one of the best – of the churches is **St-Mercurial** at the village of **VIELLE-LOURON**, containing the saint's tomb and an extraordinary *Last Supper* with Judas bearing the head of Luther. It's the only one with local key-keepers – a sign points to their house – but hours are limited to Mon–Wed 10–11.30am & 4–6.30pm. The other notable church is **St-Barthélemy**, well up the valley at **MONT**, with historical as well as sacred frescoes in the interior, but it can only be relied on to be open late afternoons in July & August – and even then there's no guarantee; otherwise console yourself with the excellent frescoes in the cemetery chapel. Here St Catherine appears in period dress, and a *Last Judgement* has some vivid devils, with the Saved beneath the Virgin, Christ and John the Baptist.

The only real **hotel** locally, and a good choice if you're car-touring, is *Hotel Les Cimes* (☎05.62.99.67.21; ③–④) above **ESTARVIELLE** on the D618, roughly halfway between Mont and Vielle-Louron. This has several balconied, en-suite rooms with valley views and a decent restaurant with some of the heartiest *garbure* around. Otherwise there's just a youth-orientated *gîte de montagne* down by the central church in Estarvielle (☎05.62.99.64.12; ①).

Approach from the east: the GR10

It's possible to walk west from **Granges d'Astau** to the **Vallée de Louron** via the GR10. Initially the way lies along the **Val d'Esquierry**, south of the ski development of Les Agudes-Peryesourde, over the **Pas de Couret** (2131m; 3hr) and then briefly along the **Val d'Aube** into the Louron valley before turning north to the hamlet of **GERM**, high up on the east flank of the valley (960m; 3hr from the pass). Most people will call it a day here after six hours of trekking, especially with the incentive to **stay** of the multi-functional *Centre de Montagne Accueil sans Frontière* (☎05.62.99.65.27, fax 05.62.99.63.22; *gîte d'étape* ①, chalets ②), with a restaurant, pool and full sports progammes summer and winter; they also do cultural tours of the surroundings, have artist-in-residence programmes and organize a small July festival. If they're full – likely if you haven't booked – you'll have to press on an hour downhill to **ARANVIELLE** overlooking the artificial Lac de Génos Loudenvielle (watersports on offer), where the welcoming *Auberge Les Isclôts* (☎05.62.99.66.21, fax ☎05.62.99.66.31; *gîte d'étape* ①, en-suite doubles ③), a restored mountain house, offers a similar sporting activities progamme, and a *table d'hôte* restaurant.

From the vicinity of the reservoir, it's four and a half hours further west to the next indoor accommodation. From Loudenvielle the GR10 climbs to the Couret de Latuhe (1586m) before dropping to the village of Azet and then the main N129 road at Vielle-Aure, with the comforts and bus connections of Saint-Lary (see p.301) 2km to the south.

Skiing: Val Louron

The local ski station of **VAL LOURON** perches high above the Lac de Génos-Loudenvielle, to the southwest. Although it's across the river from the ski complexes at Peyresourde (see p.289), and often marketed with it, Val Louron is not nearly so rigorous, with a top station of only 2100m and just one black piste out of a total of eighteen. In summer, it's a popular site for *parapente*.

South of Arreau: the upper Aure

Continuing up the Aure from Arreau, after 2km vehicles pass under the rock arch that is the porch of Nôtre-Dame-de-Pène Taillade at **CADÉAC**, a possible base with its *Hostellerie du Val d'Aure* (☎05.62.98.60.63; closed Oct to mid-Dec; ④), nicely set on the riverbank and incorporating the spa which has worked here since Roman times.

VIELLE-AURE, 9km south of Arreau and just before Saint-Lary (see below) – of which it is effectively a suburb – is the last traditional village before the ski-related developments. The central **tourist office** (summer daily 10am–12.30pm & 3–7.30pm; ☎05.62.39.50.00) sells *topo-guides* for local walks, and can help with **accommodation**. This is mostly *chambres d'hôte*, but there are two *gîte d'étapes*: one (☎05.62.39.42.31; dorms ①, rooms ②) on the west bank of the Neste d'Aure, en route to *Camping Le Lustou* (☎05.62.39.40.64; year-round), 1.5km north at Agos; the other (☎05.62.39.41.36; ②), more comfortable with doubles, up near the church. **Eating** options are pretty much down to the inexpensive *Les Gazaous*, again on the campsite road, or *Crêperie Le Martagon*, near the tourist office.

Walking: the Tour de la Vallée d'Aure

From Vielle-Aure you can take the *Tour de la Vallée d'Aure*, or follow the GR10 west to the Réserve Naturelle de Néouvielle. The well-marked **Tour de la Vallée d'Aure** runs east and west from Vielle-Aure, using sections of the GR10. Westwards, you'll initially climb steeply from the village, then more gradually across a rocky stretch before crossing the **Crête de Grascouéou**. From there the track goes north through woodland to Aulon at the base of Pic l'Arbizon, where there's a *gîte d'étape* for your first overnight stop (☎05.62.39.96.29; ①). Next you veer back across the Vallée d'Aure to **GUCHAN** (where there's a campsite), climbing up the east flank of the valley and turning sharp right shortly before the village of Lançon. The route is now predominantly through tranquil mixed woodland, the forests of Lançon and Gouaux opening up for the easy but impressive **Crête de Calamagne**. The full *tour* involves four overnight stays: *gîtes d'étapes* in Vielle-Aure and Aulon, and – depending on your starting point and timings – either in Guchan, Lançon or at the *gîte* in Azet (☎05.62.39.41.44; ①), 3km southeast of Vielle-Aure.

Saint-Lary-Soulan

SAINT-LARY-SOULAN, 12km south of Arreau, was one of the first Pyrenean resorts to be featured by package-tour operators, its rustic core now enveloped by supposedly compatible modern buildings. The **Office du Tourisme** on rue Principale (☎05.62.39.50.81) can help with accommodation in *résidences* (apartments by the week). Saint-Lary also has a *Maison du Parc National* (June–Sept & Dec–April daily 9am–noon & 2–7pm), providing guides and general information on the local flora and fauna. There are nearly a dozen **hotels** in Saint-Lary, with more at the pair of ski centres overhead, but if you're here at all, you'll have probably reserved in advance on a package. Accommodation worth trying on spec includes the town's least expensive place, *Pons Le Dahu* on rue de Coudères (☎05.62.39.53.09; ③); the two-star *Aurelia*, north of town on the old road to Vielle-Aure (☎05.62.39.56.90, fax 05.62.39.43.75; ⑤); or the two-star *La Pergola* at rue Principale 25 (☎05.62.39.40.46, fax 05.62.40.06.55; ⑤), set back from the street and with a well-regarded **restaurant**. As at so many ski resorts, restaurant choices outside the hotels aren't brilliant, though the *Crêperie La Flambée Auroise* at 20bis rue des Fougères has whole-grain bread and a good range of beers and juices offsetting rather small portions. If you have transport, it's best to head up to the village of **Sailhan**, 2km northeast, where *Chez Lulu* (closed Mon) offers filling menus for well under 100F at outdoor tables. In summer, various outdoor activities are on offer: **parapente** (☎05.62.39.41.11), **canyoning** and **caving** (☎05.62.39.44.79 or ☎05.62.39.57.51), **rafting** with Adrenaline (☎05.62.40.04.04), **climbing** with the Bureau des Guides and **horse-riding** at the Centre Equestre de Saint-Lary (☎05.62.39.41.11). Also worth remembering is that Saint-Lary has the last **banks**, with ATMs, before the Spanish frontier.

The Aure ski stations

The adjacent complexes of **PLA D'ADET** and **ESPIAUBE**, just west of Saint-Lary, have a comprehensive piste system, with the highest of the thirty lifts reaching 2400m and the 33 runs divided into eight green, twelve blue, ten red and three black. Pla d'Adet additionally features 15km of nordic skiing tracks.

PIAU-ENGALY, the last stop on the valley bus route (in winter anyway), about 20km above Saint-Lary, is probably the most futuristic ski resort in Europe. Some love the design and some hate it, but Piau-Engaly has three undeniable advantages: illuminated night-skiing (7–10pm), an excellent snow record owing to its 2500-metre top height and – for those who never mastered drag-lifts – a high proportion of chair-lifts. The mock-flying-saucer accommodation units are at 1850m, with direct access to the 21 lifts and 37 pistes, including six black.

The Rioumajou valley

Above Saint-Lary, the main river drainage begins to curl west and fray into half a dozen tributaries. The most scenic of these is the **Rioumajou valley**, which joins the Aure just over 3km upstream from Saint-Lary. The hamlet of **TRAMEZAÏGUES** (meaning "between waters") stands dramatically at the confluence of the rivers, overlooked by the ruins of an eleventh-century castle-with-church and by steep rock walls that block out the sun for much of the winter. Bears used to live in the dense surrounding forest, and a local motto, in patois, goes: *En Tramezaïgues que cridé: Qu'aouen aoucitet l'ous!*(In Tramezaïgues one shouts: We have killed a bear!). But only after the bears became locally extinct did the Rioumajou valley gain protection as a *site classé*.

To get up the valley, there's a narrow twelve-kilometre road; about halfway along, the *Auberge de l'Escalette* (co-managed with *Chez Lulu* in Sailhan), overlooking a tiny reservoir, does lunch and supper. The pavement ends at Km8, where the enormous, and enormously popular Fredançon riverside picnic meadows under the firs seem to attract half the tourists in the Vallée d'Aure of a summer weekend. The other half carry on along the final 4km of very rough track to the renovated **Hospice de Rioumajou** (1560m; aka *Rieumajou*), a traditional halt on one branch of the Santiago pilgrimage trail, and before that a stage of a Roman trade route. It's open in summer for drinks and light snacks from 11am to 6pm, but owing to lack of electricity there's no supper or overnighting. Tenting down in the vast green meadows all around will go unremarked on, however, and towards dusk you might see the *bergers* feeding rock salt to their sheep.

The environs of the *hospice* is a major crossroads of the **HRP** and its *variantes*: you can continue south across the frontier via the **Port d'Ourdissetou/Puerto de Ordiceto** (2403m; 2hr 30min–3hr) for access to Bielsa in Spain; hike east over the **Port de Madère/Puerto d'a Madera** (2526m) to the refuge at Viadós, or go west via **Pic de Lia** (2778m) and continue along the frontier, eventually reaching the *Refuge de Barroude* (see below) within a day.

Into the Parc National des Pyrénées

The approach to the **Parc National des Pyrénées** from the Vallée d'Aure is a classic alpine walk enlivened at the end by the superb Cirque de Troumouse. Get off the valley bus 13km from Saint-Lary at the stop nearest the Templar chapel (see below), where the side road for Piau-Engaly goes off to the right. From here you take the footpath up the Neste ("River" in local dialect) de la Géla, crossing the boundary of the national park almost immediately before joining the **HRP** just north of the *Refuge de Barroude* (2377m; 20 places; staffed July–Sept; part open all year; ①), perched magnificently in a namesake cirque-with-lake.

It's only a half-day hike up from the chapel, but it's best to spend the night at the refuge, retracing your steps for half an hour next morning to the HRP and then continuing northwest over the formidable, so-called "Barroude wall", via the two passes of **Hourquette de Chermentas** (2439m) and the **Hourquette d'Héas** (2608m). Descending from the second *hourquette*, often snowed up early in the summer, you find yourself in the upper reaches of the **Cirque de Troumouse**; follow the Aguila stream steeply down into the Héas valley, reached some six and a half hours from the *Refuge de Barroude*. From the valley floor the cirque reveals itself in all its glory; for a description see "The Gavarnie region", p.324.

A Templar chapel and the Túnel de Bielsa

Beyond the hamlets which comprise the *commune* of **ARAGNOUET**, just north of the D118, stands an intriguing twelfth-century Templar chapel (usually locked). Its almost windowless and plain exterior gives nothing away, though the jagged perpendicular edge of its tall *clocher-mur* suggests that there was once a large hospice here, at the base of the pedestrian route over 2429-metre Port de Bielsa.

Today most people **cross the frontier** by car, via the three-kilometre **Túnel de Bielsa** (daily April–Sept 8am–10.30pm; Oct–March 8am–7pm), the first major Pyrenean tunnel to stay open year round. Such is climate and geography here that a five-minute trip through the tunnel might take you from a damp, misty day on the northern slopes into bright Spanish sunshine, with an attendant change in vegetation from deep green to bare, scorched brown.

The Réserve Naturelle de Néouvielle

France's first protected area, created in 1935, the **Réserve Naturelle de Néouvielle** constitutes a lake-rich "annexe" at the very eastern tip of the far larger Parc National des Pyrénées. It encloses some of Europe's highest forests of mountain pine, substantial stands reaching 2400m and isolated specimens even growing at 2600m. This is due to a predominantly southern exposure, unusual for the French Pyrenees, which also encourages a riot of smaller flora. Unfortunately, *réserve* status did nothing for the region's isards, which were hunted out and had to be reintroduced in 1987. However, you should see **marmots** here, and there's a good chance of spotting **golden eagles**, and a slight chance of **lammergeier**.

Néouvielle – *Neoubieh* or *Neu Bielha* in local languages – means "old snow", perhaps a reference to the vestigial glaciers on certain peaks here. It feels similar to the Aigües Tortes-Sant Maurici park in Catalunya: tourists and dams at the lower elevations, granite walls, tarns and trekkers' passes higher up. And similar rules apply: no camping except in designated areas, and a ban on private car passage along the single road into the *réserve* from 9.30am to 6pm. During these hours a **navette** operates from the control gate at Lac d'Orédon on the south side of the *réserve* up to the car park at Lac d'Aubert. During the day, car-bound travellers can get as far as Lac d'Orédon by means of a side road, the "Route des Lacs", which climbs 14km up from Fabian in the Aure valley, lowest of the Aragnouet hamlets, but as ever in the Pyrenees it's rewarding to do most of your exploration on foot. **Trails** through the *réserve*, often the GR10 or a *variante*, are accordingly well signposted. However you arrive, the 1:50,000 IGN Carte de Randonées no. 4 "Bigorre" **map** is invaluable.

Lac d'Orédon loop hike

If you're not keen on full-pack traverse, the following popular three-hour loop, using a small portion of the GR10, gives a good sample of the *réserve*. Starting point is the Touring Club de France-owned *Chalet-Hôtel d'Orédon* (1900m; 60 places; ① dorms, ③ doubles; open & staffed June 15–Sept 15; ☎05.62.39.63.33) just above the dam of Orédon, with obliging management and excellent food, though sleeping facilities are basic. A bit of road-walking is unavoidable; head 1100m up the pavement towards Lac d'Aubert, and then bear left onto the trail marked for "**Les Laquettes**", three natural, photogenic tarns below the Aubert dam. Also just below Aubert is one of the few legal bivouac sites in Néouvielle. Next the route swings east past the car park and a defunct refuge overlooking the natural **Lac d'Aumar**. You then pick up the GR10 along a crest, affording fine views over the three southerly reservoirs of Cap de Long, Orédon and Oule, before descending back to the *chalet-hotel* from the **Col d'Estoudou** (2260m) on an unnumbered trail.

Vielle-Aure to Artigues

Hitching up the Route des Lacs from Fabian to Orédon is a pretty dubious proposition; without your own transport, a better way of beginning a traverse of the Néouvielle country is to take the **GR10** from Vielle-Aure, climbing through the Saint-Lary pistes. After about six hours you reach the simple *Cabane de Bastan*, an unstaffed shelter, where you have the choice of the *variante* towards Artigues or the main Barèges route.

For **Artigues**, hike north from the *cabane* and spend your first night at the lakeside *Refuge du Bastan* (2250m; 20 places; ☎05.62.98.48.80; staffed early June to late Sept, part always open; ①), one hour further, beyond a series of small lakes. Next day, you first climb the scree slopes up to the **Col de Bastan** (2507m), then descend between several lakes for lunch at the *Refuge de Campana de Cloutou* (2200m; 25 places; ☎05.62.91.87.47; staffed June–Sept, part always open; ①), before tackling a three-hour afternoon stage to Artigues through the wide Garet valley, which culminates in some waterfalls. Minuscule Artigues itself, on the D918 road some 10km northwest of the scenic Col du Tourmalet, has a limited number of facilities (described on p.311).

Bastan to Barèges

For **Barèges**, follow the old drovers' trail from the *Cabane de Bastan*, which skims along the eastern, then southern boundaries of the *réserve*, and spend the night either at the *Chalet-Hôtel de l'Oule* (1820m; 26 places; ① dorms; ② doubles; open & staffed mid-Dec to mid-April & early June to mid-Sept; ☎05.62.98.48.62; ①), not more than an hour away at the dammed south end of Lac de l'Oule, or at the *Chalet-Hôtel d'Orédon* (see above) two hours further. The only problem is that both of these are easily accessible by the road up from Fabian – the Lac de l'Oule via a dirt track from the **Artigousse** parking area, 6km along – and therefore highly popular. After a night at one of the *chalets*, follow the GR10 or unnumbered "Les Laquettes" trail (see above) into the heart of the *réserve* as far as the adjacent lakes of **Aumar** and **Aubert**, where there's a choice of two onward routes north.

Climb along the GR10 to the **Col de Madamète** (2509m), where you leave *réserve* territory, drop down to the basic *Cabane d'Aygues-Cluses* and then follow the idyllic Aygues-Cluses valley to join the D918 road at the Pont de la Gaubie, seven hours after leaving Orédon.

Alternatively, you can use an equally distinct, signposted but unnumbered trail departing northwest from the Lac d'Aubert, which negotiates the **Horquette d'Aubert** (2498m) before descending past half a dozen medium-sized lakes – the largest, **Coubous** – before rejoining the GR10 half an hour before the Pont de la Gaubie. The time course is the same as for the all-GR10 itinerary.

There's a small snack bar at the *pont* catering to walkers; here, you're almost exactly halfway between Barèges and the Col du Tourmalet, about 5km from either. Barèges is discussed in detail on p.322.

A Néouvielle circuit

If you have a car to leave at a trailhead, it's particularly recommended that you make a two- or three-day **circuit**, starting either from the Lac d'Aubert or the Pont de la Gaubie. Walking instructions for the sectors between the southerly lakes and the D918 are identical to the ones previously described; what makes a loop possible is a minor trail heading east from the Cabane d'Aygues-Cluses, over the **Horquette Nère** (2465m), and then southeast to the *Refuge du Bastan* (see above) – it's seven to eight hours from Pont de la Gaubie to the *refuge*.

Traverse via Pic du Néouvielle

It's possible to make a more advanced traverse to Barèges via the summit of **Pic du Néouvielle** (3091m), at the western limit of the *réserve naturelle*. Although the ascent of the peak requires no technical climbing skills, it's long and tough, requiring crampons and ice-axe. Allowing for stops, plan on twelve hours to the first attended *refuge* on the far side, from where Barèges is another three hours further on track.

Follow the clearly marked path from the car park at Lac d'Aubert westwards towards the summit, then swing north to cross the bottom of the ridge known as the Crête de Barris d'Aubert. Once over, the path peters out; ascend west again, keeping the ridge to the left, then gradually bear away northeast towards the **Brèche de Chausenque** (2790m). Before you get to the *brèche*, you swing back southwards into a wide, snow-filled valley, making your way up among huge boulders until a simple chimney takes you onto the final ridge, from which the **summit** is a short walk south (4hr from Lac d'Aubert).

To continue to Barèges, retrace your steps towards the *brèche*, climb through it this time and descend the steep slope on the other side west to the tiny **Lacs Verts**. Swing north along the shelf and gradually descend towards **Lac det Mail**, one of a succession of other lakes below to the left. Pass around its northeast shore then follow the stream down towards **Lac de la Glère** where there is the *Refuge de la Glère* (2140m; 70 places; open & staffed weekends & hols March–early June, daily early June–Sept; ☎05.62.92.69.47, fax 05.62.92.65.17; ①), reached in about six hours from the summit. From the refuge, Barèges is 10km along a track to the north; the hut warden, Philippe Trey, runs the *Gîte L'Oasis* in Barèges (see p.323) and can probably arrange transport down to spare you track-walking. He and his British wife Andrea will also be happy to reserve places in the other five staffed refuges in the area if contacted on the phone/fax numbers given.

Turon de Néouvielle

In 1787 the astronomer Vidal and the chemist Reboul became the first men to reach the summit of a Pyrenean three-thousander, when they stood on the top of **Turon de Néouvielle** (3035m). Technically it was not a great achievement – it's one of the easiest high peaks in the Pyrenees – but this and the ascent of Pic du Midi d'Ossau in the same year were instrumental in awakening interest in these mountains for research and sport.

For the ascent of Turon (actually just inside the Parc National des Pyrénées) from *Refuge de la Glère*, take the path south towards the unstaffed *Refuge Packe* and after 1km bear southeast to climb to **Lac de l'Oueil Nègre**. Just beyond, you have a choice. If you leave **Lac det Mail** to your right, you can head south between **Lacs Vert** and **Bleu** and climb the remnants of the **Glacier de Maniportet** to the summit. If you leave Mail to your left, you'll pass **Lacs de l'Estelat** and approach the **Col de Coume Estrète**; the IGN 1:25,000 map no. 275 marks the final approach through the *col*, but you can equally well leave the *col* to your right and climb to the summit via Lac Glacé. After a heavy winter, crampons, gaiters and ice-axe will be required for the final summit approach. The routes are all of a similar standard and take about ten hours there and back, including stops.

The Baronnies

One of the emptiest areas of the Pyrenees, the **Baronnies** lie between the lower valleys of the Adour and Aure, bounded to the north by the D938 Capvern–Bagnères-de-Bigorre road, and to the south by the D918 road linking Sainte-Marie-de-Campan with Arreau. This desertion is attributable to a landscape too undulating for modern agriculture, but too low for skiing and too rounded for climbing. For the casual walker and naturalist, however, the Baronnies are perfect: dense forests of beech and pine, lush, little-used pastures and a range of wildlife from desmans to griffon vultures. Monumental interest is lent by the château at Mauvezin and the abbey of Escaladieu, within a few kilometres of each other on the D938.

Public transport into the region is inevitably sparse. From the heart of the Baronnies, it's around 15km to the train station at Capvern, with the stations at Lannemezan or Bagnères-de-Bigorre slightly further. The Minibus des Baronnies company operates out of Lannemezan on Wednesdays and out of Bagnères on Saturdays, while André Pene runs a taxi service (☎05.62.39.01.14) from Esparros, the village at the centre of the region.

Otherwise you'll have to walk, hitch or drive yourself. You can get into the Baronnies from the south by hitching 13km along the D918 from Arreau to the **Col d'Aspin** (1489m) and then hiking north from the *col* itself, but the route **from the east** is more straightforward. Take a bus from Lannemezan to just north of Hèches in the Aure valley (13km); from the bus stop, stroll 4km uphill along the D26 to the **Col de Coupe** (720m), from where the view west into the Baronnies is all-encompassing: emerald pasture, forest and rolling hills. You can continue on the road to Esparros but it's better to cut off at the pass along the clear and direct horse trail, which takes half an hour.

Esparros and around

ESPARROS was the seat of an ancient *baronnie* of four parishes – hence the name of the region. Like all the villages of the Baronnies, its population has fallen dramatically since the last century: 844 inhabitants in 1851, under two hundred today. Norbert Casteret described the **Gouffre d'Esparros** as a "vast cavern of indescribable magnificence", its walls gleaming with a "hoar-frost" of gypsum flowers. Access is now restricted to protect its bat colony rather than the crystal formations, and you'll have to be an experienced caver to see it. Enquire at the **Office du Tourisme** in Laborde (☎05.62.39.03.42), 3km west of Esparros, or at *La Maison des Baronnies* at Sarlabous, 8km north, which doubles as the local *Tourisme* (summer 9am–noon & 2–5.30pm; ☎05.62.39.05.14).

Most central place to **stay** is the *gîte d'étape* at Esparros (☎05.62.39.05.96; open all year; ①), but if you're on your own and would prefer not to be, you may find the excellent *Moulin des Baronnies* at Sarlabous (☎05.62.39.05.14; ①) more sociable. There are also two simple **inns** hereabouts, both specializing in regional food: the tiny *L'Auberge d'Esparros* (☎05.62.39.02.43; closed Wed; outside of school term supper only; ③) at Esparros, and the characterful *Auberge de la Boisellerie* (☎05.62.39.05.36; dining room closed Sun evening & Mon; ③) at Laborde, 2km west of Esparros. Local **campsites** are *Le Randonneur* at Esparros (☎05.62.39.19.34; mid-June to mid-Sept), well laid-out and with a pool, and *Camping à la Ferme* (☎05.62.39.05 26) at Bulan, just over 7km northwest along the D77 from Esparros. If you're in a group and plan to stay for a week or so, the Baronnies has plenty of places to rent that can be very good value; ask for a list at the *Maison des Baronnies* in Sarlabous.

Walking: the Tour des Baronnies

Although walking in the Baronnies is not technically difficult, it can present you with tricky situations. Rainfall is high and mists often dense (some of the valley bottoms are essentially temperate rainforest), and there are vistas devoid of any sign of human habitation, except for the occasional herd of sheep or cows tended by a solitary shepherd and a mangy dog. So you'll need a compass and map, as well as rain gear and possibly rubber boots. Certain areas of this delicate and as yet untrammelled landscape are susceptible to erosion by walkers: if in a group, keep to the regular thoroughfares.

The **Tour des Baronnies**, marked on the IGN Carte de Randonnées 1:50,000 "Luchon" and "Bigorre" maps, is a lopsided figure-of-eight itinerary with its centre at **ASQUE**, 7km west of Laborde: it takes about four days, generally along tracks. The longer loop leaves Asque – where there's a *gîte d'étape* (☎05.62.39.18.21; ①), serving meals – towards the flat-topped mountain of Casque de Lhéris, then sweeps around towards Uzer, Castillon and Sarlabous; the shorter arc links Asque with Espèche, Esparros and the **Col de Couradabat**. From the *col* it is possible to walk out southwards towards **Col d'Aspin**, via **Signal de Bassia** (1921m) and the **Col de Beyrède**, but this route is unmarked, requiring some navigational skills.

Mauvezin and Escaladieu

Two of the great historical sites of this region, the château of Mauvezin and the abbey of Escaladieu, are situated conveniently close enough to each other to be seen in a single visit. If you're reliant on public transport you'll have to take the train to Capvern (there are 5 daily between Lannemezan and Pau), from where it's a five-kilometre walk to Mauvezin. It's a further three-kilometre walk to the abbey.

Mauvezin

The **Château** (*Castèth* in Gascon; May to mid-Oct daily 10am–7pm; mid-Oct to April daily 1.30–5pm; 20F) stands on the edge of **MAUVEZIN**, atop a 567-metre-high hill that was first fortified by the Romans. Between the thirteenth and fifteenth centuries it changed hands several times in the wake of protracted hostilities between the English and the French, finally passing after 1373 to Gaston Fébus (for more on whom see "Foix", p.216).

Built of grey stone, and with a crenellated tower, the square castle is particularly appealing from the outside. Inside, you're left to wander as you please, with the aid of an informative printed brochure. The now-grassy courtyard was once lined with buildings, the roofs of which funnelled rainwater into the giant cistern, built as an emergency reserve; only once was it drunk dry – during the siege of 1373. On the inside of the cistern it's possible to read the graffito *Dieu seul sera adoré et l'Antéchrist de Rome abisme* (God alone will be adored and the Antichrist in Rome cast into the abyss), carved by an imprisoned Huguenot in the sixteenth century.

The current tenant, since 1907, is the Escòla Gaston Fébus, a cultural conservation group that promotes Gascon and Occitan poetry, literature and art, including formal, medieval-themed events in August. The fully restored tower has been turned into a museum, mostly dedicated to the works of the Société Félibrée, a literary organization pledged to revive and preserve the ancient Provençal language. However, the museum is also crammed with various intriguing exhibits: sculptures, paintings, photos and bits of armour. The village itself can offer just **snacks** at the *Auberge du Château*.

The Abbaye de l'Escaladieu

Three kilometres southwest and downhill from Mauvezin in the valley bottom, towards Bagnères-de-Bigorre, you'll find the **Abbaye de l'Escaladieu** (June 15–Sept 30 daily 10am–12.30pm & 2–7pm; rest of year daily except Tues 10am–noon & 2–7pm, until 8pm May 1–June 15; free), the first Cistercian monastery in the southwest of France. Founded in the middle of the twelfth century, Escaladieu flourished for just a couple of centuries, the monks earning a living by cultivating the Baronnies, a fertile and profitable region before mechanization favoured flat fields. The monastery was plundered by Protestant forces during the Wars of Religion, and early conservationists began restoring the buildings in the seventeenth and eighteenth centuries.

Escaladieu was badly mismanaged and neglected by a private foundation between 1986 and 1993; following a court case and a token pay-out to the previous owner, the *départemental* authorities have resumed control of the place, but face a bill of 30 million francs for completing its restoration. Meanwhile, the place hosts cinema, seminars, theatre, and most accessibly, **concerts**: performances are held very sporadically from June to September, generally of Baroque music, for which the abbey makes a wonderful setting.

The showpiece of the ongoing restoration is the twelfth-to-thirteenth-century vaulted **chapter house**, opening onto a leafy inner courtyard through the sparse remnants of a cloister, all but two columns of which was shipped to California in the last century. The rest, by contrast, is typically Cistercian in its plainness, the long, white eastern facade devoid of decoration, and the enormous, echoing abbey church as bare as possible.

Bagnères-de-Bigorre

The revival of thermal resorts was something of a 1980s French fad: Luz-Saint-Sauveur did it, Ax-les-Thermes managed it, and recently **BAGNÈRES-DE-BIGORRE**, 21km southwest of Tarbes along the D935 in the Adour valley, has invested tens of millions of francs in its spa. Descended from the Roman settlement of Vicus Aquensis, Bagnères reached its apogee with the opening of the *Grands Thermes* in 1823, becoming the in-place for the likes of George Sand, Rossini and Flaubert. Today there's more to the Bagnères experience than steam rooms, being squirted with high-pressure hoses and sticking tubes up your nose – it's become more of a fusty health farm, to which the waters are only an adjunct.

From the 1830s onwards, Bagnères' British community was second in size only to Pau's, many of them having stayed on after the Peninsular War. So British was Pyrenean explo-ration at this time that of the four founders of the Société Ramond – the mountaineering club established here in 1864 and predating even the Club Alpin Français – two were Britons: the barrister-explorer Charles Packe and the photographer-inventor Maxwell Lyte. The third was Henry Russell, whose father was Irish, and only Emilien Frossard was entirely French. The society still publishes a regular bulletin and meets at the town library.

The Town

In town, beyond the market, beside the long grey *thermes* building, is the ornate **Musée Salies** (mid-May to Sept Mon–Fri 9am–noon & 3–7pm, Sat & Sun 3–7pm; rest of year ask the tourist office for keys; 20F). An elegant collection, mostly landscapes, hangs on its pink walls, but there are some more surprising artists represented, like John Jongkind, a Dutch precursor of Impressionism, and Francis Picabia, a major fig-ure of the Dada movement. Free exhibitions are often held in the downstairs gallery (same hours). The inevitable spa **casino**, next to the museum, contains what must be one of the world's most lavish cinemas, all columns and chandeliers.

The ticket for the Musée Salies also covers the **Musée du Vieux Moulin**, about ten minutes' walk away across the Adour in rue Hount-Blanque (Tues–Fri 10am–noon & 3–6pm, Sat 3–6pm); it's a typical folk museum, with exhibits of local furniture, agricul-tural tools and *Bigourdan* crafts, but is attractively laid out and well explained.

The main tourist attraction of the area is the **Grottes de Médous** (April to mid-Oct daily 9am–noon & 2–6pm; 34F), 2km south of the centre on the main road. The twelve-people-minimum-per-tour rule can mean hanging about on a quiet day, but it's worth waiting to see the wall known as the *Salle d'Orchidée* (Orchid House), rated by Norbert Casteret as one of the great limestone formations of the Pyrenees. The caves were only discovered in 1948, and thus escaped the vandalism suffered by others during the early part of the century.

Practicalities

The heart of the town lies a five-minute walk along rue de la République from the disused train station on av de Belgique where only SNCF **buses** from Tarbes stop – though they continue into the centre for a final halt by the fifteenth-century church of Saint-Vincent, within sight of the place Lafayette. Other buses up the Vallée de Campan as far as Payolle (see below) depart from next to the **tourist office** at 3 allée Tournefort (July & Aug Mon–Sat 9am–12.30pm & 2–7pm, Sun 9am–noon & 2–6pm; April–June, Sept & Oct 8.30–11.30am & 2–5.30pm; ☎05.62.95.50.71), south of the *place*. From the tourist office it's a short walk northwest to the leafy **allées des Coustous**, the main café street and also home to the *Poste*, west of which is pedestrianized **place de Strasbourg** and the covered market occupying **place Ramond**.

North of the *halles* lies the quietest area for **accommodation**; hotels facing the spa tend to be overpriced, catering for an elderly, rather sedentary clientele. In rue de l'Horloge, named for the clock in the Tour du Jacobins, the last bit of a convent destroyed during the Revolution, you'll find the funky cheapie *Hôtel l'Horloge* (☎05.62.91.00.20; ②) and the slightly more comfortable *Hôtel de Nice* (☎05.62.95.04.65; ③) – plus a **laundrette** at no. 7. Noisier, but recently modernized, is the *Hôtel de la Paix* at 9 rue de la République (☎05.62.95.20.60, fax 05.62.91.09.88; ③). **Restaurants** – in hotels or out – aren't Bagnères' strong point; about the only independent one appears to be *Le Bigourdan*, 14 rue Victor-Hugo on the corner of rue de l'Horloge, a combination pizzeria (ground floor) and regional diner (first floor) open for lunch and dinner, with well-priced *menus*.

Bagnères has a **music festival** every year, normally from mid-August to mid-September, but a more original musical tradition is the male choir, Chanteurs Montagnards, founded in the 1840s and still performing at most civic functions.

With four to six daily SNCF **buses** from Tarbes (plus several more private ones), Bagnères is easy to get to, but it's harder to move on from – only three buses daily go south past Grottes de Médous to Sainte-Marie-de-Campan (see p.311). From July to September this service covers the extra 15km east to Lac de Payolle and its picnic area (in winter a nordic skiing resort), from where you can hitch the 25km over the Col d'Aspin to Arreau in the Vallée d'Aure. In winter there are ski buses to La Mongie (see below).

Upstream from Bagnères

South of Bagnères-de-Bigorre, the valley sides of the Haute-Adour rise steeply into the Baronnies and the **Casque du Lhéris** to the east, and towards **Pic du Midi de Bigorre** to the southwest, with the **Néouvielle** Massif rising ahead to the south. Subsidies, high rainfall and a fertile soil keep the thatched farmhouses in business, three crops a year being common, much as they were in the eighteenth century when Tarbes-born politician Bertrand Barère described Haute-Adour as: "The object of admiration by all French people . . . the eye being drawn towards the majestic Pic du Midi which forms the centre-piece of a sublime tableau." Another writer of the time noted "the excellence of its butter and the beauty of its marble".

Away from the main Aure valley and its extension, the **Vallée de Campan**, two tributaries can be explored: the lush **Vallée de Lesponne**, with the much-visited Lac Bleu at its head; and the **Gripp valley**, at the top of which is La Mongie, one of the best ski resorts in the Pyrenees, and the strategically perched observatory on Pic du Midi de Bigorre.

The Vallée de Lesponne

The countryside just north of Barèges, at the head of the **Vallée de Lesponne**, is well worth a day or two. You can take a bus as far as Beaudéan, 5km along the D935, but after that you're dependent on your own resources for the 10km along the D29 sideroad to its end at **CHIROULET**. This tiny hamlet boasts a good traditional **restaurant**, *L'Isard*, featuring local dishes, and a place to stay, *La Vieille Auberge* (☎05.62.91.71.70; ③). If this is full, a plush alternative is *Domaine de Ramonjuan* (☎05.62.91.75.75, fax 05.62.91.74.54; ⑤), 7km down-valley at Lesponne hamlet, with such luxuries as a gym, sauna and jacuzzi.

From Chiroulet a popular path rises steeply for nearly three hours to **Lac Bleu**, set in a peak-ringed cirque. The Col du Tourmalet (see p.311) can be reached by climbing around the eastern side of the 120-metre-deep lake – the path in places cut into the rock – and then heading due east to the **Col d'Aoube**, from where a faint path continues down to the D918 a short distance from Tourmalet, four hours beyond Lac Bleu.

THE CAGOTS

Numerous towns in the western half of the Pyrenees – Saint-Savin, Luz-Saint-Sauveur, Cauterets and Saint-Jean-Pied-de-Port to name just four – once had sizeable populations of a mysterious people known as **Cagots**, of whom little is known for certain other than that they were persecuted. First mentioned in thirteenth-century manuscripts, Cagots were forbidden to live in the centre of towns, to kiss the Cross, to walk barefoot, to have sexual relations outside the Cagot community or to enter a mill (in case they contaminated the grain). They had to wear a distinguishing symbol on their clothes, variously described as a crow's or a duck's foot, and live in a separate ghetto at the edge of villages. Cagots had their own baptismal fonts – sometimes even their own churches – and were buried in separate graveyards.

There were compensations. Cagots were exempt from feudal duties and taxes, were subject only to ecclesiastical courts and were not permitted to bear arms, except for work. Prohibited also from owning land, many therefore became skilled woodworkers in particular, and Gaston Fébus apparently insisted on Cagot carpenters for his fortress at Montaner. But Cagots were excluded from all normal social life, and despite appeals to the pope and the secular authorities, discrimination continued for centuries. The Cagots themselves began agitating for equal rights as early as 1479, but social consciousness lagged behind legal rulings in their favour. It was not until 1789 and the Revolution that their second-class status was officially, and definitely, ended.

The measures taken against them sound like those taken against lepers, and indeed one of the many alternative names for the Cagots – *crestianas* – is almost certainly derived from *cristianaria*, the places reserved for "white" lepers – that is, those considered infected but not contagious, and whom modern medicine would probably recognize as afflicted by some minor skin disease.

So the Cagots may have been lepers or the descendants of lepers, but it also seems plausible that they were racially distinct. Some linguists derive the word Cagot from *can goth* or "dog of the Visigoths", implying a descent from the Visigoths who fled into this area after their defeat by Clovis in 507. Furthermore, the architecture of many Basque country churches – with their low "Cagot windows" through which services could be watched, and proportionally low "Cagot doors" – suggests to some commentators that Cagots were a race of less-than-average stature. It's not even certain that these features had anything to do with the Cagots. The mystery will probably never be solved – the subject was already steeped in confusion by the fourteenth century, when in contemporaneous accounts Cagots were variously described as tall, fair and blue-eyed, or short, dark and Moorish.

The Vallée de Campan

Upstream from Beaudéan, the Adour is known locally as the **Vallée de Campan**, whose east flank edges into the Baronnies. Below woods of spruce, pine and beech, the gentle valley's meadows are speckled with farms arrayed in south-facing ranks. The individual architecture is unique: house and barn are built as a unit, with the balconied living quarters always to the right as you face the sun.

It's indicative of the tenuous nature of toleration at the start of the Age of Enlightenment that when the church of **Saint-Jean-Baptiste** at **CAMPAN** (6km from Bagnères, 1km upstream from the Lesponne turning) was rebuilt after a fire in 1694, a separate Cagot door was inserted at the west end; the Cagot ghetto here was on the right bank of the Adour, in the part known as the *Quartier Charpentier* after their habitual trade. The church's personality is now defined by the ornate white-and-gilt retable by the local brothers, the Ferrérers of Asté; the fifteenth-century wooden image of Christ, originally at L'Escaladieu, is a cruder but more moving statement of faith. The village itself, with its slate-roofed houses, is attractive; for **accommodation**, the

Beauséjour (☎05.62.91.75.30; ③), opposite the market hall, represents good value. There's also the *Camping de Layris*, on the northwest side of town.

At **SAINTE-MARIE-DE-CAMPAN**, another 6km south, there's more **accommodation** at either the *Gîte L'Ardoisière* (☎05.62.91.88.88; ① gîte, ③ doubles), with advantageous half-board rates, or the more conventional *Hotel Des Deux Cols* (☎05.62.91.85.60; ③). Both are on the main through road (as is the entire town), which as it divides is designated as the D918 in either direction. To the left it climbs east to the Col d'Aspin – where half-tame horses and cows gambol, causing traffic jams – before dropping into the Vallée d'Aure at Arreau; to the right it climbs south to La Mongie (see below).

Walkers can pick up the **Tour de la Vallée de Campan** at Pont d'Arrimoula, 1km before Sainte-Marie-de-Campan; a *gîte d'étape* (☎05.62.91.81.41; ①) serves the trail at Le Peyras, 3km west, from where you can trek south to **Pic du Midi de Bigorre** (see below) and Artigues.

Up the Gripp valley: La Mongie, Tourmalet and Pic du Midi

The D918 road to La Mongie from Sainte-Marie-de-Campan rises steadily along the **Gripp valley** to **ARTIGUES**, where there's a reasonable hotel – the *Relais d'Arizes* (☎05.62.91.90.41; ③) – a campsite and not much else. Nevertheless it's a good start- or end-point for hiking in the Réserve Naturelle de Néouvielle (see p.303) and there are short walks to the nearby Cascades de l'Arises and Cascade du Garet.

La Mongie

The high-rise ski resorts of **LA MONGIE**, 6km above Artigues, together with Super-Barèges – on the opposite side of the Col du Tourmalet – constitute the largest skiing area in the Pyrenees, with 69 pistes totalling 120km. Once you get away from the buildings it's beautiful, with a combination of open bowls, runs through trees and some simple but exciting off-piste itineraries. The main development – and its satellite, **LA MONGIE-TOURMALET**, in the middle of the lower pistes – stands at 1800m, and the top lift reaches 2440m. None of the runs is difficult (there's only one black) but it's an eminently suitable place for beginners to intermediates. The descent from the top of the Télésiège de Quatre Termes, for example, is a blue run of 3km, a distance that novices rarely have the chance to sink their teeth into.

The Col du Tourmalet and the Pic du Midi de Bigorre

The **Col du Tourmalet** (2115m), 4km beyond La Mongie, ranks as the highest drivable pass in the French Pyrenees, often playing a tormenting role in the Tour de France and almost always closed between late October and the end of April. The name literally means "the bad detour", a title perhaps bestowed by the carriers of the sedan chairs that used to taxi the wealthy between the spas of Bagnères and Barèges by this long, cold road. Wheeled transport first used the *col* in 1788, when the road along the Luz valley was blocked by floods; from the La Mongie side of the pass you can still see the faint trace of the old route.

From the *col*, a **toll road** (open mid-June to mid-Oct) leads up towards the summit of **Pic du Midi de Bigorre**, stopping at 2720m, a fifteen-minute walk short of the observatory just below the summit (2872m). Bristling with antennae and radio masts, it's a fairly unsightly place, but has the virtue of being an easily accessible high-altitude look-out. On foot it's about two hours from Tourmalet to the top, from where you can see west as far as Balaïtous, south into the Néouvielle country and east as far as Andorra.

Opened in 1881, the **observatory** has been continuously staffed since, despite being cut off for many months at a time, with all provisions and equipment carted up on the back of man or mule for the first 66 years. Despite the observatory's successful history of lunar observation and current studies of Mars, Saturn and Jupiter, the future of the establishment hangs in the balance. Although major television and radio antennae have been built here, and a contract to monitor pollution and the ozone layer was awarded late in the 1980s, serious French investment has been switched to even larger installations in Hawaii, Chile and Tenerife.

Those who see the observatory's future as combining science and tourism have been opposed by the resident scientists and technicians, who maintain that the tourists cramp their style. A compromise of sorts was reached in 1996, which envisions a new year-round *téléphérique* from La Mongie, virtually all the way up to the top; an additional road from Barèges (summer only); and an enlargement of the observatory itself to include a new museum, guided tours and a restaurant. Work has begun, but meanwhile the observatory is closed to the public and unlikely to reopen before the year 2000.

Tarbes

If you're heading towards the Central Pyrenees from the northeast you'll almost certainly pass through **TARBES**, capital of medieval Bigorre and the contemporary, far larger *département* of Hautes-Pyrénées. A medium-sized, suburban sort of place, it will only appeal if you have an interest in things military. Destroyed by the Normans, then ruined by the protagonists from both sides in the Wars of Religion, Tarbes retains little evidence of its past. An overall view of the city, best obtained from the Musée Massey

---

THE TOUR DE FRANCE

Every year in July the **Tour de France** passes through the Pyrenees, on its way either to or from the Alps, and most years the riders will have to tackle the savage haul up to the Col du Tourmalet. First incorporated into the route in 1927, it has now been included in almost forty contests, forming a particularly gruelling episode in what is invariably one of the toughest days of the three-week race. In 1988, for example, the riders had to cycle through Tourmalet in the course of a 180-kilometre stage that took them over six mountains; they hit the pass having already gone over Col de Peyresourde and Col d'Aspin, with a climb to the ski station of Luz-Ardiden still before them.

Although a couple of hundred riders start each Tour de France, only a dozen or so have the all-round ability needed to win. In the early stages these star riders generally take it easy, checking out the form of their chief rivals and letting themselves be nursed along by their team-mates – the so-called *domestiques*. When they reach the mountains, however, the race changes completely. Any rider with pretensions to be wearing the leader's yellow jersey when the *Tour* finally swings into Paris has to finish each mountain stage near the front, and that requires relentless effort – even a top-class rider can lose fifteen minutes on a single bad day in the Pyrenees, and this is a race where the overall winning margin has sometimes been measured in seconds. So by the time the *Tour* moves out of the Pyrenees the leader board will have resolved itself into a chart of the race favourites.

Within the main race, there's another contest going on in the Pyrenees (and the Alps) – the one for the title **"King of the Mountains"**, awarded to the rider who records the best results in the mountain stages. Winning this competition – whose leader wears a white shirt with red polka dots – secures a reputation only marginally less illustrious than the overall winner's. Any rider who takes the polka-dot shirt more than once is assured of quasi-mythical status – the Spanish rider Federico Bahamontes, who won it six times in the 1950s and 1960s, earned himself the reverential nickname "The Eagle of Toledo" for his high-altitude prowess, and Luxembourg's Charly Gaul,

tower, gives a general impression of functional and graceless white apartment and office blocks. More inspiring and exceptional architectural efforts include the futuristic National Music School or the Parvis Cultural Centre. Arms manufacture has long been Tarbes' primary industry, but it now employs just a few thousand people compared to sixteen thousand at the end of World War I, with many of the remaining jobs threatened by automation.

The Town

The train station, north of town on av Maréchal-Joffre, is within a few minutes' walk of the three main attractions. Off rue Massey sprawls the tranquil **Jardin Massey** (daily dawn to dusk; free). Designed in the last century by the eponymous Tarbes-born Placide Massey, who also worked on the gardens at Versailles, these carefully landscaped botanical gardens are a wonderful place to shake off urban dust. Specimens – some local, some as exotic as California sequoias – are informatively labelled and discussed in French. Architectural interest is supplied by the partially reconstructed Gothic cloister from the abbey of Saint-Sever-de-Rustan, with vivid, if slightly eroded column capitals: swans attacking a bear, and a sword-brandishing angel expelling Adam and Eve from Eden.

The **Musée Massey** (July & Aug Mon–Sat 10am–noon & 2–6pm; Sept–June Wed–Sat 10am–noon & 2–6pm; 20F), housed in a rather eclectic building in the middle of the *jardin*, follows three main, rather mixed-up, themes: fine arts, archeology and the history of the Hussars regiment. The arts section groups a miscellany of pleasant

winner in 1955 and 1956, became known as "The Angel of the Mountains". The favourites for the yellow jersey of course feature strongly in the "King of the Mountains" tussle, but most teams also have a specialist climber who comes to the fore in this part of the race.

A good illustration of this is the reticent Spaniard **Miguel Indurain** (nicknamed "The Colossus of Roads" or "The Sphinx"), the only rider ever to have won five consecutive *Tours*: 1991–1995. Yet his mountain stages didn't always show him at his best, and from 1994 to 1996 Frenchman **Richard Virenque** rode off with the "King of the Mountains" jersey. However, scoring is cumulative over the numerous stages, including the important flatlands time-trials, which Indurain usually dominated.

After finishing a disappointing eleventh in the 1996 *Tour*, Indurain announced his retirement in January 1997; it was the end of an era, with no one cyclist looking set to dominate competition. The Swiss **Alex Zulle** and **Tony Rominger**, who beat Indurain for the mountain title in 1993, usually manage to get into the top six, while Britain's **Chris Boardman** has captured the first-day prologue sprint twice without ever looking likely to sustain a challenge over three weeks. In 1996, **Bjarne Riis** (Denmark) secured the yellow jersey, but it wasn't until mid-1997, when his teammate **Jan Ullrich** (Germany) powered his way to the title, that commentators were able to speculate about a possible successor to Indurain. Some years back the *Tour*'s organizers took deliberate measures to "internationalize" the contest, and must be simultaneously chagrined and pleased with the results: except for Virenque, French riders have been almost totally eclipsed, while riders from countries as diverse as Colombia, Poland and Uzbekistan have captured stages in various years since 1990.

The *Tour* passes through the Pyrenees in mid-July, bringing with it an enormous entourage of back-up teams, advertising people, television crews and journalists, who occupy every hotel room in the vicinity of each day's finishing line. Accommodation is not the only problem – actually seeing the riders at the crucial points can be tricky, as the race attracts vast crowds even on the mountain-tops. If you want to see the action at any of the major passes, take up your position at least three hours before the bikes are due.

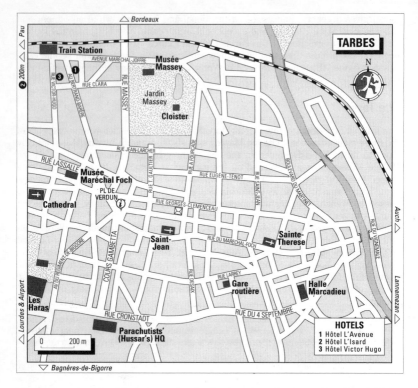

Map labels:
△ Bordeaux

TARBES

Pau △
△ 200m

Train Station

AVENUE MARÉCHAL-JOFFRE

RUE VICTOR-HUGO
RUE ARMAND-BARRÈRE

RUE CLARA

Musée Massey

RUE MASSEY

Jardin Massey

Cloister

RUE JEAN-LARCHER

RUE A-FOURCADE

RUE EUGÈNE-TÉNOT

RUE LASSALLE

Musée Maréchal Foch

RUE J. GAUTHIER

RUE SAINT-JEAN

BOULEVARD DU MARTINET

PL DE VERDUN

RUE GEORGES-CLEMENCEAU

Cathedral

RUE DU DÉNOUÉMALE

Auch △

Saint-Jean

RUE DU MARÉCHAL-FOCH

Sainte-Therese

AV DU RÉGIMENT-DE-BIGORRE

COURS GAMBETTA

RUE DESAIX

RUE LARREY

Lourdes & Airport △

Les Haras

RUE CRONSTADT

Gare routière

Halle Marcadieu

Lannemezan △

RUE DU 4 SEPTEMBRE

Parachutists' (Hussar's) HQ

0   200 m

HOTELS
1 Hôtel L'Avenue
2 Hôtel L'Isard
3 Hôtel Victor Hugo

△ Bagnères-de-Bigorre

N

pieces spanning the fifteenth to nineteenth centuries, the most attention-grabbing being a Dutch-school *Wild Boar Hunt*. Archeological exhibits include a bronze death mask of unknown date and a Roman votive altar, discovered during excavations at the train station. The Hussars section takes up the entire second floor and much of the ground floor, representing the history of the regiment, from its fifteenth-century Hungarian origins to today's parachutists, based in Tarbes, and includes military hardware and a colourful display of extravagant uniforms.

Some 300m southwest of the Jardin Massey, at 2 rue de la Victoire, is the **birthplace of Maréchal Foch** (accompanied visits only: summer daily 9am–noon & 2–6.30pm; rest of year daily except Tues & Wed 9am–noon & 2–5pm; 14F), supreme Allied commander on the western front during World War I. A traditional pitched-roof *Bigourdan* town house, it contains two floors of photos, medals and other memorabilia from the field marshal's life – including, a little morbidly, the armchair in which he died.

Tarbes' renowned stud farm, **Les Haras**, lies a couple more blocks south on rue Mouhourat (accompanied visits only, July & Aug Mon–Fri 10am–noon & 2–5pm; ☎05.62.34.44.59; 20F). Despite its relatively central location, the farm is set in acres of beautiful grounds that seem an extension of the botanical gardens. The immaculately groomed horses have impeccable manners, displayed at exercise drill, usually held at about 3pm. Founded in 1806 by Napoleon, Les Haras is best known for its *cheval Tarbais*, a cavalry breed produced by crossing English, Basque and Arabian stock.

Practicalities

From the **train station** on avenue Maréchal-Joffre there are connections with Toulouse, Lourdes and Pau. The **bus station**, on the south side of Tarbes on place au Bois, off rue Larrey, has services to Bagnères-de-Bigorre, La Mongie, Lannemezan (with onward connections to Saint-Lary) and Pau via Soumoulou. **Tarbes-Ossun-Lourdes airport**, 9km southwest of town, has daily, scheduled Air-Inter flights to and from Paris, plus numerous charters. The airport bus serves the Air-Inter flights only, but getting a taxi into the centre is no problem, and the airport has its own train station, with occasional services into the town's station.

The **tourist office** is just off the central place de Verdun at 3 cours Gambetta (Mon–Sat 9am–12.30pm & 2–7pm; ☎05.62.93.36.62), where rues Massey and Lasalle intersect. Co-publishers of the helpful IGN 1:50,000 walkers' maps, Randonnées Pyrénéenes has its headquarters at 29 rue Marcel-Lamarque (☎05.62.93.57.57), where French-language publications (as well as the maps) are sold.

There are a few reasonable **hotels** near the train station: one that comes recommended is *Hôtel de l'Avenue* at 78–80 av Bertrand-Barère (☎05.62.93.06.36; ③). In the same area, but more comfortable, you'll find the pleasant *Hôtel l'Isard*, 70 av Maréchal-Joffre (☎05.62.93.06.69; ③); the small, simple *Hotel Victor Hugo* around the corner at 52 rue Victor-Hugo (☎05.62.93.36.71; ③) would be quieter. The **youth hostel** is at 88 av Alsace-Lorraine (☎62.36.63.63; ①).

For **eating out**, again you can pretty much stay within sight of the station. The independent restaurant attached to *L'Isard* offers several *menus* ranging from subsistence to gourmet – the latter including such delights as salmon with mushrooms and *foie gras*. At 62 rue Bertrand-Barère, *Le Petit Gourmand* is a popular lunch spot, while if you're craving something exotic, *Thanh Thúy* across the street at no. 53 does very passable Vietnamese dishes à la carte for well under 100F a head, and *Le Sahara*, 21 rue Victor-Hugo, is a standard Moroccan diner. For a **drink**, *La Braisière* at 22 rue Bertrand-Barère is one of the more durable bistros in the centre.

Lourdes and around

LOURDES, just 20km south of Tarbes on the N21, is difficult to avoid if you're touring the French side of the Central Pyrenees, as it sits squarely astride the direct route up to Argelès-Gazost, Cauterets and Luz-Saint-Sauveur. And even if it weren't so pivotal, the town would be an unmissable detour. East of the main street, Lourdes is like many other small, French foothill communities. But the western part, around the *cité religieuse* on the banks of the Gave (River) de Pau, is another world – boarded up in winter, and in summer seething with the pilgrims who constitute its sole reason for existence. Whatever your views on organized religion, the huge crowds attending the Masses and the grotto make an overwhelming spectacle: over six million people come each year to this town of fewer than eighteen thousand inhabitants, and inevitably a substantial fraction disport themselves at a number of low-key attractions in the surrounding countryside.

The cult of Lourdes

The unwitting instigator of the cult of Lourdes was **Bernadette Soubirous**, daughter of a poor local miller. On February 11, 1858 she was collecting firewood near the Grotte de Massabielle when the Virgin Mary appeared and spoke to her in the *Bigourdan* dialect, asking her to return regularly to the cave. During the subsequent seventeen visitations which lasted until July, the Virgin revealed her identity to Bernadette, and commanded the girl to dig at the ground with her hands, thus releasing a spring whose

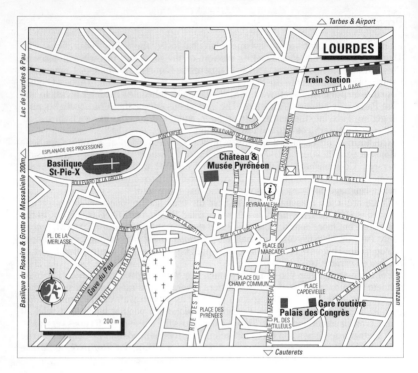

water would supposedly prove to have curative powers. Bernadette's apparition also demanded that she notify the local priests, have a chapel built and organize devotional processions to the spot.

These visions were authenticated by the church authorities in 1862, and eleven years later the first nationwide pilgrimage took place, organized by the **Assomptionistes**. This was an ultra-conservative Catholic movement founded in 1845 in response to the reigning positivism, republicanism and atheism of the era. Its ranks swelled by press agitation following the short-lived Paris Commune of 1873, the *Assomptionistes* effectively took over the town of Lourdes, dismissing the local clergy and running the pilgrimages as a going concern. Not coincidentally, from its coup dates the proliferation of hotels in Lourdes (more than 350 of them, more than any town in France bar Paris), and shops devoted to the sale of unbelievable (in all senses) religious kitsch: Bernadette and/or the Virgin emblazoned on key rings, candles, candy-bars, thermometers and illuminated plastic grottoes.

With each miraculous cure – of which there were a number, as witnessed by the discarded crutches hanging at the grotto – the pilgrimage to Lourdes gained momentum. Among early rich and famous visitors were Napoléon III and the Empress Eugénie, making the trip on behalf of their sick son. Ironically, the emperor had ordered the closure of the grotto a few years earlier, fearing public disorder. Bernadette herself had been hustled into a convent in 1866, ostensibly for her own safety, where she died thirteen years later.

No matter how cynical you may be about the authenticity of Bernadette's visions, or the motives of some who manage the pilgrim business, you cannot fail to be moved by the thousands of pilgrims, many crippled or quite obviously ill, who converge here to give their faith a chance to cure them. You see them everywhere, being wheeled about by medical personnel, amidst nuns, priests and a surprisingly heavy police presence (not least to dispense citations to those parked illegally). What impresses next is the sheer internationality of the crowds: numerous Malagasy and *Réunionais*, Africans, Spanish, Italians, Poles, Germans, Dutch and a few Anglophones.

The flamboyant, gargantuan double **Basilique du Rosaire et de l'Immaculée Conception**, built between 1871 and 1883 in "Romano-Byzantine" and Gothic styles, was no longer large enough by the centenary of the apparitions; hence the construction of the underground **Basilique Saint-Pie X**, which can hold a further twenty thousand, dominating the Esplanade des Processions, with overflow capacity of forty thousand more. But the heart of this Catholic Disneyworld is the **Grotte de Massabielle**, site of Bernadette's visions, for unbelievers merely a small, dark cavity beneath a rock overhang beside the river, below the Basilique du Rosaire. Inside stands a statue of the holy apparition, which Bernadette herself denounced as a mockery of her precise description to the sculptor. Neither the shoddy likeness or the modest dimensions of the grotto concern the pilgrims who, queuing beside signs demanding silence (in the main obeyed), circumambulate the cave clockwise, stroking the wall with their left hand. To the right of the grotto stand enormous votive candles left to prolong one's prayer, and bath-houses for immersing the sick. On the left, right under the basilica, is a row of taps channelled from the **spring**, for the collection of holy water in containers of every shape, size and material, sold in the souvenir shops and embossed with medallions depicting the Virgin and Bernadette.

The rest of the town

The Bernadette story is not the only one about Lourdes. Another tells how, during a siege of the Moorish-occupied city by Charlemagne, an eagle let drop an enormous trout into the famine-stricken town. Mirat, the Moorish chief, threw it over the walls, tricking Charlemagne into believing that the Moors still had plenty to eat, and duly lifting the siege. As with all good Christian moral parables, this one ends with Mirat being converted from his Mohammedan ways; he took the name Lorus, which in turn, subtly modified, was given to the city that now bears a giant trout on its coat-of-arms.

Lourdes' only secular attraction is its **castle**, poised on a rocky bluff on the east bank of the Gave de Pau and entered from rue du Bourg. Briefly an English stronghold in the late fourteenth century, it later became a state prison, detaining among others Lord Elgin (he of the Parthenon marbles) on his troubled way back to Britain from Ottoman territory. The main reason for the climb up is to visit the worthwhile, if unevenly labelled **Musée Pyrénéen** (guided visits only, last departure an hour before closure: April–Sept daily 9am–noon & 2–6pm; Oct–March daily except Tues & hols 9am–noon & 2–6pm, closes 5pm Fri; 26F). For the dedicated climber or walker, some of the equipment displays are intriguing, particularly the primitive axes, crampons, ropes and other expedition necessities of the pioneer *Pyrénéistes*. On show, too, are some magnificently detailed maps by Franz Schrader, who first came to the Pyrenees in 1873 on a cartographic mission; he also left paintings and drawings of the high peaks, among them an evocative view of Monte Perdido. Other exhibits include costumes and everyday items of Pyrenean life during recent centuries, plus local flora and fauna, mostly presented in tableaux form. The museum has an excellent library (which you can use with permission), containing not only books such as the 1867 edition of Charles Packe's *Guide to the Pyrenees* but also original documents (for example, the 99-year lease of Vignemale granted to Henry Russell – see feature on p.331), and hundreds of rare photographs.

Excursions

If you want to stay in Lourdes briefly before heading into the mountains, there are a number of **excursions** to be made around the town, albeit expensive and overcrowded ones. For good views with a minimum of effort, take the *téléphérique* up the 791-metre-high **Pic Béout** (Easter to mid-Oct daily 9am–noon & 2–6pm), reached from avenue Francis Lagardère, at the southern end of town. While there, you may like to visit **Gouffre Béout** (same hours), an 82-metre-deep cave discovered, with a number of prehistoric tools inside, by Norbert Casteret in 1938; but there's not a lot to see now, and it gets very busy. The other transport-assisted "climb" is up 948-metre **Pic du Jer** (daily all year 9.30–11.50am & 2–5.30pm; 44F return), a funicular ride to another panoramic view; you can walk down, following a well-marked trail.

For a short trip out of town, head 4km west to **Lac de Lourdes**, a pretty though somewhat oversubscribed picnic spot; there are local buses along the main D937 to Pau. Twelve kilometres further you come to the **Grottes de Bétharram** (March 25–Oct 25 daily 8.30am–noon & 1.30–5.30pm; Nov 20–Dec 20, Jan 3–Feb 13 & Feb 20–March 25, Mon–Fri by arrangement; ☎05.62.41.80.04; 48F), where barges and trains provide rides through 5km of underground galleries. The name of the caves derives from the *Bigourdan* phrase *Bét Arram*, meaning "beautiful branch": legend has it that the Virgin Mary saved a young girl from drowning here in the Gave de Pau by throwing a branch to her.

Practicalities

The **train station** is on the far north side of Lourdes, about ten minutes' walk from the centre; there are very frequent services to Tarbes (15min) and Pau (30min). The **gare routière** is in the central place Capdevielle, behind the Palais des Congrès, and there's a not particularly helpful **tourist office** in a new glass building on place Peyramale (Easter to mid-Oct Mon–Sat 9am–7pm, Sun 11am–6pm; mid-Oct to Easter Mon–Sat 9am–noon & 2–6pm; ☎05.62.42.77.40). **Tarbes-Ossun-Lourdes International Airport**, some 10km north, has only one regular daily bus service (departs train station 11.30am, meets Air-Inter flight, returns to train station at 1pm), but there are services to Tarbes roughly every hour along the main N21, which pass within a kilometre or so of the airport.

There's an abundance of fairly indistinguishable **accommodation** in Lourdes – some two hundred one- and two-star hotels (most ④–⑤), concentrated in the small central streets close to the castle. Establishment names like *Christ Roi*, *Golgotha* and *Calvaire* give a clue as to the usual clientele; for something in the more secular part of town, try the *Logis de France*-affiliated *Hotel d'Albret*, 21 place du Champ-Commun (☎05.62.94.75.00, fax 05.62.94.78.45; ③; closed mid-Nov to mid-Dec & Jan), opposite the *halles*, with a good attached restaurant, *Taverne de Bigorre*. Most hotels require half-board, so there are few decent independent eateries in town. **Hostel** accommodation is provided by the *Centre Pax Christi*, route de la Forêt (☎05.62.94.00.66; ①) on the western edge of town. The most central **campsite** is the *Poste* (April to mid-Oct) in rue de Langelle, just south of the train station, though it's reported to be cramped, unhygienic and lacking in hot water.

The upper Gave de Pau

The upper **Gave de Pau**, paralleled by the N21, offers a number of potential stops, such as Argelès-Gazost, the abbey-village of Saint-Savin and an aviary of raptors at Beaucens. Both road and river split in the vicinity of these attractions; the most rewarding side trip is from Argelès itself, up the joint **Vallées d'Arrens** and **d'Étaing**.

Argelès-Gazost and around

ARGELÈS-GAZOST, 13km south of Lourdes, is an innocuously dull if rather congested spa that makes a good base for touring the Gave de Pau as far as Pierrefitte-Nestalas. The town itself extends from the valley floor, quite broad here, up to the busy medieval core on a terrace to the west. The **tourist office** (summer Mon–Sat 9am–12.30pm & 2.30–7.30pm, Sun 9am–noon & 4–7.30pm; ☎05.62.97.00.25) is in the principal place de la République (aka Grande-Terrasse), three minutes south of the church. There are a number of old-fashioned but en-suite **hotels** in and around Argelès, most with attached (and good-value) restaurants: worth singling out are the comfortable *Hostellerie Le Relais*, 25 rue Maréchal-Foch (☎05.62.97.01.27; closed Oct–Jan; ④), marooned amidst car parks but with a peaceful enough front garden; *Le Soleil Levant*, just north of town on the N21, a quiet thermal establishment set back from the road (☎05.62.97.08.68; ④; closed Jan); and perhaps best of all, the *Logis de France*-member *Beau Site* at 10 rue Capitaine-Digoy near the tourist office (☎05.62.97.08.63, fax 05.62.97.06.01; ④; closed Nov), a classic French country inn with the best rooms overlooking an immense, tumbling garden.

Apart from buying mountain equipment from the excellent Lafont Sports in place du Foirail (which doubles as the main parking lot), there's little to do in or near Argelès apart from learning **rafting, kayaking** or **canyoning** at the Pavillon des Sensations (☎05.62.94.52.03), 4km back towards Lourdes at the neat, quiet village of Agos-Vidalos. Nearby **ARCIZANS-AVANT**, 2km southwest by a minor road, can offer the privately run, rather bogus **Château of the Black Prince** (mid-June to mid-Sept daily 10am–noon & 2.30–7pm; April to mid-June & mid-Sept to Oct Sun & public holidays only, same hours), most of it rather later than Edward's time; the *château* functions mainly as a restaurant, with good-value meals, and has a few **rooms** (☎05.62.97.02.79; ④). Below the church is another *Logis de France* hotel, the *Auberge Le Cabaliros* (☎05.62.97.04.31, fax 05.62.97.91.48; ④; closed mid-Oct to mid-Dec), with views south over the valley to high peaks from the restaurant's outdoor seats, and a few less expensive rooms under the mansard roof.

Saint-Savin

The twelfth-century **Romanesque abbey** at **SAINT-SAVIN**, 4km south of Argelès-Gazost, is worth visiting partly because of its unusual fortifications – the roof was raised in the fourteenth century to accommodate gun slits, the octagonal tower added simultaneously – and partly for its connection with the persecuted Cagots.

Monastic fortifications in this part of the Pyrenees generally served a double function: aiding enforcement of the *Trêves de Dieu*, the church-imposed truce days between rival *seigneurs*; and acting as a defence against Aragonese raiders. At Saint-Savin defence from irate locals may have become paramount, the abbey having grown rich, unpopular and embroiled in lawsuits stemming from ventures such as the spa at Cauterets. A monastic community existed as far back as the eighth century, and the monks quickly established a virtual mini-state here and in adjacent valleys, along with a reputation for luxury and ungodliness. The contemporary feel of the main church – perhaps the least numinous in the entire range, with little evidence of continued sacred use – seems to reflect this.

There was once a large local Cagot community, and the low opening, now blocked, to the left of the multi-lobed west portal is possibly where they listened to Mass from outside; most scholars have concluded that the two granite figures supporting the water stoup in the south transept are Cagots. The organ cabinet (1557) is carved with grotesque faces whose eyes and tongues were designed to move when the instrument was played, supposedly the grimacing visages of damned souls unable to endure the sound of heavenly music. St Savin himself, an obscure local seventh-century hermit, is supposedly entombed in the choir. The vaulted chapterhouse north of the church now serves as the entry to a **treasury** (daily summer 10am–noon & 3.30–6.30pm; 10F) whose main highlights are various twelfth-century statuettes of the Virgin.

Many visitors prefer the little **chapel of Notre-Dame-de-Piétat** (daily 10am–6pm; free), which adorns a hill amongst hay meadows 1km south of the village. Its glory is an elaborately painted ceiling, where birds perch on floral motifs covering every available space of the simple vault; you can examine them at close range from the wooden gallery.

Saint-Savin village has two **hotel-restaurants**, both on the square leading up to the church from the south: the functional *Panoramic* (☎05.62.97.08.22; ③), and *Le Viscos* (☎05.62.97.02.28; ⑤; closed Dec), whose affordable *menus* feature game; à la carte will run to at least 220F per person.

Beaucens and around

On the opposite side of the valley to Saint-Savin, there's a chance to see birds of prey in captivity at the **Donjon des Aigles**, the ruined twelfth-century keep of the château at **BEAUCENS** (Easter–Sept 2.30–6.30pm; flying displays July 3.30pm & 5pm, Aug 3pm, 4.30pm & 6pm; 30F). You might feel these magnificent raptors shouldn't be kept penned for tourists' entertainment, but seeing them close up – a trained griffon vulture actually "buzzes" the audience – should at least teach people to appreciate them.

To reach the donjon by public transport it is best to get off at **PIERREFITTE-NESTALAS**, where SNCF buses veer off for Cauterets (5–6 daily; see p.332); cross the bridge and walk the well-signposted 2km. Pierrefitte-Nestalas itself, with its belching chemical plant, has little to detain you, except for a small **aquarium** (Tues 2–6pm, Wed–Sun 9.30am–noon & 2–6pm; 35F), 50m from the bus stop, incongruously dedicated to tropical fish.

East of Pierrefitte – though the most direct road access is from Argelès – the ski station of **HAUTACAM** makes an attractive target for a sixteen-kilometre drive, the uplands being a congenial place for red and black kites, sparrowhawks and other birds of prey. The summertime hike east from here to Lac Bleu (see p.309) is recommended for lovers of solitude, but the downhill skiing in winter is not – the top station for the fourteen pistes is only 1810m, though the 12km of marked nordic tracks could be more worthwhile.

Vallée d'Arrens and Vallée d'Estaing

The D918 southwest from Argelès initially follows the Vallée d'Arrens, with a turn-off after 4km south up the D103, which serves the silky green and gentle-sided **Vallée d'Estaing**. There are some good places to **stay** and **eat** along this valley: the well-signed *Chez Begué* (☎05.62.96.44.83; ②), just off the road in **ESTAING** village, as well as a **campsite**, *Pyrénées Natura* (May–Sept), just south; a *gîte d'étape* south of the hamlet of **VIELLETTES** (☎05.62.97.14.37; ①–②), with dormitory and family rooms; and, just below the Lac d'Estaing, the *Hôtel Restaurant du Lac* (☎05.62.97.06.25; ③), whose *nouvelle-cuisine* menu draws customers from far afield. Unusually for a rural eatery, lunch is provided until 2.30pm; skip the humdrum *menus* in favour of the *carte* which features crayfish in various guises and elaborate desserts, most defying translation. The hotel rooms are simple – mostly with shared bathrooms – but tasteful. At road's end, the natural **Lac d'Estaing** is rather too popular for its own good with weekenders who rent pedaloes, patronize a pony-ride outfit and pack out a **campsite**; but the lake is also an important trailhead for the GR10, leading southeast to the Ilhéou refuge (4hr), and an unnumbered path going south to the numerous tarns around Pic d'Estradère and beyond to the Col de Portet and its lake.

The main **Vallée d'Arrens** has two fair-sized villages with facilities and points of interest. At **AUCUN**, 9km above Argelès-Gazost (2 buses daily), the **Musée Montagnard du Lavédan** (daily during school holidays 10am–noon & 3–6pm; otherwise by appointment on ☎05.62.97.12.03; 20F) has a private collection of traditional *Bigourdan* agricultural and household items. Closest places to stay are 3km upvalley at **ARRENS-MARSOUS**, where there's an excellent **gîte d'étape**, *La Maison Camélat* (☎05.62.97.40.94; ①), whose proprietors are certified guides, at least one independent **restaurant** (*Le Renaissance*), as well as the *Maison du Val d'Azun* (daily summer 9am–noon & 2–7pm; ☎05.62.97.49.49) which sells farm products and can point you in the direction of nordic skiing pistes nearby (Azun is the name of the secluded side valley just northwest). From Arrens the D918 snakes west over the beautiful *cols* de Soulor and d'Aubisque into the Ossau valley at Eaux-Bonnes; a very minor road also links the village with Estaing village in the Vallée d'Estaing, via the Col des Bordères, as does the GR10.

Luz-Saint-Sauveur

The double spa-village of **LUZ-SAINT-SAUVEUR**, in two distinct quarters straddling the confluence of the Gavarnie and Bastan rivers, lies 12km south of Pierrefitte-Nestalas. It makes a useful base if you have a car or are content to make day-trips by public transport. For the serious walker, however, it's still a bit too distant from the Gavarnie cirque – the goal of any expedition up this valley – to be ideal, despite a notional situation on the GR10. Skiing is more promising, with the small resort of Luz-Ardidens just to the west, and better ones at Barèges further east.

The Town

The oldest and most attractive part of Luz is its upper quarter, whose narrow lanes, hosting a Monday market, radiate from the fortified twelfth-century church of **Saint-André**. Surrounding houses make it difficult to get a good look at the church, a classic of medieval military architecture, with a crenellated outer wall, stout, machicolated towers and gun slits just below the roof. These were provided in the twelfth century by the Knights Templar and further modified in the fourteenth by the Knights of St John, who appropriated all of the Templars' strongholds after their suppression. A fine carved Christ in Majesty, flanked by the symbols of the Evangelists, floats on the tympanum over the north portal, and a *clocher-mur* dominates the roofline. The church interior proves disappointing and rather cluttered with three huge confessionals, but in the creaky side chapel there's a free **museum** of sacred artefacts dating back to the twelfth century, including a manuscript on procedures for exorcisms.

The **Saint-Saveur** quarter to the west consists of the startlingly elegant line of *thermes* buildings and slightly pretentious hotels on the left bank of the Gave de Gavarnie. The 21-year-old George Sand visited and was repelled, writing: "The beautiful people strut and preen and talk amongst themselves about their ailments." According to local legend, Napoléon III authorized the superfluous **Pont Napoléon** in 1860, to commemorate his illicit conception at nearby Gavarnie. He also paid for the Chapelle Solférino, south of the fortified church in the main part of the village.

You can cross the river bridge to visit the prominent, thirteenth-to-fourteenth-century **Château Sainte-Marie** (unenclosed, free), just 1km northeast in the adjoining village of Esquièze-Sère. Although the suriviving pair of round and square towers don't fulfil their promise as glimpsed from afar, the *château* provides unrivalled views over the town; it's a popular picnic spot, with a spring, and an occasional venue for concerts.

Practicalities

Buses from Lourdes drop you in place du Huit-Mai, hub of the lower part of the village, beside the helpful **Office du Tourisme** (summer Mon–Sat 9am–12.30pm & 1.30–7pm, Sun 9am–12.30pm & 4–7pm; ☎05.62.92.30.30), which can provide lists of long-term apartments for rent. Off place St-Clément, hub of the Monday market, there's a *Maison du Parc National* (summer Mon–Fri 9am–noon & 2–7pm, Sat & Sun 4–7pm; ☎05.62.92.38.38), which organizes outdoor activites and hosts an exhibition of local flora and fauna. Among **hotels**, the atmospheric *Templiers*, right opposite the fortified church (☎05.62.92.81.52; ④; closed May & mid-Oct to mid-Dec), is an excellent, quiet choice with a crêperie on the ground floor. Alternatives include *Les Cimes* (☎05.62.92.83.03; ③), 150m downhill from the *Templiers*, or the imposing *Londres* on the river bank (☎05.62.92.80.09; ④; same closing as *Templiers*), which is fine as long as you don't get a room facing the road. The well-run **gîte d'étape/youth hostel** (☎05.62.92.85.85; ①; open year-round), with a few doubles and a good restaurant, and the co-managed *Les Cascades* **campsite** above it (closed Oct & Nov) are in the southern neighbourhood, and there's another campsite, *Le Toy* (☎05.62.92.86.85; open Jan–April & June–Sept), right by place du Huit-Mai. Aside from the hotel restaurants, you can **eat** pizza and salads at *Chez Christine*, on rue d'Ossun Prolongée (supper only; closed May, Oct & Nov), or Spanish tapas and *plats de jour* at *Bodega La Tasca*, on place Saint-Clément (open noon to midnight; closed May, plus Wed & Sun off-season).

Skiing: Luz-Ardiden

The associated ski development of **LUZ-ARDIDEN**, nearly 1000m higher than Luz itself, is reached by 12km of hairpins on the D12 heading northwest. Essentially a small bowl, the resort boasts twenty lifts – highest 2450m – and 32 pistes: four green, ten blue, fourteen red and four black. The ski *randonnée* is the best thing about the place, with fine ascents of **Pic d'Ardiden** (2988m), and a possible descent to the Cauterets valley. In summer you can also **walk** in a moderate, seven-hour day from Luz to Cauterets via Luz-Ardiden on a *variante* of the GR10.

Barèges and around

The one-street village of **BARÈGES**, 8km northeast of Luz-Saint-Sauveur towards Col du Tourmalet (5–6 summer SNCF buses daily), pitches itself as a sports centre, with opportunities for bike rental (touring and mountain), riding, rafting, squash, walking, snow-shoeing, skiing – and, above all, **parapente**. Although this cross between hang-gliding and parachuting is much safer than its early days – when the accident rate exceeded that for hang-gliding – proper tuition is still a must. One of the leading schools in France is here, Air Aventure Pyrénées (☎05.62.92.91.60, mobile 06.08.93.62.02; May–Oct), with English-speaking instructors offering tandem beginner's flights (250F) and initiation days (420F).

Should you be so unlucky as to break a bone, Barèges is not a bad place to do it. It became a fashionable health resort after visits in 1677 by the Duc de Maine, the sickly son of Louis XIV, and the waters were considered particularly efficacious for gunshot wounds – a military hospital was established in 1744, and Napoleon made it one of five military *thermes*. Perhaps the spa's most significant guest was the 32-year-old **Ramond de Carbonnières**, whose passion for these mountains can be traced to Barèges, where he came in 1787 as the confidant of the disgraced Cardinal de Rohan. Today the baths have been enthusiastically incorporated into the wintertime *après-ski* routine.

Especially if you're traversing the GR10, or are interested in sampling Barèges' sporting opportunities, a top choice for **accommodation** would be the *Gîte d'Étape l'Oasis*, in a fine old building behind the thermal baths (☎05.62.92.69.47, fax 05.62.92.65.17; ①; closed two weeks Nov or May), with helpful English-speaking co-management, plumbing of some sort in all the rooms, and meals provided; it's co-run with the *Refuge de la Glère* (see p.305). Otherwise there are plenty of **hotels** in the village, all easy to find in this tiny place, the most central being the *Poste* (☎05.62.92.68.37; ③), *L'Alphée* (☎05.62.92.68.39; ③) and the *Montagne Fleurie* (☎05.62.92.68.50; ②). There is just one **campsite**, however, *La Ribère* (☎05.62.92.69.01), which you'll pass if arriving from Luz. Probably the best local independent **restaurant** is *Aubege du Lienz* (aka *Chez Louisette*; closed early May & Nov), serving hearty *menus* from 120F, including such dishes as trout, suckling pig and *garbure*. It's 2km southeast by forest track, on the wooded Plateau du Lienz, at the start of the track up to the *Refuge de la Glère*.

The **tourist office** sits right in the centre of the village (summer Mon–Sat 9am–12.30pm & 2–7pm, Sun 10am–noon & 4–6pm; ☎05.62.92.68.19), dispensing leaflets on recommended walking and VTT routes. There's also a summer-only open-air **swimming pool** (daily 11am–6pm; 14F) and **squash courts** (daily 11am–8pm; 25F for 40min) at the municipally run Hélios recreation centre.

Beyond Barèges the D918 winds up to the **Col du Tourmalet**, before dropping to La Mongie, Campan and Bagnères-de-Bigorre. Just west of the pass at Pont de la Gaubie is the **Jardin Botanique du Tourmalet** (May–Sept daily 9am–6pm; 25F), which has assembled most of the wild flora of the Pyrenees in a single two-hectare site. You can **eat** buckwheat crepes and light snacks nearby at *Auberge de la Gaubie* (lunch, June–Sept only).

Walking and snowshoeing from Barèges

The **GR10** passes through Barèges, heading southeast on an interesting traverse through the Réserve Naturelle de Néouvielle to Vielle-Aure. The ascents of either **Turon de Néouvielle** or **Pic du Néouvielle** are both challenging expeditions out of Barèges, beginning in earnest at the *Refuge de la Glère*, 10km south of Barèges by track. Both of these climbing routes, which will take the better part of twelve hours, are described on pp.304–305 – as is the traverse (in reverse sense). In winter, the valley terrain lends itself to circuits on *raquettes* or **snowshoes**; the tourist office has a leaflet describing the marked routes.

Super-Barèges

In a snowy year Barèges has some of the best skiing in the Pyrenees, due to its affiliation with La Mongie (joint pass available) and some hugely enjoyable off-piste itineraries. It had a ski school as early as 1922 and boasts a famous ski club, L'Avalanche, whose members have included French champions François Vignole and Annie Famose. The combined resort has 120km of pistes; on its own, Barèges has 50km – eight green runs, eleven blue, seven red and two black.

From Barèges the **Funiculaire de l'Ayre** rises to 2002m, but as the village is only at 1250m it is seldom possible to ski all the way back again. Better to take the ski-bus to **SUPER-BARÈGES** (1750m), a ten-minute ride east. For a great day on and off piste from there, take the Télésiège Caoubere and the Télésiège du Tourmalet and then the La Mongie lifts Coume de Pourteilh and Quatre Termes. The off-piste section begins with a short climb south into the Bassin du Bastan via a narrow gulley; from the top there is an exhilarating descent towards Lac d'Agalops, just below the Hourquette Nére, from where the GR10 leads back west to the foot of the Télésiège Caoubere.

The Gavarnie region

South of Luz-Saint-Sauveur, the D921 follows the Gave de Gavarnie 20km upstream to its source – the superlative-laden **Cirque de Gavarnie**, a glacial bowl which first sparked touristic interest in the Pyrenees. Its heyday began in the late nineteenth century, after enraptured Romantics like Victor Hugo lauded it in almost self-parodying prose – "It's the most mysterious of buildings, by the most mysterious of architects; it's Nature's Coliseum, it's Gavarnie!" – and hyperbole, estimating its height as "ten miles" and length as "ten leagues". Such publicity drew increasing crowds to the area, reaching a high of two million visitors during 1958. Since then, the annual number of visitors has fallen by 75 percent, thanks perhaps to the boom in overseas travel; the cirque and its environs have thus gained a bit of breathing space, while the creation of the national park has been the occasion of a tidying up and proclaimed, though not always effected, improvement of services in **Gavarnie village**.

It's also possible to stay 9km below Gavarnie, in the somewhat calmer village of **Gèdre**. From there you have easy road access to two other cirques: wide and ethereal **Troumouse** and lonely **Estaubé**. Most people head straight for Gavarnie (45min by bus from Luz), but anyone with a couple of days to spare can traverse all three cirques, one of the most extraordinary hiking experiences in the Pyrenees. Alternatively, two of the cirques provide acccess to the Ordesa region in Spain – via the **Brèche de Roland** from Gavarnie, and the **Brèche de Tuquerouye** from Estaubé. Gavarnie village is also the base camp for approaches to **Vignemale** peak on the westbound **GR10**, which then curves north towards Cauterets. For any, or all such explorations you'll want the 1:50,000 IGN Carte de Randonnées **map**, no. 4, "Bigorre".

Gèdre and its cirques

Purists can walk south from Luz to Gavarnie in a day along the **GR10**, but since it's mostly within sight of the D921 road you may as well take the bus (2 daily in summer, 3 a week rest of the year, on Mon, Thurs & Sat) at least as far as **GÈDRE** (12km). Almost entirely dependent on its electricity-generating installations, Gèdre has no great attraction other than convenience as a base for visiting the nearby Troumouse and Estaubé cirques, but it does hold a place in Pyrenean history as the home of Henri Cazaux and Bernard Guillembet, the guides who in 1837 became the first to climb Vignemale.

There's a central **tourist office** (summer Mon–Sat 9am–noon & 3–7pm, Sun 9am–noon; ☎05.62.92.48.05). If you want to **stay**, choose from among *Pension Les Voyageurs* (☎05.62.92.48.42; ③; closed Oct–Christmas), on the road south towards Gavarnie; *Les Pyrénées* (☎05.62.92.48.51, fax 05.62.92.49.64; ⑤; open all year) in what passes for the village centre; and the characterful, walnutwood-furnished *Hôtel La Brêche de Roland* (☎05.62.92.48.54, fax 05.62.92.46.05; ⑥; closed Oct to mid-Dec) also on the through road, which has a good attached restaurant. There are three **campsites**: one just before the village, two above it to the east. As for independent **restaurants**, *La Grotte* at a bend in the road just above *La Brêche* might look and feel like a tourist trap, but it offers an excellent buffet lunch for well under 100F, serves until 3pm and has oudoor seating with a view of the cascade and grotto of the name in the river just below.

Héas and the Cirque de Troumouse

For the **Cirque de Troumouse**, 15km from Gèdre, take the minor D922 to the east, which starts just south of the village. After 8km you reach the hamlet of **HÉAS**, a collection of farmsteads around a pilgrimage chapel. Until the road was opened in the 1950s – and the HRP was routed through here from Barroude and Gavarnie (see opposite) –

this must have been a lonely spot indeed; it's still one of the highest (1500m) permanently inhabited places in the Pyrenees.

Chambres d'hôtes, camping space and simple meals are available at *La Chaumière*, just below the hamlet (☎05.62.92.48.66; ③; May–Oct), or at *Auberge de la Munia*, in Héas proper by the church (☎05.62.92.48.39; ④; April–Nov). Beyond the toll post (22.50F), the road climbs steeply in hairpins 4km to the *Auberge de Maillet* (☎05.62.92.48.97; dorms ①, rooms ③; meals; June to mid-Oct), ending 3km later at an enormous car park, still not big enough to accommodate all visitors on a summer's day. Walkers avoid both toll and tarmac by using a clear path up the easterly Touyères ravine starting near the *Snack Bar La Refuge*, by the toll booth.

All around the car park, the desolate, wild cirque stretches 10km from end to end, not high but much bigger than Gavarnie's and, in bad weather, rather intimidating. In better conditions it's a magical spot early or late in the day, when the day-trippers have gone – and even more so in late winter, when you can get in on snowshoes or skis and have it all to yourself.

Beneath the eastern walls of the cirque are scattered a half-dozen glacial tarns, the **Lacs des Aires**; a marked path describes a circuit of them from Héas (2hr up) or the top car park (30min away), snaking through the pastures spangled with wildflowers (ranunculus, gentian and colchicum the most prominent) and divided by rivulets. The air is full of small alpine birds, and the turf, despite national-park status, is grazed by hundreds of cows and sheep as in centuries past. A 2138-metre knoll topped by a nineteenth-century statue of the Virgin, some fifteen minutes' walk northeast of the parking lot, affords the best view possible of the place.

The Cirque d'Estaubé – and hiking to Gavarnie

The relatively small **Cirque d'Estaubé** lies at the head of the next, eponymous valley west of Troumouse. You can walk there within two hours from the *Auberge de Maillet*, but the easiest and most scenic way of reaching it involves backtracking 2km from Héas to the mouth of the Estaubé valley, and the D176 side road up to the **Barrage des Gloriettes**. From there, the cirque is 4km further south along a narrow, cliff-lined glen, remote and little visited except by hikers on the HRP which goes through here, linking Gavarnie and Héas. An ice-choked gulley – approached by an easier side trail from the HRP – leads finally to the **Brèche de Tuquerouye/Brecha de Tucarroya**, at the top of the cirque at its western end (see below for detailed instructions on getting through it).

Continuing west, the **HRP** – just below the cirque and marked by a few cairns – climbs sharply in zigzags to the notch-like **Hourquette d'Alans** (2430m), from where the *Refuge des Espuguettes* can be glimpsed below (see "The Cirque de Gavarnie"); to reach it (under an hour), the path first descends slowly north, then steeply westwards in more zigzags, completing a relatively easy trekking day.

Gavarnie

At first glance **GAVARNIE**, 8km upstream from Gèdre, is nothing but a tacky collection of ramshackle souvenir kiosks, car parks and snack bars, besieged in summer by hordes scarcely less numerous than at Lourdes. Once the trippers have departed in their cars or the numerous tour coaches, Gavarnie's pavements roll up promptly at 8pm, having been first cleared of the huge piles of ordure from the horses, donkeys and mules used to carry tourists up for a quick look at the cirque. Yet almost every house and hotel here has some connection with two centuries of Pyrenean exploration, which goes some way towards justifying the village's nickname, "Chamonix of the Pyrenees". Beside the Romanesque church, last prayer stop for pilgrims along this minor branch of the Santiago route before crossing into Spain, are buried great early climbers such as Jean Arlaud and the Passet family of guides.

Practicalities

The most historic – and much the nicest – of Gavarnie's seven pricey **hotels** is the *Hôtel des Voyageurs* (☎05.62.92.48.01, fax 05.62.92.40.89; ④; closed Oct 15–Christmas & Easter–June 15), whose "Golden Book" contains the signatures of mountaineers Count Henry Russell, Charles Packe and Francis Swan, as well as those of George Sand, Gustave Flaubert, Victor Hugo and his mistress Juliette Drouet. Rumour has it that Hortense de Beauharnais conceived the future Napoléon III in one of its bedrooms on the night of August 24, 1807 – the father a Gavarnie shepherd. Even if you don't stay at the similarly illustrious if overpriced *Vignemale* (☎05.62.92.40.00, fax 05.62.92.40.08; ⑤; closed Nov–March) in the southeast corner of the village, you can still enjoy a drink in its lounge, leaning against the fireplace where, according to his memoirs, Henry Russell would stand in contemplation of Vignemale. More modest choices include the small and well-placed *Compostelle* by the church (☎05.62.92.49.43; ④; closed mid-Nov to Christmas), where most rooms face the cirque, and co-proprietor and certified guide Yvan offers day-long hiking excursions (100F) to celebrated nearby destinations, and modern *Le Taillon* (☎05.62.92.48.20, fax 05.62.92.41.13; ④), with easy parking and hearty breakfasts.

Chambres d'hôtes include *La Chaumière*, 500m from the village centre on the way to the cirque (☎05.62.92.48.08; ③; closed Nov & Dec), with an attractive breakfast bar overlooking the river; and *Jeanine Fernandes*, on the opposite (northern) outskirts, situated up on a knoll (☎05.62.92.47.41; ③). **Hostel**-type arrangements are provided by *Le Gypaète* (☎05.62.92.40.61; open all year; ①), a fancy *gîte d'étape* near the *Hôtel des Voyageurs*, and the CAF refuge *Les Granges de Holle* (☎05.62.92.48.77; ①; closed Nov), out on the road towards the ski station. This is also a convivial and reasonable place to eat or just share a fireside glass of *eau de vie*. Of other, independent **restaurants**, the appealing *La Ruade*, across the road from *Hôtel des Voyageurs* at the north end of the village, serves excellent fondues and *pierrades* (stone-grilled dishes) and has the village's favourite bar. *Le P'tit Toy*, on rue de l'Église, is an excellent alternative, open all year, with panoramic upstairs seating, quick service and two gourmet menus for under 110F.

The closest **campsite** is *La Bergerie* (☎05.62.92.48.41; mid-May to Oct) on the east bank of the river 600m above the village; facilities are basic, and the ground sloping, but there are unbeatable views up into the cirque and a breakfast bar. The other local site, *Le Pain de Sucre* (☎05.62.92.47.55; June–Sept & Christmas–Easter), is marginally more comfortable (hot water, which is charged extra) but inconvenient, 3.5km north of the village en route for Gèdre.

The Office du Tourisme forms a division of the central **Maison du Parc** (summer daily 9.30am–noon & 1–6.30pm; ☎05.62.92.49.10), which in addition to hiking and wildlife information, occasionally organizes guided walks. For **weather** and **snow conditions**, ask the CRS mountain rescue unit opposite *La Bergerie*. There's an **ATM** at the Crédit Agricole, beside the Maison du Parc.

Skiing at Gavarnie

Although it doesn't compare in size with Barèges-La Mongie, Gavarnie rates as one of the great *ski domaines* of the Pyrenees on account of its snow record and wonderful situation – when you get off the top lift at 2400m and ski out from behind the concealing summit of Pic des Tentes, you have spellbinding views towards the cirque. From the lift you can also set off on some of the best *ski-randonnées* in the range, including a tour through the Brèche de Roland (see p.328) into the Parque Nacional de Ordesa in Spain. Above the main lift station (1850m) there's normally snow from Christmas to April, but a lower lift beginning at 1460m is seldom open. In all there are thirteen lifts and nineteen runs – seven green, five blue, five red and two black.

The Cirque de Gavarnie

Approaching from the north along the D921, your first, unforgettable sight of the **Cirque de Gavarnie** comes on the road just above Gèdre, from where the Brèche de Roland – the famous gap at the west side – is clearly visible. Close up, the cirque is revealed as one of Europe's most stupendous natural spectacles, scoured by glaciation into an almost perfect semicircle, 1400m from top to bottom and 890m in diameter. Despite appearances the palisades are neither completely vertical nor uniform, actually rising in three stages – a layer of granite sandwiched between two limestone beds – separated by sloping terraces, banked by snow and ice. A main **waterfall** – a straight drop during spring, two separate cataracts later in the year – plus numerous smaller ones, embellish the great wall.

There is talk of the Cirque de Gavarnie becoming a World Heritage Site, as it ought to be, but interested parties are pressing for developments, like cable cars, that would make that classification impossible. Between Gavarnie and the cirque (a distance of 4km) the landscape is still relatively unspoiled, meadows stretching out on either side of the stream, dotted with occasional barns.

Visiting the cirque

Ever since Charles Packe wrote in 1867 of "travellers to the cirque who have the indolence and bad taste" to take horses, there has been a tendency to scorn the *muletiers*. But if you do mount up you'll at least be supporting a traditional source of employment, important to most families in a village where lack of work is driving young people away. The *muletiers* jog alongside you for safety, making up to five trips a day. If, as a hiker, you'd rather not share the trail with them – both the crowds and the manure smell can be overpowering between 9am and 5pm – you can use another trail along the west bank of the *gave*, below the pilgrim route to the pass.

Either way, on foot it takes an hour to enter the confines of the cirque. The broad, well-trodden "dung trail" climbs first to the *jardin botanique*, where there are more graves of *Pyrénéistes* – Louis Le Bondidier and Franz Schrader – and then to the **Plateau de la Prade**, a beautiful area of streams and forest – and now the setting for an open-air summer theatre, used during the annual July festival. Beyond the plateau, another short, steepish climb brings you to the *Hôtel du Cirque et de la Cascade* (1580m; 1hr from Gavarnie) – in the last century a famous meeting place for mountaineers, nowadays a heavily subscribed restaurant with reasonable meals and drinks. It's situated well within the bowl of the cirque, and should you be there during an electric storm (quite likely on summer afternoons) you're unlikely ever to forget the echoes of the thunderclaps.

From the *hôtel*, where the mule service stops and most clients just mill around, you can hike half an hour up the Oule valley to the **Grande Cascade**, the source of the Gave de Gavarnie (and ultimately the Gave de Pau) and, at 423m, the longest falls in Europe. Above you, the three-banded walls rise to a summit-ridge of nine 3000-metre-plus peaks, curving over 5km between **Astazou** (3017m) in the east and **Le Casque/El Casco** (3006m) in the west. The ridge – the border between Spain and France – is festooned by the shrunken remnants of the glaciers that formed the amphitheatre, some of the last 9 square kilometres of glacier remaining in the entire Pyrenees.

More advanced routes

Inaccessible though it may seem, the cirque is traced by **climbing routes**, and with modern rope technique, more climbers are overcome by heat-stroke than are injured in falls. In winter, the ice routes attract contemporary daredevils who jab and stab their way up the frozen waterfalls on twelve-point crampons.

Walkers can get up the walls of the cirque to the west by the trail dubbed **Échelle** (Ladder) **des Sarradets**, usually part of the passage through the Brèche de Roland (see below). Rather than retrace your steps, the most pleasant way back to Gavarnie, starting just behind and above the *Hôtel du Cirque*, is via the marked path up to the meadow-set *Refuge de Pailla* (or *Pailha*; 1760m; open & staffed July 1–Oct 15; 16 places; ☎05.62.92.48.48; ①), the way up a 45-minute corniche route through fir and black pine, with dripping rock overhangs, grotto-springs and fine views.

Just beyond the Pailla meadow, there's a fork in the path. Left and down leads in sharp zig-zags, initially beside a stream, within 45 minutes more to Gavarnie, but most prefer to head right and east a similar time uphill to the popular *Refuge des Espuguettes* (1hr 30min–2hr total from the cirque; 60 places; staffed & open weekends Easter–May & Oct, daily June–Sept; ☎05.62.92.40.63; ①), huge, grey and isolated above the tree line at 2030m. Lupines and crocus are abundant on the way up, and the detour is amply rewarded by sweeping views west along the frontier crest from Marboré to Vignemale and beyond. With a day-pack, allow an hour and a half for the total return to Gavarnie from the refuge; with full kit you should add a third to all the times given this section. From *Espuguettes* you can also continue east in less than a full day to Héas, via the Barrage des Gloriettes (see p.325).

The Brèche de Roland

Every walker in Gavarnie wants to get to, and through, the **Brèche de Roland/Brecha de Roldán** – a curious, nearly vertical gap at the top of the cirque. Tackle it in summer and you'll have company of all ages, nationalities and walking abilities. Such popularity might detract from the experience, but it does have a big advantage – a lone traveller can risk the climb knowing there's no chance of a mishap going unaided. The glaciers guarding the final approach are especially dangerous when there is no snow to cover the treacherous ice, and an ice-axe and crampons will be a big help at any time. If you're able to stay at the *Refuge de la Brèche de Roland* just below the *brèche*, you'll have the opportunity to ascend some peaks flanking it, or visit some famous ice caves just over on the Spanish side. If you do the trip as a day expedition from Gavarnie, count on a minimum of ten hours there and back.

According to legend, the 100m-by-60m gap was hacked out by the dying Roland, nephew of Charlemagne, as he attempted to smash his magic sword Durandal to prevent it falling into the hands of the Moors. The eleventh-century *Chanson de Roland* describes how:

Count Roland smites upon the marble stone;
I cannot tell you how he hewed and smote;
Yet neither does it break nor splinter,
Though groans the sword,
And rebounds heavenwards.

The battle in which Roland died actually took place nearly 100km to the west near Roncesvalles (see p.416), so the tale is pretty thin, and the startling views from the top need no legend to augment them.

Approaches to the Brèche

There are three **approaches** to the *brèche*, all converging on the *Refuge de la Brèche de Roland*. The lazy way involves driving up to the **Port de Gavarnie/Puerto de Bujaruelo** (Port de Boucharo on some maps), at the end of the road to the ski station (13km); from there a clear path climbs east under the north face of **Taillon/Tallón**, rising gradually until a gully just over an hour along, where it joins a footpath coming directly up from Gavarnie. This trail, which is the next easiest way to the *brèche*, begins by the Romanesque church, climbs steadily but manageably on the western flank of the valley, turns into the small plateau of Pouey d'Aspé and, after a time, climbs steeply again in zigzags to join the footpath from the Port de Gavarnie (2hr 45min).

Following either of these approaches, you continue on up through the Col des Sarradets to the **Refuge de la Brèche de Roland** (aka *Refuge des Sarradets*; 2587m; 57 places; staffed daily May–Sept, weekends Oct, part always open; ☎05.62.92.40.41; ①), reached in under an hour from the junction of the paths. Situated in full view of the *brèche* and just 220m below it, the refuge is understandably packed in summer, when an average of ninety walkers a night fight for places.

The third and most challenging route, the **Échelle des Sarradets**, takes about six hours from Gavarnie. Having reached the *Hôtel du Cirque* you carry on south a short distance, cross a bridge, then bear southwest on a well-trodden path to the west wall of the lower cirque, below which flourish great banks of Pyrenean irises in mid-summer. For the nonclimber the next hundred-metre section requires a lot of teeth-gritting and not too much looking down – it's not technically difficult (steps have been cut in places), but it is rather exposed, and you wouldn't want to do it downhill. The final section follows the steep Sarradets valley to the refuge.

From its namesake refuge, the **Brèche de Roland** is about forty minutes' stiff climb away, ending with the glacier crossing. Quite often, on an apparently windless day, you'll be almost bowled over as you step through the rock "doorway" and be sent rushing for something to hold onto, while flocks of calling choughs circle easily and endlessly in the gale. Looking into Spain, a high-altitude scree desert forms the summer foreground, followed by the top of the Ordesa canyon walls and then, receding into the distance, wave after wave of dense blue-green forest, turning pink, red, then purple at sunset. Back into France the summits are barer, more jagged and the light more yellow.

Climbs from the Brèche

To the west of the Brèche de Roland, towards Taillon, the rock rampart is known as **Pic Bazillac** (2975m), which ends at the so-called **Fausse Brèche** with its menhir-like finger of rock. For the ascent of **Taillon** (3144m) continue on the path beyond the Fausse Brèche and climb along the east ridge. This is considered to be one of the easiest three-thousanders in the Pyrenees but the views are no less exciting for that – and proficient climbers can opt for the almost vertical north face.

The **Casque/Casco** (3006m) forms the eastern part of the *brèche* and is climbed with only a little more difficulty than Taillon, by passing through to the Spanish side and following the path that runs hard left, keeping close to the rock wall. A steel cable gives moral and physical support over a difficult section, beyond which you bear left to the slopes that separate Le Casque and **Tour/Torre** (3009m) – next peak of the cirque – and then left again to scramble up to the summit.

The Grotte Casteret

Standing in the *brèche* and looking southeast, you can see a curious dome-shaped rock about a kilometre away. This is the entrance to **Grotte Casteret**, the most spectacular of a group of 32 ice caves of the Marboré/Monte Perdido Massif, the highest such caverns known in the world. Discovered by Norbert Casteret in 1926, the outer chamber requires no special equipment just to look in. But for the magnificent lower chamber, with the column of ice known as the *Niagara de glace*, you'll need crampons, rope and head lamp. Remember that the formations are delicate and you should do nothing that could break ice off.

It takes a good hour to get to the entrance by one of two routes: either begin as for the Casque/Casco (see above) but then, rather than bearing away left, continue around the boulder- and scree-strewn bowl; or descend into the bowl below the *brèche*, picking your way towards the domed rock and then climbing up again.

South of the Brèche: into Ordesa

Once through the *brèche* you're in the Spanish **Parque Nacional de Ordesa** (see pp.368–369). If you want to explore further – and perhaps make an ascent of **Monte Perdido** – you should head for the *Refugio de Góriz*, two to three hours away to the east. The terrain is bleak and exposed karst, but anyone who can reach the Brèche de Roland can easily get to this shelter. Keeping the bare **Pico del Descargador** to your right and the back of the Gavarnie cirque on the left, cross the **Plana de San Ferlus** and follow the valley eastwards all the way. The only difficulty is at the **Circo de Góriz**, just before the refuge, easily negotiated by a path on the north side; if you miss it you'll be confronted by an impassable succession of vertical descents. For walks from the *Refugio de Góriz*, see p.368.

Via the Brèche de Tuquerouye

An alternative access from Gavarnie to the Ordesa lies via the tougher and much less frequented **Brèche de Tuquerouye/Brecha de Tucarroya** (2660m). The first part of the approach is the reverse of the itinerary from the **Cirque d'Estaubé** to Gavarnie (described on p.325), climbing from Gavarnie village to the *Refuge des Espuguettes* and the Hourquette d'Alans. Once through the pass, the route drops eastwards in zigzags towards the floor of Estaubé, then – about halfway down – veers south-southeast, more or less along the 2200-metre contour, to the foot of the gully that leads up to the *brèche*. It's a steep ascent – 400m at an eighty-percent grade – for which crampons and axe are invariably essential. Right in the pass itself, sandwiched between the rock walls and looking like a coal bunker, stands the oldest hut in the Pyrenees, the unstaffed *Refuge de Tuquerouye* (2660m), opened – with a lavish banquet – by the Club Alpin Français in 1890. To watch over it, the Gavarnie guide François Bernat-Salles carried a 75-kilo statue of the Virgin up on his back. Basic in the extreme, the hut justifies an overnight stay by its setting and views south to glacier-hung Monte Perdido. If you have a tent or bivvy sac, you might prefer to descend on the other side to the camping area around the **Lago Helado de Marboré**, 100m or so lower – incidentally, the first reliable water since the base of the gully. A night spent at either spot is a great high-mountain experience.

West of Gavarnie: Vignemale and Russell's caves

Any visit to the **Grottes Russell** and **Vignemale** should begin at the statue of Henry Russell in Gavarnie. The statue – a replacement for one melted down by the Nazis – is beside the main bridge, gazing west up the Ossoue valley towards his beloved Vignemale.

The problem with visiting Vignemale from the east (or any direction, for that matter) is that the approach is long. With a car you can drive on road and track along the Gave d'Ossoue almost as far as the **Barrage d'Ossoue**, but on foot the GR10 from Gavarnie takes over three hours. It's a wonderful hike, though, first under spectacular cliffs where lammergeier have been nesting since the 1980s, and then across pasture where marmots whistle and isards are a frequent sight. From the simple hut at the lake, the path runs along the eastern shore to a concrete bridge over the Ossoue stream. Beyond the bridge the landscape gets even more interesting, the path zigzagging across a short section of permanent ice at one point in the climb.

About three hours above the lake you reach the dilapidated but aptly named **Grottes Bellevue**, where Russell spent some summers. The views south are sumptuous and if you're not attempting the Vignemale summit you may as well enjoy them for a bit. Another half-hour's walk brings you to the rather elderly *Refuge Bayssellance* (2651m; 58

HENRY RUSSELL

It's no exaggeration to say that Comte Henri Patrick Marie Russell-Killough – known usually as **Henry Russell** (1834–1909) – was the most original mountaineer of all time. You'll hear or read his name all over the Central Pyrenees, wherever there are mountains worth climbing: a section of the museum at Luchon is dedicated to him, and there are original photographs and letters at the Musée Pyrénéen in Lourdes. God, wrote Russell, is here a *présence palpable*, and he went to extraordinary lengths to achieve a communion with the spirit of the mountains. One August night in 1880, for instance, he had two guides cover him with scree on the summit of Vignemale, with only his head protruding above the blanket of stone.

Russell was an elegant eccentric who threw great parties and did the full social season in Pau most winters, yet who spoke of Vignemale as his wife and enjoyed nothing more than a seventy-kilometre stroll between Luchon and Bagnères-de-Bigorre. Despite a period of far-flung travel in America, Siberia, Australia and New Zealand, he seemed more than content to come home to Toulouse and explore the nearer wildernesses of the Pyrenees. In 1863, aged 29, he bagged the highest peak of the range, Pic Aneto. In the years that followed he made sixteen first ascents, including a climb of Vignemale in 1869 that was the first winter ascent of a major European peak. The bravery and the flamboyance of the man comes through in his fascinating *Souvenirs d'un Montagnard*: completely impressionist and untechnical, it contrasts strongly with the writings of his friend and fellow *Pyrénéiste*, Charles Packe, who made precise observations on everything from geology to botany.

Vignemale was always Russell's obsession. He climbed it 33 times – making his last ascent aged 70 – and his passion led him to dig several cave-homes on the peak. In 1882 work began on a set of three caves close to the head of the Ossoue glacier, which soon were joined by two others; a huge party marked their completion, with fine wines and dishes set on damask tablecloths. Within five years the caves had been made uninhabitable by the shifting glacier, so Russell moved lower, carving out the Grottes Bellevue in 1888. The position didn't satisfy him, and in 1893 his seventh and final cave, Paradis, was hollowed out by explosives only 18m below the summit. By this time the commune of Barèges had granted him a 99-year lease on the summit.

The *comte* spent much time in his mountain homes, sometimes entertaining lavishly – he insisted on guests getting up at dawn in order to witness sunrise, rewarding them with punch at 11am. He thus tempted people away from the comfort of the established resorts and into the mountains themselves, a relatively new experience for the time. His activities also boosted local commerce, especially for the hotels and guides of Gavarnie, then a poor, pastoral village. It is therefore surprising that, despite his commemorative statue in the village, the caves that Russell constructed are now completely neglected.

places; staffed mid-June to Sept, part always open; ☎05.62.92.40.25; ①), traditional base camp for the **ascent of Vignemale**.

Make an early start next morning, dropping back down the path towards the Grottes Bellevue, then cutting off west just above them to the moraine at the foot of the **Ossoue glacier**, the largest remaining one in the Pyrenees. This is dirty-looking in summer, with huge and thankfully obvious crevasses; the trodden path runs a little right of the centre. You'll need crampons and ice-axe, and you should rope up as a precaution. At the top end of the glacier is another of Russell's summer homes, the *Grotte du Paradis*: just 18m below the summit of **Pique Longue** (3289m), an easy final scramble (4hr in total from the refuge). There are several loftier peaks in Spain, but this is the highest Pyrenean point actually on the frontier.

From the *Refuge Bayssellance* you can continue on the GR10 over the **Hourquette d'Ossoue** (2734m) to the *Refuge des Oulettes* (2hr 30min further; see p.335) and thence to Cauterets.

Cauterets and around

At considerable variance from the settlements along the *gaves* de Pau and de Gavarnie, the spa and mountain-sports playground of **CAUTERETS** – 30km south of Lourdes and 10km up the D920 from Pierrefitte-Nestalas – sprouts colonnaded and iron-balconied Neoclassical buildings in its western quarter, especially on bd Latapie Flurin, facing the more traditional part on the east bank of the Gave de Cauterets. A long and narrow village, its surprisingly tall buildings prompted by the lack of flat ground, Cauterets wears a general air of elegance gone to seed; Belle Epoque follies lie abandoned or fitted with cinemas, slot machines, bowling alleys and the like. Dozens of *résidences*, apartments and pensions are only available by the week or the month, some with a seemingly permanent contingent of OAPs, though the place in fact attracts all ages and classes, intent on having a good time. All this contrasts markedly with the idyllic alpine setting, and "endorsements" by numerous notables in centuries past.

The town owes its existence to Count Raymond de Bigorre, who in 945 gave a tidy sum to the monks of Saint-Savin, enabling them to establish the baths. National fame came in the sixteenth century when Margarite d'Angoulême (see "Pau") became a regular, contented client, reputedly penning her *Heptameron*, the French equivalent of the *Decameron*, while here. In 1807 Louis Napoléon and his wife Hortense stayed for several months after the death of their first son; subsequently George Sand, Gustave Flaubert and Victor Hugo spent time in Cauterets, as did Alfred Tennyson, who with Arthur Hallam arrived in 1830 carrying dispatches for a revolutionary group plotting against the king of Spain. It was at Cauterets, too, that Châteaubriand finally met Léontine de Villeneuve, with whom he had been carrying on a torrid two-year correspondence; when she set eyes on the elderly poet, however, the affair came to an abrupt end. Later, Baudelaire, Debussy and Edward VII of England added their names to the illustrious guest list.

The lush countryside around Cauterets positively haemorrhages with waterfalls and no fewer than eleven **hot springs**, with a million and a half litres of sulphur-laden water claimed to course daily through the two surviving *thermes* of César and Rocher (open daily except Sun). Rheumatism cures are big, but the chief speciality is ear, nose and throat conditions – brochures are full of pictures of happy clients sticking devices up and down various orifices.

Cauterets' reputation as a winter sports resort is equally well deserved, with nightly discos and all the trappings of package-tour *après-ski*. As a summer resort it's perennially popular, too, offering ample opportunities for climbing, hiking and tennis. Most of the best walks depart from the massive *parc national* gatehouse at Pont d'Espagne, 6km southwest of the resort: you can explore the valley of the Marcadau further in the same direction all the way to the border and beyond, or fashion an enjoyable loop through the valleys of Gaube and Latour. The same routes are used in winter for nordic skiing, for which the Cauterets area is perhaps a better bet than downhill activities.

Practicalities

The town is small enough that you should have no trouble finding your way around. SNCF **buses** from Lourdes (4–5 daily) arrive at the *fin-de-siècle* wooden train station at the north edge of the centre; the adjacent **Maison du Parc** (summer daily 9.30am–noon & 3.30–7pm; ☎05.62.92.52.56) has a small wildlife exhibition (10F) and some helpful and enthusiastic wardens. The **Office du Tourisme** on place Maréchal-Foch (July & Aug Mon–Sat 9am–7pm, Sun 9am–noon & 4–7pm; rest of the year Mon–Sat 9am–12.30pm & 2–6.30pm, Sun 9am–noon; ☎05.62.92.50.27), sells a useful guide to local short walks, *Cauterets aux Deux Pas*; nearby in the Bureau des Guides at

5 place Clémenceau (daily mid-June to mid-Sept 10am–12.30pm & 4–7.30pm; ☎05.62.92.62.02), you can obtain current information on the condition of mountain paths and climbs, as well as the weather report. Cauterets is also an excellent place to stock up if you're on a long-haul trek; there's a fruit-and-vegetable *halle*, several super-markets and bakeries plus several sports-goods shops.

Though many of its thirty-odd **hotels** belong to an era when people took half-board by the month, Cauterets has various affordable short-term places, all pinpointed on a placard at the north end of town. In ascending order of price, there's *Le Bigorre*, 15 rue de Belfort (☎05.62.92.52.81; ③); the *Centre et Poste*, 11 rue de Belfort (☎05.62.92.52.69; ④), flanking the *Poste*; the *Lion d'Or* at 12 rue Richelieu (☎05.62.92.52.87, fax 05.62.92.03.67; ④); and two more comfortable, *Logis de France* members, *César* at 3 rue César on the way up to the eponymous baths (☎05.62.92.52.57, fax 05.62.92.08.19; ④), with TVs and phones in the rooms, or the nearby *Etche-Ona* at 2 rue Richelieu (☎05.62.92.51.43; ④). Of two **gîtes d'étape**, the hillside *Beau Soleil* at 25 rue Maréchal-Joffre (☎05.62.92.53.52; dorm beds ①, doubles ③), near the César baths, has perhaps a slight edge over the *Le Pas de L'Ours,* 21 rue de la Raillère (☎05.62.92.58.07; dorm beds ①, doubles ③). On the way into Cauterets from the north, there are several **campsites**: *Les Gleères* (☎05.62.92.55.34), *La Prairie* (☎05.62.92.54.28), *Le Pegueère* (☎05.62.92.52.28) and *Les Bergeronnettes* (no phone; June–Sept), the latter quietest by dint of its position, across the river from *Les Gleères*.

Eating out, the *Brasserie Le Paris* in place Clemenceau is the prime spot for people-watching, while a friendly place for breakfast is *La Brulerie du Gave*, on pedestrianized avenue de l'Esplanade, just east of the river. For more substantial fare, there's unfortunately very little choice outside of the hotel diners; the *Giovanni Pizzeria* in rue de la Raillère and *Casa Bodega Manolo* at no. 11 of the same street, with Spanish-style seafood and a set menu, are about the size of it.

Walking around Cauterets

There is magnificent walking around Cauterets, which lies just at the edge of *parc national* territory extending immediately southwest. Although you're still in Bigorre here, the most useful **map** for local treks is the IGN 1:50,000 Carte de Randonnées no. 3, "Béarn". Most worthwhile itineraries depart from the **Pont d'Espagne**, a scenic old stone bridge high over the confluence of the foaming *gaves* du Marcadau and du Gaube, and an important landmark on the historic route across the mountains to Spain. For those with their own car, there are 1500 spaces (20F) in the **Puntas** parking lot at the end of the D920, 7km above Cauterets, in front of the giant *parc national* visitors' centre, straddling the way to the bridge; except for vans servicing the various refuges beyond, vehicles of any sort are no longer allowed beyond this point. Otherwise six daily *navettes* from Cauterets, up the Val de Jéret (8am–6pm uphill, 9am–7pm downhill), leave you at the centre. Purists can walk there from **La Raillère**, a disused satellite spa building 3km south of Cauterets, along a fine streamside section of the GR10, pressed into double service as a *parc national* trail; it's about ninety minutes uphill along this *Sentier des Cascades*, under fine woods of beech and pine.

Next to the bridge itself, just five minutes from the Puntas car park, stands the *Hôtellerie du Pont de Espagne* (meals only); some fifteen minutes above here, past the base of the *télésiège* to Gaube (see below), the privately run, youth-orientated *Chalet du Clot* (1581m; 45 places; June–April; ☎05.62.92.61.27, fax ☎05.62.92.07.93; ①) on the broad **Plateau du Clot** offers simple meals and overnighting, as well as nordic skiing on 35km of pistes.

Refuge Wallon and the Pont du Cayan loop walk

From the plateau, signs for the **Vallée du Marcadau** and the *Refuge Wallon* point southwest along the valley, all sparkling streams, meadows and tall pines. At the **Pont**

du Cayan, some forty minutes above via either bank of the main stream at the far end of the widest part of the valley, the path climbs left through forest to the **Pont d'Estalaunque**, and then rises more steeply to the rambling, old-fashioned **Refuge Wallon** (1866m; 116 places; staffed daily early April to early May, June–Oct & winter holidays, plus March weekends; crude annexe always open; ①), which offers a full meal service as well. Although it's barely two hours from the Puntas car park, you gain a real sense of the surrounding mountains, which are ideal for walks and light scrambles of all sorts, rather than technical climbing. Owing to the mild climate, Scots and black pines, some several hundred years old, flourish up to 2000m elevation hereabouts.

If you're going back to Cauterets, rather than retrace your steps you can loop back to **Pont du Cayan** along the alternative marked footpath that heads initially northwest. After an hour, you reach rock-girt **Lac Nère** (2320m), and after twenty minutes further through a chaos of boulders, you arrive at the even more lunar **Lac du Pourtet** (2420m), a sawtooth ridge bounding it on the north. At a small notch on the lake's east shore you turn down and eastwards, passing the three smaller, turf-fringed tarns called the **Lacs de l'Embarrat** (as well as a marked side trail for the Lac d'Ilhéou – see p.335), and just over an hour an a half from the highest lake you should be back at the Pont du Cayan. This circuit does involve a stiff climb, and you should count on six hours' walking time return from the Puntas car park – as opposd to four if you backtrack entirely along the Vallée du Marcadau from *Wallon*. This is, it must be said, one of the more representative – and deservedly popular – day walks you can do around Cauterets; the lakes are all dissimilar, and wildlife surprisingly conspicuous for such a relatively accessible route.

Walks above Refuge Wallon

Above and beyond *Refuge Wallon*, there's a choice of routes in several directions, the most exciting of them along the HRP or its *variante*. You can follow the **HRP** west towards the important frontier peak of Balaïtous, using the Lac Nère approach for about 1km (25min), then veering away west-northwest up the Gave de Cambalès, through bare terrain strewn with a dozen lakes, to the **Col de Cambalès** (2706m; 3hr from the refuge). The HRP drops southwest on the other side to the very easy **Port de la Peyre-Saint-Martin/Cuello d'a Piedra de San Martin** (2295m) on the border, then goes north down the Arrens valley to the *Refuge Ledormeur* (1970m; 10 places; unstaffed but always open), a six-hour day from the *Refuge Wallon*.

If you have the time and energy, press on for an hour or so to the more comfortable *Refuge Larribet* (2070m; 62 places; staffed daily May–Sept, weekends March & April; ①) – to reach it drop northwards to the junctions of the Arrens and Larribet valleys, then curl back south along the latter. From either refuge you can descend if need be to the village of Arrens-Marsous (see p.321), mostly along 10km of dirt road.

The **HRP variante** skirts Balaïtous (3146m) to the south on a generally westward course to the next staffed alpine hut at Arrémoulit – a minimum eight-hour trekking day. It runs initially southwest from the *Refuge Wallon* along the Port du Marcadau stream, then climbs westwards to **Col de la Fache/Cuello da Facha** (2664m); once through this you're in Spain, dropping down to the north shore of the huge **Respumoso** reservoir. There's a relatively new staffed refuge (see p.374) on its banks, built to serve the Spanish **GR11**, which runs briefly in tandem with the HRP *variante* here. From Respumoso you head back into France via the **Arriel** lakes and the **Col de Palas/Cuello de Pallas** (2517m) to the *Refuge d'Arrémoulit* (2305m; 30 places; staffed June 30–Sept 30; part always open; ①) between the lakes of the same name, just beyond the southern end of Lac d'Artouste. (For more on Lac d'Artouste and Balaïtous, see p.347.)

To go **south** or **east** from *Refuge Wallon*, take the marked southerly trail beginning five minutes below the shelter at a bridge, up the Vallée d'Aratille to the **Col d'Aratille**

(2528m; 3–4hr from the refuge). From there you could either continue into the Spanish Ara valley, which drains towards the Ordesa region, or head east for a couple of hours – dropping briefly into the top of the Ara valley and then over the **Col des Oulettes/Puerto de Cauterets** (2591m), always on the **HRP** – to the *Refuge des Oulettes* in the head of the Vallée de Gaube. This is a fairly strenuous, but short traverse of five hours, with the route well marked.

Loop via the Gaube and Lutour valleys

The head of the **Vallée du Gaube** is more usually approached directly from the Pont d'Espagne, as part of the deservedly popular, two-to-three-day **loop** back to Cauterets which also takes in the **Vallée de Lutour**. To accomplish it anti-clockwise, you first head up the Gave du Gaube for an hour as far as the popular **Lac de Gaube**, with the snack bar *Hôtellerie du Lac de Gaube* at the north end of the lake. If you're exceptionally lazy, a small *télésiège* (daily summer 8.30am–6.30pm up, 9am–7.30pm down; 22F one way, 30F return) spares you about half the climb up from the bottom. Done as a day-trip, this is another "poodle walk" for the French, though dogs must be kept on a lead and are banned beyond the *hôtellerie*.

From the *hôtellerie* you continue south two hours to the *Refuge des Oulettes* (2151m; ☎05.62.92.62.97 or 05.62.46.14.72; 75 places; staffed daily April & June–Sept, according to weather in winter; part always open; ①), where an overnight stay is recommended so that you may contemplate the gaunt, breathtaking north face of Vignemale at leisure. You'd need an extra day to tackle the peak from here; most casual walkers will continue east steeply over the **Col d'Arraillé** (2583m), which permits passage to the far less crowded Vallée de Lutour, tracing the boundary of *parc national* territory.

The next suggested overnight stop is at *Refuge d'Estom* (1804m; 30 places; staffed June–Sept; ①), perched by its lake; were you to stay here an extra night, you could explore the half-dozen sizeable **Soubiran lakes** hiding under the crags defining the head of Lutour. The main itinerary carries on north along the valley for a very easy half-day back towards Cauterets, joining the Val de Jéret at La Raillère; about an hour before the latter you meet the end of the narrow but paved road in at *La Fruitière*, a popular **hotel-restaurant** (☎05.62.92.52.04; ④; closed Christmas–April) renowned for its game, trout and *garbure*. The restaurant's prices are reasonable – two menus for under 120F – though quality can vary, and reservations are suggested on summer weekends.

Traverse to Lac d'Estaing via the GR10

One exception to the pattern of walks arrayed around the Pont d'Espagne is the day-long traverse from Cauterets to **Lac d'Estaing** in the eponymous valley via the Lac d'Ilhéou, following the main **GR10**. Taking the Téléférique du Lys from just above bd B. Dulau in Cauterets up to an intermediate station (mid-June to mid-Sept every 30min 9am–5.45pm; 29F one-way) spares you the sharp initial climb, while continuing on the Télésiège du Grum (same schedule; 42F for a combined one-way ticket with the Téléférique du Lys) brings you to the Crêtes du Lys, actually higher than the Lac d'Ilhéou, with an hour on foot separating you from the refuge there (see below). For a bit extra you can haul a *parapente* or mountain bike up too. Without any assistance from mechanical lifts, it will take you the better part of three hours, heading up the Vallée du Cambasque, to draw even with the **Lac d'Ilhéou**, best seen in June when ice floes drift on its still surface and the surrounding peaks such as Grand Barbat (2813m) are still frosted with snow. The modern, PNP-built *Refuge d'Ilhéou* (1988m; 60 places; ☎05.62.92.75.07; ①) at the northeast end of the lake is staffed all summer and also offers meals and drinks on its outdoor terrace. From here the GR10 bears northwest out of the *parc national*, over the grassy **Col d'Ilhéou** (2242m), dropping down to Lac d'Estaing, with its hotel and campsite, after four more hours.

Skiing around Cauterets

With a selection of circuits from 1300m to 7500m in length, the **Pont d'Espagne** makes an excellent place to hone mountain and nordic skiing skills, and following the route from the bridge into the Marcadau valley constitutes an easy yet spectacular introduction to **ski touring**. The climb to the *Refuge Wallon* (sporadically attended in winter) totals 369m over a distance of 7km, which should take around three to four hours for beginners; count on half that to descend.

Beyond the refuge, there are possible itineraries into Spain via the **Col de la Fache/Cuello da Faxa** and the **Port du Marcadau/Puerto de Panticosa** into the Panticosa region, or the **Col d'Aratille** into the Ara valley, but these are for experts only, despite their relative ease as summer walking passes. The same goes for the winter ascent of **Vignemale** from the *Refuge des Oulettes*, subject to severe avalanche risk.

As for **downhill** skiing, Cauteret's reputation is perhaps inflated, but by Pyrenean standards it does have a good snow record. The main ski area is the **Cirque du Lys** to the west, reached by the *téléphérique* described above. A selection of mainly drag lifts continue from 1850m to a maximum of 2400m; the total length of the twenty pistes, most red and east-facing, is just under 30km.

Pau

Once capital of the medieval viscounty of Béarn, and now of the modern *département* of Pyrénées-Atlantiques, the pleasant, surprisingly cosmopolitan city of **PAU** lies an hour or less by road or rail west of Tarbes. From this major stop on the main east–west rail line along the base of the French Pyrenees, you can move on to Bayonne and the Basque country, or directly south to the *parc national* through the Vallée d'Ossau. You may well prefer to use Pau, rather than Lourdes, as a base for heading into the mountains: transportation is no problem and Pau is a far more amenable place.

The city first rose to prominence in 1464, when it became capital of Béarn (and Navarre) under Jean d'Albret and his wife Catherine of Navarre. In 1567, their descendant Henri d'Albret married the sister of the French king François I, Marguerite d'Angoulême, a writer of some gifts who turned the local court into a focus of the arts. Her daughter, Jeanne d'Albret, was by contrast a Protestant philistine, bringing ruin to Pau and its environs during the Wars of Religion, when her armies and those of Charles IX competed in the commission of various atrocities. Peace of a sort was restored only upon the accession of her son Henri IV to the French throne in 1589; but Béarn itself was not formally annexed by Paris until 1620 by Henri IV's son Louis XIII.

Pau entered the historical spotlight once more with the arrival of Wellington and his troops in 1814, following their defeat of Marshal Soult at nearby Orthez. So taken were they by the setting and mild climate that many of the officers returned for their retirement, inaugurating an English colony which would endure for nearly a century. By the early 1860s fifteen percent of the city's population was English, numbers swelled through the tireless (and ultimately wrong-headed) promotion of Pau as especially salubrious for tuberculosis sufferers, by a certain Dr Alexander Taylor. Enduring legacies of the English include the continuing pursuit of horse-racing, fox-hunting, polo, cricket, golf (the first eighteen-hole course in Europe was here), rugby and several surviving tearooms. The English weren't the only ones attracted here, though. When the train line reached Pau in 1866, the French intelligentsia followed, among them Victor Hugo, Stendhal and Lamartine, who bestowed an epigram on the place: "*Pau est la plus belle vue de ter, comme Naple est la plus belle vue de mer.*"

Although the city stands at an altitude of only a couple of hundred metres, it's the only sizeable place on this side of the Pyrenees with any palpable mountain identity.

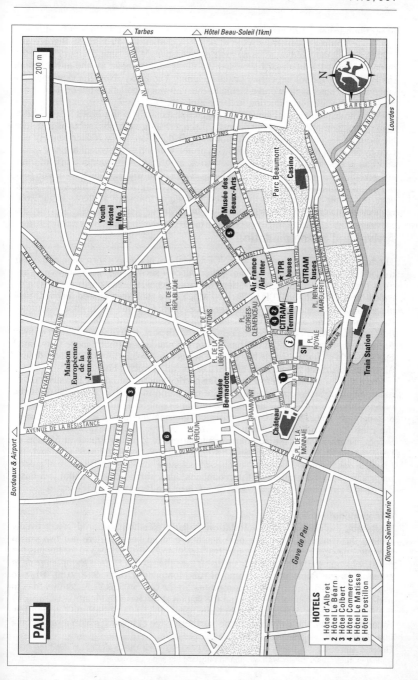

From the **boulevard des Pyrénées** which bounds downtown Pau on the south, you can see a hundred-kilometre stretch of peaks, including Pic du Midi de Bigorre and Pic d'Anie, all identified on a handy *table d'orientation*. In the time of Henry Russell – buried in Pau – the boulevard provided the finest vantage point for the north face of the Pyrenees, overlooking eighty peaks including Vignemale. Now the view is diminished by new construction and a virtually constant veil of pollution, but on a clear day it's still an evocative introduction to the mountains.

Pau's atmosphere (in all senses) changed substantially in the 1950s when a huge natural gas field opened just northwest at Lacq, creating new jobs, suburbs and spin-off industries – plus massive sulphur-dioxide air pollution, lately reduced ninety percent by filtration but still problematic. Gas production and employment are now down, and Pau is casting around for new industries, among them mountain tourism: there are several good outdoor equipment shops, stores filled with the latest climbing, rambling and environmental books, and posters advertising adventure films. The ambience is further enlivened by the presence of eight thousand students at the well-respected University of Pau, which opened in 1972.

Arrival and accommodation

The **train station** (and terminal for SNCF buses) lies at the southern edge of the centre, on the bank of the Gave de Pau. Other buses – such as the SALT service to and from Lourdes – use the **gare routière** on rue Michel-Hounau, north of the centre, except for CITRAM and TPR to Tarbes, which have their own shared terminal near place Georges-Clemenceau. Train services are plentiful along the Bayonne–Pau–Toulouse line, as are SNCF buses to Oloron-Sainte-Marie, from where buses up the Ossau and Aspe valleys are less regular. The **airport**, well to the northeast of town (information on ☎05.59.33.33.00) has flights to London and (much more frequently) Paris; there's a regular shuttle bus to the town centre (☎05.59.02.45.45 for schedules). Air-Inter/Air France have a town office at 10 rue du Maréchal-Foch.

From the train station, a free **funicular** carries you to the bd des Pyrénées on its escarpment, opposite place Royale, at the north end of which is the helpful **tourist office** (July & Aug Mon–Sat 9am–6pm, Sun 10am–5pm; Sept–June Mon–Sat 9am–noon & 2–6pm; ☎05.59.27.27.08). Other sources of information include the local chapter of the Club Alpin Français, at 5 rue René Fournets (☎05.59.27.71.81; Mon–Wed & Fri 5–7pm, Thurs 5–8pm); the southern headquarters of Gîtes de France at Maison de l'Agriculture, 124 bd de Tourasse (☎05.59.80.19.13, fax 05.59.30.60.65); and the Librairie des Pyrénées at 14 rue St-Louis, a bookstore stocking a wide range of guides, maps and general literature on the mountains. Also worth knowing about is a **laundrette** at 6 rue Gambetta (daily 7am–10pm), near the *Poste*.

Accommodation

Reasonable, salubrious **accommodation** is fairly plentiful, scattered pretty evenly around the centre of town; the best hotels are listed below. There are two **youth hostels**, one at 30 rue Michel-Hounau (☎05.59.30.45.77; ①), convenient for the bus terminal, which is well run and has a canteen; the other at the *Maison Européenne de la Jeunesse*, 18 rue Bourbaki, at the end of rue Montpensier (☎05.59.62.50.50; ①), also with a canteen. The nearest local **campsites** are *Le Coy* (☎05.59.27.71.38; mid-May to mid-Oct), fifteen minutes' walk behind the station at the Base de Plein Air, Bizanos; or the *Municipal de la Plaine*, on bd du Cami-Salié (☎05.59.02.30.49; June–Sept), off av Sallenave towards the *autoroute* on the northern edge of town. It's 5km away so take bus #4, marked "Palais des Sports".

Hôtel d'Albret, 11 rue Jeanne-d'Albret (☎05.59.27.81.58). Near the castle; never mind the floral wallpaper, the rooms, mostly with washbasin only, are big and clean. ③.

Hôtel Le Béarn, 5 rue Maréchal-Joffre (☎05.59.27.52.50). Rooms with and without bath, in a quiet alley off the above address; popular and central. ②–③.

Hôtel Beau-Soleil, 81 av des Lauriers, well to the east of the centre (☎05.59.02.40.29). Out in the former British quarter, simple en-suite rooms; a good choice if you're driving, as parking in the centre is expensive. ③.

Hôtel Colbert, 1 rue Manescau (☎05.59.32.52.78, fax 05.59.32.68.38). Two-star facilities, just north of the centre. ④.

Hôtel Commerce, 9 rue Maréchal-Joffre (☎05.59.27.24.40, fax 05.59.83.81.74). Comfortable, double-glazed rooms, all en suite, plus a decent restaurant and an interior courtyard. ⑤.

Hôtel Le Matisse, 17 rue Mathieu-Lalanne (☎05.59.27.73.80). Most rooms here are smart enough, and some have a bath. It's opposite the Musée des Beaux-Arts. ③.

Hotel Postillon, 10 cours Camou (☎05.59.72.83.00, fax 05.59.72.83.13). A pricier two-star just behind the place de Verdun car park; rooms with baths, central courtyard garden with fountain. ⑤.

The Town

Pau possesses no absolutely unmissable sights or museums, so if you choose you can merely stroll about, soaking up the city's relaxed atmosphere without feeling too guilty. The east end of bd des Pyrénées is marked by the twin-towered **casino**, now a convention/exhibition centre, surrounded by the **Parc Beaumont**, of English inspiration with its lake and waterfall. At the opposite end of the boulevard, the landmark **Château** (exterior grounds free & unenclosed) overlooks the crossing of the Gave de Pau on the vital Bordeaux–Zaragoza route. The first castle here was built by Gaston Fébus as part of his grand strategy to create a unified kingdom of the Pyrenees. More importantly for France as a whole, Henri III of Foix-Béarn, king of Navarre and later **Henri IV of France**, was born in the castle in 1553.

Pau was an important theatre of the Wars of Religion, provoked here by the virulent Protestantism of Jeanne d'Albret – Henri's mother – whose activities led to equally ruthless reprisals by the Catholic King Charles IX. Later, when Henri became the French king, switching faiths in the process, he found it necessary to accommodate the sensibilities of his Béarnais subjects by announcing that he was giving France to Béarn rather than Béarn to France. Like other Pyrenean regions that became counties and viscounties in feudal times, it retained separatist leanings even after incorporation into France, and today many of the Béarnais still speak Occitan along with French.

At the time of Henri's birth the castle was somewhat neglected, only Gaston Fébus' original brick keep remaining in an otherwise grey monolith. The d'Albrets added some sophisticated touches, like the Renaissance windows and doorways, but the most substantial alterations – including the addition of an arcade and tower close to the entrance – were carried out in the last century, first by Louis-Philippe and then by Napoléon III and Eugénie.

Within the castle, the **Musée National** or Royal Rooms (daily 9.30–11.45am & 2–5.15pm; guided visits only; 28F) consists essentially of Napoléon III's and Eugénie's apartments, notable mostly for some fabulous eighteenth-century tapestries and Henri IV memorabilia such as the turtle shell that was allegedly his cradle. In the wing opposite, the **Musée Béarnais** (daily except Christmas, New Year's Day & May Day 9.30am–noon & 2–5.30pm, last admission at 4.45pm; 10F) has a good if unexceptional collection of costumes, Pyrenean fossils and animals, musical instruments and implements of pastoral life.

Just northwest of the castle, centred on the ravine-bottom rue du Hédas, is the **quartier du Hédas**, or what remains of medieval Pau. At the base of the descending **rue Réné Fournets** is a small square with an ancient fountain and laundry – the only source of water before the Revolution. Today the nearby streets are crammed with numerous places to eat and drink, many of them listed below.

Immediately north of here, at 5 rue Tran, you'll find the mildly interesting **Musée Bernadotte** (Tues–Sun 10am–noon & 2–6pm; 10F), birthplace of the man who, having served as a commander under Napoleon I, went on to become Charles XIV of Sweden in 1818. As well as pieces of fine traditional Béarnaise furniture, the house contains some valuable works of art collected over his lifetime. At the west end of rue Tran, the arcaded **place Grammont** with its four fountains is more compelling for most, despite its use as a parking lot.

Pau's final museum, the **Musée des Beaux Arts** (daily except Tues 9am–noon & 2–6pm; 10F), lies 500m due east of the quartier du Hédas, near the Parc Beaumont. This surprisingly strong collection of paintings is drawn from several European schools spanning the fourteenth to twentieth centuries, featuring El Greco, Rubens and Degas. Local interest is provided by Eugène Devéris – one of the relatively few artists to have discovered the Pyrenean landscape – and the decidedly unromantic *Factories at Lacq* by Desnoyer.

Eating and drinking

Not too surprisingly for a university town, Pau has a fair quantity of affordable, varied places to eat and drink, concentrated in the pleasant pedestrian lanes around the château and the quartier du Hédas.

Restaurants and brasseries

Le Belvédere, 22 bd des Pyrénées. An excellent, classic *brasserie*, serving from noon until 3pm, and again 7–11pm; outdoor tables very popular at lunchtime. Seafood choices (including turtle) particularly good, but also meat dishes and *plats de jour* for under 60F.

Le Berry, rue Gachet, east side of place Georges-Clemenceau. Popular with a young crowd, who come for the reasonable *brasserie* grub.

La Brochetterie, 16 rue Henri IV. Good meat, game and fish grills on a wood fire, popular with locals. Prices from 59F lunch menu to around 110F à la carte. Open daily until 11pm, except Sat lunchtime.

Chez Maman, opposite the château. A simple but good *crêperie/cidrerie*, often with a wait for the outdoor tables. Open 11am–midnight.

Chez Olive, 9–11 rue du Château. Despite being in a heavily touristed area, reasonable *menus* with a wide choice of dishes. Closed June, plus Mon lunchtime & Sun.

La Gousse d'Ail, 12 rue du Hédas. Somewhat pricey but well-prepared traditional French cuisine. Closed Sat lunchtime and Sun; otherwise daily until 10pm.

Lotus d'Or, 1–3 place Grammont. Considered the best Chinese/Vietnamese restaurant in town, with dishes including glazed duck à l'orange. Also menus from 75F. Closed Mon & lunchtime Wed; serves until 11pm.

El Mesón, 40 rue du Maréchal-Joffre. Basque-style *tapas* diner open only in the evening. Closed Sun & Aug.

La Table d'Hote, 1 rue du Hédas. An elegant *nouvelle cuisine* restaurant in a bare-brick former warehouse; the 120F *menu* is fine, but expect long waits between courses. Closed weekends.

La Taverne du Roy, 7 rue de la Fontaine, quartier du Hédas. Basque- and Spanish-influenced cuisine, with the limited menu emphasizing seafood; good-value *menus* under 100F. Open until midnight; closed Sat lunchtime and all Sun.

Bars and tea rooms

Black Bear, 5 place Reine-Marguerite, off bd des Pyrénées. The local rugby theme pub.

Bouzoum, 6 rue Henri IV. Wide-ranging patisserie and tea room; indoor seating only.

La Cantina, 20 rue du Hédas. Student-oriented bar which serves *tapas* and has occasional live music. Closed Sun & Mon.

O'Gascon, corner rue du Château and rue Bordenave-d'Abère. A fun bar that also does ice cream and nibbles at outdoor tables.

L'Isle au Jasmin, 28 bd des Pyrénées. Tea (dozens of varieties) and muffins served outside, on chaise longues facing the view. Daily except Wed 10am–7pm.
Le Sully, 13 rue Henri IV. A relaxed, mixed gay-straight bar with clients spilling out onto the pedestrian lane.

The Ossau and Aspe valleys

The parallel north–south valleys of the **Ossau** and **Aspe,** both beginning about 20km south-southwest of Pau, are the French Pyrenees at their most *sauvage*, and the region in which the **brown bears** most tenaciously resist extinction: about a dozen survive on the slopes of the main valleys, in the **Cirque de Lescun**, and in the adjoining parts of Spain. Tourism is less developed here because of unreliable snow for skiing, but what havoc tourism has failed to wreak, a major road-widening scheme in the Vallée d'Aspe (see pp.350–351) may accomplish; even before this both valleys were major arteries into Spain. Along these main roads – the D934 through Ossau, the N134 along the Aspe – the steep, densely forested sides obscure everything other than the valley-bottom rivers and the villages directly on their banks. To see the best of the region, you should get out your map and walk, camping – with permission, of course – at the isolated farms along the way.

Currently the French train service ceases at **Oloron-Sainte-Marie**, though this may change in the wake of the controversial developments up the Aspe. Coming from Pau you bypass Oloron completely en route to the Vallée d'Ossau, which has most to offer near the border: the touristic train ride up to **Lac d'Artouste**, tough climbing on **Balaïtous** peak, and easier, classic rambles around the **Pic du Midi d'Ossau**. Highlight of the Vallée d'Aspe, and likely to remain relatively undisturbed by the road-widening project, is the **Cirque de Lescun**: not so grand as Gavarnie's, but infinitely satisfying by virtue of its unexpectedness in a much gentler landscape.

Oloron-Sainte-Marie

The Ossau and the Aspe valleys join at **OLORON-SAINTE-MARIE**, a small town reverberating with the roar of the mingling rivers; it's the traditional centre for the manufacture of the Béarn woollen **beret**, still considered the archetypal item of French male dress. Nowadays, however, it's worn far more by overseas commandos, and probably made from New Zealand, not French, wool. In the town itself, dignified old commercial properties now find themselves sandwiched between modern shops and offices. Overall it's a tolerable, if rather sprawling place, older Oloron poised opposite board-flat Sainte-Marie.

Oloron grew from the Roman *Iluro*, founded on a hill just south of the river confluence, where today's Sainte-Croix quarter is located. When barbarian hordes threatened to take the settlement, the inhabitants crossed the Gave d'Ossau to found what is now the Sainte-Marie district, which in later centuries became the episcopal seat, while Sainte-Croix evolved into a commercial and military centre.

The town's two churches are the sole points of interest for the visitor. Hilltop **Sainte-Croix**, one of the oldest Romanesque structures in Béarn, has unusual interior vaulting, created by thirteenth-century Spanish stonemasons in imitation of the Great Mosque at Córdoba; together with six massive piers, it dominates the two-aisled interior, austere in the extreme except for a few ornate capitals near the apse. The Romanesque-Gothic cathedral of **Sainte-Marie** across the Gave d'Aspe boasts an ornately sculpted portal that has escaped damage by religious vandals – even during the Revolution – thanks to the extremely durable Pyrenean marble from which it is constructed. In the upper arch, the elders of the Apocalypse play violins and rebecs, while in the second arch scenes from medieval life – hunting wild boar and fishing for salmon

THE BROWN BEAR

Local folklore might lead you to believe that the Pyrenean brown bear – *Ursos arctos* – is a fearsome creature. In fact, unlike the American grizzly or the bears of eastern Europe and Siberia, the Pyrenean species is small and timid, its diet seventy percent herbivorous. (A full-grown male can attain 300kg and females 200kg, but the average is much less.) Furthermore, its habitat is quite restricted – they do not like to go much above 1800m, they have never been sighted below 900m, and nowadays there are scarcely any signs of them at any altitude.

The **decline of the bear population** in the Pyrenees has been startlingly rapid. By 1937, when bears had probably been hunted out of every other corner of France, there were still estimated to be between 150 and 200 in the French Pyrenees. In 1954 numbers were down to about 70; by 1960 they had declined to 40, and today there are certainly less than 150 bears, concentrated in the Béarn region, almost completely outside of the Parc National de Pyrénées. No cub paw-prints have been seen around the Ossau and Aspe valleys since the late 1980s.

Such facts seem incontrovertible; what sparks heated debate is the question of exactly why the bears have disappeared. Majority opinion credits the age-old hostility of pastoral communities to the animals, who occasionally bag a stray sheep or cow, an act which in the past would lead to instant **bounty-hunting** funded by the aggrieved villagers. (This has been illegal since 1962, and the animal absolutely protected since 1981; today the government pays ample compensation for such losses.) Rural activities such as wood-cutting, berry-picking, bee-keeping and grazing are also blamed for disturbing the animals. In many parts of the Ossau and Aspe valleys such endeavours are severely restricted or banned, much to the villagers' annoyance, though there has been some co-operation; in the 1980s the villagers of Laruns were allotted 10,000F to feed the bears by helicopter and refrained from felling certain groves, the revenue thus lost being compensated by Paris. Until 1993, national policy goals envisioned the setting aside of over 1000 square kilometres of "tranquillity" – meaning off-limits to humans – enabling the bears to survive until the next century. RDP governments between then and 1997 backed off from this restrictive approach, and tried to provide incentives for local protection ordinances with grants for local economic development.

This conventional wisdom has been lately challenged by certain trackers and naturalists, who point out that bears actually thrive in proximity to humans. This group considers **depopulation of the Pyrenees** to be the main culprit in the decline of bear numbers, citing as an example the nearby Ariège, abandoned simultaneously by people and bears alike. Such revisionists maintain that bears and the country-dwellers should be left to sort themselves out by whatever means, barring shotgun massacres – preferably by fencing rogue individuals away from berry-patches and bee-hives, rather than banning humans from their traditional mountain livelihoods. Near the border between Haute-Garonne and the Ariège, two Slovenian bears released in 1997 promptly left the area, shunning prepared feeding sites in favour of sheep-bagging in the Ariège – forty dead animals at the last count, with the shepherds concerned quite literally up in arms. Unfortunately the truth of the competing arguments will in all likelihood not be established before the native bears, for whatever reason, disappear.

The bear has been exploited as a symbol by various factions in the Vallée d'Aspe. Environmental lobbies opposed to the Tunnel de Somport and road-widening schemes (see p.350) used the presumed fate of the bear as vital ammunition to slow, though ultimately not stop, these projects. Tourist brochures for the Vallée d'Aspe depict a cute cub clutching a flower, giving the frankly dishonest impression that the beasts are as common and locally loved as in America's Yellowstone Park. And the same farmers and shepherds who execrate wild bears went dewy-eyed when discussing Jojo, rescued as an orphaned cub in 1974 and long a tame resident in Borce. In 1993, Jojo died, subsequently replaced by two non-French bears rescued from maltreatment at a circus and displayed in the same enclosure as a paying tourist attraction – the time has long passed since two suitable Pyrenean bears could be found for such a dubious purpose.

– are represented. Above the left-hand door, the Persecution of the Church is balanced by the Triumph of the Church over the opposite door; the two guards above them recall the sanctioning by the Byzantine emperor Constantine of protection for Christians.

The gallant knight on horseback over the outer column on the right is Gaston IV, count of Béarn, who commissioned the portal on his return from the first Crusade at the beginning of the twelfth century, hence the inclusion of Saracens in chains amongst the sculptures supporting the portal. Inside the church, well away from the main area of worship, is a Cagot stoup, a stark reminder of the centuries-long persecution and segregation of this mysterious group.

Practicalities

The **train station** lies 200m west of the river confluence; CITRAM **buses** from Pau arrive in place de la Gare out front. The **tourist office** (mid-July to Aug daily 9am–1pm & 2–5.30pm; rest of year Tues–Sat 10am–noon & 1–7pm; ☎05.59.39.98.00) is on the east bank of the Gave d'Ossau in a booth on place de la Résistance, near the nineteenth-century church of Notre-Dame.

It's unlikely that you'll need, or want, to stay the night in Oloron, and in any case most accommodation is noisily situated. That said, there are a few reasonable **hotels**: the two-star *Hôtel de la Paix*, 24 av Sadi-Carnot, between the train station and the river (☎05.59.39.02.63; ③); the two-star *Hôtel Bristol*, rue Carrérot at the corner of rue de la Poste (☎05.59.39.43.78; ④); or if finances are tight, the faded, no-star *De la Poste* (☎05.59.39.60.97; ③), on place de la Résistance. You can **camp** at the tree-shaded *Camping du Stade* on the D919 heading southwest toward Arette (☎05.59.39.11.26; open all year). In terms of **restaurants**, choices are limited to *Le Biscondau* on rue de la Filature, overlooking the Ossau, with three *menus*; *Le Trinquet* at 3 place des Oustalots, where you can eat for under 100F (closed Sun outside of summer); and that rare thing, vegetarian *La Bio Assiette*, at 4 av Charles Moureu, by the cinema (Tues–Sat lunchtime only).

Since the closure (in 1973) of the international rail link through the Aspe valley to Canfranc-Estación in Spain, Oloron-Sainte-Marie has been the end of the line for **trains** from Pau; there are currently four daily services. Four to seven SNCF **buses** run daily south up the Vallée d'Aspe to Urdos (most of them going on to Canfranc in Spain), and four to five daily, beginning in Pau, head up the Vallée d'Ossau to Laruns, supplemented by three CITRAM buses from Pau to Gourette, east of Laruns. In July and August only, Monday to Friday, Pic Bus offers a twice-daily service all the way up to the frontier at Col du Pourtalet, via Gabas and the Fabrèges dam, with occasional diversions to the campsite below the Lac de Bious.

Along the lower Ossau

Along the **lower Ossau** between Oloron and Laruns, there are really only two places worth stopping. At **ARUDY**, the **Maison d'Ossau** (July & Aug daily 10am–noon & 3–6pm; Sept–June Mon 10am–noon, Tues, Thurs & Sat 2.30–5pm, Sun 3–6pm; 14F), housed in the village church, offers a comprehensive account of the prehistoric Pyrenees and an exhibition of the flora and fauna of the *parc national*. **ASTE-BÉON**, a few kilometres further up-valley, is home to **La Falaise aux Vautours** (daily April–Sept 10am–1pm & 2–7pm; Oct 1–Oct 24 Sun 2–6pm; Oct 25–Nov 3, Dec 28–Jan 4 & Feb Sun 3–6pm; 35F), a highly worthwhile griffon vulture breeding and viewing centre, where cameras trained on nests transmit images of vulture families going about their business to a giant viewing screen. Telescopes and binoculars are also available for more low-tech viewing, and staff lead walking safaris to pastures where the vultures feed.

If you have your own transport, a more alluring route into the Ossau starts in the Aspe valley at Escot, from where you cut across over the **Col de Marie-Blanque**

(1035m) – through thick beech forests and uplands where more vultures wheel over-head – before descending again through pines to the Ossau valley at Bielle, some 7km north of Laruns. Just over a kilometre before Bielle, in **BILHÈRES**, you can pause for a **meal** at *Chez Jean* in the village centre, where various *menus* for under 130F are served on the valley-view terrace. Here, and all along the lower Ossau, the influence of the Atlantic is strong, the fields an Irish green and the forests deciduous. Although it's still some way from the Basque country, many of the villages have a *fronton*, the court used for the Basque game of *pelota*.

Laruns

The best day in **LARUNS**, 15km upstream from Arudy and 4km from Aste-Béon, is unquestionably August 15, the main festival day when young people kitted in tradition-al red and black – the women wearing multicoloured scarves and the men the local beret – dance to a one-man band of three-holed flute and tambourine. Otherwise it's pretty dull, best kept in mind as the last place to buy provisions before heading up to the *parc national*. If you need to **stay**, try the dead-central *Hôtel D'Ossau*, place de la Mairie (☎05.59.05.30.14; ③); the *Hôtel de France*, rue de la Gare, the street leading east from the *place* to the disused train station (☎05.59.05.33.71; ④); or a **refuge**, the *Chalet-Refuge l'Embaradère*, across the street at 13 av de la Gare (☎05.59.05.41.88; ①), also offering meals until late. Among half a dozen local campsites, closest are two down in the Quartier Pon, near the old station: *Pont Lauguere* (☎05.59.05.35.99) and *Ayguebere* (☎05.59.05.38.55), both open all year. One of the very few independent **restaurants** in town is *L'Arregalet*, 37 rue du Bourguet, 250m north of the main *place* (closed Sun evening & Mon), with rather pricey specialities such as *poule au pot* and the namesake dish – garlic-bread crumbs sauteed in goose grease. The **Office du Tourisme** (sum-mer daily 9am–12.30pm & 2–7pm; rest of year Mon–Sat 9am–noon & 2–6.30pm, Sun 9am–noon; ☎05.59.05.31.41), well stocked with literature on the Ossau valley in gener-al, is in the main place de la Mairie, in the same building as the local **Bureau des Guides** (daily 2–7pm; ☎05.59.05.33.04).

The Vallée du Valentin

East of Laruns, the D918 heads up the tributary **Vallée du Valentin** to the spa of Eaux-Bonnes (4km) and the ski station of Gourette (10km), last stop (after Laruns) for most CITRAM buses out of Pau, from July to mid-September and again during ski season. **EAUX-BONNES**, yet another Second Empire watering-hole, has been spruced up of late, though the road roars through the Neoclassical central square. You're probably better off staying 1.5km northwest along a dead-end road at **AAS** with its *Auberge du Chemin de Pleysse* (☎05.59.05.38.02; ① dorms, ② doubles) installed in two old farm-houses, with meals provided.

By contrast, **GOURETTE** is not much to look at aesthetically – all of a dozen or so high-rises below the aptly named Crêtes Blanches – but there are plenty of interesting red runs from the 2380-metre top lift, making Gourette an appealing intermediate resort; the tally is 26 lifts and 19 pistes, supplemented as necessary by dozens of snow cannons.

In summer, Gourette's position on the GR10 and the *Tour de la Vallée d'Ossau* hiking routes results in a walking clientele, who stay in one of two **refuges**: either the Club Pyrénéa Sport refuge (staffed July, Aug & Dec 15–April 30; ☎05.59.05.11.35; ①), on the main through road, or that of the Club Alpin Français (staffed July 1–Sept 15 and dur-ing school holidays; ☎05.59.05.11.50; ①). En route to the Col d'Aubisque, 2km above Gourette, there's a simple **hotel**, the *Crêtes Blanches* (summer only; ☎05.59.05.10.03; ②) with shared bathrooms and a *table d'hôte* restaurant, which would be even more appealing to long-distance trekkers if it weren't slightly off the GR10. The closest **campsite** is well below the town, on the road to Eaux-Bonnes.

The Col d'Aubisque and beyond

East of Gourette, the D918 toils up to the **Col d'Aubisque** (1709m, 17km from Laruns), guarded by the Pic de Ger; so does one daily CITRAM bus, dropping you by the summertime café, from where you must hitch another 18km via the Cirque du Litor and the Col de Souler to Arrens-Marsous. The **GR10** east from Gourette shortcuts most of the road on its six-hour way to Arrens, but there's still too much narrow, dangerous tarmac for it to be a really popular stretch of the long-distance route. East of the pass, the road becomes a dramatic, one-lane corniche route, threading a succession of drippy tunnels; on the bleak moorland outside, shepherds sell ewe cheese amongst the roadside heather. It's best to enjoy the views along the way from your own car, or join the ranks of *Tour de France* wannabes who make it a point of honour to find the breath for a *bonjour* as they pedal up to the pass.

The upper Ossau

South of busy Laruns, the Gave d'Ossau narrows drastically as the D934 enters its upper reaches at **EAUX-CHAUDES**, a gloomy nineteenth-century spa that makes Eaux-Bonnes seem lively and cheerful by comparison. You'd only stop here voluntarily if everywhere else were full in season; if that happens, the *Chalet-Auberge La Caverne* (☎05.59.05.42.27; ①) will be a welcome sight.

Gabas

GABAS, 13km south of Laruns, is a one-street hamlet whose farming livelihood has long since been outstripped by its role as an important gateway to the *parc national*. At the south end of the village, the **Centre d'Écologie Montagnarde** (summer daily 9am–noon & 2–6pm), staffed by university students, has a permanent exhibition on local natural history, and cultivates rare species in its garden; there's also yet another *Maison du Parc* (☎05.59.05.32.13), with abundant walkers' information.

The best place to **stay and eat** is the *Hôtel Restaurant Chez Vignau* at the north entrance to the hamlet (☎05.59.05.34.06; ③); most rooms at the hotel, east of the road, have showers or baths, and the restaurant across the street, with such delicacies as frog's legs *persillade* and prune pie, is outstanding value. Honourable runner-up is the cheap and very cheerful *Restaurant du Pic du Midi*, where you can get trout dinners and other local specialities for well under 100F. The overpriced *Hôtel Restaurant Le Biscau* (☎05.59.05.31.37; ④) is a definite second choice in both categories. Dormitory accommodation is provided by the Club Alpin Français **refuge** above the hamlet (1035m; 46 places; staffed & open June–Oct & weekends in winter, apart from Nov–Dec 15; ☎05.59.05.33.14; ①); no cooking is allowed, but meals are available.

Around the Pic du Midi d'Ossau

An undisputed Pyrenean classic despite its modest height (2884m), the handsome, double-tipped **Pic du Midi d'Ossau** rears up in magnificent isolation above the Vallée d'Ossau, its distinctive shape recognizable from a great distance. This is one of those summits, like Canigou and Pedraforca in Catalonia, which inspire an affection bordering on reverence; nicknamed "Jean-Pierre" affectionately by the locals, it's virtually the logo of high Béarn.

The first recorded ascent of Pic du Midi was by an anonymous shepherd in 1787, who erected a summit cairn which confirmed his success. Today the peak remains a tough scramble at the very least, and is more of a mecca for rock-climbers, but the celebrated *Tour du Pic du Midi*, designed for walkers to enjoy from all angles, can be completed in a single summer's day. If you want a **map** more detailed than the 1:50,000

Carte de Randonnées, get hold of the IGN 1:25,000 "Laruns 1547 Est" *série bleue* sheet, or the IGN Parc National des Pyrénées 1:25,000 no. 1 "Aspe Ossau".

Bases

Gabas can be used as a base of activities around the Pic du Midi, but you'll get more immediately to grips with the mountain by heading 4km southwest up the very minor D231 to the dammed **Lac de Bious-Artigues**, a seasonally crowded picnic spot with desperately inadequate parking. Just beyond there's the cheerful *Cantine de Bious*, excellent for a pre-hike breakfast or post-trek celebration, and the adjacent *Refuge Pyrénéa Sport*, almost due north of the summit (1430m; 45 places; staffed & open daily mid-June to mid-Sept & weekends May to mid-June & early Oct; ☎05.59.05.32.12; ①). If both Gabas' accommodation and this refuge are full – likely in summer if you haven't phoned ahead – your only fallback is the *Camping Bious-Oumettes* (☎05.59.05.38.76; mid-June to mid-Sept), set 1.5km below the dam on grassy terraces, with a shop; this is as high as the occasional bus goes.

A remoter alternative as a local base – though still hugely popular – is the CAF-run *Refuge de Pombie* on the southeastern flank of the mountain (2031m; 55 places; staffed June 15–Sept 30; part always open; ☎05.59.05.31.78; ①), by the eponymous tarn. A well-signposted path, part of the *Tour du Pic du Midi* (see below) takes you there in about three hours from Bious-Artigues: first head east over the **Col Long de Magnabaigt** (1655m), then south through the **Col de Moundelhs** and **Col de Suzon** (2127m).

The ascent – and the Tour du Pic du Midi

The standard **ascent** begins from the Col de Suzon, a fairly easy climb, but busy in summer and plagued by loose, falling rocks – helmets are recommended. At the *col* you turn west onto a route that leads directly to the mountain; things soon start to get more serious, with movable iron pegs in one section to make the summit more accessible to non-climbers. The proper course is indicated by occasional cairns, and you'll reach the wide summit in about four hours.

You can make the classic, anticlockwise **Tour du Pic du Midi** in seven hours from Lac de Bious-Artigues, beginning by following the **GR10** along the eastern shore. About 1000m beyond the southern tip of the lake, or roughly an hour from *Refuge Pyrénéa Sport*, the trails divide; take the left-hand path, crossing the **Pont de Bious** and entering the *parc national*. Continue upstream on the true right bank, across flat, wet terrain – similar to the *artigues* (meadows) flooded by the Bious-Artigues dam lower down – until a sign reading "Pombie par Peyreget" directs you left (south). It's a steepish, zigzagging climb along a section of the HRP to the Lac de Peyreget, reached just under three hours into the day. Next, slip over the **Col de Peyreget** (2322m), between Pic Peyreget (2487m) and the southern spur of Pic du Midi, and then down past the **Pombie** lake to the *Refuge de Pombie* just east of it, well placed for a lunch stop some four hours along. From this refuge you return to Bious-Artigues via the good trail through the **Col de Suzon** and **Col de Moundelhs**, reversing the direct *Pombie* access walk described above.

West to the Vallée d'Aspe

To traverse **west** from the Pic du Midi d'Ossau region to the Vallée d'Aspe, start out on the **GR10** as described for the *tour*, but don't cross the Pont de Bious; instead, keep right at the fork, following a sign reading "Lac d'Ayous 1.30", and carry on climbing westwards, initially through forest to three successive lakes, each larger than the preceding. You arrive at the *parc national*-managed *Refuge d'Ayous* (1960m; 30 places; staffed June 15–Sept 15; part always open; ☎05.59.05.37.00; ①), well under two hours' walk from Bious-Artigues. Staying the night here – you're more likely to camp by the Lac Gentau below, as the refuge is perennially full – is rewarded by the best available vantage point for experiencing typically spectacular sunrises over the Pic du Midi, reflected in Lac Gentau.

The GR10 heads west through the **Col d'Ayous**, then curves away northwards through the **Col de la Hourquette de Larry** and then down through the Pacq woods to Etsaut in the Aspe valley (3hr; see p.351). You can get into the valley about an hour quicker by heading more directly westwards to Urdos, past the unattended *Refuge de Larry* (1724m; 6 places), less than an hour west of the Col d'Ayous.

The Tour des Lacs

If you're not confident about tackling the all-day *Tour du Pic du Midi*, the **Tour des Lacs**, a circuit of about four hours from the Bious-Artigues parking lot, makes a fine alternative; many consider that it gives better views of "Jean-Pierre". It uses the *Refuge d'Ayous* as a fulcrum and probable lunch halt, and can be combined with the best of the *Tour du Pic* to make a fine two-day loop, with the Pombie and Ayous refuges (or their environs) as overnight spots.

Begin as for the *Tour du Pic* at the Pont de Bious, where a sign"Lacs d'Ayous 2.30" hints at what you're about to do, but at the Houns de Peyreget veer southwest, following signs, towards the **Lac Casterau**, then continue northwest over a small pass to the much bigger **Lac Bersau**, and finally north to the refuge, which you should reach two-and-a-half hours along. The downhill return to the parking lot will take an hour and a half maximum. You should get to the refuge in good time for lunch, as they often run out of dishes in season, and the menu is fairly sparse to begin with.

East or south from Refuge de Pombie

You can trek to or from the *Refuge de Pombie* towards the east or south, without having to return to Gabas or the Lac de Bious-Artigues. Heading **east**, you descend by path along the Pombie stream, changing banks as necessary, until arriving after two hours at the **Callou de Soques** café in the Gave de Brousset, on the D934 road 9km north of the frontier, 7km south of Gabas. From here you can easily continue northeast on the clear **HRP** trail to the Lac d'Artouste (see below), a steep but scenic four-hour climb via the Col d'Arrious, or directly to the *Refuge d'Arrémoulit* from the *col* via the Lac d'Arrious and the somewhat exposed ledge-path called the Passage d'Orteig.

Leaving Pombie towards the **south**, you shun the Col de Peyreget route in favour of another marked trail leading in one hour to the **Col de Soum** (ca. 2100m), from where it's as long again via a heavily used path to a car-parking area 1500m north of the border at **Col du Pourtalet/Puerto de Portalet** (1794m). This is only passable for cars during snow-free months, which usually means early June to early October. If you get stuck here, there's a small, simple **hotel**, the *Col du Pourtalet* (☎05.59.05.32.00; ③; June–Sept), but the nearest habitation of any size, with onward bus service, is the ski resort of El Formigal, 8km southeast in Spain.

Around Balaïtous and Lac d'Artouste

Balaïtous, almost directly east of Pic du Midi d'Ossau across the Gave de Brousset, is, at 3145m, the most westerly Pyrenean summit to surpass the magic figure of 3000m, and one of the toughest and remotest. It was first climbed in 1825 by the military surveyors Peytier and Hossard, but they seem not to have divulged their route. Charles Packe, nearly forty years later, had to find his own way up. Balaïtous, he wrote –

> ... lies so completely away from the route of the ordinary traveller that the Eaux-Bonnes guides seem quite at a loss as to its exact whereabouts, as a friend who started from Eaux-Bonnes under their guidance found to his cost; for after passing two wretched nights in the mountain cabanes of the shepherds (a lodging which few Englishmen would prefer to the open air) he failed to attain even the foot of the Pic Balaïtous, the object of his search.

After a failed attempt in 1862, Packe made a second in 1864 with the guide Jean-Pierre Gaspard, and after a week of searching discovered a route to the summit.

The miniature train

In Packe's day, of course, there was no *téléphérique* from the giant car park and winter complex at the north end of the **Lac de Fabrèges**, 7km southeast of Gabas by a roundabout road (regular summer buses). Nor was there the miniature **tourist train** of bright-red, open carriages running the 10km southeast from the top of the lift on Pic de la Sagette to just shy of **Lac d'Artouste**. Built in 1924 to serve a hydroelectric project, the train was later converted for tourist purposes. Weather permitting, the train normally operates daily from early July until late September; first daily departure from the top of the *téléphérique* is at 8.30am in July (last return 4pm), 9am in August (last return 3pm) and 9.30am in September (last return 2pm). Reservations are suggested (☎05.59.05.34.00, fax 05.59.05.37.55); fare for the combined ten-minute lift and subsequent train ride is 82F. It's a fifty-minute trip along the sonorously named Gave de Soussouéou to the end of the line, where the train waits for ninety minutes while passengers walk down to and around the lake before heading back. Some twenty minutes above the south end of Lac d'Artouste, nearly an hour from the dam, sits the walkers' base camp of *Refuge d'Arrémoulit* (2305m; staffed June 30–Sept 30; 30 places; meal service; part always open; ☎05.59.05.31.79; ①).

The ascent of Balaïtous

The **ascent of Balaïtous** from *Refuge d'Arrémoulit* takes almost nine hours (return), and as this is very tough country indeed, you should have the IGN 1:25,000 "Balaïtous-Vignemale" map (no. 274), also issued as IGN Parc National des Pyrénées no. 2 "Balaïtous". Ascend east an hour to the **Col du Palas/Cuello de Pallàs** (2517m) on the frontier, descending southeast on the far side to skirt the **Arriel** lakes and the tarn of **Gorg Helada** (a likely lunch stop). Next follow a line of cairns to the primitive *Abri Michaud* shelter (2698m); the gully above it – full of loose, dangerous rock – leads to the western ridge and then, via more gullies, to the **summit** (3146m). From the top you can appreciate how opposite in character Balaïtous is from Pic du Midi d'Ossau: the latter showcased by a virtual parkland of lakes and grassy turf, your present vantage concealed by savage, lunar crags in every direction, with nothing to soften the landscape.

Traverse east to Refuge de Larribet

The HRP also continues **eastwards** from *Refuge d'Arrémoulit* to *Refuge de Larribet*; this is a short (4–5hr) but strenuous outing, intended for lightly laden trekkers experienced in traversing such terrain cross-country, and encountering passes relatively free of snow.

From the Col du Palas, cross the head of the Spanish Arriel valley to the **Port/Puerto de Lavedan** (2615m), dropping down on the far side to the tiny **Micoulaou** lakes; from there go northeast with a clearer path past the **Batcrabère** lakes, and finally through the **Brèche de la Garénère** (2189m) to descend on *Refuge de Larribet* (2070m; 45 places; staffed June 15–Sept 15; part always open; ①). If you've been hiking westwards from Gavarnie or Cauterets, simply reverse all of the foregoing directions to move on from the Balaïtous area to the Vallée d'Ossau.

Along the Aspe

The **Vallée d'Aspe** between Oloron-Sainte-Marie and the Col du Somport has long been an important corridor between France and Spain; the Romans had a road through it, the Saracens conducted raids along it, and lately once again the valley has become embroiled in a controversy over its role in north–south travel. In 1659, during the Wars of Religion, all the local villages but one suffered the misfortune of being burnt to the ground by Protestant forces; early the next century these settlements were reconstructed simultaneously, and – never having been altered since – they present a pleasingly homogeneous spectacle.

Escot to Cette-Eygun

The upper valley can be said to begin in earnest just south of Escot, 15km from Oloron, where a narrow namesake defile closes in on the road and river. Upstream from the gorge, along the N134, the attractive village of **SARRANCE** has the ancient monastic church of Notre-Dame de la Pierre, with a wonderfully rustic cloister – and strangely unexploited associations with Marguerite d'Angoulême, who stayed and wrote here when the weather in Cauterets turned bad. The cloister, alas, is no longer a *gîte d'étape*; the only place to stay is the no-star *Lestanguet* (no phone; ③) on the old through road, now traffic-free.

For a stay-put holiday base, you could do far worse than **LOURDIOS-ICHÈRE**, 10km away along the minor D241 over the Col d'Ichère. Here you can choose between *Estivade* (☎05.59.34.46.39), which operates both a **youth hostel** (①) and a **campsite**, and *Chez Lamothe* (☎05.59.34.41.53), which does excellent family-style meals and has just two **rooms** available (⑤ with obligatory half-board); there's another restaurant in the village, the inexpensive (under 70F) *Auberge Bellocq*.

Back in the main valley and 7km south of Sarrance, the first place of any consequence – though still resolutely rural as reflected in its traditional Thursday morning summer market – is **BEDOUS**. Here you'll find a fine church and the miniature, eighteenth-century **Château Lassalle** on the quiet Place de l'Église east of the through road. Also on this *place* is the less institutional of the two **gîtes d'étape** in town, *Le Mandragot* (☎05.59.34.59.33; ①); the other, English-speaking *Le Choucas Blanc* (☎05.59.34.53.71, fax 05.59.34.50.86; dorm ①, room ②) is on the through road opposite the main car park, and thus noisier.

There's more accommodation in a string of villages south of Bedous. Some 3km beyond **ACCOUS** – the valley capital with a **tourist office** (☎05.59.34.71.48) – the Auberge Cavalière perches high above the highway (☎05.59.34.72.30, fax 05.59.34.51.97), specializing in one-week horse-riding, nordic skiing and walking packages; the stables are on the premises. Accommodation is either at the *auberge's* attached hotel (④) or at the *Refuge des Ecuyers* (①) further up the hill, accessible by jeep track. Just before **CETTE-EYGUN**, 2km southeast from the *Auberge Cavalière* turning, *La Goutte d'Eau* (☎05.59.34.78.83; ①) is an activists' centre housed in the abandoned rail station and managed by CSAVA (see p.350), combined with a *gîte*, restaurant and bar-café. Housekeeping comes a distant second to political activity, as you might expect, but additional accommodation is provided in an old train carriage parked on the overgrown tracks, and there's **camping** space by the river.

Lescun and its cirque

Certainly the highlight of a trip along the Aspe valley is the grey limestone **Cirque de Lescun**, more intimate than Gavarnie's, contrasting sharply with the pastures and dense forest at its foot. Pyramidal, and often marbled with streaks of snow, the toothy peaks forming the cirque – such as the two Billare summits, the Aiguilles de Ansabère and storm-lashed Pic d'Anie (2504m) – rise as a semicircular screen from the quiltwork of fields ingeniously laid out by generations of farmers.

BATTLE FOR THE VALLÉE D'ASPE

Since 1990 the **Vallée d'Aspe** has been the focus of a bitter battle between advocates and opponents of a comprehensive road-widening scheme from Oloron-Sainte-Mairie to the Col du Somport, with the supplementary measure of an 8600-metre-long tunnel to be bored under the *col*. Such proposals had been mooted for years, but received additional impetus upon Spain's accession to the EC in 1986. The Spanish autonomous region of Aragón in particular, smarting over the closure of the rail line between Oloron and Canfranc, embraced the proposal as a remedy for its perceived isolation. In June 1990, the EU granted the first 98 million francs (of an eventual 210 million) towards the project, with a Franco-Spanish agreement, signed the following year, to share more or less equally the remaining 790-million-franc cost.

As originally envisaged, the plan was to facilitate the passage of one thousand heavy trucks daily, by upgrading the N134 between Oloron and the new tunnel to expressway status. This meant concreting the banks of the Gave d'Aspe, blasting away sections of mountainside or farmland, and placing the tunnel mouth in *parc national* territory. Only token provision for the reactivation of the rail link was made, and there was no consideration of the effects on the various local animal species – eagle owl, capercaillie and lammergeier, as well as the famous brown bear.

Besides the Parisian technocrats, the vast majority of local villagers and politicians favoured the scheme – most prominent among the latter the mayor of Lourdios-Ichère, **Jean Lassalle**. In his ongoing capacity as president of the Parc National des Pyrénées, he had already gained some notoriety for having proposed a nordic ski centre at the Col du Somport, a notion quashed by the Paris-based Council of State as illegal and incompatible with the goals of the park. Valley residents, meanwhile, saw the project, with its promise of improved communications north and south, as their last chance of rescuing the Aspe from complete stagnation, in particular halting the drift of young people to the cities.

Opposition to the plans crystallized quickly in the form of the **Coordination pour la Sauvegarde Active de la Vallée d'Aspe** (**CSAVA**), based at the *gîte d'étape* in Cette-Eygun and headed by **Eric Pétetin**, who came eventually to be loathed, dismissed as a misguided idealist or respected – in equal measure – by the inhabitants of the valley. Almost single-handedly, he managed to delay the project for three years.

Already by August 1991, CSAVA and its allies had appealed successfully to the ECU to halt the funding temporarily, claiming that the Canfranc–Oloron rail line could be re-opened to carry both passengers and trucks at a **cost** ten times less than the eventual projected total (one billion francs) for the road works. Next, the anti-development faction raised the spectre of massive **environmental degradation** in the wake of a projected four thousand vehicles in total per day – not just a thousand trucks – through the tunnel by 2010, and also seized on the detail of the tunnel's siting within the *parc national*.

The substantial stone houses of **LESCUN** village, wonderfully placed amidst trickling fountains on a sunny south-facing slope, lend photogenic balance in the foreground. Six steep kilometres along the minor D239 above and west of the valley floor, the village seems little affected by tourism, though it makes an excellent base for a walking tour of the cirque. The only places to **stay** are the comfortable, antique-furnished *Hôtel du Pic d'Anie* (☎05.59.34.71.54, fax 05.59.34.53.22; April–Sept; ⑤), which has the village's only **restaurant**, and the co-managed *gîte d'étape* just opposite (①). Other facilities include a **Maison de la Montagne** (July & Aug daily 9am–noon & 3–7pm), basically a guides' bureau, and a basic grocery store under the hotel. There's a medium-sized, grassy, well-equipped and incomparably sited **campsite** (*Le Lauzart*; ☎05.59.34.51.77; May–Sept) south of and below the village, also with a small *gîte d'étape*.

The national minister of environment, caught between the ecologists and the numerous *département* officials supporting the tunnel, attempted to placate the former by moving the tunnel mouth 15m out of the national park. In August 1992 the prefect of Pau signed the *déclaration d'utilé publique* (**DUP**), or go-ahead decree. But CSAVA had not yet exhausted its legal recourses; in December 1992 an administrative tribunal in Pau found for its claim that environmental impact statements had been deficient, nullifying the previous DUP. Rather than appeal against this decision, the government elected to apply for a new DUP, paying careful attention to all the points raised by the ecologists. The government succeeded in July 1993, and the final plan included provisions for bear-crossings and rehabilitation of the abandoned rail line, with work beginning over the winter of 1993 to 1994. With far less opposition, the Spanish have virtually completed the boring from their side, and their approach road – beginning in Zaragoza, bound for Huesca and Jaca – is already of the necessary standard.

CSAVA and its allies hadn't limited themselves to the courts. Throughout 1991 and 1992 they organized escalating campaigns of **civil disobedience**: graffiti, demonstrations, "Sioux" war dances in full tribal regalia around gendarmes designated as "palefaces" (a strategy which earned Pétetin the nickname "l'Indien du Somport"), road obstructions, and – ultimately – extensive vandalism to surveyors' stakes and the tunnel worksite. Their ranks were swelled by large numbers of foreign activists, particularly from Belgium and Holland, where the Pyrenees have many avid aficionados. For his pains Pétetin was arrested and detained no less than 35 times during 1991 and 1992, on the final occasion being sentenced to two years' imprisonment.

In the eyes of many *Aspois*, the eco-activists were merely carpet-baggers – as evidenced by the influx of out-of-town agitators during 1992 – who would decamp to the next fashionable cause were the issue decided in their favour, leaving the locals with the consequences. Pétetin was granted a presidential pardon and early release from prison in July 1993 just as the DUP was issued – a sure sign of the authorities' confidence that work could proceed no matter what new strategies CSAVA devised. The tunnel is now scheduled to open in 1999, and civil disobedience in the Vallée de Aspe has taken a new twist. Hundreds of activists are buying tiny plots of land along the proposed course of the approach road, in order to spin out for as long as possible the zoning and compulsory land-purchase process.

In the end the improvements and their true impact will probably prove anticlimactic, bringing neither the degree of revitalization to the area that its advocates envision – the new road will in fact bypass most Aspe villages – nor quite the environmental damage feared by opponents. However, one enduring legacy of the long campaign against the expressway and tunnel has been to open up the decision-making processes to public scrutiny, in what is historically an overly secretive and centralized nation. The whole episode also demonstrated the merits of appointing disinterested experts to evaluate whether such projects are truly in the wider public interest, and served to remind state administrators that neglecting due processes will result in expensive court actions and delays.

South of Lescun: the head of the Aspe

Once past the Lescun turning, the N134 carries on through **ETSAUT** and passes just below the attractive village of **BORCE**. In the currently disused train station of Etsaut you'll find the most westerly **Maison du Parc** (☎05.59.34.88.30; May to mid-Sept), featuring exhibits on the Pyrenean bear. Borce, poised above the valley floor on the west bank, constitutes a semifortified medieval showcase, the one place to escape the holocausts of 1659 and so graced by sumptuous fifteenth-century mansions. At Etsaut you can **stay** at *Hôtel des Pyrénées* (☎05.59.34.88.62, fax 05.59.34.86.96; ④), very much the heart of the village with the only restaurant, or across the road at *La Maison de l'Ours*, a high-quality *gîte d'étape* with only double rooms (☎05.59.34.86.38; open all year; ⑤ obligatory half-board in peak season, ③ room only out of season). In Borce there's just a *gîte d'étape* (☎05.59.34.86.40; ①; open all year) and a combination campsite-*gîte* (☎05.59.34.87.29; ①; mid-June to mid-Sept).

Both villages lie on the **GR10**, which en route southeast to Lac d'Ayous negotiates the spectacular **Chemin de la Mâture**, some 3km south. Hacked out of the sheer flank of a ravine, this path is broad enough, but the edge is not for the vertigo-prone; watch out also for ropes across the trail fastened by avid climbers abseiling down the rock face.

The grim **Fort du Portalet** (privately owned, no visits) appears atop a sheer cliff west of the N134, directly opposite the Mâture gorge. It acquired some notoriety as a political prison during and after World War II, when the Vichy government detained Léon Blum here, Socialist French premier of the 1930s; later Marshal Pétain himself was held here by the Allies.

Shortly after, **URDOS**, site of the former Customs post, is the last village on the French side of the Col du Somport. You can **stay** and **eat** at *Hôtel des Voyageurs* (☎05.59.34.88.05, fax 05.59.34.86.74; ④), a former post-house that's been in the same family for seven generations; there are also shops, petrol stations and **banks** – but nowhere to change money on a Sunday.

Beyond Urdos three or four well-spaced buses a day continue on through the beech forests and the Parc National des Pyrénées to the abandoned **frontier gate** at Col du Somport, and beyond to Canfranc, the terminus for trains from Jaca in Aragón.

Walks from Lescun

There are any number of walks for all levels of commitment in the fantastic limestone scenery south and west of Lescun, ranging from day-trips and brief circuits of the upper Aspe to long-haul traverses. Hiking is much the best way to tour the heights of the cirque, since public transport on either side of the border – which these peaks form – is almost nonexistent. Water can be a problem in these rock strata, so top up bottles wherever possible; the best map for the area is IGN Parc National des Pyrénées no. 1, 1:25,000 "Aspe Ossau".

West: the GR10, HRP and Pic d'Anie

The **GR10** to Arette-la-Pierre-Saint-Martin is the most northerly route, and is an easy day's walking. It follows a six-kilometre road – no short-cuts possible – for ninety minutes northwest of Lescun as far as the *Refuge de L'Abérouat* (1442m), eye-to-eye with 2300-metre Billare peak; the refuge specializes exclusively in boisterous children's holidays, but offers meals to all comers. This is as far as cars can go; there's a huge parking lot for those who've forgone the boring road-tramp up. Next, the route – briefly track, then path and cross-country – enters beech forest under the striking organ-pipe formations of **Orgues de Camplong** before emerging above treeline at the basic, five-person *Cabane d'Ardinet* hut. From here the GR10 climbs to another shepherd's *cabane* – and the last reliable water for the day – at Cap de la Baitch, and then steeply northwards into the **Pas d'Azuns** (1873m; 3hr from Lescun). After dropping into a slight bowl the path climbs again to the **Pas de l'Osque** (1922m), after which the GR10 crosses karst desert en route to Arette-la-Pierre-Saint-Martin (see p.400), two hours due west.

For an **ascent of Pic d'Anie** (2504m), the most westerly summit over 2000m on the French side, head south from Cap de la Baitch, curving under Pic du Soum Couy and up into the **Col des Anies** (2030m). The main HRP carries on westwards from here to Arette-la-Pierre-Saint-Martin; for Pic d'Anie, follow the easy marked path southwards. From the summit (2hr from the *col*; 4hr 30min from Lescun) you can return to Lescun in rather less than four and a half hours, making this a popular day outing from the village.

The best traverse route, though, is the **HRP variante**, which heads for the *Refugio Belagoa* in Spain, where you can pick up a bus. From Lescun you head west on track towards the toe of Petit Billare, reaching an obvious plateau at about 1100m. From here a good trail climbs steeply past a waterfall (fill up!) to the **Col d'Anaye** (2052m; 3hr), on the south flank of Pic d'Anie. On the other side of this pass you enter the twisted karst dells of Spain's *Parque Natural Pirenaico*; Belagua lies two and a half hours further west.

Tour of the border peaks

Using Lescun or Borce as a starting point, you can make a very worthwhile three-day **tour of the border peaks** which satisfactorily covers the terrain south of the preceding itineraries. Beginning in Lescun, head southwest through the Bois de Landrosque, up the *gave* draining from the **Aigulles d'Ansabère**. At the base of the lesser pinnacle (2271m) are some shepherds' huts, near which are some all-important springs and camping spots. But since you're only about three hours out of Lescun, you may wish to continue due south up to the frontier. Cross this via a nameless saddle (2030m), where you're poised to tackle the slight descent to **Ibón de Acherito** (1900m; 5hr from Lescun), just inside Spain and another scenic possibility for water and camping.

From here the topography dictates a wide skirting of the border ridge on its southeast face for about ninety minutes before crossing back into France via the **Col de Pau/Puerto de Palo** (2017m; 2hr 30min from Acherito), just northwest of the similarly low **Pic de Burcq/Pic de Burco**. (From Acherito or the Puerto de Pau in particular it's a simple matter to link up with the Spanish GR11, down in the main valley to the south.)

Back on the French side, now within the final westerly extension of the Parc National des Pyrénées, an increasingly good path hugs the ridge – except for a diversion north over the **Col de Saoubathou** to avoid **Pic Rouge/Pico Rojo** – to deposit you within five hours from the Ibón de Acherito at the PNP-administered *Refuge d'Arlet* (2000m; staffed July 1–Sept 15; 30 places; ①), beside its namesake tarn.

The most scenic way of returning to the Aspe valley involves heading east along the HRP to the small **La Banasse** cirque with its spring, and then descending north, initially via the **Baralet** valley, and then over the Col de Lagréou to change to the **Belonce** drainage, which leads out of *parc national* territory on a good if steep path into Borce (4–5hr from Arlet). If necessary, you can continue northwest along the GR10 to Lescun.

THE SOUTHERN APPROACHES

South of the Spanish **Parque Nacional de Ordesa y Monte Perdido**, in the region of **Alto Aragón**, depopulation is even more pronounced than in the French Pyrenees, as a glance at the map with its sparse villages will confirm. Among the towns only **Jaca** musters over ten thousand inhabitants, while more than four hundred mountain villages languish virtually abandoned – the highest such concentration in Spain – occupied only in summer by older people with flocks to graze, plus a handful of city-dwellers restoring ruins as holiday homes or "alternative" enterprises. This contemporary desolation is owed largely to the late General Franco and his policies. Determined to punish the *Alto Aragoneses* for their staunch support of the Republican cause, his regime withheld vital services, ignored the ravages wrought by natural disasters and dammed numerous arable valleys during the 1950s, leaving the villagers little alternative but to migrate to the cities. In the seven thousand square kilometres of Alto Aragón there are now fewer than fifty thousand inhabitants, an average density of seven per square kilometre.

The salient geographical features in the east of this region are impressive valleys or canyons and strange, wedding-cake-like mountains, both eroded from the same banded limestone. The **Valle de Ordesa** – heart of the *parque nacional* and most popular approach for an ascent of **Monte Perdido**, linchpin of the canyons – was first publicized by the French journalist and adventurer Lucien Briet, who for eight consecutive summers after 1904 traced a route from Gavarnie to Torla. (Some of his photographs can be seen at the Lourdes museum, and a Torla inn has been named in his honour.) Nowadays this landscape needs no such advertisement; in holiday periods, the gentle

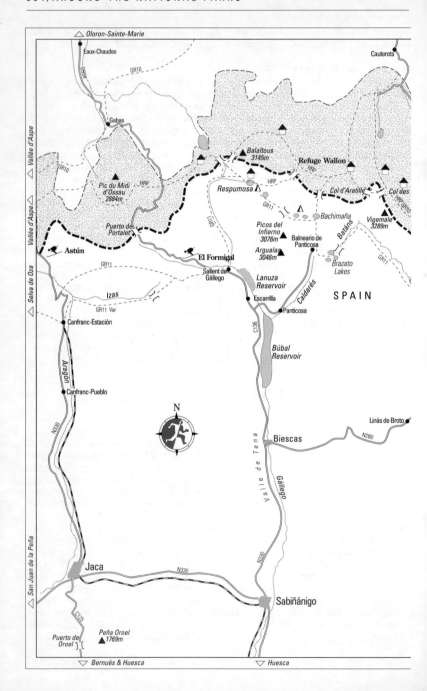

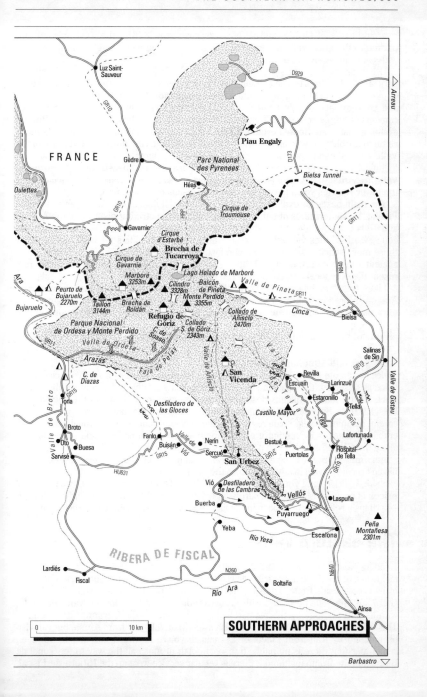

SOUTHERN APPROACHES

0   10 km

riverside paths of Ordesa and all of its approach roads from the west or south are packed to the gills, while the gateway villages becoming increasingly commercialized with each successive year.

Other canyons east or southeast of the Valle de Ordesa, wholly or partly within the park, are no less impressive in their own way but receive far fewer visitors. The absence of public transport to trailheads and limited accommodation here could be both cause and consequence of this neglect, but the extra effort required to visit these other canyons is amply rewarded. Despite having a road through it, the **Valle de Pineta**, draining east from Monte Perdido, discourages casual acquaintance with its heights by virtue of forbiddingly steep and snow-fringed walls. The **Garganta de Escuaín**, in the **Valle de Tella** south of Pineta, can only be properly appreciated on foot or as part of a technical canyoning expedition. Continuing clockwise southeast, the bottom of the **Valle de Añisclo** gets almost as crowded as Ordesa in high season, but once clear of the lower reaches you'll have only a few long-distance walkers for company.

The main bases for exploring these canyons are **Bielsa**, at the mouth of the Valle de Pineta; **Aínsa**, terminus of public transport and within striking distance of the Añisclo and Tella canyons; and **Torla**, the enduringly popular western gateway to the Ordesa country. All of these villages have an ample range of facilities for both trekkers and those more solicitous of their own comfort. Southwest of the park, **Jaca**, capital of the ancient kingdom of Aragón, and the nearby monastery of **San Juan de la Peña**, represent the only local attractions that can rival the mountains.

Like almost everywhere south of the Pyrenean watershed, the landscape of Alto Aragón is predominantly drier and less vegetated than that of French Bigorre, but towards the west, in the **Tena** and **Canfranc** valleys, the climate becomes more humid. Lakes reappear in large numbers above **Panticosa**, and in winter the nearby skiing centres of **El Formigal** and **Candanchú-Astún** do a thriving business.

Transport and accommodation

Twice as remote as the French approaches in terms of distances from major cities, and twice as deserted, the Spanish side has consequently relatively deficient **public transport**. Of the foothill villages described in this section, only those on the Sabiñánigo–Biescas–Torla–Sarvisé axis see more than one bus service a day, and many have none; careful planning is vital if you're to make the necessary connections. You'll gain considerable advantages by renting a car, or bringing your own, or by trekking east-to-west along the GR paths which run perpendicular to most roads.

Accommodation can be a serious problem in peak summer or winter seasons if you haven't reserved well in advance – even the campsites tend to fill – but with a vehicle you can simply drive until you happen upon a vacancy. Once you get settled, you'll find the **prices** of rooms and meals still surprisingly low despite the recent onslaught of tourism – perhaps a reflection of realism in the face of Spain's tenaciously severe recession.

The eastern valleys

Heading west from Posets and the Valle de Gistau on foot, you're perfectly poised to tackle any of the three major easterly valleys draining out of the national park. The GR11 or its variant leads from Viadós to **Bielsa** and the **Valle de Pineta**, while the GR19 or GR15 link the Valle de Gistau with **Lafortunada**, closest base for the **Valle de Tella**, with its tiny, photogenic villages perched on either side of the **Garganta de Escuaín**. The **Valle** (often **Cañon**) **de Añisclo** is easiest visited by car from **Aínsa**, but can also be reached by trail from Pineta or Escuaín. If you're moving south–north, however, remember that there is no public transport north of Aínsa all the way up to the Túnel de Bielsa and the frontier, although there is regular service west up the **Ribera de Fiscal**.

Aínsa

Sited above the confluence of the Ara and Cinca rivers, **AÍNSA** (L'Aínsa in Aragonese) is the natural gateway to the region, with an exceedingly attractive hilltop **old quarter**, focused on the vast, arcaded **Plaza Mayor**. The old town has recently been prettified in an attempt to cash in on some of the cross-border trade pouring down from the Bielsa tunnel, but all in the best of taste, with nowhere near the tackiness associated with Torla; traffic is banned and cars are directed to a parking lot on the west (200ptas). Just off the *plaza* stands the exceptional Romanesque church of **Santa María**, with a unique triangular cloister dictated by the sloping topography, and an ancient crypt with a forest of magnificently capitalled columns under the apse. For 200ptas you can climb the belfry for splendid views over the town, *plaza* and fifteen-to-sixteenth-century **Castillo** to the west. This is under restoration but already acts as venue for the late-July/early-August *Festival Internacional de Música*, attracting big world-music names such as Tarika and the Afro-Cuban All Stars. The only **accommodation** up here is at *Casa del Hospital* (☎974/50 97 50; ③), a *turismo rural* unit, but there's plenty of choice for **eating** and **drinking** on and near the Plaza Mayor: the *Bodegas del Sobrarbe* (closed Nov–Easter) at no. 2 is the most renowned and expensive (3500ptas per person), but there's also the less pricey *Bodegón de Mallacán* under the arches at no. 6, where you can just have coffee. Near the square, you'll find the lively *Bar Fes*, to the east at Calle Mayor 22, with affordable *menús del día* featuring grilled meat, and *Bar Restaurante El Portal*, at the easterly Portal del Abajo, with an outdoor terrace.

The unsightly and traffic-noisy **new quarter** below has the **tourist office** (summer daily 9am–2pm & 4.30–8.30pm; ☎974/50 07 67), as well as Aínsa's **hotels** and **hostales**. *Mesón de l'Aínsa*, Avda. de Sobrarbe 12 (☎974/50 00 28, fax 50 07 33; ④), *Hotel Sánchez*, Avda. de Sobrarbe 10 (☎974/50 00 14; ③), the strangely named *Hostal Apolo XI* on marginally quieter Crtra. Campo (☎974/50 02 81; ③) and *Hostal Ordesa* (☎974/50 00 09; ③) on the road west are worth singling out. The local campsite, *Camping Aínsa* (☎974/50 02 60; April–Sept), lies 1km east along the C140 towards Campo. Intersport (☎974/50 09 83) at Avda. de Sobarbe 4 comes recommended as an outfitter for **canyoning**, and Aguas Blancas next to Intersport (☎974/51 00 08) are the local **rafting** and **kayaking** specialists, while the Centro Equestre El Trío at Banastón village 3km southeast offers **horse-riding**.

Truck-drivers en route to and from the Bielsa tunnel often take refreshment in Aínsa, so it's a good bet for lifts; the town is also the last stop for the **bus** line plying the C138 road northwest towards Torla.

Bielsa

The surprisingly large town of **BIELSA**, at the entrance to the Pineta valley, hung on as a Republican stronghold long after much of Alto Aragón had been overrun by the Nationalists; when the place finally fell in June 1938, large parts of it were burned, which explains its somewhat heterogeneous appearance. Today it has become a choice, if slightly tacky summertime target for more pacific armies of French day-trippers. Nonetheless, traces of its identity as a traditional mountain county-town still persist in its old river bridge and porticoed town hall on the Plaza Mayor. Walkers heading towards the Valle de Pineta from the Posets Massif are virtually obliged to stop off here, since it's the only place close to the valley with supplies and accommodation. Bielsa is also renowned for its lively **carnival celebrations**; if you've missed it, you can get an idea of some of the rather outrageous costumes from the displays in the **Museo Etnológico** (summer daily 6–9pm, winter Mon–Fri 10am–2pm), housed in the town hall.

Practicalities

Bielsa lies well beyond all north–south public transport. Coming **from the north**, the Vallée d'Aure bus goes as far as Aragnouet-le-Plan, from where it's six steep, zigzagging kilometres to the mouth of the Bielsa tunnel; try and get a lift at the bottom of the grade, as pedestrians aren't permitted in the three-kilometre gloom. Emerging from the tunnel, Bielsa is then 11km further south. From Aínsa, the last bus stop **south** of Bielsa, you somehow have to cover 33km along the N640 highway.

Accommodation in Bielsa includes the welcoming and spotless *Hostal Habitaciones Vidaller* (☎974/50 10 04; ③), the *Hostal Pirineos* (☎974/50 10 15; ③), the *Hostal Marboré* (☎974/50 11 11; ③) and the more comfortable *Hotel Valle de Pineta* (☎974/50 10 10; fax 50 11 91; ④), all en-suite and all very easily found in the town centre or along the through road. For **eating**, the *Restaurant El Chinchecle*, very near the *Vidaller*, specializes in local mountain dishes. Bielsa also has a summer-only **tourist office** on the through highway (☎974/50 07 67).

The Valle de Pineta

A glacial trough scoured into sheer, stepped rock walls, the **Valle de Pineta** extends 15km west-northwest of Bielsa, terminating in the majestic **Circo de Pineta**; just above the *circo* looms **Monte Perdido** (3355m), one of the more celebrated summits in the Pyrenees. The idyllic floor of the valley, where reeds and birches fringe the white, boulder-flecked Río Cinca, here broadened near the lower end by a dam, contrasts drastically with the awesome cliffs of the Sierra de Espierba to the north and the even more fantastic **Sierra de las Tucas** to the south. At first glance you'll doubt that ascents of either the Circo de Pineta or the Sierra de las Tucas are possible; however, they are attainable, the rewards commensurate with the effort.

In terms of **accommodation**, there are two campsites – the reasonably priced and well-equipped *Pineta* at Km 8 of the valley road (☎974/50 10 89), and a very basic and inexpensive unnamed meadow site at Km 14 – as well as the comfortable *Parador Nacional de Monte Perdido* (☎974/50 10 11; ⑤, fax 50 11 88; ⑥) at the base of the Circo de Pineta. The *parador* has a bar and lounge from which more sedentary tourists scan the mountains through a telescope. Of more interest to trekkers, perhaps, is the 1997-built *Refugio de Pineta* nearby on the left bank of the river (1300m; 73 places; phone pending; open all year; ①).

Walking into the parque nacional

The valley's flanking palisades attract legions of technical climbers, but there are two steep, strenuous walks here, too. These classic hikes – up to the Balcón de Pineta, a shelf 1200m higher than the valley floor at the top of the Circo de Pineta, and the GR11 route climbing a similar height over the Collado de Añisclo – both lead into the northeast corner of the *parque nacional*. Once into the park, you'll appreciate having the Editorial Alpina 1:40,000 "Ordesa Vignemale Monte Perdido" map.

The Balcón de Pineta and beyond

For the **Balcón de Pineta**, take the well-marked path going left (west) just before the *parador*, which brings you to the foot of the cliffs; the subsequent series of tight zigzags gives progressively more unnerving views, as you climb through loose rock to the *balcón* in about four hours. The ascent is particularly steep in the final stages and shouldn't be attempted early in summer without crampons and ice-axe.

Thirty minutes to the northwest, a one-night tent stay is permitted at **Lago Helado de Marboré** (2632m), which on a sunny day is a welcoming blue against the hard grey rock. But most eyes will be on the mass of Monte Perdido to the south, its savage northeast wall aproned by its huge glacier. On the north side of the lake, the frontier pass of **Brecha de Tucarroya/Brèche de Tuquerouye** (2660m), with its historic but crude hut, gives access to the Estaubé cirque and the HRP down to Gavarnie (see p.330). West of the lake, it's a ninety-minute climb through snow fields and across scree to the **Cuello de Astazú/Col d'Astazou** for a magnificent view over the Cirque de Gavarnie.

Finally, you can head south from the lake over the **Cuello del Cilindro** (3052m; 3hr); this is rather more difficult than the three hundred-metre-lower Brèche de Roland, requiring year-round full snow-climbing gear including rope and, preferably, some prior experience in this sort of terrain. From this pass it takes around three hours more to descend to the *Refugio de Góriz* (see p.368); in theory you could get there in one long day from the Valle de Pineta, but it's highly advisable to break the journey with an overnight at Lago Helado.

The GR11 to Añisclo

The **GR11** climbs southwest from the valley floor up what appear to be the impossibly sheer palisades of **Las Paredes de Pineta**, through the **Collado de Añisclo** (2470m) and beyond. This is a tough walk, like the Balcón route impossible without crampons and ice-axe until late June, and completely out of bounds in spring because of the danger of avalanches. But during summer it offers marvellous scenery close to hand and a lammergeier's-eye perspective over the valley.

The start of this gruelling four-hour climb is signposted near the Capella de Nuestra Señora de Pineta, near the *parador* and the upper campsite. Once over on the other side there are no further trail ambiguities until you're up on the *collado*. Beyond this saddle, the main GR11 was rerouted during 1989 in response to walkers' complaints. If laden with a full pack, you should *not* use the *variante* heading northwest – if in fact it is still blazed – as this inches perilously, fly-on-the-wall-style, for 400m along the sheer face of **Pico de Añisclo** at the 2500m contour. Instead, descend south for about two hours along the main GR11 to the crude, unattended *Refugio de Cazadores* at the head of the **Añisclo canyon**; there is plenty of turf and water nearby if you need to camp.

Otherwise, continue west-northwest along the GR11 up the Barranco Arablo – the last reliable water being the vigorous waterfall of **Fon (Fuén) Blanca** at its mouth – where the occasionally scree-laden trail worms its way up along grassy terraces to the **Collado Superior de Góriz** (aka Arrablo; 2343m; 2hr 30min from Fon Blanca). Here you're treated to great views of Monte Perdido, Pico de Añisclo and Sum de Ramond; beyond the *collado* the *Refugio de Góriz* is less than an hour away, for a total of nine hours' walking from the Valle de Pineta.

The Ribera de Fiscal: the lower Ara Valley

The Río Ara is the major tributary of the Cinca from the west, but the lower reaches of its valley are known as the **Ribera de Fiscal** after its most important village. By Aragonese standards the valley bottom is wide and relatively fertile, yet strangely deserted; there are nearly a dozen ghost villages between Fiscal and Aínsa, within sight of the road, sporadically squatted by Spanish anarchists and alternative types who make their views known with banners stretched above the road. A principal reason for this desolation is a proposed dam at Jánovas, designed in the 1960s but yet to be built. The inhabitants were paid off with risible sums but are now demanding their homes back, even as plans for the construction of the dam are being revived.

Boltaña

BOLTAÑA, 8km west of Aínsa along the N-260, divides like its near neighbour into two parts: the ugly roadside development on the through highway, and the atmospheric hill quarter. Here the *plaza* is virtually filled by the sixteenth-century **Colegiata de San Pedro Apostol**, with its rib-vaulted ceiling, sturdy piers and carved choir stalls at the rear. Just downhill in a cul-de-sac, the *Casa Coronel* does just two things in its bar-restaurant, but well: chef's salad and garnished grills, served indoors or with mountain views in the courtyard; they also keep a few *turismo rural* **rooms** (☎974/50 21 54; ③).

Fiscal and Lardiés

FISCAL, 20km upriver from Boltaña, is the next inhabited place, and despite falling some distance short of Ordesa it's well worth considering as a base, owing to the tranquillity and high standard of its *turismo rural* facilities. Signposted 100m before the church, with very cheerful Spanish-Dutch management, *Casa del Arco* (☎974/50 30 42; ③) offers double **rooms**, triples and quads in a fine eighteenth-century mansion. Even better accommodation, provided you have your own transport, is *Los Tres Albares*, 3km west in the all-but-abandoned hamlet of **LARDIÉS** (☎974/50 30 06; ③; minimum stay two nights), with a wonderful attic sitting room and arched breakfast cellar. Proprietor Joaquín Puyuelo is a certified mountain guide, and the region just upstream is ideal for nordic skiing. For **meals**, though, you have to go to Fiscal, which also has shops and two **banks** – the only ones in the valley. There are also two **campsites** at Fiscal, *El Jabalí Blanco* (☎974/50 30 74) with its own pool, and the giant *Ribera del Ara* (☎974/50 30 35), which relies on the municipal pool adjacent.

The Valle de Tella

The **Valle de Tella**, through which flows the Río Yaga, opens northwest roughly halfway between Aínsa and Bielsa. So far unsung in conventional tourist annals, it has long been one of the favourite **canyoning** venues on the flanks of Monte Perdido. At the head of the valley, just inside *parque nacional* territory, plunges the **Garganta de Escuaín**, a series of waterfalls, smooth chutes and pools where, equipped with ropes and wet suits, devotees abseil, slide and swim – a refreshing experience on a hot summer's day.

This is great walking country too, especially when the terrain closer to Monte Perdido is snowed up. The **GR15** and **GR19** converge at Tella village, on the valley's east flank, and a PR itinerary completes a tour of most highlights; the best single base for walkers is Lafortunada, out on the main road below Tella. Scenically, the eight local villages are overshadowed, in all senses, by a landscape dappled by the interaction of soothing vegetation and blindingly bare rock. Green, lush scrub blends into low alpine forest, with two-thousand-metre **Castillo Mayor** presiding on the west, and remoter **Peña Montañesa** (2301m) dominating the skyline to the southeast.

Car access – and canyoning

The top of the valley is easily accessible by ordinary car: tracks lead to Revilla on the east bank and to the village of Escuaín on the west. The **Revilla turning** leaves the main road at Hospital de Tella, from where it's 8km on paved road and then track. As the road climbs to the hamlet of Cortalaviña there are wonderful views east to the distinctively tilted lump of Peña Montañesa; then, 2km beyond Cortalaviña, the road divides. The paved, right-hand option climbs to Tella (see below), while the left-hand dirt track continues along a ridge to Revilla, where it ends.

To get into the **Barranco de Consusa**, one of the six main canyoning courses of the area, follow an onward path towards a *mirador* inside the *parque nacional* for ten minutes. The Consusa's course includes a three-hundred-metre-long "staircase" with four thirty-metre chutes and countless smaller drops. It'll take four to six hours to cover the full length of the stream, and at the bottom it's about 45 minutes' walk back to either Revilla or Escuaín.

The **turning for Escuaín** is closer to Aínsa, 9km north on the main road just beyond Escalona, initially along the westbound HU631 towards Añisclo. After 1km on this road, take the signposted dirt track on the right to Puertolas, which continues to Escuaín, 15km in total from the main road. Some maps mistakenly indicate a nonexistent access road from Hospital de Tella. From Escuaín a track to the northwest affords access to the main canyoning area in the *garganta*.

Lafortunada and Badaín

LAFORTUNADA, on the N640, 17km north of Aínsa and 15km south of Bielsa, isn't the most prepossessing of villages, but it does make the most convenient overnight base for walkers, with congenial rooms – either en suite or sharing a bathroom – and decent meals at the *Casa Sebastian* (☎974/50 40 05; ②–③), or the plusher, adjacent *Hotel Badain* (☎974/50 40 06, fax 50 40 48; ③), where they'll prepare vegetarian meals on request. The latter hotel takes its name from the hamlet of **BADAÍN**, 500m southeast, graced by a severe eleventh-century church with a round staircase tacked onto its square belfry. Inside it's a bit over-restored, but retains its Gothic stellar vaulting and an *artesonado* gallery. Both the GR19 and GR15 pass the church: the former on its rather humdrum way along the Río Cinca to Lespuña, the GR15 more excitingly heading east through the mountains towards Saravillo and the Valle de Gistau (see p. 268).

Walking in the Valle de Tella

If you don't have transport, the quickest way into canyon country is along the westbound **GR15** trail, starting 200m north of the church in Lafortunada. This climbs initially northwest within two hours to the picturesque village of **TELLA**, bigger than it looks from afar and restored for seasonal use. There's a park **information office** (daily July–Oct 8.30am–9pm) dispensing glossy brochures, but no other facilities except for an all-important fountain. As well as the imposing Romanesque parish church, there are a clutch of *ermitas* (isolated rural chapels) to which you can detour: oldest are the eleventh-century **Virgen de Fajanillas**, an easy and obvious ten-minute walk west of the village, and **Juanipablo**, fifteen minutes further northwest on an intriguing pinnacle.

After linking up, just behind the main church, with the GR19 coming southeast from Salinas, the trail descends to a picnic area and dolmen, threads through the hamlet of **LARINZUÉ** and drops to the river at **ESTARONILLO** hamlet (4 summer inhabitants; 1hr 15min from Tella). The final track approach to Estaronillo is often jammed with cars belonging to French rafters, who delight in running the **Garganta de Marval** of the Yaga just downstream.

From Estaronillo you climb another hour and a quarter through thick woods to **ESCUAÍN**, an abandoned settlement taken over in summer by rough campers, usually technically equipped enthusiasts exploring the **Garganta de Escuaín**, which lies just upstream. If you arrive early enough, you can lunch at the *albergue* (☎974/50 09 39 or 24 09 44; ①) here, before continuing along paths into the water-sculpted ravine.

From Escuaín a very steep trail drops in twenty minutes to the Río Yaga, then continues on the far bank past a derelict mill, crosses the outflow of the Barranco de Consusa and climbs from the river. Ninety minutes out of Escuaín, five minutes shy of the road up from Tella, be extra observant: here you can veer south on a fairly clear PR trail down to Estaronillo – mistakenly shown on most maps as taking off from the road itself – or north along an overgrown twenty-minute path to **REVILLA**. Even more desolate than Escuaín, with just a few houses modernized as vacation retreats, the hamlet is well camouflaged by the orange and grey cliff immediately behind.

If you opt instead for the little-trodden PR path south, you can continue past Estaronillo and then along a shelf wedged between the Garganta de Marval and Castillo Mayor, finishing after two and a half hours in total at **Hospital de Tella**, 3km west of Lafortunada. It's possible to complete the entire figure-of-eight itinerary of Lafortunada–Tella–Escuaín–Revilla–Estaronillo–Hospital in a single, long summer's day, taking in the best this limestone region has to offer.

Escuaín to Añisclo

Escuaín itself is a good jumping-off point for walking further **into the parque nacional**, specifically the **Valle de Añisclo**. Head northwest, high up on the right (southwest) bank of the Yaga, at first on track and then on path, until you reach the **Cuello Viceto** (2010m; 3hr). From here a wide path curves south down into Añisclo, pausing at a shelf on which are the spring and unstaffed refuge of **San Vicenda** (4hr 30min along), adjacent to one of the park's few permitted camping areas.

From San Vicenda the best trail drops north into the bottom of the canyon past **Fuente de Foradiello**, and then crosses the main Añisclo watercourse just downstream from the mouth of the Capradizas ravine. Once on the far bank, you can head north to Fon Blanca and the GR11 (see above), or follow the main Añisclo canyon trail south for three and a half hours to the **Ermita de San Urbez** (San Urbano on older maps), at the very entrance to the Añisclo canyon (see the following section).

More simply, you can also follow the **GR15 southwest** from Escuaín to the *ermita* in about six hours, leaving you enough daylight to reach accommodation in Nerín. The trail initially heads west over the **Collada de Ratón** on the shoulder of Castillo Mayor; becomes track veering south to the village of Bestué (no amenities); then scenic path again for the final two and a half hours to the *ermita*, involving a steep ascent, then an equally sharp descent, rewarded by views of – and from – the banded-rock *fajas* at the top.

The Valle de Añisclo

The uninhabited **Valle (Cañon) de Añisclo**, forging due south from the Collado de Añisclo and roughly equidistant from Aínsa or Lafortunada, is on a far grander scale than the Valle de Tella and accordingly more often visited. It's a beguiling spot, more intimate and wild than its other rival Ordesa; neither is the path running through it, parallel to the Río Vellos (Bellós), a pram-pushing stroll, given its often sharp grades and vertiginous drops from unguarded edges.

If you have transport or are willing to hitch, you can reach Añisclo on the minor but paved HU631 road heading west from just north of Escalona on the N640 (9km north of Aínsa, 10km south of Lafortunada). Once past an initially unpromising landscape – where, 2km along, a large **campsite** (*Valle de Añisclo*; ☎974/50 50 96; Easter–Oct) below Puyarruego village is noteworthy only for a last chance to swim in the Río Vellos, forbidden further upstream – you enter the *parque nacional* at the dramatic **Desfiladero de las Cambras**, appetizers for the Añisclo canyon. Here the road is confined to a shelf blasted out of the rock wall, too narrow for excursion buses, and designated one-way westbound (eastbound traffic heads to Escalona along a new detour via Buerba – see opposite). At the west end of the gorge, 12km from the N640 highway, knots of parked cars announce the mouth of Añisclo just to the north.

The canyon walk

From the parking areas, two broad paths – equally good, as they form a loop around the confluence of the Vellos and Aso rivers – lead north into the canyon.

The right-hand path crosses a bridge high above the joint streams, then follows a ledge where a cave has been converted into the **Ermita de San Urbez (San Urbano)**.

Some fifteen minutes past the *ermita* you change to the west bank and climb to meet the GR15 trail coming east from Nerín on its way to Bestué. Soon you're passing through box thickets and beech woods, with the occasional conifer or yew, the locality all cool, damp and shady except at midday, thanks to the constant misting from the river. Its flashing cascades and tempting green pools glimmer far below you on the right, tantalizingly out of reach, and perhaps just as well, since you're not allowed to bathe. High, sheer walls amplifying the roar of the torrent culminate in the **Sestrales crest** to the east, which is interrupted by an uncanny keyhole-shaped cleft.

By now you'll have noticed that progress upstream is not steady – the path roller-coasters constantly, with a particularly notable climb and hairpins away from the river about two hours along, at the top of which you have the best views possible into the lower canyon. The most spectacular section finishes at the grassy expanse of **La Ripareta** (1400m), only about 500m higher than San Urbano but because of the nature of the trail nearly three hours distant. Here, you're level with the river once more, and camping is permitted; otherwise it's a good spot for a picnic, or watching the sky for birds of prey.

From La Ripareta there's a choice of onward routes, and whichever you choose you'll have more solitude, since the gradient stiffens and the trails become fainter. About 2km (40min) north you can cross the main river and follow a path up to the authorized bivouac area and shelter at **San Vicenda**. Continuing on the west bank from La Ripareta for about ninety minutes, you'll reach the Fon Blanca cascade at the Barranco Arrablo (see "Walking into the *parque nacional*" p.358), which funnels the **GR11** west to the *Refugio de Góriz*. In the opposite direction the GR11 leads over the Collado de Añisclo to the Valle de Pineta; you'll want a fairly early start from San Urbano to finish either of these traverses in a single day (the *Refugio de Góriz* is a more reasonable goal).

West from Añisclo: the Valle de Vió

West from the mouth of the Añisclo canyon, the road follows the **Valle de Vió**, a deserted district particularly hard hit by the exodus to the lowland towns; the half-dozen or so local villages have just a handful of residents, and one place is completely abandoned. But in a reversal of the situation prevailing at the Valle de Tella, the villages with their eleventh- to thirteenth-century churches are far more interesting than the valley itself, which is sun-scorched and overgrazed to barrenness on the north, though still heavily wooded on its south slope.

Vió and Buerba

The namesake village of **VIÓ**, 5km south of the Añisclo gorge parking lots, is the one village hereabouts where there are still more tractors than tourists, trundling through the surrounding hayfields. Not so at **BUERBA**, 2km further and the end of the paved road, always packed with canyoners plumbing the secrets of the **Río Yesa** to the south. For non-canyoners, the best outing from here is the two-hour **trail-walk** to Yeba village, crossing the river. Thus far the only facility is *Bar Casa Lisa*, from whose terrace you enjoy lingering views of the Añisclo cliffs, though it doesn't have food or accommodation yet.

Nerín

If you're without transport, and only committed to day-walks in Añisclo, you'll have to stay at **NERÍN**, an hour's trail-walk west of the canyon, via the forlorn, utterly deserted hamlet of Sercué. The path is marked as a sector of the **GR15**; by the road (poor hitching, not recommended to pedestrians) it's 5km away. Nerín is blessed with an incomparable setting, gazing east to Peña Montañesa, and a reliable spring, and a little life has returned to what was once a dying hamlet. The *Añisclo Albergue*, with its front garden and ravishing view (☎974/48 90 10, fax 48 90 08; dorms ①; open all year), serves meals, sells maps and guides, but requires reservations, as does the more comfortable *Pensión El Turista* (☎974/48 90 16; ③) with its panoramic *comedor*; otherwise you'll end up **camping** next to the exceptionally fine Romanesque church. Many of the dozen or so houses in the hamlet have been renovated and sold off as holiday homes.

Fanlo

The GR15 carries on west to Fanlo, curling through virtually abandoned, though beautifully sited Buisán (with a permanent population of 4), whose hilltop houses are also being restored for seasonal use. **FANLO**, 6km beyond Nerín by the more direct paved road, and again engagingly sited, is the biggest place hereabouts, with mains electricity, a nordic ski piste and forests of cranes engaged in house renovation. Although from all this activity you would expect it to have more facilities, as yet there's **no accommodation**, just a sandwich-bar (*Las Eras*; full meals by advance notice only), unimprovably perched amongst the hilltop grain barns and threshing grounds west of the village. Fanlo itself boasts a unique, turreted manor house and an equally photogenic communal laundry just south of it. There's also a **Turismo** booth (summer Tues–Fri 10am–1.30pm & 5–7.30pm, Sat & Sun 9am–1.30pm & 5–8pm) on the road below the barns.

Just northwest of Fanlo yawns the **Desfiladero de las Gloces**, a good place for a first experience of canyoning, a fact not lost on the French who throng the place. From the high point of the road, west of the information booth, a path runs north for half an hour through abandoned fields, woods and scrub to the stony riverbed. The first obstacle, a ten-metre chute, presents no problems if you've ever been to a water park, and subsequent drops are easy by comparison. Two to three hours later you emerge a little southwest of Fanlo, though well below the road.

Moving on

West of Fanlo, 12km of steep, potholed, lightly travelled road bring you down to Sarvisé on the main C138, 4km south of Broto and 6km south of Torla (see below for descriptions of all of these places). Don't try to walk this – the GR15 also emerges on the asphalt an hour out of Fanlo – but instead, either arrange a ride in Fanlo, or use a track, a bit higher than the Desfiladero de las Gloces path, heading northwest within three hours to the **Cuello de Diazas** (2133m), which overlooks the Valle de Ordesa. Once there you've a choice of paths, either north into the valley or west to Torla, the latter easily reached after another two and a half hours.

The Valle de Ordesa and around

Carved out first by glaciers and now enlarged by the east-flowing Río Arazas, the eight hundred-metre-deep trough of the superlative **Valle de Ordesa**, in the north of Alto Aragón, deservedly draws hundreds of thousands of visitors a year. It forms the showcase of the **Parque Nacional de Ordesa y Monte Perdido**, which takes the second part of its name from the imposing limestone massif lying at the centre of park territory (see the feature on pp. 368–369).

The two usual road approaches to the *parque nacional*, both served by **public transport**, are via either Sabiñánigo and Biescas (see p.372) to the west, or from Aínsa (p.357) to the southeast, along the N260 following the Río Ara, which has headwaters close to Vignemale and merges with the Cinca some 60km later at Aínsa. Along the first half of its course, before curling east, the Ara flows through the **Valle de Broto**, where villages like **Sarvisé**, **Oto** and **Broto** have been rescued by tourism from the desolation that has befallen most of those further downstream. **Torla**, 45km upstream from Aínsa and 39km northeast of Sabiñánigo, is by far the busiest of these settlements, since it's the closest to the Valle de Ordesa.

North of Torla, beyond the confluence of the Ara and the Arazas, there are just the campsites and refuge at **Bujaruelo**, beyond which is a wilderness not included in the park. Coming from the strategic *Refugio de Góriz* below Monte Perdido, the **GR11** threads through the Ordesa canyon, follows the Ara north almost to its source, then crosses west to Panticosa. Alternatively you can hike **into France** through a number of passes: the Brecha de Roldán (Spanish for Brèche de Roland) towards Gavarnie, or two others at the top of the Ara into the Cauterets basin.

The Valle de Broto

Travelling upstream from Fiscal (see p.360), the N260 turns north past gradually more forested slopes to reach **SARVISÉ**, lowest village of the **Valle de Broto**, 38km from Aínsa. In high season you could be compelled to stay in Sarvisé, rather than further north, but in consolation **accommodation** here is of a high standard, with heating in winter. In descending order of preference, choose from among the stone-built, en-suite *Casa Puyuelo* (☎974/48 61 40; ③), with an attic salon, breakfast room and broad front lawn; the new *Hotel Viña Olivan*, by itself at the edge of town on the Fanlo road (☎974/48 63 58; ④); the *Hotel Casa Frauca* (☎974/48 63 53; ③) on the main highway, which also doubles as the main **restaurant**; and finally *Hostal Pirineos* in the village centre (☎974/48 61 79; ④).

Perched high on the hillside northeast of Sarvisé, via an indirect, four-kilometre road, the beautiful, secluded village of **BUESA** consists of two *barrios* flanking a wooded vale. This is rustic Aragón as it was twenty years ago, with grilled suppers available at *Bar Merendero Balcón del Pirineo*, and rather basic rooms at *Casa Cleto* up by the church (☎974/48 61 75; ③) – no palace, but a lifesaver in August. Incidentally, between July 1 and August 31, both **buses** from Sabiñánigo call at Sarvisé: the morning one (daily) en route to Aínsa, the evening one (Mon–Sat) turning around here just before 8pm, calling at Broto and Torla before arriving back in Sabiñánigo at 9.30pm.

Broto, Oto and Linás de Broto

By the time **BROTO** itself is reached, 4km north of Sarvisé, you're in the thick of things; the **tourist information booth** (summer daily except Mon 10am–2pm & 4.30–8.30pm) can advise on who may have **accommodation** vacancies in high season. The valley's capital is a noisy, teeming place in summer, its old quarter hemmed by traffic and new construction, a plight symbolized by the collapsed Romanesque bridge just upriver, destroyed during the Civil War. Beside this is the quietest place to stay, and usually one of the last to fill: *Taberna O Puente* (☎974/48 60 72; ④). Breakfast, included in the price, is served outdoors under what's left of the bridge arch, but other meals here aren't up to much and indeed none of the restaurants in the village is worth singling out. Other accommodation, all on the through road, includes *Hostal Español* at Avda. Ordesa 20 (☎974/48 60 07; ③) and the more comfortable one-star *Hotel Gabarre* at no. 6 (☎974/48 60 52; ④), whose en-suite rooms have balconies. Aventuras Pirenaicas (☎974/48 63 92), across the road at no. 13, is the guides' bureau, specializing in rock-climbing, canyoning and caving.

Alternatively, head for the more attractive village of **OTO**, 1.5km south, which features homogeneous architecture and two notable medieval towers, one on the church, the other on a baronial mansion. More or less opposite each other in the centre are two surprisingly modern, sterile but spotless **casas rurales** – *Herrero* (☎974/48 60 93; ③), above the bar, and *Pueyo* (☎974/48 60 75; ③), which also manages the large **campsite** (*Camping de Oto*; ☎974/48 60 75) 500m beyond the village.

LINÁS DE BROTO, 10km west of Broto on the N260 towards Biescas and Sabiñánigo, would also be a reasonable spot to fetch up, as long as you have a car, with its clutch of **accommodation**, including the co-managed *Hotel Las Nieves* (☎974/48 61 09; ④) and *Hostal Cazcarro* (③) on the main through road. Without a car, you may prefer to trust to luck in Torla; a well-trodden *camino*, part of the GR15 variant II, leads there in 45 minutes from Broto's ruined bridge.

Torla

The brazenly commercialized village of **TORLA** is the most obvious gateway to the park, which lies just over 8km away by road, and besides Broto or Sarvisé is the only feasible base for anyone without their own transport. As recently as 1983 the village was the sort of place where espadrilles were inadvisable because of the amount of cow dung on the road. But a mushrooming of concrete-block construction on the outskirts since then has sullied the village's profile, though the medieval core remains intact and attractive, despite the conversion of every second building for tourist purposes.

Except in August – when even the nearby campsites fill and you must book rooms by phone three weeks in advance – **accommodation** is easy to come by. The reasonable and friendly *Hostal Alto Aragón* (☎974/48 61 72; ④) and the adjacent, co-managed *Hotel Ballarín* (☎974/48 61 55; ④) at c/Capuvita 11 received a thorough overhaul in 1997 and, especially off-season, are a bargain, with views of the village rooftops and even TVs in the rooms; the traditional home-style food served at the *comedor* in the *Ballarín* is filling and good value. Among the four other hotels, best value and character are offered by the *Villa de Torla* at Plaza Nueva 1 (☎974/48 61 56, fax 48 63 75; ④); try and get a top-floor room. It has a pool in the terrace garden, and an excllent restaurant which will outrage animal-lovers with such dishes as *sarrio* (chamois) stew. There are also two *albergues*: the French-run *L'Atalaya* (☎974/48 60 22; ①) with 21 bunks and an attached restaurant; and the friendlier, thirty-bunk *Lucien Briet* (☎974/48 62 21; ①), managed by the *Bar Brecha*, which serves good meals in its upstairs dining room.

Finally, there are three **campsites** along the road to Ordesa (all May–Oct only): the *Río Ara* by the river (☎974/48 62 48) after about 2km; the fancier, gigantic *Ordesa* (☎974/48 61 46), 3km along the road, intended mainly for cars and camper-vans, with a pool; and the smaller, more basic *San Antón* (☎974/48 60 63) 3.5km out of town up on a mountain terrace. Among **bars**, the *tapas bodega* under *L'Atalaya* vies with the more traditionally Spanish ambience of the ground-floor bars *La Brecha* and *A'Borda Samper*, which also has a good restaurant.

Rounding off the list of amenities, Torla has both a **bank** (with ATM) and a **post office**, and a *parque nacional* **information office** 4km north of the village (summer daily 9am–1pm & 4–7.30pm). Three stores sell a limited range of provisions suitable for trekking, while La Tienda on the main through lane doubles as the mountain guides' office and supplier of maps and mountaineering gear.

The year-round **bus** to Sabiñánigo, run by La Oscense, leaves Aínsa at 2.30pm, passes Sarvisé and Broto and reaches Torla at around 3.30pm, stopping at the north end of town, by the pharmacy. In high season there is also the additional service from Sarvisé (Mon–Sat), passing Torla at about 8.15pm on its way to Sabiñánigo.

Into the park from Torla

From Torla the new shuttle service rolls 4km northwest by paved road to the boundary of the **Parque Nacional de Ordesa y Monte Perdido**, at the Puente de los Navarros, at which point the road swings east for just over another 4km, where the bus leaves you at the former car-parking area, well inside the **Valle de Ordesa**. If you're on foot, you should definitely bypass the tarmac by following the *camino* marked as part of the GR15 variant II. This begins in Torla next to the *Hostal Bella Vista*, crosses the Río Ara on a cement-and-masonry bridge, then turns sharply left (north) to join the *Camino de Turieto* at the posted park boundary, 45 minutes from Torla. After that, it's an easy and beautiful hike, two hours in total from the village, signposted all the way and taking you high above the river past some voluminous waterfalls. The path, like the road, eventually leads to the former car park, where there are toilets and a restaurant, *La Pradera de Ordesa*, predictably world-weary but offering a reasonable midday menu. There is no shop, so come prepared with provisions if you're intent on trekking or picnicking. About 1km before, housed in the former *parador* above the approach road, is an **interpretation centre** detailing the geology, flora and fauna of the park.

Walks in the Valle de Ordesa

Most of the walks in the valley begin from the vicinity of the old car park, specifically at the **Puente de los Cazadores** a little way upstream. There are dozens of possibilites, encompassing all levels of enthusiasm and expertise: the following examples are just a selection. Be aware that some of the "paths" marked on maps are actually technical climbing routes; and don't underestimate the time and difficulty of the more conventional pedestrian itineraries. Once out of the shady valley floor, the sun can be taxing, and drinking water is usually unavailable en route – take plenty with you, as the various waterfalls are contaminated.

The clearest **maps** of the Valle de Ordesa are the French or Spanish 1:50,000 IGN sheets (which also cover Gavarnie, across the French border), though cheaper ones such as the Editorial Alpina 1:40,000 "Ordesa Vignemale Monte Perdido" are perfectly adequate if you're going to stick to the popular, signed paths.

Valley traverse to the Circo de Soaso

This is one of the most popular – certainly in July or August – and rewarding of the short-distance treks. It's not especially difficult: a steep, 7.5-kilometre, three-hour traverse of the entire Valle de Ordesa, along a signposted path from Puente de los Cazadores, to the **Circo de Soaso**, which is also the beginning of the route to the *Refugio de Góriz* (see p.368). From wonderful beech forest the trail climbs past the *mirador* for the **Cascada del Abanico**, 3000m from the old car park, to emerge into the upper valley pasture, with the *circo* at its head and to the left – fanning out over a cliff – the famous **Cola de Caballo** (Horse's Tail) waterfall.

Return via Faja de Pelay

Looking back from the *circo*, you have a clear view of one of the artificial-looking but entirely natural ledges known as *fajas*: a standard feature of banded-limestone terrain, they are formed where a layer of softer calcareous rock has been exploded loose by repeated cycles of freezing and thawing. The ledge running along the south side of the canyon – the **Faja de Pelay** – is negotiated along its entire length by an easy path that can be followed back to the car park. Along the way you get both more solitude than is possible in the valley bottom, and an aerial view of the canyon; opposite looms a succession of remote peaks and features – most conspicuously the Brecha de Roldán, and the peaks of Cilindro and Monte Perdido.

The route is almost level at first, then drops gently to the *mirador* and stone shelter at **Calcilarruego**. From there, you descend fiercely along the **Senda de los Cazadores** (the Hunters' Path) by a long series of tight zigzags, prone to falling rock, finally crossing the Puente de Cazadores to return to the ex-car park. The total walk back from the Circo de Soaso is four and a half hours; there's no reliable water source until just before Calcilarruego, so you must carry it the whole way. A good case could be made for doing this loop in reverse: fewer crowds, and the admittedly stiff climb up the Senda de los Cazadores (2hr 30min) done in morning shade.

THE PARQUE NACIONAL DE ORDESA Y MONTE PERDIDO

The **Parque Nacional de Ordesa y Monte Perdido** was Spain's first protected area, established in 1918 as a reserve of 21 square kilometres to protect the showcase Valle de Ordesa, which lies immediately south of France's Cirque de Gavarnie. In 1982 the *parque nacional* was extended to 156 square kilometres, incorporating half a dozen "three-thousander" summits and the entire Valle de Añisclo, plus the headwaters of the Tella and the Circo de Pineta. This made the Spanish park contiguous with France's *Parc National des Pyrénées*; in the late 1980s the two park administrations signed an agreement for joint policy formulation and management – a sensible strategy given the huge numbers of mountaineers who surge back and forth between the two parks via the Brecha de Roldán (Spanish for the Brèche de Roland; p.328).

Geomorphology

From the Ara river valley in the west to well past the Cinca drainage in the east, the Pyrenees is a great mass of **karstic limestone**, heaved up from the sea floor about fifty million years ago, its beds first tilted and folded, then diligently sculpted by glaciers into a startling backdrop of peaks, cliffs and gorges. The process continues today on a smaller scale as dozens of seasonal waterfalls pour off the *circos* of the Ordesa and Pineta valleys in particular.

Monte Perdido, roughly in the centre of the park, ranks as the highest limestone peak in Europe, and the third highest summit in the Pyrenees. This mountain forms the focus of the four major valleys – **Ordesa**, **Pineta**, **Añisclo** and **Tella** – which drain away from it; a glacier still survives on its forbidding northface. Invisible to most visitors' eyes, but no less dramatic on acquaintance, are the hundreds of sinkholes and caves riddling the rock strata here, especially in the karst dells between the French frontier and the *Refugio de Góriz*. Bleak uplands, surrounding the Valle de Ordesa on all sides, parched and cheerless in midsummer, are the delight of alpine skiers during wintertime.

Flora and fauna

Owing to the 2600-metre difference between the highest and lowest points in the park, and the consequent variation in climate, there is a full spectrum of **flora**. Beech, birch and poplar forests thrive in the moist Valle de Ordesa; in the drier Valle de Pineta pine predominates; while at the mouths of the lower, warmer Añisclo and Tella valleys, an almost Mediterranean vegetation of oaks, yew, ash and maple prevails, co-existing at slightly higher elevations with fir and black pine. Above the treeline sprawl vast moors of specially adapted pincushion-type plants, with the genus *Festuca* well represented, but tucked among all of this are nearly 1500 species of small flowering plants, scores of them endemics marooned here by the glaciers and found nowhere else.

Onward to the Refugio de Góriz

To ascend from the Circo de Soaso to the *Refugio de Góriz*, you have the choice of a gently zigzagging path to the right, or the direct assault up the cliff aided by *clavijas* (pegs and chains). The *clavijas* aren't as bad as they look, but if you've got a heavy pack, or the rocks are wet, the path is much better. Once past this point, follow the marked trail north to the **Refugio de Góriz** (90min maximum from the *circo*; 2200m; 96 places; open all year; reservations advisable on ☎974/34 12 01; ①), sometimes known as *Delgado Ubeda*, where you can stay cheaply and eat expensively. The refuge, despite its famously abrupt staff, is extremely popular and at peak times floor-space, and even food, might run out; when this happens camping is allowed nearby, but often the immediately adjacent area becomes revoltingly unsavoury – budget for extra daylight time to reach some better sites further east, towards the Collado Superior de Góriz (Arrablo).

Fauna around the *parque nacional* – including golden eagles, lammergeiers, griffon and Egyptian vultures, and chamois (*sarrios* in Aragonese; identical to izards) – is much the same as on the French side, with the added attraction of a single troupe of **ibex** haunting the impregnable cliffs of Ordesa. The *sarrios* are so prolific that at times hunters are allowed to cull the surplus; by contrast the ibex population has dwindled to a score or so despite their protected status.

Climate and seasons

Weather in the park is notoriously fickle: during some summers there's not a cloud in the sky for days on end, but at other times there's thunder and hail every afternoon. When venturing out of the valley bottoms, always go prepared. In winter the park lies under one to two metres of snow, which persists in the popular Valle de Ordesa – not to mention higher elevations – until early June. Autumn features the spectacle of turning leaves on the beech and poplar trees, yet the weather remains relatively stable, if cool, and the park is far less crowded. Unless you're equipped with snow gear, the ideal **visiting season** is June to October.

Rules and regulations

Given ever-increasing tourist numbers, the park seems in real danger of being loved to death, so a few of the **rules** are worth elaborating. **Camping is prohibited** within the confines of the park except for a few specified areas: the Balcón de Pineta; at La Ripareta, San Vicenda and Fon Blanca in the Valle de Añisclo; beside Escuaín village; and around the *Refugio de Góriz* when it's full. Even at these places, you're supposed to dismount tents and leave them lying flat during the day. The small **stone huts** marked on most maps are intended for daytime use only, as shelter from storms; the sole staffed **refuge** is the *Refugio de Góriz*, roughly at the centre of park territory. In addition to the expected bans on disturbing plant or animal life, no **fires** are allowed anywhere, even in the stone emergency huts, and **no washing or swimming** is allowed in the rivers (most of them are too cold to get in anyway except on blazing August afternoons). As at Aigües Tortes in Catalunya, there's a **peripheral zone** of varying width to the south and east of the main *parque nacional* where development is controlled but few of the above prohibitions apply – you are allowed to swim, for instance, between Torla and the park boundary.

Motorized vehicles are not admitted beyond the chained gates at various points on the park periphery, and as from early 1998 approach from Torla along the paved access road has been banned completely. The former Valle de Ordesa car park has been closed down, the only vehicles allowed now the shuttle buses which run from the new car park just below the *Villa de Torla Hotel* in Torla. A control booth has been erected at the road fork near Puente de los Navarros, to make sure that all private traffic goes north towards Bujaruel.

Ascent of Monte Perdido

The standard expedition from the refuge is the **ascent of Monte Perdido**, which you do more for the views than anything else, since the southwest flank of the mountain – facing the head of the Valle de Ordesa – is the least impressive. It's more of a walk and scramble than a climb, but Monte Perdido can kill, so take advice from the refuge wardens, who have done the climb countless times. First and foremost get an early start, since thunderstorms can break in the afternoon. Follow the path climbing steeply north up the east bank of the **Barranco de Góriz**, where cairns show the way through alternating tracts of grass and boulders. After two tough hours you reach the 3000-metre contour and the small frozen **Lago Helado**, in the shadow of **Cilindro**, Perdido's sister summit.

At the lake you almost double back for the final approach, climbing steeply southeast, often over snow and ice, the grade slackening only a little just before the summit

(5hr from the refuge). From the top you can gaze down the Pineta valley to the east; over the Tella and Añisclo canyons to the south; across Lago Helado de Marboré to the Brecha de Tucarroya to the north; and towards distant Vignemale to the west.

Once back down at Lago Helado, you don't have to return to the *Refugio de Góriz*, but can execute a traverse. This implies an extra early start, as you'll not only be climbing Monte Perdido, but negotiating the Cuello del Cilindro, dropping along the snowfields on the far side to Lago Helado de Marboré and – if you don't camp there – descending to the Valle de Pineta via the steep *balcón* trail.

To move on **west** from the *Refugio de Góriz,* trace the north side of the valley past the **Circo de Góriz** to the Brèche de Roland, the Cirque de Gavarnie and the *Refuge de la Brèche de Roland* (see p.329).

To the Cascada de Cotatuero and beyond

A popular side-trip from the valley bottom goes up to the impressive **Cascada de Cotatuero**. Starting from the wayside shrine of Virgen de Ordesa several hundred metres beyond the Puente de los Cazadores, the Cotatuero route takes you steeply but easily through the woods to a vantage point below the waterfall within an hour.

If you have a head for heights, you can continue on from here into France. With the help of more *clavijas*, you climb above the falls (2hr 30min) to reach the Gruta de Casteret and the Brecha de Roldán (4hr from the Puente de los Cazadores), the latter giving access to Gavarnie in France.

Alternatively, you can ford the stream beside the collapsed bridge here and adopt the signposted **Senda Canarrellos**, which roller-coasters up to about the 1800-metre contour on its way southeast, across the lips of hanging valleys and under rock overhangs, to a junction (3hr 30min into the day) with the main valley-bottom track at **Bosque de Haya**. This is just above the **Cascada de la Cueva**, from where the Puente de Cazadores is about an hour downhill. However, the Senda Canarrellos is now unmaintained, with lots of tree-fall and boulder slides, possibly because ibex have been reintroduced hereabouts; without actual closure of the trail, traffic is certainly being discouraged. That said, it's certainly the wildest and, after the Faja de Pelay route, the most impressive of the trails in the canyon. It's a bit easier and quicker if done in reverse from the Bosque de Haya junction (which is still signposted); coming anticlockwise around the flank of Monte Arruebo, you get impressive views of the falls. Going clockwise, allow four and a half hours for this loop, anticlockwise, slightly less.

To the Cascada de Carriata and the Faja de las Flores

Another route signposted from the former car park leads to the **Cascada de Carriata**, pouring out of the **Circo de Salarons**. You head north into the trees, fork left, and begin a steep zigzag up to the falls, which are most impressive in late spring when melted snow keeps them flowing.

If you want to continue into the *circo*, the left-hand route (at a fork on the open mountainside ninety minutes above the visitors' centre) ascends via a series of thirteen *clavijas*, not nearly as intimidating as those on the Cotatuero route and feasible for any reasonably fit walker; once up top you can carry on to the Brecha de Roldán.

The right-hand fork quickly becomes a nail-biting corniche trail along the **Faja de las Flores**. Nowhere wider than a mere 7m, this terrace runs for about 3000m horizontally along the 2100-metre contour of the valley's north wall, with an immense drop to the south. If you haven't got a head for heights you'll either have acquired one by the end, or be whimpering on your hands and knees. If you cover the entire distance, you meet up with the ascending path for the Circo de Cotatuero in about ninety minutes; reckon on an hour to descend to the Puente de los Cazadores.

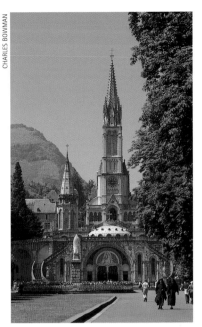

Cirque de Gavarnie, main fall

Lourdes

Boulder farmhouse, Espot

Pyrenean irises, Cirque de Gavarnie

The Respumoso reservoir

Lescun and its cirque

The old town, Aínsa

Añisclo Gorge, Ordesa National Park

Plaza Mayor, Aínsa

Bayonne

Monte Perdido area, Ordesa National Park

Walks from the upper Ara valley

To reach the **upper Ara valley** on foot from Torla, head up the GR15 variant II for just under an hour, as far as the junction with the Camino de Turieto, and then instead of continuing east into Ordesa take the **GR11** northwest. This crosses the Arazas at the **Puente de Ereta**, an anticlimactic cement aqueduct, with some icy pools beneath it (swimming permitted if you don't fear heart stoppage). Half an hour later the GR11 meets the access road for the *parque nacional* at the **Puente de los Navarros**, and then runs north along the Río Ara: first along the dirt road, and then after the Puente de Santa Elena, as an east-bank trail. About 1km above the bridge on the road, you'll find *Camping Valle de Bujaruelo* (☎974/48 61 61; April to mid-Oct), where there's a useful restaurant and shop for supplies, the highest one in the valley. Staying instead with the east-bank trail, you'll arrive (1hr 15min from Puente de los Navarros) at a wide riverside meadow with another newish, rather shadeless campsite (*San Nicolás de Bujaruelo*; ☎974/48 61 61) and several old buildings. Among these are the ruined eleventh-century church of **San Nicolás de Bujaruelo** and an old hospice refurbished as the private **refuge-restaurant** *Mesón del Labrador* (☎974/48 60 60; Easter–Sept; ①). At lunchtime especially, the *comedor* is packed for the sake of its limited but hearty four-course *menú* (about 2000ptas). From here, there are a number of possible trekking routes out of the Ara basin, all traced on current editions of the Editorial Alpina 1:30,000 "Vignemale Bujaruelo" map. You can, incidentally, proceed no further up-valley by vehicle – there's a locked barrier just past the refuge.

Trekking into France

For the **Gavarnie** basin, take the path that crosses the Ara over a beautiful Romanesque bridge and then zigzags quite steeply east to the frontier at **Puerto de Bujaruelo/Port de Gavarnie** (2270m); at the pass you pick up the HRP trail to the *Refuge de la Brèche de Roland*. Work on the dirt road which the Spanish were slowly bulldozing up to the pass appears to have been halted, the project deemed incompatible with the aims of the two national parks.

For the **Cauterets** area, hike northwest upstream beside the Ara along the **GR11**, but at the point – four hours beyond San Nicolás – where the GR climbs west towards Panticosa, continue instead to the head of the valley, where you pick up the **HRP** west through the **Col d'Aratille**, reaching the *Refuge Wallon* (see pp.333–334) after ten hours. You can also use the **HRP** east through the **Puerto de los Mulos** (2591m) to arrive at the *Refuge des Oulettes* in somewhat less time.

Trekking to Panticosa: the GR11

For **Balneario de Panticosa**, start out as for Cauterets but stay on the GR11. From the Ara valley floor, the route veers west-southwest up the **Barranco de Batáns** to the **Cuello de Brazato** (2578m; 6hr from San Nicolás) before dropping quite sharply to Balneario de Panticosa (see below), for a spectacular if full trekking day of seven and a half hours. The small tarns in the idyllic Batáns valley, plus the larger Brazato lakes, make this route a choice strategy for moving west; in any event don't make the mistake of following the **old GR11** up the Valle de Otal, which may still be marked as a *variante*. This may appear to be easier – the Collado de Tendeñera at the top of Otal is only 2327m – but it's longer and, as the GR marking committee apparently agreed, pretty tedious.

The Valle de Tena and around

The next major north–south valley west of the Ordesa region, the **Valle de Tena**, wins few beauty prizes in the judgement of many travellers. The **Rio Gállego** which waters it, starting near the Puerto de Portalet/Col du Pourtalet and the ski complex of **El Formigal**, has been extensively dammed, with the usual pipelines and high-tension lines in attendance. At **Lanuza** reservoir, many houses in the abandoned namesake villages stand poignantly half-submerged, as they have since 1954.

Consequently, if you arrive in the crossroads village of Biescas from either Torla or the transport hub of Sabiñánigo (see below), you'll need a sound pretext to head upstream along the C136 road. This is furnished by the westernmost concentration of three-thousand-metre **peaks** and **glacial lakes** in the Spanish Pyrenees, northeast of the Valle de Tena, reached either from **Sallent de Gállego**, near El Formigal, or the side valley of the Río Caldarés, which flows past **Panticosa** village from the agreeable spa of **Balneario de Panticosa**.

Biescas

An hour after leaving Torla, the bus reaches the small town of **BIESCAS**, near the lower end of the Valle de Tena, where the N260 road intersects the C136. If you have any time to spare between connections, have a look at the medieval upper quarter on the east bank of the Gállego, including a church built by the Knights Templar. Biescas comes to life between August 14 and 17, when consecutive festivities in honour of San Roque and La Virgen de la Assunción feature a "Big Heads" procession.

At other times of the year, especially if travelling under your own steam, you should at least schedule a lunch stop at the **hotel-restaurant** *Casa Ruba*, at c/Esperanza 20 (☎974/48 50 01; closed Oct & Nov; ④) on the east bank of the river. This has been in the same family for three generations, with the good-value restaurant featuring lots of game and fish, and the lively, authentic bar laying on arguably the best range of *tapas* in the mountains, plus breakfasts. Otherwise there's *Hostal la Rambla*, Rambla San Pedro 7 (☎974/48 51 77; ④), or the *Pensión Las Heras*, an old stone house with shared bathrooms at Agustina de Aragón 35 (☎974/48 50 27; ③), both in the west-bank quarter. If you take the year-round evening bus service up from Sabiñánigo to Biescas and fail to get a lift onwards, one of these establishments will certainly come in handy – and Biescas is certainly a more appealing place to spend the night than Sabiñánigo. There's also a **tourist office** by the southerly bridge (summer daily 10am–2pm & 3–9pm; ☎974/48 50 02).

Lately, Biescas has become most famous – or notorious – for one of the worst peacetime disasters ever to befall the Pyrenees. On August 7, 1996, a flash flood swept through the *Las Nieves* campsite north of town, leaving a final death toll of 87 (the last body was only found in the debris a year later). Preliminary enquiries have concluded that *Las Nieves* was unsafe, lying within the original course of the river before it was "engineered"; a new, more central **campsite**, *Edelweiss* (☎974/48 50 84; mid-June to mid-Sept), is hopefully better placed out of the flood plain.

Sabiñánigo

Unabashedly industrial **SABIÑÁNIGO**, 14km south of Biescas on the C136 and 18km east of Jaca, persuades few to linger, but almost everybody passes through at some point on their way to or from Ordesa, if only because there's an inevitable change of buses here. The **train station** is 300m northwest of the **bus terminal**, on the same boulevard.

With your own transport, make an effort to visit the remote **Museo Angel Orensanz y Artes de Serrablo** (summer Tues–Sun 10am–1pm & 5–8pm; winter Wed–Sun 11am–1pm & 4–6pm; 200ptas) at the southern edge of town by Puente Sardás, considered the best ethnological museum in Alto Aragón, with displays of traditional livelihoods alongside Señor Orensanz's sculpture.

If you're stranded for the night, there are several affordable **hostales**, all on c/Serrablo, the through road, including the *Alpino* at no. 58 (☎974/48 07 25; ③), the *Par* at no. 68 (☎974/48 01 89; ③), the *Esla* at no. 25 (☎974/48 29 35; ④) and the *Laguarta* (☎974/48 00 04; ④) at no. 21, the latter two most convenient for early-morning bus departures.

Panticosa village and spa

Fifteen kilometres upstream of Biescas, buses detour briefly at the far end of the **Embalse de Búbal** for the three-kilometre run northeast to **PANTICOSA** (Pandicosa) village, before continuing to Formigal. With its stucco exteriors and ornate windows on some of the remaining older buildings, Panticosa makes a tolerable base (though hikers might prefer Balneario de Panticosa). In recent years the small local **ski complex** has prompted a mushrooming of growth at the village outskirts. With a top station of 2005m, the runs are only just high enough – a chair lift, which also runs in summer for the benefit of mountain-bikers and walkers, links the village with 27 pistes, mostly blue- and red-rated. **Accommodation** in the village centre is heavily subscribed at peak times; best choices, in order of preference, are the one-star *Escalar* at the village entrance (☎974/48 70 98, fax 48 70 03; ④), with plush rooms, a pool and off-street parking; the one-star *Vicente* up on the road to Balneario de Panticosa (☎974/48 70 22; ④), with sweeping views across the valley; and the central *Navarro* (☎974/48 71 81, fax 48 72 20; ④) on Plaza de la Iglesia, which also has the village's original **restaurant**. You can buy trekking provisions in Panticosa, and there are three **banks**, one with an ATM.

Balneario de Panticosa

In July and August there's the option of a noon **bus** from Biescas upstream along the Río Caldarés through the **Garganta del Escalar**, whose walls are so close together that sun seldom penetrates and waterfalls often spray the road. **BALNEARIO DE PANTICOSA**, 10km beyond the village, is another one of those places claiming to be the highest (1636m) permanently inhabited spot in the Pyrenees. This attractive and traditional **spa** is fed by six mineral springs, each sampled for different, specific complaints. The emperor Tiberius supposedly visited Panticosa – the main baths are named in his honour – and there are, in fact, traces of Roman occupation in the vicinity, as well as an imposing Belle Époque casino, more restrained than its opposite numbers on the French side of the range. The several surviving **hotels** here are run as a cartel, some of them only available as part of a cure package, with a single booking agency (☎974/48 71 61, fax 48 71 37). The healthy who just want to stay the night will most likely be assigned to the *Hotel Continental* (① dorms, ④ en-suite doubles, with substantial off-peak discounts). The FAM refuge in the northwest corner of the spa, *Casa de Piedra* (☎974/48 75 71; 108 places; ①; open all year), sited to serve the GR11 which arrives here from the upper Ara valley, is unfortunately rather unwelcoming and run for the maximum convenience of the wardens; **meals** must be ordered in advance. The only independent place to eat at Balneario is the **bar** *Casa Belio*, which does *raciones*. The bus back to Biescas departs at about 3pm.

Walking from Balneario de Panticosa

You're well poised at Balneario de Panticosa for treks and climbs of all durations and difficulties: either day-hikes up scarcely trodden nearby peaks, or the two-day traverse to Sallent de Gállego along the GR11. If you're going to attempt any, or all of these routes, then get your hands on a copy of the appropriate Editorial Alpina map, the 1:25,000 "Panticosa Formigal".

Peak ascents

If you want to polish off an easy three-thousander, try **Pico d'o Argualas** (3046m), the summit immediately to the west – count on eight to nine hours there and back from the spa. Starting from a path marked "Argualas Reservoir", close to the spa's outdoor pool, you head northwest first for the **Cuello de Pondiellos** (2809m; 3hr 30min), then for the **Collado de Argualas** (2860m), gaining height by following the crest southwest towards the base of **Pico de Algas** (3021m) and finally tackling a poor footpath to complete the ascent via the west face. From here you have a wonderful view south towards the *sierras* of Telera and Tendeñera, as well as east over Balneario, Pico d'o Brazato and Vignemale.

To tackle the three summits of the **Picos del Infierno** – all of them close to 3100m – repeat the route to Cuello de Pondiellos but then head north towards the saddle that separates the central and eastern peaks, steering a middle course over the easiest terrain. From Pondiellos none of the Infierno peaks are more than ninety minutes away.

Traverse west via the GR11

To traverse west along the **GR11**, proceed north along the path behind the church, climbing to the **Ibón Bachimaña**, from where there's the option of going north through the Puerto de Panticosa/Port du Marcadau for the *Refuge Wallon*, a short trekking day of about six hours (see "Cauterets and around", p.334). To continue on the GR11 you swing west over gently rising ground to the upper **Ibón Azul** (3hr), where there's good camping.

Next you climb steeply to the double pass of **Cuello d'o Infierno** (2721m) and **Collado de Piedrafita** (2782m), problematic after snowy winters; once through this it's all downhill past the **Ibón de Llena Cantal** (another wonderful campsite) to the **Respumoso (Respomoso) reservoir** (2100m; 3hr from Ibón Azul). This is about as far as you'd comfortably get in one day from Balneario; on the north shore, reached by a detour trail, stands the *Refugio Respomoso* (2120m; ☎974/49 02 03; 105 places; open all year; ①); otherwise, there's ample turf for camping on the south shore. If you can keep your eyes off the concrete dam at the western end of Respumoso, the view north to **Balaitus/Balaïtous** and east to the triple pyramids of **Cambales** (2968m), **Petite Fache** (2947m) and **Grande Fache/Gran Facha** (3005m), more than compensates. (If you want to climb Balaïtous or head into France on the HRP, see "Around Balaïtous and Lac d'Artouste", p.347.)

To continue on the GR11, drop down the skilfully engineered path west from the lake, following the curving Aguas Limpias stream to Sallent de Gállego village (3hr), the last 45 minutes or so beyond the **Embalse de la Sarra** on asphalt road. If you've made an early start from Respumoso, it's possible and recommended to lengthen this final stage with a side trip north, on a cairned minor trail, to the **Arriel lakes** just below the HRP.

The upper Tena valley

To proceed along the **upper Tena valley** from the Panticosa turn-off you can use the onward bus service between Sabiñánigo and Sallent de Gállego, the morning departure rolling ten minutes further north to El Formigal. **ESCARRILLA**, 500m north of the junction, is the first settlement encountered, boasting a fine bridge across the Gállego and a fortified church. **Accommodation** is available at the *Hostal Sarao* (☎974/48 70 65; ④), with a popular restaurant, and at the more luxurious *Hotel Ibón Azul* (☎974/48 72 11, fax 48 72 42; ⑤), both on the main through road; there's also an enormous **campsite**, the *Escarra* (☎974/48 71 28; open all year), on the west side of the highway. A *variante* of the **GR11** heads westwards past the Escarra dam to hook up with the main GR at the **Collado de Izas**, halfway to Canfranc.

Sallent de Gállego

Once past the **Embalse de Lanuza**, a right turn and another bridge over the Gállego takes you into **SALLENT DE GÁLLEGO** (Sallén de Galligo), a sizeable old village 21km from Biescas, at the confluence of the Gállego and the Aguas Limpias. It has a dual role as winter sports and summer mountaineering centre, as well as playing host to the *Pirineos Sur* **festival** the last three weeks in July; this is one of the best world music bashes in Europe, with the likes of Manu Dibango, Youssou N'Dour and other prominent Latin/Arabic/African acts in years past.

Accordingly, **accommodation** is fairly abundant, if overpriced. Working your way from east to west along the single high street of c/Francia, you encounter *Hostal El Centro* (☎974/48 80 19; ④); *Hostal Mediodia* (☎974/48 80 71; ④), with a few cheaper rooms; *Hostal Familiar Maximina*, tucked away on a side street at c/La Iglesia 3 (☎974/48 84 36; ⑤), with suites for the price; *Hostal Faure* (☎974/48 80 07; ④), in a courtyard off the main road, with a good restaurant; and *Hotel Balaitus* (☎974/48 80 59; ⑤). If you're alone or impecunious, probably the best choice is the friendly *Albergue Foratata* near the west end of c/Francia (☎974/48 81 12; ①), with a few doubles and an inexpensive canteen on the ground floor. Sallent also has two **banks**, two or three stores, and a beguiling sixteenth-century church. Barring winter extensions to El Formigal, this is the usual terminus for bus services from and to **Sabiñánigo** (downhill services at 7am & July–Aug 3.45pm).

El Formigal

The ascending road from Sallent, with views of the pyramidal Peña Foradada on the north, weaves for almost 5km to **EL FORMIGAL**. A relatively recent ski resort of chalet-apartments, El Formigal (1550m) is neither twee nor chic, but merely sufficient for the needs of its clients, who tend to be Spanish since the winter closure of the Puerto de Portalet prevents most French skiers from getting here. The north-facing runs, much more extensive than at Panticosa, are scattered on a vast, treeless slope across the valley from the chalets; the top lift is 2250m and the 34 pistes are mostly red-rated.

During winter a regular ski-bus links Sallent with El Formigal, so you can partake of the fairly lively nightlife more or less evenly allotted between the two. Except for the two-star *Hotel Tirol* (☎974/489 03 77; ⑥), **accommodation** in El Formigal can be extremely expensive for what you get; in high season beds are hard to find anyway, in which case you'll appreciate Sallent and Escarrilla as useful fallbacks.

Beyond El Formigal, the road continues through the **Puerto de Portalet** (*Portalé* in Aragonese)/**Col du Pourtalet** (1794m), between the sharply pointed Pic d'Anéou to the west and Pic du Portalet. Once over the pass – which unlike Somport to the west is *not* kept snowploughed in winter – you're in the French Vallée d'Ossau.

Jaca and around

The approach to **JACA**, 18km west of Sabiñánigo on the N330, takes you through modern, traffic-afflicted suburbs – an unpromising introduction to this early capital and stronghold of Aragón, and the base from which the kingdom was recaptured from the Moors. The old town, however, is more characterful, overlooked by a huge star-shaped citadel and endowed with a **cathedral** that is one of the finest Spanish examples of Romanesque architecture. This, together with the monastery of **San Juan de la Peña** in the Sierra de la Peña to the southwest, are the major local sights, while in winter the proximity of **Candanchú-Astún**, the most westerly ski resort in the Spanish Pyrenees, provides an added bonus. Rail enthusiasts may be tempted by the train trip north to **Canfranc**, almost at the French border, and a good place to pick up the GR11 long-distance trail.

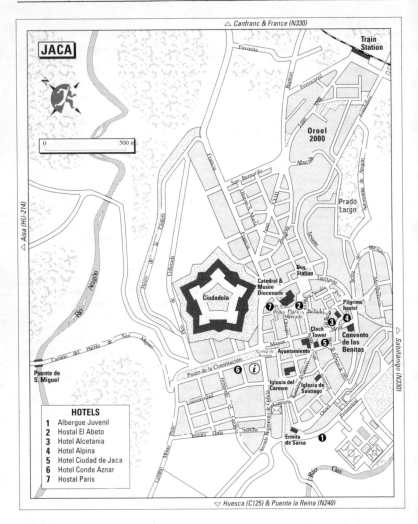

After a spell in the mountains, Jaca's relatively "big town" feel and facilities may well be an equal attraction. It's lively enough – thanks to conscripts at the large military academy and students attending a summer university – and the spring and summer calendar is punctuated by a number of boisterous festivals.

The Town

Sited at the foot of Peña Oroel, on a broad plain where the Río Aragón suddenly twists westwards, Jaca is a venerable place, called *Iacca* by the Romans after the Iaccitanii tribe who already dwelt here. The Moors occupied Jaca briefly from 715 to 760, when the Christians reconquered the town and held it, save for a brief spell, from then on.

The battle of **Las Tiendas** (4km west of town), in 795, in which a Moorish army was repulsed mostly by the local women, is still commemorated on the first Friday in May by a mock all-female battle between "Christians" and "Moors".

Even under these hard-pressed conditions an embryonic democracy of sorts prevailed from the outset among the Aragonese nobility, who stipulated comprehensive customary rights (*fueros*) limiting the power of the king to issue edicts and levy taxes. Jaca itself reached its zenith after 1035, when **Ramiro I**, son of Sancho of Navarre, established a court here and began work on the present cathedral.

The Cathedral

The **Cathedral** constitutes the principal legacy of Jaca's years as the seat of the young Aragonese kingdom, and is one of the Pyrenees' most architecturally important monuments. Rebuilt on old foundations during the middle of the eleventh century, it was the first cathedral in Spain to adopt the French Romanesque architecture and, as such, exerted considerable stylistic influence on other churches along the *Camino de Santiago*.

Ramiro's endowment of the cathedral was undoubtedly intended to confirm Jaca's role as a Christian capital in what was still almost exclusively a Moorish Iberian peninsula. Its design saw the introduction of the classic three-aisled basilica, though unhappily the original Romanesque simplicity has been much obscured by florid Renaissance decoration in the intervening centuries. It retains some of the original sculpture, however, including realistic carving on the capitals and doorway – a sixteenth-century statue of Santiago looks down from the portal. Before the central apse, the main treasure is the silver shrine of Santa Orosía, Jaca's patron saint; a Czech noblewoman who married into the Aragón royal family, she was martyred by the Moors for refusing to renounce her faith.

Installed in the dark cathedral cloisters, there's an unusually good **Museo Diocesano** (Tues–Sun: summer 8am–2pm & 4–8pm; winter 10am–1.30pm & 4–6pm; 200ptas) featuring a beautiful collection of twelfth-to-fifteenth-century Aragonese frescoes, gathered from village churches in the immediate area and from higher up in the Pyrenees. If your interest is sparked, there is a comparable, though far more extensive display of their Catalan equivalents in Barcelona.

The Ciudadela and Puente San Miguel

The **Ciudadela**, a redoubtable sixteenth-century fort built to the star-shaped plan favoured in that era, is still partly occupied by the Spanish army. You can visit parts of the interior (summer daily 11am–12.30pm & 5–6.30pm; winter daily 11am–noon & 4–5pm; 200ptas) on a guided tour – though interest is mostly confined to good views of the surrounding peaks and wooded countryside from the walls, and the herd of red deer living in the moat.

Northwest of the citadel, reached along a rough track from the end of the Paseo de la Constitución, Jaca preserves a remarkable medieval bridge, the **Puente de San Miguel**. It was across this bridge over the Río Aragón that pilgrims on the **Camino de Santiago** entered Jaca, marking the end of the arduous Pyrenean stage for pilgrims following the *Camino Aragonés*. This branch of the route, starting from Provence, entered Spain at the Puerto de Somport, and from Jaca headed west towards Navarra, where it met with the main, more popular itinerary via Roncesvalles and Pamplona. This portion of the *Camino de Santiago* – like other sections of the route – has recently experienced quite a revival and is marked as the GR65.3. Jaca is now consciously pitched as a way-station: there's a **pilgrims' hostel** in the medieval hospice on Travesía Conde Don Aznar, with route maps and pilgrimage-related souvenirs widely available.

Practicalities

The **train station** (tickets issued 10am–noon & 5–7pm) is a good 3km north of the centre, but there is a shuttle bus into town which passes the main **bus station**, around the back of the cathedral in Avda. Jacetania. Useful summer bus departures include services to Pamplona (5.30pm Mon–Fri, 11am Fri & Sat, 8pm Sun), Sabiñánigo and Biescas (10.15am & 6.15pm Mon–Sat) and Ansó via Hecho (5pm Mon–Sat); there are also more frequent services to Zaragoza and Huesca. Although timetables don't explicitly say so, hardly any buses run on Sundays.

The **old town**, where you'll spend most time, divides into a somewhat frowsy northeastern side – home to all of the budget accommodation, the roughest bars and most of the reasonable restaurants – and the flashier southwestern quarter, abutting Avenida Regimiento de Galicia, with its sidewalk cafés, restaurants and banks. On the same *avenida* you'll find the **tourist office** (summer Mon–Fri 9am–2pm & 4.30–8pm, Sat 10am–1.30pm & 5–8pm, Sun 10am–1.30pm; winter Mon–Fri 9am–2pm & 4.30–8pm, Sat 10am–1pm & 5–7pm; ☎974/36 00 98), which stocks a range of leaflets on general activities from yoga to mountain-biking, as well as comprehensive information on nearby ski resorts.

Accommodation

Although at an elevation of only 820m, Jaca counts as a Pyrenean resort and as such fills up in August or during ski season, with prices pushed up year-round by the cross-border trade.

Albergue Juvenil Escuelas Pias, Avda. Perimetral 6 (☎974/36 05 36). This youth hostel, at the very south end of town by the Zona Deportiva, has doubles, triples and quads. ①.

Hostal Residencia El Abeto, c/Bellido 15 (☎974/36 16 42). Comfortable enough, with en-suite facilities, though there may be noise from the nearby bar district. ③.

Hotel Alcetania, c/Mayor 45, but entry from c/Conde Aznar (☎974/35 61 00, fax 35 62 00). A former *hostal* refurbished in 1995 as a hotel, and good value. ⑤.

Hotel Alpina, c/Mayor 57 (☎974/35 53 69). An ex-*fonda* upgraded to en-suite hotel status. ④.

Hotel Ciudad de Jaca, c/Siete de Febrero 8 (☎974/36 43 11, fax 36 43 95). Central but quiet, with rooms with en-suite facilities. ④.

Hotel Conde Aznar, Paseo de la Constitución 3 (☎974/36 10 50). A good two-star choice: an attractive old family hotel facing a leafy parkway. ⑤.

Hostal Paris, Plaza de San Pedro 5 (☎974/36 10 20). Large if bathless rooms make this excellent value as a central choice, across from the cathedral; good attached restaurant. ③.

CAMPING

Camping Peña Oroel, 4km east on the N330 towards Sabiñánigo (☎974/36 02 15). Jumbo-sized site attractively set in a wood, with good facilities. Open Easter week, and mid-June to mid-Sept.

Camping Victoria, 1.5km west on the C134 towards Pamplona (☎974/36 03 23). A smaller, more basic affair, also in a grove, near the Río Aragón. Open all year.

Eating and drinking

There's ample choice when it comes to **eating and drinking**, with good places concentrated in the old town. The entire length of c/Gil Berges, as well as contiguous c/del Barco and c/de la Puerta Nueva, is home to most of Jaca's rowdier student bars. More sedate pubs and *tapas* bars for an older crowd concentrate on c/Ramiro Primero, a little to the southwest.

La Cabaña, c/del Pez 10. Inexpensive *menús* and à la carte dishes in unusually cheerful surroundings. It's in the same, northeastern corner of the old town as *La Fragua*.

Casa la Abuela Primera, c/de la Población 3. Unpretentious and as inexpensive as meals come in town.

Croissanterie Demilune, Avda. Regimiento de Galicia 2, by the tourist office. A wide variety of filled croissants and *batidos* (fruit shakes); a good stop for breakfast.

Cafe Dilema, Plaza del Marques de la Cadena. Coffee and alcoholic drinks outside at the foot of the Torre del Reloj (the clocktower).

La Fragua, c/Gil Berges 4. One of the best no-nonsense places for carnivores to eat, specializing in generous, reasonably priced grills cooked on an open range. Closed Wed.

Mesón Corbacho, c/Ramiro Primero 2. Regional dishes and grills (count on spending 3000ptas).

Mesón El Rancho, c/Arco 2. Tasty and good-value meals for a modest (2000ptas) outlay, one block from *La Fragua*.

Pizzeria La Fontana, c/Ramiro Primero. Upmarket pizzeria (with outdoor seating), at the end of the block where the street opens into the delightful Plaza del Marques de la Cadena, with its fountain and clocktower.

Pizzeria Polifemo, c/Dieziocho de Junio 5. Pizzeria with a loyal student clientele, down the street from *La Cabaña*.

Tomás, c/Ferrenal 8. No-nonsense bar with a vast range of *tapas* and *raciones*.

Listings

Bike rental You can usually get hold of a mountain bike at short notice for about 2500ptas daily. Reliable outlets include Alcorce, c/La Salud 5 (☎974/36 39 72), and Pirineos Aventura, c/Carmen 11 (☎974/36 39 01).

Car rental Best-value outlets are Aldecar, at the very eastern end of Avda. Jacetania at no. 60 (☎974/38 07 81), and Viajes Abad, Avda. Regimiento de Galicia 19 (☎974/36 10 81). In high season all cars must be reserved at least 24hr in advance.

Hospital The local hospital is on c/Rapitan, beyond the train station (☎974/35 82 00).

Laundrette Self-service *lavandería* next to the Superpireineos supermarket on c/Astún.

Trekking supplies Detailed maps are available only from the bookstore Abad at c/Mayor 34, and at Charli, Avda. Regimiento de Galicia 3. The latter is also good for outdoor gadgets, and is home to the local guides' bureau.

South of Jaca: San Juan de la Peña and Santa Cruz de la Serós

San Juan de la Peña, high in the hills southwest of Jaca, is the best-known monastery in Aragón. In medieval times an important "*variante*" of the pilgrim route from Jaca to Pamplona passed by, as San Juan reputedly held the Holy Grail – actually a Roman chalice which later found its way to Valencia cathedral. These days, most tourists (and there are a lot – including school parties) visit for the views and Romanesque cloister.

The most direct **route to the monastery** begins from the Jaca–Pamplona (N240) highway. A side road, 11km west of Jaca, leads south 4km to the village of Santa Cruz de la Serós with its massive Romanesque church, and from here it's a further 7km by road up to San Juan. There is no public transport, although you could take the afternoon Puente la Reina/Pamplona-bound bus from Jaca and walk from there – assuming an overnight at the upper monastery (see below). **Renting a mountain bike** would be easier: reckon on an hour's cycling from Jaca to Santa Cruz, then a further hour up the very steep road to San Juan. Returning to Jaca, you can make an enjoyable circuit rather than retracing your tire-treads: a gradual twelve-kilometre descent east to Bernués, a slight climb to Puerto de Oroel on the N330, then a fierce drop to Jaca, 17km from Bernués. This is a very scenic – and car-free – itinerary, but not something to do in reverse.

Santa Cruz de la Serós

The picturesque village of **SANTA CRUZ DE LA SERÓS**, which comes to life in summer, is dominated by its thick-set, but nonetheless stylish Romanesque **Church**

(11am–1pm & 4–6pm; 100ptas); inside, its remarkable stoup incorporates a massive central pillar holding up the vault. The sanctuary was once part of a large Benedictine convent which flourished between the eleventh and sixteenth centuries; indeed *serós* appears to be a corruption of *sorores*, after the nuns who once dwelt here, including (in their old age) the three sisters of King Sancho.

From Santa Cruz, walkers can take the old **path** up to San Juan in about an hour. The path is waymarked as variant II of GR65.3 and is signposted from near the church (where there is also a map placard). The road takes a more circuitous route of 7km around the mountainside, affording wonderful views over a vast panorama, with the peaks of the Pyrenees clearly visible to the north and the distinctive Peña Oroel to the east.

San Juan de la Peña

San Juan de la Peña actually comprises two monasteries, 1500m apart. Approaching from Santa Cruz, you reach the lower (and older) one first.

Built into a hollow under an enormous cliff, the **Lower Monastery** (mid-March to mid-Oct Tues–Sun 10am–1.30pm & 4–7pm; mid-Oct to mid-March Wed–Sun 11am–2.30pm; free, guided visits only), which contains a small museum (same days as the rest of the complex, 11.30am–1pm & 4.30–6pm), is an unusual and evocative complex, even in its partial state of survival. Entering, you pass first into a ninth-century **Mozarabic chapel**, which was adapted as the crypt of the main Romanesque **church** one level above, built two centuries later; both retain fragments of Romanesque frescoes. Here, in 1071, Cluniac monks replaced the Mozarabic Mass with the Roman rite – the first such substitution in the Iberian peninsula and made possible by the re-establishment of contact with Rome after centuries of isolation.

Upstairs, alongside the main church, is a **pantheon** of Aragonese and Navarrese nobles; reliefs on the nobles' Gothic tombs show events from the early history of Aragón. Another adjacent pantheon for the kings of Aragón was remodelled in a cold, Neoclassical style in the eighteenth century and later sacked by Napoleon's troops.

The artistic highlight, however, is the twelfth-century Romanesque **cloisters**, at the far end of the complex where the rock overhang has been left open to the sky rather than completely walled off. Only two of the bays are complete – another is in a fragmentary state – but the surviving capitals are among the greatest examples of Romanesque carving. They are the artistry of an anonymous, idiosyncratic craftsman who left his mark on a number of churches in the region. He is now known as the Master of San Juan de la Peña, and his work is easily recognizable by the unnaturally large eyes on the figures.

The surrounding cliffs are the nesting grounds of assorted **birds of prey**, and you'll be very unlucky not to see griffon vultures, or the summer-visiting Egyptian vultures. Bonelli's eagles (all year) and short-toed eagles (summer only), identifiable by their habit of soaring with dangling feet, are less frequent sights.

The late seventeenth-century **Upper Monastery**, a sizeable complex with a flamboyant Baroque facade, can be seen from the outside only – it now serves as a centre for the study of the old Aragonese kingdom – but merits the climb east from the older monastery, if only for the views of the Pyrenees from a nearby *mirador*. The former outbuildings shelter a small and rather institutional **hostal** (☎974/36 09 22; 4200ptas; April–Oct) and a bar-restaurant with a 1500-pta *menú del día*; there are seats inside the *comedor*, or buy your drinks and sit outside underneath the monastery's facade. Facing the monastery is a popular picnic ground in a huge, forest-enclosed meadow.

North of Jaca: Canfranc and Candanchú-Astún

Although it is the Río Aragón which drains south from the Puerto de Somport, its valley – extending directly **north of Jaca** – is known as the **Canfranc**. This is also the name of two settlements along the way: **Canfranc-Pueblo**, 19km out of Jaca on the N330, devastated by fire in 1944 and now with just forty inhabitants, and **Canfranc-Estación**, 23km along and (currently) the final stop for northbound trains. Just shy of the frontier, 9km beyond, the double ski resort of **Candanchú-Astún** straddles the approaches to the **Puerto de Somport**.

Canfranc: Pueblo and Estación

In keeping with its depopulation, tourist facilities in **CANFRANC-PUEBLO** are limited to the *Refugio de Canfranc* (1045m; ☎974/37 21 04; 100 places; open all year; ①), an *albergue* for pilgrims on the *Camino de Santiago*, and a single bar for meals and drink.

Since the French discontinued their part of the trans-Pyrenean line, most of the train station at **CANFRANC-ESTACIÓN** has become a badly vandalized white elephant where tall weeds grow up through the tracks. Equipped with the second longest platforms in Europe, this huge, 1928-vintage pastiche would be a listed monument anywhere else. The reopening of the line is now predicted as part of the Somport tunnel project (see p.350), but frequent services won't materialize until the prices at ski resorts on either side of the Pyrenees approach parity. Spanish undercutting of French resort rates prompted the closure of the line in 1973 after 45 years of service, though the last straw was the collapse of a bridge on the French side, left unrepaired to this day. A noticeboard at the entrance to the station tells (part of) the whole sad story.

The surrounding village, such as it is, originally sprang up to house those made homeless by the 1944 disaster, and now exists solely to lure the passing motorist trade (mostly French) with a handful of gift shops and hotels. Even if you don't continue into France, it's just about worth a day-trip from Jaca for the mountain setting, though on the train ride up you see as much tunnel as you do countryside.

If you decide to **stay**, there's the unusually expensive *Albergue Pepito Grillo* at Avda. Fernando el Católico 2, the through highway (☎974/37 31 23; ①; no cooking allowed, no meals provided), nominally serving those arriving on the GR11 (see below). Hotels include the rather gloomy one-star *Ara*, Avda. Fernando el Católico 1 (☎974/37 30 28; ④), or for roughly the same money the far quieter and superior wood-and-stone *Hotel Villa Anayet*, at the north end of town in Plaza Aragón 8 (☎974/37 31 46; ④; closed mid-April to June & mid-Sept to mid-Dec), with a well-attended *comedor*. There is also a small **campsite** (the *Canfranc*; ☎908/73 16 04; April to mid-Sept), a bit north on the road towards Candanchú. One of the few independent **restaurants**, *Casa Flores*, behind *Casa Marraco* at Avda. Fernando el Católico 27, is cheap but not especially cheerful; you'll do better tucking in with the Spanish families at the *Villa Anayet*.

Until and unless train services resume through the refurbished tunnel, the only public transport **into France** is the **bus**. There are 4 daily departures Monday to Saturday, 3 on Sunday, provided by SNCF; on weekends there's a supplemental Spanish service offered by La Oscense, passing through Canfranc-Estación at 10.15am (Sat) and 6.16pm (Sun). More information can be had from the **tourist office** (daily 9am–7.30pm, closed Wed & Thurs 1–4pm; ☎974/37 31 41), at Avda. Fernando el Católico 3.

Walking from Canfranc: the GR11

The **GR11** runs **east** from between Canfranc and Candanchú via the **Canal Roya** valley and the **Ibóns de Anayet**, while a variant goes east directly from Canfranc along the **Izas valley**, the two routes converging at El Formigal – either way an easy and (certainly near the lakes) enjoyable one-day stage. Heading west from Candanchú itself involves a somewhat longer and tougher day's trek hugging the border, enlivened by the **Ibón de Astanés**, the largest natural lake in these parts. The next significant facilities, assuming the campsite there has reopened, are at **Selva de Oza**, near the top of the **Valle de Hecho**;

if it hasn't, you'd do better to take the variant via the low Collado de Riguelo and Collado d'o Boxo to the *Refugio de Lizara*, from where Hecho is an easy stage away (see p.392).

Skiing: Candanchú-Astún

Perhaps the best Aragonese ski resort, certainly the most varied, is **CANDANCHÚ-ASTÚN**, 8km north of Canfranc (seasonal buses from Jaca). The unaesthetic but functional complexes – Astún is relatively recent, Candanchú long established – are just 4km apart, and you can alternate between them on the same pass. Astún is particularly well organized, rarely crowded and has plentiful (generally new) equipment for rent at reasonable rates.

Both resorts boast extensive north-facing runs in a treeless valley on the north side of the Aspe ridge. Given the Atlantic-influenced climate, their top lifts of 2300–2400m should ensure good snow. Candanchú has 46 pistes of all grades, more than half red or black, Astún 27, again predominately red or black. Off-piste possibilities here are considerable and a day out towards Cumbre del Aspe (2500m) or the surrounding limestone cliffs will be memorable.

Accommodation in Candanchú includes a pair of inexpensive *albergues*, the highly rated *El Aguila* (☎974/37 32 91; 60 places; ①) and *Valle del Aragón* (☎974/37 32 22; 68 places; ①), both open all year, as well as the *Pensión Somport*, Carretera de Francia 198 (☎974/37 30 09; ②). The two-star *Hotel Tobazo* (☎974/37 31 25; ⑥) and the mock-Tyrolean two-star *Candanchú* (☎974/37 30 25, fax 37 30 50; ⑥), both on the main highway, reflect the more usual hotel prices for this resort – and the lifts are two steps from their doors.

The Romans built the first road through the **Puerto de Somport/Col du Somport** (1632m) itself, below the ski slopes, and the Moors made grateful use of this handiwork during their northward invasion in 732. The recently abandoned frontier gate has for company a more venerable relic: the ruins of a twelfth-century pilgrims' hospice built by the rulers of Béarn.

travel details

French trains
Pau to: Lourdes (almost hourly; 30min); Oloron-Sainte-Marie (4 daily; 30min); Tarbes (almost hourly; 40min).

Tarbes to: Capvern (hourly; 30min); Lannemezan (7 daily; 25min); Lourdes (hourly; 20min).

Spanish trains
Jaca to: Canfranc-Estación (2 daily; 35min); Huesca (2 daily; 2hr 10min); Sabiñánigo (2 daily; 20min); Zaragoza (2 daily; 3hr 10min).

French buses
Bagnères-de-Bigorre to: Campan (3 daily July–Sept, 1 daily in term time; 20min); Lac de Payolle (3 daily July–Sept, 1 daily in term time;

45min); Sainte-Marie-de-Campan (3 daily July–Sept, 1 daily in term time; 35min).

Lannemezan to: Arreau (SNCF/Brunet buses; 5 daily Mon–Sat in term time, 3 daily summer, 4 daily weekends year-round; 40min); Bagnères-de-Bigorre (2 weekly during school term; 50min); St-Lary-Soulan (SNCF/Brunet buses; 5 daily Mon–Sat term time, 3 daily summer, 4 daily weekends year round; 1hr 5min).

Laruns to (all with SARL Canonge-Pic Bus, July & Aug Mon–Fri only): Col du Pourtalet (2 daily, 1hr 20min); Gabas (2 daily; 30min); Lac de Fabrèges (2 daily; 50min); Bious-Oumette campsite (1 daily; 50min).

Lourdes to: Bagnères-de-Bigorre (2 daily during school term, 3 daily in summer; 45min); Barèges

(SNCF bus, change at Pierrefitte-Nestalas; 7 daily July & Aug, 5 daily Sept–June; 1hr 5min); Cauterets (direct SNCF bus; 7 daily July & Aug, 5 daily Sept–June; 1hr); Luz-Saint-Sauveur (2–3 daily; 45min); Pau (4 daily; 1hr 15min); Tarbes (hourly; 30min).

Luz-Saint-Saveur to: Gavarnie (summer 2 daily with Cars Dubie, 9am & 5.30pm, return 11.40am & 6.30pm; winter 3 weekly, Mon, Thurs & Sat; 40min).

Oloron-Sainte-Marie to (all SNCF buses): Bédous (7 daily Mon–Sat, 4 on Sun; 30min); Cette-Eygun (7 daily Mon–Sat, 4 on Sun; 45min); Laruns via Buzy junction (3 daily; 1hr); Urdos (7 daily Mon–Sat, 4 on Sun; 1hr).

Pau to: Bayonne (run by TPR; 3–4 daily Mon–Sat, 2 on Sun; 2hr); Col d'Aubisque (CIT-RAM; July to mid-Sept 1 daily; 2hr); Gourette (CITRAM; 3 daily; 1hr 45min); Laruns (CITRAM; 3 daily; 1hr); Lourdes (4 daily; 1hr 15min); Oloron-Ste-Marie (Mon–Sat 2–3 daily; 45min); Tarbes (6 daily; 1hr).

Tarbes to: Argelès-Gazost (6 daily; 50min); Arrens-Marsous (Mon–Sat 1 daily; 1hr 20min); Bagnères-de-Bigorre (Mon–Sat 8–9 daily, 3 on Sun; 40min); Pierrefitte-Nestalas (6 daily; 1hr); Tarbes-Ossun/Lourdes Airport (1–2 daily; 30–45min).

Spanish buses

Aínsa to: Sabiñánigo via Torla (1 daily at 2.30pm; 2hr 40min).

Jaca to: Hecho/Ansó (1 daily except Sun at 5.30pm; 1hr/1hr 15min); Pamplona via Puente la Reina (Mon–Fri 5.30pm, Fri & Sat 11am, Sun 8pm; 1hr 35min); Sabiñánigo (2 daily at 10.15am and 6.15pm; 20min).

Sabiñánigo to: Aínsa via Torla (Mon–Sat 1 daily at 11am; 2hr 40min); Biescas (Mon–Sat 2 daily at 11am & 6.30pm; 20 min); Jaca (Mon–Sat 2 daily, 1 on Sun; 20min); Panticosa village (1 daily at 11am, plus additional service mid-July to Aug Mon–Sat at 6.30pm; 50min); Sarvisé (1 daily at 11am, plus additional service mid-July to Aug Mon–Sat at 6.30pm; 1hr 15min); Torla (1 daily at 11am, plus additional service mid-July to Aug Mon–Sat at 6.30pm; 1hr).

Sallent de Gállego to: Sabiñánigo (1 daily at 7am, plus additional departure mid-July to Aug Mon–Sat at 3.45pm; 1hr).

International buses

Jaca to (La Oscense/Hispano Ansotana buses): Lourdes via Canfranc, Pau, Tarbes (Sat at 9.45am, Sun at 5.45pm; 4hr 15min for the entire trip).

Oloron-Sainte-Marie to (SNCF buses): Canfranc via Urdos (Mon–Sat 4 daily, 3 on Sun; 1hr 30min).

CHAPTER FIVE

THE WESTERN PYRENEES

The widespread notion that the Pyrenees begin or end at Pic d'Anie, some 80km from the coast, ignores the segment of the range that contains the greatest diversity of wildlife, the densest forest, a seductively green landscape and the most tenaciously retained ethnic identity – that of the Basques. Extreme altitude is the only thing the Western Pyrenees lack: there's no peak higher than Pic d'Anie's neighbour Tres Reyes (2444m) between it and the sea, and beyond Pic d'Orhy/Pico·de Ori (2017m) the summits diminish markedly.

The **Western Pyrenees** embrace an area more extensive than **Euskal Herria**, the Basques' name for their country on both sides of the frontier. They also include a small

---

FESTIVALS

This is only a fraction of the many events, especially during summer, staged in particular on the Basque Coast and along the *Camino de Santiago*. For schedule booklets and ticket information where applicable, contact the tourist offices in Bayonne, Biarritz and San Sebastián.

JANUARY
19–20 *Tamborrada* – march with pipes and drums in honour of the patron saint of San Sebastián, with more festive action in the evenings.
Last Tuesday & Wednesday *Pottok* pony sale in Espelette.

FEBRUARY
10 Traditional dancing at Valcarlos.
Variable *Carnival* in San Sebastián.

MAY
First Sunday Start of the three-month season of *romerías* to the *Virgen de Orreaga* at Roncesvalles.

JUNE
Second Sunday Dancing, pelota, trials of strength at Itxassou.
24–26 Music, *pelota* and bonfires at Saint-Jean-de-Luz.
30 *Fiesta de San Marcial* at Irún, with the five-thousand-strong *Alarde* parade and canoeing in the Bidasoa.

JULY
6–14 *Fiesta de San Fermín* – the famous running of the bulls in Pamplona.
Second weekend *Fête du Thon*, with music and tuna-eating in Ciboure/Saint-Jean-de-Luz.
13 *Tributo de las Tres Vacas* at Belagoa.
Mid-month Surfing competitions at Biarritz and Anglet.
14–19 Folklore, parade, fireworks, bullfights and *Jazz aux Remparts* at Bayonne.
24–28 Prolonged *Fiesta de Santiago* at Isaba and Elizondo.

pocket of Alto Aragón in the paired **Hecho** and **Ansó** valleys, drainages of the same karst country as the **Haute-Soule** in France and **Isaba** in Navarra. But geographically the difference between the French and Spanish sides of the border is greater here than anywhere else in the range. In Spain the hills, often alpine in climate, extend exceptionally far from the frontier, and are often densely clad in trees; the **Irati forest**, for example, dense and extensive in Spain, has been severely reduced by exploitation on its French slopes (where it's known as the Iraty). Much of the French Basque country is strongly reminiscent of the open countryside of Scotland, especially near **Saint-Jean-Pied-de-Port**, its chief inland tourist attraction.

This western region also has the highest concentration of small gateway cities for the mountains. **Pamplona** is the largest Pyrenean town, though its attractive old town and buildings are deservedly eclipsed by the world-famous *San Fermín* festival held here every July. **Bayonne** and **San Sebastián**, near the Atlantic coast below the foothills, gracefully combine roles as commercial entrepôts, resorts and administrative centres, with either proving livelier and more exciting than anything along the Mediterranean coast of the Pyrenees.

Public transport is fairly good on the Spanish side of the Pyrenees but appalling in France except on the coast, so the easiest way of tackling the area is from the south. If

---

25 *Fiesta de Santiago*, at Valcarlos; also one including an *encierro* at Puente de la Reina de Jaca.
Variable, last two weeks *International Jazz Festival* at San Sebastián.
Variable, one Sunday *Festival des Forces Basques*, traditional sports and competitions of strength at Saint-Étienne-de-Baïgorry, repeated one Sunday in August.

AUGUST
First Wednesday *Fêtes de Bayonne*, five days of heavy drinking and concerts, plus bull-fights, at Bayonne; ten days later there's several more days of the same.
Second week *Pelota*, street parties, music, dancing and Basque sports at Cambo-les-Bains (Bas cambo) and at Saint-Étienne-de-Baïgorry.
15–23 *Semana Grande* – a folk and music festival for *Asunción* at San Sebastián, with fireworks.
13–15 *Pelota*, folklore and dancing at Saint-Jean-Pied-de-Port.
15 *Romería* to the Ermita de Nuestra Señora de las Nieves, near Ochagavía; mock Basque wedding at Saint-Étienne-de-Baïgorry.
Third weekend *Fêtes de Petit Bayonne*.

SEPTEMBER
First week More bullfights at Bayonne.
First and second weekends *Trainera* regatta in San Sebastián.
8 *Fiesta de la Virgen de Guadalupe* at Hondarribia; *romería* to the *colegiata* at Roncesvalles; *Fiesta de la Natividad de la Virgen* – folk dancing at Ochagavía.
Second Sunday Start of three-day festival at Sare, with Basque sports, singing and dancing.
Fourth week International Film Festival at San Sebastián.
Last two weeks International Film Festival at Biarritz.

OCTOBER
Third week *Festival du Théâtre* in Bayonne.
Last weekend Party, then Mass, in honour of red peppers at Espelette.

DECEMBER
17 *Fiesta de Santo Tomás* – folkloric fun in San Sebastián.
26–27 *Fiesta de San Estéban* at Yesa.

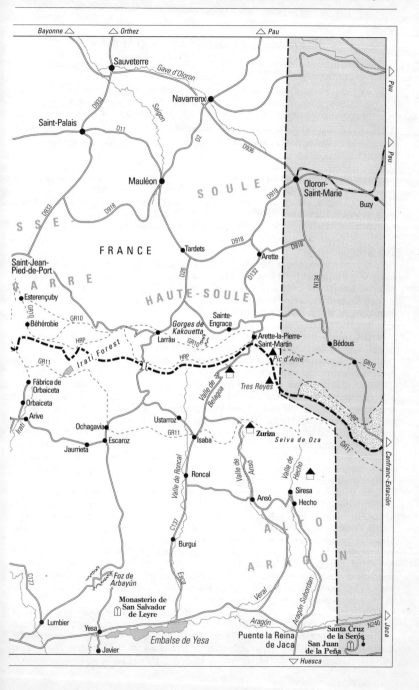

ACCOMMODATION PRICE CODES

Each place to stay in this book has been given a code which corresponds to one of the following price categories.

① Under 2500ptas/under 100F   ② 2500–3500ptas/100–140F
③ 3500–5000ptas/140–200F   ④ 5000–7000ptas/200–260F
⑤ 7000–10,000ptas/260–340F   ⑥ 10,000ptas/340F and upwards

Category ① refers to the price *per person* of a bed; the other categories correspond to the **cheapest available double room in high season**. For more details, see pp.34 & 37.

---

you're coming from Jaca you can take a bus up into the Hecho and Ansó valleys, hike west to the Roncal valley and then over its head to French attractions, like the Kakouetta gorges. Returning to Roncal or the Salazar valley enables you to catch a bus back towards Pamplona, from where you could head straight out to the coast of Gipuzkoa, or inland towards Saint-Jean-Pied-de-Port, served by French trains.

The Basques

No one knows much about the origin of **the Basques**. They are a distinct people, generally with a different build from the French or Spanish and a different blood group distribution from the rest of Europe. Certainly their **language**, the complex *Euskera* (often spelled *Euskara*), is one of the most ancient spoken in Europe, predating the migrations from the east which brought the Indo-European languages some three thousand years ago. It is now considered to be as ancient as the Basque race itself, and to be distantly related – if at all – to certain tongues of the Caucasus. Establishing certainties has been complicated by the fact that, except for one mixed Latin-Basque manuscript of the tenth century, no written examples of *Euskera* survive from before the fifteenth century. The spoken language has largely been maintained and has even evolved through the oral traditions of *bertsolariak*, or popular poets, specializing in improvised verse, a tradition still alive today. The vocabulary itself implies a way of life and belief dating back to long before the Christian era, as reflected in terms referring to ancient sites such as dolmens and cromlechs. Further evidence is an extensive Basque mythology relating to *gentiles*, the legendary giants supposedly responsible for building these sites, as well as ancient ways and bridges. Yet crucial though it has been for defining Basque identity, *Euskera* is nowadays a minority language in the region, spoken – mostly along the coastal strip – by just five hundred thousand people, roughly twenty percent of the total Basque population in France and Spain.

Some think that the Basques are the direct descendants of Europe's **aboriginal** population, a theory borne out by archeological finds earlier this century. Skull fragments of late Cro-Magnon man believed to date from around 9000 BC have been shown to be nearly identical to present-day Basque cranial formation. Much anthropological work, above all by the revered Joxe Miguel Barandiaran (who died in December 1991, aged 101), suggests that the Basques have continuously inhabited the western Pyrenees and its coastal plain, largely in isolation, for thousands of years. Indeed, in early history they had little contact with the peoples who later migrated into Europe, surrounded as they were by impenetrable mountains and considered to be mere barbarians by every invader from the Phoenicians and Romans onwards.

There are strong dialectal differences in usage, spelling and pronunciation throughout the **seven Basque regions** (four in Spain, three in France). It's worth learning to recognize the Basques' term for themselves – *Euskaldunak*, sometimes *Euskualdunak* – and their homeland, referred to as *Euskadi* or *Euzkadi* in Spain alone but more generally as *Euskal Herri(a)*. In Spain, the more or less homogeneous autonomous regions of Gipuzkoa and Bizkaia on the coast account for the bulk of *Euskera*-speakers; Alaba (Araba) and Navarra (Nafarroa), with a long history of adherence to a unitary Spanish state, experienced – until a recent, conscious revival – a steady decrease in the proportion of *Euskera*-speakers, to as little as ten percent. The weakening of *Euskera*'s hold was accelerated following the rapid industrialization of Bizkaia and Gipuzkoa during the nineteenth century and the resultant immigration of labour from the rest of Spain, a process deliberately accelerated under Franco (see feature on p.444 for more on Franco's regime and Basque nationalism). By 1975 more than fifty percent of the working class of the coastal Spanish Basque regions came from other parts of the country, whereas in Navarra the proportion of people from elsewhere in Spain was just eighteen percent. In recent labour agitation in Gipuzkoa and Bizkaia, an impulse to protect both a rapidly decreasing number of jobs from outsiders and linguistic purity had neatly coincided.

Architecturally, there's a marked difference between the French and Spanish Basque areas. The genuine Basque house – a solid stone structure that often incorporated over-hanging upper storeys – is now scarce, though some can be seen around Saint-Engrâce in Haute-Soule, and in a few other settlements. Today the popular image of the Basque house is of a white building with brown or green half-timbering, but this type of house, originally particular to the Labourd region on the French coast, has spread inland com-paratively recently, and has been adopted in Spain only along parts of the frontier.

The extended **family** – the word for which, *etxe*, is the same as that for "house" – has always been the basic social unit of Basque life, rather than the village. A farmstead or *baserri* was a multifunctional building housing up to four generations, plopped in the middle of its fields or pasturage. A yearning for such a rural idyll probably accounts for the linear, straggled appearance of the smaller Basque hamlets on either side of the border. Property was handed down intact, traditionally from one's paternal aunts, to the oldest son, compelling younger sons to seek their fortunes elsewhere, usually as sea-men or emigrants to the Americas.

Basque food is accepted as Spain's finest, and certainly garners respect even in France; the people here are prodigious eaters, whom you'll encounter seated before

---

BASQUE PLACE-NAMES

Almost everywhere in Gipuzkoa, street and road signs appear nominally in both Basque and Castilian, but the latter rendition is often painted over. Recently, many municipalities have officially chosen to prefer the Basque names and this is reflected on new tourist brochures and maps. **In Navarra** – *Nafarroa* in Euskera – the process is nearly as far advanced, to the occasional annoyance of Castilian-speakers, since only about twenty percent of the population here, mostly in the far northwest on the hilly border with Gipuzkoa, speak Euskera. Local place-names have yet to come into official use in the three French Basque regions of Labourd, Basse-Navarre or Soule.

This book makes the somewhat arbitrary decision to list the Castilian or French name first and then the Euskera rendering immediately afterwards, since international-ly produced and available maps have yet to switch over to strictly Euskera tags, except for the case of Hondarribia.

It is also worth noting a couple of key letter changes which may help to decipher ini-tially confusing words on menus and signs. The Castilian *ch* becomes *tx* (*txipirones* as opposed to *chipirones*) or *ts* (Otsagabia rather than Ochagavía), *v* becomes *b* and *y* becomes *i* (*Bizkaia* as opposed to *Vizcaya*). Above all, Euskera features a proliferation of *k*s, as this letter replaces the Castilian *c* and *qu* (*Gipuzkoa* instead of *Guipúzcoa;* Okendo, not Oquendo), and as *-ak* forms the plural. In France, Euskera names are often disguised with the French *ç* and final *y*; thus Esterençuby rather than Esterenzubi, Baïgorry rather than Baïgorri.

enormous spreads in reasonably priced roadside eateries on the outskirts of towns throughout the region. You'll also come across traditional Basque food in the form of *tapas* in virtually every bar, freshly cooked and always excellent. The tradition of **gastro-nomic societies**, unique to the Basque regions, deserves special mention: first founded in the mid-nineteenth century, they came about originally as socializing places for different craftsmen. Controversy has surrounded them due to the fact that women have traditionally not been allowed to enter (although this is changing); all the cooking is done by men who pay a token membership fee for the facilities. Members prepare elaborate dishes to perfection as a hobby and it can be said that true Basque cookery has largely retreated to these societies. The so-called *Nueva Cocina Vasca* (New Basque Cookery), heavily influenced by French cuisine, is becoming increasingly evident on menus.

THE KARST COUNTRY AND AROUND

Few landscapes in the Pyrenees have quite the same impact as that immediately to the west of Pic d'Anie. Elsewhere in the range there may be more photogenic glaciers, lakes and wildflowers, but nothing so surreal as the **karst** country around **Tres Reyes**, the highest border mountain of the Basque Pyrenees, and the Atlantic flank of **Pic d'Anie**, the westernmost peak of Béarn. Their upper slopes have been rain-carved into fantastic shapes and sluiced clean of every particle of soil; yet the heights are waterless, the Atlantic precipitation vanishing instantly through waist-deep fissures and bowl-shaped *dolines*, eroding the limestone underneath into a Swiss cheese of potholes and horizontal caverns. Between the two summits lies a zone of shattered boulders, where occasional stunted black pines erupt.

Yet the lower elevations where water reappears – sometimes weeks later, courtesy of the numerous subterranean rivers – are of an almost tropical lushness, with dense forest and pastures of brilliant green, with which a few red-tiled barns and light-grey, stone-built villages contrast markedly. These are the valleys of **Hecho** and **Ansó** in westernmost Alto Aragón, **Roncal** in Navarra, **Sainte-Engrâce** in Haute-Soule and the gorges of **Kakouetta** and **Ehujarré** which feed into the Saint-Engrâce.

So far this magnificent landscape is little protected. The French **Parc National des Pyrénées** ends at the border peak of Laraille/Ralla de las Foyas, while the less stringent forestry administration zone beyond only guarantees partial preservation of Pic d'Anie and none at all for the Sainte-Engrâce valley. Navarra has conferred *parque natural* status on the **Larra-Belagoa** area at the head of the Valle de Roncal, but it deserves more — not just to protect the dwindling fauna but to reduce wear and tear on the actual terrain, increasingly popular with Spanish city-dwellers.

The Hecho and Ansó valleys

The **Valle de Hecho** and **Valle de Ansó**, northwest of Jaca, are the most westerly valleys of Alto Aragón and, in their upper reaches, among the most beautiful, watered respectively by the Aragón Subordán and Veral rivers. They intercommunicate with each other over shallow passes between karst summits, with the Haute-Soule region in France to the north and the Valle de Roncal to the west.

Their principal villages – Hecho (833m) and Ansó (860m) – once lived (and grew wealthy) from sheep-raising. These days, timber-cutting has supplanted livestock, but despite their modest altitude on the valley floor and their manifest beauty, seasonal or weekend habitation is now the rule in both villages. Hecho and Ansó are lonely places in winter, as it's considered too arduous to commute daily to jobs in the provincial centres. Indeed until quite recently, both villages felt extremely remote all year round, and

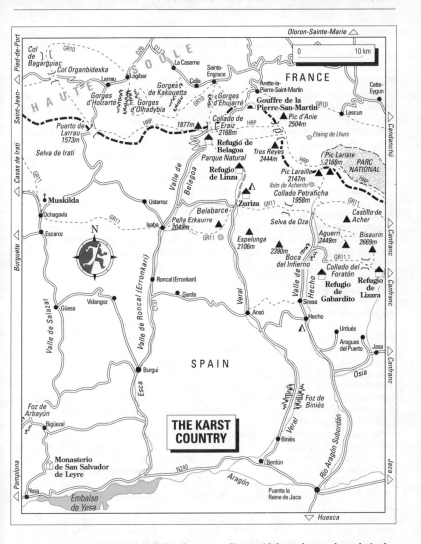

Hecho maintains an Aragonese dialect known as *Cheso*, widely spoken and taught in the school. Another holdover is the presence of the *espantabrujas*, little hoodoo figures perched atop the domed chimneys or over windows; these were believed to repel witches who were in the habit of entering houses through such orifices.

These days, Hecho and Ansó find themselves squarely on the tourist map, a favourite target for Spanish weekenders. However, in each case the local country shows its best side — and only offers anything in the way of walking — some distance upstream from the villages, though the Valle de Hecho makes a more dramatic impression within sight of its village. Developers and planners also have their eyes on the valleys. Now that a long-debated natural-gas pipeline has been shifted to the Salazar valley (see p.404), the big local environmental issue is the proposed enlargement of the Yesa reservoir downstream on the Río Aragon – you'll see (rather bizarrely for English-readers) "YESA NO" graffiti everywhere.

Access

If you don't have your own transport, renting a mountain bike in Jaca would be a good investment for exploring either valley. Otherwise, there is only a single daily **bus service** (Mon–Sat), calling first at Hecho, then Siresa, and finally continuing to Ansó. This currently departs **from Jaca** at 5.30pm, reaching Hecho at 6.30pm and Ansó half an hour later, beginning the return journey the next day at 6am. **From Pamplona** you need to take the 3.30pm bus (summer only; at 6am in winter) to the junction at Puente la Reina de Jaca – which shouldn't be confused with another Puente la Reina, 20km southwest of Pamplona – to connect with the Jaca-based bus.

By bike, reckon on around two and a half hours from Jaca to Hecho village, turning off the C134/N240 at Puente la Reina de Jaca, or much the same to Ansó village, turning off at Berdún, 7km west of Puente la Reina. The latter side road, not served by bus, is particularly spectacular, threading an unnervingly narrow course through the Foz de Biniés carved out by the Río Veral. Trans-Pyrenean trekkers can use the **GR11** to hike into and out of the area, although the trail intersects both valleys considerably above the two villages.

Hecho and Siresa

HECHO (*Echo* in the local dialect; the first "H" is silent in Castilian anyway), larger of the two villages, is a splendid old place, though historically less wealthy than – and resentful of – Ansó. Arcades ring the main double-plaza, which host the outdoor tables of its two bars, while whitewash outlines the windows and doors on some of the massive houses, with occasional peeks inside to pebble-mosaic forecourts. Although it seems ancient, Hecho in its present form is less than two centuries old; it – and Ansó – were burnt to the ground during the Napoleonic wars. Hecho can otherwise lay modest claim to fame in Aragonese history as the seat of an embryonic Aragonese feudal state under Conde Aznar Galindez in the ninth century, and as the birthplace of the "warrior king" Alfonso I.

An annual art festival, the *Simposio de Escultura y Pintura Moderna*, held every summer between 1975 and 1984, left a permanent legacy in an **open-air gallery of sculpture**, on the hillside west of the village. Created by a group of artists led by Pedro Tramullas, the 46 stone or metal pieces are not terribly stunning individually, but the aggregate effect is riveting. Unfortunately, the *simposio* was initially resisted by most of the locals, who have since come to terms with it – but now there are insufficient funds for the festival's resumption.

Near the enormous central church, there's a more conventional museum, the **Museo Etnológico** (Easter, July & Aug 11am–2pm & 6–9pm; otherwise contact the Ayuntamiento; 100ptas), with interesting collections on Pyrenean rural life and folklore.

Practicalities

In summer, or at weekends, reservations at Hecho's **hostales** are virtually mandatory (if your luck runs out, you could try the accommodation around Siresa – see below). Scheduled to open in 1998, the one above the *Restaurante Serbal de Cazadores* (☎974/37 53 35; ④) will be the most modern, with valley views. Another good choice is *Casa Blasquico*, unmarked save for an "Hs" plaque at Plaza de la Fuente 1 (☎974/37 50 07; closed Sept; ③), a wonderful and trusting establishment where locks and keys are dispensed with. Fallbacks are *Casa Chuanet*, above the *Bar Danubio* on Plaza de la

Fuente (☎974/37 50 33; ③); the modern *Lo Foratón* (☎974/37 52 47), at the north end of the village on the road to Siresa, with a somewhat shabby hostal (④) and a better hotel (⑤) with bathtubs and abundant hot water; and the nearby, adequate *Hostal de la Val* (☎974/37 50 28; ④) – ask for a room at the front, overlooking the village. There is also a **campsite**, the *Valle de Hecho* (☎974/37 53 61; year-round), 300m south of the village, which also maintains a 30-bunk *albergue* (①).

By far the most notable **restaurant** in the village is *Restaurante Gaby* (closed Sept), on the ground floor of *Casa Blasquico*. Proprietress Gaby Coarasa is often singled out in the Spanish media as the most creative chef in the Pyrenees, so naturally reservations (☎974/37 50 07; seatings at 1.30 & 8.30pm) for the tiny, six-table *comedor* are compulsory. The à la carte menu has ample choice for vegetarians and fish-eaters – the mushroom pie is ace – though these tend to be the starters; carnivore main dishes, specials and desserts like fig mousse will bump the bill up, with *Dénominación d'Origen* wine, to over 4500ptas per person. If money's tight, ask about the cheaper *menú* (not listed) and stick to the adequate house wine. The *Serbal de Cazadores* is very nearly as good, while the dining rooms at both *Hostal Lo Foratón* and *Hostal de la Val* are popular even if the food is not very elegant.

Best of several **bars** is the nocturnal *Coco's* (no sign), the closest thing to a Madrid-style nightspot with occasional live music; *Acher*, *Danubio* and *Batimala* are more conventional village hangouts, while by day people drink outside at the *Subordan* next to *Casa Blasquico*.

In terms of other facilities, Hecho has three **banks**, the only fuel pump in these hills (but no unleaded), and two **adventure companies**: the local Compañia de Guías (☎974/37 52 18), offering canyoning, rock-climbing, kayaking and nordic skiing, and the British-run walking and trekking outfit Alto Aragón (☎909/409433 in the UK). Oddly, Hecho has no pool; people just swim in a scooped-out area of the river, east of town.

Siresa

Less than two easily walkable kilometres north of Hecho stands another beautiful little village, **SIRESA**. Keeping watch over the riverside pastures is a remarkable ninth-century church, San Pedro (daily 10am–1pm & 4–6pm; free), claimed to be the oldest in Aragón and once the core of a monastery. If you can't find space in Hecho, there's a single **hotel** here, the *Castillo d'Acher* (☎974/37 53 13; ④); this also operates the **fonda** (③), over the village bar, and a reasonable **restaurant**.

If everything's full up or you desire more solitude, the good-value *Hospedería Usón* (☎964/37 53 58; ④), 5km north of Siresa, has enthusiastic young management and good Basque-style food. Immediately across the valley, 3km up the side road to the *Gabardito* refuge, *Camping Borda Bisáltico* (☎974/37 50 98) offers clean facilities and another restaurant.

Walks in the Valle de Hecho

Above Siresa, the **Valle de Hecho** constitutes a tapestry of pasture and beech forest against a backdrop of towering limestone cliffs and summits, harbingers of the karst country at the border. The best **day-walks** east of the valley are the ascents of Bisaurín (2669m), Agüerri (2449m) and Castillo de Acher (2390m), of which the finest is the climb up Agüerri, the summit of the huge bluff that forms the easternmost side of the Boca del Infierno gorge, beginning 7km north of Siresa. The usual starting point is 12km north of Siresa at **Selva de Oza**, whose eponymous campsite is scheduled to re-open in 1998 or 1999. For any outing the best **map** is the Editorial Alpina 1:40,000 "Valles de Ansó-Hecho Belagua-Zuriza", applicable also to all walks discussed up to and including "The Valle de Roncal and the Parque Natural Pirenaico" section, p.397.

Bisaurín and the Osia valley

For **Bisaurín**, make an early start along the variant GR11.1 that climbs east on the southern slopes of the Agüerri valley – this path leaves the main valley 6km north of Hecho, across the Puente de Santa Ana, and shortcuts the twisty, narrow paved road past *Camping Borda Bisáltico* to run high above the Agüerri stream. About an hour from the road, you reach the *Refugio de Gabardito* (8km in by road, 1400m; reservations ☎974/37 53 87; 50 places; open all year; ①), set on a beautiful grassy clearing near treeline – it's a popular nordic skiing centre in winter. From here the path climbs east to the **Collado del Foratón** (2032m; 2hr 30min from the refuge), and then it's a stiff two-hour climb further to the summit, rising steeply to the northeast.

You can also use the approach via the Collado del Foratón as a full-pack traverse route, finishing an hour southeast of the pass at the *Refugio Lizara* (1540m; ☎974/37 14 73; 70 places; open all year; ①), at the top of the **valley of the Río Osia**. This sits at the middle of another major nordic ski area, but in summer you can trek northeast via the Valle de los Sarrios and over **Los Puertos** pass to link up with the main GR11 route at Ibón de Estanes.The GR11.1 continues east from *Lizara* in under a day to Canfranc.

Castillo de Acher and Agüerri

Castillo de Acher and Agüerri can be tackled singly or together in one gruelling day; take plenty of water. Begin along the track that climbs east-southeast from close to the campsite at Selva de Oza; this curves back southwest after crossing the Espata stream and climbs steeply to a simple forestry hut (1740m; 2hr), just beyond which the ways divide. The summit of **Castillo de Acher** — from a distance looking exactly like a castle — now lies a little north of east, along a fairly easy path (4—5hr from Selva de Oza).

For **Agüerri**, take the right-hand path just beyond the refuge, climbing east along the **Borreguil de Achert** stream and crossing after about half an hour onto a new path that doubles back on the other side, rising west to a small saddle. Beyond this, the path swings east again, along the **Jardín** stream; at the head of the valley defined by the Collado de Costatiza, climb south for the summit (5hr 30min from Selva de Oza).

Frontier peaks and Ibón de Acherito

North of Selva de Oza, the frontier peaks of **Punta Cristian/Lariste** (2168m) and **Ralla de las Foyas/Laraille** (2147m) make classic targets, with identical approaches. Continue on the asphalt road north of the campsite, through dense forest, with the Río Aragón Subordan to the left; some 2km above Selva de Oza, the end of the pavement, you cross a bridge on a side track, beyond which the main track veers away to follow the eastward curve of the valley. Once over the Acherito side-stream via another bridge, the track ends at the locale known as **La Mina**. Here there's just a large signboard-map beside a small car park; cows graze all around, with scattered buildings for the use of the herders, plus a derelict refuge. This is the junction with the GR11, descending from the west and continuing up the main valley; it's also the trailhead for the popular day-outing to both the peaks and the **Ibón de Acherito**, second westernmost lake in the Spanish Pyrenees.

Take the path north along the stream and after five minutes turn off onto a new trail, climbing steeply northeast along the Las Foyas tributary until you reach the cirque under the frontier summits (1775m; 2hr). The routes divide here: Punta Cristian is the summit immediately north, climbed directly in another hour or so; Ralla looms to the west, reached by a route of similar duration curving to a point just southeast of the summit, then swinging back for the top. From the summit of either you look down across the idyllic pine forests and fields of the Lescun valley (see p.350) and westwards over the barren karst — an arresting contrast. The well-trodden path northwest to the *ibón* veers west from the Las Foyas route about an hour along; count on three hours maximum return.

West: the GR11

The **GR11** arrives at La Mina from Candanchú in a full day's trek along the upper reaches of the Río Aragón Subordan, a route enlivened by the large Ibón de Estanes some 2hr out, and the squelchy water-meadow of Aguas Tuertas, over halfway along. Camping is allowed at La Mina – and there are rumours of the old refuge here being restored and staffed by 1999 – and you can have a pleasant river bathe just downstream by the end of the asphalt, but as there are no reliable facilities at Selva de Oza for the moment, civilization and its comforts are a long way away, and you must provision accordingly.

A somewhat easier traverse continues west along the same path to Zuriza in the Valle de Ansó (see p.396). From the upper bridge over the Acherito described above, the GR11 climbs steeply west into the **Collado Petraficha** (1958m; 3hr uphill from Selva de Oza), from where it's all downhill along the Petraficha stream, the last hour or so of the five-to-six-hour hiking day on track.

On to Ansó by road or trail

The daily bus from Jaca to Hecho continues west to Ansó along 12km of narrow, twisting road, climbing over the Sierra de Vedao before dropping into the Valle de Ansó. Final approaches to the valley from the east are guarded by two strangely shaped rocks known locally as "the Monk and the Nun", just above a tunnel.

If you wish to walk there, shun the dangerous road in favour of the very enjoyable **PR 18 trail from Siresa to Ansó**, indicated by a sign reading "Fuen d'a Cruz" by the stream below Siresa. This is probably the most useful of the ten or so PR trails marked in the area in 1997; a descriptive booklet is now on sale locally.

Starting on the south side of the bridge, the path is initially waymarked by red arrows and purple paint splodges as well as newer PR blazes. Gaining height quickly, you collide with an unmaintained track at a saddle about 45 minutes along; turning onto this, fifteen minutes later you top out at about 1180m altitude at a T-junction in the track system, where you bear right (north). After another half-hour along the serpentine track, you'll emerge at a pass affording a first view of Ansó village; the track continues north, but you should plunge down left (southwest) on the resurgence of the old *camino*. Passing a ruined farm, continue dropping steeply into the valley running west to the village, zigzagging down to meet the stream bed, on whose right bank you should be some two hours out of Siresa. The path should have been cleaned a bit since its recent marking, so nothing substantial prevents you from reaching the fountain at the eastern outskirts of Ansó about two and a half hours after leaving Siresa. With the exception of the initial climb from Siresa, the route is shown correctly on the Editorial Alpina map; the timings given above are for those with day-packs, not full rucksacks.

Ansó

Once a more prosperous village than Hecho, **ANSÓ** fell upon hard times during the 1950s and 1960s depopulation of rural Aragón. Today, however, there are signs of a small but definite revival, with Jacan or Pamplonan professionals keeping second homes here, plus a growing stream of tourists sampling the village's attractions. It's certainly an attractive weekend base, with a little river-beach below for splashing around in the Río Veral. Without having many specific landmarks, the village outshines its setting, whose scrubby pine cover gives no hint of the splendours awaiting up-valley. The ancient church is extraordinarily rich inside and houses an interesting ecclesiastical, craft and ethnological **museum** (daily 10.30am–1.30pm & 3.30–8pm; 200ptas). In lieu of labelling you're given a plastic-laminated sheet to guide you around the exhibits, which include a video and photographic exhibition of Pyrenean wildlife and rural trades.

Practicalities

Ansó's growing popularity is reflected in five places to **stay**, somewhat less expensive than in Hecho but filling equally quickly in summer. The prominently marked *Posada Magoria* at the north entrance to the village (☎974/37 00 49; ③; reservations suggested) also serves communal vegetarian meals, though preference is given to guests. The owner Enrique himself restored the 150-year-old premises to its original palatial condition; all rooms are unique, though none are en suite. Peruvian-run, and less expensive, *La Posada Veral* at c/Cocorro 6 (☎974/37 01 19; ③) – inevitably more institutional since it's housed in the former old people's home — has, by contrast, a rather pricey restaurant. Near *Posada Magoria*, up on the main road into town, *Hostal Estanes* (☎974/37 01 46 or 43 03 31; ④) offers good-value rooms with and without baths, while the new *Hostal Kimboa* (☎974/37 01 30; ④), 200m along the same street towards Zuriza, is excellent value, with breakfast included in the rates. A final choice, if the above are full, is the wildly eccentric *Hostal Aisa*, centrally located at Plaza Domingo Miral 2 (☎974/37 00 09; ③), a cross between an Aragonese Fawlty Towers and a Victorian orphanage. There's no campsite but tents are tolerated on the grass down by the riverside municipal swimming pool, at the south end of the village; fees are collected by the adjacent restaurant when it crosses their minds.

Besides **restaurants** affiliated with the *hostales*– among which *Kimboa* gets good marks from carnivores – there's only the *Cubilarrola* at the swimming pool. Of the many **bars**, liveliest and friendliest is the spit-and-sawdust *Zuriza* on the main street; the one in the *Posada Veral* occasionally has live gigs. Ansó's two **banks** (no ATMs) round out the list of amenities.

To **leave Ansó** by public transport you have to catch the 6am bus back through Hecho towards Jaca, changing at Puente la Reina for Pamplona. Going west from Ansó, an eighteen-kilometre minor road past the village of Garde eventually joins the C137, which threads the Valle de Roncal, in Navarra. There's no bus service in this direction, and it's 21km in total to Roncal village.

Walking in the Valle de Ansó

Other than the path in from Siresa, the lower Ansó valley has little serious trekking potential; to start walking you really must go to Zuriza, 14km north. There's no bus service, and the paved road up-valley makes for tedious trudging, so try to arrange a lift if you don't have transport. In any event the scenery improves as you head upstream, with the Río Veral constantly beside the road, and the steep valley sides covered with pine, later giving way to beech. Dotted around are small stone-built farmhouses, their owners sometimes wearing cloaks of cured but otherwise untreated animal skins. The mass of **Peña Ezkaurre** (2049m) rises in front, and after 9km you enter the narrow gorge between it and **Espelunga**; there's a chance of seeing rare black vultures here, a species resembling the griffon vulture in outline, but far darker and more solitary.

Eventually the gorge widens onto the luxuriantly green basin that is **Zuriza** (1227m), less forested than the Selva de Oza in Hecho. Most obvious amenity is an enormous meadow **campsite** (*Camping Zuriza*; mid-June to early Sept) with an attached *albergue* (☎974/37 01 96; closed Feb–March; dorm ①, rooms ④), a general store and a decent restaurant. If all is full — a distinct possibility in either summer or winter peak season — you'll find another staffed refuge at **Linza** (Plano de la Casa on the Alpina map), 4km north along the track parallel to the Petrechema stream. Here the friendly, well-run *Refugio de Linza* (1320m; open year-round; 110 places; ☎ & fax 974/37 50 48; ①) is less expensive than *Camping Zuriza* in most respects and rents out nordic skis to those wishing to follow nearby prepared trails.

Tres Reyes ascent

From Plano de la Casa you can make a day-walk to **Tres Reyes**, the karst plateau astride the border with France; carry plenty of water, as there's none above the 1900-metre contour. Start by heading a little north of east along the path to the **Collado de Linza** (1906m; 2hr); from this pass the path heads north a short way then resumes its former trajectory, dropping into the shallow Hoya la Solana and then climbing out to the **Col d'Escoueste** (2114m; 3hr). You're now on the frontier — dramatically delineated by the sharp drop to the French side — and amid unbelievably barren terrain.

Follow the top of the cliffs north, at a suitably respectful distance, into a small *col* that leads to **Tres Reyes summit** (2444m; 4hr); this meeting point of France, Navarra and Aragón is adorned with a bronze statue of St Francis Xavier, the Jesuit evangelist of the Indies. Again the contrast is amazing, between the lush Lescun valley beyond the tarn of Lhurs to the east and the lunar rock and summits to the north and west, notably the pyramid of Pic d'Anie.

West to Isaba on the GR11

Zuriza straddles the **GR11**, with Selva de Oza an easy day away to the east (see p.393); west towards Isaba in the Roncal valley (14km by paved road), the GR11 was rerouted in the early 1990s. Both new and old west-bound itineraries start from the Puerto Navarra at the border between Aragón and Navarra — 700m west of Zuriza, where the difference in public-works funding between the two autonomous regions is made graphically apparent by the respective states of the asphalt.

The **new path** heads spectacularly, if strenuously, southwest up **Peña Ezkaurre/Ezcaurri** (2049m; 2hr 30min), which though not especially high impresses with its profile. Just the other side lies its namesake *ibón*, the westernmost natural tarn in the Spanish Pyrenees. Thereafter the GR11, now in Navarra, descends northwest into the **Berroeta valley**, soon becoming a track along the right bank leading to the confluence of the Berroeta and Belabarze streams. From here another track leads west to Isaba, for a six-hour walking day.

The **old itinerary** due west from Puerto Navarra is shadier and more gently graded, but difficult to find owing to inaccuracies in Spanish maps and the complete deterioration of the old waymarking. In theory it traces the length of the pastoral **Valle de Belabarze**, high up on the beech-swathed southern slopes, descending to the valley floor near the point where the namesake stream forsakes the road to flow directly towards Isaba. From Zuriza you'll need four hours to get there by this route, assuming you don't get lost, but if you are hauling a heavy load in the heat, this is to be preferred to the trans-Eskaurre route.

The Valle de Roncal and the Parque Natural Pirenaico Larra-Belagoa

The **Parque Natural Pirenaico Larra-Belagoa**, which straddles the C137 road connecting Roncal and Arette-la-Pierre-Saint-Martin in France, is the only park in the Spanish Pyrenees in which brown bears are still thought to dwell. Occupying the head of the **Valle de Belagoa**, the *parque* displays a diversity of landscapes ranging from barren karst desert to lush pasture and dense forest. Further downstream, the **Valle de Roncal** — next valley west of Ansó — is famous for the delicious, hard, cylindrical *roncalés* cheese, made from sheep's milk and widely available in the two most important villages of **Roncal** and **Isaba**.

If you're not coming by car or foot from the Ansó valley, the easiest way into the area is the 5pm daily **bus from Pamplona** run by La Tafallesa, which follows the course of the Río Esca up the Valle de Roncal. Foresters used to float logs down the Esca, a score laced together into a raft and then three or four rafts linked and controlled by a pair of huge oars; nowadays the rafts are constructed only for fun.

Roncal and Isaba

Once beyond the lowland villages of Lumbier and Burgui, the bus climbs slowly to **RONCAL** (Erronkari), capital of the valley, where the road crosses to the west bank of the river over a wrought-iron bridge in front of the old arcaded town hall. The churchyard is worth seeing for the flamboyant mausoleum of the great operatic tenor **Julián Gayarre** (1844–90), whose sarcophagus is borne heavenwards by a flight of bronze-sculpted angels.

Although you have slightly more choice in Isaba (see below), it's possible to **stay** in Roncal at either the *Hostal Zaltua* (☎948/89 50 08; ④) or a few *casas rurales*, including *Casa Txarpa* (☎948/47 50 68; ③), *Casa Indiano* (☎948/47 51 22; ③) and *Casa Pepita* (☎948/47 51 33; ③), a large mansion which also provides good **meals** at a reasonable cost.

Isaba
ISABA (Izaba), 7km north of Roncal, is larger and arrayed appealingly around a fortified hilltop church, a massive structure with a rib-vaulted nave and ornate retablo and organ inside. Unlike Roncal it's a major touring centre for the western Pyrenees, regularly descended upon by weekend trippers from the cities, and its homogeneity slightly adulterated by new apartments. Accordingly there are numerous **rooms** available, mostly under the *casas rurales* scheme. Other options include the private youth hostel *Albergue Oxanea* (☎948/89 31 53; 55 places; ①), the central *Hostal Lola*, with no single rooms, east of the through road at Mendigatxa 17 (☎948/89 30 12; ④), and *Pension Txabalkua* (☎948/89 31 01; ③), the last two both offering good **meals**; plus *Pension Txiki* (☎948/89 31 18; ④), above the bar-restaurant of that name on the through road, and the fairly comfortable *Hotel Isaba* (☎948/89 30 00, fax 89 30 30; ⑥). The **campsite**, *Asolaze* (☎948/89 31 68), sprawls at the edge of the *parque natural*, 6km up the C137 road towards the frontier.

The Valle de Belagoa

In summer, the evening bus from Pamplona continues the 18km to the comfortable **Refugio de Belagoa** (1428m; 140 places; ☎948/22 43 24 or 22 07 75; open year-round; ①), well inside the Parque Natural Pirenaico Larra-Belagoa, and you might make this, rather than Isaba, your base if you want to explore the mountains. (There is also an 8am bus up to the refuge from Isaba.) **Meals** are provided at the bar-restaurant, but you should bring at least some of your own food if you intend to stay several days. Otherwise, at the base of the switchbacks leading up to the refuge, the *Venta de Juan Pito* rates as one of the most pleasant surprises in the Valle de Belagoa, a traditional **inn** (*venta* in Spanish) serving hearty meals – including locally concocted milk-based desserts – for about 2300ptas.

The road enters the park along the Río Belagoa, flanked by forests of beech and silver fir, until the terrain opens out into flat fields and the road climbs in tight hairpins to the refuge. Standing between the road and the edge of a rock shelf, it looks out over the lower valley and, in the distance to the east, the uncompromising contours of Tres Reyes and the Pic d'Anie. The refuge provides an alternate starting-point for their ascent (see below), and serves both the GR12 – *El Sendero de Euskal Herria*, which

---

THE TRIBUTO DE LAS TRES VACAS

Beyond the *Refugio de Belagoa* the road climbs on up to the border, crossing close to the frontier cairn which has replaced the original marker of La Pedra de San Martin/Pierre-Saint-Martin. Here, every July 13, the people of the Roncal valley and the French Vallée de Barétous celebrate the **Tributo de las Tres Vacas**, a ceremony stemming from a 1375 treaty on grazing rights, the oldest of several such agreements still extant. Four representatives of Roncal, dressed in white shirts, black capes and black hats, join hands with four representatives of Barétous, whose only concession to folklore is sashes in the French national colours. With their hands linked on modern frontier cairn no. 262, they chant "Pax avant, pax avant, pax avant" while three identical blonde heifers (*las tres vacas*) are handed over to the Roncalese as tribute, securing the right of the French herdsmen to graze their charges in the Spanish valley for another year. A huge and disparate crowd of itinerant food-and-drink vendors, French gendarmes, Spanish forestry wardens, journalists, tourists and locals always turns up, even if it's raining, mainly to take part in the *fiesta* that's launched afterwards.

---

traces the Cantabrian/Mediterranean watershed throughout the Spanish Basque country – and the nearby French GR10, as well as the HRP.

Walking in the Parque Natural

The best way of seeing the eastern side of the park – where all the karst formations are – involves taking the **HRP variante** which links the *Refugio de Belagoa* with Lescun in France via the Collado de Insolo, also known as the Portillo de Lescun or Col d'Anaye. Don't confuse this pass with the Col des Anies, which is on the north side of Pic d'Anie, well in French territory – Insolo/d'Anaye is on the frontier, to the south – but you can return via the Col des Anies to make a **circuit**. Take water with you – any rain instantly disappears into the karst fissures – and in deteriorating weather, turn back. Navigating through karst badlands, which form natural mazes, is hopeless when visibility is bad – not to mention the possibility of disappearing down one of the dozens of caves and extremely deep sinkholes which pepper the terrain – and even in the finest weather you must have a compass and the recommended Editorial Alpina map.

From the refuge, the path tends slightly south of east, first making its way across pasture and then through beech forest, before arriving in the eerily beautiful Larra region, distinguished by bone-white rock and trees stunted by altitude and lack of soil. Yellow paint splodges then guide you through the boulders, until the **Collado de Insolo** (2052m) is reached in about another two and a half hours.

An ascent of Tres Reyes fills another memorable day out from the refuge. The route lies a little south of the HRP, initially close to the cliff-edge of the shelf on which the refuge stands. After climbing over **Lapazarra** (1777m; 1hr 20min), the path heads east through the Collado Larreria. This is again typical Larra scenery, littered with boulders and dotted with bonsai-sized trees in patterns so repetitious that it's easy to get lost. In autumn the landscape is brightened somewhat by the turning foliage of scattered deciduous specimens.

From Larra you continue up to the frontier ridge at the Col d'Ourtets (2182m), next turning south-southeast along it for the **Tres Reyes summit** (3hr 20min). At this altitude the karst seems more like the landscape of Sinai than the Pyrenees, but the views from the top emphasize the paradoxes of the area, where high-mountain desert is fringed by lower pasture and forest – so lush precisely because all the available water percolates down through the karst, emerging in quantity below the 1500-metre contour.

Pierre-Saint-Martin

Just on the Spanish side of the frontier despite the French name, close to the C137 road, yawns the entrance – now grilled over – of the **Gouffre de la Pierre-Saint-Martin**, among the largest underground caverns in the world. It was discovered by chance in 1950, when, on the last disconsolate night of an apparently unsuccessful expedition, a stone was thrown into an opening and clattered audibly down into a pit. In 1953, the year that Everest was conquered, speleologists reached the bottom of the cavern, at 734m the deepest anyone had ever been in a cave system. Norbert Casteret described the pioneering descent thus:

> *I came face to face with an atmospheric phenomenon which had often been observed from below during the last few days, and into which I now vanished. It was a patch of fog, a subterranean cloud, which appears at certain hours, on certain days, as a result of peculiar meteorological disturbances. The pot-hole consists of an immense vertical shaft, followed by a series of colossal chambers through which flows an icy torrent. Naturally, therefore, it possesses its own special climate, with regular changes of temperature, air currents and condensation which sometimes falls as rain or, as today, is suspended in the form of clouds. The narrow opening on the surface alternately sucks in and expels a powerful draught which causes a dull moaning sound, as it were of some great organ.*

The vertical entrance shaft of 346m remains the longest known, and its largest chamber, the *Sala de la Verna*, is an incredible 270m by 230m by 180m. Using higher entrances, subsequent expeditions during 1982 measured a total depth of 1342m and explored an overall length of interconnecting passages exceeding 50km – the second largest cave system in the world after the Jean Bernad cavern of the French Alps.

If you fancy caving in this area – including *Sala de la Verna*, which is now pierced by an electricity company tunnel – contact Aventures Nouvelles at 15 allée des Myrtilles, Arette-la-Pierre-Saint-Martin.

Skiing: Arette-la-Pierre-Saint-Martin

Some 10km beyond the *Refugio de Belagoa* and 3km into French territory from the border, **ARETTE-LA-PIERRE-SAINT-MARTIN** is a modern ski resort. In summer the main thing that counts in its favour is the presence of two convenient *gîtes d'étape* for anyone following the **GR10** between Lescun and Sainte-Engrâce (☎05.59.66.14.46 and ☎05.59.66.14.68; both ①). The Atlantic influences generally mean good snow, although the top lift is only 2140m. Of the 24 pistes, none is black and only nine are red, so it's essentially a beginner-to-intermediate resort. Nordic skiing is offered at **Boucle de Bracca**, 1km northeast, and **Issarbe**, 5km northwest.

Gorges of the Haute-Soule

Four gorges, south of the D113/D26 route linking Arette-la-Pierre-Saint-Martin in the east and Larrau in the west, are the principal reasons outsiders come to the **Haute-Soule**, easternmost and remotest corner of the French Pays Basque. Here, endless green pastures and beech groves stretch under an open, vulture-haunted sky; there are far more sheep than people about, few tourist facilities and no villages to speak of except Larrau and Sainte-Engrâce.

The superlative-laden **Gorges de Kakouetta** are the best of the managed gorges in the Pyrenees, but if you prefer a completely uncommercialized chasm, the adjacent **Gorges d'Ehujarré** constitutes a milder alternative. However, both are somewhat difficult to reach without your own vehicle, as there's no public transport on the French side, and the village of Sainte-Engrâce – at the mouth of Ehujarré – lies four hours' walk northwest of Arette-la-Pierre-Saint-Martin, along the GR10 or its *variantes*. The best way of visiting both is from the *Belagoa* refuge, trekking down the Ehujarré to Sainte-Engrâce and then up alongside the Kakouetta.

The other pair of great gorges, 18km west of Kakouetta by road, are the interconnecting **Holzarté** and **Olhadybia (Holhadubi)**, crossed at their junction by a long, terrifying and absolutely unmissable – though very touristed – suspension footbridge. By the serpentining GR10, these lie six to seven hours west of Sainte-Engrâce, with Larrau another hour or so beyond.

A walking tour of the gorges

Head up the C137 road from the *Refugio de Belagoa* for a couple of kilometres until the ridge from the summit of Lakhoura – the 1877-metre peak immediately north of the refuge – subsides at the **Collado de Eraiz**. A *variante* of the HRP goes north through this pass onto a sort of plateau above the end of the **Gorges d'Ehujarré**, where you quit the HRP and drop into the canyon. Palisades rise as high as 400m above you, but it's not a difficult walk, and this route has been used for decades for the movement of sheep from the Sainte-Engrâce valley onto the pastures around Pic Lakhoura.

Three to four hours from the refuge you emerge at the hamlet of Senta, one of three comprising the *commune* of **SAINTE-ENGRÂCE** (Urdaite, Santa Grazi). Until 1987 this was locally characterized as *le bout du monde*, "the end of the world", approachable by road only from the west and arguably the remotest spot in the French Basque country. The extension of the D113 road east to Arette-la-Pierre-Saint-Martin was supposed to change that, but despite increasing traffic the Sainte-Engrâce valley has managed to retain its rural somnolence, still surrounded by hay meadows and losing its young to the big cities.

The Sainte-Engrâce hamlets

SENTA has a combination **campsite/gîte d'étape**, *Auberge Elichalt* (☎05.59.28.61.63; ④), which serves light meals. This is found opposite the church, an exceptionally original example of twelfth-century Romanesque architecture, virtually the logo of the western Pyrenees. It's an engagingly asymmetrical structure, with a sloping-roofed belfry, a lean-to style nave and a graveyard containing some typically Basque disc-crowned headstones, much in evidence as you move further west. The interior offers graphically carved column capitals near the altar, some gaudily painted in the 1880s; look carefully and you'll find the *Adoration of the Magi*, lions devouring Christians, plus Solomon and the Queen of Sheba apparently copulating. Below this stands a rather Hindu-looking statuette of St Catherine, while grimacing owls' heads peer from the base of some columns. Beside the church, a map-placard outlines a six-to-seven-hour loop route – up the east bank of the gorge, then down its bed – for the benefit of day-trippers based here.

The middle hamlet of **CALLA** lies about 1500m downstream from Senta, where the *Hôtel Relais de la Pierre-Saint-Martin* (☎05.59.28.63.12; ③) has unfortunately become rather rude in its monopoly. The northwesternmost settlement is **LA CASERNE**, 4km beyond Calla, where there's a friendly **campsite** (*Camping Ibarra*; Easter–Oct; ☎05.59.28.73.59) on the riverbank and the only **food shop** in the valley, opposite the *Mairie*.

The Gorges de Kakouetta

The entrance to the **Gorges de Kakouetta** (March 15–Nov 15 daily 8am–dusk; 20F) lies between Calla and La Caserne. Though Kakouetta is squarely on the tourist trail, don't be put off – the gorge is genuinely dramatic and, outside high summer, not at all crowded. Its interior is essentially temperate rainforest, the air heavy with mist produced by dozens of seeps and tiny waterfalls, pampering tenacious ferns, moss and other greenery, all of which drapes vertical walls rising up to 300m high and seldom split more than 5m apart. For an organized attraction the going is often hard – sometimes along a boardwalk with a safety cable, sometimes on a narrow, slippery path right in the gorge bottom, with the stream almost lapping over your feet; come in good boots, not flip-flops. The graded path ends about an hour along at a picnic area and cave, next to which pours a twenty-metre waterfall, the accumulated percolation of a winter's precipitation through the karst strata overhead. Unfortunately it is not possible to continue up the gorge and make a circuit back to Belagoa – you'll have to retrace your steps and hike up along its edge, making for a very long nine-to-ten-hour day.

Gorges d'Olhadybia, Holzarté and Larrau

From the entrance of the Kakouetta to the entrance of the Holzarté is about four hours' walk by a new *variante* of the GR10, traced in 1993 when the Pont d'Olhadybia (see below) was temporarily washed out. But if possible it's really preferable to make a full day of it along the original **GR10** which leaves the D113 just west of the Kakouetta entrance. From there it climbs gradually southwest into the **Col d'Anhaou** (3hr), shortly after which it begins to curve northwards, almost level, towards the **Gorges d'Olhadybia (Olhadubi)**.

Owing to the steepness of the terrain, the GR handles the final approach in a giant S-bend which drops to the head of the gorge at the **Pont d'Olhadybia** (5hr). It then continues above the west bank for another hour until the intimidating Himalayan-style suspension bridge **Passerelle d'Olhadybia**, which crosses the mouth of the Olhadybia where it meets the **Gorges d'Holzarté**, swinging over a drop of 180m. Rebuilt in 1920, the bridge was originally constructed before World War I by an Italian miner to facilitate getting out of the woods to lunch hour at Logibar. Penetrating the Holzarté is for experts only – it was first achieved in 1933 and hasn't been done on more than a score of occasions since.

Once over the bridge, continue north on the corniche path along the cliff forming the east bank of the joint gorges; it's very sharply graded towards the end, with a safety cable, but within an hour you'll reach the gorge parking lot at **LOGIBAR,** where there's a good *gîte d'étape* (☎05.59.28.61.14, fax 05.59.28.61.14; ①) with reasonable meal service.

If there's no room here, leave the GR and follow the D26 road west for 2.5km to the village of **LARRAU** (Larraiñe), where the stucco walls and grey-slate roofs of the houses contrast with the green shoulder of land on which they stand. There are two friendly and simple **hotels** – the recommended *Etchémaïté* (☎05.59.28.61.45; ③; closed late Jan, plus Sun & Mon in low season), just below the through road, with an outstanding restaurant, and the *Despouey* (☎05.59.28.60.82; closed Nov–Feb; ③) on the road itself – as well as a campsite (*Ixtila*) and a good bakery.

South of Larrau the D26 road climbs to the frontier at the **Port de Larrau** (1573m), just under **Orhy/Orhi**, the first peak over 2000m as you head east from the Atlantic; on the other side the Spanish C127 drops down to Ochagavía, 33km away (see overleaf).

THE IRATI FOREST AND THE ROUTE SOUTH

Straddling the frontier between the Port de Larrau on the east and the Puero de Ibañeta on the west, the **Forêt d'Iraty/Selva de Irati** is claimed by some as the largest broadleaf forest on the continent – even if they're mistaken, it's certainly the most extensive one in the Pyrenees. The legions of trees, principally beech but interspersed with oak, fir and ancient yew, have long been exploited by boatyards on the nearby Atlantic, as beech especially makes excellent oars. Overcutting was a concern as long as three centuries ago, but only recently have systematic reforestation and controlled logging been undertaken – thus much of what you see is actually second-growth forest, if none the less attractive for that. Amazingly, none of this region yet benefits from any official protection.

Beginning from the north, a one-to-two-day traverse samples the best parts of the forest en route to attractive **Ochagavía** village at the head of the Valle de Salazar in Spain. From there it's an easy matter to follow it down towards Pamplona, perhaps pausing en route – easiest with your own transport – to sample the **Foz de Arbayún** natural reserve and the imposing **monastery of Leyre**.

Access to Iraty: The Col de Organbidexka

From the north, the Forêt d'Iraty can be reached conveniently from the **Col d'Organbidexka** (1284m), 10km west of Larrau along a minor but paved road. Between August and October the *col* is the site of amazing bird migrations, well attended by hunters and bird-watchers alike. On the pass itself rows and rows of watchers stand by tripod-mounted telescopes, while in the surrounding uplands a line of square hunting hides bristles with shotguns. During this period, millions of woodpigeons, thousands of honey buzzards, kites and cranes, and hundreds of white storks pass over the Pyrenees, the majority over the low western part of the range, and most of those through Organbidexka.

The hunters, tending more to be well-heeled city-dwellers in full "battle dress" than locals, are particularly interested in the tasty *palombes* or pigeons, with an estimated third of the annual four-million-strong flocks falling to their fire during the second half of October. Occasionally there are altercations between the gun-toters and various conservation-group members, which look set to continue since the EU will not promulgate uniform regulations against the mass slaughter of migratory birds.

At or near the **Col de Bagarguiac**, 500m northwest of the shooting-and-watching grounds, there are several places at the fringe of the forest to **stay** and **eat**: either *Les Chalets d'Iraty* (☎05.59.28.51.29, fax 05.59.28.73.28; ⑤), thirty or so wooden bungalows, which you can rent for a weekend or more; an adjacent restaurant, *Chez Jackques*; a campsite 2km west; and – 2km south along the D18, and also on the GR10 – the somewhat more elegant and well-signposted *Chalet Pedro* (weekends only Nov–April), offering such delicacies as wild trout, roast pigeon and eel.

Without your own transport, the easiest way of reaching Organbidexka/Bagarguiac is along the **old GR10** from Larrau, now a *variante*, taking three and a half hours, mostly tangled with the road. The **new routing** from Logibar is more attractive but longer at over five hours, a ridge-walk which curls around north along the thousand-metre contour before climbing slightly to Col de Bargagui.

Walking in the forest

There's enough walking here to occupy several days, but if you're in a hurry, one way to sample all the landscapes of the region is to **traverse** the forest from north to south, a two-day itinerary involving a stay at the *Casas de Irati* on the **GR11**, finishing up in Ochagavía at the head of the Valle de Salazar. With an early start, and plenty of stamina, you could make it to Ochagavía in one long day.

From Col Bagarguiac follow the road (and GR10) west as far as the **Plateau d'Iraty**, a rare flat area with a small lake and snack bar. Bear south here onto the D18 and keep going for about twenty minutes, ignoring a right turn to Esterençubi, to the *Chalet Pedro*. If you have time to spare, the summit of **Occabé** (1456m; *Okabe* in Euskera) is an easy ascent due west along the wide and clear GR10/HRP (90min from the plateau). The bare, flat top is decorated by an Iron Age cromlech (circle of low standing stones), possibly linked with contemporary graves discovered adjacent, and gives views all over the forest and the Sierra de Abodi to the south.

Back at *Chalet Pedro*, the paved road continues south for 2.5km and then becomes track. Another diversion is offered here by a path to the east, which crosses the **Pont d'Orgaté** and climbs via the Ourdanitzarreta shepherds' shelters to the summit of **Bizkarze** (1656m; 2hr 30min from the plateau), an even prettier excursion than to Occabé.

Otherwise, keep on the track along the River Iratiko Erreka (which later becomes the Spanish Río Irati), crossing the frontier after 1km. An hour after that, you reach the tiny white-painted **Ermita de Nuestra Señora de las Nieves** (where there's a religious procession on the Sunday before Aug 15) and the nearby huts of the **Casas de Irati** (880m): here there is a **refuge** (currently unstaffed) serving the GR11 and an informal camping area.

If you spend the night, you'll have sufficient daylight left to take a stroll a couple of kilometres westwards along the GR11 track to the Irabia reservoir: although there's a power dynamo at the far end, the arrangement of water, mountain and dense forest right down to the shore is eminently satisfying. The main disappointment of the forest country is that you see little wildlife, though when the mist licks around the tree-trunks you might mistake it for a *lamin*, the Basque leprechaun that is always blamed when something goes inexplicably wrong.

From *Casas de Irati*, Ochagavía lies more or less due south. The GR11 climbs sharply over the **Sierra de Abodi** via Harrizabla summit (1496m), with fantastic views over the forest and peaks, and then more gently down to the village – a four-hour march at a minimum, so not something to be attempted from the French side without an early start. Moreover, waymarking for the first hour of the route is ambiguous, so you will certainly lose some time in getting lost. *Casas de Irati* is also served by a 23-kilometre paved road in from Ochagavía, and since the *ermita* is a favourite picnic area there's some chance of a lift in peak season.

The Valle de Salazar

The **Valle de Salazar (Saraitzu)** isn't particularly spectacular but it does possess a gentle beauty, albeit one diminished somewhat by the presence of a gas pipeline, diverted here by local bigwigs from its intended route through the Valle de Hecho. The main events are very much at either end: the handsome village of **Ochagavía** near the top, and the natural reserve of **Foz de Arbayún** and the **monastery of Leyre** at the bottom. Of particular interest for anyone emerging from the Selva de Irati is the valley's daily bus service, the quickest way to Pamplona.

Ochagavía

With its white plastered walls, stone-framed windows and wrought-iron balconies, **OCHAGAVÍA** (Otxagabia, Otsagi) forms one of the showcases of Pyrenean Navarra; like Hecho and Ansó it was largely rebuilt after being sacked and burnt by the French in 1794, with pebble-mosaic entry-ways for the grander houses. The river dividing the town is crossed by a series of low bridges, and cobbled streets meander off from either streamside esplanade; to the west, on a slight rise, stands a church nearly as massive – but more graceful – than that at Isaba.

On a low hill to the north, the **Ermita de Muskilda** is much older than Nuestra Señora de las Nieves, built in stone with a multilobed entrance and a curious square half-timbered tower topped by an overhanging circular roof; every September 8 the festival of the Birth of the Virgin is celebrated by a well-attended *romería* (procession) and followed by dancing in traditional costume.

The three conventional places to **stay**, all on the east bank, are the somewhat over-priced *Hostal Auñamendi*, Plaza Gurpide 1 (☎948/89 01 89; ④), with a decent, if pricey restaurant; the good-value *Hostal Orialde*, c/Urrutia 6 (☎948/89 00 27; ②), with fine antique decor in the common areas; and, quietest of all, *Hostal Laspalas*, c/Urrutia 49 (☎948/89 00 15; ④), also home to an innovative but reasonable gourmet **restaurant**, with such goodies as carrot soup, salmon *en papillote* and decadent sweets. Additionally there are nearly a dozen **casas rurales** (③) distributed among the fine old stone hous-es; two worth singling out are *Casa Navarro* (☎948/89 03 55) and *Casa Osaba* (☎948/89 00 11), the latter one of the few survivors of the French attack. For further details con-sult the *Guia de Alojamientos: Turismo Rural*, available free of charge from the tourist office in Pamplona. If you've come from France, three **banks** (with ATMs) will be your first sight of Spanish money.

At Ochagavía the minor road from *Casas de Irati* meets the more important one com-ing from the Port de Larrau and Isaba. The **GR11** also connects Ochagavía with Isaba via the Sierra de Atuzkarratz, on a mixture of old *camino* and forest track; the altitude difference is a slight 400m, and the traverse takes under six hours in either direction, but there's no reliable water en route.

The Pamplona-based **bus**, run by La Salacenca, arrives at about 7pm, leaving the vil-lage next day at 7am (Mon–Sat); the journey takes two hours.

The Foz de Arbayún

The only really remarkable portion of the Valle de Salazar comes near its bottom end at the **Foz de Arbayún (Arbaiun)**, a six-kilometre limestone gorge carved out by the Río Salazar. Dense vegetation thrives in the shade at the base of four-hundred-metre-high cliffs; higher up, raptor nests are concealed between clumps of bushes. This is the finest place in the entire Pyrenees to see **griffon vultures**, the largest colony of Navarra's

GRIFFON VULTURES

Griffon vultures (in Castilian *buitres*, in French *vautours fauve*) occur in several other areas of Spain, but their sole French habitat aside from the Massif Central is the central and western Pyrenees, with the greatest concentrations in the Basque country. In the sky they are fairly unmistakeable, with a span of over 2.5m and fawn leading edges to the wings but almost black trailing edges. Exceeding 1m in length, they seem to have almost no head in flight, as the long, pale neck is tucked back.

Griffons live and hunt in colonies of between four and twelve couples, covering a ter-ritory radiating up to 60km from the nest, which is rarely built at an altitude of over 1100m. Nesting time is generally March to May; when they reach maturity the young birds move on to establish a new territory, perhaps within kilometres but possibly as far away as North Africa.

The vultures eat carrion only, especially dead sheep, which are plentiful in the western Pyrenees. When one of the troupe spots food it descends in spirals, thus attracting the others. The troupe seldom lands immediately but is more likely to keep the carrion under surveillance for one or two days – if the meat is too fresh it will be difficult to penetrate the skin. Once feeding starts a pecking order quite literally prevails, the dominant bird keeping the others back with menacing extensions of the neck, wings and claws; only when it is satisfied does it give way to a subordinate, who in turn gives way, and so on.

Besides the Foz de Arabayún, other reliable places to see griffon vultures include the **Foz de Burgui** in the Roncal valley, **Cumbre de Arangoiti** near the Puerto de Ibañeta and the **Cresta de Iparla** near Saint-Etienne-de-Baïgorry.

several hundred specimens being protected here by a *reserva natural* of 1200 hectares. You can see the gorge from the viewing platform just to the north of the hamlet of Iso; for the intrepid, very steep trails snake down to the river bed.

The Monasterio de San Salvador de Leyre

From the north end of the Foz de Arbayún, 3km above Iso, a narrow road climbs 4km to the hamlet of Bigüezal, from where a track rises to the **Monasterio de San Salvador de Leyre**, 11km from the gorge. With your own sturdy transport this makes a more exciting approach than the steep side-road up from Yesa on the N240 in the Aragón valley.

The monastery (daily 10am–9pm) contrasts vividly with the hermitages back in the mountains, its massive size underlining its former position as both a political and pilgrimage focus of Navarra. After languishing in ruins for over a century, it was restored and reoccupied by Benedictine monks in the 1950s and now glories in an immaculate condition. The leaflet available in English at the porter's lodge sheds useful light on the complicated sculptured facade of the church.

Although the resolutely institutional monastic outbuildings are of sixteenth- to eighteenth-century vintage, the **church** is largely Romanesque with thirteenth-century Gothic additions, its tall, severe apses and asymmetrical belfry particularly impressive. Highlights of a visit include the **west portal**, carved with images of Christ, the Virgin, St Peter, St John and assorted monsters. Inside, the sturdy little columns of the **crypt** are so short that the capitals are at knee height; they can be illuminated by putting a coin in the slot. Try to catch a service if you can; the Benedictine community here employs the Gregorian chant.

The former pilgrims' hospice adjacent is now run as a two-star **hotel**, the *Hospedería de Leyre* (☎948/88 41 00, fax 88 41 37; ⑤; closed Dec–March), and although far more expensive than staying in Yesa (see below), it is still a remarkable bargain, providing **meals** as well. Men can stay at the monastery itself for a nominal fee, but anyone wanting to do this should write or phone ahead. The monastery is still, as it has long been, an important halt on the Aragonese variant of the *Camino de Santiago*, today codified as the GR65.3, last encountered at San Juan de la Peña.

Yesa – and on to Pamplona

A good four-kilometre road drops south from the monastery, down the Sierra de Leyre mountains, to join the N240 in **YESA** (Esa), at the western end of the **Embalse de Yesa**, whose enlargement has long been mooted. Yesa has several **hostales**, the best being *El Jabalí* (☎948/88 40 42; ④) on the main road, with a pool and restaurant. At least one daily bus links Yesa with both Pamplona and Jaca.

PAMPLONA

PAMPLONA (Iruñea, sometimes Iruña) has been the capital of Navarra since the ninth century, and long before that was a powerful fortress town defending the northern approaches to Spain at the foothills of the Pyrenees. Even now it has something of the appearance of a garrison city, with its hefty walls and elaborate pentagonal citadel. However, much of the fortification that made this clifftop fortress on the Río Arga the strongest in northern Spain has been levelled during the past century to make way for urban expansion. Pamplona was designated as a model town during the Francoist era, when new districts with wide boulevards and green belts were amply designed for an

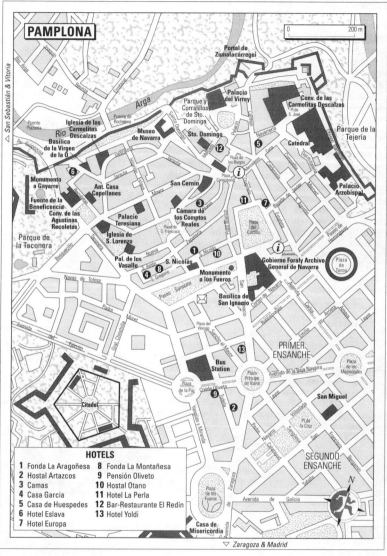

PAMPLONA

0   200 m

Portal de Zumalacárregui

Palacio del Virrey

Conv. de las Carmelitas Descalzas
Pl. de S. José

Parque y Corralillos de Sto. Domingo

Parque de la Tejería

Arga

Iglesia de las Carmelitas Descalzas

Museo de Navarra

Sto. Domingo

12

5

Catedral

Puente de Rochapea

Río

Basílica de la Virgen de la O

Puente Plazaola

Av. Guipúzcoa

Plaza de los Burgos

Plaza Consistorial

Palacio Arzobispal

Monumento a Gayarre

6

Ant. Casa Capellanes

San Cernín

3

11

7

Fuente de la Beneficencia

Conv. de las Agustinas Recoletas

Palacio Teresiana

Cámara de los Comptos Reales

Plaza de San Francisco

Plaza del Castillo

Parque de la Taconera

Iglesia de S. Lorenzo

1

i

Pal. de los Vasallo

S. Nicolás

4 **8**

S. Gregorio

10

S. Nicolás

Monumento a los Fueros

Gobierno Foral y Archivo General de Navarra

i

Plaza de Toros

Navas de Tolosa

Basílica de San Ignacio

Plaza del Vínculo

PRIMER ENSANCHE

Plaza de las Merindades

13

Bus Station

Plaza Príncipe de Viana

Avenida de la Baja Navarra

Plaza de la Paz

Conde Oliveto

9

2

San Miguel

Pl. de la Cruz

SEGUNDO ENSANCHE

Citadel

Plaza de los Fueros

Avenida de Galicia

N

HOTELS

1 Fonda La Aragoñesa
2 Hostal Artazcos
3 Camas
4 Casa García
5 Casa de Huespedes
6 Hotel Eslava
7 Hotel Europa
8 Fonda La Montañesa
9 Pensión Oliveto
10 Hostal Otano
11 Hotel La Perla
12 Bar-Restaurante El Redín
13 Hotel Yoldi

Casa de Misericordia

△ San Sebastián & Vitoria

▽ Zaragoza & Madrid

eventual population of two hundred thousand; thus the effects of the current fierce recession are all the more poignantly visible in the form of boarded-up premises and occasionally unkempt public spaces.

With a long history as capital of an often semi-autonomous state, Pamplona has plenty to offer around its old centre, the *Casco Viejo*: enticing Gothic and Baroque churches, a beautiful park and the massive citadel. It's an enjoyable place to be throughout the

---

SAN FERMÍN - THE FACTS

Accommodation and security

During the *fiesta*, the town's normal accommodation is packed to the gills; you'll need to book well in advance. However, the tourist office opposite the bullring fills with old women willing to let **rooms** for the night at exorbitant prices. If you have no luck, accept that you're going to sleep on the ramparts, in the park or on the plaza (along with hundreds of others), and deposit your luggage at the bus station on c/Conde Oliveto – it's inexpensive (though these lockers fill early in the week too), you can have daily access, and there are also showers here.

Probably the **best plan**, though, is to find a room somewhere else (Vitoria or Estella for instance), leave your luggage there, and arrive in Pamplona by bus, staying as long as you can survive on naps in the park before escaping for some rest and a clean-up. The first few days are best – by the end of the town is getting pretty filthy.

Alternatively, there's a **campsite**, *Ezcaba* (☎948/33 03 15), 7km out of town on the road to France. You have to be there a couple of days before the *fiesta* starts to get a place. Facilities include good toilets and showers but they can't really handle the numbers during San Fermín – be prepared for long queues. The main bonus is that security is tight – admission is by pass only and there's a guard who patrols all night. During the *fiesta* there is another, **free campsite**, by the river just below *Ezcaba*. Security at this is dubious, however. The bus service, which goes to both the campsites, is poor (about 5 a day, first at 9am, last at 1am), but it's easy to hitch or get a lift on one of the tour buses that stay at the official campsite.

Wherever you sleep, keep an eye on everything you have with you – there's a very high rate of **petty crime** during the festival; vehicles are broken into with alarming frequency and people are often robbed as they sleep, occasionally with violence.

El Encierro

To watch the *encierro* it's essential to arrive early (about 6am) – crowds have already formed an hour before it starts. The best **vantage places** are near the starting point around Plaza Santo Domingo or on the wall leading to the bullring. If possible, get a spot on the outer of the two barriers – don't worry when the one in front fills up and blocks your view, as all these people will be moved on by the police before the run. The event divides into two parts: there's the actual running of the bulls, when the object is to run with the bull or whack it with a rolled-up newspaper. It can be difficult to see the bulls amid all the runners but you'll sense the sheer terror and excitement down on the ground; just occasionally this spreads to the watching crowd if a bull manages to breach the wooden safety barriers. Then there's a separate event after the bulls have been through the streets, when bullocks with padded horns are let loose on the crowd in the bullring. If you watch the actual running, you won't be able to get into the bullring (too many people), so go on two separate mornings to see both things. For the bullring you have to arrive at about 6am to get the free lower seats. If you want to pay for a seat higher up, buy from the

---

year, but for anyone who has been here during the thrilling week of the **Fiesta de San Fermín**, a visit at any other time can only be an anticlimax.

San Fermín

From midday on July 6 until midnight on July 14 the city gives itself up entirely to riotous nonstop celebration. The centre of the festivities is the **encierro**, or the **running of the bulls**, which draws tourists from all over the world, but this has become just one aspect of a massive fair replete with bands, parades and dancing in the streets 24 hours a day. You could have a great time here for a week without ever seeing a bull,

ticket office outside, not from the touts inside, who will rip you off. On Sunday you have to pay for any seat.

We advise against it, but if you do decide to **run**, remember that although it's probably less dangerous than it looks, at least two people get seriously injured every year, and that thirteen have been killed since 1924 – the first year statistics were kept. Don't try any heroics; bulls are weighed in tons and have very sharp horns. Don't get trapped hiding in a doorway and don't get between a scared bull and the rest of the pack. Traditionally women don't take part, though more and more are doing so; if you do, it's probably best to avoid any officials, who may try to remove you.

The only official way in is at the starting point, Plaza Santo Domingo, entered via Plaza San Cernin: shortly before the start the rest of the course is cleared, and then at a few minutes before 8am you're allowed to make your way along the course to your own preferred starting point (you should walk the whole course beforehand to get familiar with it). To mark the start, two rockets are fired: one when the bulls are released, a second when they are all out (it's best if these are close together, since the bulls are far less dangerous if they're running as a herd rather than getting scared individually). As soon as the first signal goes you can start to run, though if you do this you'll probably arrive in the ring well before the bulls and be booed for your trouble; if you wait awhile you're more likely to get close to the bulls. Although there are plenty of escape points, these are only for use in emergency – if you try to get out prematurely you'll be shoved back.

Other events

There are plenty of other hazardous things to do in Pamplona, especially once the atmosphere has got the better of a few people's judgement. Many people (chiefly tourists) have fun hurling themselves from the fountain in the centre of town and from surrounding buildings (notably *La Mesillonera* – the mussel bar), hoping their friends will catch them below. Needless to say, several people each year are *not* caught by their drunken pals.

Other events include **music** from local bands nightly from midnight in the bars and at Plaza de Castillo, continuing until about 4am in the fairground on the Avenida de Bayona, where local political groups and other organizations set up stands. There are **fireworks** every evening in the citadel (about 11pm), and a **funfair** on the open ground beside it. Competing **bands** stagger through the streets all day playing to anyone who'll listen. When things calm down a bit you can sunbathe, take a shower, catch up on sleep and even swim at the public **swimming pool** outside the walls below the Portal de Zumalacárregui.

Bullfights take place daily at 6.30pm, with the bulls that ran that morning. Tickets can get expensive, at between 2000ptas and 12,000ptas, and if you have no choice but to buy from the touts, wait until the bullfight has begun, when you can bargain better (the price drops with each successive killing). You can also buy tickets the day before from the ticket office in Plaza de Toros (opens 8am), but be prepared to queue. At the end of the week (midnight, July 14) there's a mournful candlelit procession, the **Pobre De**, at which the festivities are officially wound up for another year.

and even if you are virulently opposed to bullfighting, the *encierro* – in which the animals decisively have the upper hand – is a spectacle not to miss.

Six bulls are released each morning at eight (traditionally it was an hour earlier, so that the festival started on the seventh hour of the seventh day of the seventh month) to run from their corral near the Plaza San Domingo to the bullring. In front of, around and occasionally under them run the hundreds of locals and tourists who are foolish or drunk enough to test their daring against the horns. Hemingway's *The Sun Also Rises* really put "Los San Fermines" on the map, and the area in front of the Plaza de Toros has been renamed Paseo de Hemingway by a grateful municipal council. His description of the week as "a damned fine show" still attracts Americans by the thousands. No outsiders, though, could outdo the locals in their determination to have a good time, and it's an indescribably exhilarating event in which to take part.

Arrival, information and accommodation

Although Pamplona is a sizeable city, the old centre is remarkably compact – nothing you're likely to want to see is more than five minutes from the main Plaza del Castillo. The **train station** is 1500m northwest of the centre on Avda. de San Jorge; bus #9 runs every ten minutes from here to the citadel end of the Paseo de Sarasate, a few minutes' walk from the Plaza del Castillo. There's a handy central RENFE ticket office at c/Estella 8 (Mon–Fri 9.30am–2pm & 4.30–7.30pm, Sat 9.30am–1pm; ☎948/22 72 82). The **bus station** is more central, on c/Conde Oliveto, just at the edge of the citadel to the east. Schedules are confusing, given the number of companies operating from here; check the large timetable posted overhead at the station.

The **tourist office** (summer daily 10am–7pm; winter Mon–Fri 10am–2pm & 4–7pm, Sat 10am–2pm; ☎948/22 07 41) is at c/Duque de Ahumada 3, just off Plaza del Castillo. A municipal **information bus** (June–Sept 10am–2pm & 5–8pm; longer hours at San Fermín), selling an accurate folding map, also parks in Plaza del Castillo over the summer.

Banks are scattered throughout the central area, with much-restricted morning-only hours during the festival – one that also opens in the afternoons (4–6pm) is the Caja de Ahorros de Navarra in c/Roncesvalles, though there are plenty of ATMs. There's a central **post office** at Paseo Sarasate 9 (Mon–Fri 8am–9pm, Sat 9am–7pm). A **laundry** (in case your clothes have borne the brunt of the festivities) can be found at c/de Descalzos, a couple of minutes' walk from the Plaza de San Francisco. If you're headed towards the mountains, fairly sophisticated **trekking gear and supplies** can be had at the bizarrely named Coronel Tapioca, on c/Francisco Bergamín, at the southeast corner of town in the Segundo Ensanche district.

Accommodation

Most of the budget *fondas* and *hostales* are in c/San Nicolás and c/San Gregório, off Plaza del Castillo. Even outside San Fermín, when prices can double or triple, rooms fill up quickly in summer, and it might be easier to accept that you'll have to pay a little more to avoid the hassle of trudging around. If you want to continue looking, the streets around the cathedral, across the Plaza del Castillo, yield other possibilities. Further away from Plaza del Castillo and the old town, there are several *hostales* and *hoteles* in the more modern *ensanches* (extensions) southwest of the central area. All listings following are in the Casco Viejo unless otherwise specified.

Fonda La Aragoñesa, c/San Nicolás 32 (☎948/22 34 28). Reasonable doubles with washbasins. ②.
Hostal Artazcos, c/Tudela 9, 2°, Primer Ensanche (☎948/22 51 64). A well-established *hostal* going back five decades; recently renovated to give all rooms en-suite facilities. ③.
Camas, c/Nueva 24, 1° (☎948/22 78 25). Next to the upmarket *Hotel Maisonnave*; well-furnished doubles and singles. ③.
Casa García, c/San Gregoório 12 (☎948/22 38 93). Double rooms without bath above a restaurant; it's worth considering their reasonable full-board rate. ③.
Casa de Huéspedes Santa Cecilia, c/Navarrarería 17, 1° (☎948/22 22 30). Spacious rooms in a former palace right by the fountain much splashed in during San Fermín. The place looks forbidding with a massive heavy door and grey facade, but the owner is extremely welcoming. ③.
Hotel Eslava, Plaza Virgen de la O 7 (☎948/22 22 70 or 22 51 57). Very cosy and comfortable hotel run by the Eslava family in a quiet corner of the old city – views from balconies overlooking the plaza extend west over the plain beyond. Singles and doubles with all facilities and a bar in the basement. ⑤.

Hotel Europa, c/Espoz y Mina 11 (☎948/22 18 00). Just off Plaza del Castillo before the tourist office; a good 3-star hotel with restaurant of the same repute. ⑥.

Fonda La Montañesa, c/San Gregório 2 (☎948/22 43 80). Doubles and singles; nothing special, but you might be thankful for the room during San Fermín. ③.

Pensión Oliveto, Avda. de Conde Oliveto 3, Primer Ensanche (☎948/24 93 21). Just across the road from the bus station; nice rooms without bath but with satellite TV and plenty of hot water. ④.

Hostal Otano, c/San Nicolás 5 (☎948/22 50 95). Very well-run and popular *hostal* above a bar and restaurant which have been in the same family since 1929. The bar originally served as a watering hole for those working in the cattle yard that once stood on this site. ④.

Hotel La Perla, Plaza del Castillo 1 (☎948/22 77 06). Great character, and a few rooms with balcony overlooking the street (prices triple during San Fermín). Hemingway stayed in Room 217. ⑤.

Bar-Restaurante Redín, c/del Mercado 5 (☎948/22 21 82). Well located in the street by the market and within a stone's throw of the start of the *encierro*. Mostly double rooms with a bar-restaurant downstairs; full board available. ④.

Hotel Yoldi, Avda. de San Ignacio 11, Primer Ensanche (☎948/22 48 00). The hotel where the bull-fighters and VIPs from the *taurino* world stay during San Fermín, when there's no chance of a room. Garage parking. ⑥.

The Town

Founded as Roman *Pompeiopolis* in 77 BC, and later occupied by the Vascones – the ancient Basques – Pamplona's period of illustriousness began in 738 AD, when the Muslims took the place and renamed it *Bambilonah*. Although Pamplona returned to Christian rule ten years later, an understanding reached with the still surrounding Muslims, gave Charlemagne a pretext for a vicious attack on the city in 778. The Basque counter attack came at Roncesvalles, as Charlemagne headed home (see "Roncesvalles", p.417). By 905 Navarra had become a kingdom of which Pamplona was the capital. Its relative tranquillity was threatened in the twelfth century by both Castilla and Aragón, but it was not until 1512 that Navarra was forced to accept integration into Fernando V's unified state – and even then it remained a semi-autonomous kingdom.

Navarra's ancient customary laws – the **fueros**, usually taking the form of numerous written charters granted by a king – instilled a strong sense of independence, but coexisted with the innate conservatism of the rural landowners, which explained Navarra's support for the pretender Don Carlos (1788–1855), brother of King Fernando VII, then recently deceased. The initial defeat of the religious, ultra-traditionalist Carlists in 1841 resulted in the punitive suppression of the Navarran *fueros*, finalized after the second unsuccessful rebellion in 1876. In June 1926, Hemingway witnessed a vast Carlist mob chanting "Viva Christo Rey" in response to a call by Don Jaime, the new pretender to the throne. This enduring Carlist tendency ensured Navarra's support for the Nationalists at the outbreak of the Civil War, while the other Basque provinces stayed loyal to the government; as a reward Franco reinstated most of the Navarran *fueros* after 1939. For better or worse, this gave Navarra a considerable headstart in the scramble for home-rule in post-Franco Spain, with long experience managing some of its own affairs resulting in its autonomous parliament reconvening as early as 1978.

Plaza del Castillo and the cathedral

The **Plaza del Castillo**, a tree-lined square ringed with fashionable cafés, is the centre of Pamplona and much of its activity. The narrow streets of the former *Judería* fill the area to the northeast, towards the city walls by the cathedral – virtually the only trace of a large Jewish community that thrived here before the persecutions, executions and expulsions of the Inquisition. From the opposite side of the square, c/San Nicolás runs down towards the citadel and the most modern area of the city to the west. It's in c/San Nicolás and its continuation, c/San Gregório, that you'll find many inexpensive *hostales* and *fondas,* a number of excellent small restaurants and loads of raucous little bars.

Originally Romanesque, the **Cathedral** is now basically Gothic, rebuilt over a period of 130 years from the late fourteenth to the early sixteenth century, with an unattractive facade added in the eighteenth. It doesn't look promising, but the interior, containing the tomb of Carlos III and Eleanor in the nave, and the ancient *Virgen de los Reyes* above the high altar – before which the kings of Navarra had to swear allegiance to the *fueros* – is fine, and the cloister magnificent. The **Museo Diocesano** (Tues–Sat 9–10.30am & 6–8pm, Sun 9–10.30am; free) is entered via the cloisters and housed in two superb buildings, the refectory and the kitchen – both rather overshadowing the exhibits. Don't miss the many sculpted doorways and side chapels in the **cloister**, particularly the Puerta de la Preciosa, intricately carved with scenes from the life of the Virgin, and the **Barbazán chapel** with stellar vaulting, built by a fourteenth-century bishop to house his own tomb.

La Navarrería and the citadel

Northwest of the cathedral lies one of the oldest parts of the city, an area known as **La Navarrería**. Here you'll find the best section of the remaining **city walls** with the Baluarte de Redín and Portal de Zumalacárregui (or de Francia) looking down over a loop of the Río Arga. If you head out through the gate, paths lead down to the river from where you'll fully appreciate the impregnability of these defences.

Follow the inside of the walls west for 350m and you'll come to the **Museo de Navarra** (Tues–Sat 10am–2pm & 5–7pm, Sun 11am–2pm; 300ptas) in the magnificent sixteenth-century hospital building on c/Santo Domingo. Inside there's a display of material on the archeology and history of the old kingdom of Navarra, along with some good Roman mosaics and an art collection that includes *Portrait of the Marqués de San Adrián* by Goya. Heading back towards Plaza del Castillo via c/Santo Domingo and the Plaza Consistorial you'll pass the **market** and the fine Baroque **Ayuntamiento**, from one of whose balconies the mayor used to announce the opening of the *San Fermines*.

There's much more to be seen along the streets of the old town, with ancient churches and elegant buildings on almost every corner. In particular, have a wander around the parks and gardens that surround and include the semi-ruinous **Citadel**, missing two of its bastions since 1890. From here you can follow the line of the old walls northwest through the **Parque de la Taconera** and down to the river by an alternative route.

Eating and drinking

For **breakfast** in peaceful surroundings and a chance to read the paper, there's no better place than *Café Alt Wien*, known to the locals as *El Vienés*, in the Jardines de la Taconera. The elegant *Café Iruña* on Plaza del Castillo is the place to nurse a leisurely **coffee** and survey the action, or try the more modern yet equally enjoyable *Café Niza* opposite the tourist office on c/Duque de Ahumada.

For good inexpensive *menús*, c/San Nicolás is the best venue; a wide range of bars serving **tapas** and *bocadillos* are scattered to either side of c/Major, in particular c/San Lorenzo.

Restaurants

Alhambra, c/Bergamín 7. Good for local dishes, especially stuffed lamb.

La Campana, c/Campana 12, near San Cernino (Saturnino) church. One of the best *menús* in town.

Casa Otano, c/San Nicolás. Popular *menú del día* at this restaurant which excels in *cocina Navarra*. Closed Sun night.

La Cepa, c/San Lorenzo 2. Wide selection of *tapas* and *bocadillos*.

Deportivo, c/Tafalla 34. Reasonably priced, tasty home cooking. Closed Thurs.

Ibañeta, c/San Nicolás 15. Basically prepared but good-value dishes at this lively restaurant. Closed Sun evening & Mon.

Josexto, Plaza Príncipe de Viana (☎948/22 20 97). One of the best – and priciest – restaurants in town.

Mesón del Caballo Blanco, at the end of c/Redín, by the city walls behind the cathedral. Lots of character at this surprisingly inexpensive restaurant dishing up a good selection of *raciones* and traditional Navarran food (evenings only).

Sarasate, c/San Nicolás 19. Very decent vegetarian restaurant.

ALONG THE CAMINO DE SANTIAGO

An obvious itinerary from Pamplona entails moving northeast along the principal branch of the **Camino de Santiago** into France, via the fabled **Puerto de Ibañeta**. It's a route easily covered by bus, car, mountain bike or – for purists or pilgrims – on foot along the **GR65** long-distance trail. (In the opposite direction out of Pamplona, the *camino* continues southwest a day's journey to Puente la Reina – recently renamed Gares – where it joins the Aragonese variant coming west from Jaca and Leyre.)

Leaving Pamplona, the C135 road follows the Río Arga upstream until Zubiri, at which point it veers east over two ridges to the valley of the Río Urrobi. **Burguete**, a village on a wide plain at the foot of the frontier peaks, is an obvious and comfortable staging-point. A short distance north of Burguete, the abbey of **Roncesvalles** has long been a hallowed stop on the pilgrim route to Santiago de Compostela, and occupies a central location in the legend of **Roland**. The famous ambush of Charlemagne's rearguard, supposedly under Roland's command, took place close by – possibly after the Franks emerged from the thick, gloomy beech forest onto the barren expanse of the Puerto de Ibañeta.

This pass notches the main Pyrenean watershed, but an anomalous finger of Spanish territory encompassing **Valcarlos** protrudes north and down halfway to **Saint-Jean-Pied-de-Port**, touristic mecca of the French Pays Basque since its days as a pilgrimage way-station. From here the *camino* – now paralleled by the modern road and rail line – heads northwest along the valley of the River Nive to the attractive cathedral city of **Bayonne**, with relatively little to compel a stop before then. In doing so the pilgrim route transects the two westerly historic divisions of the French Basque country; after **Soule** it passes through **Basse Navarre** and **Labourd** – respectively *Zuberoa*, *Nafarroa Beherra* and *Lapurdi* in Euskera.

THE CAMINO DE SANTIAGO IN NAVARRA

Following the European Parliament's decision to designate the *camino* as Europe's first "cultural itinerary", Navarra has invested considerably in improving facilities along the route. There are now a total of eleven pilgrims' *hostales* within Navarra which bona fide pilgrims can use – to qualify you must show a letter of introduction from your parish church at home, or the town hall at the place where you plan to start the route (in Spain this is usually Roncesvalles or Somport, or the church of San Cernino (Saturnino) or the archbishop's palace in Pamplona). You'll be given a "passport" as an accredited pilgrim which is then stamped at each *hostal* along the route. Most of the *hostales* have hot showers, some have kitchens and are either free or charge only a nominal 500-peseta fee. A few of the *hostales* may only be open during the summer months, but regional tourist offices in Navarra can provide up-to-date details.

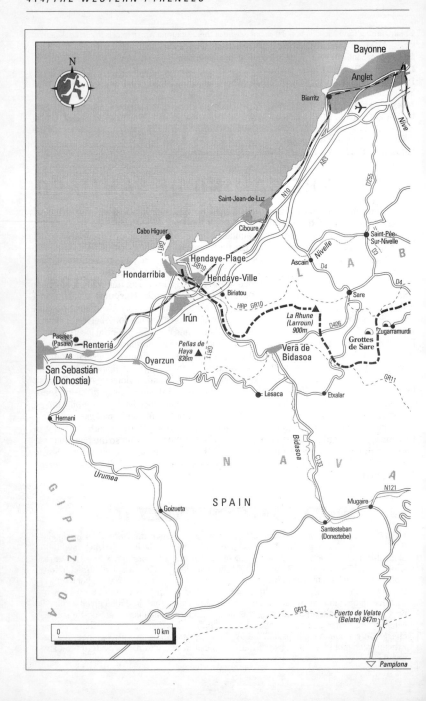

N

Bayonne

Anglet

Biarritz

Nive

A63

N10

D255

Saint-Jean-de-Luz

Cabo Higuer

Ciboure

Saint-Pée-
Sur-Nivelle

Nivelle

L   A   B

Hendaye-Plage

Ascain

D4

D3

GR11

GR10

Hondarribia

Hendaye-Ville

Biriatou

Sare

D4

HRP   GR10

La Rhune
(Larroun)
900m

D406

Irún

Zugarramurdi

Grottes
de Sare

Pasajes
(Pasaia)

Renteriá

Peñas de
Haya
836m

GR11

Vera de
Bidasoa

A8

Oyarzun

San Sebastián
(Donostia)

Lesaca

Etxalar

GR11

Hernani

Bidasoa

Urumea

N   A   V   A

C133

G   I   P   U   Z   K   O   A

Goizueta

SPAIN

Mugaire

N121

Santesteban
(Donoztebe)

GR12

Puerto de Velate
(Belate) 847m

0   10 km

▽ Pamplona

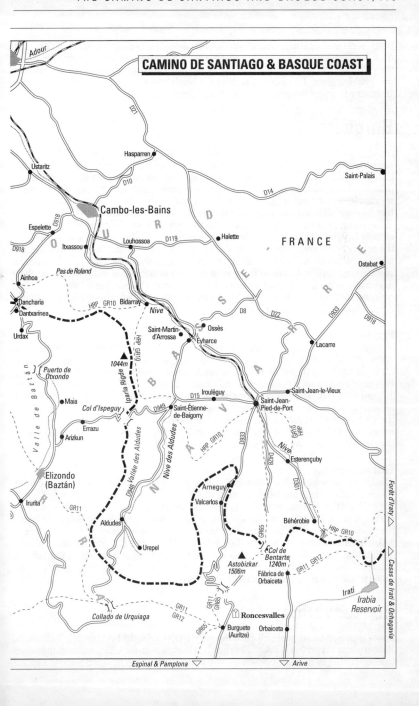

CAMINO DE SANTIAGO & BASQUE COAST

Although not strictly on the *Camino de Santiago*, it's worth considering an alternate route northwest of Pamplona to Saint-Jean-Pied-de-Port, initially along the N121. Once over the Cantabrian watershed, beyond which all rivers flow into the Atlantic rather than the Mediterranean, you're in the **Valle del Baztán**, where **Elizondo** makes a good halting place. From here a minor road heads east via pastoral **Saint-Étienne-de-Baïgorry** to rejoin the pilgrim route at Saint-Jean.

Burguete

Arriving on the La Montañesa bus, you virtually have to stay in **BURGUETE** (Auritze) since the only daily service leaves Pamplona at 6pm and arrives ninety minutes later. This is no great hardship, as the one-street village is a typically pleasant Basque Pyrenean settlement, surrounded by fields, cattle barns and wooded ridges on the horizon. Burguete appears to be not much bigger than in Hemingway's time – he (and his fictional characters Jake and Bill) used to come trout fishing nearby before or after San Fermín.

The GR65, the GR12 and GR11 all pass through here on the same right-of-way just outside Burguete to the west, a somewhat confusing fact when it comes to interpreting the cryptic waymarks of the old GR11 and its *variantes* to the east; the shared GR11 and GR12 in particular trace a very circuitous route north, then east toward Ochagavía, for two walking days with little in the way of facilities or habitation in between. For short day-strolls along streams and through the woods, with Burguete as a base, the rolling countryside immediately east of the village is your best bet. The pertinent Editorial Alpina **map** is "Roncesvalles".

Practicalities

The most comfortable place to **stay** – though usually busy – is the recently renovated *Hotel Loizu* (☎948/76 00 08, fax 79 04 44; ⑤) on the main road. Others include the *Hostal Burguete* (☎948/76 00 05; ③) and *Hostal Juandeaburre* (☎948/76 00 78; ③). Alternatively, Burguete has a handful of *casas rurales*, including *Casa Loigorri* (☎948/76 00 16; ③), *Casa Vergara* (☎948/76 00 44; ③) and the characterful and spotless *Casa Lopirini* (☎948/76 00 68; ③), right above the **bank**, the next-to-last before the frontier. There is also a **campsite**, the *Urrobi* (☎948/76 02 00), 3km south near Espinal (Auritzberri). Food is available at most of these places, and there are two independent **restaurants** as well: *Bar Garate*, inexpensive but rather unwelcoming, or the marginally pricier *Txiki Polit*.

East of Burguete

The afternoon bus from Pamplona first calls in at Roncesvalles (see below) and then continues 10km east past attractive Gerralda to **ARIVE**, an equally appealing little village on the banks of the Río Irati, with a lovely stone bridge. From there a tiny tarmac road heads north along the upper Valle de Aezkoa, becoming track and crossing the GR11 just before the Irabia reservoir. The bus carries on eastwards from Arive, terminating 18km later at **JAURRIETA**, another attractive village with a good deal of half-timbering and a reasonable **fonda**, the *Sario* (③). With your own vehicle, you're just 6km shy of the Valle de Salazar at Escaroz, 2km below Ochagavía, but road-walking there is not suggested – the grade to Escaroz is stiff and the right-of-way narrow.

Roncesvalles

It would indeed be surprising if contemporary **RONCESVALLES** (Orreaga in Euskera, Roncevaux in French), a hamlet 2.5km north of Burguete on the C135, matched the expectations spurred by its semi-legendary history. As you approach from Burguete the impact of its **Collegiata**, an Augustinian abbey founded by Sancho VII el Fuerte (the Strong) of Navarra in 1219, is considerably diminished by the ramshackle associated buildings and sheets of bright zinc roofing. Sancho was one of the heroes of the battle of Las Navas de Tolosa (1212), a decisive defeat for the Almohadan Moors symbolized by the broken chain – which had guarded the Muslim chieftain's tent – in the Navarran coat-of-arms. Sancho's **tomb** lies in a side chapel, topped by a massive 2.25-metre-long effigy of the man, said to be life size.

The best of the architecture is the Gothic cloister, rebuilt after a fire in 1400. In the small **museum** (summer daily and weekends all year 11am–1.30pm & 4–6pm; otherwise by appointment on ☎948/76 00 00), housed in the former chapter-house, an array of religious treasure includes a fragment of the chain from Las Navas de Tolosa, and memorabilia of centuries of pilgrimage to Santiago de Compostela. But the history that interests most tourists is the ambush of Charlemagne's troops in the mountains above, an event here commemorated by a clutch of bogus exhibits, such as a pair of sixteenth-century velvet slippers purported to have belonged to the eighth-century Bishop Turpin, killed in the battle.

Yet the original role of the abbey was as a beacon on the *Camino de Santiago*; after all, its founding – centuries after the battle – was motivated by the need for a strategically placed pilgrims' hospice a day's journey south of Saint-Jean-Pied-de-Port. Had it really been intended as a memorial to Roland, the *collegiata* would have been sited (rather impractically) up on the Puerto de Ibañeta. The tale of the attack merely provided a general endorsement by exemplary defenders of Christianity.

THE LEGEND OF ROLAND

In 778 the Frankish emperor Charlemagne briefly besieged and demolished the fortifications of Pamplona on his way out of Spain, which he had invaded – the only time he ever crossed the Pyrenees – to assist one faction during an outbreak of inter-Moorish strife. He was continuing homeward, laden with booty from various other raids in the Ebro valley, when on August 15, 778, the rear of his army was ambushed somewhere in the area of the Puerto de Ibañeta, by Basques determined to avenge the attack on Pamplona.

The episode hasn't much historical significance, but it achieved international prominence through the myth of Roland, supposedly the greatest of Charlemagne's paladins, who is said to have commanded the rearguard and been killed in the battle. The precise source of the Roland tale is impossible to determine, but its distant origins lie in knightly ballads that were popular at the time of the battle. By the ninth century, *cantilènes* (chanted stories) were being told throughout the Ariège and Andorra about this brave companion of Charlemagne's. He was held up as an example of bravery to the Norman battalions at the Battle of Hastings, and the legend worked its way around Europe to Germany and Italy. But it was during the twelfth century that the legend really took off, with the appearance of the mysterious epic called **La Chanson de Roland** (The Song of Roland).

In 1130 the archbishop of Pamplona, Sancho de Rosa, relived the ambush in a dream that pinpointed its location at the Puerto de Ibañeta. The vision was well publicized, and elaborated in 1170 by the anonymous clerk who wrote the *Chanson de Roland*, the ultimate medieval heroic epic. The Catholic Church eagerly exploited the story, not just as a propaganda device against the Infidel – ignoring the minor detail that Roland's final, Basque adversaries were also Christians – but also to promote the sales of souvenirs and relics along the *camino*. Although the geographical and historical accuracy of the poem is open to question, its evocation of chivalric valour adds poignancy to a visit to Roncesvalles; the Penguin edition in English fits easily into a backpack.

In the years immediately following its establishment, the abbey enjoyed a meteoric success, ranking among the most wealthy and powerful of the thirteenth century; it was said that a pilgrim of the era beginning in London could travel to Roncesvalles entirely on lands belonging to the *collegiata*. Today the place is more commonly the destination of numerous local *romerías*, from both the French and Spanish valleys, by virtue of its thirteenth-century image of the *Virgen de Orreaga*, honoured with special fervour on September 8.

Practicalities

There are **dormitory beds** in the abbey, intended for bona fide pilgrims following the *Camino de Santiago*; for permission to spend the night ask for Padre Javier Navarro. As a mere tourist it's more appropriate to stay at *La Posada* (☎948/76 02 25; ④; closed Nov), with en-suite facilities and **meals** served, or at the simpler *Hostal Casa Sabina* (☎948/76 00 12; ③). All this seems a mere echo of the medieval hospice here, which for seven centuries listed its services rendered to the (predominantly male) pilgrims as follows: a bath, haircut, shave and mending of shoes or clothes, performed – as various manuscripts attested – "by women solicitous and far from ugly".

Over the Puerto de Ibañeta

A better way to get a sense of the Roland legend is to make the half-hour walk up through the beech woods from the back of the abbey to the **Puerto de Ibañeta** (1057m), the trail marked by the red/white paint marks of the joint GR65/12/11. According to many scholars, you'll be walking through the site where Roland's defeat occurred.

On a misty day – and there are many of those – the pass can be suitably melancholy. An ugly modern chapel stands in the pass, on the site of the ancient chapel of San Salvador, whose bell used to guide pilgrims in foggy weather. There are also a couple of small medieval stone monuments to Roland and the vestiges of another built by a doctor from Pamplona in 1934.

From the Puerto de Ibañeta, you can continue along the *Camino de Santiago* to Saint-Jean-Pied-de-Port, a long, seven-to-eight-hour day through beautiful countryside with a chequered history. Thirty-two years after Charlemagne followed approximately this route, his son, Louis le Débonnaire, avoided a repeat performance of the Basque ambush by forcing the wives and children of local villagers to accompany his troops through the pass. It was also the route taken by Edward the Black Prince to the battle-ground of Navarrate in 1367; Napoleon's troops retreated this way after the Peninsular War; and the defeated Republicans fled in thousands through the sombre scenery here as the Spanish Civil War drew to a close.

A lot of the way is on asphalted road but some is on Roman-era cobbles. From the chapel at the Puerto de Ibañeta pass, follow a narrow paved road east for about 4km to a junction; because of a three hundred-metre climb it takes a couple of hours. At the junction you head north off the paved road into the **Collada Lepoeder**, flanked by the rounded summits of Astobizkar (1506m) and Menditxipi (1401m).

Beyond these hills, the route – now trail – swings round to the east again, passing the ruins of the Elizacharre chapel before attaining the **Col de Bentarte/Collado de Betartea pass** (1240m) – which some insist was the more likely place for the ambush. The joint GR11/12 heads east here, parting company with the GR65, which heads north again across the frontier to meet the paved D428 road for Saint-Jean after about half an hour. Alternatively, you can walk eastwards on the marked path to the **Urkulu burial tower** (dating from about 1500 BC), and join the road there, a diversion which will cost you another hour. Once on the road, Saint-Jean is about 16km away, although the GR provides a few short cuts across woods and farmland.

Alternatively, you can drive from Roncesvalles – beyond which there's no public transport – along the main road into France down the Valcarlos valley, a narrow salient of Spanish territory jutting north from the usual frontier ridge.

Valcarlos

VALCARLOS (Luzaide) itself, 16km below the Ibañeta pass, is a reasonably attractive village with the souvenir trappings of most border halts. Should logistics require an overnight **stay**, there's the *Hostal Maitena* on the main through road (☎948/79 02 10; ④) and, on the side of town towards France, the excellent *Casa Etxezuria* (☎948/79 00 11; ③). The latter, offering just a pair of luxuriously furnished rooms, is a bargain, and accordingly a big hit with modern *Camino de Santiago* pilgrims, so phone ahead if possible.

ARNEGUY, 3km on, is the last Spanish village before the frontier. There's no public transport from the French side of the border but at least there are a couple of cafés here where you might be able to organize a lift.

Saint-Jean-Pied-de-Port

SAINT-JEAN-PIED-DE-PORT (Donibane Garazi), 8km from the frontier on the young River Nive, is a much-loved tourist attraction, its highly photogenic old quarter enveloped in pink sandstone walls and watched over by an imposing fortress. Once capital of Basse-Navarre, Saint-Jean thrived until the sixteenth century on the pilgrimage traffic to Santiago de Compostela, and all over town you'll see the scallop-shell emblem of the shrine. The three main pilgrim routes across France converge some 20km northeast at Ostabat, from where caravans of travellers used to descend on Saint-Jean, singing in reply to the church bells that would ring when a group was spotted on the horizon. From the north, they entered by **Porte de Saint Jacques** in the town walls and left by **Porte d'Espagne**, heading up to the Puerto de Ibañeta – hence the suffixed *Pied-de-Port*, meaning "Foot-of-the-Pass".

The oldest neighbourhood lies on the right bank of the River Nive, behind the medieval fortifications, and consists essentially of a single street. This begins life as the rue d'Espagne, heading north from Porte d'Espagne, and lined on both sides with souvenir shops and pastel-painted houses, some with carved lintels dating them to as far back as the sixteenth century. Crossing the **Vieux-Pont**, which offers the best photo opportunities in town – balconied houses, decked in washing and flowers, handsomely reflected in the placid, trout-filled waters of the Nive – you pass through the well-preserved **Porte Nôtre-Dame** to reach the plain, largely Gothic **Nôtre-Dame-du-Bout-du-Pont** on the right. Here the street becomes the cobbled rue de la Citadelle, climbing steeply past the long and narrow **Prison des Evêques** (Bishops' Prison; open daily Easter–Oct; 10F), separated by a garden from the episcopal residence. The pilgrimage to Santiago inevitably attracted a few shady characters who preyed on the occasionally gullible genuine pilgrims; the con-men, when discovered, were arrested by the guards furnished by the Church and flung into dungeons such as this. Accordingly you are shown, in addition to a small gallery of knick-knacks, a subterranean earth-floored chamber still complete with chains for restraining the prisoners.

At the top of the rise, above the Porte de Saint-Jacques, looms the classical **citadel**, built in 1628 on the orders of Richelieu, and redesigned by Vauban in 1685. It's now a college, but the lower, grassy ramparts have unrestricted access, and are worth the climb up for the sweeping views west and north.

Practicalities

The **train station** is north of the centre, a ten-minute walk into town along av Renaud. You emerge on place du Général-de-Gaulle, under the old walls, where the **tourist**

office (July & Aug Mon–Sat 9am–12.30pm & 2–7pm, Sun 10.30am–12.30pm & 3–6pm; rest of year Mon–Sat 9am–noon & 2–7pm; ☎05.59.37.03.57), with information on *chambres d'hôtes*, occupies a kiosk opposite the *Mairie*.

Several affordable **hotels** are close by: the seventeenth-century *Les Remparts* at 16 place Floquet (☎05.59.37.13.79, fax 05.59.37.33.44; ④), below the ramparts park and the covered market at the south end of town; the equally venerable *Ramuntcho* at 1 rue de France (☎05.59.37.03.91, fax 05.59.37.35.17; ⑤) up in the old town, with a decent restaurant; the refurbished *Itzalpea*, 5 place du Trinquet (☎05.59.37.03.66; ③), which offers good-value meals; or the luxurious *Central* on place du Général-de-Gaulle (☎05.59.37.00.22; ⑤), whose gourmet restaurant enjoys a riverside terrace setting. There's a **gîte d'étape** at 9 route d'Uhart, the Bayonne road (☎05.59.37.12.08; ①), and for bona fide pilgrims, a **hospice** at 55 rue de la Citadelle. The municipal **campsite** *Plaza-Berri* (☎05.59.37.11.19; April to mid-Oct) is quite a way upstream on the south bank of the Nive, towards the *fronton* – which hosts a barehanded **pelota** match, the most macho variety, every Monday at 5pm (tickets 40–50F).

If you've drawn a blank for accommodation, the village of **Ascarat**, 2km west towards Saint-Étienne, has the *Chambres d'Hôte Irigaray* (☎05.59.37.00.49; ②), which does wonderful home-style meals, and *Camping de la Truite* (☎05.59.37.31.22; July & Aug), by the Nive on the Bayonne road.

Eating out, there's no better place to rid yourself of money burning a hole in your pocket than at the **restaurant** of the *Hôtel des Pyrénées* at 19 place du Général-de-Gaulle (closed Jan & mid-Nov to mid-Dec), reckoned to be one of the best in the Pyrenees: count on 350–500F for the works, which often include dishes like fillet of salmon, roast pigeon with mushroom ravioli and decadent sorbets. Otherwise, there are a dozen rather less expensive, and fairly indistinguishable sidewalk *brasseries* and *crêperies* – packed out in August particularly – and a lively **Monday food market**, continuing for most of the day.

The only ways of moving on by public transport are the **train** west to Bayonne or the **bus** west to Saint-Étienne-de-Baïgorry. You can enquire about **bike rental** at Steunou (☎05.59.37.25.45), next to the SI, or at Garazy (☎05.59.37.21.79) for mountain bikes.

Southeast: the upper Nive valley

Heading southeast of Saint-Jean, the D301 secondary road – and, higher up, running roughly parallel, the GR10 – furnishes access to the upper reaches of the **Nive valley**, in the case of the road penetrating almost all the way to its source, with the final approach on foot. There seems little in this progressively deepening valley at first glance other than vast hay meadows, scythed and raked by entire families in early summer, and equally extensive tracts of bracken fern, also prized for animal bedding. Yet there are a few hamlets with excellent places to eat and stay, these often booked out during the autumn hunting season.

SAINT-MICHEL, 4km along the D301, has the excellent *Hôtel Xoko-Goxoa* (☎05.59.37.06.34, fax 05.59.37.34.63; ④; closed Jan–March) to prompt a halt, with a panoramic, well-regarded restaurant and rooms with country views. Proceeding 4km further – four hours from Saint-Jean along the meandering GR10 – brings you to tiny **ESTERENÇUBY** with its medieval galleried church. Some 3km upstream from Esterençuby there's the *Hôtel Artzain Etchea* (☎05.59.37.11.53, fax 05.59.37.20.16; ③; closed mid-Nov to mid-Dec), with a popular restaurant; 2km further, at the minuscule hamlet of **BÉHÉROBIE**, virtually the only building is the *Hôtel des Sources de la Nive* (☎05.59.37.10.57; ④; closed Jan & Tues out of season, full with hunters in Oct), again with a highly regarded restaurant, serving up Basque treats such as trout and *piperade* (a pepper-and-tomato stir-fry with eggs), as well as a fair cross-section of whatever the hunters bring down. The terrace overhangs the river and when the guns aren't blasting away it's a relaxing hideaway.

Walking from the upper Nive

A road twists up from Béhérobie to the border at the Col d'Arnostéguy; more worthwhile is the ninety-minute walk up to the **Sources de la Nive**, though the path is deteriorated and slippery, only practicable with any enjoyment in dry weather. There are in fact various other walking possibilities in the area, most of them utilizing the old GR10 and current HRP, very close to the frontier; during the late 1980s the GR10 was rerouted, rather dully on roads, to head from Estérençuby to *Chalet Pedro* (see p.403) via Phalgacette village and Iraukotuturru peak.

The old trail follows a tributary of the Nive southeast, high up the side of the valley to emerge into lush grasslands about an hour out. Another hour should see you at the Col d'Errozaté (1076m), just north of which is Errozaté peak (1345m); if you're traversing rather than dayhiking, it's possible to continue east, via Occabé (see p.403), to the vicinity of *Chalet Pedro* in the Forêt d'Iraty – six to seven hours from Béhérobie.

West: Saint-Étienne-de-Baïgorry

Although the little town of **SAINT-ÉTIENNE-DE-BAÏGORRY** lies only 11km west of Saint-Jean-Pied-de-Port by the D15, it's a different world, where agriculture rather than tourism is the focus of life. Market centre of the Vallée des Aldudes, the town basks in an air of plump contentment, its highly profitable farming co-operatives presenting their public face through several sales outlets in town. The local **Irouléguy wines**, the only *appelation* red and rosé produced in the Pays Basque, are worth stocking up on; you can taste them at the vintner's outlet on the road back towards Saint-Jean (mid-June to Aug Mon–Sat 9am–noon & 2–6.30pm; July–Aug also Sun 10am–12.30pm). Other local specialities include ham, sheep's-milk cheese and preserved mushrooms.

There are few great sights here – a hump-backed medieval bridge juxtaposed with the small castle of the Etchaux (Etxauz) quarter, and a seventeenth-century church with a gloriously overdone gilded retable. Instead it's the wonderfully bucolic atmosphere that brings visitors to Saint-Étienne-de-Baïgorry. The Euskera suffix to the town's name translates as "beautiful view" and from the outlying quarters, which clamber up pastured and vine-clad hills, you do indeed get a marvellous panorama of the gentle lower slopes of the Pyrenees.

Practicalities

Saint-Étienne has any amount of **accommodation** for all pockets, most of it good value. For long stays in apartments or *chambres d'hôtes*, you might start a search at the **tourist office** on place de l'Église (☎05.59.37.47.28; July & Aug Mon–Sat 9am–12.30pm & 2.30–7pm, Sun 10am–noon & 3–6pm; Sept–June Mon–Sat 9am–noon & 2–6pm), or just keep an eye out for signs on the approach roads and in the town itself. **Hotels** include the *Hargain* (☎05.59.37.41.46; ③) in what passes for the main quarter of the scattered town, or the more rural *Manechenia* (☎05.59.37.41.68; ④), at the north end of things beyond Lespars district, which includes an excellent **restaurant** featuring lots of game and Basque specialities. On the Chemin d'Ispéguy, 3km west of town, you'll find the friendly, English-run *Maison Guerecietenia* (☎05.59.37.47.77; ④), a B&B specifically pitched at walkers and cyclists. The municipal river-bank **campsite**, *Camping Irouléguy* (☎05.59.37.40.80; open all year), is quite central, while at Lespars there's another rather lively campsite/*gîte d'étape*, *Camping à la Ferme Mendi* (☎05.59.37.42.39; year-round).

Regular **bus** services connect Saint-Étienne with the train stations at Saint-Jean-Pied-de-Port and Ossès-Saint-Martin-d'Arrossa, 8km northeast along the D948.

Walking from Saint-Étienne

The GR10 arrives circuitously in Saint-Étienne from Saint-Jean in about six hours, curling southwest via 1021-metre Monhoa hill, then north. Continuing northwest – and this is the more popular, rewarding outing – the GR saunters off between the castle and Lespars district for the stiff, two-and-a-half-hour climb, first through woods and then along a bare ridge, to the **Col de Buztanzelhay** (843m), at the southern end of the **Iparla crest**, which here forms the border. Iparla offers the classic ridge-walk of the French Pays Basque, and indeed one of the best in the entire Pyrenees.

Once up, it's hard to get lost: you simply follow the ridge due north, as close to the eastern face as you dare. Griffon vultures commonly circle overhead and there's the possibility of spotting the rare black vulture, too. Although the highest point, **Pic d'Iparla** (under 3hr from Buztandelhay), is only 1044m, it's as impressive a walk as you could hope for, with France precipitously below to the east, and a gentler decline towards a much less developed, almost secret corner of Spain below to the west.

Bidarray

About an hour beyond Pic d'Iparla, the ridge begins to descend noticeably and incline northeast, towards the attractive village of **BIDARRAY**, reached nearly three hours beyond Pic d'Iparla. As you walk down into it, inevitably late in the day, you'll pass a *gîte d'étape* (☎05.59.37.71.34; ①), one possibility for staying the night. Alternatively, there's the *Hôtel Noblia* (☎05.59.37.70.89; ③), on the main road by the bridge over the River Nive, or the nearby *Hôtel Erramundeya* (☎05.59.37.71.21; ④). Opposite the medieval bridge, with rooms overlooking the river, *Pont d'Enfer* (☎05.59.37.70.88, fax 05.59.37.76.60; ④) is reckoned the town's fanciest, with an outdoor terrace restaurant. From the **train station** – right by the old, humpbacked Pont-Noblia – there are three to four trains daily in each direction: southeast to Saint-Jean-Pied-de-Port, northwest towards Bayonne.

The Valle de Baztán

Heading more or less due north of Pamplona, the N121 provides an alternate, non-pilgrims' approach to Basse-Navarre, and to Saint-Étienne-de-Baïgorry in particular. This road first climbs over the **Puerto de Velate** (Belate), on the watershed separating Mediterranean- from Cantabrian-draining rivers, descending to Oronoz. Here, a left fork follows the scenic valley of the Río Bidasoa to Irún, Hendaye and Hondarribia. Bearing right or upstream, you enter the **Valle de Baztán** ("Rat's Tail" in Euskera) with its string of tiny villages, beautiful countryside and caves.

Elizondo

Centre of a joint municipality composed of fifteen villages, **ELIZONDO** is the capital of this most strongly Basque of Navarran valleys. The town boasts fine Basque Pyrenean architecture, especially alongside the river, but serves primarily as a comfortable base for exploring the area.

Among several places to **stay** in Elizondo, the best options are *Casa Jaén* (☎948/58 04 87; ③), but with only two rooms, or *Pensión Eskisaroi*, c/Jaime Urrutia 40 (☎948/58 00 13; ③). If you have your own transport, then *Casa Urruska* (☎948/45 21 06; ③), a wonderful farmstead 6km east by dirt track at Bearzun de Elizondo, is an even better choice. Considerably more expensive are the three-star *Hotel Baztán* (☎948/58 00 50, fax 45 23 23; ⑤) on the Pamplona road south of town, complete with garden and swimming pool, and in the town itself, *Hostal Saskaitz*, c/María Azpilikueta 10 (☎948/58 04 88, fax 58 06 15; ⑤). For **eating out**, the *Galarza* at c/Santiago 1 (closed Tues in winter) offers a range of valley specialities for 2000 to 2500 pesetas per person. Three

buses arrive daily from both Pamplona and San Sebastián, but there is no public transport to most of the smaller villages covered below.

Elizondo also lies astride the **GR11**, which heads west out of Burguete, then turns north along the border (about 10hr). It's worth getting a dawn start from Burguete and trying to polish off this stretch in a day, as there's little in the way of facilities in between. If you have to break the journey in two, **Puerto de Urkiaga** (912m), about halfway, offers water and the possibility of camping.

The Saint-Étienne turning

Nearby **ARIZKUN**, just off the N121 on the minor road **east to Saint-Étienne**, is graced by the seventeeth-century convent of Nuestra Señora de los Angeles with its striking Baroque facade. Just beyond the village stands a typical example of a fortified house (very common in the valley) where Pedro de Ursua, the leader of the Marañones expedition up the Amazon in 1560 in search of El Dorado, was born. You can **stay** in Arizkun at the friendly and well-run *Pensión Etxeberria* (☎948/45 30 13; ③), which serves good meals.

Some 8km before the spectacular, narrow **Col d'Izpegui/Ispéguy** on the frontier stands the last Spanish village of **ERRAZU**, another gem, with a couple of well-preserved *casas rurales*: one is a fourteenth-century palatial home, *Casa Etxebeltzea* (☎948/45 31 57; ③④), and the other, *Casa Marimartinenea*, (☎948/45 31 17; ③③), still keeps livestock on the ground floor.

Zugarramurdi: village and caves

North of Elizondo, the main N121 climbs over the **Puerto de Otxondo** at the top of the Valle de Baztán to Urdax, Zugarramurdi and the double village of Dantxarinea/Dantxaria (the latter just inside France), any of which make good stopovers between Pamplona and the French Basque coastal towns of Biarritz and Bayonne. The only **public transport** on this stretch is the noon mail bus from Elizondo – check in town to confirm the exact time.

ZUGARRAMURDI, 4km southwest of the border hamlet of Dantxaria, off the N121, is famous for its **caves**, whose highlight is the giant natural arch under which the *Regata de Infierno* (Hell's Stream) flows. The cavern was a major venue for witchcraft during the Middle Ages and consequently the area bore the brunt of persecution by the Inquisition. Underneath the arch, *akelarres* or witches' sabbaths allegedly took place; these seem to have survived, in a tame derivative, as the *zikiroyate* rite every August 18, which features a "love-feast" of roast meat held in the grotto. The appealing village itself makes a good base for excursions into the surrounding countryside; one possibility is to walk 3km along the track beyond the caves into France to another set of caves, the **Grottes de Sare**.

Zugarramurdi is well supplied with **casa rurales**, although they often fill up at weekends; *Casa Sueldeguía* (☎948/59 90 88; ③) and *Casa Teltxegu* (☎948/59 91 67; ③) are both in the centre of the village, or there is a **campsite**, *Camping Josenea* (☎948/59 90 11) right on the border in **DANTXARINEA**. Surprisingly, considering the lowest-common-denominator enterprises that usually monopolize frontier crossings, there's also a good **restaurant** at Dantxarinea: *Menta* (closed Mon dinner and Tues). There are low-priced menus at 1500 to 2500 pesetas, but it's advisable to order the more expensive à la carte seafood if you want to see what the chef can really do.

Through Labourd to the coast

Beyond Bidarray, travelling along the Nive by road or train, you enter **Labourd** (Lapurdi), the westernmost of the three traditional French Basque regions which are now gathered into the *département* of Pyrénées-Atlantiques. The Basque farm- and town-houses get even more sumptuous as you approach the coast, and the soft, rolling hills maintain their electric-green livery even in the summer.

The spa of **Cambo-les-Bains** is the biggest place between Saint-Jean-Pied-de-Port and Bayonne; here also, with your own vehicle, you forsake the Bayonne-bound artery for the westerly D918, which passes through or near such tourist-friendly villages as **Espelette** and **Ainhoa** on its way to Saint-Jean-de-Luz. A bus based in the latter town serves Espelette several times daily in summer.

Itxassou

The small, spread-out village of **ITXASSOU**, 11km northwest of Bidarray in a bowl of wooded hills, makes a good introduction to the region, and a great place to hide away. A quintessentially Basque graveyard of ancient, keyhole-shaped tombstones surrounds the church of **Saint Fructueux**, 1km south of the centre on the Laxia road; inside you'll find the typical French Basque three-tiered galleries, constructed to deny the Devil mischievous opportunites arising from the mingling of the sexes during Mass: the men sat upstairs, the women down in the nave. Another kilometre southeast along this minor road (and rail line), the River Nive loops through a narrow defile at the **Pas-de-Roland**, yet another element in the Roland legend. Merely a hole in a roadside boulder, it's claimed to have been punched out by the hooves of the great knight's horse.

There are four reputable places to **stay** and **eat** in or around Itxassou: *Hôtel Arza Mendi* on place du Fronton (π05.59.29.75.29; ③–④), with attractive, old-fashioned rooms in all sizes and shapes, as well as several variably priced *menus* and English-speaking management; the more formal *Hôtel du Fronton* across the way (π05.59.29.75.10, fax 05.59.29.23.50; ④; closed Jan to mid-Feb & Wed low season), with an outdoor terrace for its excellent, reasonably priced *Restaurant Bonnet*; the simpler *Hôtel Etchepare*, again on the same square (π59.29.75.1405.59.29.75.14, fax 05.59.29.80.59; ③; closed Nov–March), with a decent restaurant; and – a bit out of town towards the Pas-de-Roland – *Hôtel du Chêne* (π05.59.29.75.01, fax 05.59.29.27.39; ④; closed Jan–March & Mon–Tues low season).

Cambo-les-Bains

Ten minutes downstream by train, the spa of **CAMBO-LES-BAINS** ranks as one of the largest towns in the Labourd region. An attractive mixture of town and country, with plentiful shops, bars and hotels encircled by richly rural landscape, it makes an appealing (if somewhat stuffy) place to break the journey. Long a magnet for sufferers of respiratory ailments, the thermal establishment here is the focal point of the ornate houses and hotels that radiate out along the heights above the Nive. The original town of **Bas Cambo**, typically Basque with its square, whitewashed houses and galleried church, lies down in the valley, right beside the river and train station.

The most famous resident was Edmond Rostand, author of *Cyrano de Bergerac*, who from 1900 to 1918 lived in the huge **Villa Arnaga**, a couple of kilometres west of Bas Cambo. Today the house is a museum (April–Sept daily 10am–noon & 2.30–6.30pm; Feb, March & Oct to mid-Nov Sat & Sun 2.30–6.30pm; 28F), surrounded by a bizarre formal garden defined by topiary hedges and reflecting pools, and crammed inside with kitsch decor and memorabilia of the writer's career.

The **tourist office** is in Parc St-Joseph in the upper town centre (July & Aug Mon–Sat 9am–noon & 2.30–6.30pm, Sun 10am–12.30pm; rest of year Mon–Sat 9am–noon & 2.30–5.30pm; π05.59.29.70.25).If you plan to **stay**, and **eat** something other than café snacks, make for the old town, Bas Cambo, where you'll find the *Auberge Chez Tante*

Ursule (☎05.59.29.78.23, fax 05.59.28.57; ③; closed mid-Jan to mid-Feb) by the *fronton*, virtually the only "non-cure" establishment. The nearest year-round campsite is *Ur-Hégia* on route des Sept-Chênes (☎05.59.29.72.03), also in Bas Cambo; *Camping Bixta Eder* is the other side of town along av d'Espagne (☎05.59.29.94.23; April to mid-Oct).

Espelette

From Cambo it's a five-kilometre trip southwest on the D918 to **ESPELETTE**, a village of wide-eaved houses, with a church notable for its heavy, square tower and fine wrought-ironwork. Pimentos are the principal crop here, and in summer the streets are garlanded with strings of colourful peppers, hanging in the sun to dry; on the last Sunday in October a special Mass is preceded by a Saturday-night party celebrating the various Basque culinary uses of the pepper. Espelette is primarily a market town, holding a regular Wednesday livestock and general market, and the major event of its social calendar is the annual January fair for trading **pottok** (pronounced *potiok*) ponies. An ancient, stocky breed of Paleolithic origins, apparently little changed from the horses depicted in prehistoric Pyrenean cave paintings, *pottoks* were once exported to work in British mines, but are now reared locally for both riding and meat.

Eating out, a treat is in store for you at Espelette: the *Hôtel Euzkadi* (☎05.59.93.91.88, fax 05.59.93.90.19; ⑤) has what is reckoned among the best traditional Basque restaurants in Labourd – reservations thus mandatory – and very reasonable for what you get at 95F to 175F (restaurant closed Mon year-round; Tues in low season; & mid-Nov to mid-Dec). Otherwise, the *Hôtel Chilar*, on the same main street, has slightly less expensive **rooms** (☎05.59.29.90.01, fax 05.59.93.25; ③).

West to Saint-Jean-de-Luz

The D918 curls west from Espelette via Saint-Pée-sur-Nivelle en route to Saint-Jean, a 25-kilometre distance served occasionally by bus. You might, however, veer south along the D20 to Ainhoa, 8km from Espelette and just 3km shy of the frontier at Dantxaria.

Ainhoa – and the end of the GR10

Yet another showcase village in a region not lacking in them, **AINHOA** gets understandably busy in season, when tourists fill its single street lined with substantial houses, whose lintel plaques offer mini-genealogies as well as foundation dates. The bulky-towered church is worth a look for the sake of its extravagantly Baroque altarpiece of prophets and apostles in niches, framed by ornate columns.

Among places to **stay**, *Maison Elissaldia* by the church is a *gîte d'étape* geared to walkers (☎05.59.29.25.29; ①). The quaint, though unheated rooms in the *Hôtel-Bar Irubera* (☎05.59.29.91.49; ②) represent excellent value; for a bit more comfort, there's the somewhat overpriced *Hôtel Oppoca* on the main square (☎05.59.29.90.72, fax 05.59.29.81.03; ⑤; closed Nov–March & Mon in low season). The latter two establishments serve **meals**. Alternatively, up on the frontier at Dantxaria you'll find the small, shady, well-run *Camping Xokoan* (☎05.59.29.90.26, fax 05.59.29.73.82), also with a handful of rooms (③) available.

The frontier to either side of the campsite hosts several little **ventas**, relics of pre-EU times when these rough-and-ready Spanish-run inns, essentially the retail outlets of smugglers, did a roaring trade in the many items – mainly booze and canned goods – which were far cheaper in Spain than in France. Today, with price parity being approached for many items, they would seem to have a bright future only as snack bars for hikers on the GR10.

Speaking of which, if you've hiked west seven hours from Bidarray on the GR10, Ainhoa is a logical stop. From here towards the Atlantic, the GR meanders over to Sare

---

BASQUE SPORTS

The Basque sport of *jaï alaï*, or **pelota** (*pelote* in France), is played all over both Spanish Euskadi and the French Pays Basque. Even the smallest village has a *fronton* or *pelota* court and betting on the sport is rife. Nearly twenty different versions of the game are played throughout the Basque country. In essence it resembles a high-risk version of squash, the players smashing the ball against the *fronton* either with their bare hands, or with a sort of wooden bat (the *pala*) or with a *chistera*, a narrow wicker basket that extends the player's forearm. The largest *chisteras* launch the ball at speeds of around 200km an hour, making *pelota* one of the most dangerous games in the world. The *pelotas* themselves are balls of fibre wound tightly around a rubber core and then encased in two layers of leather; tedious to make, they are phenomenally expensive and quite sensitive to extremes of temperature and humidity.

Other unique Basque sports include *palankaris* (tossing an iron bar), *aizkolaritza* (log-chopping), *harri-jasotzea* (stone-lifting), *soka-tira* (tug-of-war) and *segalaritza* (grass-cutting). The finest exponents of the first two in particular are popular local heroes; the world champion stone-lifter Iñaki Perurena's visit to Japan resulted in the sport being introduced there – he remains the only lifter to surpass the legendary 315-kilo barrier. All form an important part of the many local *fiestas*.

---

within three to four hours, brings you to the base of La Rhune (see p.436 for both these spots) and reaches civilization again at Biriatou, a very long walking day of nine to ten hours. Only purists do the final urban stretch through Hendaye; for detailed reverse directions to La Rhune, see below.

THE BASQUE COAST

For a region with such a long maritime tradition, the **Basque coast** – *Côte Basque* in French, *Costa Vasca* in Castilian – is surprisingly short and devoid of good natural harbours. It's scarcely more than 120km from the mouth of the River Adour, separating Bayonne and Biarritz from the dunes of the Landes to the north, to the Cantabrian border just past Bilbao in the west. Of that only about 50km – between Bayonne and San Sebastián – can be considered, by any stretch of the imagination, to be Pyrenean shoreline, and only at the mouths of the rivers Nivelle, Bidasoa and Oyarzun is there evidence of past Basque prowess in whaling, navigating and piracy.

The all-enveloping carpet of green vegetation, so unlike the Mediterranean coast, bespeaks a damp, often misty climate, without sharp differences between winter and summer temperatures. Yet the sun does shine, just enough in season to attract hordes of holiday-makers, and if you've been up in the hills for any length of time, the sea comes as a very welcome sight. Unfortunately it *is* often just for looking: frequently dangerous and wave-lashed – to the delight of hardy surfers – always turbid and, anywhere near a major river-mouth, so polluted that your skin may begin to itch or burn suspiciously after any time spent in the water.

This last detail is regrettable, since otherwise the Basque coast has all the ingredients for a perfect vacation: excellent food and drink, seductive scenery, characterful architecture and a handful of not-too-demanding inland side-trips. The two defining cities of **Bayonne** and **San Sebastián** are the biggest attractions, though the small ports of **Pasajes** and **Saint-Jean-de-Luz**, the historic border town of **Hondarribia** and the period-piece resort of **Biarritz** also have considerable appeal. Once you've sampled the best of the coast, it's possible to return to inland Navarra by the valley of the **Río Bidasoa**, with a trio of handsome villages in its lower reaches.

Bayonne

Although virtually contiguous with the fashionable resort of Biarritz (see p.431), the inland position of **BAYONNE** has protected it from the ravages of mass tourism – which makes it a far more interesting place to visit. Built astride the confluence of the rivers Adour (navigable) and Nive (less so), 6km inland and roughly 60km down the Nive from Saint-Jean, the city has long served as an important commercial port, its future guaranteed by some determined engineering works four hundred years ago to fix the wandering mouth of the Adour. Bayonne is both a Gascon city and the capital of the Pays Basque, but the tall white houses, their shutters and beams picked out in the distinctive brownish-reds and greens of the Basques, betray the major influence.

The place was founded by the Romans as the garrison town of *Lapurdum*. The name, corrupted to *Lapurdi* (Euskera) or *Labourd* (French), was later extended to signify the

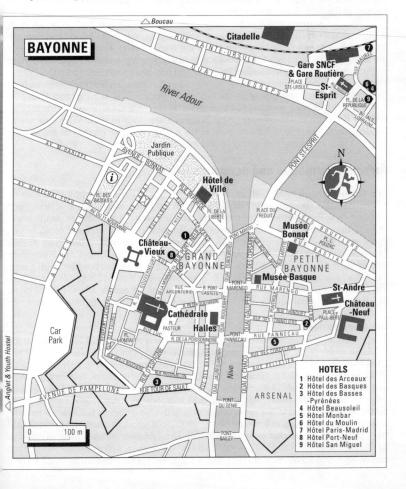

entire westernmost French Basque province; the current Euskera-derived name – *Baiona* in the vernacular – means "good river". For three centuries until 1451, it enjoyed prosperity and relative peace under English domination, until falling to the French in the course of the Hundred Years' War. Some fifty years later, Sephardic Jews fleeing the Iberian Inquisitions arrived, bringing with them their knowledge of chocolate-manufacturing; the city's heyday came during the eighteenth century, based on the dubious underpinnings of armaments manufacture (the word *bayonet* derives from the place) and a judicious amount of piracy. After the French Revolution, it lost considerable status when the Parisian regime merged the three traditional French Basque regions into the single modern *département* of Pyrénées-Atlantiques, governed from Pau.

Just as Perpignan became a refuge for Catalans who opposed Franco, so did Bayonne for the Spanish Basques, seeking refuge among their own. For decades the Petit Bayonne quarter was a haven for extreme Basque nationalist practitioners (ie ETA fugitives), until a recent clampdown by Parisian authorities. Wall posters in the neighbourhood still demand freedom for imprisoned ETA members and urge *insumisoa* (disobedience) in the face of new measures.

Economically there are also parallels between Bayonne and Perpignan, as both hope to gain from the single European market, sitting as they do beside increasingly busy truck and train routes between Spain and northwestern Europe. Bayonne needs the business, for although the aerospace industry is a big employer and electronics companies are growing in number, this area still has unemployment above the French average. Traditional footwear and clothing industries have declined severely, as have the chemical plants processing by-products from the gas field at Lacq, near Pau.

None of this is likely to affect you as a visitor, however, and initial favourable impressions of Bayonne as a small-scale, easy-going city are likely to stick. Wherever you're headed you're likely to at least stop in, as it's a major transport hub; you might even consider it as a relatively inexpensive and quiet base for a seaside holiday.

Arrival, information and accommodation

The **airport**, also serving Biarritz, is 6km southwest at Parme (flight information on ☎05.59.23.90.66; taxi link only). Bayonne's **train and bus stations** are adjacent, just off place de la République in the somewhat frowsy district of Saint-Esprit on the north bank of the Adour; there are city buses into the centre on the opposite bank, or you could walk the 700m across the Pont Saint-Esprit. The **tourist office** (July & Aug Mon–Sat 9am–7pm, Sun 10am–1pm; rest of year Mon–Fri 9am–6.30pm, Sat 10am–6pm; ☎05.59.46.01.46, fax 05.59.59.37.55) is inside the park in place des Basques, with a summer annexe at the train station (July & Aug Mon–Sat 9.30am–12.30pm & 2–6.30pm). They're useful for accommodation information, city plans and details of guided tours, like that to the Izarra liqueur distillery on Quai Bergeret in Saint-Esprit.

Accommodation

The most desirable accommodation is in the main quarter of **Grand Bayonne**, on the left bank of the Nive. Start with the classic and central *Hôtel des Arceaux*, 26 rue Port-Neuf (☎05.59.59.15.53; ③), on a pedestrian lane, the minuscule *Hôtel Port-Neuf* nearby at no. 44 (☎05.59.25.65.83; ③), with a breakfast terrace, or the quiet, comfortable *Hôtel des Basses-Pyrénées*, at 14 place des Victoires, on the corner of rue Tour-de-Sault (☎05.59.59.00.29; ④; closed mid-Dec to mid-Jan), where some rooms have rampart views. In **Petit Bayonne**, on the opposite side of the Nive, there's the spartan but adequate *Hôtel des Basques* at 4 rue de Lisses (☎05.59.59.08.02; ②), with quieter rooms at the back, or the somewhat more comfortable *Hôtel Monbar* within hailing distance at 24 rue Pannecau (☎05.59.59.26.80; ④). If all else fails – and it well might without a reservation from mid-July to September – there are some useful fallbacks in **Saint-Esprit**, including three acceptably quiet budget options in pedestrianized rue Sainte-Catherine: *Hotel du Moulin* at no. 12 (☎05.59.55.13.29; ②); the *Beausoleil* opposite at no. 23 (☎05.59.55.00.10; ②), with a pleasant breakfast salon, and *Hôtel San Miguel* at no. 8 *bis* (☎05.59.55.17.82; ③). *Hôtel Paris-Madrid*, in place de la Gare (☎05.59.55.13.98; ②), would do if you are catching a dawn train, and it's recently been renovated, with double glazing on the most noise-prone rooms.

A luxury **campsite**, *La Chêneraie* (☎05.59.55.01.31; mid-April to mid-Oct), lies well north of the Adour, through the Saint Frédéric quarter on the D117 towards Fontaine des Anges. For the **Anglet youth hostel** (see p.433), take the Ligne Bleue bus # 4 for Biarritz-La Négresse from outside the Hôtel de Ville, getting off at Cinq Cantons; from there turn left down promenade de la Barre, then fifth left along promenade des Sables and finally right along route des Vignes – a 25-minute walk.

The City

Bayonne is more a wandering town than one offering great sights, but it does have a handful of diversions scattered throughout the three central quarters. You'll spend most of your time south of the Adour, in the quarters of **Grand Bayonne** (in turn on the west bank of the Nive tributary) or **Petit Bayonne** (the east bank). The less compelling neighbourhood of **Saint-Esprit** spreads out on the Adour's north bank.

Grand Bayonne

The **Cathedral**, abutting place Pasteur at the summit of **Grand Bayonne**, looks best from a distance, with its twin towers and steeple rising with airy grace above the houses. Up close, the yellowish stone reveals bad weathering, with most of the decorative detail lost to post-revolutionary vandalism as well. The interior is more impressive, thanks to the height of the nave and some sixteenth-century glass set off by the prevailing gloom. Like other southern French Gothic cathedrals of the period (about 1260) it was based on more famous northern models, in this case Soissons and Rheims. On the south side is a fourteenth-century **cloister** (daily except Sat 9.30am–12.30pm & 2–5/6pm; 14F) with a lawn, cypress trees and beds of begonias: a quiet, secretive spot affording a rather flattering view of the church.

From place Pasteur, rue de la Monnaie and its continuation, rue du Port-Neuf, lead downhill to the main **place de la Liberté**, where you'll find the much-frequented *Café du Théâtre*. The square is flanked by *pâtisseries* and *confiseries* exuding a strong aroma of chocolate, a Bayonne speciality on a par with its famous air-cured hams. Most of it is still made in the Saint-Esprit quarter, but the most prestigious retail outlets are Cazenave and Darenatz, arcade shops at nos. 19 and 15 respectively in rue du Port-Neuf.

The Nive Quais and Petit Bayonne

Heading upstream from the place de la Liberté, the **Nive Quais** are a lively and authentic part of town, the tall houses on the right bank reflected appealingly in the placid Nive. The *halles* on the Grand Bayonne side host a comprehensive market on Tuesdays, Wednesdays and Saturdays. Near one end of Pont Marengo, installed in a four- hundred-year-old town-house, is the **Musée Basque**, at the time of writing set to reopen – and possibly move to the Château Neuf – after nearly a decade of "restoration" (really an arcane political dispute). Whenever and wherever it operates again, exhibits illustrating Basque life through the centuries will include reconstructed farm buildings, house interiors, tools and the *makhilas* – a sort of walking stick often elaborately carved from medlar wood. There should also be a section on Basque seafaring (Columbus' skipper was Basque, and another Basque, Sebastian de Caro, navigated the first circumnavigation of the world in 1519–22), and a wing on the history and stars of *pelota*.

The painting collection of the **Musée Bonnat** (daily except Tues 10am–noon & 2.30–6.30pm, Fri until 8.30pm; 25F), nearby at 5 rue Jacques-Laffitte (plus an annexe at 9 rue Fredéric-Bastiat), provides a welcome variance from the usual dross of provincial galleries. Thirteenth- and fourteenth-century Italian art is well represented, as are most periods up to (but not including) Impressionism; highlights include Goya's *Self-Portrait* and *Portrait of Don Francisco de Borja*, Rubens' powerful *Apollo and Daphne* and *The Triumph of Venus*, plus works by Murrillo, El Greco and Ingres. A whole gallery is devoted to high-society portraits by Léon Bonnat (1833–1922), whose personal collection formed the original core of the museum. There are also frequent temporary exhibits of the work of prominent artists, well worth catching.

North of the river: Saint-Esprit

There's little reason to venture north of the river. A deliberately inconspicuous **synagogue** at 35 rue Maubec, founded by sixteenth-century refugees from Spain and Portugal, denotes a dwindling Jewish presence. The church of **Saint-Esprit** opposite the train station is all that remains of a hospice for pilgrims on the *Chemin de Saint-Jacques*; the interior is worth a look for a fifteenth-century wood sculpture of *The Flight into Egypt*. Just above the train station, the massive **Citadelle** was built by Vauban in 1680; constructed to defend the town against Spanish attack, it didn't see much action until the Napoleonic wars, when its garrison held out against Wellington for four months in 1813.

Eating, drinking and entertainment

A summary of eating possibilities in **Grand Bayonne** has to start (in all senses) with *Bar du Marché* at 39 rue des Basques (closed Sat evening & Sun), a family-run outfit that begins serving food and drink at 5am to assorted market-sellers and bar-flies heading home for bed, continuing with economical *plats de jour* at lunchtime. *La Chistera* at 42 rue Port-Neuf (closed Mon–Wed evenings in low season) offers more sophistication and choice, with Basque fare at about 100F a head; this same street is lined with several **oyster bars**, a local treat.The area can also provide all kinds of exotic food, notably Japanese, Vietnamese or Egyptian; good options are the *Gandhi* at 29 rue d'Espagne, for north Indian meals, and *El Mosquito*, 12 rue Gosse, with Latin American *menús* from 80F.

For more traditional food and drink, you're best off in the **Petit Bayonne** area, where you can dine on seafood under the arcades by the Nive at *Le P'tit Chalut*, 24 quai Galuperie, with menus from 85F. More rough-and-ready choices around the corner on rue des Cordeliers include *Xan Xan Gorri* at no. 9 (closed Mon), which is more bar than restaurant (though *tapas* and *plats de jour* are available), with live music on Friday night; and its near neighbour at no. 13, *Bar des Amis*, where locals eat abundantly and cheaply (until 9.30pm). Close to the Musée Bonnat at 68 rue Bourg-neuf, one-star Michelin excellence is yours for as little as 130F at the *Auberge du Cheval Blanc* (☎05.59.59.01.33), where decadent desserts are a speciality.

Saint-Esprit is pretty much a culinary desert except for *Le Bistrot Sainte-Cluque* at 9 rue Hughes (reservations suggested on ☎05.59.55.82.43; closed Mon Oct–July), with very good-value (under 100F) *nouvelle cuisine*. On a more modest note, don't be put off by the appearance of *Au Gourmet* at 7 rue Sainte-Catherine; it's good for savoury-crêpe breakfasts, with friendly service.

Nightlife and entertainment

Ordinary Bayonnais **nightlife** is poor, but the city makes up for it with a vengeance during a summer season of almost back-to-back **festivals**. These kick off with *Jazz aux*

Remparts, usually four days from July 14, with a mix of local and international acts topped by fireworks and street parties. August events include the *Fêtes de Bayonne*, five days of street partying and booze-ups from the first Wednesday, continuing non-stop with the *Faire de l'Assomption* until at least August 15, this followed by the *Fêtes de Petit Bayonne* over the third weekend in August. There's also a theatre festival in October, with numerous foreign troupes appearing.

Besides *pelota*, **rugby** is the sport that commands the greatest loyalty in Bayonne, and the town's top-class rugby team has produced many members of the national squad. You might catch a view of them in action by following the Vauban fortifications to the Parc des Sports south of Grand Bayonne, where the solid walls act as grandstands.

Biarritz

BIARRITZ, 8km west of Bayonne, makes no secret of its identity as a resort that expects a little refinement from its guests. Much of this hotch-potch of giant ocean-liner-style hotels and mock-Gothic châteaux wears a bygone air that appeals to more traditional middle-class visitors, while the town's newer neighbourhoods are aimed at a younger but no less prosperous market. The surviving casino does a roaring trade, the *de rigueur* black ties and cocktail dresses lending the desired Monte Carlo touch (the other, the massive Art Deco Casino Municipal behind the Grande Plage, is now an exhibit and conference hall).

Biarritz burst into prominence during the mid-nineteenth century when the Spanish-born Empress Eugénie, wife of Napoléon III – whom she met here – brought the entire court of the Second Empire to what had been the favourite seaside watering-hole of her childhood. Others soon followed, including Edward VII, who virtually held a second court here, nominating Asquith as prime minister in Biarritz in 1908. After World War I had destroyed the existing European social order, high fashion moguls like Hermès and Lanvin, and film stars like Douglas Fairbanks and Gloria Swanson, replaced the crowned heads and nobility. Biarritz reached the nadir of its fortunes after the next global convulsion, but has slowly recovered since, thanks to the way it has embraced less elitist pursuits like golf, surfing, conferences and even a small cinema festival. Yet it's inevitably a come-down, the overriding impression being the uneasy coexistence of the chic and the shabby, the geriatric and the adolescent – while one-third of Biarritz's inhabitants are retirees, it has also become Europe's biggest wave-surfing mecca.

The Town

Most specific attractions are strung out along the landscaped, clifftop terraces just inland from the promontories and coves around which the town grew. Nostalgia buffs might attempt to recover past glories at the **Musée du Vieux Biarritz**, installed in a disused Anglican church on rue Broquedis (Mon–Wed, Fri & Sat 10am–noon & 2.30–6pm): mostly knick-knacks and documents relating to Belle Époque royalty.

Like so many spots on the coast hereabouts, Biarritz started life as a whaling centre, a local industry which collapsed late in the eighteenth century, and whose only remnants are a whale-spotting tower near place de l'Atalaya and some memorabilia in the **Musée de la Mer** (July to mid-Sept daily 9.30am–8pm, until midnight mid-July to mid-Aug; rest of year daily 9.30am–12.30pm & 2–6pm; 45F), on the claw-shaped promontory west of town. Completely refurbished in 1992, it now has a small aquarium and seal-frolicking section as well, making it – if not exactly a must – at least a good place to take kids. At the tip of the promontory, an iron catwalk leads out to the **Rocher de la Vierge**, a rocky islet bearing a white statue of the Virgin – a work of Eiffel, he of the tower – that has become Biarritz's landmark. Other rocky islets are scattered about in the surf, and the view seems irresistible to lovers – and film-makers such as Eric Rohmer, the scenery figuring largely in his *Le Rayon Vert*. Just east of the promontory, the tamarisk-and-hydrangea-fringed **Port des Pêcheurs** no longer sees any fishing, but is merely a picturesque venue for snacks in one of the waterfront *tapas* bars.

As for the town itself, only the streets immediately inland from the museum bluff are worth a passing glance. Place Clemenceau is fronted by prissy, high-nosed establishments like Salons de Thé Miremont and Pâtisserie Dodin; further west, above the old fishing port, the places Sainte-Eugénie and Atalaye can muster a number of whimsically turreted and balconied hotels and villas. In recent years, any number of these have fallen to the wrecker's ball, but in 1997, under threat of a fifty-acre development proposed to replace the Casino Municipal by Gaullist councillors in cahoots with developers, the rest of the council resigned, forcing the resignation of the mayor. He was replaced by a centrist acceptable to conservationists, who immediately slapped a preservation order on the town's surviving 230 follies, not coincidentally guaranteeing work for restoration architects and maintenance men for the next generation.

The beaches

The wave-pounded **beaches** to either side of the promontory are generously sandy and, according to the fickle weather, either carpeted with a mix of beautiful people and middle-class families tanning themselves or abandoned to wet-suited Californian and Australian surf bums. Served by a special *navette* bus in summer, the strands extend 5km from the southern **Plage de la Milady** to the lighthouse (visits daily April–Sept 10am–noon & 2–6.30pm; rest of year daily 2–5pm) at **Pointe Saint-Martin** to the north. The main sections are Plage Marbella; Côte des Basque; Plage du Port Vieux, closest to the promontory; and the Grande Plage, backed by the domes of a Russian Orthodox church dating from 1908, and also overlooked by the former **Villa Eugénie**, a present of Napoléon III to his wife in 1855. Now the luxury *Hôtel du Palais*, it was twice gutted by fire between 1881 and 1905, so that little remains of the original fabric. Beyond Pointe Saint-Martin begin the even wilder, broader beaches of Anglet (see below).

Practicalities

The **train station** lies an inconvenient 3km east of the centre, in the quarter called La Négresse; city bus #2 or #9 links it with the *Hôtel de Ville*. **Buses** from Bayonne and Anglet call at the more central place Bellevue. The **tourist office** is behind the *Hôtel de Ville* and Casino Municipal in place d'Ixelles (summer daily 8am–8pm; rest of year Mon–Fri 8.30am–12.30pm & 2–6.45pm; ☎05.59.24.20.24), and has information in particular about the various festivals. Given Biarritz's sprawling layout, **bike or scooter rental** is worth considering for longer stays; enquire at So-Bi-Lo, 24 rue Peyroloubilh (☎05.59.24.94.47).

Accommodation

Contrary to most expectations, there are a handful of affordable **hotels** in town, though obviously during July or August advance reservations are all but mandatory. Start with the friendly, family-run *Hôtel de la Marine*, just off place de l'Atalaye at 1 rue des Goélands (☎05.59.24.34.09; ③), or the *Hôtel Atalaye* at 6 rue des Goélands

(☎05.59.24.06.76; ④), dating from 1912. Heading towards the Plage du Port Vieux, you'll find the old-fashioned *Hôtel Palym*, 7 rue du Port-Vieux (☎05.59.24.16.56; ④), or well sited right above the *plage*, the *Hôtel Le Welcome* (☎05.59.24.10.42; ⑤), with an English-speaking proprietress, plus a sea-view pizzeria-bar. Much further inland, but quieter, the small *Hôtel Maïtagaria* at 34 av Carnot (☎05.59.24.26.65; ⑤) has a garden in its favour.

Otherwise you're best advised either to stay in Bayonne or Anglet (see below) and travel in by bus, or find a place in one of the heavily subscribed **campsites** which dot the coast to the south – these also require reservations in season. *Le Biarritz* (☎05.59.23.00.12; May–Sept) and *Le Splendid* (☎05.59.23.01.29; April–Sept), both in route d'Harcet, are about 500m from Plage de la Milady.

Eating and drinking

As with accommodation, so with **food and drink**: a bit of hunting around in less obvious spots is rewarded; for once in France it's possible to eat after 10pm. *Le Bistrot des Halles*, 1 rue du Centre (☎05.59.24.21.22; closed Sun evenings low season, & Mon), features daily-changing specials for about 110F per person; reservations advisable. *Bar Jean*, at 5 rue des Halles, offers *plats du jour* for about 50F or seafood *tapas* until midnight. True night-owls gather at *Le Morgan*, 4 rue du Helder, where you can down oysters or basically prepared dishes until 4am. Down at the Port des Pêcheurs, *La Crampotte* is probably a better bet for light grilled seafood snacks than the adjacent, rather overpriced *Chez Albert*. Finally, 2km southwest of the train station, beyond Chapelet on the road to Arcangues, the moderately priced *L'Auberge de Chapelet* keeps more usual hours and is worth the considerable detour for its well-prepared Basque food.

Anglet

Sprawling north and east from Biarritz, amorphous **ANGLET** (pronounced *Anglett*) occupies most of the triangular territory between the Pointe Saint-Martin, the mouth of the Adour and Bayonne. There is nothing here of note except half a dozen excellent beaches – the most famous being **Chambre d'Amour**, so named after two lovers trapped and drowned here by the rising tide, and the surfers' mecca of **Sables d'Or**. As the pair's fate indicates, swimming here is generally dangerous owing to treacherous currents and you should heed the warning signs and lifeguards.

Buses run to Anglet from the Hôtel de Ville in Biarritz; alternatively you can walk here in about half an hour along av de l'Imperatrice, becoming av MacCroskey, then second left down to the seaside bd des Plages. The spacious, friendly and well-run **youth hostel** in quartier Chiberta at the north end of route des Vignes (☎05.59.63.86.49; no curfew; ①), offers a full programme of sporting activities – including, of course, surfing – and operates a cafeteria from June to September. Using the #6 bus, alight near the (not especially recommended) Fontaine-Laborde campsite, bear up the road by the site, then left onto promenade des Sables and left again into route des Vignes. There are few other noteworthy options for eating or staying in Anglet, aside from the *Camping de la Chambre d'Amour* on route de Bouney (☎05.59.03.71.66; open May–Sept), 600m inland from Plage de l'Océan. This is a bit pricier than normal for a campsite but has its own store and restaurant, as well as being close to other shops.

Saint-Jean-de-Luz and around

Just fifteen minutes and 20km south of Biarritz by one of the many fast trains, **SAINT-JEAN-DE-LUZ** (Donibane Lohitzun – "Saint John of the Marshes" – in Euskera) rates as one of the most popular, though still attractive resorts on the Basque coast. It has been an active fishing port for centuries, whose tuna, sardine and anchovy catches still find their way onto the menus of countless eateries around town.

Previously the fishermen were mainly preoccupied with whales and cod; local sailors travelled as far as Newfoundland, which the Basques claim to have discovered one hundred years before Columbus reached America. In the seventeenth century, Dutch and English whalers drove them from their habitual ports in Arctic waters, so the enterprising Basques devised a method of boiling down the blubber on board, enabling the ships – essentially the first factory whalers – to stay at sea much longer. Later, by the provisions of the eighteenth-century Treaty of Utrecht, the local skippers lost their cod-fishing grounds off Newfoundland and only saved themselves from ruin by becoming pirates. The more respectable pursuit of anchovies, tuna and sardines only resumed in the nineteenth century.

The Town

Wrecked by a fire set by invading Spanish in 1558, Saint-Jean itself has since developed into a solid and pleasant place, its seafaring wealth transmuted into the seventeenth- and eighteenth-century homes of the merchants and shipowners. Apart from loitering in the partly pedestrianized streets of the old quarter, you can visit one of these homes, the so-called **Maison Louis XIV** (guided tours June–Sept daily 10.30am–noon & 2.30–5.30pm, until 6pm in July & Aug), actually built for the shipowning Lohobiague family in 1635 but temporary residence of the Sun King in 1660 when he came to Saint-Jean for his marriage of political convenience to Maria-Teresa, the Infanta of Castile. (Oddly perhaps, the couple managed to fall in love, and the widowed king years later remarked that her death was "the only annoyance she ever caused me".) The stately interior is authentically Basque, with heavyweight wooden fixtures, some more delicate pieces of furniture and fine examples of tableware and glass. Maria-Teresa lodged in the equally imposing pink Italianate villa overlooking the harbour on quai de l'Infante.

Their sumptuous wedding took place in the church of **Saint-Jean-Baptiste** on rue Gambetta, and the door through which the couple left was permanently sealed immediately afterwards. Even without this curiosity, the church deserves a look: the largest French Basque church, it has magnificent tiered oak galleries, reached by wrought-iron staircases. Hanging from the ceiling is an *ex voto* model of the Empress Eugénie's paddle-steamer, *Eagle*, which narrowly escaped running aground near Saint-Jean in 1867.

Practicalities

Buses arrive in the outdoor terminal at place du Maréchal-Foch, also home to the **tourist office** (July & Aug Mon–Sat 9am–8pm, Sun 10.30am–1pm & 3–6.30pm; rest of year Mon–Sat 9am–12.30pm & 2–6.30pm; ☎05.59.26.03.16). **Bikes** can be rented from ADO on nearby avenue Labrouche, or Luz-Evasion on place Maurice-Ravel. The **train station** lies at the southern edge of the centre, within a short walk of a few affordable **hotels**; half-board is almost universally obligatory in high summer. Try *Hôtel Toki-Ona*, 10 rue Marion-Garay (☎05.56.26.11.54; ③; closed Nov–March); *Le Trinquet Maïtena*, in the centre by the *fronton* at 42 rue du Midi (☎05.59.26.05.13; ④); or *Hôtel Verdun*, 13 av Verdun (☎05.59.26.02.55; ③). A little way north of the centre in Le Lac neighbourhood, *Hôtel Kopa-Gorry*, 9 rue Paul-Gelos (☎05.59.26.04.93; ③; closed Oct), is a final mid-range possibility. There are numerous **campsites**, all gathered in a *zone des campings* about 3km northeast of town in the Acotz and Erromardie districts.

Eating and drinking

Every Tuesday and Friday morning there's a lively street **market** on avenue Victor-Hugo, just outside the permanent *halle*. Otherwise, the social centre is **place Louis XIV**, near the harbour, with its bandstand (free concerts) under the plane trees and various cafés.

The obvious **restaurants** on picturesque rue de la République, leading northwest from the square toward the beach, are by and large tourist traps, though if you insist, *La Taverne Basque* at no. 7 is the most reasonable, with menus from around 100F. There's ample scope elsewhere in Saint-Jean for fair-value eating. For just **seafood**, look no further than the harbour and the market district: *Grillerie des Sardines* (mid-June to mid-Sept), right on the quay across from the tourist office, is always packed and reasonable value, at 55F to 60F for a somewhat small-portioned meal. *Olharroa*, at 16 rue Marion-Garay (corner of bd Victor-Hugo), charges 70 to 80F for a simple but well-prepared meal of mussels or fish, including a drink, in congenial surroundings. Alternatively *La Buvette des Halles* – a tiny hole-in-the-wall joint installed in a corner of the market building and identified only by a sign reading *Sardines Grillées Crustacées* – offers similar food at similar prices at sidewalk tables (lunchtime only). In the old town, several streets near rue de la République feature reasonable establishments: *La Vieille Auberge* at 21 rue Tourasse (closed Wed, and either lunchtime or evening Tues) for more seafood at 72F and up; *Le Tourasse* at no. 25 for a wider range of dishes from 110F and up; *Ramuntcho* at 24 rue Garat (closed Nov–Feb & Mon); and *Le Prisme* at 65 rue Saint-Jacques for inexpensive *plats de jour* which attract a local clientele.

Across the river: Ciboure

Saint-Jean shares the Nivelle estuary with **CIBOURE** on its south bank, both *communes* taking maximum advantage of one of the very few sheltered anchorages along the Atlantic coast south of Bordeaux. By comparison, Ciboure is calm and untouristy, with two beautiful streets opposite the end of the bridge over from Saint-Jean: the waterfront **quai Maurice-Ravel** (a plaque commemorates the composer's birth at no. 12), and the parallel **rue Pocolette** behind, an exquisite terrace of wide-fronted, half-timbered and balconied town houses, many built by seventeenth-century traders who did business with the West Indies and the Orient. Near the south end of rue Pocolette protrudes the octagonal tower of the sixteenth-century church of **Saint-Vincent**, inside which are particularly good examples of a Basque-country altarpiece and three-tiered gallery, as well as yet another model-ship *ex voto* suspended in the middle.

If Saint-Jean-de-Luz is full up, Ciboure makes a possible fallback base, with the **hotels** *Bakea* on place Camille Julian, opposite the bridge (☎05.59.47.34.40; ④), with a moderately priced seafood **restaurant**, and *La Caravelle*, bd Pierre Benoit, the continuation of quai Maurice-Ravel (☎05.59.47.18.05; ⑤), the most reasonable possibilities.

Standing on the bridge, you look over the dock stacked with fishing paraphernalia, towards the extremely narrow harbour entrance. In the opposite direction the view inland over small craft beached in the river mud at low tide is dominated by the 900-metre landmark peak of La Rhune (see below), astride the border and the westernmost Pyrenean summit of note.

Inland from Saint-Jean: Ascain, La Rhune and Sare

Heading southwest from Saint-Jean, perhaps on one of the three or four summer weekday buses towards Sare from the train station, you reach **ASCAIN** after 6km, doll's-house cute and thus inevitably a target of the overspill from Saint-Jean in season. There are several expensive hotels here, in one of which – *De la Rhune* – Pierre Loti stayed while writing *Ramuntcho* (see below); the most reasonable is *Des Chasseurs*, place Pierre-Loti by the church (☎05.59.54.00.31; ④), with a good attached restaurant.

La Rhune

To reach **La Rhune** (from the Euskera *larre dun*, meaning "good pasture"), stay on the bus for 4km more until the **Col de Saint-Ignace**, from where you can pick up the La Rhune **rack-and-pinion railway** (July–Sept daily departures every 30min 10am–5pm; May, June & Oct to mid-Nov, weekends and holidays at 10am & 3pm only; rest of year 10am & 3pm daily during school holidays only; information on ☎05.59.54.20.26). The 4200-metre journey to the top takes just half an hour, but allow two hours for the queues – time possibly filled at the eminently reasonable *Restaurant Col de Saint-Ignace*, right opposite the train terminal, where you can dine for under 100F. Even with a meal to work off, it's a fairly easy climb – you can walk from the pass to the top in two hours. From the summit – topped by a radio transmitter – there are fine views over most of the Basque provinces, Spanish as well as French.

Sare

It's worth walking the extra 3km from the Col de Saint-Ignace, or along the GR10 from the intermediate station below La Rhune's summit, to **SARE**, from where you can catch the bus back to Saint-Jean (or stay the night). This proves to be another perfectly proportioned Basque village, with a galleried church, *fronton* and tree-shaded streets. Pierre Loti used it, disguised as "Etchezar", for the setting of his 1897 romance *Ramuntcho*. Animal lovers might avoid the place in autumn, when Sare earns its nickname of *l'enfer des palombes* – "woodpigeon hell" – as thousands of the creatures are both shot and trapped live in nets strung between trees.

Among a selection of fairly pricey local **hotels**, two of the more reasonable are *Lastiry*, place du Fronton (☎05.59.54.20.07; ③), or – in the Ihalar neighbourhood, on the D4 – the *Baratchartea* (☎05.59.54.24.48; ④), with a well-regarded **restaurant**. Failing this, there are no fewer than three **campsites** south of the village, on the way up towards the border: *Telletchea* (☎05.59.54.20.12; July & Aug); *La Petite-Rhune* (☎05.59.54.23.97; April–Sept), and the highest one, *Goyenetche* (☎05.59.54.21.71; April–Oct), along the D306 towards the Grottes de Sare.

Hendaye

Running parallel, the D912 and *Chemin Piétonnier Littoral* footpath follow the cliffs of the so-called Corniche Basque 15km west from Saint-Jean-de-Luz to **HENDAYE** (Hendaia), the road cutting inland a little only at the Pointe Sainte-Anne. The path cuts through the Domaine d'Abbadia, a vast nature reserve around a privately built and owned nineteenth-century château. Neither **Hendaye-Ville** nor the coastal annexe of **Hendaye-Plage** have much contemporary intrinsic interest despite a significant past, including the long-time residence (and death) of **Pierre Loti**, author of the locally set *Ramuntcho* as well as assorted orientalist romances. Now half-forgotten, Loti was vastly popular in his time for syrupy, exotic romances, their settings – including Istanbul and Tahiti as well as the Pays Basque – gleaned from a lifetime of far-flung postings in the service of the French navy.

For the best **beaches**, drivers should bear right at the promontory, where there's also a road going inland; if you're walking you have the choice of the superb route around the rocky point, or of cutting across the peninsula to rejoin the road. The main road and rail line continue a couple more kilometres to Hendaye-Ville, which has another well-protected sandy beach fronting the Chingoudy estuary, but a somewhat dull atmosphere.

If you're taken with the place, be warned that while Ville is marginally less expensive than Plage, there's little short-term **accommodation**; if you've come this far, it's probably best to carry on into Spain for the night. In the way of **restaurants**, there's the surprisingly good-value and popular *La Petite Marée*, 2 av des Mimosa (reservations on ☎05.59.20.77.96; closed Wed in term time), serving seafood until 10.30pm.

Hendaye-Ville lies on the River Bidassoa, with the border running down the middle for about 8km at this point. Just upstream from the town, the tiny wooded island known as **Île des Faisans** or Île de la Conférence is administered jointly by the two countries; it looks insignificant now, but was once used for meetings between their respective monarchs, the best known of which was the signing of the **Treaty of the Pyrenees** in 1659. The following year it again became the centre of attraction when the marriage contracts between Louis XIV and the Spanish Infanta Maria-Teresa were signed here. The great painter Velázquez reputedly died of a chill caught while painting the interior of the negotiations room.

Hendaye almost made history once more on October 23, 1940, when Spanish *Caudillo* Franco met Hitler in the Hendaye train station. Despite the blandishment of a guaranteed Moroccan mini-empire, Franco refused the Fuehrer's invitation to join the war on the Axis side, and Hitler was later overheard saying that he would rather go to the dentist than meet his potential ally again.

Walking from Hendaye

The **GR10** and **HRP** both start their trans-Pyrenean course beside the casino at Hendaye-Plage. The early part of the walk is dull: along avenue Général-Leclerc, through Hendaye-Ville on rue des Citronniers, under the rail line, then 50m east on the N10 before following waymarks towards the A63 highway. A cattle track passes underneath and continues to the tiny hilltop village of **BIRIATOU**, where the walking starts to get interesting. (If you've got access to transport, or can splash out on a taxi, start at Biriatou.)

A short, steep section leads to a Basque church with a collection of weather-worn Celtic-type tombstones, next door to the fifteenth-century *Auberge Hirribarren*, a temporary haven for many Allied soldiers during World War II and now an excellent **restaurant** (meals for 90–160F a head until 9pm). From here the main footpaths and a number of local variations rise rapidly above the coast to semi-isolation, with only the buzzing power lines (which you soon leave behind) and the occasional long-distance walker or local jogger to disturb the peace.

There are a couple of day-long circuits: looping west of the main path at the **Col des Joncs** and descending along the frontier to follow the Bidassoa back to Biriatou, or circling east by cutting away shortly after the *col*, at frontier stone 11. Both alternatives are well waymarked, but it is advisable to have handy the Randonnées Pyrénéennes 1:50,000 "Pays Basque Ouest" map.

Another alternative would be to follow the GR10/HRP **east** to La Rhune (see previous page), a 27-kilometre walk from Hendaye (8–9hr) with no shelter available until the *gîte d'étape* in the hamlet of **MENTO BAYTA** (☎05.59.54.00.98; ①), shortly before La Rhune; in good weather a bivouac is a better alternative.

Irún and around

The Spanish Basque coastal province of Gipuzkoa adjoins the French frontier, and its border town, **Irún**, is one of the major road and rail entry points into Spain. There are fast public transport connections on to San Sebastián, although if you're travelling more slowly or under your own power, the fishing ports of **Hondarribia** and **Pasajes** are worth a stop. The main C133 road to the south crosses almost immediately into Navarra and leads via the beautiful Valle de Bidasoa to the N121 highway, and thence eventually to Pamplona. The **GR11**, traversing northwest from Elizondo, finally finishes its 700-plus-kilometre course from the Catalan Costa Brava, expiring in the Atlantic surf at Cabo Higuer.

Irún

Like most border towns, **IRÚN**'s chief concern is how to make a quick buck from passing travellers, and the main point in its favour is the ease with which you can leave; there are trains to Hendaye in France and to San Sebastián throughout the day, and regular long-distance and international connections. If arriving by train from Paris (or elsewhere in France) at Hendaye, note that it is far quicker to take the local *topo* (mole train, so called because of all the tunnels it goes through) from the separate platform on the right outside Hendaye main station; it runs every thirty minutes to Irún (to the station at Avda. de Colón 52) and San Sebastián.

If you do need to spend the night, there are plenty of bars and places to eat, and prices are markedly lower than in France or San Sebastián (which is no place to arrive late with nowhere to stay). In the vicinity of Irún's main train station are several small, reasonably priced **hostales** and **restaurants** specializing in good local food. *Hostal Irún*, c/Zubiaurre 5 (☎943/61 16 37; ③), and *Bar Pensión los Fronterizos*, c/Estación 7 (☎943/61 92 05; ③), have some of the lowest-priced rooms; for more comfort try the nearby *Lizaso*, c/Aduana 5–7 (☎943/61 16 00; ④), or *Matxinbenta*, Paseo Colón 21 (☎943/62 13 84; ④). For a modest outlay, the *Asador Baserri* at c/Berrotarán 5 (closed Sun evening and Mon), serves Basque, farm-style meat dishes.

Hondarribia

The fishing port and fortified stronghold of **HONDARRIBIA** (formerly Fuenterrabía), 6km north of Irún and opposite Hendaye, is a far more attractive place than either of these two. The cobbled streets of the original fishing village run from the heights topped by the castle down to the harbour. Calle San Pedro, the tamarisk-lined main promenade, is flanked with traditional, wood-beamed Basque houses, interspersed with bars offering some of the best seafood and *pinchos* around. In summer, the fine **beaches** just beyond the town are an escape from ultra-crowded Playa de la Concha in San Sebastián.

Hondarribia has a picturesque, walled old town entered via the fifteenth-century **Puerta de Santa María**, carved with the town coat of arms and angels paying court to Our Lady of Guadalupe, who is said to have saved the town in a two-month French siege in 1638. Calle Mayor, leading up to the Plaza de Armas, has further fine examples of wood-beamed houses adorned with wrought-iron balconies and studded doors, some displaying the family coats of arms above doorways. At the end of c/Mayor stands the church of **Santa María**, predominantly Gothic though extensively and misguidedly renovated in the seventeenth century. The proxy wedding between Louis XIV and the Maria-Teresa which confirmed the 1659 Treaty of the Pyrenees took place here in 1660, six days before the official signing ceremony on the Île des Faisans. The plaza itself is dominated by the **Palacio de Carlos Quinto**, started originally in the tenth century by Sancho el Fuerte of Navarra and subsequently extended by Carlos V in the sixteenth. It is now a luxurious *parador* (see below), and it's worth at least having a drink at the bar inside.

Practicalities

There is a helpful **tourist office** on c/Javier Ugarte 6 (☎943/64 54 58; July & Aug Mon–Sat 9am–8pm, Sun 10am–2pm; rest of year Mon–Fri 9am–1.30pm & 4–6.30pm, Sat 10am–2pm). Good, if sometimes pricey **accommodation** includes *Hostal Alvarez Quintero*, c/Bernat Etxepare 2, in the Edificio Miramar (☎943/64 22 99; ④), or *Txoko-Goxua*, c/Miguel María Ayestaran 19 (☎943/64 46 58; ③), in the old town. The *Hotel Rio Bidasoa,* c/Nafarroa Behera (☎943/64 54 08; ⑤), ⑥), has its own pool, while the *Parador Nacional El Emperador* (☎943/64 21 40; ⑥⑥) is stunningly located in the town's fortified castle. The **youth hostel**, *Juan Sebastián Elkano*, is on Carretera Faro (☎943/64 15 50; ①); fork left beyond c/San Pedro on the way to the beaches. The closest **campsite**, *Camping Jaizkibel* (☎943/64 16 79; open all year), is 2km west of town along Carretera Guadalupe towards Pasajes. Also outside town, just by the chapel of Nuestra Señora de Guadalupe, is a signposted turn-off to *Artzu* (☎943/64 05 30; ④) in Montaña hamlet, an *agroturismo* offering accommodation in an old restored farmhouse.

The bars along c/San Pedro are the best hunting ground for **food and drink**. In the old town, tucked away in a narrow cobbled alley two streets behind c/Mayor, the *Mamutzar* restaurant serves a good value *menú del día*, and next door is the tiny *Hamlet* bar, a popular haunt for radical Basque punks.

Moving west

Frequent **buses** leave from c/San Pedro to San Sebastián. The stretch of coastline from here as far as the port of Pasajes is particularly rugged and has long been a haven for smugglers. With your own transport you should foresake the busy highway inland in favour of the initially wiggly minor road towards the chapel of **Nuestra Señora de Guadalupe** (5km), target of a September 8 festival; the road continues climbing more gradually through pine forests to the 543-metre-high peak of **Monte Jaizkibel**, where there are wonderful views along the Basque coastline. You then descend to Pasajes de San Juan, a total of 16km.

Pasajes

The one place you might consider stopping for any length of time en route between Irún and San Sebastián is the port of **PASAJES**, consisting of three separate settlements built around the sheltered mouth of the Río Oyarzun. Pasajes Ancho and Pasajes San Pedro on the south bank are modern, industrial ports, considered the least problematical on a stretch of coast known for its difficult swells; it was from here that the Marquis de Lafayette, general and statesman, sailed to America to fight for the colonists in the War of Independence. But the old quarter of **PASAJES SAN JUAN** (Pasaia Donibane) on the north bank retains its charm. The narrow cobbled c/San Juan (Victor Hugo once lived at no. 65, the house built over the tunnel) leads to Plaza de Santiago, with its colourful, wood-fronted merchant houses. Pasajes San Juan is also famous for its waterside **fish restaurants**, many of which offer good-value *menús del día*. A **launch** (*txalupa*) runs throughout the day until 10.30pm across the Oyarzun to Pasajes San Pedro, from where frequent buses run to San Sebastián's Alameda del Boulevard.

Towards Pamplona

If you're heading straight down to Pamplona, you'll pass through the **Valle de Bidasoa** with its succession of beautifully preserved towns, the best of which are Vera de

Bidasoa, Lesaka and Etxalar. At Mugaire, the road intersects the N121; right (south) leads over the Puerto de Velate to Pamplona, while the left (easterly) turning takes you up to the Baztán valley (see p.422). The Bidasoa valley lies along a direct bus route between San Sebastián/Irún and Pamplona.

Vera de Bidasoa

The first substantial place beyond the Gipuzkoa/Navarra border, **VERA (BERA) DE BIDASOA** offers some of the finest examples of old wood-beamed and traditional stone houses in the region; the brightly painted buildings along c/Altzarte and the main square are particularly attractive. About 100m off the square, just past the old Customs post, is the former house (no. 24) of the Basque writer Pio Baroja, which used to house a small museum. It's now closed indefinitely following a burglary; for current information, contact the **tourist office** (summer only) in c/Altzarte or phone ☎948/63 00 20.

If you want to **stay**, there's the small *Fonda Chantre*, c/San Estéban 15 (☎948/63 02 39; ③) or the higher-standard *Euskalduna*, c/Bidasoa 5 (☎948/63 03 92; ④), with a good restaurant offering a *menú del día* and local specialities. Alternatively, there's a **casa rural** just outside town, *Casa Etxebertea*, Barrio de Zelain (☎948/63 02 72; ③), which also has bicycles to rent.

Lesaka

South of Vera just 4km up the Río Bidasoa, a turn to the right leads within a couple of kilometres more to **LESAKA**. Despite the eyesore of a large factory on the outskirts of the town, it's a beautiful place dominated by the hilltop parish church in which the pews bear family names of the local farms and mansions. On the banks of the irrigation channel which flows through town stands one of the best remaining examples of a *casa torre* (fortified private house) of a design peculiar to the Basque provinces, dating back to the days when the northwestern marches of Navarra were in the hands of a few powerful and constantly feuding families.

For **accommodation** try *Pensión Tolareta*, Plaza Berria 2 (☎948/63 71 06; ②), above a shop just off the main square, or the more upmarket *Hotel Berean* (☎948/62 75 09, fax 62 76 47; ④) near the main road.

Etxalar

ETXALAR is an even tinier place, 4km east of the main C133, but is perhaps the best-preserved town of the valley, famous for the impressive array of Basque disc-topped headstones in the churchyard. There's an excellent **casa rural**, *Casa Domekenea* (☎948/63 50 31; ③) in the centre, and another, *Casa Herri-Gain* (☎948/63 52 08; ③), perched on a steep, panoramic hill.

Walking: the end of the GR11

Heading northwest from Elizondo, the **GR11** finishes its course by passing through or very near many of the places above. The penultimate day of a trans-Pyrenean traverse, from **Elizondo to Vera de Bidasoa**, is the tougher and more interesting of the two, crossing deserted country to skim the frontier between Etxalar and Sare; count on seven hours to reach Vera. The final half-day is more perfunctory, skirting rather than climbing the **Peñas de Haya**, and then unrelentingly urban in character once you enter Irún and Hondarribia. Only at the end is there a bit of drama, as you emerge beyond the beach of Hondarribia onto **Cabo Higuer**, the promontory marking the terminus of both the GR route and the Spanish Pyrenees.

San Sebastián

Capital of Gipuzkoa (Guizpúzcoa) autonomous region, and the undisputed queen of the Basque resorts, **SAN SEBASTIÁN** (Donostia) is a picturesque seaside town with good beaches and frequent transport connections with Irún and Hondarribia. It has long been among Spain's most fashionable places to escape the heat of the southern summers, and in July and August it's always packed. Although San Sebastián tries hard to be chic, it's still too much of a family resort to compete in those terms with the Catalan Mediterranean fleshpots of Roses or Cadaqués.

Set around the deep, still bay of La Concha and enclosed by rolling low hills, the town is beautifully situated. The old quarter sits between the bay and the Río Urumea which divides the town, its back to the wooded slopes of Monte Urgull, while newer development has spread onto the east bank of the Urumea, around the edge of the bay to the foot of Monte Igeldo and on the hills overlooking the bay.

Arrival and information

Most **buses** arrive at Plaza Pio XII, fifteen minutes' walk up the river from the centre, but from Pasajes they call at the Alameda del Boulevard, and from Hondarribia they stop on Plaza de Gipuzkoa. The mainline train station, the **Estación de Atocha**, for arrivals from Pamplona via Alsasua or further afield, is across the Urumea on the Paseo de Francia; local lines from Hendaye and Bilbao via Zarauz and Zumaya (which do not accept rail passes) use the **Estación de Amara** on c/Easo.

The **municipal Turismo** (Mon–Sat 8am–8pm, Sun 10am–1pm; closed Sat afternoon out of season; ☎943/48 11 66) is on c/Reina Regente in the Teatro Victoria Eugenia. For a greater selection of pamphlets there is also the very useful Gipuzkoan **regional tourist office** (Mon–Sat 9.30am–1.30pm & 3.30–6.30pm, plus Sun 9.30am–1.30pm in July & Aug) at Paseo de los Fueros 1, just off the main Avda. de la Libertad.

San Sebastián is something of a travel hub for the region. Viajes TIVE, c/Tomás Gros 3 (☎943/27 69 34) is a youth/student **travel agency** that sells tickets for international buses and discount plane tickets. Another good travel agency is Viajes Aran, c/Elkano 1 (☎943/42 90 09 or 42 90 11). For travel books and maps (both local and elsewhere), and for **books** on all things related to the Basque provinces, the best is Graphos on the corner of Alameda del Boulevard and c/Mayor. Also recommended are Bilintx, c/Esterlines 10, and Dr. Camino, c/XXXI de Agosto 32–36, which has a small reading room.

Accommodation

Accommodation, though plentiful, can be expensive and hard to find in season – if you arrive without a reservation in July or (worse) August, or during the film festival in September, you'll have to start looking early in the day. There is little difference in rates between the cheapest places in the **Parte Vieja** (old quarter) and elsewhere, although *hostales* along the Alameda del Boulevard do tend to be more expensive. There is often more chance of finding space in the cathedral – **Centro** – area around c/Easo, c/San Martín, c/Fuenterrabia and the lively c/San Bartolomé, or on the other side of the river in **Gros**, behind the main train station in **Egia**, or in the new part of town, **Amara Nuevo**, on the way to the Anoeta sports complex. Asking in bars in any of the above-mentioned areas about unofficial private rooms will often also produce results – though the Turismo strongly recommends sticking to licensed establishments.

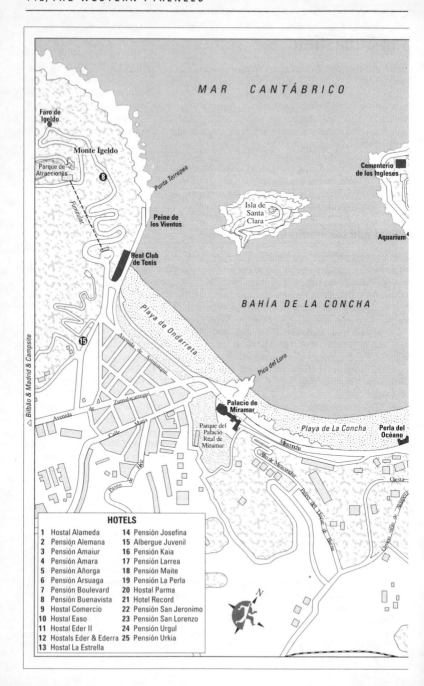

MAR CANTÁBRICO

Faro de
Igeldo

Monte Igeldo

Parque de
Atracciones

Punta Torrepea

Cementerio
de los Ingleses

Isla de
Santa
Clara

Peine de
los Vientos

Aquarium

Real Club
de Tenis

BAHÍA DE LA CONCHA

Playa de Ondarreta

◁ Bilbáo & Madrid & Campsite

Avenida de Satúregui

Pico del Loro

Zumalacárregui

Palacio de
Miramar

Playa de La Concha

Perla del
Océano

Avenida de

Calle Maira

Parque del
Palacio
Real de
Miramar

Río de Miraconcha

Paseo de

Paseo del Duque de Baena

Cuesta

N

HOTELS

1	Hostal Alameda	14	Pensión Josefina
2	Pensión Alemana	15	Albergue Juvenil
3	Pensión Amaiur	16	Pensión Kaia
4	Pensión Amara	17	Pensión Larrea
5	Pensión Añorga	18	Pensión Maite
6	Pensión Arsuaga	19	Pensión La Perla
7	Pensión Boulevard	20	Hostal Parma
8	Pensión Buenavista	21	Hotel Record
9	Hostal Comercio	22	Pensión San Jeronimo
10	Hostal Easo	23	Pensión San Lorenzo
11	Hostal Eder II	24	Pensión Urgul
12	Hostals Eder & Ederra	25	Pensión Urkia
13	Hostal La Estrella		

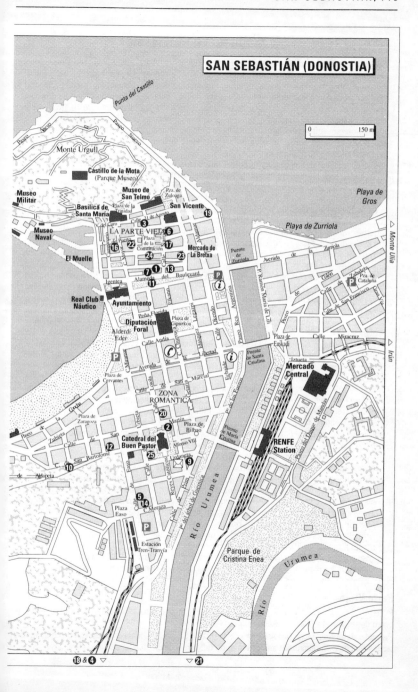

SAN SEBASTIÁN (DONOSTIA)

0   150 m

Punta del Castillo

Paseo Nuevo

Monte Urgull

Castillo de la Mota
(Parque Museo)

Museo
Militar

Museo de
San Telmo

Pza. de
Zuloaga

Playa de
Gros

Basilíca de
Santa María

Plaza de la
Trinidad

San Vicente

19

Playa de Zurriola

Museo
Naval

LA PARTE VIEJA

3

6

Mercado de
La Bretxa

Monte Ulia

El Muelle

16

22

Plaza
de la
Constitución

17

23

Puente
de
Zurriola

Avenida   de   la   Zurriola

Calle   de   Colón

Pza. de
Cataluña

24

Irún

Real Club
Náutico

Ayuntamiento

7   1   13

Alameda   del   Boulevard

11

Calle   de   San Francisco

Diputación
Foral

Peña Florida

Plaza de
Gipuzkoa

Alderdi
Eder

Calle Andía

Calle   Libertad

Plaza de
Euskadi

Calle   Miracruz

Plaza de
Cervantes

Avenida   de   San   Marcial

Puente
de Santa
Catalina

Mercado
Central

ZONA
ROMÁNTICA

20

Iztueta

RENFE
Station

Catedral del
Buen Pastor

12

2

25

Plaza de
Bilbao

9

Plaza de
Zaragoza

San   Martín

Alfonso VIII

10

San Bartolomé

de   Aldapeta

5   14

Plaza
Easo

C. Moraza

Puente
de María
Cristina

Río   Urumea

Estación
Tren-Tranvía

Parque de
Cristina Enea

Río   Urumea

18 & 4 ▽   ▽ 21

BASQUE NATIONALISM

Despite the high-profile activities of **ETA** (*Euskadi ta Askatasuna* – "Freedom for the Basques"), **Basque nationalism** is not an especially recent phenomenon. Richard Ford wrote in the nineteenth century that "these highlanders, bred on metal-pregnant mountains, and nursed amid storms in a cradle indomitable as themselves, have always known how to forge their iron into arms, and to wield them in defence of their own independence." The Visigoths perceived the *Vascones* as being a "dangerous rural population emerging from the mountains to threaten the settled inhabitants of the valleys". The Visigoth king, Recared, unable to completely subdue the region, used to send his troops out here just to keep them fit.

For almost the entire history of both France and Spain, the Basques jealously defended their *fors* or *fueros* – ancient customary privileges guaranteeing them effective autonomy – against constant pressure from Paris and Madrid, and guarded the wealth brought by seafaring skills, mineral riches and industrial enterprise. After the Revolution in 1790, the French Basques' millennium-old *fors* were abolished as part of the general centralizing strategy of the Jacobins, and the three traditional French Basque regions were lumped together with Béarn in a new administrative *département*. In Spain, it was not until 1876 and the second, final defeat of the Carlists, whom the Basques supported as upholding their own traditionalist values, that the victorious Liberals finally abolished the *fueros* altogether to punish the rebellious Basques.

Although the conservative, traditionalist **Basque National Party** (PNV) emerged in Spain towards the end of the nineteenth century, it is only in this century that Basque nationalism has become associated with the political left, mostly in reaction to Franco's regime. Cut off from their Republican allies by predominantly rural Navarra and Alava, whose conservative landowners sided with the Nationalists, the urbanized Basque coastal provinces of Gipuzkoa and Vizkaia were conquered in a vicious campaign that included the infamous German bombing of **Gernika** (Guernica) in 1937. Franco's vengeful boot went in hard, and as many as twenty-one thousand people died in his attempts to tame the Basques after the war. Public use of the language was forbidden, and central control was asserted with the gun.

But Spanish state violence failed signally, succeeding only in nurturing a new resistance based on ETA, which took to the field in 1968. Their terrorist activities have included scores of bombings, with nearly eight hundred victims to date, the most spectacular success being the 1973 assassination in Madrid of Franco's right-hand man and probable successor, Admiral Carrero Blanco. Even now the military and the *Guardia Civil* are regarded – and behave – as an army of occupation, and the more radically minded Basques of the *Abertzale* (nationalist) movement continue to support ETA's aims, if not their methods.

Following the **return to democracy**, however, things have changed substantially. The Spanish Basque parliament has been granted a fair degree of autonomy in its own affairs (it's the only autonomous community allowed to collect its own taxes), and there's a Basque police force, the *ertzaintza* (distinguished by its red berets) much in evidence in the streets. The Basque **language** is flourishing again and is taught in at least half of all primary schools in the coastal regions. The Basque flag (the *Ikurriña*) flies everywhere.

Since gaining home rule, Spanish Euskadi has, like Catalunya and Galicia, been controlled by the political right. When the conservative *Partido Popular* failed to gain an outright majority of seats in the Madrid parliament in March 1996 elections, they were forced into a coalition pact with Catalan and Basque conservative parties. Among the

Parte Vieja

Pensión Amaiur, c/XXXI de Agosto 44, 2° (☎943/42 96 54). A pleasant and friendly place with carpeted doubles and a few triples. ④.

Pensión Arsuaga, c/Narrica 3, 3° (☎943/42 06 81). Simple, spacious doubles; can be chilly in winter but has its own restaurant and offers good full-board deals. ③.

concessions made was the transfer of 32 convicted ETA terrorists (out of more than 600) to jails in or close to the Basque country, a persistent demand of **Herri Batasuna** (Popular Unity), ETA's political wing. Otherwise, *Herri Batasuna* has little influence in a Basque parliament dominated by the PNV and the Socialists; their electoral support rarely tops ten percent except in the heartland of Gipuzkoa and parts of Vizkaia. Polls show that while wanting increased autonomy, many Basques oppose forming a breakaway state.

The economic recession no doubt has much to do with this – the former industrial glories of Vizkaia in particular have, since the 1930s, been reduced to rusty, outdated factories and idle steel foundries and shipyards. Terrorism keeps away needed new investment, and unemployment is extremely high. In January 1988 a historic pact was signed by all the Basque parties except *Herri Batasuna*, condemning ETA's tactics while upholding their goals. HB's credibility has been further dented in 1997 by its organization of street marches in support of ETA, undermining its previous claims to act independently of the terrorists.

The Spanish government has offered an **amnesty** to activists who publicly renounce ETA's methods – though the few who have done so are prone to assassination from their former comrades – and until 1989 engaged in secret negotiations with ETA leaders. But Madrid often wielded a big stick while granting these concessions: a rightist death squad known by the acronym **GAL** which liquidated over twenty ETA fellow travellers between 1983 and 1988 in a clandestine "dirty war", has been demonstrated to consist mainly of certain off-duty members of the *Guardia Civil*, who considered government anti-terrorist policies to be inadequate. Their operations were even carried out in the French Basque regions, while an extradition treaty with France has also denied gunmen their former safe refuges across the border. In early 1992 the French police arrested the three top-ranking ETA members in one swoop on a house near Biarritz, probably kept by ETA's French counterpart, **Iparreterrak**. Despite the existence of this group, there is no real desire among rank-and-file French Basques for unity with the Spanish community in an independent country, and French sympathy for ETA has largely evaporated since Franco's death and the institution of home rule across the frontier.

Despite all the foregoing, ETA terror continues, a strategy seen by many as a desparate, last-ditch attempt to force a government return to negotiation; it appears that since 1994 young hard-liners, especially from the radical-left faction **KAS**, have seized control from the historic leadership. Premier Aznar himself narrowly escaped death from a 1996 car bomb detonated by ETA in Madrid, and summer of that year saw numerous small devices – designed more to scare than kill – set off in southeastern coastal resorts popular with Britons. New tactics, such as extorting "revolutionary taxes" from Basque-run businesses and kidnapping VIPs for ransom, have emerged of late to fund the estimated $8 million annual ETA "budget". Money can be laundered in a vast network of front businesses, including Basque hotels and restaurants not only in France and Spain but also in the expatriate communities of Mexico, Venezuela and Uruguay. But each outrage generates increasing revulsion, none more so than when a *Partido Popular* municipal counsellor, **Miguel Ángel Blanco**, was kidnapped in July 1997 and soon found mortally wounded with two bullets in the neck when ransom demands were ignored. The kidnapping, and funeral, prompted street demonstrations a million strong in the Basque country and across Spain. ETA and *Herri Batasuna* have both been effectively marginalized and, in the former case, made socially unacceptable on its home turf; evidently an overwhelming majority of the Basque population feels that more will be achieved through the newly available democratic channels than by ETA violence.

Hostal La Estrella, Plaza de Sarriegi 1 (☎943/42 09 97). Attractive old place, offering rooms with or without shower, either overlooking the plaza or Alameda del Boulevard. ④.

Pensión Kaia, c/Puerto 12, 2° (☎943/43 13 42). Recently refurbished rooms with bath. ④.

Pensión Larrea, c/Narrica 21, 1° (☎943/42 26 94). Clean, modern rooms but on a busy street corner, and a bit cramped and noisy. ④.

Hostal Parma, c/General Jauregi 11 (☎943/42 88 93). Comfortable rooms with all amenities, some overlooking the sea. Well located between the Parte Vieja and Paseo Nuevo. ⑤.

Pensión San Jerónimo, c/San Jerónimo 25, 2° (☎943/42 08 30). Adequate though spartan rooms with crumbling hallway and stairs. ③.

Pensión San Lorenzo, c/San Lorenzo 2, 1° (☎943/42 55 16). A small place where guests can use the kitchen to prepare food. ③.

Pensión Urgul, c/Esterlines 10, 3° (☎943/43 00 07). Airy, spotless and tastefully furnished rooms – only five of them, so arrive early or phone ahead. ③.

Alameda del Boulevard

Hostal Alameda, Alameda del Boulevard 23 (☎943/42 16 87). An old, characterful building showing its age; rooms are without bath and not particularly good value. ④.

Pensión Boulevard, Alameda del Boulevard 24, 1° (☎943/42 94 05). Big, comfortable modern rooms, but only one is en suite. ④.

Hostal Eder II, Alameda del Boulevard 16, 2° (☎943/42 64 49). Elegant hallway with fine wood panelling leads to spacious rooms, some with bath. ④.

Centro

Pensión Alemana, c/San Martín 53, 1° (☎943/46 48 81). An excellent central location by the cathedral; highly recommended. ⑤.

Pensión Añorga, c/Easo 12, 1° (☎943/46 79 45). A large *pensión* on two floors; fairly plain but clean rooms, some with bath. ③.

Hostal Comercio, c/Urdaneta 24 (☎943/46 44 14). Simply furnished but reasonable rooms with washbasins and fan heaters. ④.

Hostal Easo, c/San Bartolomé 24 (☎943/46 68 92). Relatively low-priced rooms with washbasin or shower. ④.

Hostal Eder and **Hostal Ederra**, c/San Bartolomé 33 and 25 (☎943/42 46 96). Two smart *hostales* run by the same management as the *Eder II* in Alameda del Boulevard; open Easter and summer only. ④.

Pensión Josefina, c/Easo 12, 3° (☎943/46 19 56). Has a couple of large rooms facing the street, otherwise offers only cramped singles and doubles with little or no natural light. ④.

Pensión La Perla, c/Loiola 10 (☎943/42 81 23). Excellent-value, spotless rooms with bath. Close to Buen Pastor cathedral and the food market. ③.

Pensión Urkia, c/Urbieta 12, 3°(☎943/42 44 36). Run by the sister of *La Perla*'s owner, this has equally good rooms with bath. ④.

Out of the centre

Pensión Amara, Isabel II 2, 1° (☎943/46 84 72). Clean, comfortable rooms in a highly recommended outfit. ④.

Hotel Buenavista, Barrio de Igeldo (☎943/21 06 00). Typical Basque chalet on the main road to Monte Igeldo. Great sea views and a good restaurant. ④.

Pensión Maite, Avda. de Madrid 19, 1°, Amara (☎943/47 07 15). Good, clean rooms with bath and TV; handy for bus station, Astoria cinema and Anoeta football stadium. The owners also run the *Bar Maite* opposite. ④.

Hotel Record, Calzada de Ategorrieta (☎943/27 12 55 or 28 57 68). Situated at the far end of Gros and a pleasant alternative to the bustle of the Parte Vieja and Centro; well connected by bus or a 15-min walk from the centre with plenty of parking. All rooms with shower or bath and larger rooms with terraces. ⑤.

Camping and hostelling

Albergue Juvenil, Paseo de Igeldo (☎943/31 02 56). Known also as *La Sirena*, this is just a few minutes' walk from the end of Ondarreta beach. ①.

Igeldo, Barrio Igeldo (☎943/21 45 02). San Sebastián's campsite is excellent, although it's a long way from the centre on the landward side of Monte Igeldo, reached by bus #16 from the Alameda del Boulevard.

The Town

A fire destroyed most of the **Parte Vieja** (old quarter) in 1813, but its narrow streets were renovated so expertly that you would never guess the comparative modernity of most buildings. The defensive wall of the old city was demolished later in the century to make way for expansion of the new town; Alameda del Boulevard marks the former course of the wall. The cramped and noisy streets of the Parte Vieja remain the focus of interest, where crowds congregate in the evenings to wander among the many small bars and shops, or sample the shellfish from the street traders down by the fishing harbour.

Here, too, are the town's chief sights: the elaborate Baroque facade of the eighteenth-century church of **Santa María**, and the more elegantly restrained sixteenth-century Gothic church of **San Vicente**. The centre of the old quarter is **Plaza de la Constitución** (known by the locals simply as *La Consti*) – the numbers on the balconies of the apartments around the square remain from the days when it was used as a bull-ring, and the balconies served as paying seats. Situated just off c/XXXI Agosto (the only street to survive the great fire of August 31, 1813), behind San Vicente, is the excellent **Museo de San Telmo** (Tues–Sat 9.30am–1.30pm & 4–7pm, Sun 10am–2pm) whose displays – around the cloisters of a former convent – include a fine Basque ethnographic exhibition on the first floor and the largest collection of keyhole-shaped funerary steles in the Spanish Basque provinces. There are regular exhibitions of work by modern Basque painters and the convent chapel is decorated with a series of frescoes by José Sert, depicting scenes from Basque life. In the same square as the side entrance to the museum is the oldest surviving gastronomic society in the city, the **Artesana**.

Behind the plaza rises **Monte Urgull**, crisscrossed by winding paths through the park here (daily 7am until 1hr after sunset). From the mammoth figure of Christ on its summit, a 45-minute climb, there are great views out to sea and back across the bay to the town; also up here stand the dilapidated remains of the castle. On the way down you can stop at the **Aquarium** (May–Sept Mon–Sat 10am–1.30pm & 3.30–8pm; Oct–April Tues–Sat 10am–1.30pm & 3.30–7.30pm; 200ptas) on the harbour – containing the skeleton of a whale caught in the last century and an extensive history of Basque navigation, although not a great deal of fish. Close by, at Paseo de Muelle 24, is the **Museo Naval** (mid-June to mid-Sept Mon–Sat 10am–1.30pm & 5–8.30pm, Sun 11am–2pm; rest of year Tues–Sat 10am–1.30pm & 4–7.30pm) with video facilities and exhibits tracing the tradition and history of Basque fishing.

Still better views across the bay can be had from the top of **Monte Igeldo**: take the bus marked *Igeldo* from the boulevard or walk 2km around the bay to its base near the tennis club, from where a funicular will carry you to the summit.

Beaches

There are four **beaches** in San Sebastián: Playa de la Concha, Playa de Ondarreta, Playa de Zurriola and Playa de Gros. **La Concha** is the most central and the most celebrated, a wide crescent of yellow sand stretching around the bay from the town. Despite the almost impenetrable mass of flesh here during most of the summer, this is the best of the beaches, enlivened by sellers of peeled prawns and cold drinks and offering great swimming out to the sand bars and boats moored in the bay. Out in La Concha bay is a small island, **Isla de Santa Clara**, which makes a good spot for picnics; a boat leaves from the port daily in summer every half-hour from 10am until 8pm.

Ondarreta, the best beach for swimming and even in summer somewhat less crowded than La Concha, is a continuation of the same strand beyond the rocky outcrop which supports the **Palacio de Miramar**, once a summer home of Spain's royal family. Set back from Ondarreta are large villas, some of the most expensive properties in Spain, mostly owned by wealthy families from Madrid who vacation here. This area is known as *La Diplomática* for this reason and has a reputation for being rather more staid than the central area, although the lively district of **El Antiguo** with its many bars is only a few minutes' walk beyond.

Far less crowded, and popular with surfers, **Playa Zurriola** and the adjacent **Playa de Gros** have recently been rearranged to shield them from dangerous currents and river pollution. One of the best views of the whole town and bay may be had by climbing up the steps to the cider house on the side of **Monte Ulia** from the far end of the beach. This stroll can easily be extended for about 5km along the coast to the lighthouse overlooking the entrance to Pasajes harbour.

Eating, drinking and entertainment

San Sebastián has plenty of lively bars and good places to eat, arrayed around the Parte Vieja and offering international or local cuisine. Prices tend to reflect the old quarter's popularity, especially in the waterside restaurants, but it's no hardship to survive on the delicious *pinchos* and *raciones* which are laid out in all but the fanciest bars.

Restaurants and tapas bars

If you're in the mood for a gastronomic treat, San Sebastián has some of the best **restaurants** in Spain – although most are closed Sunday evening and Monday. Inclusion of a phone number below means that reservations are suggested. On a less exalted level, the lunchtime *menús del día* in the Parte Vieja are generally good value, and the *pinchos* and *raciones* in the bars are a great way to eat cheaply in the evenings.

Akelarre, Paseo de Padre Orcolaga in Barrio Igeldo (☎943/21 20 52). One of the city's top restaurants, with wonderful sea views. Budget for over 5000ptas a head.

Arzak, Alto de Miracruz 21 (☎943/27 84 65). A shrine of Basque cuisine, with three Michelin rosettes and a superb *menú* for nearly 8000ptas.

Casa Maruxa, Paseo de Bizkaia 14, Amara. Specializes in food from Galicia and attracts the cinema crowd on their way to the Astoria cinema complex just around the corner.

Casa Nicolasa, c/Aldamar 4 (☎943/42 17 62). Specializes in classic Basque cookery. Expensive (5000–7000ptas).

Domenico's, c/Zubieta 3. Upmarket Italian restaurant, very popular with the locals.

SIDRERIAS

If you're in San Sebastián between late January and early May, a visit to one of the many **sidrerías** (*sagardotegiak* in Euskera, or cider houses) in the area around **Astigarraga**, about 6km southeast of town, is a must – take the red Hernani-bound bus from the Alameda del Boulevard or a taxi for about 1000ptas.

Cider production is one of the oldest traditions in the Basque provinces. Until the Spanish Civil War and subsequent industrialization, practically every farmhouse in Gipuzkoa and, to a lesser extent, the other provinces produced cider, which was a valuable commodity for barter. Barter remained the main form of exchange in rural communities here until comparatively recently, and the larger farms were practically open houses where local people socialized – the *bertsolariak* tradition of oral poetry originated in these places – and drank cider.

Cider houses are again flourishing, and for 1500 to 3000 pesetas you can also feast on enormous steaks, grilled fish and codfish omelette followed by local cheese and walnuts, drink unlimited quantities of cider and in general enjoy the raucous atmosphere. Of the fifty or so *sidrerías*, some of the most accessible include *Petritegi* and *Gartziategi*, just a few kilometres out of town, while many of the more rustic (ie authentic) ones, such as *Sarasola* and *Oiarbide,* are on the so-called *Ruta de las Sidrerías* (the Cider Trail) beyond Astigarraga. Check in the Turismo for a full list with phone numbers.

Bar Etxadi, c/Reyes Católicos 9. A lively place for *raciones* and inexpensive *menús*.

Gaztelu, c/XXXI de Agosto 22. A good bar in the Parte Vieja where you can choose from a selection of reasonably priced *raciones*.

Mama Mia's, c/Triunfo 8. Good, inexpensive Italian restaurant serving vegetarian dishes.

Morgan Jatetxea, c/Narrica 7. Specializes in the French-influenced new Basque school of cookery and also has dishes suitable for vegetarians – especially tasty first courses. It's quite normal to order two of these instead of the meat- and fish-based main courses.

Oriental, c/Reyes Católicos 6. Best of seven Chinese restaurants in terms of quality food, price and an extremely friendly atmosphere.

Cafetaria Ubarrechenea, c/San Martin 42. Excellent and economical *menús*.

Bars and clubs

In the evenings, you'll find no shortage of action, with clubs and bars everywhere. The two main areas are the **Parte Vieja**, where you'll find most of the punk and heavy-metal bars – including *Akerbeltz* or *Iguana* – and the area around **c/Reyes Católicos**, where a large number of the city's more expensive music pubs are located. In the latter zone *El Nido* plays a wide selection of music, or there's *Pokhara, Kalima* and *La Bodeguilla*. Carrer San Bartolomé a few streets back from the Concha promenade, attracts a very young crowd with (among other outfits) San Sebastián's only karaoke bar. For **jazz**, try *BeBop* or *Etxekalte*, both on the edge of the Parte Vieja. In Gros there are also a couple of excellent German-style pubs, *El Chofre* and *Bidea*, with a range of imported beers.

Once the pubs close, usually by about 3.30am, the night continues at *Komplot* in c/Pedro Egaña and at *La Piscina* and *Tenis*, both at the far end of Ondarreta beach, where there is often live music (especially *salsa*) well into the small hours.

Festivals

Throughout the summer there are constant **festivals**, many involving Basque sports, including the annual rowing (*trainera*) races in September between the villages along the coast. The International Jazz Festival, at different locations throughout the town for five days in July, invariably attracts top performers as well as hordes of people on their way home from the *fiesta* in Pamplona. The second week in August sees the *Aste Nagusia* festival, with folkloric events, concerts and fireworks. There is also the one-week film festival during mid-September and frequent theatrical and musical performances throughout the year at both the Teatro Victoria Eugenia and the Teatro Principal. The Turismo produces a monthly guide to what's on.

Listings

Banks Most banks have their main branches along Avda. de la Libertad including Banco Central Hispano at no. 17 and Banco Bilbao Bizkaia on the corner with c/Hernani.

Bike rental You can rent mountain bikes from Comet, Avda. de la Libertad 6 (☎943/42 66 37).

Car rental Atesa, c/Amezketa 7 (☎943/46 30 13); Avis, c/Triunfo (☎943/46 15 27 or 26 15 56); Europcar, c/San Martín 60 (☎943/46 17 17); and Hertz, c/Zubieta 5 (☎943/46 10 84).

Hiking information Contact Club de Montaña de Kresala, c/Euskalerría 9 (☎943/42 09 05), or Noresta, c/María Lili (☎943/29 35 20), a travel and map bookstore that also rents skis and trekking gear.

Post office The *Correos* is on c/Urdaneta, just south of the cathedral (Mon–Fri 8am–9pm, Sat 9am–2pm).

Swimming pools The sports centre in Anoeta, Polideportivo de Anoeta (☎943/45 87 97), has an open-air pool, track, tennis courts and a gym. There's a newer pool, Termas La Perla, at Paseo de la Concha (☎943/45 88 56), which also has a gym and sauna.

Telephones There is a *telefónica* on c/San Marcial 29, one block from Avda. de la Libertad (Mon–Sat 9.30am–11pm).

travel details

Spanish trains

Pamplona to: San Sebastián via Alsasua (6 daily; 2hr 30min–3hr); Zaragoza (7 daily; 2hr 30min).

San Sebastián to: Bilbao (9 daily; 2hr 30min–3hr); Hendaye, France (every 30min 7am–10pm; 35min); Irún (every 30min 5am–11pm; 30min).

French trains

Bayonne to: Biarritz (13 daily; 10min); Hendaye (at least 15 daily; 35min); Irún (4–5 daily; 1hr); Lourdes (5–6 daily; 1hr 45min); Pau (5–6 daily; 1hr 20min); Saint-Jean-de-Luz (13 daily; 30min); Tarbes (5–6 daily; 2hr).

Saint-Jean-Pied-de-Port to: Bayonne (3–4 daily; 1hr); Cambo-les-Bains (3–4 daily; 40min); Itxassou (3–4 daily; 35min).

Spanish buses

Pamplona to: Burguete (Mon–Sat 1 daily at 6pm; 1hr 30min); Elizondo (Mon–Fri 3 daily, Sat & Sun 1 daily; 2hr); Irún (3 daily; 2hr); Isaba (Mon–Fri 1 daily at 5pm; 2hr); Jaca (Mon–Sat 1 daily at 3.30pm year-round, additional 6am departure in summer; 2hr 30min); Jaurríeta (Mon–Sat 1 daily at 6pm; 2hr 30min); Ochagavía (Mon–Fri 1 daily at 6pm, Sat at 1.30pm; 2hr); Roncesvalles (Mon–Sat 1 daily at 6pm; 1hr 35min); Yesa (Mon–Sat 1 daily at 5pm; 1hr).

San Sebastián to: Elizondo (3 daily; 2hr); Hondarribia (every 15min; 20min); Pamplona (5–6 daily; 3hr).

French buses

Bayonne to: Biarritz (hourly; 15min); Cambo-les-Bains (4–5 daily; 30min); Pau (up to 4 daily; 2hr 15min); Saint-Jean-de-Luz (hourly; 30min); San Sebastián (2 daily; 1hr 45min).

Saint-Jean-de-Luz to: Cambo-les-Bains (3–4 daily in summer; 45min); Espelette (3–4 daily in summer; 35min); Hendaye (hourly; 35min); Sare (3–4 daily in summer; 20min).

PART THREE

THE
CONTEXTS

HISTORY

The history of the Pyrenees inevitably draws 'on that of both France and Spain, although through the ages the border region has often found itself well out of the social and political mainstream. The following summary highlights the salient events and trends which directly impinged on the mountains and their people.

PREHISTORIC HABITATION

The history of the Pyrenees begins man who died aged twenty some 455,000 years ago near what is now the village of Tautavel in Roussillon. Excavated from the floor of a limestone cave in 1971, the bones of the so-called "Tautavel Man" rank as some of the earliest human remains found anywhere in Europe. However, the trail then grows cold until late Paleolithic times (35,000–10,000 BC), the period of the paintings left by cave-dwelling hunter-gatherers in various parts of the Pyrenees. The most spectacular discoveries date from the end of the Paleolithic era – known as the Magdalenian period – and include the painted caves of Niaux and Bédeilhac in France. At around 5000 BC appear **dolmens**, either stone burial chambers or – as recently conjectured – seasonal shelters for shepherds, found throughout most of the Pyrenees. No habitations from this period have been discovered, but it can be assumed that perishable huts of some sort were erected, and farming had certainly begun by this time.

EARLY INVASIONS

Before the start of the **Bronze Age** (around 2000 BC), the Pyrenean people – as elsewhere in Europe – began to move into fortified villages, and from then until the thirteenth century AD, when the Moors were effectively driven out of Spain, the area experienced an almost endless succession of **invasions**. First, around 1000 BC, came a mix of Celtic and Germanic peoples. The **Celtic** "urnfield people" settled in Catalonia, and later mingled with the Iberians from the south to become the **Celtiberians**. The mysterious **Vascones**, whose origins remain unclear, probably occupied what is now the Basque country at around the same time.

Later, by 550 BC, the **Greeks** established a trading post at Roses, on the Catalan coast. In the third century BC the **Carthaginians** occupied Catalonia, with their effective headquarters in the Spanish part, from where their most famous commander, Hannibal, crossed the Pyrenees in 214 BC on his way to Italy. But after the Second Punic War (218–201 BC) the Carthaginians were expelled from the peninsula by the **Romans**, who despite strong resistance from the Celtiberian tribes – and never-complete dominance of the Vascones – succeeded in making the Pyrenees, as well as Iberia and Gaul to either side, an integral part of their empire. Although a political backwater, the Pyrenean foothills were endowed by the Romans with a network of roads, bridges, villas and garrison towns.

Roman rule soon began to be eclipsed – a process not completed for several centuries – with raids by **Franks** and **Suevi** (Swabians), who overran the Pyrenees between 262 and 276 AD. Two centuries later followed new invasions of **Alans** and **Vandals**, eventually superseded by the fifth-century incursions of the **Visigoths** from Gaul, former Romanized allies of Rome who had been pushed out of France by the Franks under King Clovis. The Visigoths established a capital first at Toulouse and then another at Barcelona in 531 AD. By the end of the sixth century, the Visigothic kingdom extended from the Pyrenees to include most of modern Spain and half of modern France, although the Basque region retained its independence. Apparent strength and unity were spurious, however: the Visigothic monarchy was elected, leading to constant factional strife; adherence by many to the Arian heresy forfeited the kingdom support from the Byzantines; and the bulk of the population lived in a state of virtual serfdom.

THE MOORS AND THE RECONQUEST

With the Visigothic state in terminal decline, the **Moorish conquest of Spain** was – in contrast to Rome's protracted campaigns – startlingly rapid. In 711, less than a century after Mohammed had left Mecca, governor of Tangier Tariq the Berber led a force of seven thousand across the Straits of Gibraltar and defeated the Visigothic army of King Roderic. Little effective resistance was mounted elsewhere, and within ten years the Moors controlled most of the peninsula, including the foothills of the Pyrenees. By the standards of its time, Moorish administration was remarkably tolerant: virtual autonomy was conceded to remoter communities in return for regular payment of tribute, while Jews and Christians were allowed to continue in their faith, those who did not convert being called Mozarabs.

The Moors called the area they controlled **al-Andalus**, whose borders expanded and contracted over the next eight centuries. Their authority soon stretched beyond the Pyrenees, a progress only halted at Poitiers in 732 by the Frank, **Charles Martel** – so named because he crushed the invaders like a *marteau* (a hammer). A scion of the Merovingian dynasty which then dominated what is now modern France, he drove the Moors south out of Aquitaine, a fight continued by his son Pepin, and his more famous grandson **Charlemagne** (768–814), whose empire at its height effectively included the southern slopes of the Pyrenees as well as the northern, most of modern Catalonia and much of Navarra. But Charlemagne endured setbacks, most notably the massacre of his rearguard near Navarran **Roncesvalles** in 778. No reliable, unbiased contemporary account of this event exists, but it seems he had crossed the Pyrenees to assist a Catalan Moorish faction opposed to the Umayyad emir of Cordoba. His putative ally defeated, Charlemagne contented himself with raiding and sacking most of the important towns of the Ebro valley, slighting their fortifications for good measure. By demolishing the walls of Pamplona as well, he antagonized its Basque inhabitants; as his army

retreated over the Pyrenees, the Pamplonans retaliated by wiping out his rearguard.

After Roncesvalles, Charlemagne again switched his attention to the Mediterranean side of the Pyrenees in an attempt to defend his empire against the Moors. He took Girona in 785, and his son Louis le Débonnaire directed the successful siege of Barcelona in 801. Continued Frankish military success meant that any influence the Moors had wielded in the Pyrenees waned long before the turning point for the whole peninsula, the battle of **Las Navas de Tolosa** in 1212, won by the united Christian kings of Leon, Castile, Aragón and Navarra.

To secure the territory recaptured from the Moors, castles were built in strategic places south of the Pyrenean crestline from Barcelona to the hills of western Aragón. A vassal who held a castle in fief for his lord was variously known as a *castellanus, castlá* or *catlá*, from which is possibly derived the name **Catalonia** – or, in Catalan, Catalunya. To the west, the Navarran capital of Pamplona remained an important strategic town, and from the ninth century onwards was just northeast of the meeting point for the two main pilgrim routes to the shrine of ·Santiago de Compostela in Galicia. Protected by the castles and made wealthy by the patronage of kings and pilgrims, **monasteries** flourished throughout the Pyrenees. Benedictine monks established themselves in Rousillon, Catalunya, Aragón and the Comminges, beginning in the tenth century and taking advantage, of lands and funds granted by the local Pyrenean leaders to build on a grand scale. Thus there are numerous surviving **Romanesque churches** across the range, the cathedral at Jaca being one of the finest examples.

Although Islamic influence lingered in Spain until as late as the sixteenth century, when the last *mudéjars* – Moors living under Christian rule – were expelled from Andalucía, there is a continuing debate as to whether or not any remained on the north side of the Pyrenees. Partisans in favour point to apparent versions of the word "Moor" in the names of mountains and places – Moreau, Serre Mourène and Pouey-Morou, for example. But these are more easily explained as variations on the old French word *moreau*, meaning brown. If they colonized any of the high ground, it could only have been briefly: by 920 Jaca was out of Moorish hands for the last time, Huesca was reconquered in 1096, and Barbastro returned to Christian rule in 1100.

EARLY NATION-BUILDING

Charlemagne's grandsons divided his empire between them after 843, and it was only a matter of time before the Frankish empire fell apart. In the face of destabilizing attacks by Normans and Norsemen during the ninth century, the **Carolingian kings** were forced to delegate more power and autonomy to provincial governors, whose lands already had acquired strong identities of their own. With the death of the last Carolingian in 987, **Hugues Capet** was elected king of what was left of the empire, founding a dynasty of Paris-based rulers that was to last until 1328.

The **Capetians** were initially no more than first among unequals, surrounded by nominal vassals who were often more powerful than the king. In feudal France, such provincial *seigneurs* spent their time fighting each other, occasionally besieging each other's castles but more usually destroying crops, stealing cattle and burning villages. Things got so out of hand that the bishops introduced *La Trêve de Dieu* (God's Truce), which banned fighting from Wednesday evening until Monday morning – but they fortified their own monastic churches as a precaution, as at Saint-Savin and Luz near Lourdes.

The situation began to change when **Eleanor**, daughter of the powerful William VIII, duke of Aquitaine, married the future Louis VII, thus bringing that duchy under Parisian control. But Eleanor divorced him and immediately – in 1152 – remarried Henry of Normandy, who shortly became Henry II of England. Thus the English gained control of a huge chunk of what would become modern France, with the vast **Angevin empire** stretching from the Channel to the Pyrenees. The most notorious British personality was **Edward the Black Prince**, whose harsh tactics – thus the epithet – provoked revolts in Bigorre late in the fourteenth century.

At the same time, Catalunya and Aragón were also active in "French" territory. In 1137 the betrothal of Count Ramon Berenguer IV of Catalunya to Petronella, the two-year-old daughter of King Ramiro II of Aragón, united the two kingdoms. His son Alfonso I added Roussillon and much of southern France to his territories, and fancied himself as the "Emperor of the Pyrenees".

Philippe Auguste (1180–1223) began to reverse the Angevin gains, undermining English

rule by exploiting the bitter relations between Henry II and his sons, one of whom was Richard the Lionheart. By the end of his reign, the Capetian royal lands were for the first time greater than those of any other French lord, a process assisted by the support given to the pope's crusade against the **Cathars**, which began in 1209. The Cathars – also known as the Albigensians – were an heretical religious group who had rapidly gained support in Languedoc and the eastern Pyrenees. By convention, the lands and other property of defeated heretics went to the victors, which explains the enthusiasm of Paris for the venture.

First Béziers fell to the papal crusade, then Carcassonne. In 1213 Pedro (or Pere), son of Alfonso I and king of Aragón and Catalonia, intervened on the Cathar side, but was killed besieging the papal general Simon de Montfort at Muret. His defeat signalled the end of Catalan aspirations north of the Pyrenees: had he won, Languedoc might be Spanish today. The outcome of the crusade was the virtual extinction of Catharism and the strengthening of French influence in the Pyrenean foothills. Much of the property of Raymond VII, defeated count of Toulouse, was forfeited to the Crown, and the walls of Toulouse and many other fortified places were razed. Indirectly, the success of the crusade also spelt the end of patronage for the **troubadour poets**, with whom the Cathars had been associated, and consequently the decline of the *langue d'oc*, the southern French language that they had championed. From this period also date the first **bastides**, some three hundred fortified new towns scattered across the Pyrenean foothills by the victors, built to a grid plan around proportioned central squares.

With the death of Pedro, **Jaume I of Aragón**, nicknamed "the Conqueror" (1208–76) succeeded to the throne at the age of five. The 63 years of his reign were a period of concerted expansion for the joint kingdom of Aragón and Catalunya: he drove the Moors from Mallorca in 1229, took Minorca in 1231 and Ibiza in 1235, and reached Valencia in 1238. Realizing that the Catalan future lay to the south and east, he was less determined north of the Pyrenees and in 1258 signed the **Treaty of Corbeil**, by which he renounced all territorial rights in France (except Montpellier, the Cerdagne and Roussillon), in return for King Louis' of France's renunciation of claims on Catalunya.

PYRENEAN LIFE IN THE MIDDLE AGES

Before the Black Death struck the Pyrenees in the middle of the fourteenth century, the **population** in the mountains was bigger than it is today, with a well-developed social structure. Each village of any size had its minor aristocracy acting as military agents for the local count, plus a bailiff to collect rents and dues, and settle small disputes. However, there was little of the rigid class distinction of the major towns in Spain and France, and aristocrats, clergy and villagers met on fairly equal terms.

There were no taverns, so socializing was limited to the fireside, the village square and Sunday Mass. Though knowledge of religious teaching was rudimentary, the **Church** was an enormously significant force for social cohesion, and all people were highly God-fearing. The local priest was accepted as one of the villagers, but the distant bishop was despised as the one who imposed unjust tithes – though outright opposition to these was a recipe for trouble with the **Inquisition**. The poorest houses, and even the shepherds' summer huts, were repositories of ancestral superstition, maintained by years of continuous habitation by the same families, who would keep fingernail clippings and locks of hair as household talismans.

It was an introverted society. Most people married within the village and spent their entire lives there, except for visits to the nearest **market** town to buy or sell produce. Money was little used: villagers survived on their own farm produce and craft, by bartering and swapping favours. Only the shepherds moved freely, sometimes over surprisingly long distances: it was not uncommon to winter the flock in the very south of Catalonia, but to spend the summers in the lush upland pastures of Ariège.

Little is known about the general **health** of people in the Pyrenees in the late Middle Ages, but all social classes were certainly infested with parasites such as lice. Bathing was unheard of, except for medical reasons at one of the spas. The lot of **women** was correspondingly harsh. Treated as chattel, they were married off for social gain and could expect frequent beatings. Apart from the inevitability of regular childbearing, a woman's duties included fetching water and kindling, tending the fire and the garden, cooking, weeding the fields and harvesting.

FROM THE HUNDRED YEARS' WAR TO THE WARS OF RELIGION

The northern part of the Angevin empire was lost by King John in 1204, and from then on the Capetians chipped away steadily at English rule in Aquitaine. When the Capetian male line expired in 1328, the French throne went to Philippe VI of Valois, nephew of Philippe the Fair, but this succession was quickly disputed by Edward III of England, Philippe the Fair's grandson. Thus began the **Hundred Years' War** (1338–1453), with Paris aiming to take Aquitaine and Gascony – which included much of the western Pyrenees – and the English attempting to recover what John had lost.

Against this background **Gaston Fébus**, count of Foix, disputed with the powerful house of Armagnac for the part of Gascony known as Bigorre. Fébus' defeat of the Armagnacs at the **Battle of Launac** in 1362 was the first step towards the creation of a small **kingdom of the Pyrenees**, and at its zenith the area ruled by Fébus included Foix, Bigorre, Béarn and Soule. However, he died without an heir in 1391, and the chance of an independent northern Pyrenees went with him.

Roussillon was taken from an increasingly united Spain by Louis XI of France in 1463, but Perpignan revolted against the French a decade later. Although the city was recaptured in 1474 after a harsh siege followed by brutal repression, Charles VIII – who succeeded Louis in 1483 – decided there were richer pickings to be had in Italy and handed Roussillon back to Spain in 1493.

Despite coming out on top in the Hundred Years' War, France was eventually forced by the Spanish to relinquish most of its interest in the Pyrenean-straddling kingdom of **Navarra/Navarre**, which it had held since the early thirteenth-century election of Theobald (Thibaut), count of Champagne, as king of Navarre. Later Navarre passed first to the Fébus clan of Foix, and then early in the sixteenth century to the French house of Albret, which was shortly to embrace Protestantism. All of Navarra was conquered by Fernando of Aragón in 1512, though the region of Basse-Navarre north of the watershed was returned to the French in the person of

Henri II d'Albret in 1530, who ruled – as did his descendants – from Pau.

His daughter, the militantly Calvinist **Jeanne d'Albret**, created an important secondary the-atre in the **Wars of Religion** wracking France at this time, defeating the Catholic troops of Charles IX at nearby Navarrenx. Like the Cathars before them, the Protestants were especially strong in the south of France, but also claimed a considerable number of adherents in the west. Jeanne's more easy-going son, Henri III of Béarn and Navarre, put himself in line for the French Crown by marrying Marguerite of Valois in 1572. Accordingly when he acceded to the throne of France in 1589 as **Henri IV**, his inheritance of Foix-Béarn and Basse-Navarre was de facto incorporated into France, and the Pyrenean boundary of southwestern France was thus finalized. But as a Protestant, Henri was unacceptable in the Catholic north, and it was only after four years of fighting against the ultra-Catholic league led by the Guise family, and his own eventual conversion to Catholicism ("Paris is worth a Mass", he is reputed to have said) that he could truly claim to be king of all France.

Commendably, Henri set about reconstruct-ing the country and attempting to accommodate the religious factions that had been at war since 1562. By the 1598 **Edict of Nantes** the Huguenots – as the Protestants were also called – were accorded freedom of worship in specified places, the right to education and pub-lic office on the same basis as Catholics, their own courts and the retention of certain fortress-es as a guarantee against renewed attack. But Henri's assassination in 1610 ended royal pro-tection for the growing numbers of Protestants in the French Pyrenees. The new King Louis XIII's agent **Cardinal Richelieu**, having crushed the Protestant strongholds of La Rochelle and Montpellier, then set about razing Pyrenean fortresses such as Miglos in Ariège.

FRANCO-SPANISH WAR AND THE PYRENEES TREATY

In 1635 an ascendant France and a greatly weakened Spain were again at war, and by 1640 the Catalans had taken advantage of this state of affairs to declare themselves an **inde-pendent republic**, under the presumed protec-tion of Louis XIII. Their marching song, *Els Segadors* (The Reapers), was later to become

the Catalan national anthem. Louis annexed Roussillon from the Spanish Crown and came personally to supervise the siege of Perpignan, which fell on September 9, 1642. The inhabi-tants were grateful, and looked forward to an independent Catalonia, but this was never to be: Barcelona fell to Spanish forces in 1652 and Catalonia was effectively split in two. In July 1654, the French besieged Villefranche-de-Conflent, which capitulated after eight days, and in October the key Cerdanyan town of Puigcerdà also fell to France. The French razed the walls of Villefranche in 1656 fearing that the Spanish might retake the city, which was somewhat rash, since the town soon became theirs by the **Treaty of the Pyrenees**. This, negotiated by the respective foreign ministers of France and Spain on a neutral island in the River Bidasoa near Bayonne during late 1659, provided for permanent French control of Roussillon and part of the Cerdagne. The Spanish paid a heavy price when the details were thrashed out the following year at Llívia, ancient capital of the Cerdanya/Cerdagne. They lost Perpignan – then one of the most important towns in Europe – and the fortified port of Collioure. Puigcerdà and Llívia itself remained Spanish, but the surrounding territory became French, leaving Llívia as an enclave. As for the Catalans, they forever lost the prospect of a united, independent country.

With **Louis XIV,** the *Roi Soleil* or "Sun King", reigning alone after the death of Cardinal Mazarin in 1661, **Sébastien le Prestre de Vauban** began fortifying dozens of towns for the king along the north slopes of the Pyrenees, his most famous work being **Mont-Louis** in the Cerdagne. Even Vauban, however, was to fall out of favour for his criticism of Louis' war-mongering and wealth-amassing, financed by taxation from which aristocrats and clergy were exempt.

Although the boundary envisioned by the treaty was not formally delineated until the mid-nineteenth century, it has long been one of the most stable and peaceable in Europe. For the Pyrenean population, especially in the upland of Cerdanya/Cerdagne, the treaty's terms conferred dubious benefits: age-old local customs were superseded by centralizing states; the power of the Church – whose dioce-ses frequently overlapped the new boundaries – was severely challenged; and smuggling was an inevitable consequence of the zealously re-energized customs services. For the first time many Pyreneans, especially on the French side, became liable to conscription and thus saw parts of the wider world, often settling far away in the lowlands – the beginning of the massive mountain depopulation that continues to this day. Not only the Catalans, but the Basques at the opposite end of the range suffered progressive erosion of the *fors/fueros*, charters which had guaranteed some degree of home rule.

WAR OF THE SPANISH SUCCESSION

With the death of the Habsburg King Charles II of Spain in 1700, the throne was offered to the grandson of Louis XIV, Philippe d'Anjou, provided he renounce his rights to the throne of France. Louis XIV's acceptance of the deal, which put a Bourbon on the throne of Spain and gave him indirect control there, guaranteed war with Habsburg Austria, whose Archduke Charles had already been named as successor. England too was drawn into the conflict, fearing a combined French-Spanish power. The **War of the Spanish Succession** lasted thirteen years from 1701, with the Netherlands, Portugal and Denmark on the side of Austria and England, arrayed against France, Spain and Bavaria. Peace was eventually achieved by the treaties of **Utrecht** (1713) and **Rastatt** (1714), with Philippe remaining as **King Felipe V** of Spain, but his realm was divested of all territory in Belgium, Luxembourg, Italy and Sardinia, with Gibraltar and Menorca being ceded to England. In revenge for its support of the Austrian claimant, Felipe V suppressed what little remained of Catalunya's autonomy. The war effort had effectively bankrupted the French, and Louis XIV, his sun well and truly set, died in 1715.

THE FRENCH REVOLUTION AND THE PENINSULAR WAR

On the evening of July 28, 1789, a group of strangers arrived in the *Roussillonais* town of Prades, sounded the alarm bell and forced the doors of the salt store, instrument of the hated *gabelle* (salt tax). The **French Revolution** had reached the Pyrenees, and within a few days all the crown agents and tax-gatherers had been beaten up and ejected from Roussillon. But the euphoria was short-lived. After the solidarity of the anti-tax riots, the Revolution degenerated into a settling of old personal scores, of village against village; peasants went armed just to tend their vines. People soon realized that they had swapped a despised but distant monarchy for a system of government that would far more effectively pervade every aspect of their lives, not least in the suppression of the traditional regions such as Bigorre and Béarn and their replacement with new, gerrymandered *départements* designed to sever all old loyalties.

When six customs officers returned to Perpignan in 1791 after a two-year absence they were attacked, and one was killed. **Land reform**, with its abolition of feudal dues and tithes, was popular on the plains but less significant in the mountains where there was already a complex system of communal grazing rights. There was no support for the war with the royalist empires of Prussia and Austria who were determined to crush the Revolution, and men became fugitives rather than be conscripted, turning instead to smuggling. The **Terror** of 1792–95 claimed few Pyrenean lives, but when it did peasants suffered disproportionately. In Tarbes, for example, six people who had been overheard to criticize the new regime were guillotined: one naval officer, one priest and four peasants.

THE PENINSULAR WAR

Soon after becoming emperor of France in 1804, **Napoleon** saw an opportunity to take over Spain. The Spanish fleet was defeated at the Battle of Trafalgar in 1805, precipitating the abdication of Carlos IV. In April 1808 Napoleon summoned the disgraced Spanish royal family to Bayonne, deported Carlos IV and his wife to Italy and imprisoned their sons Fernando and Carlos in France. Napoleon then installed his own brother, Joseph Bonaparte, as king of Spain. Among Spanish intellectuals, opposition was initially muted by the hope that French rule would serve as a liberalizing force, but optimism quickly evaporated, and Britain and Portugal joined Spain against France in the **Peninsular War** (1808–14). Napoleon organized hospitals for his troops at Bagnères-de-Bigorre, Cauterets, Barèges and Capvern, a move that led to the revitalization of these spa towns. The emperor also planned various civil engineering projects in the Pyrenees to support his troops in Spain, including roads across passes above Marcadau and Gavarnie, but his army was forced back before anything came of them. His men retreated along the famous pilgrim route via Roncesvalles and were pursued eastwards along the Pyrenees by **Wellington**. Wellington's armies were rapturously received by a people sick of Napoleonic bellicosity – scoring extra points by paying for supplies rather than just requisitioning them – and many of his officers returned after the war to settle at Pau.

SEEDS OF THE SPANISH CIVIL WAR

Between 1810 and 1813 a *Cortes* or Spanish parliament attempted to found a liberal regime, envisioning ministers answerable to it in the framework of a constitutional monarchy. But Fernando VII, upon being restored to the throne in 1814, immediately abolished the embryonic parliament and remained an implacable opponent of any liberalization, presiding at the same time over the loss of most of Spain's colonies in South America. Upon his death in 1833 the crown was claimed both by his daughter Isabella II (a child under the regency of her mother), and by his brother Carlos, backed by the Church, the conservatives and the Basques. The **First Carlist War** (1833–39) ended with victory for the relative liberals supporting Isabella, who came of age in 1843. Her reign was a long record of scandal, political crisis and constitutional compromise, until liberal army generals forced Isabella to abdicate in 1868. The experimental **First Republic** (1873–75) failed, and following the **Second Carlist War** the throne went to Isabella's son Alfonso XII.

Thereafter, attempts to balance monarchism with parliamentary government were only partly successful. Working-class **political movements** such as the Socialist Workers' Party were developing apace; the socialist trade union, the UGT, formed in 1888, took hold in the industrialized Basque country. The anarchists' rival union, the CNT, was especially well represented in Catalunya. The loss of Cuba, Puerto Rico and the Philippines to the USA in 1898, and the "Tragic Week" of rioting in Barcelona in 1909 – following a call-up of army reserves to fight in Morocco – represented significant blows to national morale.

During World War I Spain was neutral but inward turbulence continued, and in 1923 **General Primo de Rivera** overthrew the government to establish a dictatorship. After his death in 1930, the success of anti-monarchist parties in the municipal elections of 1931 led to the abdication of the king and the foundation of the **Second Republic**.

Catalunya declared itself an independent republic two days after the municipal elections on April 14, 1931, but had to settle for a statute of limited autonomy granted by Madrid the following year. A relatively dynamic region, it had long felt itself exploited by the rest of Spain. Meanwhile the Madrid government was too entangled by the expectations of left-wingers and the potential of right-wing reaction to accomplish anything substantial in the way of agrarian or tax reform. Additionally, all the various brews of extreme political ideology that had been fermenting in Spain over the course of the previous century were ready to explode. Anarchism, communism and socialism all derived some impetus from the Russian Revolution, while at the other end of the spectrum were the **Falangists** – founded in 1923 by José Antonio Primo de Rivera, son of the dictator.

The **army** was divided between the anti-monarchists, monarchists who supported the Bourbon dynasty and monarchists who supported the Carlist line – whose power base was conservative Navarra. But they were sufficiently united in their opposition to left-wing government, and though General José Sanjurjo's 1934 coup attempt failed, it spawned the infamous **Spanish Military Union**, whose members included General Manuel Goded, General Emilio Mola and **General Francisco Franco**, all openly talking of another rebellion should the Catholic right fail to win the coming election. When the left-wing *Frente Popular* (Popular Front) won the election of February 1936 by a tiny majority, the stage was set.

EVENTS IN FRANCE 1810–1938

Following the end of Napoleonic rule, France endured over half a century of turbulence despite nominal restoration of the monarchy in 1815. There were reversals of revolutionary tenets under a series of reactionary kings or self-styled emperors, alternating with growing popular discontent and periods of liberal retrenchment, all taking place against a backdrop of growth in industrial and economic power.

The trauma of defeat in the 1870 Franco-Prussian War resulted in the definitive declaration of a **republic**, and indirectly to the growing influence of the political left; the Spanish UGT had a near-exact counterpart in the French CGT, which eschewed political organization in favour of "direct action". As in Spain, the various socialist and communist parties found it difficult to co-operate, even amidst the opportunity presented by the aftermath of World War I, whose 25 percent casualty rate among the French ranks and massive devastation on French soil had dealt the old social order a huge blow. The Catholic right, whose shock troops the *Action Française* dated from the early years of the century, mirrored the analogous groupings in Spain.

Faced by the growing threat of both Nazism across the Rhine and homegrown fascist activism, the French Left papered over its internal differences and – in the same year as the Spanish Popular Front victory – won a rather more convincing mandate in the Parisian Chamber of Deputies. "Encouraged" by a wave of spontaneous sit-ins and wildcat strikes celebrating the poll triumph, the first **Front Populaire** government of 1936–37, headed by **Léon Blum**, nearly succeeded in ratifying the sorts of reforms which the Spaniards were only able to contemplate. But within a year these had been stymied by a corollary proposal on currency exchange control. Similarly blunted by "reasons of state" (for which read "fear of the English and the Germans") were Blum's ineffectual attempts, despite his evident personal sympathy with the Spanish *Frente Popular*, to intervene openly in the Civil War – or even just supply armaments to the Republicans – until the fall of his second government in 1938.

THE SPANISH CIVIL WAR

On July 17, 1936, the military garrison in Morocco rebelled under the leadership of Franco, the agreed signal for revolt throughout Spain. Sanjurjo, by now in exile in Portugal, was the Military Union's choice for provisional head of state but was killed when his plane crashed between Portugal and Burgos. Another Franco rival, Goded, was captured by Republican loyalists in Barcelona and shot, leaving the way open for Franco to be proclaimed commander of the rebels – and "Head of State" – in October 1936.

The Nationalists, as the rebels styled themselves, had expected a short campaign but the **Spanish Civil War** (1936–39) turned out to be long and bloody. In the Pyrenees, only Navarra immediately came out in favour of the Nationalists, who had convinced the heirs of the Carlists to allow themselves to be absorbed into Franco's Falange. Gipuzkoa and Bizkaia, which had recently benefited from a home-rule statute similar to Catalunya's, remained devoutly Republican as did Catalunya and Aragón, where the mountain villages were particularly attracted by anarchism, an ideology that shared their traditional values of equality and personal liberty. Although the Nationalists initially had little popular support, they gradually swept the country by a mixture of audacity and deliberate terror, backed by a flood of arms and men from Nazi Germany and Italy; the Republicans were less effectively supplied by Russia, and very sporadically by France. An international arms embargo and declaration of non-intervention was universally and selectively winked at by interested parties. Nominally a civil war, the Spanish conflict was really the opening act of World War II, and the first "modern" campaign: Italian and German airmen demonstrated the efficacy of terror bombings on civilian targets, and radio saw service as a propaganda weapon.

In the north, their foothold in Navarra allowed the Nationalists to attack both east and west. The Basque country was overwhelmed by the end of 1937, paving the way for a major Aragonese offensive in March 1938. As the Nationalists advanced eastwards, **Republican** soldiers, marooned in the valleys of Alto Aragón and Catalunya, fled north across the high passes into France, joined or preceded by their families, and others fearful of a Falangist victory. Many Republicans believed, or perhaps deluded themselves, that theirs was a tactical withdrawal, and hoped to be saved by a pan-European war in the wake of Hitler's provocations in Czechoslovakia. But by the beginning of 1939 it was all over, and the majority now arrived quite openly at ordinary road frontier crossings like Le Perthus, sometimes in columns of thousands. The Republican *Cortes* held its last meeting at Figueres on February 1, 1939.

WORLD WAR II

Ironically, the outbreak of **World War II** soon led to a refugee movement in the opposite direction. With the capitulation of France in 1940, small numbers began making their way over the

Pyrenees, intent on reaching England via neutral Spain, in response to de Gaulle's June 1940 radio appeal to join the Free French forces. There was also a weekly movement from France into Spain of Swiss gold ingots, two truckloads at a minimum, as payment for humanitarian food aid to occupied Europe from America.

The Germans were initially content to leave the south of France, including the Pyrenees, under the control of the collaborationist **Vichy** government, but the Allied landings in North Africa in November 1942, only briefly opposed by Vichy troops in Morocco and Algeria, left them vulnerable to attack from across the Mediterranean. Hitler immediately ordered the formal occupation of the south, leading to a new wave of escapes over Pyrenean passes.

ESCAPEES AND ESCAPE ROUTES

These later refugees fell into four categories: **Allied personnel**, mainly airmen who had been shot down; **évadé(e)s**, who had escaped prison or internment in France (though the word *évadé(e)s* tends to be applied to all escapees); **réfractaires**, French people who were in trouble with the Vichy or German authorities for falling foul of Occupation rules; and, of course, **Jews**.

Their guides were known as **passeurs** in French, **passadores** in Castilian. Some of these knew the old contraband trails from lengthy experience, but the majority were ordinary people, working in hotels and cafés and perhaps smuggling occasionally for a little extra money. Another contingent was made up of Spanish Republicans who, having fled from the frying pan into the fire, lived in hiding along the border, especially around the Cerdanya/Cerdagne. Some clergy were involved, as well as a few shepherds, a handful of mountaineering guides, and even a scattering of officials such as mayors and customs officers. Altogether, three thousand French were active in the Pyrenean escape routes including two hundred women, and five hundred Spaniards.

Until the **German occupation** of the French Pyrenees on November 11, 1942, it was left to the French themselves to patrol the frontier, a task entrusted to no more than eight hundred customs officers, policemen and support staff, and these were easily circumvented by well-established methods. Fugitives and their guides, for example, could take the Sunday afternoon train to Latour-de-Carol, stroll up to the frontier to mingle with the local Spanish and French who by custom gathered there to chat, and then just drift away onto the Spanish side. In Vichy Marseilles, the American and Mexican consulates simply put escapees on the train to Spain via Cerbère and Port Bou.

However, from the end of 1942 the frontier was patrolled by over a thousand military police, backed by mobile units that doubled their number. In addition, there were about a hundred Nazi agents working covertly in the region, assisted by French volunteer forces and informers motivated by money, anti-Semitism or both. Though the Germans were mostly older men considered unsuitable for the rigours of a combat front, these frontier guards were nevertheless formidable – tough Bavarian or Austrian mountaineers, well trained and well equipped, using reconnaissance aircraft to track their quarry. The Spanish had about eight hundred border guards and police on their side, and additionally 30,000 troops were also stationed not more than 30km south of the frontier.

The **escape organization** that developed to counter this intensified border security was run like a business, and an occasionally ruthless one. Known by the code-name **MAURICE**, it had an annual income of more than 16,000,000 francs to be used for transport, false documents, food, the hiring of a guide and other expenses. Much of the money was raised by loans from sympathizers, for whom coded messages were broadcast on the BBC to acknowledge the receipt of funds and confirm later repayment. The cost of each crossing depended on the negotiating skill of the organizer and the difficulties of the route involved: if transport had to be arranged to the start of a crossing, the cost shot up astronomically as fuel was difficult to obtain. As particularly "hot" items, Jews had to pay – or be paid for – at many times the normal going rate to be guided out of the country, whether individually or in a group. Those who demurred, and attempted to flee via the normal daily rail link between Oloron and Canfranc, were liable to be returned by the Spanish authorities or sent to an internment camp (see below).

M.R.D. Foot, in his *SOE in France*, describes the methods of the covert escape chain: "The security measures taken . . . for the bodies passing down the line are very strict. They change hands as many times as possible, and each courier acts as a cut-out, not knowing where the bodies come from or where they are going. The bodies are kept in a park or other public place until nightfall, when they are taken to the house where they are to sleep. They are not told the address of the house, however, and seldom have any idea where they are, or which courier is in charge of them. Safe houses and contacts are changed every three months, regardless of whether they are blown or not."

In the early days of the war the cost of arrest on the French side was not too strict: imprisonment, a fine or perhaps "volunteering" for the Vichy Foreign Legion. Later, the penalties became more severe: about 1000 escapees died in concentration camps in France or elsewhere, as did 150 of the 500 *passeurs* who were caught. Arrival in Spain did not mark the end of danger; Spain might have been neutral but it was a pro-Fascist country, and no official could be trusted. Anyone captured on the Spanish side would be sent to one of the local **internment camps**, where conditions were so bad as sometimes to be fatal – and approximately one out of seven escapees ended up in internment. Despite these hazards, about 35,000 people succeeded in escaping into Spain, including approximately 5000 Jews, 2000 Belgians, 500 Dutch, 800 Poles and around 1000 members of the Resistance.

THE PYRENEES AFTER THE WARS

Although the Spanish Civil War had left more than half a million dead, destroyed a quarter of a million houses and sent a third of a million Spaniards into exile in France and Latin America, Franco was in no mood for reconciliation. He set up **war tribunals** which sentenced thousands of Republicans to death and interned nearly two million others in concentration camps until "order" had been restored. The Falange was the only permitted political organization, and censorship was rigidly enforced.

By the end of World War II, during which Spain was too weak to be anything but neutral, Franco was the last remaining fascist head of state in Europe, and had in fact sanctioned more judicial deaths than any other ruler in Spanish history. Spain remained politically and economically isolated into the early 1950s, despite diplomatic recognition of Franco's regime by most of Europe. With the economy at a standstill, Pyrenean villagers began to drift down to the towns in a usually fruitless search for work, accelerating the **depopulation** of the mountains. Mismanagement of the economy was so blatant that by 1953 the country was exporting less than it had twenty years earlier. The traditional livelihood of **smuggling** across the Pyrenees mushroomed into a major enterprise, but even this was dwarfed by the corruption of army officers and customs officials who imported luxury goods on false documents, an illicit trade that was equal to half the official imports.

Franco's otherwise probable overthrow was only averted in 1953 by the acceptance of **American aid**, on condition that he provided land for American air bases. The economy was revitalized not only by US loans, but remittances from tourism and Spaniards working in northern Europe, resulting in a growth rate during most of the 1960s second only to Japan's. Such investment, however, merely brought forward the death of traditional Pyrenean agriculture, as the **mechanization of farming** on the plains marginalized mountain life even further. A Spain of increasing urbanization and lowland agriculture required massive amounts of water and power, supplied by a burgeoning number of dams in Catalunya and Aragón; their flooding of Pyrenean pastoral valleys, combined with the punitive neglect of Madrid in failing to provide the most basic services to the overwhelmingly pro-Republican mountaineers, pretty well finished off any hope of subsistence in various parts of the Pyrenees.

Meanwhile in **France**, with **Charles de Gaulle** emerging as the undisputed leader of the Free French government-in-exile, the Allies had little choice but to co-operate with him; following D-Day and the liberation, an uneasy coalition of right and left, the *Conseil National de la Résistance*, emerged as a provisional government for the demoralized, bankrupt nation. By 1947, thanks to the Cold War and the Marshall Plan, the left – as well as (temporarily) de Gaulle – had been excluded from what became the Fourth Republic, though not before a new constitution had been agreed upon, providing for women's suffrage, the nationalization of key industries, trade union rights and the rudiments of a welfare state.

In the French Pyrenees themselves, hundreds of communities had been destroyed by the German burning of villages in reprisal for supporting the Resistance. Thousands of villagers who had been driven out decided to remain in the valley towns after the war, and even today villages are still abandoned entirely or in part – though this changed somewhat after 1968 (see below).

If thoroughgoing political reform had been thwarted, France during the 1950s transformed itself from a primarily agricultural country to a modern industrial giant, its growth rate often rivalling that of West Germany, with whom it established in 1957 the European Coal and Steel Community, predecessor to the Common Market/EC/EU. Although the country, like Spain, was a member of NATO, much of France's military resources soon became embroiled in the **Algerian colonial rebellion**, which coming on the heels of the 1954 catastrophic defeat at Dien Bien Phu in Indochina proved to be an eight-year experience nearly as traumatic as the German occupation. By 1958, hard-line rightists among the army and the so-called **pieds noirs** – a million civilian settlers in Algeria virulently opposed to its possible independence – threatened to take on both loyal army units and the native rebels. de Gaulle returned from political limbo, dissolving the Fourth Republic and demanding extraordinary powers to settle the Algerian mess. For his pains as president of the Fifth Republic, de Gaulle provoked an even more serious military revolt in 1961, with the **OAS** – a rogue army faction intent on preventing any settlement – mounting several attempts on his life. But Algerian independence was finally granted in 1962, prompting a flood of refugees – mostly *pieds noirs*, Jews and Arabs who had fought for the central government – into France. The *pied noirs* in particular, many of them settling in the south of France, would later lend considerable support to a resurgence in assorted racist and fascist activities, including the *Front National* of the 1990s.

CRACKS IN THE OLD ORDER

De Gaulle's style in diplomacy was idiosyncratic, to put it mildly; by the mid-Sixties he had ruffled numerous feathers abroad by blocking British entry to the Common Market, rebuking the US for its policy in Vietnam, withdrawing from the central command structure of NATO and refusing to sign any nuclear test ban treaties. Even at home he was far from universally popular, and not just among the rightist fringe; a young challenger on the Left, **François Mitterrand**, nearly upset him in the 1965 presidential elections.

Yet despite these rumblings of discontent, the events of **May 1968** took everyone by surprise. What started as a provincial student protest against the paternalistic matriculation system quickly escalated into a broad spectrum of agitation by both blue-collar and white-collar workers as well as academics, culminating in a protracted general strike. *Autogestion* – workers' self-management – was the dominant slogan; rather than specific demands for reform, there was general sentiment that all French institutions were too hierarchical and elitist. De Gaulle dropped out of sight for two weeks, consulting with army commanders; upon his return, he dissolved parliament and demanded a fresh electoral mandate to quell the "revolution" from the frightened silent majority – who complied.

Although the protesters could point to few specific gains except in education, the events of 1968 changed French society in subtler ways over the next two decades; there was a perceptible lessening in the formality and authoritarianism of French society, and various homegrown alternative movements can trace their start to the "days of May". Numerous self-employed professionals – not just hairy hippies – who felt themselves thwarted by the return to normality in the main power centres fled south, as had generations of dissidents before them, to the shelter of the Cevennes and the Pyrenees, forming the advance guard of the **nouveaux ruraux** (new rurals) who would slowly repopulate the abandoned villages and eventually set up tourism-related enterprises.

Spain's increasing prosperity as the 1960s proceeded merely underlined the intellectual and financial bankruptcy of Franco's regime, and its inability to cope with popular demands. Higher incomes, the need for contemporary education and skills, plus a creeping invasion of outside culture made the anachronism of the Falange starkly clear. The *generalissimo's* only reaction was an attempt to withdraw what few traces of increased liberalism had emerged, and his last years mirrored the repression of the early 1940s. Basque nationalists, whose 1973 assassination of Admiral Carrero Blanco effectively destroyed Franco's last hope of a like-minded successor, were singled out for particularly harsh treatment. When Franco finally died in November of that year, few expected much of his second-choice heir as head of state, the Bourbon prince **Juan Carlos**, cynically nicknamed *El Breve* (The Brief) for the anticipated duration of his reign.

In the event, and much to his credit, over the next seven years the new Spanish king oversaw a cautious, gradual but steady progress towards "democracy without adjectives", the demand of street activists in the late 1970s. The first **free elections of 1977** returned a coalition government, with the extreme left and right marginalized. Recognizing that his own future depended on the maintenance of the fledgling democracy, Juan Carlos declined to support the **attempted coup** of February 1981 by disaffected elements of the *Guardia Civil* and the army; its collapse, and attendant further discreditation of those nostalgic for the old order, set the stage for the landmark elections of October 1982.

Meanwhile, **in France**, the 1970s had been dominated by the two presidential terms of the centre-rightist **Valéry Giscard d'Estaing**, who defeated Mitterrand twice in 1974 and 1978. Despite a series of embarrassing scandals – most remarkably Giscard's acceptance of gifts from cannibal "Emperor" Bokassa of Central Africa – the political left seemed incapable of presenting a united front for the 1978 polls in particular. As in Spain of the late 1970s, few would have predicted the decisive result of the French elections of May 1981.

THE SOCIALIST GOVERNMENTS

In May 1981, Parisians gathered spontaneously at the Place de Bastille to celebrate the victory of Mitterrand's Socialists, the first left-of-centre triumph in France since the 1930s. Just over a year later, on October 28, 1992, Felipe González's PSOE – the Spanish Socialists, second-finishers in 1977 – also came to power with massive support, an even more dramatic reversal considering the nearness of the Falangist past. Despite enjoying substantial goodwill at the outset, both movements subsequently foundered on domestic and international realities, amidst increasingly acrimonious accusations of unprincipled betrayals of campaign promises and party manifestos. As a result, the French Socialists lost power between 1986 and 1989, and again between 1993 and 1997, while their Spanish counterparts only just squeaked back into office in 1993 before being eased out in 1997.

The presence of four Communist ministers in the first post-1981 French cabinet reflected the inital commitment to an aggressively leftist agenda; by 1984, in the face of capital flight and bureaucratic foot-dragging, Mitterrand had been compelled to eat large quantities of humble pie as a centrist cabinet was cobbled together under Prime Minister **Laurent Fabius**. 1986 saw the return of the right under **Jacques Chirac**'s Gaullists, an uneasy arrangement under a sitting Socialist president – because parliamentary and presidential elections are out of sync in France – referred to as **cohabitation**. Chirac's monetarist fumblings and flirtations with **Jean-Marie Le Pen**'s overtly racist *Front National* resulted in a centre-left parliamentary coalition returning by a bare margin in 1989, under social-democrat prime minister **Michel Rocard**. Though some of Chirac's privatization programmes were stalled, the unpopularity of Rocard's own austerity measures resulted in **Édith Cresson** replacing him in 1991. Her abrasiveness and numerous gaffes prompted her sacking in 1992 in favour of **Pierre Bérégovoy**, a confidant of Mitterrand's. All these comings and goings virtually guaranteed a landslide coalition victory of the RPR and the UDF, the two conservative parties, in 1993; two months later, Bérégovoy – accused of accepting a private loan from a dubious character – shot himself, leaving no explanatory note.

This thumbnail summary of French elections and regimes to the early 1990s gives just a hint of the malaise which still grips the French political scene. Scandal – blood supplies knowingly contaminated with HIV, deal-cutting with the Iranian regime as it stalks its opponents in France and the secret service's bombing of Greenpeace's ship *Rainbow Warrior* in New Zealand – has been a near-constant feature of public life since 1981. Equally disappointing, perhaps, was the Socialists' failure to affect the traditional, all-pervasive secrecy, militarism and environmental-unfriendliness in one of the most centralized states in the world. In the Pyrenees in particular, despite lip service to planning policy sympathetic to ecological considerations, mega-projects such as the Somport tunnel were usually only slowed or modified rather than reversed.

Spain by contrast enjoyed a certain amount of stability throughout the 1980s; the PSOE was convincingly re-elected in 1986, and only began to falter visibly in 1989 as the recession – and scandals pertaining to PSOE campaign contributions by large corporations – started to bite.

Yet there was a similar pattern of compromise on core issues, which often made the PSOE government seem indistinguishable from Britain's contemporaneous Conservative government or from Germany under Chancellor Kohl. **Felipe González** swept into office in 1982 partly on an anti-NATO platform, but campaigned for continued membership in the hard-fought 1986 referendum on the issue, which went narrowly in favour. Control of inflation, supposedly in deference to EC-stipulated goals, had a higher priority than employment, and loss-making state-owned industries were drastically overhauled, and many privatized. **Anti-labour measures** such as cuts in already meagre unemployment benefits, a pay freeze for civil servants and a differential minimum-wage law for under-25s resulted in general strikes coordinated by the PSOE's own trade union, the powerful UGT (resurrected after the Franco years).

By the early 1990s, it became increasingly obvious that prolonged time in office had made the PSOE not just corrupt but complacent, with only the lack of compelling alternatives to "Felipe" (as the prime minister was universally called) and the enduring suspicion of the right combining to maintain something like the status quo. The PSOE barely survived a strong 1993 challenge by the centre-right *Partido Popular* (PP) under its uncharismatic chief **José María Aznar**, and continued to govern only by dint of support from the Catalan nationalist party, having fallen short of an outright majority. As in France, spectacular scandals regularly punctuated the news, eroding the PSOE's position still further: the director of the *Guardia Civil*, a 1986 González appointee, fled the country in 1995 with $18 million in bribes and kickbacks salted away in Switzerland (he was extradited back to Spain, tried and jailed in 1997); the governor of the Bank of Spain was also caught with his hand in the cookie jar to the tune of millions. But most damaging of all was the discovery of **GAL** (*Grupo Antiterrorista de Liberación*), a semi-autonomous anti-terrorist unit which had been waging a "dirty war" throughout the 1980s, kidnapping and/or assassinating suspected ETA members. The press and an independent judiciary – both interfered with by the PSOE government – exposed police participation in these acts and a clear chain of command extending up to the highest echelons of the PSOE.

Despite all the foregoing, the **elections of late 1996** yielded yet another **hung parliament**, though this time Aznar's PP had a bare plurality of fifteen seats over the PSOE. González seemed not to have drawn the proper conclusion from the result: "A couple more weeks of campaigning and we would have won" was his off-the-cuff reaction. The close finish denied the PSOE a period of urgently needed self-reflection that a crushing defeat and González' resignation as leader (which eventually occurred in mid-1997, with Joaquín Almunia replacing him) would have permitted. Aznar failed to win an outright majority for two principal reasons: memories of the long and repressive Franco era, which at the last moment unnerved many voters wary of losing hard-won decentralization and the PSOE-established social benefits system; and the electoral weight of Andalucía, González' power base, which fulfilled its traditional role of offsetting the right-leaning north by supplying many of the PSOE's surviving MPs. Aznar currently governs in **coalition** with the Catalan, Basque and Canary Islands nationalist parties, who in return for their support expect continued benefits to their regions from a government committed to traditional unitary nationalism.

FRANCE: THE RIGHT IN POWER – AND OUT AGAIN

The first major crisis for Prime Minister **Edouard Balladur**'s centre-right government in early 1994 was the violent reaction on the part of students and trade unionists to his proposal of reduced wages for young people. A similar response by Air France workers, farmers and fishermen to further monetarist measures caused Balladur to back down, losing the respect of his natural constituency. Corruption scandals, both in government and business, and political violence in the south of France, continued unabated, adding – along with stubbornly high unemployment – to the support for fringe parties on the left and right (especially the racist *Front National*).

Meanwhile **Mitterrand**, terminally ill with prostate cancer, clung to office until mid-1995 despite various assaults on his reputation. Two months after Bérégovoy's suicide, Réné Bosquet, head of police in the Vichy government and responsible for the deportation of Paris Jews in 1942, was murdered before he could be tried for his crimes; a close friend of Mitterrand, he was thought to have carried damning secrets about the president to his grave. Worse was to come near the end of Mitterand's term, with revelations about his war record as an official in the Vichy regime before he belatedly joined the Resistance. Yet when he **died** in January 1996, after fourteen years as head of state, he was mourned as a man of culture and vision, a tenacious political operator and a committed European.

The **May 1995 presidential elections** saw the Socialist Lionel Jospin – backup choice after Jacques Delors, who refused to run – pitted against a rightist field split between Balladur, Chirac, Le Pen (who scored 15.5 percent) and the anti-European Philippe de Villiers, a French equivalent to James Goldsmith. In the second round, **Jacques Chirac** stole the Left's thunder by mouthing comforting noises about unemployment and social exclusion, narrowly edging Jospin.

One of Chirac's first decisions was to delay signing the Nuclear Non-Proliferation Treaty until France had carried out a new series of **nuclear tests** in the South Pacific. These provoked almost universal condemnation (Britain and China being the exceptions), boycotts of French goods, attacks on French embassy buildings in Australia and New Zealand, plus full-scale riots in Tahiti. The French navy captured Greenpeace's *Rainbow Warrior II*, almost ten years to the day after French secret service agents sank *Rainbow Warrior I* in Auckland harbour.

On the domestic front, Chirac's new prime minister was **Alain Juppé**, a clever but rather clinical technocrat. It was left to him to square the circle of Chirac's election pledges of job creation, maintenance of pensions and welfare benefits and reducing the number of homeless, with promised tax cuts, a continued strong franc and a reduction of the budget deficit with an eye to European monetary union. Juppé also promised to clean up corruption but ironically enough became immediately involved in an uproar concerning his municipally subsidized luxury flat in Paris. This, and continued business-as-usual on the scandal front, contributed to a feeling of ever-widening distance between the political elite and ordinary people, who had hitherto accepted nest-feathering as a perk of power but now, pressed to the wall by austerity programmes, were in no mood to brook double standards.

The last straw came in autumn 1995, when Chirac announced that fiscal rectitude would have to take precedence over social comfort, and Juppé proposed changes in social security and "downsizing" of the rail network. The response was all-but-general **strikes** in November and December, when five million public-sector workers, including most of the transport, energy, post and telecom industries, took to the streets with considerable support from becalmed private-sector commuters – the strongest show of protest in France since May 1968. Amazingly, Juppé survived this storm, abandoning some proposals and postponing others. A new tax to pay off the social security deficit was imposed, and cuts in the health service proceeded; some of the heat came off the prime minister as the three main trade unions fell to bickering as usual.

The UDF-RPR coalition stumbled along through 1996, fulfilling predictions by Mitterrand and Giscard d'Estaing that Chirac's opportunism and impetuousness would make him and his government a laughing stock within months of assuming power. Although Chirac and Juppé enjoyed a four hundred-seat parliamentary majority, valid until spring 1998, hanging on to the bitter end, like Britain's John Major, was not Chirac's cup of tea. Incredibly, in April 1997 he called **snap elections** for late May, perhaps hoping for a smaller but less fractious majority – and an end to future potential *cohabitation* by making the start of the next parliamentary and presidential terms coincide in 2002.

In the event Chirac had totally miscalculated the public mood and the Socialists' ability to reach accommodation with potential coalition partners; his arrogant ploy to strengthen the presidency backfired spectacularly. The agony was prolonged over two rounds, with Juppé hastily replaced by parliamentary speaker Phillipe Séguin in the interim, but to no avail. **Jospin** and his allies, the Communists, the Greens and the anti-Maastricht Citizens' Movement, swept back to power in June on a programme featuring a proposed 35-hour week, minimum wage hikes, an emergency youth employment programme and a more humane policy on immigration and naturalization. Thirty-eight Communists, seven Greens and more than a hundred women took seats. The *cohabitation* Chirac had gone to such lengths to avoid had come to pass a year earlier than it otherwise would have.

THE CONTEMPORARY OUTLOOK

Despite ongoing political turmoil **in France** since the 1980s and continual (often self-inflicted) damage to the country's international reputation, the **French economy** remains sounder – with an unemployment rate of just under thirteen percent – and the standard of living higher than in Spain. Jospin's victory has inevitably raised unrealistic expectations of just what a left-of-centre government can accomplish, when its room for manoeuvring is severely limited by Brussels and the globalization of industrial economies. But to its credit, the new government has in its first five months adopted a consensual style of government, with decisions reached only after debate and monitoring of public opinion, markedly in contrast to Juppé's high-handed from-the-top-down style. In so doing it has engendered enough public support and confidence to be able to propose a 15-billion franc **increase in taxation** for social programmes in 1998, borne equally by corporations and individuals, without seriously denting its popularity.

The other riveting contemporary issues in France are the interrelated ones of **racism**, general xenophobia (most obvious during the 1992–93 GATT negotiations), remorse (or lack thereof) for the fate of its **Jews** during World War II and **immigration control**. The main exploiter of these concerns is the quasi-fascist *Front National*, which although it has long since lost its parliamentary seats through some creative gerrymandering, has captured four municipalities in Provence since 1995, and consistently polls about fifteen percent nationwide (on one occasion thirty percent around Perpignan). Other politicians of various stripes have seen fit to jump on the nativist bandwagon at critical times, usually in the wake of the latest Algerian terrorist outrage. Charles Pasqua, Balladur's minister of the interior, considerably tightened up procedures for granting right of residence, let alone citizenship, to immigrants and their descendants and introduced random street identity checks. Under Juppé, matters worsened when police evicted hundreds of Malians, whose petitions for asylum had been denied, from the Paris church where they had sought refuge. In a welcome gesture which temporarily at least has reduced tension, Jospin's government almost immediately regularized the position of the Malian church-occupiers, and in a one-off amnesty granted residence to thousands of other illegals who had been working and paying taxes in France for years. While the *Front National* considers Jews, in particular those of North African descent, no better than Muslims, in September 1997 French Catholic bishops formally apologized for the Church's complicity in the 1942 rounding-up of local Jews.

In Spain, despite the level of domestic discontent since the economic bubble burst in the late 1980s, a certain confidence still lingers. The country's voice is now listened to with respect in international circles, and her cities are conceded to be some of the art and entertainment beacons of Europe. But three extravaganzas held during 1992 – the Barcelona Olympics, Sevilla's Expo, and Madrid's tenure as European City of Culture – as well as the much-publicized high-speed rail link between Madrid and Sevilla, seemed to many to be inexcusable profligacy in the light of the country's desperate need for more sustained investment in its infrastructure and human resources. While Barcelona has been able to build on the momentum left by the Olympics, the still-abandoned Expo pavilions in Sevilla furnish stark evidence of a wider need to concentrate on long-term issues.

In accordance with the constitution of 1978, there has been an appreciable **devolution of powers** to the seventeen autonomous regions into which Spain is divided. Each of the **autonomías** as they are called now has its own president, parliament and civil service, an enormously expensive duplication of functions. In the Pyrenees, statutes of autonomy in varying degrees have been granted to Catalunya, Aragón, Navarra and the Basque provinces. However, Madrid has reserved too many powers – most notably tax collection, followed by proportional disbursement – for the system to have yet approached true federalism, though Catalunya's president **Jordi Pujol** has extracted from the central government the concession of collecting, and spending, thirty percent of its own budget. Elsewhere, especially in Aragón, the political authority has been present for local Pyrenean initiatives, but funds have often proved to be insufficient. Another obvious downside to decentralized control is the tendency of *autonomías*, when they do get hold of cash, to subsidize benefit payments to buy votes, rather

BASQUE AND CATALAN NATIONALISM: A COMPARISON

Although the **Basque and Catalan separatist movements** share certain concerns – resistance to exploitation from central governments, and the preservation of a distinctive language and culture – they also differ markedly. In Catalunya, demands for autonomy haven't acquired the same dimension as in large parts of the Basque country; the notion of an independent Catalan nation has very few adherents aside from the extremists of the *Terra Lliure* group. Whereas the Catalan complaint is of a relatively successful province milked by the rest of Spain, and therefore draws support from all social classes, the Basque protest remains fundamentally motivated by fears over non-Basque immigrant labour and is predominantly lower-middle-class and working-class in character. Finally, there are sharp political differences within the Basque provinces: urbanized, industrialized Bizkaia and Gipuzkoa are Basque-nationalist, but more rural Navarra and Araba are conservative and Spanish-loyalist, while the French Basque areas see themselves as separate from both their Spanish counterparts and the rest of France.

Tension between Madrid and the Spanish Basques first arose in the eighteenth century, with the abrogation of the region's *fueros*, the age-old charters guaranteeing a measure of self-government. The situation worsened considerably after Franco's victory in the Civil War, when the October 1936 statute of autonomy granted by the Republicans to Gipuzkoa and Bizkaia was rescinded, the Basque language banned outside the home and "politically unreliable" teachers dismissed. The Catholic Church's opposition to supposedly atheistic socialism had made it pro-Falangist during the war, but the reality of Franco's victory prompted a gradual change. From the 1950s onwards, the Church encouraged part-time Basque schools or *Ikastolas*, and by the end of the Franco era there were 33,000 pupils enrolled in them.

The nature and prevalence of Euskera is an index of the distinctness – and precariousness – of Basque culture. While a Catalan-speaker stands a chance of being understood in the rest of Spain and even in France, someone speaking only the archaic Basque language cannot communicate with outsiders. A poll in 1970 highlighted the relative strengths between the two principal minority languages of the Pyrenees: 90 percent of Catalan housewives were found to understand Catalan, 77 percent to speak it, 62 percent to read it and 38 percent to write it; for the Basque country the figures were 50 percent, 46 percent, 25 percent and 11 percent respectively.

The failure of the **Basque National Party** (PNV or *Partido Nacionalista Vasco*), founded in the late nineteenth century, to gain lasting political autonomy for the coastal Basque provinces, followed by the Francoist repression, led to the emergence by the early 1950s of ETA (*Euskad Ta Azkatasurra* – "Basque Homeland and Freedom"). Originally a middle-class student movement whose methods included – and still embrace – bank robberies, kidnappings for ransom, protection rackets and assassinations, it eventually split into two factions: the violent *ETA-Militar* and the *ETA-Politico-Militar*, the latter being socialists first and Basque nationalists second. Although full-time ETA membership has never exceeded one thousand, its methods provoked widespread reprisals, including mass arrests, torture and show trials as at Burgos in 1970, which backfired internationally, and closer to home caused Catalan intellectuals to stage a sympathy sit-in at the monastery of Montserrat. Meanwhile, there was little violence in Catalunya itself and no counterpart of the ETA: a 1963 petition against language restrictions, or a pointed rendition of the traditional anthem in Franco's presence, was more typical of the Catalan approach.

than fund economic development. Striking a healthy balance between peripheral self-determination and fiscal responsibility is the task confronting Madrid governments of any complexion, and one that goes against the grain of the national impulse to live for the moment and let tomorrow take care of itself.

The stubbornly high Spanish **unemployment** rate – over twenty percent in most of the country – means that petty crime is on the rise, even

in isolated areas. Only Catalunya, especially Girona, is markedly better off for work; many of the young people you'll see in seasonal jobs at Catalan Pyrenean resorts are migrants from distant provinces, working with little in the way of employment contracts or security, and considering themselves fortunate for what they've found.

Mountain agriculture is no longer viable on either slope of the Pyrenees, so the ancient terraces are crumbling back into wilderness.

Following the restoration of democratic process by referendum in 1976, the free elections of the following year gave **Pacte Democratico per Catalunya** – an alliance of pro-Catalan parties – ten seats in the lower house of the Spanish parliament; among the Basques, the reconstituted PNV won eight seats and a new left-wing nationalist party, **Euskadi Eskerra**, won one. The PNV and *Euskadi Eskerra* remain theoretically committed to independence but seek change by constitutional means – in contrast to **Herri Batasuna** (United People), linked to *ETA-Militar*. In the 1980 elections, HB won eleven seats in the Basque regional parliament, in 1984 eleven again and in 1986 thirteen, but in all cases the deputies refused to take up their seats, leaving the PNV in control. Subsequently, the PNV divided: Carlos Garaikoetxea, the first Basque premier, decamped with half his regional deputies to form the centralist *Eusko Alkartasuna* (EA), leaving the PNV to the decentralist José Antonio Ardanza.

Although Catalunya's experiences earlier this century paralleled those of the Basque country – the granting of a statute of autonomy by the Republicans, followed by severe cultural repression after 1939 – relations with Madrid are curently more cordial. Catalunya is now effectively run day-to-day by its **Generalitat**, the regional government, which controls education, health, social security, tourism, commerce, agriculture and cultural matters. Curiously, in light of the Republican past, centre-right regional parliaments have been consistently returned by Catalunya voters since 1978; they are apparently seen as better able to look after Catalan business interests, and – by participating in the coalition governments of 1993 and 1997 – to extract fiscal concessions from Madrid.

For many Basques the wounds of large-scale immigration, exploitation by a non-Basque elite and denial of significant independence still fester. Yet alone thus far among Spain's autonomous regions, the Basque provinces have the right to collect and disburse all of their own revenues, and the *Guardia Civil* has been replaced by a home guard, the *Ertzainza*.

Continuing **ETA outrages**, apparently designed to provoke centralist repression which will convince waverers to support the extreme solution of independence, garner less and less approval, and would seem to be a desperate rearguard action by a fringe group that perceives its support to be waning. The kidnapping and eventual murder of PP municipal councillor Miguel Ángel Blanco in July 1997 – his release alive had been contingent on the PP's meeting the impossible demand of relocating six hundred ETA prisoners to Basque-province jails – sparked an unprecedented wave of anti-ETA street demonstrations across the country. Subsequently the non-violent Basque local parties have moved to oust HB mayors in certain ETA strongholds, in conjunction with Madrid's efforts to break up the front-business networks (often hotels and restaurants) which finance ETA. But at the same time PP-inspired calls to "socially isolate" HB in the Basque country, for example by boycotting its supporters' shops, have been denounced, somewhat hyperbolically, as reminiscent of early Nazism.

ETA was much slower to take root in the overwhelmingly rural **French Basque regions**, where – except in Bayonne – an urban proletariat is almost nonexistent. Grievances here have more to do with a perceived Parisian policy of relegating the Pays Basque to "Third World" status, promoting only tourist-related industries at the expense of others. Peaceful protests against this in 1983 involved deliberate "go-slows" on the coastal highway to Spain, and mass picnics on the beach at Biarritz. As for cultural identity, the 61 teachers in the *ikastolak* or Basque-language primary schools around Bayonne were finally recognized as state employees in November 1989.

Repopulation is therefore left to the *nouveaux ruraux*/*neo-rurales* in search of alternative lifestyles, and to people renovating second homes. France in particular offers a range of grants for permanent mountain-dwellers, but full-time Pyrenean residence remains a precarious business.

The **single European market** is already having a discernible impact in towns like Perpignan and Bayonne, which will handle much of the freight moving north and south. Spanish membership of the EU is showing its effects in the Pyrenees, as grant money funds civil engineering projects otherwise beyond the means of the autonomous regions. Much of this development is highly unsympathetic to the environment, with the Pyrenees at risk of transformation into a series of tame theme parks, where genuine indigenous culture and wildlife have been destroyed.

WILDLIFE

There is plenty of wildlife to observe in the Pyrenees, despite the effects of hunting and environmental damage (see "The Environment", p.476). The range is especially rewarding for bird-spotters, with a variety of magnificent resident indigenous species, and enormous numbers of migrating birds to be seen flying over the western Col d'Organbidexka and, in the east near Canigou, the Col d'Eyne.

The round-up below picks out the major animal species that you might encounter (as well as the declining species that you probably won't), and details some of the more interesting types of Pyrenean flora. However, it can only be a general guide to occurrence and habitat. For something more specific, see the list of recommended wildlife titles on p.485.

BIRDS

The **lammergeier** or bearded vulture (*gypaète barbu* in French; *quebrantahuesos* in Castilian) was persecuted almost out of existence by herdsmen fearing for their livestock, but lately has made a slight recovery. It is easily identified by the wonderful pinkish-gold breast of the adult, a long wedge-shaped tail, narrow wings and enormous size – weighing up to 6kg, with a wingspan of almost 3m. Still rare enough to be a thrill when spotted, lammergeiers can most reliably be seen in several places: at Gavarnie, in the Aspe/Ossau region, in the Valle de Ordesa and in their principal strongholds of the Hecho, Ansó and Roncal valleys to the northwest of Jaca.

The lammergeier's diet consists mainly of bone marrow, which it exposes by dropping bones onto a rocky surface from a height of 30–50m (hence the Castilian name, meaning "breaks-bones"). To locate its meal, the solitary lammergeier often works in conjunction with a flock of **griffon vultures** (*vautour fauve* in French; *buitre común* in Spanish), which are similar in size, but lack the wedge-shaped tail and streamlining, and have a distinctive white head and neck. Only when the griffons have finished stripping the flesh from the carcase does the lammergeier move in. Flocks of griffon vultures patrol much of the Pyrenees, especially in the Basque country and the Aspe/Ossau valleys.

Occasionally, the rare **black vulture** is seen in the western Pyrenees, particularly the Valle de Hecho and the Iparla ridge, either with griffons or on its own. This bird can be distinguished from the griffon by its longer and more rounded tail, its much darker plumage and a black area around the eye.

Unlike the above species, the **Egyptian vulture** (*percnoptère* in French; *acantilados alimoche* in Castilian) is found in the Pyrenees only during the breeding season, when it can be seen in the Aspe, Ossau and Soule valleys or around the Ordesa region. The smallest of the vultures – with a wingspan of about 150cm – the Egyptian has white plumage and black wingtips. Nicknamed *Marie-Blanque* or *La Dame Blanche* in the French valleys, its arrival in the April skies announces the start of spring.

The **golden eagle** (*aigle royal* in French; *aguila real* in Castilian) is glimpsed everywhere in the high mountains, each breeding pair having a territory of between 90 and 130 square kilometres. You can identify juveniles by the white patches on the wing underside, but for adult birds over five years old, identification is more by size (around 80cm from beak to tail, with a wingspan of 3m) and the open V-shape of its upturned wings as it soars. Whereas the golden eagle and the scarcer Bonelli's eagle – dark on top; paler underneath, with a dark, striped tail – are seen all year round, the **booted eagle** and the **short-toed eagle** settle here only during the summer breeding season. The booted is the smallest of the European eagles, with a wingspan of up to 120cm. It has a long, narrow tail and is either pale with an almost white front and white-flecked head, or uniformly mahogany-coloured with slender white stripes along the front of the wings. The short-toed eagle is often almost pure white with darker banding all round the wings, and has a head that seems disproportionately large. A unique characteristic is its habit of hovering motionless over its intended prey, commonly snakes, with its legs dangling freely.

The acrobatic kites are perhaps the most entertaining birds to watch. The **red kite** (*milan royal* in French; *milano* in Castilian) has a deeply forked tail, and continuously twists in the air as it manoeuvres over carrion. The **black kite** (*milan noir* in French; *milano negro* in Castilian) is darker than the red kite, its tail shorter and straighter-edged, and its wingspan smaller at around 115cm. It is most often seen circling over municipal rubbish dumps, unconcerned by the comings and goings of the trucks. The autumn migration swells the numbers that have been in the Pyrenees during the summer.

The turkey-like **capercaillie** (*grand tétras* in French; *urogallo* in Castilian), hunted and harassed to extinction in the French Alps, survives in small numbers in the Pyrenees, protected – though not entirely effectively – in the national parks and in Andorra. Despite its size it is a very elusive bird, but you might see one breaking noisily from cover, or witness the late-winter mating display of the cock, when it throws back its green-ringed neck, and dances and sings. The hen is duller, mostly brown flecked with white, and with smaller bright red "eyebrows" than the male.

Since it is also seldom seen in flight, except when flushed out of hiding, the **ptarmigan** (*lagopède alpin* in French; *perdiz blanca* in Castilian) is also difficult to spot. It's found in pairs around the central Pyrenees during summer, and in winter in flocks, when the birds are almost totally snow-camouflage white, except for a black tail and red "eyebrows".

Three smaller but distinctive birds of high altitude are the playful and acrobatic **alpine chough**, a slim crow with a curved yellow beak, sometimes seen with its red-beaked cousin, the **common chough**; the **snow finch**, like a large sparrow, but noticeably black and white in flight; and the **wall-creeper**, red, grey and black, with a thin curved beak and usually found on or near cliffs. Lower down, the **white-backed woodpecker** has its only western European home in the woodlands of the Pyrenees.

MAMMALS

The most agile and conspicuous wild mammal of the high mountains is the **izard** or **Pyrenean chamois** (*isard* in French or Catalan; *rebeco* or *camuza* in Castilian; *sarrio* in Aragonese), a member of the antelope family and a close relative of the larger Alpine chamois. Living among the peaks in summer and descending in the winter, they are numerous in the Parc National des Pyrénées and the contiguous Parque Nacional de Ordesa y Monte Perdido. Individuals around Port d'Espagne, near Cauterets, as well as in Ordesa are uncharacteristically tame because of their contact with tourists. Gavarnie, the Sierra del Cadí, Canigou and Aigües Tortes are other good places to see them (for further information, see "The Environment", p.476).

The **mouflon** (same in French; *muflón* in Castilian), which resembles a very large and sturdy sheep with curling black horns, is a recently reintroduced species. Bones found at Tautavel, near Perpignan, show that they inhabited the region thousands of years ago, but Corsica, Sardinia and Cyprus were this sheep's only modern natural strongholds. Mouflon are now doing well in the Carlit massif and on Pic Pibeste, near Lourdes, where the arid, Mediterranean-like microclimate allows them to thrive.

The dark-bristled **wild boar** (*sanglier* in French; *jabalí* in Castilian) is nocturnal, and nomadic when under hunting-season pressure, covering up to 40km between dusk and dawn. You may see it at its mud-bath, to which the beast may return regularly, but are more likely to notice signs of its presence than the animal itself; large areas of disturbed earth are often indicative that a wild boar has been rooting around with its tusks, especially in woodland where it forages for beech nuts and acorns.

Red deer and the much smaller, slim-horned **roe deer** live in the central Pyrenees, both favouring calcareous zones where open pasture meets forest and the necessary combination of food and cover is provided. Dawn and dusk are the best times to view deer, when feeding activity is most intense; they are elusive animals, though, and local advice will usually be needed to find them.

Throughout much of the high Pyrenees you will hear, though not see, the **marmot** (*marmotte* in French; *marmota* in Castilian), a now-common dweller above the tree line that once disappeared from the Pyrenees after centuries of hunting, mostly for dog food but partly for its fur. This robust rodent – reaching a length of 75cm – was reintroduced to the French central Pyrenees earlier this century, and has now spread to both sides of the range. The shrill alarm whistle emitted by "sentry" individuals sends the colony scurrying to its extensive tunnel system, which is generally dug on warm, south-facing scree slopes at around 2000m – a habitat where its fawn-grey fur makes the marmot almost invisible. Despite their cuddly appearance and anthropomorphic habit of standing on two legs, marmots can be fierce, fighting to the death over territorial disputes.

The Pyrenean **wildcat** (*chat sauvage* in French; *gato montés* in Castilian) is genetically much the same as that found in other parts of Europe; it looks like a domestic tabby, only much larger, with a distinctively thick tail. Pyrenean wildcats prefer south-facing forests well below alpine habitats, where their preferred prey of fieldmice and voles is abundant; they dislike snow, and descend as necessary in winter. Wildcats are protected on both sides of the Pyrenees, and are actually increasing in numbers and expanding their range, but are shy and seldom seen.

Stoats are small, sinuous carnivores of the weasel family which prey on small rodents and rabbits. In their reddish-brown summer fur with a black-tipped tail they are fairly conspicuous, but in winter they change colour to white to camouflage themselves in the snow, at which time they are called **ermines**. A larger relative is the **pine marten** (*martre* in French; *marta garduña* in Castilian), which remains a warm brown colour all year round, and is found up to the treeline in the Pyrenees in coniferous and mixed woodland. The **red squirrel** (*ardilla roja* in Castilian; *écureuil rouge* in French) favours much the same habitat and, not subject to competition from greys as in Britain, is relatively abundant.

ENDANGERED SPECIES

The Spanish **ibex** (*bouquetin* in French; *cabra montés* in Castilian), a stocky species of wild goat, is almost extinct in the Pyrenees. The slopes of the Valle de Ordesa support the range's single troupe, and they are rarely seen by tourists. Hunting has been the principal

cause of their destruction, their distinctive ribbed horns a much-esteemed trophy during the nineteenth century. Although ibex live in large numbers in other parts of Spain, particularly the Gredos where there are some five thousand, they are not precisely the same as those formerly native in the Pyrenees. The larger Pyrenean subspecies seems doomed, since the genetic pool has become too reduced to stage a recovery; an additional threat may be posed by the appearance of a debilitating, and possibly contagious, eye disease among the more numerous izards.

The small, unaggressive Pyrenean subspecies of **brown bear** (*ours* in French; *oso pardo* in Spanish) is even closer to extinction. No one knows precisely how many bears remain in the Pyrenees but the top figure is only around twenty, and some experts put it as low as four. Bears are most likely to survive in an area straddling the border around the Aspe, Ossau and Roncal valleys; there may still be some in the border area between Luchon and Benasque; and there is an outside chance that there are still a few in the Haute Ariège and Couserans. Experience with other species shows that so small a population seldom retains sufficient genetic diversity to reproduce successfully. Effectively, therefore, the brown bear of the Pyrenees is finished as a distinct subspecies, though there might still be time to cross the remaining specimens with stock from other European brown bear populations; Slovenia was the source of a few individuals introduced into the Couserans in 1997. Once again, the decline is directly attributable to hunting and the degradation of its habitat – subjects discussed in "The Environment", p.477.

The only other large carnivore of the area is the rare **lynx** (same in French; *pardelo* in Castilian), which like the bear has been widely persecuted. Some remain in the western French Pyrenees, but are vulnerable to loss of habitat through deforestation. Wildcats (see above) are sometimes mistaken for them.

Few have heard of the **desman** (same in French; *almizclera* or *desmán* in Castilian), yet this trunk-nosed, aquatic, mole-like mammal is one of the great curiosities of the Pyrenees. All attempts to study the creature have failed, since in captivity specimens die almost immediately, and it is extremely scarce in the wild. Needing undisturbed and unpolluted streams to survive, the desman has been sighted in the Baronnies, in the Aspe and the streams of the eastern Pyrenees, which are the cleanest in the range; the parks and reserves south of the watershed are promising too, especially Aigües Tortes and Roncal's Parque Natural Pirenaico.

AMPHIBIANS, REPTILES AND BUTTERFLIES

The slow-moving **fire salamander** (*salamandre jaune et noire* in French; *salamandra común* in Spanish), is like a soft-skinned lizard, with brilliant yellow-and-black markings that warn potential predators of its toxic skin secretions. They are primarily nocturnal, and usually only seen by day in damp weather, when heavy rain can lure them out onto paths and roads. The smaller, camouflaged Pyrenean **brook salamander** is endemic to the mountains, and found in cold lakes and streams.

A true reptile, the **Iberian rock lizard** can be found, unlike most of its sun-loving relatives, at surprisingly high altitudes in the Pyrenees. Several snakes occur in the area, none of them poisonous except the **asp viper**. Like most snakes, this species, with a dark wavy or zigzag pattern along the spine, only bites if under threat of attack and needs merely to be left alone.

Numerous **butterflies** (French *papillon*; Castilian *mariposa*) make a home in the Pyrenees, even to quite high altitudes, with July and August being the best months; the Vall d'Aran is one of the best locales for them. Apollo butterflies are white, with distinctive red or yellow eyespots on the wings, whereas the humbler clouded apollo could be mistaken for a small cabbage white. The endemic Gavarnie blue is a rather disappointing shade of grey, but the slightly more widespread Eros blue can equal the colour of the gentians it feeds among. Ringlets are a group of medium-sized brown butterflies, with wings marked by black eyespots. They are difficult to distinguish, even for experts, but two species and seven subspecies are endemic to the Pyrenees.

FLORA

Pyrenean high-altitude flora resembles that of the Alps in many ways, but with the higher average temperatures, the treeline of the Pyrenees can be much higher in a few favoured positions,

reaching 2600m on southern slopes of the Néouvielle massif, or 2100m in the Marcadau valley. The highest-altitude **trees** are Pyrenean mountain pines (either *Pinus uncinata* or *Pinus mugo*, and hybrids), with distinctive hooked tips to the cone scales – thus the French name of *pin crochet*. Black pines (*Pinus nigra, ssp salzmanii*) are the next most tolerant of alpine conditions, occurring up to about 2100m; lower down, in roughly descending order of occurrence, Scots pine, beech, silver fir, birch and poplar form dense forests, with some of the finest being in the Ordesa National Park. Lower still (below about 1000m) grow maple, hornbeam, sweet chestnut and various deciduous oaks. To the east, near the Mediterranean coast, appear groves of umbrella-shaped stone pine, whose edible seeds are gathered as pine nuts.

Because of the rainfall disparity between some of the dry Spanish slopes and the much wetter French slopes, the vegetation in one country is often very different to that at a similar altitude on the opposite side of the border. The underlying igneous and metamorphic rocks are hard and slow-weathering, but often overlaid with more plant-friendly limestone. The range's altitude has made the mountains an effective barrier, preventing the spread of many lower-altitude Spanish species northward into France, and vice versa.

More than 3300 species of **plants** are recorded for the Pyrenees, about 180 of them endemic – found growing wild nowhere else. The two unspectacular and very similar species of **Pyrenean yam**, with tiny green flowers, a swollen starchy root and tropical relatives, are ancient relics of a warmer climate. Both are confined to the Pyrenees, with the rarer living only in the Noguera Ribagorçana gorge. A much more attractive relict from the Tertiary period is the **ramonda**, named after Ramond de Carbonnières, the doyen of Pyrenean exploration in the late eighteenth century. Although not rare, it is endemic to limestone slopes in northeastern Spain and the Pyrenees. Resembling its distant relative, the African violet, it has fleshy wrinkled leaves and, in summer, small purple flowers with a central yellow cone of stamens.

Other endemics attract attention: the long-leaved **butterwort**, which is spectacular on the cliffs at Gavarnie, has flypaper leaves that trap and digest insects; the large purple **storksbill** has bright, almost garish flowers, while the ashy and western **cranesbills** have far more subtle shades of soft pink on their trumpet-shaped flowers; more delicate still are the little **horned pansies**, with fragrant violet blooms. The rare **silvery vetch** has spikes of pea flowers that are white with thread-like violet veining; the Pyrenean and Aragonese **columbines** have long-spurred flowers of a wonderful blue, while their relative, the Pyrenean **adonis** or pheasant's eye produces huge golden bowl-shaped flowers over feathery foliage in early summer. The higher areas of the Pyrenees are home to tussocky **fescue** grasses (genus *Festuca*), many species of which are endemic to these mountains.

Several **primroses** in subtle shades of lilac to red can be found in rocky or marshy places, but their small, compact and more delicate relatives the **rock jasmines** are mostly restricted to high-altitude cliffs and screes – *Androsace ciliata* and *A. cylindrica* are two of the rarest, confined to the central areas such as Gavarnie and on the Monte Perdido massif. The **Pyrenean snowbell** has deeply fringed violet flowers and favours damp, shady conditions in the west of the range.

Growing mostly above the treeline, though sometimes in shady woodland, are many species of **saxifrage**, five of them endemic to the Pyrenees. Their flowers are usually small, numerous and starry, coloured white or pinkish in loose sprays. The endemic **water saxifrage** grows in mountain bogs and along streams up to about 2200m, its white flowers appearing in mid-summer; the cliff-dwelling **Pyrenean saxifrage** has a large rosette of lime-encrusted leaves, which eventually produces a tall red-stemmed spike of flowers before dying. The **paniculate** (or livelong) **saxifrage** is similar to the Pyrenean but has a smaller, more ragged rosette, with yellow and white flowers only at the top. The most spectacular of this group, the **purple saxifrage**, has large, stemless flowers over carpets of tiny leaves, and grows on the highest peaks.

Succulent **stonecrops** (*Sedum* spp.), with yellow, white or pink flowers, and frequently red leaves, grow in dry, open places, often where there is little soil. The equally fleshy, but neatly rosetted, **houseleeks** produce occasional spikes of reddish flowers, and are capable of growing at altitudes of nearly 3000m. A smaller, pale pink flowered species of houseleek is endemic to the Sierra del Cadí.

Globularias are dwarf shrubs, with spherical tufted heads of blue or purple flowers and a long flowering period of May to August. There are numerous types of **daisy**, some with large flowers, like the endemic purple **Pyrenean aster**, and the even larger shasta daisy – the latter now widely cultivated elsewhere as a garden plant. The huge **cardoon knapweed** has spectacular purple thistle heads, to 7cm across, in late summer meadows; parts of this plant, a close relative of the artichoke, are edible and sometimes appear stewed in restaurants.

Members of the heather family cover large areas, and add colour to the slopes all through the summer. **Bilberries** (April–July), **bearberries** (June–Sept) and **cowberries** all have greenish-white or pinkish, often bell-shaped flowers, followed by edible berries. The prostrate, mat-forming creeping **azalea** (May–July) produces tiny pink flowers, but its bigger cousin the **wild rhododendron** (May–Aug) or alpenrose has clusters of conspicuous red flowers. Various species of **heather** itself provide colour from May to October.

The higher alpine meadows are home to some gorgeous members of the lily family, such as the chocolate or deep purple bells of the **Pyrenean fritillary**; the large white trumpets of **Saint Bruno's lily**; the yellow **Turk's-cap lily**; the **dogstooth violet**, which takes its name from the white oval bulb, not the blossom; and *Brimeura*, a small amethyst **hyacinth**. Belonging to the same family, but crocus-like in shades of pink and white, are *Bulbocodium*, *Colchicum* and pink-purple *Merendera*, most of these autumn-blooming. The **true crocuses** appear both in early summer amongst receding snow-patches, and in autumn as the season cools. During spring, half a dozen small members of the **daffodil family** appear, usually in damp meadows and often in great quantity; the rush-leaved narcissus, rock narcissus and lesser wild daffodil are among the more common. **Buttercups** are also well represented, for example the glacier crowfoot *(Ranunculus glacialis)*, conspicuous as shiny white or pink flowers on high-altitude glacial moraines or screes, to 3000m and beyond. They are followed, in summer, by the deep blue so-called "English" **iris** (*Iris latifolia*, ex-

xiphioides), which despite its name is more or less confined in the wild to the Pyrenees, forming spectacular clusters on treeless slopes between 1900 and 2100m elevation. This species is the parent of many cultivated forms in northern Europe, and shouldn't be confused with the more widespread Spanish iris (*Iris xiphium*).

Twelve types of **gentian** are recorded for the Pyrenees, at elevations over 1500m, and can sometimes be tricky to identify. Most species are small and delicate, with starry or trumpet-shaped flowers of a piercing blue that can mirror the sky or mountain tarns, but the more robust yellow gentians can attain a metre in height. The most common are the large, deep-blue trumpet gentians, *Gentiana acaulis* (ex-*kochiana*) and closely related species. Another legendary alpine which may grow with them is the **edelweiss**, though the fuzzy whitish flowers can be disappointing up close and lack the gentian's charisma.

Numerous **bellflowers** occur, including a number endemic to the Pyrenees. The taller ones grow in open or woodland areas, but the real gems grow nestled into crevices of the limestone, or running delicate stems through the debris of scree slopes. With them, but in contrasting shades of purplish-red through to pale pink, are **wild carnations** and **pinks** (*Dianthus* spp), which often have powerful fragrances according to the kind of soil rooted in; the fringed pink, thriving up to 2000m, is one of the most attractive.

A number of alpine or central European **orchids** grow in woodland and meadows on the French side, while lower areas on the Spanish side and at the hotter eastern and western ends of the range, are home to more Mediterranean species. *Epipactis parviflora* and *Dactylorhiza caramulensis* are two specialities of the area, but the endangered **lady's slipper** still survives in a few places in the east.

During late summer and autumn local people harvest the abundant **wild fungi**. Robust ceps, crinkly yellow chanterelles and saffron milk-caps are favourites, but most in demand are the brown honeycombed morels of springtime, scarce but almost worth their weight in gold when gathered and dried.

THE ENVIRONMENT

Human populations may be lower in most of the Pyrenees than they were a century ago, but the landscape is nonetheless threatened, and since the early 1980s French and Spanish conservationists have turned considerable attention to the region. Concerns are numerous: the potential extinction of endangered species, massacres of migrating birds, obstruction of waterways by hydroelectric schemes, the death from pollution of thousands of hectares of trees. Their arguments might not be changing developmental priorities yet, but environmental protests get a hearing these days, at least on the French side, and occasionally succeed in stopping or altering destructive projects. At (literally) ground level, the standard of rural tidiness has improved, especially on the Spanish side of the range: dumpster bins are ubiquitous and well used, and public education campaigns on environmental matters seem slowly to be having an effect.

However, there are still formidable obstacles to be overcome, not least the mind-set of top governmental officials in post-1996 Spain, where vice-president Álvarez Cascos has proclaimed more or less verbatim that environmental considerations are the concern of a few smelly hippies, and that any opposition to developmental projects must be ignored or brushed aside. Such attitudes are echoed at all levels of regional and local government, compounded by corruption and often wilful ignorance among those officials directly responsible for the welfare of the Pyrenean environment.

NATURAL RESERVES

Among the qualifications for national park status, as defined by the International Union for the Conservation of Nature and Natural Resources (IUCN), are that there should be no hunting and no exploitation other than that consistent with the "natural" way of life of mountain people, such as grazing or wild-food gath-

ering. So far there are just three **national parks in the Pyrenees**, and only two of those actually meet the IUCN criteria – the Parc National des Pyrénées in France and the adjoining Parque Nacional de Ordesa y Monte Perdido in Spain. The Parc Nacional d'Aigües Tortes in Catalunya is not officially recognized by the IUCN because of its numerous hydroelectric installations, which are a source of constant friction with conservationists.

Other areas of the Pyrenees are administered under lesser categories of conservation schemes. In Spain there are the *parques naturales* of Cadí-Moixeró, Maladeta-Posets, the Garrotxa and Larra-Belagoa; and France has various *réserves naturelles* – but these do not entirely protect wildlife from hunting.

HUNTING

Hunting in the Pyrenees is **controlled** in a number of ways besides the outright ban in the national parks. Various private reserves keep the numbers of hunters down by charging high fees; permits are limited by auction or the drawing of lots; certain animals are designated as protected species; the number of hunting days is restricted; and voluntary management plans have been implemented by (French more than Spanish) hunting associations.

In some instances these restraints have been effective. There are around fifteen thousand izards on the French side of the range and probably a similar number on the Spanish, a reasonably healthy situation that leads hunters to insist that further kill-limits are unnecessary. However, permitted hunting has taken a heavy toll of this species in places: the Néouvielle region's population, for example, has had to be restocked after being depleted. Herds have territories of around one square kilometre, so those within the protected areas are fairly safe; the animals at risk – solitary old males, youngsters rejected by their mothers and mature males driven off by rivals – are those that stray outside the protected reserves.

But the hunters' main interest is in smaller **game animals**, and for these species the situation is far from satisfactory. For instance, there is no explicit protection for capercaillie in the management plans of many hunting associations, even where it is on the verge of local extinction. And management plans have not always been thoroughly thought out: the one for Mantet, in the eastern Pyrenees, calls for a reduction in the numbers of predators, a scheme that will adversely affect the marten, a species on which no authoritative conservation research has yet been done.

Even if an animal is classified as a protected species, it isn't necessarily safe. The twenty-five thousand hunters who account for one and a half million pigeons each year often illegally kill other species, such as vultures and kestrels, in the same barrages of shot. The one avian bright spot is a steady increase in lammergeier populations in the western Pyrenees, thanks to EU-funded conservation projects and growing awareness amongst country people that these raptors feed only on already-dead livestock.

THE BROWN BEAR

A *cause célèbre* of environmentalism has been the **brown bear** (see also the feature on p.342), whose survival became a badge of political mettle when former French president François Mitterrand pledged to save the species. Accordingly a **Plan Ours** was announced in 1984, but since then nothing effective has happened – there are too many commercial interests in the Pyrenees to make saving the bear anything other than a pipe dream. In 1990 the *Office National des Forêts* announced the creation of a reserve near Luchon, but by then there were no more than one or two bears left in the area. Forestry and ski development pose threats to the species, but hunting has been the bear's nemesis, either for "sport" (2 were shot as recently as 1982), or killed by angry shepherds, or for bear fat – which once sold as a cure for baldness under the title *Pommade de Lion*. Shepherds, the traditional enemies of the bear, continued to destroy them even after the total prohibition of bear-hunting in 1972. Indemnity payments for lost livestock were introduced after World War II and increased under the *Plan Ours*, but not enough to keep shepherds from mounting resolute opposition to any further plans to protect the bears – only overcompensation, costing very little in relative terms, would gain their support for bear-protection measures.

The hunting of animals other than bear has also adversely affected them. According to some experts, the wild boar hunt – involving large and noisy parties – has scared the bears away by ruining the calm they prefer, as has the use of helicopters during the seasonal Andorran izard hunt.

SKI DEVELOPMENT

Given the relatively poor snow record of the Pyrenees, **ski development** here has lagged far behind that of the Alps, especially on the Spanish side of the range. However, despite projections showing that the number of skiers is not set to grow and that global warming could make investment in the Pyrenees highly risky, funds continue to trickle in. On the Spanish side, new resorts are projected for the thus far untouched Valle de Gistau and Valle de Aisa, while Formigal, Astún and Candanchú are to be united into one "macro"-station; the main potential beneficiaries of such plans are developers of hundreds of apartments in Jaca, built during the speculative boom of the 1980s and worth very little since the recession struck. Existing stations frantic over recent poor winters are looking to the highest slopes of the range to alleviate their problems or, worse, are proposing to drain natural lakes to feed snow-cannons. At least two proposed French schemes have demanded exemption from the ban on development in the Parc National des Pyrénées, and on the Spanish side none of the various proposals or accomplished projects has been subject to an environmental impact study. One particularly lunatic scheme proposes blasting away part of the Pico d'Aspe to "improve" ski runs.

Such projects have repercussions beyond the obvious visual disturbance, increase in traffic densities and disruption of natural habitats. There is growing awareness, for example, that the clearance of forests for the construction of pistes and resorts can lead to a higher incidence of snow and mud **avalanches**, with devastating effects on hitherto protected settlements.

FORESTS

In 1989 research institutes at Toulouse and Lannemezan in France and Vitoria in Spain reported that 21 percent of Pyrenean trees were sick, with the worst-affected forest being the silver firs of the Luchon valley. Several causes have been identified, including repeated dry periods, late frosts and errors of forestry management, but **acid rain** emerges as a major culprit, with the gas field at Lacq, near Pau, particularly singled out. A filtration system at Lacq has drastically cut the release of sulphur into the air, but emissions remain high here and in the industrial conglomerations of Catalunya,

Aragón and the Basque country. Andorra's main power station launches 324 tonnes of sulphur into the air each day, while the factories of western Euskadi produce 490 tonnes – more than twice as much as the whole city of London. On the north flank of the Pyrenees 79 percent of forest environments register a pH factor of between 4 and 5 (pH7 is neutral), which ranks with the level in the Vosges, long considered the worst-affected area of France.

Forest **fires** have so far had less impact along the Pyrenees than in Provence, but ominously the Aude suffered a forest fire in February 1990, a time of year when such problems are almost unknown. There is now some suggestion of planting the nearby Albères with more cork oak, a species highly resistant to fire. Improved husbandry of vineyards and olive groves through the clearance of undergrowth and the construction of firebreaks has given some protection to vegetation in the vulnerable Alt Empordà region, behind Catalunya's Mediterranean coast, but the nearby Cap de Creus promontory in Catalunya seems to burn with depressing regularity every few years.

Destructive **logging practices**, especially in the Spanish Hecho and Ansó valleys, are responsible for massive erosion and habitat depletion. Instead of sustainable, selective extraction using mules or horses along existing tracks and paths, clear-cutting and haulage with heavy machinery are the rule. Compounded by the absence of any replanting programmes, such methods are still leaving behind ever-worsening erosion scars, plus the prospect of floods and altered rainfall patterns.

THE SEA AND RIVERS

The 1975 Directive of the European Community requires designated **swimming beaches** to be tested every other week during the summer, and sets a standard of 2000 fecal coliform per 100 millilitres of water for 95 percent of samples. (Coliform is a bacterium found in the human gastro-intestinal tract and therefore an indicator of the level of sewage pollution.) To put this into perspective, the United States Environmental Protection Agency sets a standard ten times more stringent, and Canada is twenty times stricter. To be within the EC/EU standard is hardly a guarantee of safe bathing and to exceed it is disgusting; even at the recommended levels, swimming in such water may provoke skin, eye and ear infections, or (if you swallow any) gastro-intestinal distress.

Upon testing, numerous beaches on the Mediterranean and (especially) the Atlantic coast habitually fail to meet the relatively lax EU standards, though there have been significant improvements since increased investment in sewage treatment plans on both sides of the frontier.

Of the **rivers** of the French Pyrenees, the Nive, the Gave d'Oloron, the Gave de Pau, the Adour, the Agly and the Aude historically have failed pollution tests at most measuring points; only the higher reaches of the Garonne, the Ariège, the Tech and most of the Têt were essentially satisfactory. The less-inhabited valleys on the Spanish side fare better, with only about twenty percent of samples falling short of requirements in the recent past.

HYDROELECTRIC POWER

Although **hydroelectric power** is much more acceptable than fossil-fuelled or nuclear alternatives, and can be almost benign environmentally, neither Spain nor France has made much effort to make it so in the Pyrenees. Valleys have been scoured and flooded in an entirely unaesthetic way, with almost no money spent on landscaping or tidying up, and construction has often occurred with no thought given to the impact on wildlife – the Laparan dam project near Ax-les-Thermes, for example, helped hasten the local extinction of the bear. Tunnel-sized feed pipes have been routed through once-wooded areas, and substations send out their rhythmic roar day and night even in the remotest locations. Cable cars and high-tension pylons are strung across otherwise empty sky, while leftover construction and maintenance materials deface the most unexpected places. Virtually no major river is untouched, and warning notices advise you to keep away from the banks downstream from dams in case the power company instigates sudden changes in water level.

The pace of hydroelectric development on the French side, which hit its stride between the world wars, has now slowed down considerably as France enjoys a kilowatt surplus (often sold abroad). The Spaniards were latecomers to the game: while the very first dams appeared in the hills of Catalunya at the turn of the century, the most Spanish projects were commissioned after World War II, and **new proposals** are still on the drawing boards for depopulated Alto Aragón and Navarra – with the bulk of accumulated water and power to be sent, in all cases, down to the flatlands. Mooted projects include reservoirs at Itoiz, Biscarrués, Jánovas on the Río Ara (the last undammed Spanish Pyrenean river) and Santa Liestra on the Río Ésera, and the enlargement of the Yesa dam.

BOOKS

This list is a sample of general and specific books that will enrich a visit to the range. Not all are concerned exclusively with the Pyrenees, but certain titles that deal with the whole of France and Spain have been chosen because they contain much that is relevant to the mountains and their cultures. For all books in print, publishing details are given in the form "UK publisher; US publisher", where they differ; if books are published in one country only, this follows the publisher's name; "o/p" means out of print – consult a library or specialist second-hand bookdealer.

GENERAL ACCOUNTS & TRAVEL

Alain Bourneton *Rivages Pyrénéens* (Éditions Milan, Toulouse, France). Expensive but beautifully photographed tour around a thousand Pyrenean lakes. Covering geography, wildlife and legends, it makes a wonderful souvenir.

Alastair Boyd *The Essence of Catalonia* (André Deutsch, UK & US; o/p). Part history, part guide, this is strong on the art and architecture of the obvious towns and monuments, but weaker on the Pyrenean mountain side of things.

Norbert Casteret *The Descent of Pierre Saint-Martin* (Dent, UK o/p). English translation of Casteret's *Trente Ans sous Terre*, dealing with the exploration of what was then the world's deepest known cave system. Other translations of books by Casteret, the greatest of Pyrenean speleologists, include *Ten Years Under the Earth* (Mendip; Cave Books, Missouri), *Cave Men New and Old* (Dent, UK o/p) and *The Darkness Under the Earth* (Dent, UK o/p).

Eleanor Elsner *Romance of the Basque Country and the Pyrenees* (Herbert Jenkins; Dodd, Mead & Co; o/p). Published in 1927, but still a treasure for its old photographs and anecdotes.

Nina Epton *The Valley of Pyrene* (Cassell, UK o/p). Record of a tour through the Ariège in the 1950s, with copious anecdotes and reflections. Encounters with luminaries – including Dalí – give added depth to the account.

Norman Lewis *Voices of the Old Sea* (Penguin, UK & US). Set in the early 1950s, this ingenious blend of novel and social record charts the lives of two remote Costa Brava villages and the breakdown of the old ways in the face of tourism.

Rose Macaulay *Fabled Shore* (Oxford UP, o/p). The Spanish coast as it was in 1949 (read it and weep), travelled and described from Catalunya to the Portuguese Algarve.

Edwin Mullins *The Pilgrimage to Santiago* (o/p). While just a brief section of the medieval pilgrims' route from Paris to the shrine of St James (Santiago) passes through the Pyrenees, this is by far the best history of the Santiago legend and the pilgrimage it sparked. Mullins points out churches along the way, giving incisive accounts of their social and architectural background.

Henry Myhill *The Spanish Pyrenees* (Faber & Faber; Transatlantic; o/p). The Spanish side as it was in the early Sixties; excellent for its historical speculation and human anecdotes, less commendable for an obvious pro-Francoist bias.

John Sturrock *The French Pyrenees* (Faber & Faber, UK & US; o/p). Another absorbing and detailed historical travelogue, but one in which the author rarely gets out of his car. Sturrock starts at the west coast and works east, stopping abruptly at borders with the exception of a detour to Roncesvalles.

HISTORY, SOCIETY AND POLITICS

John Ardagh *France Today* (Penguin, UK & US). Journalistic overview up to 1987 – covering food, film, education and holidays as well as politics and economics.

Alfred Cobban *A History of Modern France* (3 vols: 1715–99, 1799–1871 & 1871–1962; Penguin; Viking Penguin). Complete and very readable account of the main political, economic and social strands in French history from the death of Louis XIV to the middle of the de Gaulle era.

John A. Crow *Spain: The Root and the Flower* (University of California Press, UK & US). Cultural and social history from Roman Spain to the present.

Natalie Zemon Davis *The Return of Martin Guerre* (Harvard University Press, UK & US). A man presents himself as a woman's long-lost husband, and persuades many that he is who he claims to be, despite his extremely tenuous resemblance to the missing spouse. A perplexing and titillating hoax which actually occurred in the Pyrenean village of Artigat during the sixteenth century; even better than the movie or the musical.

J.H. Elliot *Imperial Spain 1469–1716* (Penguin, UK & US). Best introduction to the centuries immediately after unification – academically respected and a gripping tale.

Ian Gibson *Fire in the Blood: the New Spain* (Faber-BBC, UK; o/p). This Madrid-based writer, García Lorca scholar and naturalized Spaniard is a passionate enthusiast and critic of the country, which comes across in this 1993 book written to accompany a TV series. More dated than Hooper's revision (see below), but a fine overview of Spanish attitudes and quirks.

Christopher Hibbert *The French Revolution* (Penguin; Morrow). Good, concise popular history of the period and salient events.

John Hooper *The New Spaniards* (Penguin, UK & US). A 1995 update of a perceptive 1987 portrait of post-Franco Spain and the new generation by the *Guardian*'s long-time Madrid correspondent. The best one-volume introduction to contemporary Spain.

S.J. Keay *Roman Spain* (British Museum Publications o/p; University of California Press). Recent and definitive survey of a neglected subject, well illustrated and with a logical layout that makes it easy to use en route.

Paul Preston *Franco* (HarperCollins, UK & US). Penetrating, monumental biography of Franco and his regime, demonstrating how he won the civil war, how he survived in power so long, and – two decades after his death – what his ultimate significance was.

Peter Sahlins *Boundaries: The Making of France and Spain in the Pyrenees* (University of California Press, UK & US). Using the partition of the Cerdanya/Cerdagne as a model, this explores the process of instilling French and Spanish national identities in a formerly unified area of the Catalan Pyrenees; academic and replete with charts and tables, but has its readable moments.

Alexander Worth *France 1940–55* (Beacon Press, US o/p). Excellent and emotionally engaging portrayal of the most taboo period in French history: the Occupation, followed by the early Cold War and colonial-struggle years in which the same political tensions and heart-searchings were under way.

THE CATHARS

In its anti-centralist, anti-clerical essentials, the Cathar issue still fascinates the French. The publication of material on the Cathar era is something of a major industry in the Pyrenean provinces in particular, with two Toulouse publishers – Éditions Privat and Éditions Loubatières – specializing in it. The following are just some of the titles currently available in French and English.

Catherine Bibollet and Michel Roquebert *Ombre et Lumière en Pays Cathare* (Editions Privat). Attractive coffee-table effort, available also in an English edition.

Anne Brenon *Petit précis de catharisme* (Éditions Loubatières). Short summary of the sect's beliefs, drawn from a course given at the University of Montpellier. Her *Le vrai visage due catharisme* (Éditions Loubatières) discusses its flourishing in the Occitan-speaking areas and the details of its suppression.

Jean Duvernoy *Histoire et Religion des Cathars* (2 vols, Éditions Privat). Over forty years, Duvernoy completed the original translation from Latin of the Inquisition's records, which made Le Roy Ladurie's work possible; this is his own history. Vol. 1 analyses the records; Vol. 2, more interestingly, tallies all the medieval sects, from Asia Minor to Britain, allied with Catharism.

Emmanuel Le Roy Ladurie *Montaillou* (Penguin; Vintage). Life in a Cathar village in the Pays de Sault, as recorded by the Inquisition in the fourteenth century, and stored away until the 1970s in the Vatican archives. Hard going in places but a fascinating insight.

Zoé Oldenbourg *Massacre at Montségur* (Phoenix, UK). English translation of the 1961 classic history of the Cathar crusades, dense but vivid, stressing the connection between the suppression of the heresy and that of Languedoc separatism.

Michel Roquebert *L'Epopée Cathare* (4 vols, Éditions Privat). Exhaustive but readable history, 31 years in the making, drawing on nearly everything known about the sect. His more focused *Montségur, Les Cendres de la Liberté* (Éditions Privat) may be more accessible.

Steven Runciman *The Medieval Manichee* (Cambridge UP, UK & US). Classic account of the evolution of the dualist heresy from the Bogomils and Paulicians up to the Cathars.

SPANISH CIVIL WAR

Gerald Brenan *The Spanish Labyrinth: An Account of the Social and Political Background of the Spanish Civil War* (Cambridge UP, UK & US). As the subtitle says: not a straight history of the war, but one of the best non-academic studies on Spanish rural society of the time.

Ronald Fraser *Blood of Spain* (Penguin; Pantheon). Subtitled *The Experience of Civil War*, this oral history of 1936–39 gives a voice to the people who fought in and lived through the war. As a record of ordinary lives in extraordinary times, it's more immediately accessible than Hugh Thomas's tome.

George Orwell *Homage to Catalonia* (Penguin; Harvest Books). Orwell the journalist cut his teeth in this – if not his most celebrated book, it's certainly the best of his reportage. A forthright account of the fighting on the Aragón front, followed by Orwell's injury and subsequent disillusionment with the factional fighting among the Republican forces.

Hugh Thomas *The Spanish Civil War* (Penguin; Touchstone). Massive, exhaustive political study of the period, and still the best single telling of the convoluted story.

WORLD WAR II: FRENCH OCCUPATION AND RESISTANCE

Max Bloch *Strange Defeat* (Norton, US). Moving personal study of the reasons for France's defeat and subsequent caving-in to Nazism. Found among the papers of this Sorbonne historian after his death at the hands of the Gestapo in 1942.

Philippe Burin *Living with Defeat* (Arnold, UK). Excellent French account of the Occupation that focuses in particular on the experiences of ordinary people.

Emilienne Eychenne *Les Pyrénées de la Liberté* (Editions France-Empire, France). History of World War II escapes over the Pyrenees into Spain, by a historian who has made this her special subject. She has also written other titles dealing with specific segments of the range.

H.R. Kedward *In Search of the Maquis: Rural Resistance in South France 1942–44* (Oxford UP, UK & US). Slightly dry, but full of fascinating detail about the brave and often mortal struggle of the countless ordinary people in the region who fought to drive the Germans from their country.

Ian Ousby *Occupation: The Ordeal of France 1940–1944* (John Murray, UK). Somewhat revisionist 1997 account by a non-academic historian, which shows how relatively late resistance was and how widespread collaboration was and why.

Paul Webster *Pétain's Crime: The Full Story of French Collaboration in the Holocaust* (Papermac; I.R. Dee). The fascinating and alarming story of the Vichy regime's more than willing collaboration with the deportations of Jews and the bravery of those, especially the Communist resistance in occupied France, who attempted to prevent it.

ETHNOGRAPHY, NATIONALISM AND FOLKLORE

Luis Nuñez Astrain *The Basques: Their Struggle for Independence* (Welsh Academic Press, UK). The Basque case for independence argued passionately by a journalist.

Claude Bailhé *Autrefois les Pyrénées* (Éditions Milan, Toulouse, France). The French Pyrenees as they were from the latter half of the nineteenth century until World War I, in early photos. Organized by topic (mountaineering, family life, local industries) with intelligent text.

Roger Collins *The Basques* (Basil Blackwell, UK & US o/p). Except for a section on the *fueros*, this is disappointingly dull but there's little currently available that's any better.

Daniele Conversi *The Basques, the Catalans and Spain* (Hurst, UK). Scholarly exploration of the differing evolutions of Basque and Catalan nationalism.

Antoine Lebègue *Lieux Insolites et Secrets des Pyrénées* (Éditions Sud Ouest, Bordeaux, France). Inexpensive miscellany of legends, odd rites and semi-mythic personalities, organized by region. Sketchy (quite literally, with reproductions of old engravings) but fun.

Severino Pallaruelo *Pastores del Pireneo* (Spanish Ministry of Culture; o/p). A thorough – though rather specialist – research into the arts and popular traditions of Pyrenean mountain people, with good photographs.

ART AND ARCHITECTURE

Jean Clottes and David Lewis-Williams *Les Chamanes de la Prehistoire* (Editions Seuil, France). Revisionist view of the Ariège cave art, declaring that designated shamans rendered the art from their visions; see box on p.214.

Kenneth J. Conant *Carolingian and Romanesque Architecture, 800–1200* (Yale UP, UK & US). Fastidious, scholarly treatment of the subject, with excellent material on the French side of the St-Jacques (Santiago) pilgrim route.

John Golding *Cubism: A History and an Analysis 1907–1914* (Faber & Faber; Harvard University Press). The standard work on the years of purist Cubism – essential reading to get the most out of a trip to Céret.

Meyer Schapiro *Romanesque Art* (Thames & Hudson; George Braziller) An excellent illustrated survey of Spanish Romanesque art and architecture – and its Vizigothic and Mozarabic predecessors.

Ann Sieveking *The Cave Artists* (Thames & Hudson, UK & US; o/p). A comprehensive introduction to late Paleolithic cave painting, with an explanation of the theories on meaning and layout, plus two chapters devoted to the Pyrenees.

Sarah Whitfield *Fauvism* (Thames & Hudson, UK & US). Although its reproductions can't do justice to the vibrant colours of Matisse and the artists in his orbit, this serves well as an introduction to the preoccupations of the Fauves.

LITERATURE

Victor Català (pseudonym of Caterina Albert i Paradís) *Solitude* (Readers International, UK & US). This tragic tale of a woman's life and sexual passions in a mountain village is regarded as the most important pre-civil war Catalan novel.

Ernest Hemingway *Fiesta/The Sun Also Rises* (Cape; Scribner). First – though by no means the best – novel from the American macho-maniac. Its account of the San Fermín festival at Pamplona put the town on the world tourism circuit.

Pierre Loti *Ramuntcho* (in French). Cloyingly tragic romance, a sort of early, high-class Mills & Boon-type affair, set in the French Basque country.

The Song of Roland (Penguin, UK & US). The most famous French epic, translated by Glyn Burgess. Written around the end of the eleventh century, this mini-saga conjures up the whole legend of Roland and the famous ambush near Roncesvalles in the Basque Pyrenees.

Colm Toibin *The South* (Picador, UK). Toibin's wonderful first novel follows a woman fleeing her boring, middle-class family life in Ireland for a lover and new life in the Spanish Pyrenees.

SPECIFIC GUIDES

Abbé G. Bernes, George Veron and L. Laborde Balen *The Pilgrim Route to Compostela* (Robertson McCarta, UK o/p). The most practical of the many guides to the route: thorough on the paths, clear on maps and with basic details of accommodation. Translated rather woodenly from the French, however.

Hal Bishop *The Way of St James: GR65* (Cicerone; Hunter). Monument-fixated guide to the French side between Le Puy and Saint-Jean-Pied-de-Port, with no maps and little in the way of route directions.

Alan Castle *The Pyrenean Trail: GR10* (Cicerone; Hunter). Despite nominal 1997 revision, only slightly more current than *Walking the Pyrenees* (see p.484); fairly accurate time-courses from west to east, good pocket size, but no maps, and obsolete refuge/gîte details.

The Confraternity of Saint James publishes two *Pilgrim Guides to the Roads through France to Santiago de Compostela*, which are more useful and current than the Cicerone guides. Volume 1, *The Camino Francés 1997*, despite the name, covers the stretch from Saint-Jean to Pamplona; volume 4, *Arles to Puenta la Reina*, goes via Jaca and Pamplona. Both have good route and facilities details, but no maps.

Marc Dubin Trekking in Spain (Lonely Planet, UK & US). Good general trekking guide by the author of this volume, covering the entire peninsula but with a long section on the Pyrenees. Good maps, though trail and facilities accounts are now a decade old.

GR11, Senderos de Gran Recorrido/Senda Pirenaica (PRAMES, Zaragoza, Spain). In Castilian. Comes in two packagings: the complete range, covered in a two-ring binder – you extract sections and carry them about in the provided case – or paperbound in three separate volumes: Andorra/Catalunya, Aragón, Navarra/Gipuzkoa. Invaluable, and updated regularly (current pages available for the binder edition).

Paul Lucia Through the Spanish Pyrenees, GR11: A Long-Distance Footpath (Cicerone, UK). Better and more current than the same company's GR10 volume, with accurate time-courses, altitude profiles and tables of available facilities, but poor maps and coverage of variants.

Pierre Merlin Guide des Raids à Skis (Denoël, France). Guide, in French only, to the Pyrenean traverse on skis.

Pierre Minvielle Randonnées en Aragon (Diffusion Randonnées Pyrénéennes, France). A well-illustrated pocket-sized walking guide devoted to one of the least known though most spectacular walking areas of the Pyrenees.

J-P Pontroué and Fernando Biargue Au coeur des Sierras du Haut Aragón (Editions J-C Bihet, Pau, France). French-language guide to the canyons, best on Ordesa area walks and canyoning but also with sketchy summaries of the Valle de Gistau, Hecho/Ansó and Panticosa/Sallent. Also by the same authors, Canyons et Barrancos du Haut Aragón and Parc National d'Ordesa et du Mont Perdu (Randonnées Pyrénéennes, France), though currently out of print, are much better than Biargue's later solo effort Parque Nacional de Ordesa y Monte Perdido, 100 Itinerarios (self-published).

Por los Valles de Ansó, Echo y Aragües (PRAMES, Zaragoza, Spain). Everything you would want to know (in Castilian) about the valleys and their settlements, plus tips for walking, rock-climbing and canyoning.

Pyrenees West, Pyrenees East (o/p), **Pyrenees Central** (West Col, UK). More detailed than the single-volume Cicerone guides, though shabbily produced.

Alison Raju The Way of St James: Spain (Cicerone; Hunter). Covers the pilgrim route only from the Puerto de Ibañeta to Pamplona and beyond; some useful route maps.

Kev Reynolds Walks and Climbs in the Pyrenees (Cicerone; Hunter). Now in its third edition, this is the standard English-language guide for trekkers and scramblers, covering the most spectacular parts of the range. His Classic Walks in the Pyrenees (Oxford Illustrated Press, UK o/p) is a bit more clearly presented when route-planning, if rather purple in the prose.

Sua Edizioak is a Bilbao-based mountaineering publisher with several guides (unfortunately in Castilian and Euskera only) pertaining to the Pyrenees. They include Navarra Paso a Paso, a topoguía for every GR trail in Navarra; GR11, Pirineo Vasco, a topoguía describing the trail from Zuriza to Hondarribia; La Alta Ruta de los Pirineos en Bici, for mountain-biking close to the HRP; El Camino de Santiago en Bici, rather less strenuous touring-bike itineraries along the pilgrim route; and Rutas y Paseos por Belagoa, selected excursions in the parque natural at the head of the Roncal valley.

Georges Véron Pyrenees High Level Route (West Col Publications, UK). English translation of the standard mountaineer's traverse of the Pyrenees (original published by Gastons), by the Frenchman who knows the range better than anyone.

Rafael Vidáller Tricas Guía del Valle de Benasque (Editorial Pirineos, Huesca, Spain). More rigorous than the Aragonese government's and mountain club's co-published PR booklet (see p.261); this one grades the progressively more difficult walks.

Derek Walker Rock Climbs in the Pyrenees (Cicerone; Hunter). The first English guide for climbers; serious stuff, including Pic du Midi d'Ossau and the palisades of the Valle de Ordesa.

Walking the Pyrenees (Robertson McCarta, UK o/p). English translation of the French topoguide to the GR10, including IGN maps in colour. Useful, but timings are often optimistic, and many route and accommodation details are woefully out of date. You're probably better off buying the current French original and putting your school French to work.

WILDLIFE FIELD GUIDES

Most of the following titles are best ordered through specialist dealers; a good one in the UK is F & M Perring, Green Acre, Wood Lane, Oundle, Peterborough PE8 5TP (☎01832/273388, fax 274568). Note that the system of Linnaean classification is in a constant state of flux in the case of small flora, where entire families have been suppressed in recent years, and various species have been renamed or even assigned to a different genus. Thus it's as well to have the most up-to-date manual you can lay hands on, but while you may find photos of the live specimens in front of you, don't expect to always have a currently correct identification.

Marjorie Blamey and Christopher Grey-Wilson *The Alpine Flowers of Britain and Europe* (HarperCollins, UK). Comprehensive field guide to mountain flowers, shrubs and trees.

Bertel Brun *Birds of Britain and Europe* (Hamlyn, UK). Well illustrated, and includes species range maps.

John A. Burton *Field Guide to the Mammals of Britain and Europe* (Kingfisher, UK). A bargain: well illustrated and thorough.

John A. Burton, E. N. Arnold and D. W. Ovenden *Field Guide to the Reptiles and Amphibians of Britain and Europe* (HarperCollins, UK). For all those alpine newts, lizards and frogs.

Pierre Delforge *Orchids of Britain and Europe* (HarperCollins, UK). The best and most up-to-date guide, but still not completely error-free; the author is less than happy with the translation from the French.

L. G. Higgins and N. D. Riley *Field Guide to the Butterflies of Britain and Europe* (HarperCollins, UK). Not specific to the Pyrenees, but an excellent start.

D. Macdonald and P. Barrett *Field Guide to the Mammals of Britain and Europe* (HarperCollins, UK). A good alternative to the Burton volume.

Miniguides Nathan Tout Terrain (Nathan, Paris). Full-colour pocket series by various authors in French, covering specific wildlife subjects such as flowers, birds, mushrooms and butterflies; identifying photos are labelled with French and botanical names.

Oleg Polunin and B. E. Smythies *Flowers of Southwest Europe* (Oxford UP, UK & US o/p). Another possibility for the Pyrenees, especially the lower altitudes. Their *Flowers of the Mediterranean* (Chatto, UK) is a useful, if by no means exhaustive, field guide.

A.W. Taylor *Wildflowers of the Pyrenees* (Chatto, o/p). Rare – published in 1972 – and difficult to find, but worth the effort as this is the only guide specifically dedicated to the range.

LANGUAGE

One of the characteristics of the Pyrenees is the number of regional languages – linguists recognize Catalan, Aranés, Aragonese and Euskera – and the strong dialects which seemingly exist in every French valley. There will be little opportunity to learn any of these on a short visit, though a smattering of French and Castilian Spanish should serve you adequately for most purposes.

FRENCH

French is far from an easy language, despite the number of words and structures it shares with English, but the bare essentials are not difficult to master, and they make all the difference. Even just saying "Bonjour Monsieur/Madame" when you enter a shop will usually get you a smile and helpful service. People working in tourist offices, hotels and so forth almost always speak better English than you do French, and so tend to reply in it when you're struggling to stammer out something in French – be grateful, not insulted.

Differentiating words is the initial problem in understanding spoken French, as it's very hard to get people to slow down – if all else fails, get them to write what they've said, as you are bound to recognize more words that way. Even outside the Basque and Catalan areas, there are districts where the language of daily life is a strong dialect of French or, in places, something more like a different species. Don't be dismayed – though you'll probably never understand an overheard conversation, any attempt to make yourself understood in school-book French will

---

A BRIEF GUIDE TO SPEAKING FRENCH

PRONUNCIATION

One easy rule to remember is that **consonants** at the ends of words are usually silent. *Pas plus tard* (not later) is thus pronounced "pa-plu-tarr". But when the following word begins with a vowel, you run the two together: *pas après* (not after) becomes "pazapray".

Vowels are the hardest sounds to get right. Roughly:

a	as in t**a**r		*i*	as in mach**i**ne
e	as in g**e**t		*o*	as in h**o**t
é	between g**e**t and g**a**te		*ô, au*	as in **o**ver
è	between g**e**t and g**u**t		*ou*	as in f**oo**d
eu	like the **u** in h**u**rt		*u*	as in a pursed-lip version of **u**se

More awkward are the **combinations** in/im, en/em, an/am, on/om, un/um at the ends of words, or followed by consonants other than n or m. Again, roughly:

in/im	like the **an** in **an**xious	*on/om*	like the **don** in **Don**caster said
an/am, en/em	like the **don** in **Don**caster when		by someone with a heavy cold
	said with a nasal accent	*un/um*	like the **u** in **u**nderstand

Consonants are much as in English, except that: ch is always "sh", ç is "s", c is "s" before i or e only, but always hard at the end of a word, h is silent, th is the same as t, ll is like the y in yes, w is "v", and r is growled (or rolled).

GENDER

French nouns are divided into masculine and feminine. This causes difficulties with adjectives, whose endings generally have to change to agree with the gender of the nouns they qualify. If you know some grammar, you will know what to do. If not, stick to the masculine form, which is the simplest – it's what we have done in the glossary.

BASICS

Today	*Aujourd'hui*	At midday	*À midi*	Less	*Moins*
Yesterday	*Hier*	Man	*Un homme*	A little	*Un peu*
Tomorrow	*Demain*	Woman	*Une femme*	A lot	*Beaucoup*
In the morning	*Le matin*	Here	*Ici*	Cheap	*Bon marché*
In the afternoon	*L'après-midi*	There	*Là*	Expensive	*Cher*
In the evening	*Le soir*	This one	*Ceci*	Good	*Bon*
Now	*Maintenant*	That one	*Celà*	Bad	*Mauvais*
Later	*Plus tard*	Open	*Ouvert*	Hot	*Chaud*
At one o'clock	*À une heure*	Closed	*Fermé*	Cold	*Froid*
At three o'clock	*À trois heures*	Big	*Grand*	With	*Avec*
At ten-thirty	*À dix heures et demie*	Small	*Petit*	Without	*Sans*
		More	*Plus*		

TALKING TO PEOPLE

When addressing people you should always use *Monsieur* for a man, *Madame* for a woman, *Mademoiselle* for a girl. Plain *bonjour* by itself is not enough. This isn't as formal as it seems, and it has its uses when you've forgotten someone's name or want to attract someone's attention.

Excuse me	*Pardon, excusez-moi*	OK/agreed	*D'accord*
Do you speak English?	*Parlez-vous anglais ?*	Please	*S'il vous plaît*
How do you say it in French?	*Comment ça se dit en Français ?*	Thank you	*Merci*
What's your name ?	*Comment vous appelez-vous ?*	Hello	*Bonjour*
		Goodbye	*Au revoir*
My name is . . .	*Je m'appelle . . .*	Good morning/afternoon	*Bonjour*
I'm English	*Je suis anglais[e]*	Good evening	*Bonsoir*
Irish	*irlandais[e]*	Good night	*Bonne nuit*
Scottish	*écossais[e]*	How are you?	*Comment allez-vous?/ Ça va?*
Welsh/American	*gallois[e]/américain[e]*	Fine, thanks	*Très bien, merci*
Australian	*australien[ne]*	I don't know	*Je ne sais pas*
Canadian	*canadien[ne]*	Let's go	*Allons-y*
a New Zealander	*néo-zélandais[e]*	See you tomorrow	*À demain*
Yes	*Oui*	See you soon	*À bientôt*
No	*Non*	Sorry	*Pardon / Je m'excuse*
I understand	*Je comprends*	Leave me alone (aggressive)	*Fichez-moi la paix!*
I don't understand	*Je ne comprends pas*		
Please speak slower	*S'il vous plaît, parlez moins vite*	Please help me	*Aidez-moi, s'il vous plaît*

FINDING THE WAY

Bus	*Autobus, bus, car*	Railway station	*Gare (SNCF)*
Bus station	*Gare (routière)*	Platform	*Quai*
Bus stop	*Arrêt*	What time does it leave?	*À quelle heure part-il?*
Car	*Voiture*		
Train/taxi/ferry	*Train/taxi/ferry*	What time does it arrive?	*À quelle heure arrive-t-il?*
Boat	*Bâteau*		
Plane	*Avion*	A ticket to . . .	*Un billet pour . . .*

FINDING THE WAY (CONTINUED)

Single ticket	*Aller simple*	Near	*Près/pas loin*
Return ticket	*Aller retour*	Far	*Loin*
Validate your ticket	*Compostez votre billet*	Left	*À gauche*
Valid for . . .	*Valable pour . . .*	Right	*À droite*
Ticket office	*Vente de billets*	Straight on	*Tout droit*
How many kilometres?	*Combien de kilomètres?*	On the other side of	*À l'autre côté de*
How many hours?	*Combien d'heures?*	On the corner of	*À l'angle de*
Hitchhiking	*Autostop*	Next to	*À côté de*
On foot	*À pied*	Behind	*Derrière*
Where are you going?	*Où allez-vouz?*	In front of	*Devant*
I'm going to . . .	*Je vais à . . .*	Before	*Avant*
I want to get off at . . .	*Je voudrais descendre à...*	After	*Après*
The road to . . .	*La route pour . . .*	Under	*Sous*
The path to . . .	*Le sentier pour . . .*	To cross	*Traverser*
Beware! Field set with animal traps	*Attention! Piégé*	Bridge	*Pont*

ACCOMMODATION

A room for one/two people	*Une chambre pour une/deux personnes*	Do laundry	*Faire la lessive*
A double bed	*Un lit double*	Sheets	*Draps*
A room with a shower	*Une chambre avec douche*	Blankets	*Couvertures*
		Quiet	*Calme*
A room with a bath	*Une chambre avec salle de bain*	Noisy	*Bruyant*
		Hot water	*Eau chaude*
For one/two/three nights	*Pour une/deux/trois nuits*	Cold water	*Eau froide*
		Is breakfast included?	*Est-ce que le petit déjeuner est compris?*
Can I see it?	*Puis-je la voir?*	I would like breakfast	*Je voudrais prendre le petit déjeuner*
A room on the courtyard	*Une chambre sur la cour*		
A room over the street	*Une chambre sur la rue*	I don't want breakfast	*Je ne veux pas le petit déjeuner*
First floor	*Premier étage*	Can we camp here?	*On peut camper ici?*
Second floor	*Deuxième étage*	Campsite	*Un camping/terrain de camping*
With a view	*Avec vue*		
Key	*Clef*	Tent	*Une tente*
To iron	*Repasser*	Tent space	*Un emplacement*
		Youth hostel	*Auberge de jeunesse*

DAYS AND DATES

January	*janvier*	November	*novembre*	August 1	*Le premier août*
February	*février*	December	*décembre*		
March	*mars*	Sunday	*dimanche*	March 2	*Le deux mars*
April	*avril*	Monday	*lundi*	July 14	*Le quatorze juillet*
May	*mai*	Tuesday	*mardi*		
June	*juin*	Wednesday	*mercredi*	November 23	*Le vingt-trois novembre*
July	*juillet*	Thursday	*jeudi*		
August	*août*	Friday	*vendredi*	1998	*dix-neuf-cent-quatre-vingt-dix-huit*
September	*septembre*	Saturday	*samedi*		
October	*octobre*				

CARS

To park the car	*Garer la voiture*	Oil	*Huile*
Car park	*Un parking*	Inflate the tyres	*Gonfler les pneus*
No parking	*Défense de stationer/*	Battery	*Batterie*
	stationnement interdit	The battery is dead	*La batterie est morte*
Service station	*Garage*	Spark plugs	*Bougies*
Filling station	*Poste d'essence*	To break down	*Tomber en panne*
Fuel	*Essence*	Traffic lights	*Feux*
To fill it up	*Faire le plein*	Insurance	*Assurance*
Gas can	*Bidon*		

NUMBERS

1	*un*	11	*onze*	21	*vingt et un*	95	*quatre-vingt-quinze*
2	*deux*	12	*douze*	22	*vingt-deux*	100	*cent*
3	*trois*	13	*treize*	30	*trente*	101	*cent et un*
4	*quatre*	14	*quatorze*	40	*quarante*	200	*deux cent*
5	*cinq*	15	*quinze*	50	*cinquante*	300	*trois cent*
6	*six*	16	*seize*	60	*soixante*	500	*cinq cent*
7	*sept*	17	*dix-sept*	70	*soixante-dix*	1000	*mille*
8	*huit*	18	*dix-huit*	75	*soixante-quinze*	2000	*deux mille*
9	*neuf*	19	*dix-neuf*	80	*quatre-vingts*	5000	*cinq mille*
10	*dix*	20	*vingt*	90	*quatre-vingt-dix*	1,000,000	*un million*

QUESTIONS

Where?	*Où?*	How many/	*Combien?*	At what time?	*À quelle heure?*
How?	*Comment?*	how much?		What is.../	*Quel est...?*
When?	*Quand?*	Why?	*Pourquoi?*	which is...?	

FRENCH LEARNING MATERIALS

Rough Guide French Phrasebook (Rough Guides, UK & US). Mini dictionary-style phrasebook with both English–French and French–English sections, along with cultural tips for tricky situations, and a menu-master.

Dictionary of Modern Colloquial French (Routledge, UK & US). A bit bulky to carry in the mountains, but the key to all you ever wanted to understand. The **Collins Gem** (HarperCollins, UK) is a far more compact dictionary, cheap and adequate for beginner's needs.

Breakthrough French (Pan Macmillan, UK; book and 2 cassettes). Excellent teach-yourself course.

A Vous La France; Franc Extra; Franc-Parler (BBC Publications, UK; EMC Publishing, US; each course a book and 2 cassettes). BBC radio courses, running from beginners' to fairly advanced levels.

meet with a sympathetic response and a fairly comprehensible reply.

CASTILIAN SPANISH

Although Spain, like France, has its regional dialects and six recognized written languages, **Castilian** Spanish – the language of the central *meseta* – is understood over most of the penin-sula. Once you get into it, Castilian is the easiest language there is, and you'll be helped everywhere by people who are eager to try and understand even the most faltering attempt. English is spoken, but only in the main tourist areas to any extent, and wherever you are you'll get a far better reception if you at least try communicating with Spaniards in their own tongue.

A BRIEF GUIDE TO SPEAKING SPANISH

PRONUNCIATION

The rules of **pronunciation** are pretty straightforward and, once you get to know them, strictly observed. Unless there's an accent, words ending in d, l, r and z are **stressed** on the last syllable, all others on the second last. All **vowels** are pure and short.

A	as in f**a**ther	**N**	is as in English unless it has a tilde (accent) over it (**Ñ**), when it becomes NY: *mañana* sounds like "manyana"
E	as in g**e**t		
I	as in pol**i**ce		
O	as in r**o**le		
U	as in r**u**le	**QU**	is pronounced like an English K
C	is a theta before E and I, hard other wise: *cerca* is pronounced "thairka"	**R**	is rolled, RR doubly so
		V	sounds like B, *vino* becoming "beano"
G	works the same way, a guttural "H" sound (like the *ch* in loch) before E or I, a hard G elsewhere – *gigante* becomes "higante"	**X**	has an S sound before consonants, normal X before vowels. More common in Basque, Gallego or Catalan words where it's "sh" or "zh"
H	always silent		
J	the same sound as a guttural G: *jamón* is pronounced "hamon"	**Z**	is the same as a soft C, so *cerveza* becomes "thairvaitha". Catalan does not lisp c or z before i or e
LL	sounds like an English Y: *tortilla* is pro nounced "torteeya"		

GENDER

Spanish nouns are divided into masculine and feminine. This causes difficulties with adjectives, whose endings generally have to change to agree with the gender of the nouns they qualify. If you know some grammar, you will know what to do. If not, stick to the masculine form, which is the simplest – it's what we have done in the glossary.

BASICS

Yes, No, OK	*Sí, No, Vale*	Hello, Goodbye	*Hola, Adiós*
Please, Thank you	*Por favor, Gracias*	Good morning	*Buenos días*
When, Where	*Cuando, Dónde*	Good afternoon/night	*Buenas tardes/ noches*
What, How much	*Qué, Cuánto*		
Here, There	*Aquí, Allí*	See you later	*Hasta luego*
This, That	*Este, Eso*	Sorry	*Lo siento/disculpeme*
Now, Later	*Ahora, Mas tarde*	Excuse me	*Con permiso/perdón*
Open, Closed	*Abierto/a, Cerrado/a*	How are you?	*¿Como está (usted)?*
With, Without	*Con, Sin*	You're welcome	*De nada*
Good, Bad	*Buen(o)/a, Mal(o)/a*	I (don't) understand	*(No) entiendo*
Big, Small	*Gran(de), Pequeño/a*	Do you speak English?	*¿Habla (usted) inglés?*
More, *Less*	*Mas, Menos*	I don't speak Spanish	*No hablo español*
Today, Tomorrow	*Hoy, Mañana*	My name is . . .	*Me llamo . . .*
Yesterday	*Ayer*	What's your name?	*¿Como se llama usted?*

DAYS

Monday	*Lunes*	Thursday	*Jueves*	Saturday	*Sábado*
Tuesday	*Martes*	Friday	*Viernes*	Sunday	*Domingo*
Wednesday	*Miércoles*				

HOTELS AND GETTING ABOUT

I want	Quiero	Left, right, straight	Izquierda, derecha,
Do you know . . . ?	¿Sabe . . . ?	ahead	derecho
I don't know	No sé	Old inter-village track	Camino
There is (is there)?	(¿)Hay (?)	Trail	Sendero, senda
Give me . . .	Deme . . .	Forest road	Pista forestal
(one like that)	(un tal)	Where is . . . ?	¿Dónde esta . . . ?
Do you have . . . ?	¿Tiene . . . ?	. . . the bus station . . .	la estación de auto-
. . . the time . . .	la hora		buses
. . . a room . . .	una habitación	. . . the train station . . .	la estación de ferrocar-
. . . with two beds/	con dos camas/		riles
double bed . . .	cama matrimonial	. . . the nearest bank . . .	el banco mas cercano
It's for one person	Es para una persona	. . . the post office . . .	el correo (la oficina de
(two people)	(dos personas)		correos)
. . . for one night	. . . para una noche	. . . the toilet . . .	el baño/sanitario
(one week)	(una semana)	Where does the bus	¿De dónde sale
It's fine, how	¿Está bien,	to . . . leave from?	el autobús para . . . ?
much is it?	cuanto es?	Is this the train for Jaca?	¿Es este el tren para
It's too expensive	Es demasiado caro		Jaca?
Don't you have	¿No tiene algo	I'd like a (single/	Querría un billete
anything cheaper?	más barato?	return) ticket to . . .	(sencillo/de ida y
Can one . . . ? . . .	¿Se puede . . . ?¿ . . .		vuelta) para . . .
camp (near) here?	acampar aquí	What time does it ¿	A qué hora sale
	(cerca)?	leave (arrive at . . .)?	(llega en . . .)?
Is there a hostel/	¿Hay una albergue/	What is there to eat?	¿Qué hay para comer?
fonda/hostal nearby?	fonda/hostal aquí	What's that?	¿Qué es eso?
	cerca?	What's this called	¿Cómo se llama
How do I get to . . . ?	¿Cómo se va a . . . ?	in Spanish?	este en espanol?

NUMBERS

1	un/uno/una	14	catorce	80	ochenta
2	dos	15	quince	90	noventa
3	tres	16	diez y seis or dieciséis	100	cien(to)
4	cuatro	17	diez y siete or diecisiete	101	ciento uno
5	cinco	18	diez y ocho or dieciocho	200	doscient(os)/(as)
6	seis	19	diez y nueve or diecinueve	500	quinient(os)/(as)
7	siete	20	veinte	700	setecient(os)/(as)
8	ocho	21	veintiuno	1000	mil
9	nueve	30	treinta	2000	dos mil
10	diez	40	cuarenta	1998	mil novecientos
11	once	50	cincuenta		noventa y ocho
12	doce	60	sesenta	first	primer(o)/(a)
13	trece	70	setenta	second	segund(o)/(a)
				third	tercer(o)/(a)

Being understood, of course, is only half the problem – and getting the gist of the reply, often rattled out at a furious pace, may prove more difficult.

The boxes above contain lists of a few useful words and phrases that will enable you generally to get you what you want. Anyone travelling for any length of time, however, would be well advised to invest in a decent dictionary or phrase book. A cursory glance at a Spanish **dictionary** might be perplexing – bear in mind that until 1994 CH, LL and Ñ

MOUNTAIN TERMINOLOGY

CATALAN PRONUNCIATION

IG or **TG** sound like "tch" in scratch; thus *Contraig* is pronounced "con-traytch", *Mitg* sounds like "meetch"

Ç is like S; *plaça* is pronounced "plassa"

C followed by E or I is a soft S-sound, not a TH as in Castilian

G followed by E or I is like the "zh" in Zhivago; otherwise hard

J is soft as in French, unlike the Castilian *jota*

LL as in Castilian, except when final (eg Ripoll), when it's merely an emphatic "l" sound

L.L pronounced as two separate "l"s

L-L pronounced as two separate "l"s

NY replaces the Castilian Ñ

T can sound like D, as in the words *viatge* (pronounced "veeadzheh") or *dotze* (pronounced "dodzeh")

X is like SH or soft CH in most words, but as in English in *excursionista*

EASTERN AND CENTRAL PYRENEES

Agua/aigue/aygue	Water
Aigüeta	Small stream
Artigue/artiga	Pasture, meadow
Bal/ball/bat/ batch/val/vall	Valley
Borde/borda	Isolated cottage
Boum	Deep lake
Caillaouas	Rocky
Campana	Pointed rock
Can, cal	Isolated lowland farmhouse
Cap	Highest point on a ridge; also means coastal cape, or the rear/back side of something
Cirque/circ/cirro	Alpine amphitheatre
Clot	A depression or narrow valley
Col/coll/collado/cuello	A pass or saddle
Corral	Enclosure for animals
Cortal	Shepherd's hut
Coma/Coume	Bare incline between trees
Desfiladero/garganta/ congosto/foz	Gorge
Eras/Eres	Grain barns, usually by a threshing *cirque*
Estanyet/estanyol	Small lake, pond
Estibe/estive	Pasture
Étang/estany /llac	Lake
Faja/faxa/feixa	Natural terrace in limestone
Farge /fragua	Forge
Font/fount /fuente	Source of a river
Gave	River (Béarn)
Gorg	Tarn

Grange/granja/ grangera	Barn
Grau	Pass
Hont/hount	Source of a river
Hourquette/ forqueta/horcado	Steep pass
Ibón	Tarn, small lake
Mas/masia	Farm
Né/ner/nère	Black
Neste	River (Bigorre)
Noguera	River (Catalunya)
Oule/oulette	Small bowl
Pántano/Pantà	Reservoir
Passerelle/passarella	Suspension bridge, catwalk
Peña/Peyre	Prominent rock out-crop
Port/porteille/puerto	Pass (implies long use as a trade or pilgrim-age route)
Prat/prado/pradère	Meadow
Pic/puig	Peak
Pujol/puy/puyo/pouey	High point
Raillère/ralhère	Avalanche gallery
Ribera/ribèra	River bank or river valley
Rio/riu	River
Salhèt	River bank
Salto	Waterfall, cascade
Seilh	Glacier
Serre/serra	Serrated, tooth-like ridge
Soula/solana/soulane	South-facing slope
Soum/turon/turoun	Rounded summit
Tartera/tartère	Scree slope
Tozal/tuc/tuca	Peak
Ubago/obaga/umbría	North-facing slope

BASQUE PYRENEES

Aran	Valley	*Çuby/Zubi*	Bridge	*Ichouri /itxurri*	Slope
Ardi	Sheep	*Erreka*	River	*Ithourri*	River source
Arri	Stone	*Etche/etxe*	House	*Kayolar/cayolar*	Pastoral hut
Artz	Bear	*Etchola/etxda*	Hut	*Larra/larria*	Moor, pasture
Artzain	Shepherd	*Gain/gagna*	Summit	*Lepo*	Pass
Beltz	Black	*Gorri*	Red	*Orri/orry*	Pastoral hut
Bide	Route	*Goyen/gora*	High	*Mendi*	Mountain
Celhay/selhai	Plateau	*Handi*	Big	*Oyhan*	Forest
Chara	Wood	*Harri*	Stone	*Portilloua*	Pass
Chipi	Small	*Hegi*	Hill	*Tchipi/txipi/ttipi/tiki*	Small
Churi/chouri/txuri White		*Ibar*	Valley	*Ur*	Water

counted as separate letters, and in older dictionaries will still be found after the C, L and N words respectively.

EUSKERA AND CATALAN

After French and Castilian, the two most prevalent languages of the Pyrenees are Euskera and Catalan. There are no written records of **Euskera**, the Basque tongue, before the Middle Ages, even though it had been spoken for at least a thousand years by then. Its origins are contentious: some scholars propose that it can be traced to a language spoken on the Iberian peninsula before the Roman occupation, while others maintain that it bears a familial resemblance to certain Caucasian languages, such as Georgian. There are currently about half a million Euskera-speakers in Spain and France, at the western end of the Pyrenees.

Catalan, a Romance language evolved from medieval Provençal, survived centralist campaigns either favouring Castilian or actively suppressing *Català* (as it calls itself), from the fifteenth to the twentieth centuries. Although the teaching, printing and broadcasting of Catalan was prohibited under Franco, it is again a flourishing language, spoken by between three and four million people around the eastern part of the range. Since the early 1990s, all signposting in Catalunya (as well as rural restaurant menus) is solely in Catalan, the official language.

To the outsider, **written** Catalan is a far easier language to comprehend than Euskera – with a knowledge of both high-school Castilian and French you can get the gist of most tourist pamphlets or trekking booklets in *Català*. **Spoken** *Català*, with its harsh sound and strong dialects, is much harder to follow. Though the Catalans in particular are always delighted if you make some attempt to use their language, all Basques and most Catalans understand and speak Castilian or French as the case may be, if sometimes grudgingly. Thus the basic French and Spanish vocabularies given in this section

CASTILIAN AND CATALAN LEARNING MATERIALS

Spanish Rough Guide Phrasebook (Rough Guides, UK & US) Mini dictionary-style phrasebook, with Castilian–English and English–Castilian sections, cultural tips and menu-masters.

Breakthrough Spanish (Pan Macmillan, UK). Excellent teach-yourself course comprising a book and 2 cassettes.

Collins Gem Spanish Dictionary (HarperCollins, UK). Compact, cheap and good enough for most beginner's queries.

Teach Yourself Catalan (Hodder & Stoughton, UK; David Mackay, US). A not very ambitious primer, presented in English.

Parla Català (Pia, Spain). The only available English–Catalan phrasebook.

Digui Digui (Generalitat de Catalunya). The best total-immersion course if you're serious about learning Catalan, comprising a series of books and tapes. In Britain, it's most easily available at Grant & Cutler, 55 Great Marlborough St, London W1 (☎0171/734 2012).

should be sufficient to make yourself understood as you travel through either end of the Pyrenees. However, a few local words can be useful for interpreting maps and signs in the Basque and Catalan regions (as well as those French valleys with strong dialects), so a comprehensive "Mountain Language" section appears on p.492. Also, the sounds of letters in Catalan are often completely different from those of Castilian; the most important points of divergence are summarized there, enabling you to at least pronounce place-names accurately.

GLOSSARY

APSE Often multiple, semi-circular or polygonal terminations at the east end of a church.

AYUNTAMIENTO In Spain, the town hall; *ajuntament* in Catalan.

BAROQUE Late Renaissance period of art and architecture, distinguished by extreme ornateness.

BARRIO (Castilian) Suburb or quarter.

BASTIDE One of the grid-plan fortified towns established in southern France during the thirteenth century.

CAMINO DE SANTIAGO/CHEMIN DE SAINT-JACQUES The medieval pilgrim's route to the shrine of St James at Santiago de Compostela in northwest Spain, with several branches crossing the Pyrenees west of Luchon.

CATHARISM Heretical religion of the thirteenth century, with strongholds in the Ariège and Pays de Sault.

CLAVIJAS A fixed peg-and-chain for hauling yourself up rock faces.

CLOCHER-MUR A triangular bell wall, either free-standing or at one end of the church, often topped with decorative detail and often attributed to the Knights Templar.

CLOISTER Colonnaded walled courtyard, usually Romanesque and square, adjoining a monastic church on its south side.

COLEGIATA (Castilian) Large parish church, not quite ranking with a cathedral.

COMARCA/COMARQUE (Castilian/Catalan). Equivalent to an English county.

CORREOS/CORREUS (Castilian/Catalan) Post office.

DÉPARTEMENT One of the French administrative provinces created after the Revolution of 1790, replacing the traditional feudal duchies.

DOLMEN Neolithic stone monument, consisting of two or more upright slabs and a capping stone, thought to be either tombs or – from their frequent position on ridgelines – shepherds' shelters.

ERMITA/ERMITAGE (Spain/France). A wayside chapel, usually (but not always) out in the country.

FRESCO A wall painting made more durable by being applied to wet plaster.

FRONTÓN The playing court for *jaï alaï*, found in most villages of the Basque country.

GOTHIC Architectural style prevalent from the twelfth until the sixteenth century, distinguished by pointed arches and ribbed vaulting.

HALLE(S) In France, a covered produce market.

HOSPICE/HOSPITAL/HÔPITAU Medieval travellers' hostel built by religious or chivalric orders, often at the foot of strategic passes.

HÔTEL DE VILLE The town hall of a larger town in France.

ISARD French or Catalan for the Pyrenean chamois or izard, ubiquitous at higher elevations; known as *rebeco* in Castilian, *sarrio* in Aragonese.

JAÏ ALAÏ The spectacular, high-speed ball game played in numerous versions by teams of two; *pelota* in Castilian, *pelote* in French.

MAIRIE The municipal office of a village in France.

MIRADOR A viewing point or platform intended for trekkers or motorists in the mountains.

MOZARABIC Pertaining to the religion, art or culture of Mozarabs, medieval Spanish Christians living under Muslim rule.

NAVE Main body of a church.

NAVETTE In France, a shuttle bus.

PARADOR Luxury hotel in Spain, often installed in a minor historical monument.

(LA) POSTE (French) The post office.

ROMANESQUE Unadorned, squat architectural style prevalent from the eighth to the thirteenth century; characterized by rounded arches and naively sculpted column capitals.

ROMERÍA In Spain, a religious procession to a rural shrine, often with a venerated image in tow.

SALLE CAPITULAIRE (French) Chapterhouse off a Romanesque cloister, often with fine rib vaulting.

TRANSEPT Transverse arms of a church, perpendicular to the nave.

TYMPANUM The vertical, half-circular space above a Romanesque church portal, often decorated with a relief of Christ in Majesty.

VARIANT(E) An alternate routing of the long-distance trails GR10, GR11 and HRP.

ACRONYMS

CAF *Club Alpin Français*, the French Alpine Club, administering many staffed refuges.

CEC *Centre Excursionista de Catalunya*, rival to the FEEC (see below).

FAM *Federación Aragonesa de Montañismo*, the Aragonese alpine club and refuge-managing entity.

FEEC *Federació de Entitats Excursionistes de Catalunya*, important alpine club and refuge operator in Catalunya.

FNM *Federación Navarra de Montaña*.

GR *Gran recorrido* (Castilian), *grande randonnée* (Fench), long-distance trekking trails for which you must have overnighting/mountaineering gear.

HRP *Haute Randonnée Pyrénéenne*, strenuous, longitudinal traverse of the range, sticking close to the watershed.

ICONA *Instituto Nacional Para la Conservación de la Naturaleza*, the Spanish natural resources administrator, responsible for certain picnic grounds, unrestricted campsites and unstaffed shelters.

PNP *Parc National des Pyrénées*, administering most staffed mountain refuges within its area.

PR *Pequeño recorrido* (Castilian), *petite randonnée* (French), resort-based walking itineraries which take a day or less, without special experience or equipment.

RENFE *Red Nacional de Ferrocarriles*, the Spanish state rail corporation.

SNCF *Société Nationale des Chemins de Fer*, the French state rail corporation.

INDEX

Stay in touch with us!

ROUGH*NEWS* is Rough Guides' free newsletter. In four issues a year we give you news, travel issues, music reviews, readers' letters and the latest dispatches from authors on the road.

I would like to receive ROUGH*NEWS*: please put me on your free mailing list.

NAME . . . .

ADDRESS . . . .

Please clip or photocopy and send to: Rough Guides, 62–70 Shorts Gardens, London WC2H 9AB, England or Rough Guides, 375 Hudson Street, New York, NY 10014, USA.

the perfect getaway vehicle

low-price holiday car rental.

rent a car from holiday autos and you'll give yourself real freedom to explore your holiday destination. with great-value, fully-inclusive rates in over 4,000 locations worldwide, wherever you're escaping to, we're there to make sure you get excellent prices and superb service.

what's more, you can book now with complete confidence. our £5 undercut* ensures that you are guaranteed the best value for money in holiday destinations right around the globe.

drive away with a great deal, call holiday autos now on **0990 300 400** and quote ref RG.

holiday autos miles ahead

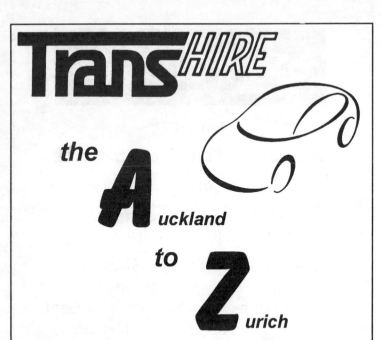